How to put a phone call on air.

The Radio Station

WCRA must be in delay.

Push "Dump" and hold it for a second.

Ø Prog 1 FM AIR.

on the Right.

Tel 1 + Tel 2

Dumping ~~Caccie~~

In case of swear.
Pod down.

Auto vault on
Press dump.

The Radio Station

Broadcast, Satellite & Internet

EIGHTH EDITION

Michael C. Keith

ELSEVIER

AMSTERDAM • BOSTON • HEIDELBERG • LONDON
NEW YORK • OXFORD • PARIS • SAN DIEGO
SAN FRANCISCO • SINGAPORE • SYDNEY • TOKYO

Focal Press is an imprint of Elsevier.

Focal Press is an imprint of Elsevier
30 Corporate Drive, Suite 400, Burlington, MA 01803, USA
Linacre House, Jordan Hill, Oxford OX2 8DP, UK

Library of Congress Cataloging-in-Publication Data

Application submitted

British Library Cataloguing-in-Publication Data

A catalogue record for this book is available from the British Library.

ISBN: 978-0-240-81186-4

For information on all Focal Press publications
visit our website at www.elsevierdirect.com

Typeset by: diacriTech, Chennai, India

09 10 11   5 4 3 2 1

Printed in the United States of America

Contents

11 Consultants and Syndicators   303

Preface

What was said in the preface of the last edition remains true in this newest incarnation. To the understandable chagrin of all but a few radio executives, the industry now includes other forms of the medium besides terrestrial or broadcast outlets. Added under the rubric "radio" (or radio media) are satellite and web stations – thus the subtitle of this book. Says Larry Rosin, President, Edison Media Research, "Regardless of the platform, consumers see all these [audio] options as merely being new forms of 'radio.'" This author agrees. In point of fact, there are now many different types of radio stations, not just AM and FM.

The industry has literally metamorphosized since the start of the new millennium, and to be sure it barely resembles the description in the book's first edition in the 1980s. Why? Succinctly stated, the rollout of new audio technologies and the elimination of station ownership caps. For good or bad, these have altered the very nature of the industry. For example, in the case of the near obliteration of ownership caps, today one radio company can own hundreds, even thousands, of stations, whereas it could own only a handful (a few dozen) little more than a decade ago.

Indeed, since the first publication of this book, the radio industry has witnessed seismic change. In addition to the significant regulatory revamping of the last decade, radio has undergone unprecedented technical overhauling. The advent of high-definition radio – HD Radio – promises to revolutionize broadcast signal transmission and reception, or at least, that is the hope of station owners and operators. Meanwhile, critics argue that HD is already a bust. Of course, with such transformations come challenges and concerns, and these will doubtlessly occupy the thoughts of broadcasters well into the foreseeable future.

When this book was initially published in the mid-1980s, radio was enjoying unprecedented prosperity. The prices being paid for radio properties were soaring, and station revenues were at exceptional levels. Life was good for almost everyone in the industry, or so it seemed. Many AM station owners were not in on the opulent banquet, and a growing number were pulling the plug on their operations. Yet on the whole, the 1980s were auspicious years for the magic medium.

The tide shifted as the final decade of the twentieth century began. The nation had slipped into a nasty recession, taking radio with it on its downward slide, but soon the medium's fortunes were on the upswing and broadcast properties were again attracting gargantuan sums. The catalyst of this unparalleled resurgence was the Federal Communications Commission, which eliminated station ownership caps through the groundbreaking legislation of its Telecommunications Act of 1996.

The industry has certainly experienced many ups and downs since its modest inception over 80 years ago, however, and it will doubtlessly know the thrill of ascent and the angst of decline again. (As this edition was being prepared, the economic crisis on Wall Street and in the banking and housing markets was causing the industry to brace itself for another likely downturn in its fortunes.) Radio was, is, and hopefully will continue to be a wonderfully alive and dynamic medium with a seemingly incalculable life span. It is impossible to imagine a world without David Sarnoff's radio music box, but that is not necessary – it is safe to assume that radio in some form (broadcast, satellite, Internet) will continue to be an integral part of our lives for a very long time to come.

The mission of this book has not changed. This edition, like the previous seven, is the result of a desire and effort to provide the student of radio with the most complete account of the medium possible, from the insider's view, if you will. It is presented from the perspective of the radio professional, drawing on the insights and observations of those who make their daily living by working in the industry.

What continues to set this particular text apart from others is that hundreds of radio people have contributed to this effort to disseminate factual and relevant information about the medium in a way that captures its reality. These professionals represent the top echelons of network and corporate radio, as well as the rural daytime-only outlets spread across the country.

I have sought to create a truly practical, timely, illustrative (a picture can be worth a thousand words – stations explain and reveal themselves through visuals), and accessible book on commercial radio station operations; a book that reflects through its structure and organization the radio station's own organization. Therefore, the departments and personnel that comprise a radio station are our principal focus. I begin by examining the role of station management and then move into programming, sales, news, engineering, production, and traffic, as well as other key areas that serve as the vital ingredients of any radio outlet.

Because my strategy was to draw on the experience of countless broadcast and allied professionals, my debt of gratitude is significant. It is to these individuals who contributed most directly to its making that I also dedicate this book.

Therefore, I would like to express my sincere appreciation to the many individuals and organizations that assisted me in so many important ways. Foremost among

them are Jay Williams, Jr., and Lee Abrams. It also goes without saying (but I'll say it again) that the help of the following individuals was invaluable: Valerie Geller, Ed Shane, Ralph Guild, David Reese, Jason Insalaco, Bill Siemering, Lynn Christian, Erwin Krasnow, Dick Oppenheimer, Chris Sterling, Donna Halper, Ed Cohen, Jeff Smulyan, Ty Ford, Dave Neugesser, Tom Taylor, Luke Russert, John Gehron, George Capalbo, Mark Ramsey, Darryl Pomicter, Larry Shannon, John David, Michael A. Krasner, Gregg Cassidy, Matt Grasso, Tripp Eldridge, Andrew Curran, Tom Severino, Brian Buckley, Robin Martin, Larry Miller, Juan Carlos Hidalgo, Robert Dunlop, Bruce DuMont, Paul Fiddick, Doug Ferber, Norm Feuer, Ward Quaal, Frank Bell, Allen Myers, Gary Berkowitz, Jim Robertson, Robin Martin, Tom Severino, Andrew Curren, Rob Dunlop, Dave Scott, Ken Mills, Ted Bolton, Gary Begin, Doug Erickson, Rebecca Schnall, Thomas Gibson, Rob Vining, Stephen Winzenburg, et al. – the list is endless. My hat is off to every individual and organization cited in this book, as well as my first-class editors at Focal Press, foremost among them Michele Cronin.

Countless companies and organizations contributed to the body of this work. They include the ABC Radio Networks, Air America, Apple Corporation, Arbitron Ratings Company, Auditronics Inc., Backbone, The Benchmark Company, Bolton Research, BMI, Boston Acoustics, BPME, Broadcast Electronics, *Broadcasting and Cable*, Broadcast Programming, Burkhart Douglas and Associates, C-SPAN Radio, CBS, CIPB, Clear Channel Communications, Clear Channel Sucks.com, Coleman Research, Communication Graphics, CFM, CRN, Cumulus, David Sarnoff Library, Denon, Deer River Group, Direct Marketing Research, Edison Media Research, Emmis, Erickson Media Consultants, ESPN Radio, the FCC, *FMQB*, FMR Associates, Geller Media International, Global Radio News, Goldwave Inc., Greater Media, Halper and Associates, HD Radio, Hear2.0, Holland Cooke Media, iBiquity Digital, IGM Inc., Infinity Broadcasting, Inside Radio, Interep Radio Store, International Demographics, iTunes, Jacobs Media, Jefferson Pilot Data

Systems, Jones Radio News, Katz Media Group, KD Kanopy, Kelton Agency, Library of American Broadcasting, Lund Consultants, *The Mancow Show*, Marketron Inc., Mediabase, Metro Traffic Network, MMR, Ken Mills Agency, Moose Lake Products Company, Museum of Broadcast Communications, National Association of Broadcasters, Orban, Oxysys, Pandora Radio, Premiere Radio Networks, Prophet Systems, Public Radio International, QuikStats, Radeo, Radio Advertising Bureau, *Radio and Internet News*, *Radio Business Report*, *Radio Daily News*, *Radio Ink*, Radiolandia, *Radio and Records*, *RTNDA*, Radio Computer Systems, Radio SAWA, RCA, Satellite Music Network, Shane Media, 360 Systems, SiriusXM Radio, Skyline Satellite Services, Society of Broadcast Engineers, Jim Steele, Annette Steiner, Superaudio, Sysndication. net, *Talkers Magazine*, Talk Radio Network, Tapscan, 360 Sysytems, TM Century, Westinghouse Broadcasting, Westwood One, and WOR-AM.

Since the publication of earlier editions, it is certain – in an industry noted for its nomadic nature – that a significant number of contributors have moved on to positions at other stations (or in some cases left the industry). Moreover, it is equally certain that many stations have changed call letters, because that is the name of the game, too. Because of the sheer volume of contributors, it would be difficult to establish the current whereabouts or status of each without employing the services of the FBI, CIA, NSA, Secret Service, and CNN. Therefore, I have usually let stand the original addresses and call letters of contributors except when new information has become available; in those cases, changes have been made.

As this new edition goes to press, radio's greatest writer, Norman Corwin, nears his 100th birthday. Therefore, it seems fitting that his homage to radio be carried over in this new edition as an homage to him for all he contributed to the glory of the medium.

In any case, good evening or good afternoon, good morning or good night,
Whichever best becomes the sector of the sky
Arched over your antenna.
We wish some words with you
Concerning magic that would make a
Merlin envious
The miracle, worn ordinary now, of just such business as this
Between your ears and us, and oceantides of ether.
We mean the genii of radio
Kowtowing to Aladdins everywhere,
As flashy on the run as light, and full of services to ships at sea and planes in the air and people in their living rooms, resembling you.

—Norman Corwin, *Seems Radio Is Here to Stay*

Foreword to the Eighth Edition

by Lee Abrams

Windows are rolled down as you blaze down the open road . . . a hot radio station screams out of the speakers. A cold wintry night at 2 A.M., a distant AM station speaks to the American vista, or a controversial beacon of the mainstream keeps you company with arguable dialogue. These are just a few of the reasons that radio is the soundtrack of the nation. An indescribable experience that when executed with passion and purpose is timeless, intoxicating, and magical.

Oddly enough, the obituary for radio has been written time and time again. In the 50s, it was TV. After all, who would listen to the Lone Ranger when you could now watch it? In the 70s, it was home taping. Why bother waiting for your favorite song when you could tape it on your cassette player and listen at your convenience? Nowadays, it is the Internet that is the "culprit."

But time and time again, radio reinvents itself and continues to prevail as the Teflon medium. Radio doesn't "kill" other media, it just exists . . . and prospers, as reliably as a sunrise.

With that said, there are red flags of concern. I don't think radio has anything to fear but itself. As radio ownership has evolved from individuals and relatively small broadcast-centric companies into giant corporations, there's a fear that radio is losing its soul. That its passion, its desire to create fans instead of users, and its vision-impaired broadcasters are to blame. The FCC has liberal guidelines for inventive radio, yet too many stations are innovation-adverse as if there was this mysterious FCC law that guided the sound, preferring to maintain a dated playbook as the standard, at a time when the competitive landscape has never been denser. Fortunately, there are answers but it's going to be the new generation of thinkers that create and execute a new vision.

Radio needs to go into creative hyper drive and aggressively challenge traditional thinking – not only in programming, but in literally every area of radio station operation. While at XM Radio, I was amazed at the denial among so many broadcasters who wrote off satellite radio for all the wrong reasons. Forty years ago, the same denial existed among many AM broadcasters who trumpeted that FM was a fad for hippies and classical music fans. The twenty-first century is a bad time for denial. A better approach is accepting that there are new forms of audio entertainment emerging and that radio, from a position of strength, needs to refocus its energy and fight back . . . with passion, character, and muscle. Satellite radio, Internet radio, iPods, and whatever new technologies are created in the next few years, are all competition for the world's ears. The economic viability is still a question mark, but there's no shortage of compelling sound being created by nontraditional audio providers.

Radio needs to mobilize its benefits: theater of the mind production; immediate and credible information; the bible of music, old, new, and of all genres; voices that you become addicted to; and the list goes on. But if you listen to many stations today, that edge is being lost. Production using tired old-school voices with *Star Wars* sound effects, stale news presentations, limited playlists that are behind the curve and generic voices with little character. Radio needs to accept these facts . . . and aggressively attack them . . . and write the new playbook for the twenty-first century.

Although the scenario is daunting, never has there been an opportunity to rethink and reinvent. To look at radio as a living and breathing entity that needs to be fed and nurtured with extreme invention and confidence. With all of the challenges that face radio in this century, that's all the more reason to be excited about the possibilities. It's up to those inside the stations to manufacture magic . . . and turn listeners into fans. With that said, there's no reason radio cannot and will not enter another golden age. It's in your control.

What's New to This Edition of *The Radio Station*

The 8th edition strives to be more universal and timely in its approach to its subject by incorporating material about ALL radio stations – broadcast, satellite, and Internet. The entire text has been updated and revised to include dozens of new figures. Some of the highlights include:

Chapter 1 — Digital radio is discussed more extensively in terms of its prospects for competing with satellite radio and helping revive a sagging terrestrial radio market. Likewise, the sections on satellite and Internet radio are embellished in terms of programming, marketing, and policy and their relationship with broadcast radio and other forms of audio, namely, mobile multimedia devices.

Chapter 2 — The impact of station clustering on management is expanded and several new contributors weigh in on a host of topics related to running broadcast, satellite, and Internet operations and the overseeing of the integration of new technologies in a difficult economy.

Chapter 3 — New and evolving formats are discussed as well as programming in the cluster environment. Sections on satellite and Internet programming are expanded and the uses and applications of podcasts and blogs are considered. Station Web site content is examined in this context as well.

Chapter 4 — New contributions by key industry sales executives refresh this chapter. Selling in the cluster setup and in a volatile economy is assessed more extensively. Updated figures include new rate cards and sales software programs.

Chapters 5, 7, 8, and 11 — The content in these chapters has been updated to reflect the expanding presence of computers and use of the Internet and station websites. How station consolidation has impacted these areas is further considered.

Chapter 6 — The section on Arbitron's Portable People Meter is expanded and updated and how the Internet is used to enhance station research is examined.

Chapter 9 — Stronger emphasis on the digital studio highlights this significantly revised chapter. Information on the expanding array of new audio tools – equipment and Internet applications – is presented in the context of studio production.

Chapter 10 — New and expanded data on station classifications and governmental regulations and the influence of technology give this chapter a timeliness as does updated information on satellite and Internet radio.

Also by

Michael C. Keith

Norman Corwin's "One World Flight:" The Lost Journal of Radio's Greatest Writer (with Mary Ann Watson)

Radio Cultures: The Sound Medium in American Life

Sounds of Change: The History of FM Broadcasting in America (with Christopher H. Sterling)

The Quieted Voice: The Rise and Demise of Localism in American Radio (with Robert L. Hilliard)

The Next Better Place: Memories of My Misspent Youth

Dirty Discourse: Sex and Indecency in American Radio (with Robert L. Hilliard)

Sounds in the Dark: All Night Radio in American Life

Queer Airwaves: The Story of Gay and Lesbian Broadcasting (with Phylis Johnson)

Talking Radio: An Oral History of Radio in the Television Age

Waves of Rancor: Tuning in the Radical Right (with Robert L. Hilliard)

The Hidden Screen: Low-Power Television in America (with Robert L. Hilliard)

Voices in the Purple Haze: Underground Radio and the Sixties

Signals in the Air: Native Broadcasting in America

Global Broadcast Systems (with Robert L. Hilliard)

The Broadcast Century and Beyond: A Biography of American Broadcasting (with Robert L. Hilliard)

Radio Programming: Consultancy and Formatics

Selling Radio Direct

Broadcast Voice Performance

Radio Production: Art and Science

Production in Format Radio

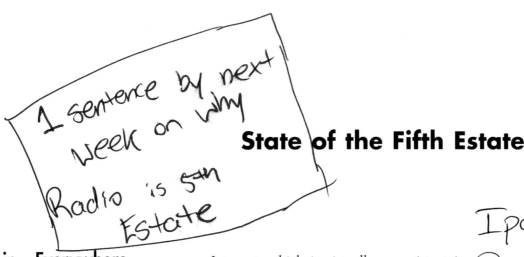

[handwritten note: 1 sentence by next week on why Radio is 5th Estate]

State of the Fifth Estate

[handwritten note: Ipod Fatigue. Radio is not dying.]

In the Air – Everywhere

The competitive landscape of broadcast radio has changed dramatically in the last few years. New audio technologies, such as satellite and Web radio, as well as music downloading media (MP3s and iPods) and mobile music services or mobile multimedia devices (cell phones and PDAs), have transformed the listening environment. Yet, in the first decade of the new millennium, broadcast radio continues to hold its own in the face of the many new competing audio technologies and the seismic shifts in its management and operational structure due to the elimination of long-standing ownership caps and the subsequent consolidation and clustering of thousands of stations. Station owner and communications entrepreneur Jay Williams, Jr., states: "Buoyed by deregulation, consolidation and Wall Street money, then buffeted by increased competition and new technology, terrestrial radio executives are bracing for a challenging future by exploring programming and format options, more sophisticated advertiser relationships, and new digital distribution platforms to more robustly compete and grow."

Although overall listening has declined (over 15% between 1990 and 2008 according to recent estimates and mainly among younger listeners), as has the actual time people spend tuned to broadcast radio (one report in 2006 had time spent listening (TSL) down by nearly 4% since 2003) due to increased competition from other audio choices and legislative changes, radio continues to be one of the most pervasive media on earth, even more so than the Internet, which is virtually nonexistent in many parts of the world, especially in Third World countries.

Observes Tribune Company's COO, Randy Michaels, "Listening may be down, but radio use remains very high, with over 90% of everyone over the age of 6 hearing the radio every week." There is no patch of land, no piece of ocean surface untouched by the electromagnetic signals beamed from the more than 40,000 radio stations worldwide. Over a quarter of these broadcast outlets transmit in America alone. Today, more than 13,500 stations in this country reach 99% of all households, and less than 1% have fewer than five receivers (most have at least eight). There are nearly a billion working radios in the United States.

Modern radio's unique personal approach resulted in a shift of the audience's application of the medium: radio went from family or group entertainer before 1950 to individual companion after the debut of the video medium. Although television usurped radio's position as the number one home entertainment source over five decades ago, radio's total reach handily exceeds that of the video tube. More people rely on radio for its multifaceted offerings than on any other medium – print or electronic, although the Internet is quickly gaining ground. Practically every automobile (96%) has a radio. "There are twice as many car radios in use (approximately 140 million) as the total circulation (50 million) of all daily newspapers, and four of five adults are reached by radio each week," contends Kenneth Costa, former vice president of marketing for the Radio Advertising Bureau (RAB).

1

FIGURE 1.1
In 2008, satellite
radio merged.
Courtesy SiriusXM.

[Handwritten margin note: Localism – Know audience. Keep them close to you.]

Eight of 10 adults are reached weekly by car radio. According to Arbitron's annual report "Radio Today," the medium "reaches more than 94% of the U.S. 12+ population each week, [and] on average, Americans spend around 18 hours per week listening to their favorite stations." As the new millennium proceeded, this computed to well over 230 million Americans, although some recent audience studies have suggested that listening figures for radio, in particular TSL, are on a noteworthy decline due to new competing audio media. A Radio's All Dimensional Audience Research (RADAR) report also found that working women account for nearly 60% of radio listening by women, a statistic that reflects the times. Meanwhile, radio continued to be tremendously popular among African Americans and Hispanics, where the medium's weekly reach is about 95% of that population. The number of radio receivers in use in America has risen by more than 50% since 1970, when 325 million sets provided listeners with a wide range of audio services. In recent years, technological innovations in receiver design alone have contributed to the ever-increasing popularity of the medium. According to the *New York Times*, Americans bought nearly 60 million radios annually in the last years of the 1990s, but that trend slowed in the new century, due to mobile music services. Radio's ability

to move with its audience has never been greater. Out-of-home listeners account for over 60% of the average audience Monday through Friday. In addition, the RAB concluded that 7 of 10 computer purchasers and wine and beer drinkers tune into the medium daily.

Radio appeals to everyone and is available to all. Its mobility and variety of offerings have made it the most popular medium in history, while this popularity has been on the wane in recent years, it continues to be high. To most adults, radio is as much a part of their day as morning coffee and the ride to work. It is a companion that keeps us informed about world and local events; gives us sports scores; provides us with the latest weather and school closings and a host of other information, not to mention our favorite music; and asks for nothing in return. A Katz Radio Group study concluded "only radio adapts to the lifestyle of its audience." The report dispelled the belief that radio listening drops during the summer, as does TV viewing, proving that radio is indeed a friend for all seasons.

It is difficult to imagine a world without such an accommodating and amusing cohort, one that not only has enriched our lives by providing us with a nonstop source of entertainment, but has also kept us abreast of happenings during times of national and global crisis. To most Americans, radio continues to be an integral part of daily life.

FIGURE 1.2
Courtesy Arbitron.
Source "Radio Today,"
2008 © Copyright
Arbitron.

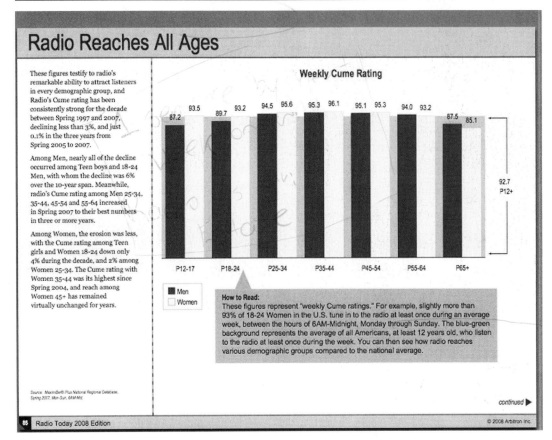

A Household Utility

Although radio seems to have been around for centuries, it is a relatively recent invention. Many people alive today once lived in a world without radio – hard to imagine, yet true. The world owes a debt of gratitude to several "wireless" technologists who contributed to the development of the medium. A friendly debate continues to be waged today as to just who should rightfully be honored with the title "father of radio." There are numerous candidates, some who date as far back as the nineteenth century. For example, there is physicist James Clerk Maxwell, who theorized the existence of electromagnetic waves, which later in the century were used to carry radio signals. Then there is German scientist Heinrich Hertz, who validated Maxwell's theory by proving that electromagnetic waves do indeed exist.

The first choice of many to be anointed grand patriarch of radio is Guglielmo Marconi, who is credited with devising a method of transmitting sound without the help of wires – thus the name wireless

telegraphy. A host of other inventors and innovators can, with some justification, be considered for the title. Nikola Tesla experimented with various forms of wireless transmission and although he has been largely neglected by historians, today there are Tesla Societies that maintain he is responsible for the invention of wireless transmission and modern radio. Lee De Forest, Ambrose Fleming, Reginald Fessenden, and David Sarnoff are a few others whose names have been associated with the hallowed designation. (A further discussion of radio's preeminent technologists can be found in Chapter 10.) However, of the aforementioned, perhaps the pioneer with the most substantial claim is Sarnoff. A true visionary, Sarnoff reportedly conceived of the ultimate application of Marconi's device in a now-famous memorandum. In what became known as the "radio music box" memo, Sarnoff supposedly suggested that radio receivers be mass-produced for public consumption and that music, news, and information be broadcast to the households that owned the appliance.

FIGURE 1.3
President Coolidge
tests car radio.
Courtesy Library of
Congress.

According to legend, at first his proposal was all but snubbed. Sarnoff's persistence eventually paid off, and in 1919 sets were available for general purchase. Within a very few years, radio's popularity would exceed even Sarnoff's estimations. Recently, some scholars have argued that Sarnoff's memo may have been written several years later, if at all, as a means of securing his status in the history of the radio medium. However, the latest consensus gives Sarnoff credit for proposing radio as we know it.

A Toll on Radio

Though not yet a household word in 1922, radio was surfacing as a medium to be reckoned with. Hundreds of thousands of Americans were purchasing crude, battery-operated crystal sets of the day and tuning the two frequencies (750 and 833 kc) set aside by the Department of Commerce for reception of radio broadcasts (a third frequency was soon added). The majority of stations in the early 1920s were owned by receiver manufacturers and department stores that sold the apparatus. Newspapers and colleges owned nearly as many. Radio was not yet a commercial enterprise. Those stations not owned by parent companies often depended on public donations and grants. These outlets found it no small task to continue operating. Interestingly, it was not one of these financially pinched stations that conceived of a way to generate income, but rather AT&T-owned WEAF in New York.

According to most broadcast historians, the first paid announcement ever broadcast lasted 10 minutes and was bought by

FIGURE 1.4
Courtesy Arbitron.

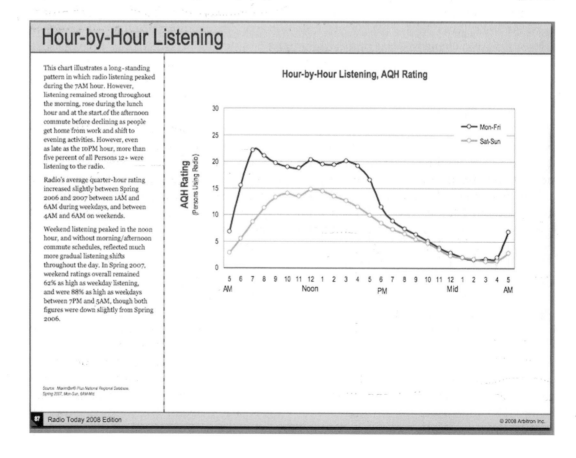

Hour-by-Hour Listening

This chart illustrates a long-standing pattern in which radio listening peaked during the 7AM hour. However, listening remained strong throughout the morning, rose during the lunch hour and at the start of the afternoon commute before declining as people get home from work and shift to evening activities. However, even as late as the 10PM hour, more than five percent of all Persons 12+ were listening to the radio.

Radio's average quarter-hour rating increased slightly between Spring 2006 and 2007 between 1AM and 6AM during weekdays, and between 4AM and 6AM on weekends.

Weekend listening peaked in the noon hour, and without morning/afternoon commute schedules, reflected much more gradual listening shifts throughout the day. In Spring 2007, weekend ratings overall remained 62% as high as weekday listening, and were 88% as high as weekdays between 7PM and 5AM, though both figures were down slightly from Spring 2006.

Source: Maximize® Plus National Regional Database, Spring 2007, Mon-Sun, 6AM-Mid

Radio Today 2008 Edition

© 2008 Arbitron Inc.

Hawthorne Court, a Queens based real estate company. (Radio scholar Donna Halper contends that Boston's WGI actually aired a commercial before WEAF.) Within a matter of weeks other businesses also paid modest "tolls" to air messages over WEAF. Despite AT&T's attempts to monopolize the pay-for-broadcast concept, a year later in 1923 many stations were actively seeking sponsors to underwrite their expenses as well as to generate profits. Thus, the age of commercial radio was launched. It is impossible to imagine what American broadcasting would be like today had it remained a purely noncommercial medium as it has in many countries.

Birth of the Networks

The same year that Pittsburgh station KDKA began offering a schedule of daily broadcasts, experimental network operations using telephone lines were inaugurated. As early as 1922, stations were forming chains, thereby enabling programs to be broadcast simultaneously to several different areas. Sports events were among the first programs to be broadcast in network fashion. Stations WJZ (later WABC) in New York and WGY in Schenectady linked for the airing of the 1922 World Series, and early in 1923 WEAF in New York and WNAC in Boston transmitted a football game emanating from Chicago. Later the same year, President Coolidge's message to Congress was aired over six stations. Chain broadcasting, a term used to describe the earliest networking efforts, was off and running.

The first major broadcast network was established in 1926 by the Radio Corporation of America (RCA) and was named the National Broadcasting Company (NBC). The network consisted of two dozen stations – several of which it had acquired from AT&T, which was encouraged by the government to divest itself of its broadcast holdings. Among the outlets RCA purchased was WEAF, which became its flagship station. Rather than forming one exclusive radio combine, RCA chose to operate separate Red and Blue networks. The former comprised the bulk of NBC's stations, whereas the Blue network

FIGURE 1.5
David Sarnoff, the man who helped put radio into the home. Courtesy RCA.

remained relatively small, with fewer than half a dozen outlets. Under the NBC banner, both networks would grow, the Blue network remaining the more modest of the two.

Less than 2 years after NBC began operation, the Columbia Broadcasting System (CBS, initially Columbia Phonograph Broadcasting System) began its network service with 16 stations. William S. Paley, who had served as advertising manager of his family's cigar company (Congress Cigar), formed the network in 1928 and would remain its chief executive into the 1980s.

A third network emerged in 1934. The Mutual Broadcasting System went into business with affiliates in only four cities – New York, Chicago, Detroit, and Cincinnati. Unlike NBC and CBS, Mutual did not own any stations; its primary function was that of program supplier. In 1941, Mutual led its competitors with 160 affiliates. The network left the air in April 1999 following a long series of financial difficulties.

Although NBC initially benefited from the government's fear of a potential monopoly of communication services by AT&T, it also was forced to divest itself of a part of its holdings because of similar apprehensions. When the Federal Communications Commission (FCC) implemented more stringent chain broadcasting rules in the early 1940s, which prohibited one organization from operating two separate and distinct networks, RCA sold its Blue network, retaining the more lucrative Red network.

The FCC authorized the sale of the Blue network to Edward J. Noble in 1943. Noble, who had amassed a fortune as owner of the Lifesaver Candy Company, established the American Broadcasting Company (ABC) in 1945. In the years to come, ABC would eventually become the largest and most successful of all the radio networks.

By the end of World War II, the networks accounted for 90% of the radio audience and were the greatest source of individual station revenue. Today, most of the major networks are under the auspices of megacorporations. In 1995, Disney purchased Cap Cities/ABC and Westinghouse bought CBS. A few years earlier, GE reclaimed NBC.

Conflict in the Air

The 5 years that followed radio's inception saw phenomenal growth. Millions of receivers adorned living rooms throughout the country, and more than 70 stations were transmitting signals. A lack of sufficient regulations and an inadequate broadcast band contributed to a situation that bordered

on catastrophic for the fledgling medium. Radio reception suffered greatly as the result of too many stations broadcasting, almost at will, on the same frequencies. Interference was widespread. Frustration increased among both the listening public and the broadcasters, who feared the strangulation of their industry.

Concerned about the situation, participants of the National Radio Conferences (1922–1925) appealed to the secretary of commerce to impose limitations on station operating hours and power. The bedlam continued, however, because the head of the Commerce Department lacked the necessary power to implement effective changes. However, in 1926, President Coolidge urged Congress to address the issue. This resulted in the Radio Act of 1927 and the formation of the Federal Radio Commission (FRC). The five-member commission was given authority to issue station licenses, allocate frequency bands to various services, assign frequencies to individual stations, and dictate station power and hours of operation.

Within months of its inception, the FRC established the Standard Broadcast band (500–1500 kc) and pulled the plug on 150 of the existing 732 radio outlets. In less than a year, the medium that had been on the threshold of ruin was thriving. The listening public responded to the clearer reception and the increasing schedule of entertainment programming by purchasing millions of receivers. More people were tuned to their radio music boxes than ever before.

FIGURE 1.6
The radio becomes the centerpiece of the living room. Courtesy David Sarnoff Library.

Radio Prospers during the Depression

The most popular radio show in history, *Amos 'n' Andy*, made its debut on NBC in 1929, the same year the stock market took its traumatic plunge. The show attempted to lessen the despair brought on by the ensuing Depression by addressing it with lighthearted humor. As the Depression deepened, the stars of *Amos 'n' Andy*, Freeman Gosden and Charles Correll, sought to assist in the president's recovery plan by helping to restore confidence in the nation's banking system through a series of recurring references and skits. When the *Amos 'n' Andy* show aired, most of the country stopped what it was doing and tuned in. Theater owners complained that on the evening the show was broadcast, ticket sales decreased dramatically.

As businesses failed, radio flourished. The abundance of escapist fare that the medium offered, along with the important fact that it was provided free to the listener, enhanced radio's hold on the public. Not one to overlook an opportunity to give his program for economic recuperation a further boost, President Franklin D. Roosevelt launched a series of broadcasts on March 12, 1933, which became known as the "fireside chats." Although the president had never received formal broadcast training, he was completely at home in front of the microphone. The audience perceived a man of sincerity, intelligence, and determination. His sensitive and astute use of the medium went a long way toward helping in the effort to restore the economy.

In the same year that Roosevelt took to the airwaves to reach the American people, he set the wheels in motion to create an independent government agency whose sole function would be to regulate all electronic forms of communication, including both broadcast and wire. To that end, the Communications Act of 1934 resulted in the establishment of the FCC.

As the Depression's grip on the nation weakened in the late 1930s, another crisis of awesome proportions loomed – World War II. Once again radio would prove an invaluable tool for the national good. Just as the medium completed its second decade of existence, it found itself enlisting in the battle against global tyranny. By 1939, as the great firestorm was nearing American shores, 1465 stations were authorized to broadcast.

Radio during World War II

Before either frequency modulation (FM) or television had a chance to get off the ground, the FCC saw fit to impose a wartime freeze on the construction of new broadcast outlets. All materials and manpower were directed at defeating the enemy. Meanwhile, existing amplitude modulation (AM) stations prospered and enjoyed increased stature. Americans turned to their receivers for the latest information on the war's progress. Radio took the concerned listener to the battlefronts with dramatic and timely reports from war correspondents, such as Edward R. Murrow and Eric Sevareid, in Europe and the South Pacific. The immediacy of the news and the gripping reality of the sounds of battle brought the war into stateside homes. This was the war that touched all Americans. Nearly everyone had a relative or knew someone involved in the effort to preserve the American way of life. Broadcast news emerged as a major programming factor during the war and would play a central role in every subsequent conflict.

Programs that centered on concerns related to the war were plentiful. Under the auspices of the Defense Communications Board, radio set out to do its part to quash aggression and tyranny. No program of the day failed to address issues confronting the country. In fact, many programs were

FIGURE 1.7
Sponsors of kids' shows during radio's golden age offered prizes, known as premiums, to develop and strengthen listener loyalty.

FIGURE 1.8
In the 1930s, radio offered an impressive schedule of programs for children.

expressly propagandistic in their attempts to shape and influence listeners' attitudes in favor of the Allied position.

Programs with war themes were popular with sponsors who wanted to project a patriotic image, and most did. Popular commentator Walter Winchell, who was sponsored by Jergen's Lotion, closed his programs with a statement that illustrates the prevailing sentiment of the period: "With lotions of love, I remain your New York correspondent Walter Winchell, who thinks every American has at least one thing to be thankful for on Tuesday next. Thankful that we still salute a flag and not a shirt."

Although no new radio stations were constructed between 1941 and 1945, the industry saw profits double and the listening audience swell. By war's end, 95% of homes had at least one radio.

Television Appears

The freeze that prevented the full development and marketing of television was lifted within months of the war's end. Few radio broadcasters anticipated the dilemma that awaited them. In 1946 it was business as usual for the medium, which enjoyed newfound prestige as the consequence of its valuable service during the war. Two years later, however, television was the new celebrity on the block, and radio was about to experience a significant decline in popularity.

Although still an infant in 1950, television succeeded in gaining the distinction of being the number one entertainment medium. Not only did radio's audience begin to migrate to the TV screen, but many of the medium's entertainers and sponsors jumped ship as well. Profits began to decline, and the radio networks lost their prominence.

In 1952, as television's popularity continued to eclipse radios, 3000 stations of the faltering medium were authorized to operate. Several media observers of the day predicted that television's effect would be too devastating for the older medium to overcome. Many radio station owners around the country sold their facilities. Some reinvested their money in television, and others left the field of broadcasting entirely.

Recalling this bleak period in radio's history in a 1958 magazine article in *Wisdom*, David Sarnoff wrote: "In the Spring of 1949, the cry went up that 'radio is doomed.'" Some of the prophets of doom predicted that within 3 years sound broadcasting over national networks would be wiped out, with television taking its place.

"I did not join that gloomy forecast in '49,' nor do I now. Years have passed, and radio broadcasting is still with us and rendering nationwide service. It plays too vital a role in the life of this nation to be canceled out by another medium. I have witnessed too many cycles of advance and adaptation to believe that a service so intimately integrated with American life can become extinct."

"We would be closing our eyes to reality, however, if we failed to recognize that radio has been undergoing fundamental changes. To make the most of its great potentials, it must now be operated and used in ways which take cognizance of the fact that it is no longer the only broadcast medium. A process of adjustment is necessary, and it is taking place."

A New Direction

A technological breakthrough by Bell Laboratories scientists in 1948 resulted in the creation of the transistor. This innovation provided radio manufacturers the chance to produce miniature portable receivers. The new transistors, as they were popularly called, enhanced radio's mobility. Yet the medium continued to flounder throughout the early 1950s as it attempted to formulate a strategy that would offset the effects of television. Many radio programmers felt that the only way to hold onto their dwindling audience was to offer the same material, almost program for program, aired by television. Ironically, television had appropriated its programming approach from radio, which no longer found the system viable.

By 1955, radio revenues reached an unimpressive $90 million, and it was apparent to all that the medium had to devise another way to attract a more formidable following. Prerecorded music became a mainstay for many stations that had dropped their network affiliations in the face of decreased program schedules. Gradually, music became the primary product of radio stations, and the disc jockey (deejay, jock) their new star.

Radio Rocks and Roars

The mid-1950s saw the birth of the unique cultural phenomenon known as rock 'n' roll, a term invented by deejay Alan Freed to describe a new form of music derived from rhythm and blues. The new sound took hold of the nation's youth and helped return radio to a position of prominence.

In 1955, Bill Haley's recording of *Rock Around the Clock* struck pay dirt and sold over a million copies, thus ushering in a new era in contemporary music. The following year Elvis Presley tunes dominated the hit charts. Dozens of stations around the country began to focus their playlists on the newest music innovation. The Top 40 radio format, which was conceived by Todd Storz (while at his favorite watering hole in Omaha) and developed by a slew of programming innovators about the time rock made its debut, began to top the ratings charts. In its original form, Top 40 appealed to a much larger cross section of the listening public because of the diversity of its offerings. At first artists such as Perry Como, Les Paul and Mary Ford, and Doris Day were more common than the rockers. Then the growing penchant of young listeners for the doo-wop sound figured greatly in the narrowing of the Top 40 playlist to mostly rock 'n' roll

records. Before long the Top 40 station was synonymous with rock and teens.

A few years passed before stations employing the format generated the kind of profits their ratings seemed to warrant. Many advertisers initially resisted spending money on stations that attracted primarily kids. By 1960, however, rock stations could no longer be denied because they led their competitors in most cities. Rock and radio formed the perfect union.

FM's Ascent

Rock eventually triggered the wider acceptance of FM, whose creator, Edwin H. Armstrong, set out to produce a static-free alternative to the AM band. In 1938 he accomplished his objective, and 2 years later the FCC authorized FM broadcasting. However, World War II and RCA (which had a greater interest in the development of television) thwarted the implementation of Armstrong's innovation. Construction on FM stations did not begin until 1946. Yet FM's launch was less than dazzling. Television was on the minds of most Americans, and the prevailing attitude was that a new radio band was hardly necessary.

More than 600 FM outlets were on the air in 1950, but by the end of the decade the number had shrunk by 100. Throughout the 1950s and early 1960s, FM stations

FIGURE 1.9
Pioneer radio operator Mary Loomis ran a radio school at the dawn of the medium. Courtesy Library of Congress.

directed their programming to special-interest groups. Classical and soft music were offered by many stations. This conservative, if somewhat highbrow, programming helped foster an elitist image. FM became associated with the intellectual or, as it was sometimes referred to, the "egghead" community. Some FM stations purposely expanded on their snob appeal image in an attempt to set themselves apart from popular, mass appeal radio. This, however, did little to fill their coffers.

FM remained the poor second cousin to AM throughout the 1960s, a decade that did, however, prove transitional for FM. Many FM licenses were held by AM station operators who sensed that someday the new medium might take off. An equal number of FM licensees used the unprofitable medium for tax write-off purposes. Although many AM broadcasters possessed FM frequencies, they often did little when it came to programming them. Most chose to simulcast their AM broadcasts. It was more cost-effective during a period when FM drew less than 10% of the listening audience.

In 1961, the FCC authorized stereo broadcasting on FM. This would prove to be a benchmark in the evolution of the medium. Gradually, more and more recording companies were pressing stereo disks. The classical music buff was initially considered the best prospect for the new product. Since fidelity was of prime concern to the classical music devotee, FM stations that could afford to go stereo did so. The "easy listening" stations soon followed suit.

Another benchmark in the development of FM occurred in 1965 when the FCC passed legislation requiring that FM broadcasters in cities whose populations exceeded 100,000 break simulcast with their AM counterparts for at least 50% of their broadcast day. The commission felt that simply duplicating an AM signal did not constitute efficient use of an FM frequency. The FCC also thought that the move would help foster growth in the medium, which eventually proved to be the case.

The first format to attract sizable audiences to FM was Beautiful Music, a creation of program innovator Gordon McLendon. The execution of the format made it particularly adaptable to automation systems, to which many AM/FM combo operations

resorted when the word came down from Washington that simulcast days were over. Automation kept staff size and production expenses to a minimum. Many stations assigned FM operation to their engineers, who kept the system fed with reels of music tapes and cartridges containing commercial material. Initially, the idea was to keep the FM as a form of garnishment for the more lucrative AM operation. In other words, at combo stations the FM was thrown in as a perk to attract advertisers – two stations for the price of one. To the surprise of more than a few station managers, the FM side began to attract impressive numbers. The more-music, less-talk (meaning fewer commercials) stereo operations made money. By the late 1960s, FM claimed a quarter of the radio listening audience, a 120% increase in less than 5 years.

Contributing to this unprecedented rise in popularity was the experimental progressive format, which sought to provide listeners with an alternative to the frenetic, highly commercial AM sound. Rather than focusing on the best-selling songs of the moment, as was the tendency on AM, these stations were more interested in giving airtime to album cuts that normally never touched the felt of studio turntables. The progressive or album rock format (also called underground and freeform), conceived by Larry Miller and Tom ("Big Daddy") Donahue, slowly chipped away at Top 40's ratings numbers and eventually earned itself part of the radio audience.

The first major market station to choose a daring path away from the tried and true chart hit format was WOR-FM in New York. On July 30, 1966, the station broke from its AM side and embarked on a new age in contemporary music programming. Other stations around the country, foremost among them KMPX in San Francisco, did not take long in following its lead.

The FM transformation was to break into full stride in the early and mid 1970s. Stereo component systems were a hot consumer item and the preferred way to listen to music, including rock. However, the notion of Top 40 on FM was still alien to most. FM listeners had long regarded their medium as the alternative to the pulp and punch presentation typical of the Standard

Broadcast band. The idea of contemporary hit stations on FM offended the sensibilities of a portion of the listening public. Nonetheless, Top 40 began to make its debut on FM, and for many license holders it marked the first time they enjoyed sizable profits. By the end of the decade, FM's profits would triple, as would its share of the audience. After three decades of living in the shadow of AM, FM achieved parity in 1979 when it equaled AM's listenership. The following year it moved ahead. In the late 1980s, studies demonstrated that FM attracted as much as 85% of the radio audience.

With nearly as many AM stations (4784) as FM stations (5720) and only a quarter of the audience, the older medium was faced with a unique challenge that could determine its very survival. In an attempt to retain a share of the audience, many AM stations dropped music in favor of news and talk. WABC-AM's shift from music radio to talk radio in 1982 clearly illustrated the metamorphosis that AM was undergoing. WABC had long been the nation's foremost leader in the pop/rock music format.

In a further effort to avert the FM sweep, hundreds of AM stations went stereo in the latter part of the last century. AM broadcasters hoped this would give them the competitive edge they urgently needed. It was hoped that music would return to the AM side, bringing along with it some unique format approaches. A number of radio consultants believed that the real programming innovations in the years ahead would occur at AM stations. "Necessity is the mother of invention," said Dick Ellis, programming consultant and former radio format specialist for Peters Productions in San Diego, California. "Expect some very exciting and interesting things to happen on AM," predicted Ellis over a decade ago. In some respects, his vision was on target, but the full realization of his prediction did not come to pass.

AM Stereo

Hoping to help AM radio out of its doldrums, in the early 1980s the FCC authorized stereocasting on the senior band. However, the commission failed to declare a technical standard, leaving that task to the marketplace. This resulted in a very sluggish conversion to the two-channel system, and by the 1990s only a few hundred AM outlets offered stereo broadcasting. Those that did were typically the more prosperous metro market stations that ultimately featured talk and information formats.

Eventually, the FCC declared Motorola the industry standard-bearer, but by the mid-1990s the hope that stereo would provide a cure for AM's deepening malaise had dimmed considerably. By this time, many AM outlets, which may have benefited by having a stereo signal, were in a weaker financial state and unable to convert or were less than enthusiastic about any potential payback. Many were just holding on in the hope that the impending conversion of radio to digital would help level the playing field for AM.

Noncommercial/Public Radio

More than 1500 stations operate without direct advertiser support. Noncommercial stations, as they are called, date back to the medium's heyday and were primarily

NPR VOICES

FIGURE 1.10
NPR News reaches millions of listeners and is regarded by many as the medium's foremost news service.

run by colleges and universities. The first "noncoms" broadcast on the AM band but moved to the FM side in 1938. After World War II, the FCC reconstituted the FM band and reserved the first 20 channels (88–92 MHz) for noncommercial facilities. Initially, this gave rise to low-power (10-W) stations known as Class D's. The lower cost of such operations was a prime motivator for schools that wanted to become involved with broadcasting.

In 1967, the Corporation for Public Broadcasting (CPB) was established as the result of the Public Broadcasting Act. Within 3 years National Public Radio (NPR) was formed. Today, more than 400 stations are members of NPR, which provides programming. Many NPR affiliates are licensed to colleges and universities, and a substantial number are owned by nonprofit organizations.

Member stations are the primary source of funding for NPR. They contribute 60% of its operating budget. Affiliates in turn are supported by listeners, community businesses, and grants from the CPB. Program underwriting (the equivalent of sponsorships) is a primary way that public stations meet their operating budgets. These on-air announcements run approximately 15 seconds and include sponsor name and information but no direct selling or hype. They are purchased by sponsors in much the same way that spots are sold on commercial stations – from a rate card based on ratings. (Public radio station Web sites usually provide more detail on this subject.)

The CPB claims that 22.2 million listeners tune into public radio stations on a weekly basis. NPR claims that over 13 million Americans tune into their member stations. Their literature states that "NPR's news and performance programming attracts an audience distinguished by its level of education, professionalism, and community involvement." (Programs such as *All Things Considered* and *Morning Edition* have become the industry's premier news and information features, achieving both popular and critical acclaim.) Public radio consultant Ken Mills declares, "The growth of public radio news listening is one of the biggest success stories in terrestrial radio of the past two decades. Since the early 1990s, listening to NPR News stations has more than doubled. As of 2005, more than 26 million listeners hear NPR News each week. NPR News stations are often among the most-listened-to stations in most markets. The growing demand for public radio news has created an opportunity for public radio consultants such as myself. News/talk programming and documentaries – the types of programming I specialize in – will likely continue to be in demand."

Research shows that NPR listeners are consumers of information from many sources and are more likely than average Americans to buy books. They are motivated citizens involved in public activities, such as voting and fund-raising. They address public meetings, write letters to editors, and lead business and civic groups.

Public Radio International (formerly American Public Radio) debuted in 1983 and operated much like NPR. It provided listeners with additional noncommercial

FIGURE 1.11
A Public Radio International promotional piece. Courtesy PRI.

PRI Public Radio International℠

Public Radio International (PRI) is the source of more public radio programming than any other distributor in the United States. Founded in 1983 as American Public Radio, PRI is steadily moving forward with its second decade goal to "provide expanded global perspectives on world news, current events, and culture to public radio audiences."

In addition to acquiring finished programming from station-based and independent producers around the globe, PRI actively shapes and develops new programs and program formats. PRI also seeks to expand the reach, impact, and relevancy of public radio for audiences who have not traditionally been public radio listeners.

The network emphasizes programming in three general areas:
• News and information
• Classical music
• Comedy/Variety and contemporary music

PRI also distributes an average of four special programs per month.

Keep us in mind and on file. We look forward *to talking with*

"@"
PRI Public Radio International™

Public Radio International
100 North Sixth Street, Suite 900A
Minneapolis, Minnesota 55403
Telephone: 612.338.5000
Facsimile: 612.330.9222

This recycled paper is made from 50% waste paper and contains 10% postconsumer waste.

options, airing popular programs like Garrison Keillor's *A Prairie Home Companion* and many others.

Noncommercial stations can be divided into at least three categories: public, college (noncommercial educational), and community. A fourth category, noncommercial religious stations, has emerged during the last couple of decades and continues to grow in the second half of the 2000s.

Many public radio stations, especially those affiliated with NPR, choose to air classical music around the clock; others opt to set aside only a portion of their broadcast day for classical programming. According to the preeminent association of college broadcasters, the Intercollegiate Broadcasting System (IBS), more than 800 schools and colleges hold noncommercial licenses. The majority of these stations operate at lower power, some with as little as 10 W. Since the late 1970s, a large percentage of college stations have upgraded from Class D and now radiate hundreds of Watts or more. Most college stations serve as training grounds for future broadcasters while providing alternative programming for their listeners.

Community noncoms are usually licensed to civic groups, foundations, school boards, and religious associations. Although the majority of these stations broadcast at low power, they manage to satisfy the programming desires of thousands of listeners.

In some instances, noncoms pose a ratings threat to commercial stations. However, this threat is usually in the area of classical music and news programming. Consequently, commercial and noncommercial radio stations manage a fairly peaceful and congenial

---

William Siemering | On Public Radio

FIGURE 1.12
William Siemering.

Although the distance between commercial and public radio has narrowed in recent years, they remain notably different. As the largest single source of income for public radio stations is listener contributions, the programming is listener-driven and the program directors read the Arbitron ratings just as their commercial colleagues do. However, their programming must be significantly different in content and quality from commercial programs to elicit freewill contributions. (In many European countries, public service broadcasting is supported by a tax on receivers, not voluntary contributions.) Commercial stations, though often involved in community service, have one goal: make a profit. Public stations have a mission to serve unmet cultural, information, and community needs.

The most listened-to programs on public radio are news and information programs: *Morning Edition*, *All Things Considered*, and *Fresh Air*. These are characterized by both the thoroughness of their coverage and the breadth of subjects. They regard news of the arts/popular culture to be as important to understanding the world as news of politicians. No commercial network comes close to replicating these programs. Local stations frequently sponsor town meetings on important public affairs issues or sponsor concerts in the community to strengthen their local links. Local stations may broadcast jazz, Triple A (Adult Alternative Album), blue grass, acoustic, classical music, or an array of talk programs. Some stations are directed to specific audiences such as Hispanic or Indian.

Public radio listeners tend to be educated and to include decision makers and influentials in their communities, so their influence is great. Eight of 10 newspaper editors rely on it as an important source of information, as do network television producers and anchors. *Publishers Weekly* said public radio is the single most important medium for the book business.

In addition to support from listeners, public radio also receives corporate and business underwriting, and grants from foundations and the CPB, which was created in 1967 to distribute federal funds and protect stations against political pressure on programming. Managing a public radio station is, therefore, more complex because it's funding is so diverse. At the same time it must protect the independence of the programming from the funder influence.

Recently, some politicians have questioned continued federal funding for public broadcasting, and various alternative systems of this support are being explored.

FIGURE 1.13
Some popular radio
program formats
from 1960 to the
present. New formats
are constantly
evolving.

Acid Rock	Jazz
Adult Contemporary	Lite
Album-Oriented Rock	MAC
Arena Rock	Mellow Rock
Beautiful Music	Middle-of-the-Road
Big Band	Mix
Black	Modern Rock
Bluegrass	Motown
Bubble Gum	News
Children's	News/Talk
Classical	New Wave
Classic Hits	Nostalgia
Classic Rock	Oldies
Contemporary Country	Pop
Contemporary Hits	Progressive
Country and Western	Punk Rock
Chicken Rock	Religious
Dance	Rhythm and Blues
Disco	Soft Rock
Easy Listening	Southern Rock
Eclectic	Standards
English Rock	Talk
Ethnic	Top 40
Folk Rock	Urban Contemporary
Free Form	Urban Country

coexistence. (See "Suggested Further Reading"
for additional information on noncommercial
radio.)

Proliferation and Frag-Out

Specialization – *narrowcasting* or *nichecast-ing* as it came to be called – salvaged the
medium in the early 1950s. Before that time,
radio bore little resemblance to its sound
during the age of television. It was the video
medium that copied radio's approach to programming during its golden age. "Sightradio,"
as television was sometimes ironically called,
drew from the older electronic medium its
programming schematic and left radio hover-
ing on the edge of the abyss. Gradually, radio
station managers realized they could not
combat the dire effects of television by programming in a like manner. To survive they
had to change. To attract listeners they had to
offer a different type of service. The majority
of stations went to spinning records and presenting short newscasts. Sports and weather
forecasts became an industry staple.

Initially, most outlets aired broad-appeal
music. Specialized forms, such as jazz,
rhythm and blues, and country, were left off
most playlists, except in certain regions of
the country. Eventually, these all-things-to-
all-people stations were challenged by what
is considered to be the first popular attempt

at format specialization. As legend now has
it, radio programmer Todd Storz and his
assistant Bill Steward of KOWH-AM in
Omaha, Nebraska, decided to limit their
station's playlist to only those records that
currently enjoyed high sales. The idea for
the scheme struck them at a local tavern
as they observed people spending money
to play mostly the same few songs on
the jukebox. Their programming concept
became known as "Top 40." Within months
of executing their new format, KOWH
topped the ratings. Word of their success
spread, inspiring other stations around the
nation to take the pop-record approach.
They too found success.

By the early 1960s other formats had
evolved, including Beautiful Music, which
was introduced over San Francisco station
KABL, and All-News, which first aired
over XETRA located in Tijuana, Mexico.
Both formats were the progeny of Gordon
McLendon and were successfully copied
across the country.

The diversity of musical styles that
evolved in the mid-1960s, with the help of
such disparate performers as the Beatles and
Glen Campbell, gave rise to myriad format
variations. Although some stations focused
on 1950s rock 'n' roll ("blasts from the past,"
"oldies but goodies"), others stuck to current
hits, and still others chose to play more
obscure rock album cuts. The 1960s saw
the advent of the radio formats of soft rock
and acid and psychedelic hard rock. Meanwhile, country, whose popularity had been
confined mostly to areas of the South and
Midwest, experienced a sudden growth in
its acceptance through the crossover appeal
of artists such as Johnny Hartford, Bobbie
Gentry, Bobby Goldsboro, Johnny Cash,
and, in particular, Glen Campbell, whose
sophisticated country-flavor songs topped
both the Top 40 and country charts.

As types of music continued to become
more diffused in the 1970s, a host of new
formats came into use. The listening audience became more and more fragmented.
Frag-out, a term coined by radio consultant
Kent Burkhart, posed an ever-increasing
challenge to program directors (PDs) whose
job it was to attract a large enough piece
of the radio audience to keep their stations
profitable.

The late 1970s and early 1980s saw the rise and decline of the disco format, which eventually evolved into urban contemporary, and a wave of interest in synthesizer-based electropop. Formats such as soft rock faded from the scene only to be replaced by a narrower form of Top 40 called contemporary hit. New formats continue to surface with almost predictable regularity. Among the most recent batch are Adult Standards, New AC/Smooth Jazz, Eclectic-Oriented Rock, All-Weather, Churban, All-Motivation, and All-Business.

Although specialization saved the industry from an untimely end a half century ago, the proliferation in the number of radio stations (which more than quadrupled since 1950) competing for the same audience has brought about the age of hyperspecialization. Today, there are more than 100 format variations in the radio marketplace, compared to a handful when radio stations first acknowledged the necessity of programming to a preselected segment of the audience as the only means to remain in business. (For a more detailed discussion on radio formats, see Chapter 3.)

Profits in the Air

Although radio has been unable to regain the share of the national advertising dollar it attracted before the arrival of television, it does earn far more today than it did during its so-called heyday. About 7% of all money spent on advertising goes to radio. This computes to billions of dollars.

Despite the enormous gains since WEAF introduced the concept of broadcast advertising, radio cannot be regarded as a get-rich-quick scheme. Many stations walk a thin line between profit and loss. Although some major market radio stations demand and receive more than $1000 for a 1-minute commercial, an equal number sell time for the proverbial "dollar a holler."

Though the medium's earnings have maintained a progressive growth pattern, it also has experienced periods of recession. These financial slumps or dry periods have almost all occurred since 1950. Initially, television's effect on radio's revenues was devastating. The medium began to recoup

U.S. Ownership of Radio Receivers: 1925–1975

Year	Percent of Households Owing Radio	Average Receiver Cost	Percent of Households With FM Sets	Percent of Cars with Radio	Total Produced (Thousands)
1925	10	$83	–	–	2,000
1935	67	55	–	9	6,026
1945	88	40	N/a	23	500
1955	96	20	N/a	60	14,190
1965	99	N/a	48% [1966]	79	41,7126
1975	99	N/a	93	95	34,515

(Source: Sterling and Kittross (2002), pp. 862–863, citing various industry sources, chiefly Electronic Industries Association. Final column from Sterling (1984), pp. 212–213.)

its losses when it shifted its reliance from the networks and national advertisers to local businesses. Today, 70% of radio's revenues come from local spot sales as compared to half that figure in 1948.

By targeting specific audience demographics, the industry remained solvent. In the 1980s, a typical radio station earned $50,000 annually in profits. As the medium regained its footing after the staggering blow administered to it by television, it experienced both peaks and valleys financially. In 1961, for example, the FCC reported that more radio stations recorded losses than in any previous period because it began keeping records of such things. Two years later, however, the industry happily recorded its greatest profits ever. In 1963, the medium's revenues exceeded $636 million. In the next few years earnings would be up 60%, surpassing the 1.5 billion mark, and would leap another 150% between 1970 and 1980. FM profits have tripled since 1970 and have significantly contributed to the overall industry figures.

The AM daytimer segment of the industry has found it the most difficult to stay in the black. The FCC requires these radio stations to cease broadcasting around sunset so as not to interfere with other AM stations. Of the 2000 daytimers in operation, nearly a third reported losses at one time or another in the 1980s.

Concerning the challenges of programming an AM daytimer, station manager Dan Collier observes, "You don't have the

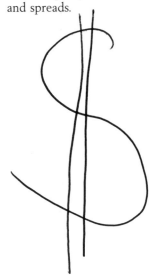

FIGURE 1.14
Radio receiver ownership expands and spreads.

money for staff. You don't have the budget for talented people. You don't have the resources for new equipment or to even maintain the equipment you have, which is typically in disrepair. These stations are a very tough sell to advertisers, so they lapse into decline and many eventually go silent. It doesn't have to be that way, but good management of this type of station is almost as scarce as advertising dollars."

The unique problem facing daytime-only broadcasters has been further aggravated by FM's dramatic surge in popularity. The nature of their license gives daytimers subordinate status to fulltime AM operations, which have found competing no easy trick, especially in the light of FM's success. Because of the lowly status of the daytimer in a marketplace that has become increasingly thick with rivals, it is extremely difficult for these stations to prosper, although some do very well. Many daytimers have opted for specialized forms of programming to attract advertisers. For example, religious and ethnic formats have proven successful.

Over the years, the FCC has considered a number of proposals to enhance the status of AM stations. One such proposal suggested that the interference problem could be reduced if certain stations shift frequencies to the extended portion (1605–1705 kHz) of the AM band. FCC Docket 87-267, issued in the latter part of 1991, cited the preceding as a primary step in improving the AM situation. It inspired many skeptics who regarded it as nothing more than a bandage. Other elements of the plan included tax incentives for AM broadcasters who pull the plug on their ailing operations and multiple AM station ownership in the same market.

As a consequence of the formidable obstacles facing the AM daytime operation, many have been put up for sale, and asking prices have been alarmingly low.

However, many full-time metro market AMs have sold for multimillions, for the simple reason that they continue to appear in the top of their respective ratings surveys. Meanwhile, the price for FM stations has skyrocketed since 1970.

In general, individual station profits have not kept pace with industrywide profits due to the rapid growth in the number of outlets over the past two decades. To say the least, competition is keen and in many markets downright fierce. It is common for 30 or more radio stations to vie for the same advertising dollars in large cities, and the introduction of other media in recent years, such as cable, satellite, and web radio, intensifies the skirmish over sponsors.

Economics and Survival

Following the general financial euphoria and binge-buying of the 1980s, the early 1990s experienced a considerable economic downturn, which had a jarring impact on the radio industry. Had the medium become a "top-down" industry, to use the vernacular of the day? (See Figure 1.15.)

FIGURE 1.15 In the early 1990s stories like this revealed the downside of one of radio's most turbulent years. Courtesy *Broadcasting*.

FCC SAYS RADIO IS IN 'PROFOUND FINANCIAL DISTRESS'

"Small [radio] stations—the bulk of the industry—are in profound financial distress."

That's the first line and bottom line of an internal FCC report on the state of the radio business distributed to Chairman Alfred Sikes and other commissioners last week.

"Radio today is a world of large haves and little have-nots," the report says. "Industry revenue and profits are overwhelmingly concentrated in the small number of large radio stations, while most small stations struggle to remain solvent."

One indicator of the "distress": by the FCC's count, 287 radio stations have gone dark, 53% in just the last 12 months.

Not surprisingly, the findings undergird pending proposals to relax the radio ownership rules, which prohibit a company from owning more than one AM or FM in a market and from owning more than 12 AM's and 12 FM's. (A minority-controlled company may own up to 14 stations of each type.) The FCC may vote on the ownership proposal in March or April.

"The potential economies from consolidation would materially improve industry profitability," the report says. "If a conservative 10% of general and administrative costs could be eliminated, for example, the savings would raise industry profitability by 30%," the report continues. "Alternatively, these savings could immediately boost flat per-station programing outlays by 5% and still raise industry profits by 15%," the report says.

The top-50 large-market stations, just one-half of 1% of the some 10,000 stations now on the air, account for 11% of industry revenue and 50% of industry profit in 1990, the report says. Yet stations with less than $1 million in annual revenues—75% of all stations—on average, lost money in 1990, it says. —MJ

Many people consider 1991 to have been one of the worst years ever for radio. "As a result of the proliferation of stations, the excessively high prices paid for them during the deregulatory buying and selling binge of the late 1980s, and the recession, more than half of the stations in the country ran in the red," observed Rick Sklar of Sklar Communications. (Mr. Sklar passed away shortly after this interview.)

Producer Ty Ford agreed with Sklar, adding, "The price fallout of the late 1980s and early 1990s was due in great part to the collapse of the property-value spiral that was started by deregulation and the negative effect that investors had on the broadcasting business. This resulted in depressed or reduced salaries and an inability to make equipment updates due to the need to pay off highly leveraged station loans."

According to leading radio consultant Kent Burkhart, "The recession in the first third of the 1990s crippled financing of radio properties. The banks were under highly leveraged transaction (HLT) rules regarding radio loans; thus the value of stations dropped by one-third to one-half. The recession created advertising havoc too. Instead of five-deep buys, we were looking for one through three deep. Emotional sales pitches were rejected. Stations streamlined costs due to the economic slump. Airshifts were expanded and promotion budgets slashed. The top ten to fifteen markets did reasonably well in the revenue column, but those markets outside of the top majors went searching for new ad dollars, which were difficult to find." The total value of radio station sales declined 65% in a 6-month period between 1990 and 1991, and radio revenues dropped 4% during the same period, according to statistics in *Broadcasting* magazine (September 9, 1991). All of this took place during a time when operating expenses rose. These were troubling figures when compared to the salad days of 1988 when $5.8 billion was paid for 955 radio stations.

Cash flow problems were the order of the day, and this resulted (as Ty Ford pointed out) in significant budgetary cuts. This was made very evident by a report in the December 1991 issue of *Broadcast Engineering* magazine that stated, "All radio budgets

show a decrease." The survey showed that budgets for equipment purchases were being delayed and that "planned spending for most areas is somewhat below last year's."

To counter the sharp reversal of fortunes, many broadcasters formed local marketing (also called *management*) agreements (LMAs) whereby one radio station leases time and/or facilities from another area station. The buzzword in the early 1990s became LMAs.

LMAs allowed radio stations to enter into economically advantageous, joint operating ventures, stated the editors of *Radio World*. They believed that LMAs should remain the province of the local marketplace and not be regulated by the federal government. The publication asserted that LMAs provide broadcasters a means of functioning during tough economic times and in a ferociously competitive marketplace.

Those who opposed LMAs feared that diversity would be lost as stations combined resources (signals, staffs, and facilities). A few years later, the relaxation of the duopoly rules would raise similar concerns. Proponents argued that this was highly improbable given the vast number of frequencies that light up the dial. In other words, there is safety in numbers, and the public will continue to be served. However, radio station general manager Pat McNally presciently observed, "In the long run LMAs and consolidation may cause a loss of available jobs in our business and help to continue the erosion of creative salesmanship and conceptual selling. Radio station sales staffs will become like small rep firms."

In the 1990s, Century 21 Programming's Dave Scott observed that LMAs had inspired some interesting arrangements. "Some of the novel partnerships include a suburban station north of Atlanta that bought a suburban station south of Atlanta and created one studio to feed them both. A similar situation occurred in San Francisco/San Jose, and I believe they're on the same frequency (or maybe a notch apart). Around Los Angeles, someone got two or three stations on the same frequency. Necessity is the mother of invention, they say."

Although many industry people were guardedly hopeful about the future of radio, many saw change as inevitable. "Major adjustments are being made as the consequence of the recent mini-crash. In the future, we will depend on fewer nonrevenue producers at stations. We'll see less people per facility. The belt will be tightened for good," notes Bill Campbell, former vice president and general manager of WSNE-FM in Providence, Rhode Island.

Rick Sklar accurately predicted that satellite-supplied stations would have a role in this. "To save money and stay in business, large numbers of stations are going satellite and others are turning to suppliers of twenty-four-hour formats for their programming because of the economic environment." (See Chapter 11 for more on syndicated programming.)

Fred Jacobs, president of Jacob's Media, assessed the state of the Fifth Estate: "In the first third of the 1990s, everything seemed to be converging, and radio's future was up in the air. Many operators were in debt and were feeling the pressures of a long economic recession. Similarly, the FCC was not providing regulatory focus. There was no consensus about the legality of LMAs, multiple station ownership in the same market, and so on. Format fragmentation had made for a more competitive environment in most cities, including medium markets. The available revenue pie was now being split among more players. Like cable television, radio has become very niche-oriented. To make matters even more uncertain, Digital Audio Broadcasting (DAB) was and remains a murky issue. It's coming, but we don't really have a fix on when and in what form. Will it create even more outlets? If so, where will existing broadcasters end up and what will be the value of their properties? Will there be enough advertising revenue to go around?"

Despite the medium's shaky start in the 1990s, publisher Eric Rhoads possessed a positive outlook. "I believe that radio is poised for a strong future over the next ten years. Cable is floundering in its local sales efforts, and TV is having huge problems. Nationally the networks are still high-priced and have reduced viewing. In the end, radio is the only stable medium. It is targeted and cost-effective. This fact will keep the industry alive for a long time. Radio will survive and thrive."

Then came the financial crash of 2008. The dramatic downturn in the economy impacted radio station values and brought a decline in advertisers, who were adjusting their budgets in light of the recession. Among the casualties was the Tribune Company. Observed its COO, Randy Michaels, at the time this text was being revised, "We aren't quite on the ropes yet. We're restructuring our debt, so we'll be around for a while yet." In the end, observes Entercom's Operations Manager, Dave Neugesser, "While the economy may be wreaking havoc, just as important are the new audio platforms that have grown over the past 5 years. Radio has the unfortunate and unfair image of being viewed as 'old' media. There are newer, shinier objects that have become even sexier than radio, so the tide has turned away from the medium on multiple fronts. Hard work and ingenuity are key to its future success and survival."

As 2008 came to an end, Nielsen's "Media Week" reported, "For the second consecutive year, radio revenue is expected to drop 7% this year to $16.7 billion, the lowest total in more than five years. And that's not even the bottom. Next year radio revenue could plummet 10%, going as low as $15 billion."

Consolidations, Downsizings, and Clusters

As the medium entered the middle of the 1990s, it was doing more than just fine. The headlines in the industry trade publications revealed exactly how well the medium had recovered: "Radio Draws Advertisers as Economy Strengthens" (*Broadcasting*, May 1994), "Recovery" (*Radio Ink*, December 1993), "Radio Revenues Hit One Billion in May" (*Radio World*, August 1994), "National Spot Revenue up 38%" (*Broadcasting*, May 1995).

The primary cause of this dramatic upsurge was the relaxation of FCC rules, foremost among them station ownership caps and duopoly. With the advent of the Telecommunications Act of 1996, individual companies could own several stations in the same market (up to eight in large markets and no limits on national totals – at this writing, radio station ownership limits were being reviewed by the FCC), and this spurred active trading and mergers of broadcast properties. (See Figure 1.16.) The idea was to reduce competition and thus overhead. The consolidation and downsizing prompted by LMAs would pick up steam with the elimination of the duopoly rule, which prevented dual station ownership in the same market. Greater Media's David Pearlman says, "The Telecommunications Act of 1996 is the biggest piece of legislation in radio history. It has changed everything."

Telecommunications Act of 1996

FCC Home | Search | Updates | E-Filing | Initiatives | For Consumers | Find People

FCC > 1996 Telecom Act   site map

Search:
[   ] Go
Help | Advanced

Act Text

FCC Materials

Implementation Proceedings

Other Resources

Telecommunications Act of 1996

The Telecommunications Act of 1996 is the first major overhaul of telecommunications law in almost 62 years. The goal of this new law is to let anyone enter any communications business -- to let any communications business compete in any market against any other.

The Telecommunications Act of 1996 has the potential to change the way we work, live and learn. It will affect telephone service -- local and long distance, cable programming and other video services, broadcast services and services provided to schools.

The Federal Communications Commission has a tremendous role to play in creating fair rules for this new era of competition. At this Internet site, we will provide information about the FCC's role in implementing this new law, how you can get involved and how these changes might impact you.

This page will include information listing the proceedings the FCC will complete to open up local phone markets, increase competition in long distance and other steps. You will find copies of news releases summarizing action, announcements of meetings where these items will be discussed, and charts describing the work ahead of us and where (within the FCC) and when it will be completed. **Please note:** some of the links on this page lead to resources outside the FCC. The presence of these links should not be taken as an endorsement by the FCC of these sites or their content.

For more information about the referenced documents, contact the person listed on the document.

Please let us know what topics most interest you or where you have questions about this new law. We will soon begin to post a series of Questions & Answers with Commission officials designed to answer your questions.

Text of the Act

The FCC maintains ASCII Text and Adobe Acrobat versions *(128 pages)* of the Telecommunications Act of 1996, as well as WordPerfect and Adobe Acrobat versions *(335 pages)* of the completely updated Communications Act of 1934, as amended by the 1996 Act. The official citation for the new Act is: Telecommunications Act of 1996, Pub. LA. No. 104-104, 110 Stat. 56 (1996). The official printed slip law is available from the Government Printing Office.

Materials from the FCC

- Revised schedule of proceedings to implement the Act. This implementation schedule is an outline of statutory requirements pursuant to the Telecommunications Act of 1996 and is a guide to the actions taken by the FCC to implement the Act. The schedule is divided into five sections. The first section identifies the specific issues and the bureau handling those issues. The second section contains the statutory language and page references to S. Rept. 230, 104th Cong. 2nd Sess. (1996). The third section identifies the FCC proceeding to implement the statutory requirement including the bureau docket number and the FCC number of the documents released related to the proceeding. The fourth and fifth sections contain information regarding the timetable and status of the proceeding. (Revised January 13, 1997)

- The Report on FCC Implementation of Telecommunications Act of 1996 is a cumulative report of all actions taken since February 8, 1996, by the FCC to implement the Act. This report has two sections: (1) Commission Actions and (2) Facilitating Public Information.

- Transcript of Proceedings from the FCC Telemedical Advisory Committee meeting on September 17, 1996 [Text Version | WordPerfect Version].

- Transcript of Proceedings from the FCC Telemedical Advisory Committee meeting on July 11, 1996 [Text Version | WordPerfect Version].

- Chairman Hundt's Statement and related Report on the FCC Implementation of the Telecommunications Act presented to the Subcommittee on Telecommunications and Finance, Committee on Commerce of the U.S. House of Representatives on July 18, 1996.

- Transcript of Proceedings from the FCC Telemedical Advisory Committee meeting on June 12,

FIGURE 1.16
Telecommunications Act of 1996 as outlined on the FCC's Web site and a Web site inspired by the impact it inspired.

Observes Lynn Christian, "Consolidation – market by market – is the word best describing what was happening in commercial radio in the 1990s. The legal authority to own and operate several radio stations in almost every market has rapidly changed radio's landscape. Radio station operators have become more like local cable operators, offering a variety of formats on the FM and AM dials."

One alarming effect of consolidation and subsequent downsizing for aspiring broadcasters is the reduction of available jobs. "Individual station staffs get small as companies grow in station holdings. A direct result of duopoly softening and the increase in ownership limits is fewer jobs, more generalization, and less specialization. Jacks and Jills of all trades will be valuable. Group presidents will be taking jobs as station managers, especially in clusters or multiple station operations," observes Ed Shane, president of Shane Media.

Another concern inspired by consolidation is the potential loss of programming diversity. Christian adds, "While cost savings and profits are central to the concept behind downsizing and multiple ownership, the creative forces in radio are taking a hit. In point of fact, in the past few years no exciting new programming ideas have been developed."

On this topic, Jay Williams, Jr., observes,

Many argue that consolidation is bad, charging that radio programming has become less innovative and diverse, that local radio news is in decline, and the lack of competition within each local market has driven up rates for advertisers. Others counter that radio "research" combined with the demand for higher ratings had already eliminated programming innovation. Proponents for consolidation point to the stations previously competing in the same format head-to-head that are now co-owned allowing one of the stations to carve out a new format. They suggest that television and 24-hour cable news competition, plus the rising costs of radio news programming, had already precipitated the decline of radio news well before consolidation, and that new technologies, such as the continuous news updates on the Internet, have only accelerated the pace. And they point to the increasing variety of other media and promotional options open to advertisers as the reasons that radio rates will always remain competitive. It might be better if consolidation were viewed as being neither good nor bad but as a reaction to the changing realities of business.

Williams gives a brief overview of a major West Coast cluster inspired by the consolidation approach:

Clear Channel's greater San Diego cluster consists of 13 stations. They also oversee two additional suburban stations in Temecula, California about 50 miles away. The Temecula stations simulcast two of the San Diego stations but add local content. The two suburban stations have a local sales manager and local sales staff. In addition to the stations, they also operate Clear Channel Traffic (similar to, but competitors of, Shadow and Metro traffic) and the Padres sports network as separate business entities out of this facility.

Despite the many concerns, business improved after the mid-1990s. The dollar volume of station transactions (number of stations changing hands) approved by the FCC soared. Entering the new millennium, the radio business was robust, to say the least. Annual revenues were heading toward the

FIGURE 1.17
AM/FM share of listening. Courtesy National Database.

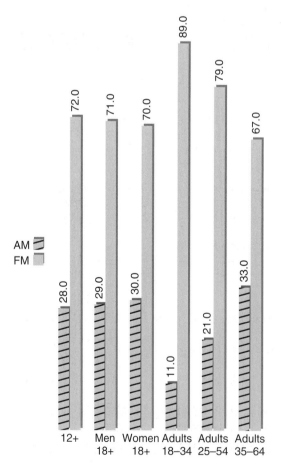

AM
FM

72.0   71.0   70.0   89.0   79.0   67.0

28.0   29.0   30.0   11.0   21.0   33.0

12+   Men   Women   Adults   Adults   Adults
       18+   18+   18–34   25–54   35–64

$20 billion mark. A handful of radio corporations, many owning hundreds of stations, recorded yearly earnings in the billion-dollar range. However, by 2006, due to a variety of factors – namely increased competition, *Radio Business Report* and other industry publications were charting the downward trajectory of the medium's annual revenues.

Meanwhile, the large radio station holdings groups began downsizing the number of properties they owned. In fact, many mega radio groups (like Clear Channel) returned to private ownership forsaking Wall Street. The trend in what is called "de-consolidation" was well underway as this new edition was being prepared.

Buying and Selling

Today, brokerage firms handle the sale of many radio stations. "It's difficult to overlook the importance of Wall Street and the financial community in the future of radio," notes Ed Shane. Bill Campbell, co-owner of Blue River Communications, says the future is now. "Wall Street is where much of the buying and selling of radio outlets occurs nowadays. Things have changed to where stations are sold through lawyers and brokerage houses more than they are from broadcaster to broadcaster. Those are pretty much bygone days, and that is kind of sad. It became the 'three-piece-suiters' game in the 1990s. There is little direct negotiating, no bargaining between owners over a drink at the corner pub. Stations are commodities to be bought and sold by people who sometimes have little appreciation or understanding of what radio is really all about. Of course, the economic inertia of the first part of this decade inspired more direct negotiations (strategic alliances) between owners, and I think that is good. I'm also detecting a move to drive the MBAs out of our business. Broadcasters who gain general experience beyond just management are the future."

Money And Finance

RADIO INK DEAL TRACKER

PROPERTY	BUYER	SELLER	PRICE	BROKER
WEVD-AM New York	ABC Radio Inc.	Forward Broadcasting	$78 M	Media Venture Partners
Brill Media stations	Regent Communications	Brill Media	$62 M	
Sabre Communications stations	Backyard Broadcasting	Sabre Communications	$42 M	Patrick Communications
WKSM-FM, WNCV-FM, WYZB-FM, WZNS-FM, WFTW-AM	Cumulus Media	East Mississippi Broadcasters	$30 M	
KKRG-FM Albuquerque, KIOT-FM Los Lunas, KOSZ-FM Rio Rancho, KKSS-FM & KRQS-FM Santa Fe	Hispanic Broadcasting	Simmons Media Group	$22 M	Star Media Group
KURS-AM San Diego	Hi-Favor Broadcasting	Pacific Spanish Network	$8.5 M	
WZBR-FM Kinston, WHRT-FM Morehead City, WNBR-FM Oriental, WCBZ-FM Williamston, NC	Archway Broadcasting	Eastern Carolina Broadcast	$6.5 M	Snowden Assoc.
KJON-AM Carrollton, TX	Family Worship Center	Monroe-Stephens Broadcasting	$4.2 M	MGMT Services/ The Connell Co.
WKCL-FM Pekin, IL	AAA Entertainment	Kelly Communications	$4 M	Media Services Group
WKCD-FM Pawcatuck, CT	John Fuller	AAA Entertainment	$3.75 M	Media Services Group
KFIG-AM Fresno	Radio Central LLC	Big Dawg Broadcasting	$2 M	
KSLK-FM Visalia	Nelson Gomez	New Visalia Broadcasting	$1.2 M	
WBYA-FM Islesboro, ME	Mariner Broadcasting LP	Gopher Hill Communications	$1.15 M	

SOURCE: BIA MEDIA ACCESS PRO

FIGURE 1.18
The price for stations continued to climb in the early 2000s. Courtesy Radio Ink.

For their services, brokers receive an average commission of 7–8% on sales, and in some cases they earn additional incentives based on the size of the transaction. In recent years, brokers have been very successful in negotiating large profits for their clients (see Figure 1.18).

Brokerage firms promote the sale of stations through ads in industry trade magazines, direct mailings, and appearances at broadcast conferences. Interested buyers are provided with all the pertinent data concerning a station's geographical location, physical holdings, operating parameters, programming, and income history, as well as economic, competitive, and demographic information about the area within reach of the station's signal.

Another recent approach to the buying and selling of radio properties is the auction method, although this means of selling a station is perceived by some as a kind of last-resort effort at getting rid of profitless stations, most of which are AM. Owing to the upsurge in radio's fortunes, this approach has declined.

The average price of an AM station in the late 1980s was $450,000, with some selling for as little as a few thousand dollars and others for as much as several million. In 1986 New York station WMCA-AM sold for $11 million, and in 1992, WFAN-AM received a bid of $70 million, proving that AM stations can still command enormous sums. In 2000, Clear Channel paid $24 billion for AMFM's group of radio stations.

The average price for FM stations is higher than it is for AM. In the early 1990s the average price for an FM station exceeded several million, and in the mid-2000s was in the tens, if not hundreds, of millions. Meanwhile, at this writing, many AM outlets sell in the hundreds of thousands. For example, in the spring of 2006, *Inside Radio* reported that KJRG in Newton, Kansas, sold for $600,000 and WADA in western North Carolina went for $350,000.

Many AM broadcasters look for fulltime status, improved reception, and stereo to increase the value of their properties in the coming years, although the stereo conversion of the band is hardly seen as the panacea it once was. Perhaps most important is the fact that many await the conversion to digital audio broadcasting to level the playing field with FM.

Despite the bullishness of the past decade in the station acquisition market, Robin Martin, CEO of the Deer River Group, expresses concerns about the tactics used by station owners to keep property values high, "The radio industry is too defensive and is not pursuing innovative strategies for creating new streams of revenue. How the industry in general is responding to more competition and new technologies does not inform the average owner (not a major group owner) about how to succeed in this changing environment on a local level. Each market, each owner, and each station will have unique sets of circumstances that would define the optimal strategies for that situation. As I visit different markets and talk with station owners and managers, I find that there are creative plans for success of many different types in markets of all size and characteristics. Forget what the overall industry pundits and reports say. Study the specific target market to understand how to develop the strategies that will begin or continue to generate advertiser loyalty and the willingness to commit with more advertising and promotion money on the station. Radio generates enough revenues in most markets to give individual owners opportunities to make good returns on their investments. Regardless of the dire news on the national level, there are successes to be earned in many markets. The difficult truth is that, with some exceptions for turnarounds, gone are the days of easy double-digit increases in sales from traditional ad revenues. Cost control and the generation of creative concepts to increase advertiser stickiness and new types of revenues are necessary ingredients for financial stability, growth, and enhanced station values."

Media broker Doug Ferber offers some closing thoughts on the state of radio station values in the mid-2000s as well as an interesting prediction, "Overall, things are down because advertising revenue is flat with no sign of growth rates getting back to mid-to-upper single digits any time soon. Listening levels of young demos are about the same despite views to the contrary (there's recent research to support this). Satellite is dead as it exists today. It's had a negligible effect on mainstream radio revenue. Check the stock prices."

Digital and HD Radio Revolution

DAB makes analog AM and FM outmoded systems. With the great popularity of home and portable digital music equipment (CD, MP3s, iPods), broadcasters are forced to convert their signals to remain competitive. Thus, DAB, or High Definition (HD) as it is more popularly called, looms large in the future of radio. The days of analog signal propagation are numbered. (For an explanation of both digital and analog signaling, see Chapters 9 and 10.)

In the mid-1980s, compact disc players were introduced to the consumer market. Today, CD players no longer rank as the top consumer item for home music reproduction, because they have all but been replaced by iPods and MP3s. Turntables have long gone by the board, and the analog tape cassette market is consigned to the history books. Digital is here to stay, at least until something better comes along.

At first broadcasters viewed DAB as a threat. The National Association of Broadcasters (NAB) looked at the new sound technology adversarially. In an interview in the July 23, 1990, issue of *RadioWeek*, John Abel, NAB's executive vice president of operations, stated, "DAB is a threat and anyone who plans to stay in business for a while needs to pay careful attention."

As time went on, DAB was regarded as a *fait accompli*, something that was simply going to happen. Soon broadcasters assumed a more proactive posture regarding the technology, and then the concern shifted to where to put the new medium and how to protect existing broadcast operations.

Early on, NAB proposed locating DAB in the L-band portion of the electromagnetic spectrum. It also argued for in-band placement. Eventually the FCC saw fit to recommend that DAB be allocated room in the S-band, and it took its proposal to the World Administrative Radio Conference (WARC) held in Spain in February 1992. This spectrum designation is expected to help in-band terrestrial development. In-band, on-channel (IBOC) digital signaling, developed by iBiquity Digital Corporation's Glynn Walden, permits broadcasters to remain on their existing frequencies. This is something they favor, as satellite DAB signal transmission is regarded as a significant threat to the local nature of U.S. broadcasting. On the other hand, many countries are fully supportive of a satellite DAB system because they do not have the number of stations the United States possesses and thus lack the coverage and financial investment.

Of course, digitized terrestrial radio (called HD Radio) renders existing analog receivers obsolete. This is cause for some anxiety among broadcasters who wonder how quickly the buying public will convert. However, considerable confidence exists since consumers' huge appetitite for new and improved sound shows no sign of abating. As of this writing, several manufacturers are offering HD receivers at prices that are becoming more and more affordable and competitive and a number of car manufacturers provide HD Radio in their latest models. Digital converters are also available at a modest price.

Considered another plus of digital radio is its capacity to do other things. For example, iBiquity has developed a technology that allows those stations broadcasting digitally to transmit data to portable digital services, including cell phones. This is attractive to the station operator's bottom line. The ability to multicast (provide side-channel transmissions) is yet another major plus for HD Radio. Known as HD2, it allows the medium to provide additional program streams (two to eight channels) to the listening audience.

America is a nation of audiophiles, demanding high-quality sound. Analog broadcasting cannot compete with the interference-free

FIGURE 1.19
HD Radio advertisement. Courtesy iBiquity.

reception and greater frequency dynamics of digital signals. Digital signaling heralds a new age in radio broadcasting. Jeff Tellis, former president of the IBS, explains why. "The reason for the great interest in digital broadcasting is its considerable number of advantages." Among them are:

- Significantly improved coverage using significantly less power
- Dramatic improvement in the quality of the signal; compare CD to vinyl
- More precise coverage control using multiple transmitters similar to cellular phone technology
- No adjacent channel reception problems
- On-channel booster capabilities eliminating the need to use separate frequencies to extend the same signal
- Easy transmission of auxiliary services, including format information, traffic, weather, text, and selective messaging services
- Sharing of transmitting facilities – common transmitter and antenna

Telecommunications professor Ernest Hakanen expands on the cost advantages of digital broadcasting. "DAB also promises to be economically efficient. Since there is no interstation interference between digital signals and because of the appeal of the spectrum efficiency provided by the interleaved environment, all of the channel operators in an area could utilize the same transmitter. The transmission facilities could be operated by a consortium for the construction, operation, and maintenance of the common transmission plant. Antenna height for DAB systems is also lower than current FM standards. Electrical power conservation and savings are a huge advantage of DAB."

Picking up on Hakanen's point about consolidating broadcast operations, Lynn Christian says, "The consortium (radio station malls or clusters) approach to maintaining and operating a station is commonplace because of economic reasons, and HD Radio is very conducive to a collaborative relationship among broadcasters."

Prior to the WARC meeting in 1992, NAB's DAB Task Force proposed a set of standards to ensure that the technology would operate effectively. The specifications included:

- CD-quality sound
- Enhanced coverage area
- Accommodation of existing AM and FM frequencies
- Immunity to multipath interference
- Immunity to stoplight fades
- No interference to existing AM and FM broadcasters
- DAB system interference immunity
- Minimization of transmission costs
- Receiver complexity
- Additional data capacity
- Reception area threshold

After nearly a century of analog signal transmission, radio is venturing into the digital domain, which will keep it relevant to the demands of a technologically sophisticated listening marketplace as it embarks on its next 100 years. As of this writing hundreds of radio stations across the country offer digital signals, and the majority are also providing expanded listening options with HD2 service. At several industry gatherings in the first half of the 2000s, former NAB president Eddie Fritts presciently proclaimed HD Radio as the wave of the medium's future, saying "Transitioning to digital will give radio even better opportunities to serve [its] listeners."

Today, not all industry observers see HD/HD2 as the solution to the drop in music radio listening. Observes Mark Ramsey of Mercury Media Research, "Will digital help reverse radio's declining audience? Absolutely not." Counters Dave Neugesser, "It's not something that's going to happen overnight. HD2 gives radio an infinite dial with incalculable choices, but it won't impact the market as fast as some would like. Before this happens, it has to be standard equipment in new cars, and people have to buy HD radios. It's a steep hill, but it can be surmounted."

Satellite and Cable Radio

Radio broadcasters retain a wary eye on the ever-evolving digital audio services being made available by satellite companies (see Figure 1.20). It is the threat of increased

Reader poll: Will Sirus-XM Satellite Radio be in business by this time next year?

No	49.13%
Yes	46.51%
No opinion	4.37%

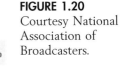

FIGURE 1.20
Courtesy National Association of Broadcasters.

competition that inspires concern for the new and evolving audio options. Although broadcasters have long employed satellite programming and network services to enhance their over-the-air terrestrial signals, the idea of a direct-to-consumer alternative has not been greeted with enthusiasm, especially since these nonterrestrial signals are available in digital sound, something broadcasters are just beginning to offer. For several years, the FCC debated the question of satellite radio. In the waning years of the 1990s, the feds gave licenses to companies, such as CD Radio and XM Satellite Radio, to launch their services. Meanwhile, the NAB vociferously argued against its introduction into the local marketplace. Despite all the brouhaha, XM Satellite launched its service in September 2001 and a year later claimed nearly a quarter of a million subscribers. Less than a year after XM Satellite rolled out its audio service, Sirius Satellite Radio debuted. It quickly became clear to terrestrial broadcasters that there was a new kid in town, one who would further accelerate the splintering of the radio listening audience. In 2008, both satellite radio services merged, with Mel Karmazin at the helm of the renamed SiriusXM.

Over the air broadcasters contend that their local orientation betters the services of the satellite audio companies, which are nationally based programmers. Former Infinity Broadcasting senior vice president, David Pearlman, says, "Broadcast radio is locally rooted and the satellite companies can't fulfill that need at the present time. This will be its saving grace and aid in its ability to withstand this frontal attack. With its selling of local news, traffic, weather, events, personalities, and services, the product differentiation will work in the industry's favor."

Satellite radio is fee driven and offers a wide array of program options, which include an array of famous personalities, among them Howard Stern, Bob Dylan, and Martha Stewart. In all, satellite radio provides some 200 channels to subscribers. A monthly cost of $12.95 is charged for the coast-to-coast signals (continuously in receiver range), but subscribers also have to invest money for receiver equipment. SiriusXM has signed contracts with car manufacturers to install their digital receivers and predicts the acquisition of an impressive segment of the drivetime listening audience in the not too distant future. At this writing, satellite radio was approaching 14 million subscribers, which for a company whose primary revenue is based on "signups" is encouraging.

In the mid-2000s, many longtime broadcast radio listeners were making the switch to satellite for reasons similar to those articulated by media scholar and author Christopher Sterling: "Like many older Americans, I used to listen to radio, especially in the car . . . but in the past year here in Washington, the medium has left me in the lurch. I used to listen to three stations (usually one at a time), but all have dumped friendly formats to slave after programming already available on other outlets in this market. The main public radio station dropped a decades-long classical music and talk format to rely totally on the latter – including British talk shows that keep giving me numbers I can call in London (I note with an 'I told you so' feeling that their audiences and donations are down as a result). The remaining commercial classical music station got caught in a shift of Clear Channel station frequencies and now uses a fringe transmitter that can't put a decent signal into downtown. And most recently, the oldies station that had played music from the 60s and 70s 'moved ahead' and now focuses on the late 70s and the 80s. Why do programmers presume nobody of 55 matters? Thank heaven for satellite radio where genuine choice thrives. I almost never turn on a radio anymore."

Former XM programming chief Lee Abrams discounted the potential impact on his medium of terrestrial HD Radio. "I'm pretty sure these guys will screw up HD. They'll add a Blues channel but it'll play 200 blues songs and be run by guys who don't know much about the blues beyond Stevie Ray Vaughn." And about the potential of increased local programming on broadcast radio stations influencing the fate of his medium, Abrams said, "I doubt local radio will ever get back to the so-called 'community.' In fact, they're going the other way by cutting costs and taking on more remote voice track and syndicated programming."

To compound the competition for the listening audience, cable companies provide in-home music services for most of their subscribers. For example, Comcast cable users receive more than 50 channels of music that are often quite niche specific. These commercial-free channels of diverse nonstop music, replete with on-screen information about what is being played, are very attractive to subscribers and frequently result in the loss of yet another portion of traditional radio's listening audience.

That said, many media observers believe satellite radio's prospects for succeeding in the face of myriad new audio competitors and mounting debt is not good. Jason Insalaco of The Kelton Agency says, "Satellite radio's subscription-based model has not yet reach critical mass, and I'm not sure it ever will."

Internet Radio

In the early 2000s, many listeners accessed their favorite radio station via their computers. However, with the specter of costly copyright royalty fees imposed on stations streaming music, their numbers dwindled and the future of Internet radio was cast in doubt. To mollify the situation,

a proposed royalty rate compromise bill, known as the Small Webcaster Settlement Act (H.R. 5469), was passed by Congress. It was designed to mitigate the burden, so the future for the medium has brightened. Rates established by the Digital Millennium Copyright Act of 1998 had forced many radio broadcasters – both commercial and noncommercial – to reconsider their plans to Web cast. At the time radio industry publisher Eric Rhoads made this observation, "With the current fees, the economics do not make sense for anyone intent on building a business from this. Unless Congress steps in and makes a change, the RIAA fees are unreasonable and will kill the music side of online radio."

Despite the upheaval resulting from the "pay for play" issue, most broadcasters felt that it was important to retain a Web presence, even if it meant offering no music programming. It was thought that stations broadcasting news, sports, talk, and other nonmusic forms of programming were the likeliest to remain in the webcasting business. Maintaining a Web site for promotional purposes, even without audio streaming, was perceived as a worthwhile endeavor. Commented Jay Williams, Jr., "In the initial surge of the dot.com boom, radio stations rushed to create web sites that included station, music and local event information as well as billboard ads. After the Internet bloom faded in 2001, many stations stopped streaming audio and many radio web sites languished. Station web sites are again considered essential, and streaming over the Internet is seen as a critical, additional distribution platform for terrestrial radio stations. As more national and local advertisers demand a web site presence as part of their radio buys, stations have also learned the benefits of using these sites to relate programming and promotion information. Station web sites can give listeners direct and immediate access to personalities and can be used for listener research, both of which can improve a station's connection with the audience and the on-air product."

In spite of the formidable issues confronting webcasters, the RAB determined that over 4000 stations were streaming their content as of April 2002, and Arbitron/

Edison Media Research calculated that online radio listening actually grew from 14% in 1999 to 23% in 2001. Meanwhile, Measure-Cast reported that Internet radio listening was continuing to grow a year later, so the practice was far from moribund. *Radio Ink* magazine cited Jazz FM and Virgin Radio in London, L-Love Radio in Sacramento, ESPN Radio in Connecticut, and WQXR/FM Radio in New York as the top five simulcast streamers during the summer of 2002.

Indeed, today stations continue to view the Internet as a viable supplement to their on-air signals, especially for promotion and audience research purposes. Interactive radio is a growing reality, as is the opportunity for everyone with the right computer and software to be a broadcaster or cybercaster. With an Internet encoder, the home user can transmit to an international audience. This prospect prompts a collective sigh from station managers, who are losing track of the new forms of competition.

Notes longtime broadcaster Lynn Christian, "The major concern regarding the future of radio is centered on new competi-tion from satellite, cable, and online sources. Those companies that are planning to partner with these new media choices, and develop data services, will undoubtedly be the big winners in the twenty-first century. Broadcast radio, as I have known it during the past 50 years, will not be the same in the next few years. But what American business is the same now? These are revolutionary times in radio and in the world."

Jason Insalaco, observes:

Radio executives programming in the rapidly changing media landscape must embrace the technological revolution that is upon them. Cell phones, the Internet, MP3 players, the iPod, and videogames are vying for the audience's attention. Programmers must heed these encroachments on terrestrial radio or else accept extinction. Rather than fear the new and evolving audio media, traditional radio needs to embrace it for its own benefit. Radio websites are great places for listeners to find out about the station's personalities, music, contests, and events. Websites are cyber-extensions of the over the air station brand. Station websites also enhance audience interactivity and constitute another revenue source for a station.

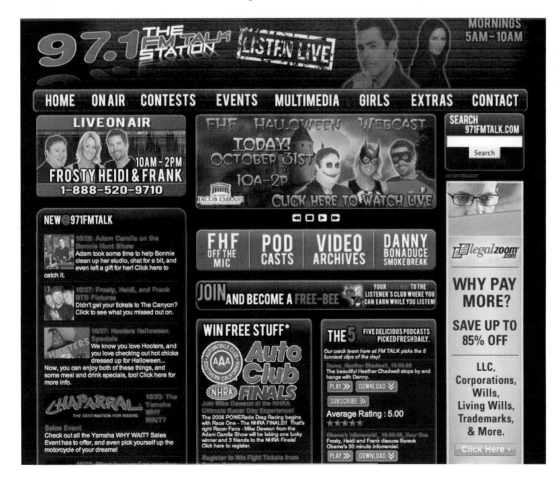

FIGURE 1.21
Stations employ websites to extend their brand. Courtesy 971FMTalk.

In 2009, the biggest challenge confronting Internet presence related to fees charged to provide music. States Paul Kemp of Backbone Networks, an Internet radio software provider:

> The performance royalty rates is probably the largest obstacle. Currently, in the US, there are a number of different rates and laws that apply to internet performance royalty rates. This includes the Small Webcasters Settlement that requires stations of a certain size to pay a percentage of their revenue. There is also the commercial Copyright Review Board (CRB) rate that requires internet radio stations to track performances of a particular piece. This rate escalates through next year [2009] when it is up for renewal again. The reason this is a big challenge for internet radio is that the rate is higher than for other broadcast mediums, like terrestrial and satellite broadcasts. If the rate was equal across all broadcast media we suspect there would be a rush to internet broadcasting because of the more precise listener statistics that can be generated and the opportunity to more precisely advertise to a particular target. The royalty rate discussion masks a broader issue that needs to be confronted. The strength of the internet is that it is worldwide. As such an internet broadcaster would have to pay performance royalties to all of the Professional Rights Organizations where a connection terminates (the country from where the listener connects).

Cognizant of the many obstacles and challenges that exist in the age of the Internet, most radio broadcasters forecast a long-term relation between the two mediums, one that will benefit both. As radio heads warp speed into this "future world," it is obvious that aspiring broadcasters will have to know their way around a computer, because the audio studio will exist both in the ether and in cyberspace. For those interested in this aspect of the medium, Radio and Internet Newsletter (RAIN) provides a daily update on the key issues involving radio and the Internet.

Mobile Music Services

Cell phones, with music downloading capabilities, and MP3s and iPods constitute the biggest competitive challenge to radio, and with the ever-expanding WiFi and WiMax universe, this will only increase. Mark Ramsey says, "We are fast-entering a time when 'radio' will become a feature of other things rather than simply a destination unto itself, as it has been up until now." Although many media observers predict that downloading will continue to draw huge numbers of young listeners away from traditional radio, Emmis Communication's VP of Programming, Jimmy Steal, thinks otherwise:

> I don't agree that there is a mass exodus of young people away from radio to downloading media. According to the Paragon Media Youth Radio and New Media study conducted earlier this year (Spring 2008), 14–24 year old males and females who "listen to music on FM over the air more than they listen to music from other sources" surged from 27% in 2007 to 41% in 2008. All MP3 players need to be fed new music! Check out the latest generation Microsoft Zune model w/the built in FM receiver. You can bet Microsoft did a lot of research Before making this radio upgrade. Can we be doing an even better job of attracting young listeners? Absolutely, in the future radio needs to permeate cell phones as well as all mobile media.

Steal's boss at Emmis, Jeff Smulyan, agrees:

> While there has been a migration to iPods, recent research indicates that most new music is discovered by traditional radio (65%). That's why Zune has added a tagging device to its new Zunes, which lets people buy songs they hear on the radio included in the Zune. Our goal as an industry is to have a radio embedded in all portable devices (iPods, PDAs, and all cell

FIGURE 1.22
The Apple iPod represents yet another competitive threat to broadcast radio. The youth listening market has enthusiastically embraced the new audio alternative, causing further anxiety among already besieged radio station programmers and managers.

phones) within the next five years We think radio is a perfect complement to portable music consumption in the future. Nearly half of all cell phones sold outside the United States include radios. There is a Paragon research study that was featured in The New York Times recently the showed that among younger listeners, radio consumption has actually increased in the last year as iPod fatigue begins to occur.

Michael A. Krasness, head of Oxysys, a mobile music networking service, expands on the virtues of his enterprise:

> For the listener, traditional music radio – both over-the-air and Internet delivery – is about listening to tracks the user already knows, plus music discovery by the radio station's playlist, driven by an ad-based revenue model. Mobile music services add to that by allowing interactive user selection of music, active participation in the music discovery process, and social networking. As similar ad-based revenue model may be augmented by e-commerce through integration of a store. Traditional radio certainly provides complementary services for our users. As a feature for our users, Oxy phling! includes simple, integrated access to a number of Internet radio stations. For the radio station, they now have access to our community of mobile users.

With Pandora Radio, Slacker, and other Internet-based mobilized audio services likely venturing into nonmusic areas, such as talk and sports, the competitive threat to broadcast and satellite radio looms larger than ever. On the upside, Consultant Ed Shane says, "these services have new apps for mobile phones that allow reception of terrestrial radio."

LPFM (Low-Power FM)

A microradio movement surfaced in the 1990s and raised the ire of both broadcast regulators and the industry. The debate positioned the NAB against what it labeled radio "pirates." After lengthy reflection, FCC Chairman William Kennard proposed rule-making designed to legitimize these unauthorized, tiny wattage outlets. The argument used to justify support of LPFMs cited the erosion of programming diversity in commercial radio as the consequence of widespread consolidation and mergers. According to Kennard this new species of

broadcaster would give voice to those alienated or disenfranchised by mainstream corporate radio. The FCC's proposal sought to create two types of new licenses on the FM band. Power would span 10 (LP10) to 100 (LP100) watts with service areas restricted to three to nine miles. Among many stipulations, the FCC requires that LPFM licensees be nonprofit organizations. This rule helped placate commercial broadcasters' concerns that the new category of stations would represent yet another competitive threat. The LPFM rules further require that this "sub" or "secondary" category of radio stations not interfere with the signals of regular full power outlets. As the FCC states, "LPFM stations are not protected from interference that may be received from other classes of FM station."

Perhaps the greatest threat to the existence of microstations is the looming conversion of regular radio outlets to IBOC digital. This will all but squeeze out any chance for the continued survival of the community-centric medium. Meanwhile, many proponents of LPFM have been alarmed by the micromedium's takeover by conservative religious broadcasters, which have been scooping up as many noncommercial frequencies (both primary and secondary) and translators as possible to spread their gospel.

Former executive director of now defunct Allston-Brighton Free Radio, Stephen Provizer, gives this view of the threatened medium. "As an open platform for all voices, we had two goals: to disseminate programming that would otherwise be unavailable and to empower our participants which, to the greatest extent possible, encompassed the entire community. The first goal becomes increasingly important as the range of consumer choice becomes narrower due to ongoing corporization and an obsession with demography-driven advertising. The second goal, participation, is driven by our belief that direct participation is the key to empowerment. If an individual in our media-drenched culture is going to be able to exercise critical judgment toward mainstream media, he or she must have the process demystified and clarified. Perhaps if media literacy education was more available in lower school this would not be necessary, but such is not now and has never been the case."

Radio and Government Regulations

Almost from the start it was recognized that radio could be a unique instrument for the public good. This point was never made more apparent than in 1912, when, according to legend (which was recently challenged by scholars who contend that others were involved), a young wireless operator named David Sarnoff picked up the distress signal from the sinking *Titanic* and relayed the message to ships in the vicinity, which then came to the rescue of those still alive. The survivors were the beneficiaries of the first attempt at regulating the new medium. The Wireless Ship Act of 1910 required that ships carrying 50 or more passengers have wireless equipment on board. The effective use of the medium from an experimental station in New York City's Wanamaker Building helped save 700 lives.

Radio's first practical application was as a means of communicating from ship to ship and from ship to shore. During the first decade of the twentieth century, Marconi's wireless invention was seen primarily as a way of linking the ships at sea with the rest of the world. Until that time, when ships left port they were beyond any conventional mode of communications. The wireless was a boon to the maritime services, including the Navy, which equipped each of its warships with the new device.

Coming on the heels of the *Titanic* disaster, the Radio Act of 1912 sought to expand the general control of radio on the domestic level. The secretary of commerce and labor was appointed to head the implementation and monitoring of the new legislation. The primary function of the act was to license wireless stations and operators. The new regulations empowered the Department of Commerce and Labor to impose fines and revoke the licenses of those who operated outside the parameters set down by the communications law.

Growth of radio on the national level was curtailed by World War I, when the government saw fit to take over the medium for military purposes. However, as the war raged on, the same young wireless operator, David Sarnoff, who supposedly had been instrumental in saving the lives of passengers on the ill-fated *Titanic*, was hard at work on a scheme to drastically modify the scope of the medium, thus converting it from an experimental and maritime communications apparatus to an appliance designed for use by the general public. Less than 5 years after the war's end, receivers were being bought by the millions, and radio as we know it today was born.

As explained earlier, the lack of regulations dealing with interference nearly resulted in the premature end of radio. By 1926 hundreds of stations clogged the airways, bringing pandemonium to the dial. The Radio Act of 1912 simply did not anticipate radio's new application. It was the Radio Act of 1927 that first approached radio as a mass medium. The Federal Regulatory Commission's five commissioners quickly implemented a series of actions that restored the fledgling medium's health.

The Communications Act of 1934 charged a seven-member commission with the responsibility of ensuring the efficient use of the airways, which the government views as a limited resource that belongs to the public and is leased to broadcasters. Over the years the FCC has concentrated its efforts on maximizing the usefulness of radio for the public's benefit. Consequently, broadcasters have been required to devote a portion of their airtime to programs that address important community and national issues. In addition, broadcasters have had to promise to serve as a constant and reliable source of information, while retaining certain limits on the amount of commercial material scheduled.

The FCC has steadfastly sought to keep the medium free of political bias and special-interest groups. In 1949, the commission implemented regulations making it necessary for stations that present a viewpoint to provide an equal amount of airtime to contrasting or opposing viewpoints. The Fairness Doctrine obliged broadcasters "to afford reasonable opportunity for the discussion of conflicting views of public importance." Later, it also stipulated that stations notify persons when attacks were made on them over the air.

Although broadcasters generally acknowledge the unique nature of their business, many have felt that the government's involvement has exceeded reasonable limits in a society based on a free-enterprise system. Because it is their money, time, and energy they are investing, broadcasters feel they should be afforded greater opportunity to determine their own programming.

In the late 1970s, a strong movement headed by Congressman Lionel Van Deerlin sought to reduce the FCC's role in broadcasting, to allow the marketplace to dictate how the industry conducted itself. Van Deerlin actually proposed that the Broadcast Branch of the commission be abolished and a new organization with much less authority be created. His bill was defeated, but out of his and others' efforts came a new attitude concerning the government's hold on the electronic media. President Reagan's antibureaucracy, free-enterprise philosophy gave impetus to the deregulation move already under way when he assumed office. The FCC, headed by Chairman Mark Fowler, expanded on the deregulation proposal that had been initiated by his predecessor, Charles Ferris. The deregulation decision eliminated the requirement that radio stations devote a portion of their airtime (8% for AM and 6% for FM) to nonentertainment programming of a public affairs nature. In addition, stations no longer had to undergo the lengthy process of ascertaining community needs as a condition of license renewal, and guidelines pertaining to the amount of time devoted to commercial announcements were eliminated. The rule requiring stations to maintain detailed program logs was also abolished. A simplified postcard license renewal form was adopted, and license terms were extended from 3 to 7 years. In a further step the commission raised the ceiling on the number of broadcast outlets a company or individual could own from 7 AM, 7 FM, and 7 television stations to 12 each. As of March 1992, the FCC saw fit to raise the caps on ownership again, this time to 30 AM and 30 FM. Later in the year, these were reduced to 18 AM and 18 FM. Three years later, with a Republican Congress in place, a new telecommunications bill proposed to eliminate ownership caps completely. The bill also sought to relax the cross-ownership rule, which kept a single entity from possessing a radio, TV, and newspaper company in the same market. Meanwhile, radio license terms were to be raised to 10 years.

On August 4, 1987, the FCC voted to eliminate the 38-year-old Fairness Doctrine, declaring it unconstitutional and no longer applicable to broadcasters. A month before, President Reagan had vetoed legislation that would have made the policy law.

The extensive updating of FCC rules and policy was based on the belief that the marketplace should serve as the primary regulator. Opponents of the reform feared that with their newfound freedom, radio stations would quickly turn their backs on community concerns and concentrate their full efforts on fattening their pocketbooks.

Those who support the position that broadcasters should first serve the needs of society are concerned that deregulation (unregulation) has further reduced the medium's "good citizen" role. "Radio, especially the commercial sector, has long since fallen down on its 'interest, convenience, and necessity' obligation born of the Radio Act of 1927. While a small segment of the industry does exert an effort to address the considerable problems facing society today, the overwhelming majority continue to be fixated on the financial bottom line. There needs to be more of a balance," observes Robert Hilliard, former FCC chief of public and educational broadcasting. Proponents of deregulation applauded the FCC's actions, contending that the listening audience would indeed play a vital role in determining the programming of radio stations, because the medium has to meet the needs of the public to prosper.

Although the government continues to closely scrutinize the actions of the radio industry to ensure that it operates in an efficient and effective manner, it is no longer perceived as the fearsome, omnipresent Big Brother it once was. Today, broadcasters more fully enjoy the fruits of a laissez-faire system of economy, although they are not immune to commission actions (see Figure 1.24).

In the spring of 1996, the Telecommunications bill (made a Telecommunications Act) mentioned earlier became a

FIGURE 1.23
A new kind of radio via the Internet. Courtesy Pandora.

PANDORA®
internet radio

reality, and ownership caps were all but eliminated. The act opened the floodgates for those radio groups wanting to vastly expand their portfolios. For example, by 2002, Clear Channel Radio had acquired nearly 1400 stations. Consequently, by the mid-2000s, localism had taken a substantial hit, as many of the major radio groups had replaced the indigenous broadcasts of their stations with voice-tracking and "out-of-town" programming.

In terms of what interests the FCC most regarding station acquisition, radio group CEO Robin Martin offers the following view: "Over the last decade and more, the Commission has relaxed the bureaucratic requirements for approval of the transfer of licenses to new owners. Most of the questions on the forms can be answered by checking boxes. However, simple as this process might seem, the check marks a new owner places in the boxes represent legal certifications by the proposed licensee and should not be taken lightly. The FCC has great interest in a certain few areas that qualify as threshold questions of eligibility to be a license holder. The percentage of foreign ownership is but one example. If the answers to these questions do not comply with FCC rules and regulations, the transfer will not be approved. However, all the non-threshold questions, while not necessarily individually disqualifying, may in the aggregate lead the FCC staff to inquire further about the response to clarify the details or to understand if the application is fatally defective or can be corrected or amended with supplemental information. The most important issue for the FCC is honesty. If an applicant answers a question dishonestly, the Commission will take swift action against the applicant should it discover falsehoods. The consequences of not being truthful with the Commission are more dire than if the answer was truthful and required more explanation or even a waiver of the rules. It's therefore important to understand the meaning or implications of the questions to avoid unwittingly answering incorrectly. Attorneys need to be consulted before applications are submitted."

Prominent broadcast attorney Erwin Krasnow provides the following summary pertaining to the downsizing trend of the past two decades in FCC regulations for radio broadcasters. "The world of FCC regulation has changed dramatically. No more ascertainment. No more Fairness Doctrine (William Paley once quipped that the Fairness Doctrine was like the Holy Roman Empire, which was neither Holy, Roman, nor an Empire). No regulation of call signs or submission of Annual Financial Reports. Virtually all applications and forms are now filed electronically, many without the assistance of a communication lawyer. Rather than terms of three years, licenses are now renewed for eight years (that's a long time; a common law marriage results after only seven years)."

Mr. Krasnow waxes poetically about the situation in "Deregulation: A Lawyer's Lament":

Martin, Tate, and McDowell are proceeding with deregulation en masse,
But nobody's thought of the lawyers who subsist on the present morass.
When Arcane comparative hearings
Have been paying the partnership's bills
It will not be an easy conversion to torts and divorces and wills.
Plain language rules will be all that are left
No "wherefores" and "hereins" and such
Treasured old forms will be thrown on the fire
And for lunch we'll be forced to go Dutch.
So pity your struggling lawyer
Who has served at your side for so long
And write to your Congressman promptly to tell him that "deregulation" is wrong.

Jobs and Equality in Radio

Today, the radio industry continues to employ tens of thousands, but with all the downsizing and consolidation and the increase in new and competitive audio media, this figure has eroded and likely will continue to do so in the coming years. WBZ/WODS general manager, Ted Jordan, says, "Consolidation is causing a lack of a career path because so many middle and upper management positions have been eliminated." Jim Robertson, vice president of Dix Communication, concurs and adds, "Consolidation has affected employment for on air positions and promotion jobs due to staffing cutbacks. However, if graduates are willing to hit the streets selling, things are better." Since 1972, 75,000 individuals have found full-time employment in radio. Today, opportunities for women and minorities are greater than ever. Until fairly recently, radio has been a male-dominated profession (and in some respects still is). In 1975, men in the industry outnumbered women nearly four to one. But that has changed. Now women are being hired more than ever before, and not just for office positions. Women have made significant inroads into programming, sales, and management positions, and there is no reason to think that this trend will not continue. Ed Shane says, "Females have made exceptional inroads, especially in sales." It will take a while, however, before an appropriate proportion of women and minorities are working in the medium. The FCC's insistence on equal opportunity employment within the broadcast industry makes prospects good for all who are interested in broadcasting careers.

Still there is room for improvement in the participation levels of different ethnic groups in the radio industry. NAB's former vice president for human resources, Dwight Ellis, says, "Current employment trends reported by the FCC reveal very little growth between 1980 and 1999 in Native American broadcast employment, for example. Other groups have experienced slow growth too. The NAB is committed to assisting the growth of employment and station ownership for minorities in the industry. The NAB has been a vanguard for minority progress in broadcasting. Nevertheless, more must be done."

A common misconception is that a radio station consists primarily of deejays with few other job options available. Wrong! Nothing could be farther from the truth.

Fine Guide	
Violation	Fine
Construction/operation without authorization	$10,000
Failure to comply with prescribed lighting/marking	$10,000
Violation of public file rules	$10,000
Violation of political rules (reasonable access, lowest unit charge, equal opportunity, discrimination)	$9,000
Unauthorized substantial transfer of control	$8,000
Violation of children's television commercializaiton or programing requirements	$8,000
Emergency Alert System equipment not installed or operational	$8,000
Alien ownership violation	$8,000
Failure to permit inspection	$7,000
Transmission of indecent/obscene materials	$7,000
Interference	$7,000
Importation/marketing of unauthorized equipment	$7,000
Exceeding of authorized antenna height	$5,000
Fraud by wire, radio or television	$5,000
Use of unauthorized equipment	$5,000
Exceeding power limits	$4,000
Failure to respond to FCC communications	$4,000
Violation of sponsorship ID requirements	$4,000
Unauthorized emissions	$4,000
Using unauthorized frequency	$4,000
Failure to engage in required frequency coordination	$4,000
Construction/operation at unauthorized location	$4,000
Violation of requirements pertaining to broadcasting of lotteries or contests	$4,000
Violation of transmitter control/metering requirements	$3,000
Failure to file required forms or information	$3,000
Failure to make required measurements or conduct required monitoring	$2,000
Failure to provide station ID	$1,000
Unauthorized pro forma transfer of control	$1,000
Failure to maintain required records	$1,000
Failure to implement rate reduction or refund order	$7,500
Violation of cable program access rules	$7,500
Violation of cable leased-access rules	$7,500
Violation of cable crossownership rules	$7,500
Violation of cable broadcast carriage rules	$7,500
Violation of pole attachment rules	$7,500
Failure to maintain directional pattern within prescribed parameters	$7,000
Violaiton of main studio rule	$7,000
Violaiton of broadcast hoax rule	$7,000
AM tower fencing	$7,000
Broadcasting telephone conversations without authorization	$4,000
Violation of enhanced underwriting requirements	$2,000

Granted, deejays comprise an important part of a station's staff, but many other employees are necessary to keep the station on the air.

An average-size station in a medium market used to employ between 18 and 26 people, but today due to consolidation, a fraction of that number may be used where several stations form a cluster or radio mall, and on-air personnel may comprise most of that figure. Stations are usually broken down into three major areas: sales, programming, and engineering. Each area, in particular the first two, requires a variety of people for positions that demand a wide

FIGURE 1.24
FCC Fine Guide. Courtesy *Broadcasting and Cable.*

FIGURE 1.25
Selling receivers was a brisk business in early radio. Courtesy Library of Congress.

How FCC Rules Are Made

I. Initiation of Action

Suggestions for changes to the FCC Rules and Regulations can come from sources outside of the Commission either by formal petition, legislation, court decision or informal suggestion. In addition, a Bureau/Office within the FCC can initiate a Rulemaking proceeding on its own.

II. Bureau/Office Evaluation

When a petition for Rulemaking is received, it is sent to the appropriate Bureau(s)/Office(s) for evaluation. If a Bureau/Office decides a particular petition is meritorious, it can request that the Dockets department assign a Rulemaking number to the petition.

A similar request is made when a Bureau/Office decides to initiate a Rulemaking procedure on its own. A weekly notice is issued listing all accepted petitions for Rulemaking. The public has 30 days to submit comments. The Bureau/Office then has the option of generating an agenda item requesting one of four actions by the Commission. If a Notice of Inquiry (NOI) or Notice of Proposed Rulemaking (NPRM) is issued, a docket is instituted and a docket number is assigned.

III. Possible Commission Actions

Major changes to the Rules are presented to the public as either an NOI or NPRM. The Commission will issue an NOI when it is simply asking for information on a broad subject or trying to generate ideas on a given topic. An NPRM is issued when there is a specific change to the Rules being proposed.

If an NOI is issued, it must be followed by ei-

ther an NPRM or a Memorandum Opinion and Order (MO&O) concluding the inquiry.

IV. Comments and Replies Evaluated

When an NOI or NPRM has been issued, the public is given the opportunity to comment initially, and then respond to the comments that are made. When the Commission does not receive sufficient comments to make a decision, a further NOI or NPRM may be issued.

It may be determined that an oral argument before the Commission is needed to provide an opportunity for the public to testify before the Commission, as well as for the Bureau(s)/Office(s) to present diverse opinions concerning the proposed Rule change.

V. Report and Order Issued

A Report and Order is issued by the Commission stating the new or amended Rule, or stating that the Rules will not be change. The proceeding may be terminated in whole or in part.

The Commission may issue additional Report and Orders in the docket.

VI. Reconsideration Given

Petitions for reconsideration may be filed by the public within 30 days. They are reviewed by the appropriate Bureau(s)/Office(s) and/or by the Commission.

VII. Modification Possible

As a result of its review of a petition for reconsideration, the Commission may issue an MO&O modifying its initial decision or denying the petition for reconsideration.

Provided by FCC

FIGURE 1.26
Courtesy Radio World.

schools and colleges offer courses in radio broadcasting, and most award certificates or degrees. As in most other fields today, the more credentials a job candidate possesses, the better he or she looks to a prospective employer.

Perhaps no other profession weighs practical, hands-on experience as heavily as radio does. This is especially true in the on-air area. On the programming side, it is the individual's sound that wins the job, not the degree. However, it is the formal training and education that usually contribute most directly to the quality of the sound that the program director is looking for when hiring. In reality, only a small percentage of radio announcers have college degrees (the number is growing), but statistics have shown that those who do stand a better chance of moving into managerial positions.

Many station managers look for the college-educated person, particularly for the areas of news and sales. Before 1965, the percentage of radio personnel with college training was relatively low. But the figure increased as more and more colleges added broadcasting curricula. Thousands of communications degrees are conferred annually, thus providing the radio industry a pool of highly educated job candidates. Today, college training is a plus (if not a necessity) when searching for employment in radio. The job application or resume that lists practical experience in addition to formal training is most appealing. The majority of colleges with radio curricula have stations. These small (low-power) outlets provide the aspiring broadcaster with a golden opportunity to gain some much needed on-air experience. Some of the nation's foremost broadcasters began their careers at college radio stations. Many of these same schools have internship programs that provide the student with the chance to get important on-the-job training at professional stations. Again, experience is the key, and it rates high to the prospective employer. Small commercial stations often are willing to hire broadcast students to fill part-time and vacation slots. This constitutes professional experience and is an invaluable addition to the resume.

range of skills. Subsequent chapters in this book will bear this out.

Proper training and education are necessary to secure a job at most stations, although many will train people to fill the less-demanding positions. Hundreds of

Entry-level positions in radio seldom pay well. In fact, many small-market stations pay near minimum wage. However, the experience gained at these small-budget operations more than makes up for the small salaries. The first year or two in radio constitutes the dues-paying period, a time in which a person learns the ropes. The small radio station provides inexperienced people with the chance to become involved in all facets of the business. Rarely does a new employee perform only one function. For example, a person hired as a deejay will often prepare and deliver newscasts, write and produce commercials, and may even sell airtime.

To succeed in a business as unique as radio, a person must possess many qualities, not the least of which are determination, skill, and the ability to accept and

FIGURE 1.27
Native-owned stations provide radio jobs for American Indians. Courtesy KTNN.

benefit from constructive criticism. A career in radio is like no other, and the rewards, both personal and financial, can be exceptional. "It's a great business," says Lynn Christian, former senior vice president of the Radio Advertising Bureau. "No two days are alike. I recommend it over other career opportunities."

CHAPTER HIGHLIGHTS

1. With nearly 14,000 radio stations in the United States, radio is the most available source of entertainment, companionship, and information.

2. Guglielmo Marconi is generally considered the father of radio, although David Sarnoff and Lee Deforest are likely contenders.

3. As early as 1922, the Department of Commerce set aside two frequencies for radio broadcasts. WEAF in New York and WGI in Boston aired the first commercials.

4. Today, most radio networks have been subsumed by major corporations (Disney, GE, Viacom, Westwood One).

5. Station networks, first called chain broadcasting, operated as early as 1922. Radio Corporation of America (RCA) formed the first major network in 1926, the National Broadcasting Company (NBC). Columbia Broadcasting System (CBS) was

formed in 1928, and Mutual Broadcasting System (MBS) followed in 1934. American Broadcasting Company (ABC), formed in 1945, became the largest and most successful radio network.

6. Early station proliferation led to overlapping signals. Signal quality decreased, as did listenership. The Radio Act of 1927 formed the Federal Radio Commission (FRC), a five-member board authorized to issue station licenses, allocate frequency bands, assign frequencies to individual stations, and dictate station power and hours of operation. The FRC established the Standard Broadcast band (500–1500 kc).

7. Radio prospered during the Depression by providing cost-free entertainment and escape from the harsh financial realities. *Amos 'n' Andy*, which made its debut in 1929, was the most popular radio show in history. President Franklin D. Roosevelt's fireside chats began on March 12, 1933. The Communications Act of 1934 established the seven-member Federal Communications Commission (FCC).

8. World War II led the FCC to freeze construction of new broadcast outlets; therefore, existing AM outlets prospered.

9. Two years after the end of the war, television usurped the home entertainment leadership.

10. The Bell Lab scientists' invention of the transistor in 1948 helped save radio by providing portability. Music became radio's mainstay.

11. The Top 40 radio format, conceived about the same time as the emergence of rock music, became the most popular format with younger audiences.

12. Edwin H. Armstrong developed the static-free FM band in 1938. The FCC

authorized stereo FM broadcasting in 1961, and in 1965 it separated FM from AM simulcasts in cities with populations in excess of 100,000. Beautiful Music was the first popular format on FM, which relied heavily on automation. The progressive format focused on album cuts rather than Top 40. By the mid-1980s, FM possessed 70% of the listening audience.

13. Today, FM often commands up to 80% of the audience, although some AM stations top their market ratings.

14. The Corporation for Public Broadcasting was established in 1967. Three years later, National Public Radio began providing funding and programming to member stations. More than 800 schools and colleges hold noncommercial radio licenses.

15. Narrowcasting is specialized programming. Frag-out refers to the fragmentation of audience because of numerous formats.

16. Highly leveraged transactions (HLTs) created economic problems for many stations. Local marketing agreements (LMAs) allowed broadcasters to form contracts with one another for mutually beneficial purposes.

17. Consolidation, downsizing, and mergers have been prompted by the FCC's relaxation of the duopoly and ownership rules.

18. Seventy percent of radio's revenues come from local spot sales.

19. Brokerage firms handle the sale of most radio stations. Brokers receive a commission of between 7 and 8% on sales.

20. Digital audio broadcasting (DAB), popularly called High-Definition (HD) Radio, is in the process of replacing the conventional analog system of signal transmission and reception.

21. Satellite and cable radio services are providing listeners with options besides traditional terrestrial signal reception.

22. Radio Web sites, once beset by copyright issues, have become an central part of station operations and are used to promote programming and interact with listeners.

FIGURE 1.28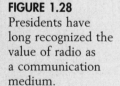
Presidents have long recognized the value of radio as a communication medium.

Station Web sites also provide secondary revenue opportunities.

23. Mobile music services spawned by the Internet, WiFi, and cell phones draw listeners away from traditional radio, although it is anticipated that broadcast and satellite radio will become an integral part of these audio sources.

24. Micro- or low-power FM stations constitute a new category of noncommercial radio outlets, but the conversion to IBOC digital by regular broadcast outlets and the takeover by religious broadcasters may mean the end to the community (neighborhood)-oriented medium.

25. In 1949, the FCC formulated the Fairness Doctrine, which obligated broadcasters to present opposing points of view. In 1987 the FCC declared the doctrine unconstitutional and eliminated it. In 2009, with a new democratic administration in the White House, there was speculation the Fairness Doctrine may be restored.

26. The Republicans wrote a new telecommunications bill designed to lift significant sanctions from broadcasters. The Telecommunications Act of 1996 all but eliminated radio station ownership ceilings, resulting in the reduction in the level of local programming.

27. The radio industry employs fewer people today due to consolidations and the subsequent downsizings. Women and minorities have made significant gains in recent years. A combination of practical experience and formal training remains the best preparation for a career in broadcasting.

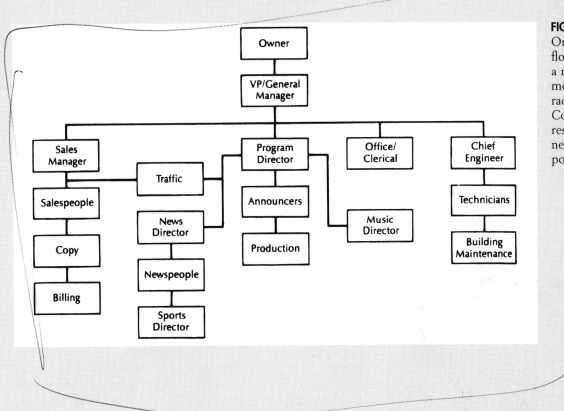

FIGURE 1.29
Organizational flowchart for a nonclustered medium-market radio station. Consolidation has resulted in many new and revised positions.

Lynn Christian

On Radio in the Twenty-First Century

FIGURE 1.30
Lynn Christian.

Today's broadcast radio has lost several of its former major components. First, the introduction of new popular music is being overtaken by the Internet and other personal electronic media choices. Large segments of the radio audience no longer go to the radio to discover a new recording artist, a new release or experimental alternative bands or singers. This is a big loss for program directors and on-air talent. Second, local news is still important to radio listeners, but national news has been moving away from both radio and television networks for the last 10 years. Cable and satellite networks are now, combined, the major source for both National and International news programming. Only NPR News seems to be growing. Third, talk radio

remains very important to the media, especially on the AM dial, but it's being marginalized by the services of the half-dozen 24-hour news, sports, financial, and weather cable networks and by the general national opinion that most of talk radio is controlled by conservative or right-wing commentators and networks. Talk radio is becoming stagnant. The only politically liberal network, Air America, has had a rocky life and short life. Christian radio on FM and AM is also diluting much of AM's talk radio audience, too. Troublesome times for radio in the midst of an economic recession, yet challenging for those entrepreneurial professionals who believe radio's problems as we near the end of the millennium's first decade are bottoming out.

FIGURE 1.31
Mobile music services compete with broadcast and satellite radio. Courtesy Oxy Systems.

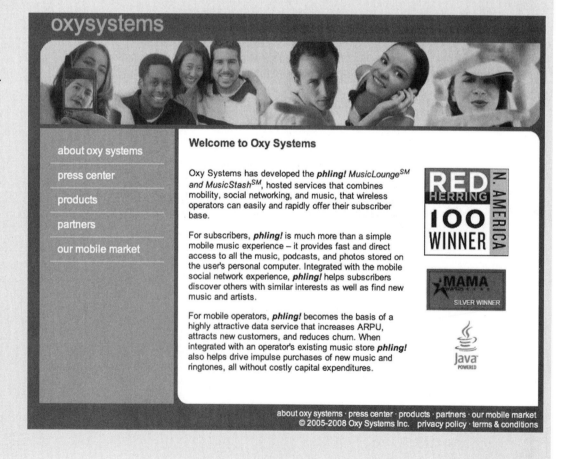

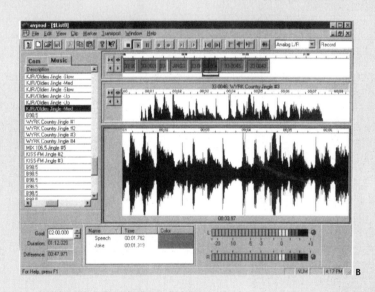

FIGURE 1.32
(A) The look of radio at its inception. (B) The look of radio today. Courtesy Broadcast Electronics and Westinghouse.

FIGURE 1.33
This Internet player makes thousands of broadcasts, webcasts, and podcasts available to listeners. Courtesy Radio Internet Player.

SUGGESTED FURTHER READING

Aitkin, H.G.J., *Syntony and Spark*, John Wiley and Sons, New York, 1976.

American Women in Radio and Television, *Making Waves: The 50 Greatest Women in Radio and Television*, Andrews McMeel Publishing, Chicago, IL, 2001.

Archer, G.L., *History of Radio to 1926*, Arno Press, New York, 1971.

Aronoff, C.E., editor, *Business and the Media*, Goodyear Publishing Company, Santa Monica, CA, 1979.

Baker, W.J., *A History of the Marconi Company*, St. Martin's Press, New York, 1971.

Balk, A., *The Rise of Radio, from Marconi to the Golden Age*, McFarland, Jefferson, NC, 2005.

Barlow, W., *Voice Over: The Making of Black Radio*, Temple University Press, Philadelphia, PA, 1999.

Barnouw, E., *A Tower of Babel: A History of Broadcasting in the United States to 1933*, vol. 1, Oxford University Press, New York, 1966.

Barnouw, E., *Media Marathon: A Twentieth-Century Memoir*, Duke University Press, Durham, NC, 1996.

Barnouw, E., *The Golden Web: A History of Broadcasting in the United States 1933 to 1953*, vol. 2, Oxford University Press, New York, 1968.

Barnouw, E., *The Image Empire: A History of Broadcasting in the United States from 1953*, vol. 3, Oxford University Press, New York, 1970.

Barnouw, E., *The Sponsor: Notes on a Modern Potentate*, Oxford University Press, New York, 1978.

Bergreen, L., *Look Now, Pay Later: The Rise of Network Broadcasting*, Doubleday, Garden City, NY, 1980.

Bianchi, W., *Schools of the Air*, McFarland, Jefferson, NC, 2008.

Bittner, J.R., *Broadcasting and Telecommunications*, 2nd edition, Prentice Hall, Englewood Cliffs, NJ, 1985.

Bittner, J.R., *Professional Broadcasting: A Brief Introduction*, Prentice Hall, Englewood Cliffs, NJ, 1981.

Blake, R.H., and Haroldsen, E.O., *A Taxonomy of Concepts in Communications*, Hastings House, New York, 1975.

Brant, B.G., *College Radio Handbook*, Tab Books, Blue Ridge Summit, PA, 1981.

Broadcasting Yearbook, Broadcasting Publishing, Washington, DC, 1935 to date, annual.

Brown, R.J., *Manipulating the Ether: The Power of Broadcast Radio in Thirties America*, McFarland Publishing, Jefferson, NC, 1998.

Browne, B., and Coddington (consultants), *Radio Today — and Tomorrow*, National Association of Broadcasters, Washington, DC, 1982.

Buono, T.J., and Leibowitz, M.L., *Radio Acquisition Handbook*, Broadcasting and the Law, Miami, FL, 1988.

Campbell, R., *The Golden Years of Broadcasting*, Charles Scribner's Sons, New York, 1976.

Cantril, H., *The Invasion from Mars*, Harper & Row, New York, 1966.

Carpenter, S., *40 Watts from Nowhere: A Journey in Pirate Radio*, Scribner, New York, 2004.

Chapple, S., and Garofalo, R., *Rock 'n' Roll Is Here to Pay*, Nelson-Hall, Chicago, IL, 1977.

Coe, L., *Wireless Radio: A History*, McFarland Publishing, Jefferson, NC, 2006.

Cox Looks at FM Radio, Cox Broadcasting Corporation, Atlanta, GA, 1976.

Craig, D.B., *Fireside Politics: Radio and Political Culture in the United States, 1920–1940*, Johns Hopkins University Press, Baltimore, MD, 2000.

Delong, T.A., *The Mighty Music Box*, Amber Crest Books, Los Angeles, CA, 1980.

Ditingo, V.M., *The Remaking of Radio*, Focal Press, Boston, MA, 1995.

Douglas, S.J., *Inventing American Broadcasting, 1899–1922*, Johns Hopkins University Press, Baltimore, MD, 1987.

Douglas, S.J., *Listening In*, Times Books, New York, 1999.

Dreher, C., *Sarnoff: An American Success*, Quadrangle, New York, 1977.

Dunning, J., *Tune in Yesterday*, Prentice Hall, Englewood Cliffs, NJ, 1976.

Edmonds, I.G., *Broadcasting for Beginners*, Holt, Rinehart, and Winston, New York, 1980.

Erickson, D., *Armstrong's Fight for FM Broadcasting*, University of Alabama, Birmingham, AL, 1974.

Eskanazi, G., *I Hid It Under the Pillow: Growing Up with Radio*, University of Missouri Press, Columbia, MO, 2005.

Fang, I.E., *Those Radio Commentators*, Iowa State University Press, Ames, IA, 1977.

Fisher, M., *Something in the Air: Radio, Rock, and the Revolution That Shaped a Generation*, Random House, New York, 2007.

Fones-Wolf, E., *Waves of Opposition*, University of Illinois Press, Champaign-Urbana, IL, 2006.

Fornatale, P., and Mills, J.E., *Radio in the Television Age*, Overlook Press, New York, 1980.

Foster, E.S., *Understanding Broadcasting*, Addison-Wesley, Reading, MA, 1978.

Fowler, G., and Crawford, B., *Border Radio*, University of Texas Press, Austin, TX, 2002.

Geller, V., *The Powerful Radio Workbook*, M Street Corporation, Washington, DC, 2000.

Grant, A.E., editor, *Communication Technology Update*, Focal Press, Boston, MA, 1995.

Hall, C., and Hall, B., *This Business of Radio Programming*, Hastings House, New York, 1978.

Halper, D., *Invisible Stars*, M.E. Sharpe, Armonk, NY, 2001.

Hasling, J., *Fundamentals of Radio Broadcasting*, McGraw-Hill, New York, 1980.

Head, S.W., and Sterling, C.H., *Broadcasting in America: A Survey of Television, Radio, and the New Technologies*, 7th edition, Houghton Mifflin, Boston, MA, 1993.

Hilliard, R.L., *The Federal Communications Commission: A Primer*, Focal Press, Boston, MA, 1991.

Hilliard, R.L., editor, *Radio Broadcasting: An Introduction to the Sound Medium*, 3rd edition, Longman, New York, 1985.

Hilliard, R.L., and Keith, M.C., *Dirty Discourse: Sex and Indecency in Broadcasting*, Blackwell Publishing, Boston, MA, 2006.

Hilliard, R.L., and Keith, M.C., *Global Broadcasting Systems*, Focal Press, Boston, MA, 1996.

Hilliard, R.L., and Keith, M.C., *The Broadcast Century: A Biography of American Broadcasting*, 4th edition, Focal Press, Boston, MA, 2005.

Hilliard, R.L., and Keith, M.C., *Waves of Rancor: Tuning the Radical Right*, Focal Press, Boston, MA, 1999.

Hilmes, M., *Radio Voices: American Broadcasting, 1922–1952*, University of Minnesota Press, Minneapolis, MN, 1997.

Horten, G., *Radio Goes to War*, University of California Press, Berkeley, CA, 2002.

Hunn, P., *Starting and Operating Your Own FM Radio Station*, Tab Books, Blue Ridge Summit, PA, 1988.

Inglis, A.F., *Behind the Tube*, Focal Press, Boston, MA, 1990.

Keirstead, P.O., and Keirstead, S.K., *The World of Telecommunication*, Focal Press, Stoneham, MA, 1990.

Keith, M.C., *Signals in the Air: Native Broadcasting in America*, Praeger Publishing, Westport, CT, 1995.

Keith, M.C., *Sounds in the Dark: All Night Radio in American Life*, Iowa State University Press, Ames, IA, 2001.

Keith, M.C., *Talking Radio: An Oral History of Radio in the Television Age*, M.E. Sharpe, Armonk, NY, 2000.

Keith, M.C., *Voices in the Purple Haze: Underground Radio and the Sixties*, Praeger Publishing, Westport, CT, 1997.

Keith, M.C., editor, *Radio Cultures: The Sound Medium in American Life*, Peter Lang, New York, 2008.

Ladd, J., *Radio Waves*, St. Martin's Press, New York, 1991.

Lazarsfled, P.F., and Kendall, P.L., *Radio Listening in America*, Prentice Hall, Englewood Cliffs, NJ, 1948.

Leinwall, S., *From Spark to Satellite*, Charles Scribner's Sons, New York, 1979.

Lenthall, B., *Radio America*, University of Chicago Press, Chicago, IL, 2007.

Levinson, R., *Stay Tuned*, St. Martin's Press, New York, 1982.

Lewis, P., editor, *Radio Drama*, Longman, New York, 1981.

Lewis, T., *Empire of the Air: The Men Who Made Radio*, HarperCollins Publishers, New York, 1991.

Lichty, L.W., and Topping, M.C., *American Broadcasting: A Source Book on the History of Radio and Television*, Hastings House, New York, 1976.

Looker, T., *The Sound and the Story*, Houghton Mifflin, Boston, MA, 1995.

Loviglio, J., *Radio's Intimate Public*, University of Minnesota, Minneapolis, MN, 2005.

MacDonald, J.F., *Don't Touch That Dial: Radio Programming in American Life, 1920–1960*, Nelson Hall, Chicago, IL, 1979.

Matelski, M., *Vatican Radio*, Praeger Publishing, Westport, CT, 1995.

McCauley, M., *NPR: The Trials and Triumphs of National Public Radio*, Columbia University Press, New York, 2005.

McLuhan, M., *Understanding Media: The Extensions of Man*, McGraw-Hill, New York, 1964.

Mitchell, J.W., *Listener Supported: The Culture and History of Public Radio*, Praeger Publishers, Westport, CT, 2005.

Morrow, B., *Cousin Brucie*, Morrow, New York, 1987.

NAB, *Radio Station Salaries*, National Association of Broadcasters, Washington, DC, 2004.

Nachman, G., *Raised on Radio*, University of California Press, Berkeley, CA, 2000.

Naughton, J., *A Brief History of the Future: From Radio Days to Internet Years in a Lifetime*, Overlook Press, Woodstock, NY, 2000.

O'Donnell, L.B., et al., *Radio Station Operations: Management and Employee Perspectives*, Wadsworth Publishing, Belmont, CA, 1989.

Orlik, P.B., *Electronic Media Criticism*, Focal Press, Boston, MA, 1994.

Paley, W.S., *As It Happened: A Memoir*, Doubleday, Garden City, NY, 1979.

Pease, E.C., and Dennis, E.E., *Radio: The Forgotten Medium*, Transaction Press, New Brunswick, NJ, 1995.

Phillips, L.A., *Public Radio: Behind the Voices*, CDS Books, New York, 2006.

Pierce, J.R., *Signals*, W. H. Freeman, San Francisco, CA, 1981.

Podber, J., *The Electronic Front Porch*, Mercer University Press, Macon, GA, 2007.

Pusateri, C.J., *Enterprise in Radio*, University Press of America, Washington, DC, 1980.

Radio Facts, Radio Advertising Bureau, New York, 1988.

Ramsey, M., *Making Waves: Radio on the Verge*, iUniverse, 2008.

Rhoads, B.E., *Blast from the Past*, Streamline Press, West Palm Beach, FL, 1996.

Richter, W.A., *Radio: A Complete Guide to the Industry*, Peter Lang, New York, 2006.

Routt, Ed., *The Business of Radio Broadcasting*, Tab Books, Blue Ridge Summit, PA, 1972.

Rudell, A., *Hello, Everybody! The Dawn of American Radio*, Harcourt, New York, 2008.

Sarnoff, D., *The World of Television*, Wisdom, Agoura Hills, CA, 1958.

Schiffer, M.B., *The Portable Radio in American Life*, University of Arizona Press, Tucson, AZ, 1991.

Seidle, R.J., *Air Time*, Holbrook Press, Boston, MA, 1977.

Settle, I., *A Pictorial History of Radio*, Grosset and Dunlap, New York, 1967.

Shapiro, M.E., *Radio Network Prime Time Programming, 1927–1967*, McFarland, Jefferson, NC, 2002.

Siegel, S., and Siegel, D.S., *A Resource Guide to the Golden Age of Radio*, Book Hunter Press, Yorktown Heights, NY, 2006.

Sipemann, C.A., *Radio's Second Chance*, Little, Brown, Boston, MA, 1946.

Sklar, R., *Rocking America: How the All-Hit Radio Stations Took Over*, St. Martin's Press, New York, 1984.

Smith, F.L., *Perspectives on Radio and Television: An Introduction to Broadcasting in the United States*, Harper & Row, New York, 1979.

Soley, L., *Free Radio*, Westview Press, Denver, CO, 1999.

Sterling, C.H., editor, *Encyclopedia of Radio*, Fitzroy Dearborn, New York, 2003.

Sterling, C.H., and Keith, M.C., *Sounds of Change: FM Broadcasting in America*, University of North Carolina Press, Chapel Hill, NC, 2007.

Utterback, A.S., *Broadcasters Survival Guide*, Bonus Books, San Francisco, CA, 1997.

Vowell, S., *Radio On: A Listener's Diary*, St. Martin's Press, New York, 1997.

Wertheim, A.F., *Radio Comedy*, Oxford University Press, New York, 1979.

Whetmore, E.J., *MediaAmerica*, 4th edition, Wadsworth Publishing, Belmont, CA, 1989.

Whetmore, E.J., *The Magic Medium: An Introduction to Radio in America*, Wadsworth Publishing, Belmont, CA, 1981.

Winn, J.E., and Brinson, S.L., editors, *Transmitting the Past: Historical and Cultural Perspectives on Broadcasting*, University of Alabama Press, Tuscaloosa, AL, 2005.

Woolley, L., *The Last Great Days of Radio*, Republic of Texas Press, Dallas, TX, 1995.

Yoder, A., *Pirate Radio Stations*, McGraw-Hill, New York, 2001.

Station Management 2

Nature of the Business

Radio station management has changed dramatically in just the past few years. Indeed, in most markets, especially in larger ones, things have gone from managing a single or combo outlet to overseeing the operations of a half dozen or more, often clustered in the same building. On top of that, the station manager must now compete with new audio media that did not exist at the start of this century. Were these not enough, compounding the manager's challenge is a host of other external factors, foremost among them being the up-and-down economy (mostly down at this writing) and changes in the regulatory landscape.

Of course, some things remain the same. As has always been the case, the medium's unique character requires that the manager deal with a broad mix of people, from on-air personalities to secretaries and from sales personnel to technicians. Few other businesses can claim such an amalgam of employees. Even the station manager of the smallest outlet with as few as six or eight employees must direct individuals with very diverse backgrounds and goals. For example, radio station WXXX in a small Maine community may employ three to four full-time air people, who likely were brought in from other areas of the country. The deejays have come to WXXX to begin their broadcasting careers with plans to gain some necessary experience and move on to larger markets. Within a matter of a few months, the station will probably be looking for replacements.

Frequent turnover of on-air personnel at small stations is a fact of life. As a consequence, members of the air staff often are regarded as transients or passers-through by not only the community but also the other members of the station's staff. Less likely to come and go are a station's administrative and technical staff. Usually they are not looking toward the bright lights of the bigger markets, since the town in which the station is located is often home to them. A small station's sales department may experience some turnover but usually not to the degree that the programming department does. Sales people also are likely to have been recruited from the ranks of the local citizenry, whereas air personalities more typically come from outside the community.

Running a station in a small market presents its own unique challenges (and it should be noted that half of the nation's radio outlets are located in communities with fewer than 25,000 residents). Stations in larger markets, however, typically are faced with stiffer competition and fates that are often tied directly to ratings. In contrast to station WXXX in the small Maine community, where the closest other station is 50 miles away and therefore no competitive threat, an outlet located in a metropolitan area may share the airwaves with 30 or more other broadcasters. Competition is intense, and radio stations in large urban areas usually succeed or fail based on their showing in the latest listener surveys. The metro market station manager must pay close attention to what surrounding broadcasters are doing, while striving to maintain the best product possible to retain a competitive edge and prosper.

Meanwhile, the government's perception of the radio station's responsibility to its consumers also sets it apart from other industries. Since its inception, radio's business has been Washington's business, too. Station managers, unlike the heads of most other enterprises, have had to conform to the dictates of a federal agency especially conceived for the purpose of overseeing their activities. Failing to satisfy the Federal Communications Commission (FCC)'s expectations can result in stiff penalties such as fines and even the loss of an operating license; as a result, radio station managers have been obliged to keep up with a fairly prodigious volume of rules and regulations.

The 1980s and 1990s deregulation actions designed to unburden the broadcaster of what had been regarded by many as unreasonable government intervention have made the life of the station manager somewhat less complicated. Nevertheless, the government continues to play an important role in American radio, and managers who value their license wisely invest energy and effort in fulfilling federal conditions. After all, a radio station without a frequency is just a building with a lot of expensive equipment.

The listener's perception of the radio business, even in this day and age when nearly every community with a small business district has a radio station, is often unrealistic. Film and television's portrayal of the radio station as a hotbed of zany characters and bizarre antics has helped foster a misconception. This is not to suggest that radio stations are the most conventional places to work. Because it is the station's function to provide entertainment to its listeners, it must employ creative people, and where these people are gathered, be it a small town or a large city, the atmosphere is certain to be charged. "The volatility of the air staff's emotions and the oscillating nature of radio itself actually distinguishes our business from others," observes Kentucky station manager J.G. Salter.

Faced with an audience whose needs and tastes sometimes change overnight, today's radio station has become adept at shifting gears as conditions warrant. What is currently popular in music, fashion, and leisure-time activities will be nudged aside tomorrow by something new. This, says broadcast manager Randy Lane, forces radio stations to stay one step ahead of all trends and fads. "Being on the leading edge of American culture makes it necessary to undergo more changes and updates than is usually the case in other businesses. Not adjusting to what is currently in vogue can put a station at a distinct disadvantage. You have to stay in touch with what is happening in your own community as well as the trends and cultural movements occurring in other parts of the country." The complex internal and external factors that derive from the unusual nature of the radio business make managing today's station a formidable challenge. Perhaps no other business demands as much from its managers. Conversely, few other businesses provide an individual with as much to feel good about. It takes a special kind of person to run a radio station.

FIGURE 2.1
Newspaper listing of radio stations in a major market. Large cities such as New York, Chicago, Los Angeles, and Philadelphia often have more than 60 stations.

Station	AM	FM	Station	AM	FM
WABC	770		WLIR		92.7
WADB		95.9	WLIX	540	
WADO	1280		WLTW		106.7
WALK	1370	97.5	WMCA	570	
WAPP		103.5	WMCX		88.1
WAWZ	1380	99.1	WMGQ		98.3
WBAB		102.3	WMJY		107.1
WBAI		99.5	WMTR	1250	
WBAU		90.3	WNBC	660	
WBGO		88.3	WNCN		104.3
WBJB		90.5	WNEW	1130	102.7
WBLI		106.1	WNJR	1430	
WBLS		107.5	WNNJ	1360	
WBRW	1170		WNYC	830	93.9
WCBS	880	101.1	WNYE		91.5
WCTC	1450		WNYG	1440	
WCTO		94.3	WNYM	1330	
WCWP		88.1	WNYU		89.1
WDHA		105.5	WOBM	1170	92.7
WERA	1590		WOR	710	
WEVD		97.9	WPAT	930	93.1
WFAS	1230	103.9	WPIX		101.9
WFDU		89.1	WPLJ		95.5
WFME		94.7	WPOW	1330	
WFMU		91.1	WPRB		103.3
WFUV		90.7	WPST		97.5
WGBB	1240		WPUT	1510	
WGLI	1290		WQXR	1560	96.3
WGRC	1300		WRAN	1510	
WGSM	740		WRCN	1570	103.9
WHBI		105.9	WRFM		105.1
WHLI	1100		WRHU		88.7
WHN	1050		WRKL	910	
WHPC		90.3	WRKS		98.7
WHTG	1410	106.3	WRTN		93.5
WHTZ		100.3	WRVH		105.5
WHUD		100.7	WSBH		95.3
WHWH	1350		WSIA		88.9
WICC	600		WSKQ	620.0	
WINS	1010		WSOU		89.5
WIXL		103.7	WSUS		102.3
WJDM	1530		WTHE	1520	
WJLK	1310	94.3	WUSB		90.1
WKCR		89.9	WVIP	1310	106.3
WKDM	1380		WVOX	1460	
WKJY		98.3	WVRM		89.3
WKMB	1070		WWDJ	970	
WKRB		90.9	WWRL	1600	
WKTU		92.3	WXMC	1310	
WKWZ		88.5	WYNY		97.1
WKXW		101.5	WYRS		96.7
WLIB	1190		WZFM		107.1
WLIM	1580				

Valerie Geller | The Manager's Challenge

In these uncertain economic times managing and motivating people are the challenges. It is easier to run *any* business when there is money around, when cost cuts and belt tightening are not the emphasis. But while the "fat" years may be in the past, radio still continues to thrive. And these are exciting times for the medium. Managing is a talent in its own right. It takes talent to lead, and it takes talent to find good people. If you find you get a kick out of leading people and are excited by other people's good work, as much as from your own work, you may be a good candidate for management. There are many jobs in radio. Some people are naturally better "actors" than "directors." Those people should probably *not* be in management. But if you enjoy motivating others and running a team then management is something you should consider. The keys to managing staff include honesty, enthusiasm, creativity, and empathy.

FIGURE 2.2
Valerie Geller.

The Manager as Chief Collaborator —nonexistent

There are many schools of thought concerning the approach to managing a radio station. For example, there are the standard X, Y, and Z models or theories of management (which admittedly oversimplify the subject but give the neophyte a basic working model). The first theory embraces the idea that the general manager is the captain of the vessel, the primary authority, with solemn, if not absolute, control of the decision-making process. The second theory casts the manager in the role of collaborator or senior advisor. The third theory forms a hybrid of the preceding two; the manager is both a coach and a team player, or the chief collaborator. Of the three models, broadcast managers tend to favor the third approach.

Lynn Christian, who has served as the general manager of several major market radio stations, preferred working for a manager who used the hybrid model rather than the purely authoritarian model. "Before I entered upper management, I found that I performed best when my boss sought my opinion and delegated responsibility to me. I believe in department head meetings and the full disclosure of projects within the top organization of the station. If you give someone the title, you should be prepared to give that person some authority, too. I respect the integrity of my people, and if I lose it, I replace them quickly. In other words, 'You respect me, and I'll respect you,' is the way I have always managed."

Randy Bongarten, network chief, concurs with Christian and adds, "Management styles have to be adaptive to individual situations so as to provide what is needed at the time. In general, the collaborator or team leader approach gets the job done. Of course, I don't think there is any one school of management that is right 100% of the time."

Jim Arcara, former radio network head, also is an advocate of the hybrid management style. "It's a reflection of what is more natural to me as well as my company. Employees are capable of making key

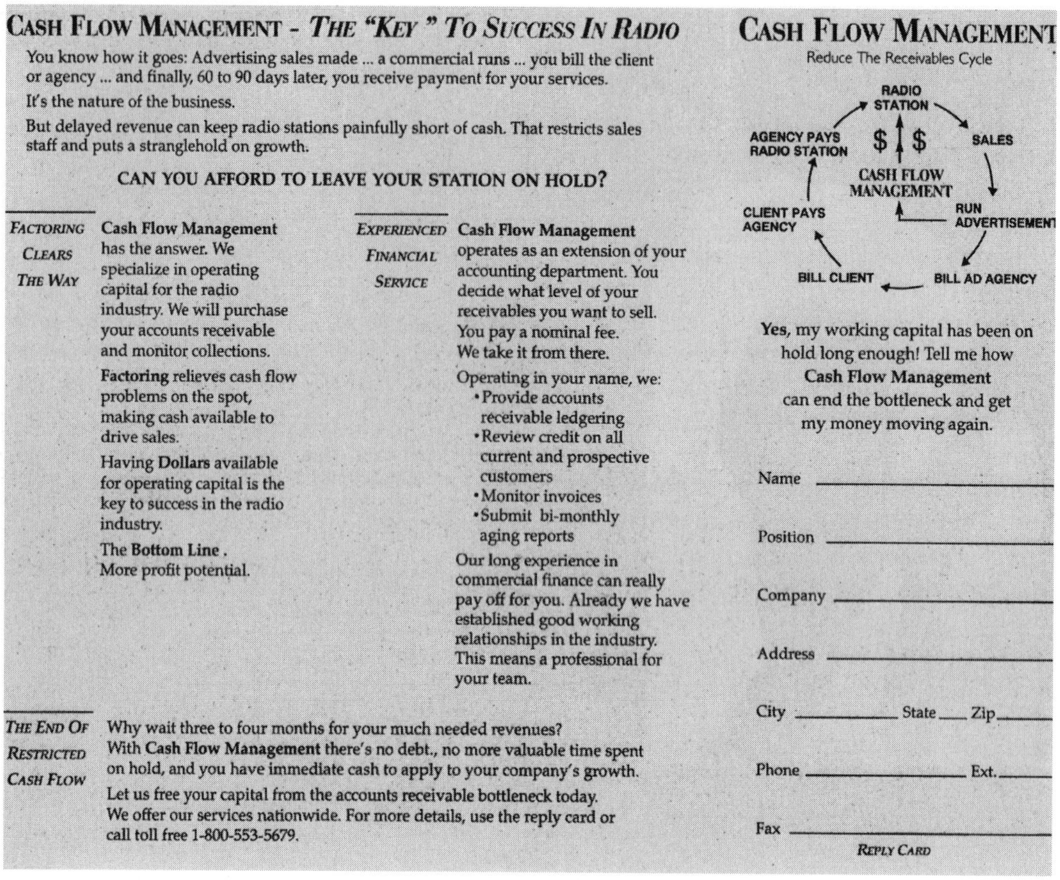
CASH FLOW MANAGEMENT - THE "KEY" TO SUCCESS IN RADIO
You know how it goes: Advertising sales made ... a commercial runs ... you bill the client or agency ... and finally, 60 to 90 days later, you receive payment for your services.
It's the nature of the business.
But delayed revenue can keep radio stations painfully short of cash. That restricts sales staff and puts a stranglehold on growth.
CAN YOU AFFORD TO LEAVE YOUR STATION ON HOLD?
FACTORING CLEARS THE WAY
Cash Flow Management has the answer. We specialize in operating capital for the radio industry. We will purchase your accounts receivable and monitor collections.
Factoring relieves cash flow problems on the spot, making cash available to drive sales.
Having Dollars available for operating capital is the key to success in the radio industry.
The Bottom Line. More profit potential.
EXPERIENCED FINANCIAL SERVICE
Cash Flow Management operates as an extension of your accounting department. You decide what level of your receivables you want to sell. You pay a nominal fee. We take it from there.
Operating in your name, we:
• Provide accounts receivable ledgering
• Review credit on all current and prospective customers
• Monitor invoices
• Submit bi-monthly aging reports
Our long experience in commercial finance can really pay off for you. Already we have established good working relationships in the industry. This means a professional for your team.
THE END OF RESTRICTED CASH FLOW
Why wait three to four months for your much needed revenues?
With Cash Flow Management there's no debt., no more valuable time spent on hold, and you have immediate cash to apply to your company's growth.
Let us free your capital from the accounts receivable bottleneck today.
We offer our services nationwide. For more details, use the reply card or call toll free 1-800-553-5679.
CASH FLOW MANAGEMENT
Reduce The Receivables Cycle
RADIO STATION
SALES
RUN ADVERTISEMENT
BILL AD AGENCY
BILL CLIENT
CLIENT PAYS AGENCY
AGENCY PAYS RADIO STATION
$ $
CASH FLOW MANAGEMENT
Yes, my working capital has been on hold long enough! Tell me how Cash Flow Management can end the bottleneck and get my money moving again.
Name
Position
Company
Address
City State Zip
Phone Ext.
Fax
REPLY CARD

FIGURE 2.3
Keeping the station solvent is the manager's primary task. Companies like this one help the manager do this. Courtesy CFM.

decisions, and they should be given the opportunity to do so. An effective manager also delegates responsibility."

General manager Pat McNally finds the collaborative approach suitable to his goals and temperament. "My management style is more collaborative. I believe in hiring qualified professional people, defining what I expect, and allowing them to do their job with input, support, and constructive criticism from me. My door is always open for suggestions, and I am a good listener. I consider this business something special, and I expect an extra special effort."

This also holds true for general manager Steven Woodbury. "I hire the best people as department heads and then work collaboratively with these experts. Department heads are encouraged to run their areas as if they had major ownership in the company. That instills a sense of team spirit too. Their energy level and decision-making efforts reflect this."

The manager/collaborator approach has gained popularity in the past two decades. Radio functions well in a team-like atmosphere. "Since practically every job in the radio station is designed to support and enhance the air product, establishing a connectedness among what is usually a small band of employees tends to yield the best results," contends station manager Jane Duncklee. "I strongly believe that employees must feel that they are a valid part of what is happening and that their input has a direct bearing on those decisions which affect them and the operation as a whole. I try to hire the best people possible and then let them do their jobs with a minimum of interference and a maximum of support."

Marlin R. Taylor, founder of Bonneville Broadcasting System and former manager of several major-market radio outlets, including WRFM, New York, and WBCN, Boston, believes that the manager using the collaborative system of management gets the most out of employees. "When a staff member feels that his or her efforts and contributions make a difference and are appreciated, that person will remain motivated. This kind of employee works harder and delivers more. Most people, if they enjoy the job they have and like the organization they work for, are desirous of improving their level of performance and contributing to the health and well-being of the station. I really think that many station managers should devote even more time and energy to people development."

Station general manager Paul Aaron believes that managers must first assert their authority; that is, make it clear to all that they are in charge, before the transition to collaborator can take place. "It's a sort of process of evolution. Actually, when you come right down to it, any effective management approach includes a bit of both the authoritarian and collaborative concepts. The situation at the station will have a direct impact on the management style I personally deem most appropriate. As the saying goes, "different situations call for different measures." When assuming the reins at a new station, sometimes it is necessary to take a more dictatorial approach until the organization is where you feel it should be. Often a lot of cleanup and adjustments are necessary before there can be a greater degree of equanimity. Ultimately, however, there should be equanimity."

Surveys have shown that most broadcast executives view the chief collaborator or hybrid management approach as compatible with their needs. "It has pretty much become the standard *modus operandi* in this industry. A radio manager must direct as well as invite input. To me it makes sense, in a business in which people are the product, to create an atmosphere that encourages self-expression, as well as personal and professional growth. After all, we are in the communications business. Everyone's voice should at least be heard," contends Lynn Christian.

What Makes a Manager?

As in any other profession, the road to the top is seldom a short and easy one. It takes years to get there, and dues must be paid along the way. To begin, without a genuine affection for the business and a strong desire to succeed, it is unlikely that the position can ever be attained. Furthermore, without the proper training and experience, the top

General Sales Manager - WPLJ	
Categories:	**Radio**
Ad Number:	**8770**
Date Posted:	**06/14/2006**
Contact:	Linda Wnek WPLJ, 2 Penn Plaza - 17th Floor New York, NY 10121 US
Telephone:	
E-Mail:	nyradiojobs@abc.com
Web Site:	http://www.wplj.com/jobs.asp

Description

Strong hands on manager responsible for complete fiscal responsibility of a high volume sales department. Candidate must be competent with inventory management and pricing, staffing, problem solving, expense control and new business development. Candidates must have strong agency relationships and a minimum of 5 years of radio sales management experience in a medium to large market. Interested applicants should contact: Linda Wnek, Diversity Recruitment Coordinator, 2 Penn Plaza 17th Floor, New York, NY 10121 or at nyradiojobs@abc.com or by fax (212) 613-8956. EOE. Application deadline 6/28/06

FIGURE 2.4
Courtesy
TVandRadioJobs.com

job will remain elusive. So then what goes into becoming a radio station manager? According to Jim Robertson, vice president of Dix Communications, the main personal and professional qualities a station manager should possess are honesty and integrity. As Robertson says, "Everything else is mute without that to start. You must be willing to lead by example. Be a part of the process not just an overseer. We are not a huge operation, which allows me to be much more a participant. As the size of the staff and the number of stations gets larger, the challenge of participation grows, and that brings us right back to honesty and integrity. These are core ingredients. Add to these the importance of leading a balanced life. One that allows you to share time with family, engage in leisure activities, participate in community, and so on. It is very important that a manager knows how to balance and prioritize these things."

Emmis Communications chief, Jeff Smulyan, says the current times require special skills. "A radio manager must be flexible. The media world is changing daily. Providing leadership that understands a rapidly changing world is the most important attribute. None of us understands how technology will change the industry. We have to provide content that can be deployed in several different ways. Content that creates a unique listening experience and provides adequate results for advertisers. Being able to adjust to the shifting market scene is crucial for any manager."

Entercom's Dave Neugesser observes, "A station manager has to have a complete understanding of the three legs that support the body of radio – the listener, the client, and the station. While much of what we do in programming supports the station and listener, radio is a business and the client is just as crucial. A manager must have a clear vision, tight focus, and solid strategy to succeed. He or she must have a great team to be a great leader."

Longtime broadcast executive John Gehron shares his perspective on what makes for a successful manager. "He or she must understand what channels the audience is using and then match content to fit the channel. Deciding how to allocate resources among the many distribution sources is of utmost importance. At the same time the manager must not pull too many resources from the primary channel and diminish its popularity."

First and foremost, a prospective manager needs a good foundation, and formal education plays a strong role in this background. Hundreds of institutions of higher learning across the country offer programs in broadcast operations. The college degree has achieved greater importance in radio over the last decade or two, and, as in most other industries today, it has become a standard credential for those vying for management slots. Anyone entering broadcasting in the 2000s with aspirations to operate a radio station should acquire as much formal training as possible. Station managers with master's degrees are not uncommon. However, a bachelor's degree in communications gives the prospective station manager a good foundation from which to launch a career.

In a business that stresses the value of practical experience, seldom, if ever, does an individual land a management job directly out of college. In fact, most station managers have been in the business at least 15 years. "Once you get the theory nailed down you have to apply it. Experience is the best teacher. I've spent 30 years working in a variety of areas in the medium. In radio, in particular, hands-on experience is

what matters," says station general manager Richard Bremkamp, Jr.

To radio station manager Roger Ingram, experience is what most readily opens the door to management. "While a degree is kind of like a union card in this day and age, a good track record is what wins the management job. You really must possess both."

Jane Duncklee began her ascent to station management by logging commercials for airplay and eventually moved into other areas. "For the past 17 years I have been employed by Champion Broadcasting Systems. During that time I have worked in every department of the radio station, from traffic, where I started, to sales, programming, engineering, and finally management on both the local and corporate levels."

Many radio station managers are recruited from the sales area rather than programming. Since the general manager's foremost objective is to generate a profit, station owners usually feel more confident hiring someone with a solid sales or business background. Consequently, three out of four radio managers have made their living at some point selling airtime. It is a widely held belief that this experience best prepares an individual for the realities encountered in the manager's position. "I spent over a decade and a half in media sales before becoming a station manager. In fact, my experience on the radio level was exclusively confined to sales and then for only eight months. After that I moved into station management. Most of my radio-related sales experience took place on the national level with station rep companies," recalls Norm Feuer of Force Two Communications.

Station manager Carl Evans holds that a sales background is especially useful, if not necessary, to general managers. "I spent a dozen years as a station account executive, and prior to entering radio I represented various product lines to retailers. The key to financial success in radio exists in an understanding of retailing."

It is not uncommon for station managers to have backgrounds out of radio, but almost invariably their experience comes out of the areas of sales, marketing, and finance. Broadcaster Paul Aaron worked as a fundraiser for the United Way of America before entering radio and contends that many managers come from other fields in which they have served in positions allied to sales, if not in sales itself. "Of those managers who have worked in fields other than radio, most have come to radio via the business sector. There are not many former biologists or glass blowers serving as station managers," says Aaron.

Although statistics show that the station salesperson has the best chance of being promoted to the station's head position (more general managers have held the sales manager's position than any other), a relatively small percentage of radio's managers come from the programming ranks. "I'm more the exception than the rule. I have spent all of my career in the programming side, first as a deejay at stations in Phoenix, Denver, and Pittsburgh, and then as program director for outlets in Kansas City and Chicago. I'll have to admit, however, that while it certainly is not impossible to become a GM [general manager] by approaching it from the programming side, resistance exists," admits station manager Randy Lane.

Many in the industry consider the programmer's role to be more an artistic function than one requiring a high degree of business savvy. However accurate or inaccurate this assessment is, the result is that fewer managers are hired with backgrounds exclusively confined to programming duties. Programmers have reason to be encouraged, however, since a trend in favor of hiring program directors (PDs) has surfaced in recent years, and predictions suggest that it will continue.

In its useful (albeit aging) text pertaining to how PDs become station managers, *Up the Management Ladder: From Program Director to General Manager*, the National Association of Broadcasters (NAB) states:

> The biggest obstacle facing the program director with an eye on management is image.
>
> Programming is an operational expense. To create the "sound" of the station, the program director must spend money to pay staff salaries, to buy programming aids, and to maintain studio equipment. Where does the money come from? Sales.
>
> And it used to be that only those who were in sales were considered for promotion. The reasoning? Those in sales, through the very

nature of their jobs, had a solid understanding of the radio rule: Time = Money.

> Those in sales, through the very nature of their jobs, also enjoyed the pursuit of more money.
>
> "I get turned on," said one general sales manager, "when people tell me 'no.' I love getting them to say 'yes.'"
>
> Program directors, it was believed, lacked that basic grounding. Concerned with creating the station's image, program directors inadvertently created an image for themselves as "creative" types without concern or respect for the "business" aspects of radio.
>
> So how is the program director to compete?
>
> By presenting skills you already possess in the most positive, business-oriented format and by getting the skills you don't already possess.

In reality, the most attractive candidate for a station management position is the one whose experience has involved both programming and sales responsibilities. No general manager can fully function without an understanding and appreciation of what goes into preparing and presenting the air product, nor can he or she hope for success without a keen sense of business and finance.

Today's highly competitive and complex radio market requires that the person aspiring to management have both formal training, preferably a college degree in broadcasting, and experience in all aspects of radio station operations, in particular sales and programming. Ultimately, the effort and energy an individual invests will bear directly on the dividends he or she earns, and there is not a single successful station manager who has not put in 15-hour days. The station manager is expected to know more and do more than anyone else, and rightfully so, since he or she is the person who stands to gain the most.

Radio group president Dan Mason relates the qualities he sees in the most successful station managers: "A keen sense of what is 'good business,' humility to take the blame in bad times and to give staff credit in good times, fairness and passion for all, responsiveness to situations (not reactionary), passion for the industry, recognition and knowledge of staff (know by first name), and ability to keep personal problems out of the station."

The Manager's Duties and Responsibilities

A primary objective of the station manager is to operate in a manner that generates the most profit, while maintaining a positive and productive attitude among station employees. This is more of a challenge than it may seem at first, claims radio broadcaster Cliff Shank. "In order to meet the responsibility that you are faced with daily, you really have to be an expert in so many areas: sales, marketing, finance, legal matters, technical, governmental, and programming. It helps if you're an expert in human nature, too." Jane Duncklee puts it this way: "Managing a radio station requires that you divide yourself equally into at least a dozen parts and be a 100% whole in each situation." In the new Telecommunications Act of 1996 environment, consultant Ed Shane observes, "The duties for station managers have changed radically. For example, Chris Wegmann, manager of the Capstar cluster at Baton Rouge, has responsibility for several AM and FM stations in other parts of Louisiana and Texas. Talk about dividing yourself."

In today's consolidated environment, this is more common than not; says Jay Williams, "Mike Glickenhaus, a Clear Channel vice president and market manager, originally oversaw nine FM stations in the San Diego cluster."

Station owner Bill Campbell says that the theme that runs throughout the classic Tom Peters's book, *In Search of Excellence*, is one that is relevant to the station manager's task today. "The idea in Peters's book is that you must make the customer happy, get your people involved, and get rid of departmental waste and unnecessary expenditures. A station should be a lean and healthy organism."

Station managers themselves generally must answer to a higher authority. The majority of radio stations, roughly 85%, are owned by companies and corporations that both hire the manager and establish financial goals or projections for the station. It is the station manager's job to see that corporate expectations are met and, ideally, exceeded. Managers who fail to operate a facility in a way that satisfies the corporate hierarchy may soon find themselves looking for another job.

Fewer than 15% of the nation's stations are owned by individuals or partnerships. At these radio outlets, the manager still must meet the expectations of the station owner(s). In some cases, the manager may be given more latitude or responsibility in determining the station's fate, whereas in others, the owner may play a greater role in the operation of the station.

A basic function of the manager's position is to formulate station policy and see that it is implemented. To ensure against confusion, misunderstanding, and possible unfair labor practices that typically impede operations, employees often receive a station policy manual. This manual states the station's positions on a host of issues, such as hiring, termination, salaries, raises, promotions, sick leave, vacation, benefits, and so forth. As standard practice, a station may require that each new employee read and become familiar with the contents of the policy manual before actually starting work. Job descriptions, as well as organization flowcharts, commonly are outlined to make it abundantly clear to staff members about who is responsible for what. A well-conceived policy book may contain a statement of the station's programming philosophy with an explanation of the format it employs. The more comprehensive a policy book, the less likely there will be confusion and disruption.

Hiring and retaining good people are other key managerial functions. "You have some pretty delicate egos to cope with in this business. Radio attracts some very bright and highly talented people, sometimes with erratic temperaments. Keeping harmony and keeping people are among the foremost challenges facing a station manager," claims Norm Feuer.

Steve Woodbury agrees with Feuer, adding, "You have to hire the right people and motivate them properly, and that's a challenge. You have to be capable of inspiring people. Actually, if you are unable to motivate your people, the station will fail to reach its potential. Hire the best people you can and nurture them."

Cluster market manager Mike Glickenhaus says, "You make sure you have a lot of great people. You need more key people who you can give lots of responsibility to because you don't have time to micromanage them. It's important to hire the right people and then clearly lay out the vision, goals, and many of the steps that will be necessary and agree on them. You need people who understand what it takes, what they have to do, and have the direction to get there. Then as manager you have to decide what (projects or problems) you're going to apply your time to."

NAB's executive vice president for radio, John David, adds, "There is no longer just one key to running successful radio stations. My advice would be to find as many creative people who have a real connection to the people in the audience. Hire them, treat them with respect, listen to their input, and pay them. Managers can hire people all day that agree with them. Hire people who have different ideas but are smart enough to carry out the plan with enthusiasm once the direction is determined. That goes for all departments of the team, including management. With this formula, you won't be constantly looking for people."

As mentioned earlier, managers of small-market radio stations are confronted with a unique set of problems when it comes to hiring and holding onto qualified people, especially on-air personnel. "In our case, finding and keeping a professional-sounding staff with our somewhat limited budget is an ongoing problem. This is true at most small market stations, however," observes station manager J.G. Salter.

The rural or small-market station is where the majority of newcomers gain their experience. Because salaries are necessarily low and the fledgling air person's ambitions are usually high, the rate of turnover is significant. Managers of small outlets spend a great deal of time training people. "It is a fact of the business that radio people, particularly deejays, usually learn their trade at the 'out-of-the-way,' low-power outlet. To be a manager at a small station, you have to be a teacher, too. But it can be very rewarding despite the obvious problem of having to rehire to fill positions so often. We deal with many beginners. I find it exciting and gratifying, and no small challenge, to train newcomers in the various aspects of radio broadcasting," says Salter.

Randy Lane also enjoys the instructor's role but notes that the high turnover rate affects product continuity. "With air people coming and going all the time, it can give the listening public the impression of instability. The last thing a station wants to do is sound schizophrenic. Establishing an image of dependability is crucial to any radio station. Changing air people every other month doesn't help. As a station manager, it is up to you to do the best you can with the resources at hand. In general, I think small market managers

Change in Stations Owned by the Top Companies
1999-2005

	Clear Channel	Cumulus Broadcasting	Citadel Communications	CBS Radio*	Entercom	Salem
1999	520	303	175	161	91	0
2000	1157	226	210	181	96	0
2001	1211	243	204	183	101	82
2002	1211	258	207	182	103	84
2003	1207	268	218	184	105	93
2004	1194	305	220	183	103	103
2005	1184	300	223	179	103	106
	☑	☑	☑	☑	☑	☑

Source: BIAfn Media Access Pro

*Due to restructuring within the Viacom Corportation, Infinity is now CBS Radio

Top companies by number of stations whose holdings include news format stations

FIGURE 2.5
Courtesy BIAfn.

do an incredible job with what they have to work with."

Managers of small-market stations must wrestle with the problems stemming from diminutive budgets and high employee turnover, whereas those at large stations must grapple with the difficulties inherent in managing larger budgets, bigger staffs, and, of course, stiffer competition. "It's all relative, really. While the small town station gives the manager turnover headaches, the metropolitan station manager usually is caught up in the ratings battle, which consumes vast amounts of time and energy. Of course, even larger stations are not immune to turnover," observes KGLD's Bremkamp.

It is up to the manager to control the station's finances. Knowledge of bookkeeping and accounting procedures is necessary. "You handle the station's purse-strings. An understanding of budgeting is an absolute must. Station economics is the responsibility of the GM. The idea is to control income and expenses in a way that yields a sufficient profit," says Roger Ingram.

The manager allocates and approves spending in each department (in cluster operations this means each station). Heads of departments must work within the budgets they have helped establish. Budgets generally cover the expenses involved in the operation of a particular area within the station for a specified period, such as a 6- or 12-month period. No manager wants to spend more than what is absolutely required. A thorough familiarity with what is involved in running the various departments within a station prevents waste and overspending. "A manager has to know what is going on in programming, engineering, sales, actually every little corner of the station, in order to run a tight ship and make the most revenue possible. Off course, you should never cut corners simply for the sake of cutting corners. An operation must spend in order to make. You have to have effective cost control in all departments. That doesn't mean damaging the product through undernourishment either," says Evans.

David Saperstein, president of Metro Networks, observes that, "In the early days, radio was a mom-and-pop type of business. With the huge dollars in radio today, one mistake could cost a station hundreds of thousands or even millions of dollars in revenue."

To ensure that the product the station offers is the best it can be, the station manager must keep in close touch with every department. Since the station's sound is what wins listeners, the manager must work closely with the program director and engineer. Both significantly contribute to the quality of the air product. The program director is responsible for what goes on the air, and the engineer is responsible for the way it sounds.

Meanwhile, the marketing of the product is vital. This falls within the province of the sales department. Traditionally, the general manager works more closely with the station's sales manager than with anyone else.

An excellent air product attracts listeners, and listeners attract sponsors. It is as basic as that. "The formula works when all departments in a station work in unison and up to their potential," contends Marlin R. Taylor. "In radio our product is twofold – the programming we send over our frequency and the listening audience we deliver to advertisers. A station's success is linked to customer/listener satisfaction, just like a retail store's. If you don't have what the consumer desires, or the quality doesn't meet his standards, he'll go elsewhere and generally won't return."

In a fast-moving, dynamic industry like radio, where both cultural and technological innovations have an impact on the way a station operates, the manager must stay informed and keep an eye toward the future. New technologies employed by stations compound the manager's task. For example, determining how best to employ a station's Web site is ultimately the decision of the station manager. Radio manager Jim Robertson notes, "In terms of Web sites, they have to be established based on a plan. Our country station Web site, 93.7kcountry.com, is much more advanced at this point than our classic rock station WIND-FM. K Country's site is streaming and gets more attention every day. WINDFM.com is coming along and will be streaming in the next few months. Both stations do interactive work with their listeners. We do everything possible on air to get people to go to our sites, including Web site only contesting.

FIGURE 2.6
Publications such as these keep managers informed of industry developments and issues.

The Web sites, as good as they are now, deserve more attention and resources to improve. That is high on my list of things to get done over the next couple of years. It's important to keep the sites as uncluttered with sales-related material as possible and make it more hands on with the really important things that our listeners want and need. Too many sites, including ours at times, look like a laundry list of the clients currently on the air rather than an interactive fun site. It's another important element of today's radio station management."

In terms of other new technologies, such as HD and its side-channels features, Robertson says that effective strategies for the implementation of such things are a part of what is expected of station managers. "You have to know what is going to enhance your product in the face of mounting competition. We are

very excited about offering new opportunities for listening with our HD channels, and as manager you have to stay abreast of things all the time."

Financial projections for future needs must be based on data that include the financial implications of prospective and predicted events. An effective manager anticipates change and develops appropriate plans to deal with it. Industry trade journals (*Broadcasting and Cable, Radio and Records, The Radio Ink, Radio Business Report*, and a host of Internet newsletters) and conferences conducted by organizations such as the NAB and the Radio Advertising Bureau (RAB) help keep the station manager informed of what tomorrow may bring.

About industry trade journals, Ed Shane observes, "The consultant (not the comedian) George Burns once said 'Never has

Norman Feuer | The Qualities That Make a Station Manager

1. *Smart/intelligent*. This is something that I cannot teach or help someone with; they are either smart or they are not.
2. *Organized*. A GM or GSM [general sales manager] has a lot on his or her plate, especially with the limited time available to accomplish what has to be done. An unorganized person will waste that time.
3. *Good communicator*. As a group head, I too have a lot on my plate. I must rely on my managers to communicate with me quickly and efficiently. If they can do that, I have the comfort that they are able to communicate effectively with their staff on the station's missions and goals to be accomplished.
4. *Strategic thinker*. In today's world there's no such thing as a quick fix. Therefore, I need to have

someone who can think through the long-term effects of each major decision that he or she makes.
5. *Motivated*. In my opinion, you cannot motivate people; they are either self-motivated or not. All I can do is set a work environment that motivates them to do their best.
6. *Businesslike*. I need people who understand that this is a business, not a hobby, and that every decision that they make has a return on investment and will lead to a successful business conclusion.
7. *Leader*. I want a person who is a winner, for whom people want to work, with the ability to read personnel, hire the best people, and be able to maximize the potential of all his or her people.
8. *Has a good track record*. Although it is nice to be able

to find someone who has a winning track record on all or most of his or her previous assignments, we also understand that no one is born a GM or GSM. Therefore, it is not always a criterion.
9. *Has a high energy level*. I've always felt that you can determine a successful person by watching the way he or she walks down the hallway. I believe a person with a high energy level tends to get his or her people to move at a higher level also.
10. *Honest and has integrity*. It is absolutely critical that you trust your manager, and trust that he or she won't try to make excuses and place blame on other people. This is a very hard ingredient to determine up front and may have to be acquired eventually.

so much been written by so many about so few.' The differences in today's trades compared to just a few years ago are significant. *Inside Radio, Radio Only, Radio Business Report's Radio News Today, R&R's Hot Wax,* and *Alternative Radio Confidential* are all paperless papers. *Broadcasting* is now *Broadcasting and Cable.* What does that say to the student of radio as a career? *R&R* [*Radio and Records*] claims that more company executives subscribe to it than any other trade, which was formerly *Broadcasting's* forte. Nonetheless, you have to read them to be up to date."

Station consultants and "rep companies," which sell local station airtime to national advertising agencies, also support the manager in his or her efforts to keep on top of things. "A station manager must utilize all that is available to stay in touch with what's out there. Foresight is an essential ingredient for any radio manager. Hindsight is not enough in an industry that operates with one foot in the future," says Lynn Christian, who

summarizes the duties and responsibilities of a station manager: "To me the challenges of running today's radio station include building and maintaining audience ratings, attracting and keeping outstanding employees, increasing gross revenues annually, and creating a positive community image for the station, not necessarily in that order." Richard Bremkamp is more laconic. "It boils down to one sentence: Protect the license and turn a profit."

Managing the Cluster

In the latter half of the 2000s, a huge percentage of the nation's radio stations exist in cluster configurations. That is to say, several stations owned by the same company are gathered together in one location. This has resulted in the downsizing of station staffs and the ultimate enhancement of the bottom line for the corporations licensed to operate these outlets. The latter is what has motivated this sweeping reorganization of the broadcast radio landscape. The long-time model of a single station run by a single manager is being eclipsed in major and medium markets by the post-Telecommunications Act of 1996 "cluster" paradigm in which a single market manager oversees the operation of many stations – in some cases up to eight. This creates a whole new set of challenges for radio managers. Perhaps the biggest challenge for the person responsible for the stations in a cluster is providing the appropriate amount of focus on each.

Tom Severino, Emmis Indianapolis Radio Market Manager, observes, "While managing a single station or even two, you have more time to get involved with more detail in each department. When you manage a cluster of four or more, you have to stay focused on the biggest issues that move you toward goals. The right people have always been your most important asset, and that is even more critical in cluster management. You have to make sure you have the absolute right person in the right position because you have to rely on leadership at all levels more in a cluster situation. To manage this effectively everyone in the organization must know what the goals are, how they contribute to those goals, how we are doing in reaching those goals. Everyone needs to be familiar with the values of the company as well."

Dix Communications vice president Jim Robertson shares many of Severino's views regarding the management of a station cluster. "The on-going balancing act of time and resources is by far top of the list from my perspective. I am fortunate to have two stations (93.7K Country/WOGK) and our three station classic rock simulcast (WNDD/WNDT/WNDN) that are capable of being number one in all of the key demographics. Each station rightfully demands and deserves equal attention. Admittedly, each station at times feels like the other is favored. I think that is good in a competitive environment. Good communication is essential in a cluster operation, especially at the department-head level. It allows each station's program director to understand why things are happening across the hall at the other station. A cluster has to function organically.

Severino offers a list of the pros and cons of the station cluster concept:

Pros: As a manager, you can use each entity to cross promote each other (events, programming specials, news, formats, etc; you can spread expenses); you can cross utilize personnel; you can expand what is offered to advertisers; you can utilize each station's audience delivery and events to best serve the customer; you can combine resources to get better pricing from vendors (promotional items, outside marketing); and you can reduce expenses on support staff (business office, sales, and so forth).

Cons: As a manager, you cannot get involved in the day-to-day detail of each entity; you cannot devote full focus on a single station; you cannot engage in long-term strategic thinking of each station enterprise.

Organizational Structure

Radio stations come in all sizes and generally are classified as small-, medium-, or large (metro)-market outlets (see Figures 2.7–2.9). The size of the community that a station serves usually reflects the size of its staff. That is to say, the station in a town of 5000 residents may have as few as three or four full-time employees. It is a question of economics. However, some small-market radio outlets have staffs that rival those of larger-market stations because their income warrants it. Few small stations earn enough to have elaborate staffs, however. Out of financial necessity, an employee may serve in several capacities. The station's manager also may assume the duties of sales manager, and announcers often handle news responsibilities. Meanwhile, everyone, including the station's secretary, may write commercial copy. The key word at the small station is flexibility, since each member of the staff is expected to perform numerous tasks.

Medium-market stations are located in more densely populated areas. An outlet in a city with a population of between 100,000 and a half million may be considered medium sized. Albany, New York; Omaha, Nebraska; and Albuquerque, New Mexico,

FIGURE 2.7
Organizational
structure of a small-
market station.

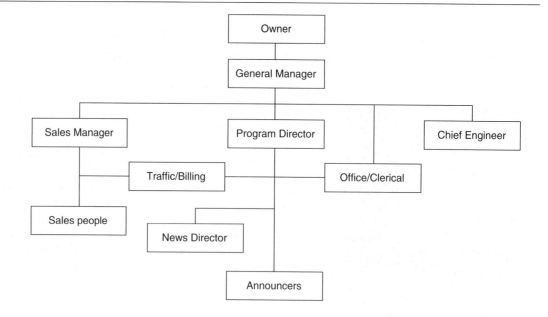

FIGURE 2.8
Organizational
structure of former
XM Satellite Radio.
Courtesy Lee
Abrams.

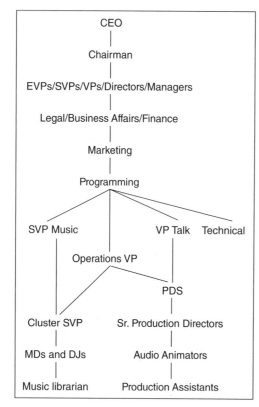

to specific areas of responsibility. Seldom do announcers substitute as news people. Nor do sales people fill airshifts, as is frequently the case at small outlets. (Reexamine Figure 1.29, a medium-market flowchart.)

Large (also referred to as major or metro)-market radio stations broadcast in the nation's most populated urban centers. New York, Los Angeles, and Chicago rank first, second, and third, respectively. The top 20 radio markets also include cities such as Houston, Philadelphia, Boston, Detroit, and San Francisco. Competition is greatest in the large markets, where as many as 70 stations may be dividing the audience pie.

When stations are purchased by large radio companies, positions are typically consolidated and centralized. For example, middle management slots (sales manager, program director, etc.) may be eliminated at the local station.

Market manager Tom Severino offers this view of how his particular station cluster is organized:

Market Manager – general manager of cluster; reports to corporate headquarters.
Director of Sales (DOS) – oversees the cluster's sales operation, including the individual stations' sales managers. The DOS reports directly to the market manager.
General Sales Manager (GSMs) – supervises the sales department of an individual station; reports to the DOS.
Director of Operations for AM – responsible for all programming elements, including

are typical medium markets. Greater competition exists in these markets, more than in the small market where only one or two stations may be vying for the listening audience. Each of the medium markets cited has over a dozen stations.

The medium-market radio station averages 12–20 employees. Although an overlapping of duties does occur even in the larger station, positions usually are more limited

Ward Quaal

My Management Philosophy

1. To succeed, radio stations must rededicate themselves to "localism" and their involvement in every possible phase of activity within their respective community (this applies regardless of format).
2. Regardless of the size of the market involved, those people who are making the news, whether in the world of academia, government, politics in general, and civic leadership, must become a part of a radio station's total operation. In short, management must encourage and develop their participation so as to add to the richness and the superior culture of the property.
3. Basic to every radio operation and ultimate success is policy control over commercial material – its length, its acceptability to a station of the type involved, and passing of the "test" as to whether the commercial and the station complement one another.

FIGURE 2.9
Ward Quaal.

marketing for WIBC and Network Indiana; reports to market manager.

Director of Operations for FM – responsible for all programming elements, including marketing for 97.1 Hank–FM (WLHK), B 105.7 (WYXB), and 93.1 RadioNow (WNOU). The program director for WNOU reports to the director of operations FM.

Controller – responsible for the business office, financial reporting, and office staff. Reports to market manager.

Network Indiana Operations/Building Operation – responsible for the Engineering and IT departments, building operations, and Network Indiana operations and affiliates. This position reports to market manager.

It should be kept in mind that each radio group or corporation designs its organizational elements in a manner it perceives to be most effective and efficient, although the preceding is fairly representative of station cluster organizational structure around the country.

Major-market stations employ as many as 50–60 people and as few as 20, depending on the nature of their format. Stations relying on automation, regardless of the size of their market, usually employ fewer people. Also keep in mind that station clustering and consolidation have changed the personnel landscape at many stations, as radio groups often concentrate the operation of several stations in one center. Station clusters often employ over 100 people.

The following brief descriptions of department head duties and responsibilities are explained more fully in later chapters. These individuals are regarded as station middle management and generally report directly to the station's manager. In cluster operations, these positions are often expanded or eliminated all together.

Operations Manager

In noncluster operations, this person is second only to the general manager in level of authority; the operations manager (not all stations have such a slot) is sometimes considered the station's assistant manager. The operations manager's duties include the following:

- Supervising administrative (office) staff
- Helping to develop station policies and see that they are implemented

- Handling departmental budgeting
- Keeping abreast of government rules and regulations pertaining to the entire operation
- Working as the liaison with the community to ensure that the station provides appropriate service and maintains its "good guy" image.

Duties tend to be more skewed toward programming and may even include the job of station programmer, or, as in the age of station clustering, the operations manager may be responsible for a radio group's programming and direct its individual station program director. In such cases, the operations manager's duties are designed with a primary emphasis on on-air operations. Assistant program directors commonly are appointed to work with the operations manager to accomplish programming goals. Not all stations have established this position, preferring the department head reporting to station manager approach.

Program Director

As one of the three key department head positions at a radio station, the program director is responsible for the following:

- Developing and executing format
- Hiring and managing air staff
- Establishing the schedule of airshifts
- Monitoring the station to ensure consistency and quality of product
- Keeping abreast of competition and trends that may affect programming
- Maintaining the music library
- Complying with FCC rules and regulations
- Directing the efforts of the news and public affairs areas.

Sales Manager

The sales manager's position (called director of sales in cluster operations) is a pivotal one at any radio station, and involves the following:

- Generating station income by directing the sale of commercial airtime
- Supervising sales staff
- Working with the station's rep company to attract national advertisers

- Assigning lists of retail accounts and local advertising agencies to sales people
- Establishing sales quotas
- Coordinating on-air and in-store sales promotions
- Developing sales materials and rate cards.

In cluster situations, a group general sales manager may direct the efforts of individual sales managers or account executives.

Chief Engineer

The chief engineer's job is a vital station function. Responsibilities include the following:

- Operating the station within prescribed technical parameters established by the FCC
- Purchasing, repairing, and maintaining equipment
- Monitoring signal fidelity
- Adapting studios for programming needs
- Setting up remote broadcast operations
- Working closely with the programming department.

Human Resources

The management of station personnel constitutes one of the manager's greatest challenges. Following is prominent radio executive Dick Oppenheimer's perspective on the subject: "One of the oldest sayings I can remember is that the more things change, the more they stay the same. Perhaps, but that adage certainly does not apply to the radio industry any longer."

"Before there were LMAs, duopolies, and super-duopolies, you were the manager of one or, at most, two radio stations. Now the norm is to manage at least six in your market. This is an industry where the inventory is time and the commodity is people. In fact, radio is a business totally driven by people."

"I can remember the days when almost anything was acceptable. The radio station was a totally male-dominated environment, except for the few female administrative assistants (clerks and secretaries). As a male manager you flattered, pampered, complimented, and cajoled the women employees. The station was a close-knit family whereby if you did not make notice of the appearance of a female worker she was insulted. If you did not put your arm around her, it meant you did not care. Likewise, if you did not insult or intimidate a male employee, something was wrong. Now, any and all of that can and probably will inspire a lawsuit – one you cannot win no matter what the outcome."

"The typical radio station had perhaps 15 employees and although you had middle managers you were truly 'hands-on.' The manager was more than just the boss, he was priest, rabbi, psychologist, big brother, confidant, and so on. Today, with upward of 100 employees, you can no longer be 'hands-on.' You are now a corporate figurehead. You are responsible to and for your corporation for the day-to-day operations of your slew of radio stations."

"Today's radio station is far different from the one of 10 or 20 years ago. Now there's a host of considerations you as manager must keep a watchful eye on, including sexual harassment, job discrimination, hostile work environment, disabilities acts, and race, religion, and gender issues. That's for starters."

"The first thing a manager must do is learn all the rules and laws concerning areas that impact human resources. You shouldn't attempt this yourself. Hire and retain an attorney who specializes in labor law. Have the attorney write an employee manual and establish the policies that are necessary for you to be a competent personnel manager. Once you have done this, have an initial meeting with your management staff and your attorney to convey the information necessary to assist your people in their management of other people."

"Next have your employees acknowledge receipt of the manual, and each and every quarter have reviews with your management staff regarding the various policies outlined in the manual as a means of detecting and assessing any potential problems."

"Document everything. *Remember, if it is not in writing, it did not occur.* When an employee comes to you with a complaint, have someone else present to verify the discussion and its content. Keep in mind that in a courtroom, you are the defendant. All the employee has to say is that it happened. The burden of proof is yours."

"Of course, one of the best ways to prevent problems is through proper hiring. It has been my experience that, often times, the employee who files charges against you is a marginal or questionable employee, that is to say, an employee who should not have been hired in the first place. Unfortunately, it is not until a suit has been filed that you learn about an employee's history of filing complaints. However, there are times when a complaint is legitimate. Real problems can and do exist. You have to be mindful of this."

"Handling people is one of the significant challenges of any manager. It is also one of the most rewarding."

Whom Do Managers Hire?

Managers want to staff their stations with the most qualified individuals. Their criteria go beyond education and work experience to include various personality characteristics. "A strong resume is important, but the type of person is what really decides it for me. The goal is to hire someone who will fit in nicely with the rest of the station's members. A station is a bit like a family in that it is never too large and people are in fairly close contact with one another. Integrity, imagination, intelligence, and a desire to succeed are the basic qualities that I look for when hiring," says Maine station manager Christopher Spruce.

Ambition and a positive attitude are attributes that rank high among most managers. "People with a sincere desire to be the best, to win, are the kind who really bolster an operation. Our objective when I headed Viacom Radio was to be number one at what we did, so any amount of negativity or complacency was viewed as counterproductive," says Norm Feuer. Lynn Christian, who once served as Feuer's boss while manager of a Miami radio station, says that competitiveness and determination are among the qualities he, too, looks for, and adds loyalty and dedication to the list. "Commitment to the station's philosophy and goals must exist in every employee or there are soft spots in the operation. In today's marketplace you have to operate from a position of strength, and this takes a staff that is with you all the way."

Stability and reliability are high on any manager's list. Radio is known as a nomadic profession, especially the programming end. Deejays tend to come and go, sometimes disappearing in the night. "A manager strives to staff his station with dependable people. I want an employee who is stable and there when he or she is supposed to be," states Duncklee.

A station can ill afford to shut down because an air person fails to show up for his or her scheduled shift. When a no-show occurs, the station's continuity is disrupted both internally and externally. Within the station, adjustments must be made to fill the void created by the absent employee. At the same time, a substitute deejay often detracts from efforts to instill in the audience the feeling that they can rely on the station.

Managers are wary of individuals with fragile or oversized egos. "No prima donnas, please! I want a person who is able to accept constructive criticism and use it to his or her advantage without feeling that he is being attacked. The ability to look at oneself objectively and make the adjustments that need to be made is very important," observes manager Cliff Shank. Carl Evans echoes his sentiments. "Open-mindedness is essential. An employee who feels that he can't learn anything from anyone or is never wrong is usually a fly in the ointment."

Honesty and candor are universally desired qualities, says Bremkamp. "Every station manager appreciates an employee who is forthright and direct, one who does not harbor ill feelings or unexpressed opinions and beliefs. An air of openness keeps things from seething and possibly erupting. I prefer an employee to come to me and say what is on his or her mind, rather than keep things sealed up inside. The lid eventually pops

and then you have a real problem on your hands."

Self-respect and esteem for the organization are uniquely linked, claims J.G. Salter. "If an individual does not feel good about himself, he cannot feel good about the world around him. This is not a question of ego, but rather one of appropriate self-perception. A healthy self-image and attitude in an employee makes that person easier to manage and work with. The secret is identifying potential problems or weaknesses in prospective employees before you sign them on. It's not easy without a degree in Freud."

Other personal qualities that managers look for in employees are patience, enthusiasm, discipline, creativeness, logic, and compassion. "You look for as much as you can during the interview and, of course, fill in the gaps with phone calls to past employers. After that, you hope that your decision bears fruit," says Spruce.

The Manager and the Profit Motive

Earlier we discussed the unique nature of the radio medium and the particular challenges that face station managers as a consequence. Radio, indeed, is a form of show business, and both words of the term are particularly applicable since the medium is at once stage and store. Radio provides entertainment (and information) to the public and, in turn, sells the audience it attracts to advertisers.

The general manager or market manager is answerable to many: the station's owners and corporate heads, listeners, and sponsors. However, to keep his or her own job, the manager must first please the owner or corporate manager. More often than not, this person's first concern is profit. As in any business, the more money the manager generates, the happier the owner.

Ed Shane observes, "The new radio paradigm is 'manager as financial expert.' Pressure from corporate ownership to feed stock prices has changed the way managers think about their stations. Budgets, once an annual affair, are reevaluated quarterly and even monthly. Managers now must be prepared at a moment's notice to cancel planned advertising expenditures or to move the expenditures into another quarter if the local cluster (or the company's region) is not making budgets. 'Budgets' does not mean breaking even. It means achieving the percentage increase over the previous year's cash flow. Margins of 45–50% are not uncommon."

Critics have chided the medium for what they argue is an obsessive preoccupation with making money, which has resulted in a serious shortage of high-quality, innovative programming. They lament too much sameness. Meanwhile, station managers often are content to air material that draws the kind of audience that advertisers want to reach.

Marlin Taylor observes that too many managers overemphasize profit at the expense of the operation. "Not nearly enough of the radio operators in this country are truly committed to running the best possible stations they can, either because that might cost them more money or they simply don't understand or care what it means to be the best. In my opinion, probably no more than 20% of the nation's stations are striving to become the IBM of radio, that is, striving for true excellence. Many simply are being milked for what the owners and managers can take out of them."

The pursuit of profits forces the station manager to employ the programming format that will yield the best payday. In several markets certain formats, such as classical and jazz, which tend to attract limited audiences, have been dropped in favor of those that draw greater numbers. In some instances, the actions of stations have caused outcries by unhappy and disenfranchised listeners who feel that their programming needs are being disregarded. Several disgruntled listener groups have gone to court in an attempt to force stations to reinstate abandoned formats. Since the government currently avoids involvement in programming decisions, leaving it up to stations to do as they see fit, little has come of their protests.

The dilemma facing today's radio station manager stems from the complexity of having to please numerous factions while earning enough money to justify his or her continued existence at the station. Marlin Taylor has suggested that stations reinvest more of their profits as a method of upgrading the overall quality of the medium. "Overcutting can have deleterious effects. A station can be too lean, even anemic. In other words, you have to put something in to get something out. Too much draining leaves the operation arid and subject to criticism by the listening public. It behooves the station manager to keep this thought in mind and, if necessary, impress it upon ownership. The really successful operations know full well that money has to be spent to nurture and develop the kind of product that delivers both impressive financial returns and listener praise."

Although it is the manager who must deal with bottom-line expectations, it is also the manager who is expected to maintain product integrity. The effective manager takes pride in the unique role radio plays in society and does not hand it over to advertisers, notes station manager Bremkamp. "You have to keep close tabs on your sales department. They are out to sell the station, sometimes one way or the other. Overly zealous sales people can, on occasion, become insensitive to the station's format in their quest for ad dollars. Violating the format is like mixing fuel oil with water. You may fill your tank for less money, but you're not likely to get very far. The onus is placed on the manager to protect the integrity of the product while making a dollar. Actually, doing the former usually takes care of the latter."

Conscientious station managers are aware of the obligations confronting them and are sensitive to the criticism that crass commercialism can produce a desert or "wasteland" of bland and uninspired programming. They are also aware that while gaps and voids may exist in radio programming and that certain segments of the population may not be getting exactly what they want, it is up to them to produce enough income to pay the bills and meet the ownership's expectations.

Paul Fiddick

What Makes a Successful Radio Manager?

In reflecting on "what qualities . . . make a radio manager successful," I've considered the dozens of managers who have worked for me in my stints running the Multimedia radio group (when they had one) and the last nine years with Heritage. And I've decided that there are two indicators that are essential (among others, I'm sure) for high performance. The first of these is a bias for action, or what industrial psychologists describe as task orientation. The concept of entrepreneurism is closely related to this, as is the quality of decisiveness. The radio manager must be innately tuned to the notion of taking the initiative if opportunities are to be exploited or – at a minimum – order is to be maintained.

The other quality is harder to describe. The term I have used is that successful managers take things personally. This may seem counterintuitive. Shouldn't managers retain a kind of cool objectivity with regard to their work?

What I've found is that the job is too demanding for that – at least at the highest levels. In order to overcome the frustrations that come from so many aspects of your performance being outside of your direct control (i.e., ratings, competitive changes, the fact that a music station's primary product is produced by someone else), the successful manager must be a driven personality, and that drive comes from an inner, personal need. I do not believe it is coincidental that success and obsessiveness go hand in hand in the radio business.

FIGURE 2.10
Paul Fiddick.

The Manager and the Community

In the early 1980s, the FCC reduced the extent to which radio stations must become involved in community affairs. (This deregulation process continued into the 1990s with the Republicans' creation of a sweeping telecommunications bill.) Ascertainment procedures requiring that stations determine and address community issues have all but been eliminated. If a station chooses to do so, it may spin the hits 24 hours a day and virtually divorce itself from the concerns of the community. However, a station that opts to function independently of the community to which it is licensed may find itself on the outside looking in. This is especially true of small-market stations, which, for practical business reasons, traditionally have cultivated a strong connection with the community. Therefore, most stations do make an attempt to ascertain community

issues and do so on a quarterly basis, maintaining the results of these surveys (often a list of the top 10 issues confronting the community of license) in their Public File to attest to their good citizenship. This looks particularly positive at license renewal time.

A station manager is aware that it is important to the welfare of his or her organization to behave as a good citizen and neighbor. Although the sheer number of stations in vast metropolitan areas makes it less crucial that a station exhibit civic mindedness, the small-market radio outlet often finds that the level of business it generates is relative to its community involvement. Therefore, maintaining a relationship with the town leaders, civic groups, and religious leaders, among others, enhances a station's visibility and status and ultimately affects business. No small-market station can hope to operate autonomously and attract the majority of local advertisers. Stations that remain aloof in the community in which they broadcast seldom realize their full revenue potential.

One of the nation's foremost figures in broadcast management, Ward Quaal, president of the Ward L. Quaal Company, observes, "A manager must not only be tied, or perhaps I should say 'married' to a station, but he or she must have total involvement in the community. This is very meaningful, whether the market is Cheyenne, Cincinnati, or Chicago. The community participation builds the proper image for the station and the manager and concurrently aids, dramatically, business development and produces lasting sales strength."

Cognizant of the importance of fostering an image of goodwill and civic mindedness, the station manager seeks to become a member in good standing in the community. Radio managers often actively participate in groups or associations, such as the local Chamber of Commerce, Jaycees, Kiwanis, Rotary Club, Optimists, and others, and encourage members of their staff to become similarly involved. The station also strives to heighten its status in the community by devoting airtime to issues and events of local importance and by making its microphones available to citizens for discussions of matters pertinent to the area. In so doing, the station becomes regarded as an integral part of the community, and its value grows proportionately.

Surveys have shown that over one-third of the managers of small-market radio stations are native to the area their signal serves. This gives them a vested interest in the quality of life in their community and motivates them to use the power of their medium to further improve living conditions.

Medium- and large-market station managers realize, as well, the benefits derived from participating in community activities. "If you don't localize and take part in the affairs of the city or town from which you draw your income, you're operating at a disadvantage. You have to tune in your audience if you expect them to do likewise," says Bremkamp.

The manager has to work to bring the station and the community together. Neglecting this responsibility lessens the station's chance for prosperity, or even

survival. Station consolidation has influenced localism across the country, but most managers continue to recognize that community involvement is a key to their success.

The Manager and the Government

Earlier in this chapter, station manager Richard Bremkamp cited protecting the license as one of the primary functions of the general manager. By "protecting" the license he meant conforming to the rules and regulations established by the FCC for the operation of broadcast facilities. Since failure to fulfill the obligations of a license may result in punitive actions such as reprimands, fines, and even the revocation of the privilege to broadcast, managers have to be aware of the laws affecting station operations and see to it that they are observed by all concerned.

An article in *Radio Ink* in the early 2000s summarized the FCC's punitive actions against stations for rules violations. Here are some examples:

- Construction or operation without authorization: $20,000
- Unauthorized transfer of control: $20,000
- Failure to permit FCC inspections: $18,750
- Failure to respond to FCC communications: $17,500
- Exceeding power limits: $12,500
- EBS equipment broken or not installed: $12,500
- Broadcasting indecent/obscene material: $12,500
- Violation of EEO or political broadcast rules: $12,500
- Violation of main studio rule: $10,000
- Public file violations: $7500
- Sponsor ID or lottery violations: $6250.

Since then, fines in some areas have increased significantly, especially in the area of indecency and obscenity.

The manager delegates responsibilities to department heads who are directly involved in the areas affected by the commission's regulations. For example, the program director will attend to the legal station identification, station logs, program content, and myriad other concerns of interest to the government. Meanwhile, the chief engineer is responsible for meeting technical standards, and the sales manager is held accountable for the observance of certain business and financial practices. Other members of the station also are assigned various responsibilities applicable to the license. Of course, in the end, it is the manager who must guarantee that the station's license to broadcast is, indeed, protected.

All rules and regulations pertaining to radio broadcast operations are contained in Title 47, Part 73, of the *Code of Federal Regulations* (CFR). The station manager keeps the annual update of this publication accessible to all employees involved in maintaining the license. A copy of the CFR may be obtained through the Superintendent of Documents, Government Printing Office, Washington, DC 20402, for a modest fee. Specific inquiries concerning the publication can be addressed to the Director, Office of the Federal Register, National Archives and Records Service, General Services Administration, Washington, DC 20408.

To reiterate, although the station manager shares the duties involved in complying with the FCC's regulations with other staff members, he or she holds primary responsibility for keeping the station out of trouble and on the air.

As noted in Chapter 1, many of the rules and regulations pertaining to the daily operation of a radio station have been revised or rescinded. Since the CFR is published annually, certain parts may become obsolete during that period. Martha L. Girard, director of the Office of the *Federal Register*, suggests that the *Federal Register*, from which the CFR derives its information, be consulted monthly. "These two publications must be used together to determine the latest version of any given rule," says Byrne. A station may subscribe to the *Federal Register* or visit the local library.

Since the FCC may, at any time during normal business hours, inspect a radio station to see that it is in accordance with the rules and regulations, a manager makes certain that everything is in order. An FCC inspection checklist is contained in the CFR, and industry organizations, such as the NAB, provide member stations with similar checklists. Occasionally, managers run mock inspections in preparation for the real thing. A state of preparedness prevents embarrassment and problems.

The Public File

Radio stations are required by the FCC to maintain a Public File. This, too, is ultimately the manager's responsibility. However, other members of a station's staff typically are required to update certain elements of the file. The purpose of the file is to provide the general population with access to information pertaining to the way a station has conducted itself during a license period. Interest in a station's Public File often increases around license renewal periods, when members of a community may choose to challenge a station's right to continue broadcasting.

The FCC expects a station's Public File to contain the following (this is subject to change as rules and regulations are revised):

- The Public and Broadcasting – A Procedural Manual (revised edition)
- Annual employment reports
- Copies of all FCC applications (power increases, original construction permit (CP), facilities changes, license renewals)
- Ownership reports
- Political file
- Letters from the public
- Quarterly issues
- Local public notices.

The Public File must be located in the community in which the station is licensed. Most stations keep the file at their main studio facility rather than at another public location, which is also permissible. The Public File is often the first place FCC agents look when they inspect a station, so it must be readily available. It is imperative that the file be kept up-to-date. As a general rule, files are retained for a period of 7 years.

More detailed information pertaining to a station's Public File may be found in Section 73.3526 of the FCC's *Rules and Regulations*.

The Manager and Unions

The unions most active in radio are the American Federation of Television and Radio Artists (AFTRA), the National Association of Broadcast Employees and Technicians (NABET), and the International Brotherhood of Electrical Workers (IBEW). Major-market radio stations are the ones most likely to be unionized. The overwhelming majority of American stations are nonunion and, in fact, in recent years union membership has declined.

Dissatisfaction with wages and benefits, coupled with a desire for greater security, are often motivators that prompt station employees to vote for a union. Managers seldom encourage the presence of a union since many believe that unions impede and constrict their ability to control the destiny of their operations. However, a small percentage of managers believe that the existence of a union may actually stabilize the working environment and reduce personnel turnover.

It is the function of the union to act as a bargaining agent working in good faith with station employees and management to upgrade and improve working conditions. Union efforts usually focus on salary, sick leave, vacation, promotion, hiring, termination, working hours, and retirement benefits.

A unionized station appoints or elects a shop steward who works as a liaison between the union, which represents the employees, and the station's management. Employees may lodge complaints or grievances with the shop steward, who will then review the union's contract with the station and proceed accordingly. Station managers are obliged to

✍ tactics: direct marketing
A Management Report from Shane Media

WWW.YOUR STATION

What's the first step in getting radio clients to spend money on your Web site? Getting them to accept the Web as a viable medium to reach customers, according to iRADIO, the Internet newsletter.

The advice: Let advertisers know that your Web site is part of your station's overall marketing artillery and that you have a reason for net surfers to check your site and come back for more.

Here are priorities iRADIO recommends for radio station Web sites:

- Station line-up and schedule
- Sound bites from station programming
- Live audio using Audio Net
- Monthly promotion calendars with event details
- Loyal listener club registration
- Station merchandise sales
- Contest information including tips on winning
- Station phone numbers, addresses, etc.
- E-mail feedback to personalities and management
- Listener testimonials
- Advertiser testimonials
- Promos for programs and features
- "Virtual Mall" of advertisers (by category)
- Weekly music charts
- New music releases and reviews
- Concert and entertainment calendar

Should your Web site include links to other sites? Yes, but be careful. Your Web site should be a promotional vehicle for your station. Links take your customer out of reach of your message and put someone else's message in front of them.

For example, a news station that links to CNN undermines its own news credibility. On the other hand, a Country station that links to the Garth Brooks fan club is doing its listeners a service. Avoid links to the competition.

Don't forget that your Web site is first and foremost -- a promotional vehicle for your station. The best use of the Internet is to motivate surfers to turn on the radio. Consider a "silent contest" that rewards net surfers when they log on to radio.

Another use for the Web: It's the ultimate "at work network." Set up regular e-mail to office workers with the same contest and event news you distribute through at-work faxes.

© SHANE MEDIA   HOUSTON, TX   (713) 952-9221

work within the agreement that they, along with the union, helped formulate.

As stated, unions are a fact of life in many major markets. They are far less prevalent elsewhere, although unions do exist in some medium and even small markets. Most small operations would find it impractical, if not untenable, to function under a union contract. Union demands would quite likely cripple most marginal or small-profit operations.

Managers who extend employees every possible courtesy and operate in a fair and reasonable manner are rarely affected by

FIGURE 2.11
Sourcing nontraditional revenue is a management goal. Courtesy Shane Media.

FIGURE 2.12
FCC ownership and
license application
form.

Federal Communications Commission
Washington, D.C. 20554

APPLICATION FOR NEW BROADCAST STATION LICENSE
(Carefully read instructions before filling out Form)
RETURN ONLY FORM TO FCC

Approved by OMB
3060-0029
Expires 9/30/90

For Commission Fee Use Only

FEE NO:

FEE TYPE:

FEE AMT:

ID SEQ:

For Applicant Fee Use Only

Is a fee submitted with this application? ☐ Yes ☐ No

If No, indicate reason therefor (check one box):

☐ Nonfeeable application

Fee Exempt (See 47 C.F.R. Section 1.1112)

☐ Noncommercial educational licensee

☐ Governmental entity

SECTION I — GENERAL DATA

For Commission Use Only

File No.

Legal Name of Applicant

Mailing Address

City | State | Zip Code

Telephone No. (include area code)

1. Facilities authorized by construction permit

This application is for: ☐ Commercial ☐ Noncommercial

☐ AM Directional ☐ AM Non-Directional ☐ FM Directional ☐ FM Non-Directional ☐ TV

Call Letters	Community of License	Construction Permit File No.	Modification of Construction Permit File No(s).	Expiration Date of Last Construction Permit

2. Is the station now operating pursuant to automatic program test authority in accordance with 47 C.F.R. Section 73.1620? ☐ Yes ☐ No

If No, explain.

3. Have all the terms, conditions, and obligations set forth in the above described construction permit been fully met? ☐ Yes ☐ No

If No, state exceptions.

4. Apart from the changes already reported, has any cause or circumstance arisen since the grant of the underlying construction permit which would result in any statement or representation contained in the construction permit application to be now incorrect? ☐ Yes ☐ No

If Yes, explain.

5. Has the permittee filed its Ownership Report (FCC Form 323) or ownership certification in accordance with 47 C.F.R. Section 73.3615(b)? ☐ Yes ☐ No ☐ Does not apply

If No, explain.

FCC 302
June 1988

unions, whose prime objective is to protect and ensure the rights of station workers.

The Manager and Industry Associations

Every year, the NAB and a variety of specialized and regional organizations conduct conferences and seminars intended to generate industry awareness and unity. At these gatherings, held at various locations throughout the country, radio managers and station personnel exchange ideas and share experiences, which they bring back to their stations.

The largest broadcast industry trade organization is the NAB, which was originally conceived out of a need to improve operating conditions in the 1920s. Initially only a lobbying organization, the NAB has maintained that focus while expanding considerably in scope. The primary objective of the organization is to support and promote the stability and development of the industry.

FY 2005 AM FM Reg. Fees

FY 2005 AM AND FM RADIO STATION REGULATORY FEES							
					Fee		
Facility Id.	Call Sign	Service	Class	Code	Amount	State, Community	Population
57172	82052OAT	FM Station	CP	0516	550	CA LOS OSOS-BAYWOOD PK	
57771	820524BD	FM Station	CP	0516	550	CA LOS OSOS-BAYWOOD PK	
70709	880217NG	FM Station	CP	0516	550	RI WAKEFIELD-PEACEDALE	
83423	960916ME	FM Station	CP	0516	550	GA GIBSON	
89056	971030ML	FM Station	CP	0516	550	WI MOUNT HOREB	
89615	971226MA	FM Station	CP	0516	550	SD WESSINGTON SPRINGS	
129788	DKACE	AM Station	CP	0515	310	UT FILLMORE	
7749	DKIIS	AM Station	B	0527	2975	CA THOUSAND OAKS	500,000 to 1.2 million
36167	DKQXX	AM Station	B	0526	1950	TX BROWNSVILLE	150,001 to 500,000
79024	DKRZB	FM Station	CP	0516	550	TX ARCHER CITY	
72785	DWBIT	AM Station	B	0523	475	GA ADEL	up to 25,000
129309	DWKKK	AM Station	CP	0515	310	CT OAKVILLE	
129354	DWKTT	AM Station	CP	0515	310	FL SILVER SPRINGS	
54464	DWREY	AM Station	CP	0515	310	FL MULBERRY	
54768	DWVUV	AM Station	B	0523	475	AS LEONE	up to 25,000
25819	DWVZN	AM Station	D	0536	675	PA COLUMBIA	25,001 to 75,000
54328	DWWTM	AM Station	C	0530	550	AL DECATUR	25,001 to 75,000
55492	KAAA	AM Station	C	0530	550	AZ KINGMAN	25,001 to 75,000
39607	KAAB	AM Station	D	0536	675	AR BATESVILLE	25,001 to 75,000
63872	KAAK	FM Station	C1	0549	2300	MT GREAT FALLS	75,001 to 150,000
17303	KAAM	AM Station	B	0580	5475	TX GARLAND	above 3 million
31004	KAAN	AM Station	D	0535	450	MO BETHANY	up to 25,000
31005	KAAN-FM	FM Station	C2	0547	725	MO BETHANY	up to 25,000
63882	KAAP	FM Station	A	0542	1125	WA ROCK ISLAND	25,001 to 75,000
18090	KAAQ	FM Station	C1	0547	725	NE ALLIANCE	up to 25,000
8341	KAAT	FM Station	B1	0542	1125	CA OAKHURST	25,001 to 75,000
33253	KAAY	AM Station	A	0521	3950	AR LITTLE ROCK	500,000 to 1.2 million
33254	KABC	AM Station	B	0580	5475	CA LOS ANGELES	above 3 million
44000	KABG	FM Station	C	0550	3000	NM LOS ALAMOS	150,001 to 500,000
18054	KABI	AM Station	D	0535	450	KS ABILENE	up to 25,000
26925	KABL	AM Station	B	0527	2975	CA SALINAS	500,000 to 1.2 million
36032	KABL-FM	FM Station	A	0544	2375	CA WALNUT CREEK	150,001 to 500,000
13550	KABN	AM Station	B	0527	2975	CA CONCORD	500,000 to 1.2 million

FIGURE 2.13
First page of the FCC's AM/FM regulatory fees document. Note that the larger a licensee's market, the higher the annual fee.

In the mid-1990s, however, the National Radio Broadcasters' Association, which merged with the NAB in the 1980s, threatened to break from the organization for its alleged overemphasis on non-radio matters.

Thousands of radio stations also are members of the RAB, which was founded in 1951, a time when radio's fate was in serious jeopardy owing to the rise in television's popularity. "The RAB is designed to serve as the sales and marketing arm of America's commercial radio industry. Members include radio stations, broadcast groups, networks, station representatives, and associated industry organizations in every market in all 50 states," explains Kenneth J. Costa.

Dozens of other broadcast trade organizations focus their attention on specific areas within the radio station, and regional and local broadcast organizations are numerous. The following list is a partial rundown of national organizations that support the efforts of radio broadcasters. A more comprehensive list may be found in *Broadcasting Yearbook*, the definitive industry directory, or in local area directories.

FIGURE 2.14
NAB's David Rehr heads the nation's foremost commercial broadcaster's association.

- National Association of Broadcasters, 1771 N Street, N.W., Washington, DC 20036
- Radio Advertising Bureau, 304 Park Avenue, New York, NY 10010
- National Association of Farm Broadcasters, 26 E. Exchange Street, St. Paul, MN 55101
- American Women in Radio and Television, 1101 Connecticut Avenue, N.W., Suite 700, Washington, DC 20036
- Broadcast Education Association, 1771 N Street, N.W., Washington, DC 20036
- Broadcast Pioneers, 320 W. 57th Street, New York, NY 10019
- Clear Channel Broadcasting Service, 1776 K Street, N.W., Washington, DC 20006
- Library of American Broadcasting, University of Maryland, College Park, MD 20742
- Native American Public Telecommunications, Box 83111, Lincoln, NE 68501
- National Association of Black Owned Broadcasters, 1730 M Street, N.W., Suite 412, Washington, DC 20036
- National Religious Broadcasters, 299 Webro Road, Parisippany, NJ 07054
- Radio Network Association, 1700 Broadway, 3rd Floor, New York, NY, 10019
- Radio-Television News Directors Association, 1000 Connecticut Avenue, N.W., Washington, DC 20006
- Society of Broadcast Engineers, Box 20450, Indianapolis, IN 46220.

NAB membership dues are based on a voluntary declaration of a station's annual gross revenues. The RAB and others take a similar approach. Some organizations require individual membership fees, which often are absorbed by the radio station as well.

Buying or Building a Radio Station

The process involved in the purchase of an existing radio facility is fairly complex. There is much to take into consideration. For one thing, it is rarely a quick and easy procedure because the FCC must approve of all station transfers (sales).

The FCC examines the background of any would-be station owner. Licensees must be U.S. citizens and must satisfy the following criteria, among others:

- Must not have a criminal record
- Must be able to prove financial stability
- Must have a solid personal and professional history.

Anyone interested in purchasing a radio property should employ the services of an attorney and/or broker who specializes in this area (consult *Broadcasting and Cable Market Place* for listings or contact the NAB).

The following points should be carefully considered before taking definitive action to purchase a station:

- Analyze the market in which the station is located.
- Evaluate the facilities and assets.
- Hire a technical consultant.
- Assess existing contracts, leases, and agreements.
- Research financial records.
- Examine the Public File.
- Probe the FCC's file.

According to radio station acquisition expert Erwin G. Krasnow, "The due diligence process involved in the acquisition of a radio station typically includes a review of the general economic and operational conditions, as well as such areas as the financial and accounting systems, programming, technical facilities, legal matters, marketing, employee benefits, and personnel and environmental matters. The objective of due diligence is to obtain information that will (a) influence the decision of whether or not to proceed with the acquisition; and (b) have an effect on the purchase price or working capital adjustment."

Purchasing a broadcast property is unlike any other kind of acquisition because of the unique nature of the business. It is important to keep in mind that in the end a station owner does not own a frequency. An operator is merely granted permission (a license) to propagate a signal for a prescribed period of time (7 years) and then must reapply to continue broadcasting.

If an individual wishes to create a station from scratch, an application for a CP must be filled out and submitted to the FCC. This too is quite involved and requires special expertise; it is necessary to determine whether a new station can be accommodated on the existing broadcast bands in the area of proposed operation.

If it can be proven that an available frequency exists and that no interference will occur, a CP may be granted. The applicant is then given a specified amount of time (usually 18 months) to commence and complete construction.

Before proceeding with a CP request, it is incumbent on the applicant to meet all of the criteria for station ownership set by the FCC. A new station must apply to the FCC for call letter acquisition. The station may request a particular set of calls, offer an existing station (possessing the calls it wants) a deal to transfer their calls to it, or take whatever the FCC issues it. Meanwhile, a station receives its frequency (kHz/MHz) from the FCC based on what is available in the allocation table for a particular market.

Radio company CEO Robin Martin offers the following criteria for station acquisition.

1. *The attractiveness and strength of the market*: I view this criterion from the perspective of general economic health and growth, the number of outlets and competitiveness of radio and other media in the market, and the general livability of the market (a measure of whether the owner would like to visit often or live in the market).

2. *The signal coverage of the station*: Not every station must be a Class B or C FM facility or a 50,000-W AM, but to be competitive in the target market, the tower location and height, combined with the authorized power, must be sufficiently optimized for the signal to reach the business and residential areas of the market with a signal that penetrates buildings and overcomes topographical obstructions so the average listener, in a car, at work, or home can listen on an average or subpar receiver. If listeners or advertisers can't hear the station clearly, the station can't expect to earn their loyalty even under the best of management.

3. *The reputation and legacy of the station*: A key test of success in my due diligence

FIGURE 2.15
Job one: "Protect the license." Courtesy *Broadcasting and Cable*.

FCC judge moves to pull radio licenses

By Chris McConnell

An FCC administrative law judge has decided to revoke the license of a broadcaster convicted of

of a station is the longevity of the sales force. The longer the average tenure of the incumbents and the more people on the sales force with over 5 years of service with the station, the greater the likelihood the station is well-regarded and successful in the marketplace. Another measure of this same success is the compensation of the middle half of the sales force. Disregarding both the best performers and the new recruits, higher compensation of the middle of the pack sales people indicates that the station has strong relationships with its advertisers as evidenced by their high renewal rate and great number of success stories (i.e., the station's advertising brings customers to the store). The success of the station and its competent management, along with the resulting good compensation, means that sales people like working at the station.

4. *The consistency of financial and ratings performance*: Long and steady growth in sales, cash flow, and ratings are a better predictor of future performance than recent or occasional sales spikes that propel performance up over a short period. Numerous changes in programming or promotional strategy, in rate philosophy, or in staff all indicate an unstable organization in search of the next new thing to

the detriment of listeners and advertisers. The results of station performance will be uneven and unpredictable.

If the target station is a startup or a turnaround, however, only the first two criteria apply meaningfully. The other main considerations for this type of purchase would be the strength of the management team, the reasonableness of the well-researched business plan, and the depth of finances the new owner brings to the deal.

CHAPTER HIGHLIGHTS

1. Radio managers face greater challenges than ever due to new audio competition and station consolidation. In addition, radio's unique character requires that station managers deal with a wide variety of talents and personalities.

2. The authoritarian approach to management implies that the general manager makes all of the policy decisions. The collaborative approach allows the general manager to involve other station staff in the formation of policy. The hybrid or chief-collaborator approach combines elements of both the authoritarian and collaborative management models. The chief-collaborator management approach is most prevalent in radio today.

3. To attain management status, an individual needs a solid formal education and practical experience in many areas of station operation – especially sales.

4. Key managerial functions include operating in a manner that produces the greatest profit, meeting corporate expectations, formulating station policy and seeing to its implementation, hiring and retaining good people, inspiring staff to do their best, training new employees, maintaining communication with all departments to ensure an excellent air product, and keeping an eye toward the future, especially in terms of how new technological applications, such as Web sites and HD, can enhance profitability.

5. Station clustering and consolidation have changed the personnel landscape at stations as radio groups often concentrate the operation of several stations in one central location. Some of the positions in a station cluster include a market manager, director of sales, general sales manager, director of operations, and controller.

6. In noncluster station environments, the operations manager is second only to the general manager at those outlets that have established this position. This individual supervises administrative staff, helps develop and implement station policy, handles departmental budgeting, functions as regulatory watchdog, and works as liaison with the community.

7. The program director is responsible for format, hires and manages air staff, schedules airshifts, monitors air-product quality, keeps abreast of competition, maintains the music library, complies with FCC rules, and directs the efforts of news and public affairs. The sales manager heads the sales staff, works with the station's rep company, assigns account lists to sales people, establishes sales quotas, coordinates sales promotions, and develops sales materials and rate cards. The chief engineer operates within the FCC technical parameters; purchases, repairs, and maintains equipment; monitors signal fidelity; adapts studios for programming needs; sets up remote broadcasts; and works closely with programming.

8. Managers hire individuals who possess a solid formal education, strong professional experience, ambition, a positive attitude, reliability, humility, honesty, self-respect, patience, enthusiasm, discipline, creativity, logic, and compassion.

9. Says consultant Ed Shane, "The new radio paradigm is 'manager as financial expert.'"

10. Radio provides entertainment to the public and, in turn, sells the audience it attracts to advertisers. It is the station manager who must ensure a profit, but he or she must also maintain product integrity.

11. To foster a positive community image, the station manager becomes actively involved in the community and devotes airtime to community concerns – even though the FCC has reduced a station's obligation to do so.

12. Although the station manager delegates responsibility for compliance with FCC regulations to appropriate department heads, the manager is ultimately responsible for protecting the license. Title 47, Part 73, of the *Code of Federal Regulations* contains the rules pertaining to radio broadcast operations. Updates of regulations are listed monthly in the *Federal Register*.

13. Radio stations are required to maintain a Public File and to make it available to the public during normal business hours.

14. The American Federation of Television and Radio Artists (AFTRA), the National Association of Broadcast Employees and Technicians (NABET), and the International Brotherhood of Electrical Workers (IBEW) are the unions most active in radio.

15. The National Association of Broadcasters (NAB) and the Radio Advertising Bureau (RAB) are among the largest radio trade industry organizations.

16. A person must be a U.S. citizen to hold a broadcast license. The FCC investigates all would-be station owners. To put a new station on the air, a construction permit (CP) application must be submitted to the FCC.

17. Call letters and frequencies are issued by the FCC.

18. Radio group CEO Robin Martin says the following must be weighed during the station acquisition process: strength of market, coverage area of the signal, station's reputation, and financial and ratings performance.

SUGGESTED FURTHER READING

Agor, W.H., *Intuitive Management*, Prentice Hall, Englewood Cliffs, NJ, 1984.

Albaran, A., *Management of Electronic Media*, 5th edition, Wadsworth, Los Angeles, CA, 2005.

Appleby, R.C., *The Essential Guide to Management*, Prentice Hall, Englewood Cliffs, NJ, 1981.

Aronoff, C.E., editor, *Business and the Media*, Goodyear Publishing Company, Santa Monica, CA, 1979.

Boyatzis, R.E., *The Competent Manager*, John Wiley and Sons, New York, 1983.

Brown, A., *Supermanaging*, McGraw-Hill, New York, 1984.

Coleman, H.W., *Case Studies in Broadcast Management*, Hastings House, New York, 1978.

Cottrell, D., *Monday Morning Leadership*, Cornerstone Leadership, New York, 2002.

Creech, K.C., *Electronic Media Law and Regulation*, 4th edition, Focal Press, Boston, MA, 2003.

Czech-Beckerman, E.S., *Managing Electronic Media*, Focal Press, Boston, MA, 1991.

Elimore, R.T., *Broadcasting Law and Regulation*, Tab Books, Blue Ridge Summit, PA, 1982.

Goodworth, C.T., *How to Be a Super-Effective Manager: A Guide to People Management*, Business Books, London, 1984.

Kahn, F.J., editor, *Documents of American Broadcasting*, 4th edition, Prentice Hall, Englewood Cliffs, NJ, 1984.

Kobert, N., *The Aggressive Management Style*, Prentice Hall, Englewood Cliffs, NJ, 1981.

Krasnow, E.G., and Werner, E.T., *Radio Deals: A Step by Step Guide*, RBR Publications, Springfield, VA, 2002.

Lacy, S., et al., *Media Management: A Casebook Approach*, Lawrence Erlbaum Associates, Hillsdale, NJ, 1993.

McCluskey, J., *Successful Broadcast Station Management and Ownership*, Pearson Custom Publishing, Boston, MA, 1999.

McCormack, M.H., *What They Don't Teach You at Harvard Business School*, Bantam, New York, 1984.

Miner, J.B., *The Management Process: Theory, Research, and Practice*, Macmillan, New York, 1978.

Mogel, L., *The Business of Broadcasting*, Billboard Books, LA, 2004.

National Association of Broadcasters. *Political Broadcast Catechism*, 16 edition, NAB, Washington, DC, 2007.

Pember, D.R., *Mass Media in America*, Science Research Association, Chicago, IL, 1981.

Pringle, P.K., Starr, M.F., and McCavitt, W.E., *Electronic Media Management*, 5th edition, Focal Press, Boston, MA, 2005.

Quaal, W.L., and Brown, J.A., *Broadcast Management*, 2nd edition, Hastings House, New York, 1976.

Rhoads, B.E., et al., editors, *Management and Sales Management*, Streamline Press, West Palm Beach, FL, 1995.

Routt, E., *The Business of Radio Broadcasting*, Tab Books, Blue Ridge Summit, PA, 1972.

Schneider, C., *Starting Your Career in Broadcasting*, Allworth Press, New York, 2007.

Schwartz, T., *Media, the Second God*, Praeger, New York, 1984.

Shane, E., *Cutting Through: Strategies and Tactics for Radio*, Shane Media, Houston, TX, 1990.

Shane, E., *Selling Electronic Media*, Focal Press, Boston, MA, 1999.

Townsend, R., *Further up the Organization*, Alfred A. Knopf, New York, 1984.

Wicks, J.L., et al., *Media Management: A Casebook Approach*, LEA, Mahwah, NJ, 2003.

Programming 3

Program Formats

"The devil is in the details," wrote famed French author Gustave Flaubert, and for our purposes in this chapter, we could say that the devil is in the *programming*. Indeed, designing a radio station's sound continues to be a bedeviling task, even as large radio companies cluster their outlets in the age of station consolidation. There is double the number of stations today competing for the audience's attention than existed in the 1960s, and more continue to enter the fray. Other media have proliferated as well, resulting in a further distraction of radio's customary audience. The government's laissez-faire, "let the marketplace dictate" philosophy, concerning commercial radio programming gives the station great freedom in deciding the nature of its air product, but determining what to offer the listener, who is often presented with dozens of audio alternatives, involves intricate planning. In the end, proffers Randy Michaels, "Programming is the key. Yes, I can hear my favorite songs on an iPod, but 'sometimes you like to drive, sometimes you like to ride.' A good programmer can create an experience that 'shuffle' cannot. The iPod won't bring play by play sports, breaking news, or introduce me to something new. It won't put events in context."

The bottom-line, of course, is to air the type of format that will attract a sizable enough piece of the audience demographic to satisfy the advertiser. Once a station decides on the format it will program, then it must know how to effectively execute it.

Ultimately, says Emmis programmer Jimmy Steal, "Great programming remains a constant regardless of amount/source of competition and the type of ratings methodology. The core of successful programming has always been unique content, passionate/knowledgeable/distinctive/engaging personalities, a consistent source of new music (format applicable, of course), and an overall presentation that eschews a sense of fun, a sense of energy, a sense of drama (positive drama – maybe suspense is a better word here), and an overall friend to, or oasis from, the daily challenges in the lives of our listening constituencies."

That said, programming in today's daunting marketplace is no easy task, observes consultant Ed Shane. "The staff reductions in postconsolidation radio cause national chains to fill the time with something – often syndication or repurposed content from another market. Ryan Seacrest is a perfect example. Seacrest does his morning show at KISS in Los Angeles, then portions of the program are edited and repackaged for other stations, mostly in the Clear Channel family (CC owns KISS), although the show is available to stations owned by companies other than Clear Channel. That reduces local radio to 'repeater,' not originator."

Brief descriptions of some of the most frequently employed formats in radio today follow. There are a host of other formats, or subformats – more than 100, in fact. Many are variations of those listed. The reader should keep in mind that formats morph as new trends in lifestyle and culture emerge. Radio formats are anything but static.

Adult Contemporary

In terms of the number of listeners, Adult Contemporary (AC; also referred to as The Mix, Hot AC, Triple A, Urban AC, Soft AC, Spectrum AC, and Lite AC) was the most popular format in the 1980s and continues to draw impressive audiences in the new millennium (number 3 most tuned format according to Arbitron), although some subcategories have lost ground since the last edition of this book. Says consultant Ed Shane, "Because the AC target audience is so diverse, the format has been most prone to fragmentation and competition."

AC is very strong among the 25–49-year age group, which makes it particularly appealing to advertisers, since this demographic group has significant disposable income. Also, some advertisers spend money on AC stations simply because they like the format themselves. The AC format is also one of the most effective in attracting female listeners.

AC outlets emphasize current and not so current (all the way back to the 1970s at some AC stations) pop standards, sans raucous, or harsh beats – in other words, no hard rock. Some AC stations could be described as soft rockers. However, the majority mix-in enough ballads and easy listening sounds to justify their title. The main thrust of this format's programming is the music. More music is aired by deemphasizing chatter. Music is commonly presented in uninterrupted sweeps or blocks, perhaps 10–12 minutes in duration, followed by a brief recap of artists and song titles. High-profile morning talent or teams became popular at AC stations in the 1980s and remain so today. Commercials generally

FIGURE 3.1
Courtesy Arbitron.

National Radio Format Shares and Station Counts

Radio Format Rankings and Station Counts
Ranked by Mon-Sun 6AM-Mid,
Persons 12+, AQH Share

Format	AQH Share 12+	Stations	Format	AQH Share 12+	Stations
Country	12.7	1,683	Soft Adult Contemporary	0.9	142
News/Talk/Information	10.7	1,553	Spanish Adult Hits	0.9	46
Adult Contemporary	7.2	798	Adult Standards	0.8	294
Pop Contemporary Hit Radio	5.6	381	Classic Country	0.8	299
Classic Rock	4.5	514	Rhythmic AC	0.7	26
Rhythmic Contemporary Hit Radio	4.0	156	Spanish Tropical	0.7	48
Urban Adult Contemporary	3.7	170	Contemporary Inspirational	0.6	99
Urban Contemporary	3.7	154	Modern Adult Contemporary	0.6	31
Mexican Regional	3.4	302	Educational	0.4	126
Hot Adult Contemporary	3.2	451	Jazz	0.4	75
Classic Hits	2.8	288	New Country	0.4	102
Oldies	2.6	750	Spanish News/Talk	0.4	63
All Sports	2.3	560	Latino Urban	0.3	12
Contemporary Christian	2.2	724	Rhythmic Oldies	0.3	18
Album Oriented Rock	2.1	174	Spanish Variety	0.3	146
Alternative	2.1	315	Easy Listening	0.2	46
Adult Hits	2.0	172	Ethnic	0.2	97
Classical	2.0	275	Southern Gospel	0.2	194
Active Rock	1.9	149	Spanish Religious	0.2	82
New AC/Smooth Jazz	1.8	72	'80s Hits	0.1	19
Talk/Personality	1.8	202	Nostalgia	0.1	63
Religious	1.5	993	Spanish Oldies	0.1	26
Spanish Contemporary	1.5	126	Tejano	0.1	21
All News	1.4	31	Urban Oldies	0.1	20
Variety	1.0	750	Children's Radio	0.0	29
Album Adult Alternative	0.9	154	Family Hits	0.0	26
Gospel	0.9	304	Other	0.0	78

Source: Format definitions are from Arbitron. Data come from Maximiser® Plus National Regional Database, Spring 2007.

are clustered at predetermined times, and midday and evening deejay talk often is limited to brief informational announcements. News and sports are secondary to the music. In recent years, ACs have spawned a host of permutations, such as Adult Hits and Adult Standards, as well as the iPod wannabe formats, known as Jack and Mike, which typically distinguish themselves from their AC counterparts by featuring a broader playlist, sometimes venturing as far back as the 1960s for music selections. In the late 2000s, according to Arbitron, the AC subgenre showing the most growth was Urban AC.

Contemporary Hit Radio

Once known as Top 40, Contemporary Hit Radio (CHR) stations play only those records that currently are the fastest selling. CHR's narrow playlists are designed to draw teens and young adults. The heart of this format's demographic is the 12–18 year olds, although in the mid-1980s it enjoyed a broadening of its core audience. Like AC, it too has experienced erosion in its numbers in recent years. In the *Journal of Radio Studies* (1995–1996), Ed Shane observed that the format "was a statistical loser in the 1990s. What futurist Alvin Toffler called 'the demassification of media' affected CHR the most. There were too many types of music to play. No one radio station could create a format with elements as diverse as rapper Ice T, rockers like Nirvana, country artists like George Strait and Randy Travis, or jazz musicians like Kenny G or David Benoit. Each of those performers fits someone's definition of 'contemporary hit radio.' CHR lost its focus."

Consultant Jeff Pollack believed that CHR had lost ground because it was not in tune with what he called the "streets," and he predicted that the format would embrace a more dance-rap sound as well as develop more appreciation for alternative rock hits. The format is characterized by its swift and often unrelenting pace. Silence, known as "dead air," is the enemy. The idea is to keep the sound hot and tight to keep the kids from station hopping, which is no small task since many markets have at least two hit-oriented stations.

In the 1995 interview in *Radio Ink*, programmer Bill Richards predicted that the high-intensity jock approach would give way to a more laid-back, natural sound. "The days of the 'move over and let the big dog eat', sweepers are over. Top 40 will look for more jocks who sound like real people and shy away from the hyped deejay approach." CHR deejays have undergone several shifts in status since the inception of the chart music format in the 1950s. Initially, pop deejay personalities played an integral role in the air sound. However, in the mid-1960s, the format underwent a major change when deejay presence was significantly reduced. Programming innovator Bill Drake decided that the Top 40 sound needed to be refurbished and tightened. Thus, deejay talk and even the number of commercials scheduled each hour were cut back to improve the flow. Despite criticism that the new sound was too mechanical, Drake's technique succeeded at strengthening the format's hold on the listening audience.

In the mid- and late 1970s, the deejay's role on hit stations began to regain its former prominence, but in the 1980s, the format underwent a further renovation (initiated by legendary consultant Mike Joseph) that resulted in a narrowing of its playlist and a decrease in deejay presence. Super or Hot Hit stations, as they also are called, were among the most popular in the country and could be found either near or at the top of the rating charts in their markets.

At the moment, at least, CHR has a bit less of a frenetic quality to it and perhaps a more mature sound. Undergoing an image adjustment, the format is keying in on improving overall flow while pulling back on jumping aboard the fad bandwagon. The continued preening of the playlist will keep the format viable, say the experts.

News is of secondary importance on CHR stations. In fact, many program directors (PDs) consider news programming to be a tune-out factor. "Kids don't like news," they claim. However, despite deregulation, which has freed stations of nonentertainment program requirements, most retain at least a modicum of news out of a sense of obligation. CHR stations are very promotion minded and contest oriented.

FIGURE 3.2
In the mid-2000s,
radio conceived a
format emulating
iPod diversity.
Courtesy Jack
FM 105.9.

Fewer than 500 stations (nearly all FM) call themselves CHR. Many of these stations prefer to be called Rhythm Hits (Churban fell out of favor in the late 1990s), which combines urban and rock hits, or Pop CHR/ Modern Hits, a narrower-based version of Top 40 that draws its playlist from MTV/ VH1 and college stations.

Country

Since the 1970s, the Country format has been adopted by more stations than any other. Although seldom a leader in the ratings race until recent years, its appeal is exceptionally broad. An indication of country music's rising popularity is the fact that there are over 10 times as many full-time Country stations today than there were 25 years ago. Although the format is far more prevalent in the South and Midwest, most medium and large markets in the North have Country stations. Due to the diversity of approaches within the format – for example, traditional, middle-of-the road (MOR), contemporary hit, and so on – the Country format attracts a broad age group, appealing to young as well as older adults. "The Country format has scored very high among 25–54-year-olds," adds Burkhart.

Says Shane, "In spite of predictions, Country has not fragmented. There are ways to skew the format for older or younger demos, but each group demands essentially the same music. The difference is in presentation and content between the songs."

Country radio has always been particularly popular among blue-collar workers. According to the Country Music Association

FIGURE 3.3

Market format breakdown. Courtesy Mix 105.1.

PROGRAMMING PROFILES
Tuning around
the Orlando Radio Dial

AM	540	580	740	990	1030	1140	1270	1440	1600
	WQTM	WDBO	WWNZ	WHOO	WONQ	WRMQ	WRLZ	WPRD	WOKB

FM	92.3	93.1	94.5	95.3	96.5	97.5	98.1	98.9	100.3	101.1	101.9	103.1	104.1	105.1	105.9	106.7	107.7
	WWKA	WKRO	WCFB	WTLN	WHTQ	WPCV	WGNE	WMMO	WSHE	WJRR	WJHM	WLOQ	WTKS	WOMX	WOCL	WXXL	WMGF

JAMMIN OLDIES

WOCL

OLDIES

WSHE

ROCK

WJRR

ADULT STANDARD

WHOO

COUNTRY

WWKA
WPCV
WGNE

NEWS/TALK

WWNZ
WTKS
WDBO

CHR

WXXL

ADULT CONTEMPORARY

WOMX

URBAN

WJHM
WCFB

JAZZ

WLOQ

SPANISH

WONQ
WRMQ
WRLZ
WOKB
WPRD

CHURBAN

WTLN

SPORTS

WQTM

CLASSIC ROCK

WHTQ

SOFT ROCK

WMMO

LITE ROCK

WMGF

ALTERNATIVE

WKRO

and the Organization of Country Radio Broadcasters, the Country music format is drawing a more upscale audience today than it did in the past. As many FM as AM stations are programming the Country sound in the 2000s, which was not the case just a few years ago. Until the 1980s, Country was predominantly an AM offering. Depending on the approach they employ, Country outlets may emphasize or deemphasize air personalities, include news and public affairs features, or confine their programming almost exclusively to music.

According to some programming experts, the Country format peaked in the mid-1990s, but Arbitron's "National Radio Format Share and Station Counts" in 2008 indicated otherwise, as the format led all others in terms of audience size (12.7 share) and station's claiming to be Country – 1683.

Soft Adult/Easy Listening/Smooth Jazz

The Beautiful Music station of the 1960s became the Easy Listening or Soft Adult station of the 2000s. Playlists in this format have been carefully updated in an attempt to attract a somewhat younger audience. The term *Beautiful Music* was exchanged for *Easy Listening* in an effort to dispel the geriatric image the former term seemed to convey. Easy Listening is the ultimate "wall-to-wall" music format. Talk of any type is kept minimal, although many stations in this format concentrate on news and information during morning drive time.

Instrumentals and soft vocals of established songs are a mainstay at Soft Adult/ Easy Listening stations, which also share a penchant for lush orchestrations featuring

FIGURE 3.4
Two top formats. Courtesy Arbitron.

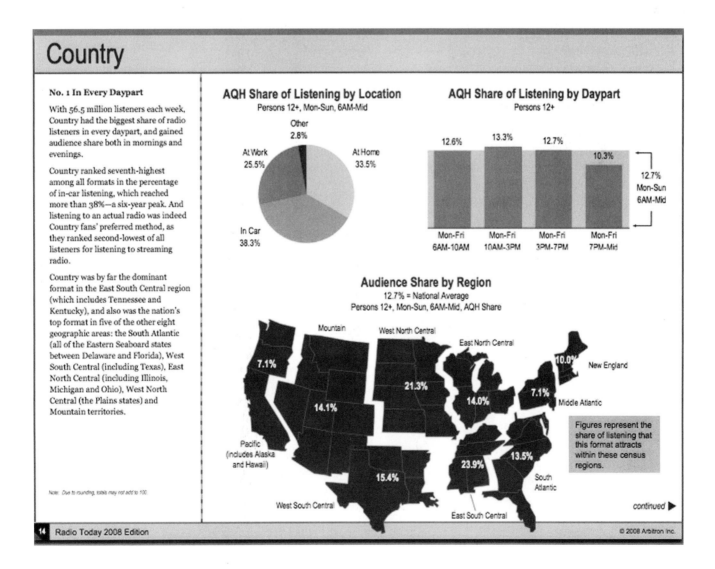

Country

No. 1 In Every Daypart

With 56.5 million listeners each week, Country had the biggest share of radio listeners in every daypart, and gained audience share both in mornings and evenings.

Country ranked seventh-highest among all formats in the percentage of in-car listening, which reached more than 38%—a six-year peak. And listening to an actual radio was indeed Country fans' preferred method, as they ranked second-lowest of all listeners for listening to streaming radio.

Country was by far the dominant format in the East South Central region (which includes Tennessee and Kentucky), and also was the nation's top format in five of the other eight geographic areas: the South Atlantic (all of the Eastern Seaboard states between Delaware and Florida), West South Central (including Texas), East North Central (including Illinois, Michigan and Ohio), West North Central (the Plains states) and Mountain territories.

Note: Due to rounding, totals may not add to 100.

AQH Share of Listening by Location
Persons 12+, Mon-Sun, 6AM-Mid

- Other 2.8%
- At Home 33.5%
- At Work 25.5%
- In Car 38.3%

AQH Share of Listening by Daypart
Persons 12+

| Mon-Fri 6AM-10AM | Mon-Fri 10AM-3PM | Mon-Fri 3PM-7PM | Mon-Fri 7PM-Mid |
| 12.6% | 13.3% | 12.7% | 10.3% |

12.7% Mon-Sun 6AM-Mid

Audience Share by Region
12.7% = National Average
Persons 12+, Mon-Sun, 6AM-Mid, AQH Share

Mountain 7.1%
Pacific (includes Alaska and Hawaii) 14.1%
West North Central 21.3%
East North Central 14.0%
New England 10.0%
Middle Atlantic 7.1%
West South Central 15.4%
East South Central 23.9%
South Atlantic 13.5%

Figures represent the share of listening that this format attracts within these census regions.

continued ▶

© 2008 Arbitron Inc.

plenty of strings. These stations boast a devoted audience.

Station hopping is uncommon. Efforts to draw younger listeners into the Easy Listening fold have been moderately successful, but most of the format's primary adherents are over 50 years. Music syndicators provide prepackaged (canned) programming to approximately half of the nation's Easy Listening/Soft Adult/Smooth Jazz stations, and over three-quarters of the outlets within this format utilize computer-automated systems to varying degrees. Easy Listening has lost some ground in the 1990s and 2000s to AC and other adult-appeal formats such as Album Adult Alternative and something called New Age, which some media critics describe as Easy Listening for Yuppies.

Soft Adult, Lite and Easy, Smooth Jazz, Adult Standards, and Urban AC have become replacement nomenclatures for Easy Listening, which, like its predecessor, Beautiful Music, began to assume a geriatric connotation.

Rock and Alternative

The birth of the Album Oriented Rock (AOR) format in the late 1960s (also called Underground and Progressive) was the result of a basic disdain for the highly formulaic Top 40 sound that prevailed at the time. In the summer of 1966, WOR-FM, New York, introduced Progressive radio, the forerunner of AOR. As an alternative to the super-hyped, ultra-commercial sound of the hit song station, WOR-FM programmed an unorthodox combination of nonchart rock, blues, folk, and jazz. In the 1970s, the format concentrated its attention almost

FIGURE 3.4
Continued

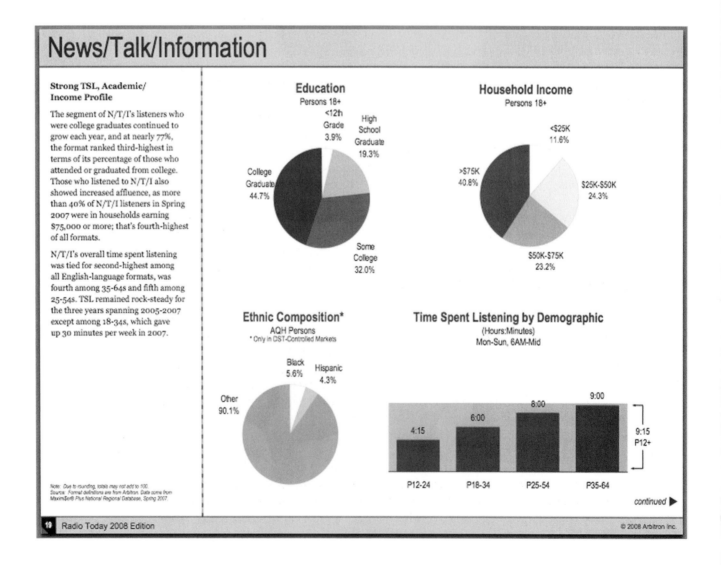

exclusively on album rock, while becoming less freeform and more formulaic and systematic in its programming approach.

Today, AOR often is simply called Rock, or more specifically Modern Rock or Classic Rock, and although it continues to do well in garnering the 18–34-year-old male, this format has always done poorly in winning female listeners, especially when it emphasizes a heavy or hard-rock playlist. This has proven to be a sore spot with certain advertisers. In the 1980s, the format lost its prominence owing, in part, to the meteoric rebirth of hit radio. However, as the decade came to an end, AOR had regained a chunk of its numbers, and in the 1990s, it renamed itself Modern Rock.

Generally, Rock stations broadcast their music in sweeps or at least segue two or three songs. A large airplay library is typical, in which 300–700 cuts may be active. Depending on the outlet, the deejay may or may not have "personality" status. In fact, the more-music/less-talk approach particularly common at Easy Listening stations is emulated by many album rockers. Consequently, news plays a very minor part in the station's programming efforts.

Rock (also called Active Rock) stations are very lifestyle-oriented and invest great time and energy developing promotions relevant to the interests and attitudes of their listeners. Reflecting the considerable drift away from the AOR nomenclature and model, WBCN's longtime PD, Oedipus, declared to the world in 1995, "We're Modern Rock!"

The Alternative Rock format tries for distinctiveness. That is to say, it attempts to provide a choice that is in contrast to the other Rock radio approaches. Creating this alternative sound is a challenge, says Stephanie Hindley, PD of Buzz 99.9: "The Alternative format is a great challenge for programmers. Think of the music you liked and the things you did when you were 18. Now think of the music you liked (or will like) and the things you did (or will do) at age 34. Despite the vast differences in taste in the 18–34 demographic, we need to play music that will appeal to as many people as possible within this diverse group. It's a constant balancing act. We have to play a lot of new music without sounding too unfamiliar. We

have to be cool and hip without sounding exclusive. We have to be edgy without being offensive. Be smart without sounding condescending. Young and upbeat without sounding immature. As long as those balances are maintained on a daily basis, we will continue to have success in this format."

News and Talk

There are News, News/Talk, News Sports, News Plus, and Talk formats, and each is distinct and unique unto itself. News stations differ from the others in that they devote their entire air schedule to the presentation of news and news-related stories and features. The All-News format was introduced by Gordon McLendon at XETRA (known as XTRA) in Tijuana, Mexico, in the early 1960s. Its success soon inspired the spread of the format in the United States. Because of the enormous expense involved in presentating a purely News format, requiring three to four times the staff and budget of most music operations, the format has been confined to larger markets able to support the endeavor.

The News/Talk format is a hybrid. It combines extensive news coverage with blocks of two-way telephone conversations. These stations commonly "daypart" or segmentalize their programming by presenting lengthened newscasts during morning and afternoon drive time hours and conversation in the midday and evening periods. The News/Talk combo was conceived by KGO in San Francisco in the 1960s and has gradually gained in popularity so that it now leads both the strictly News and the Talk formats. Talk radio began at KABC-AM, Los Angeles, in 1960. However, talk shows were familiar to listeners in the 1950s, since a number of adult music stations devoted a few hours during evenings or overnight to call-in programs. The motivation behind most early Talk programming stemmed from a desire to strengthen weak time slots while satisfying public affairs programming requirements. Like its nonmusic siblings, Talk became a viable format in the 1960s and does well today, although it too has suffered due to greater competition. In contrast to All-News, which attracts a slightly younger and more upscale audience, All-Talk amasses a large following among blue-collar workers and retirees, and in 2008 was classified as the second most popular format in radio.

One of the recent news and information-oriented formats calls itself News Plus. Even though its emphasis is on news, it fills periods with music, often AC in flavor. News Plus stations also may carry a heavy schedule of sporting events. This combination did well for a while in several medium and large markets but began to fizzle in favor of newer permutations in the early 2000s.

News and/or Talk formats are primarily located on the AM band, where they have become increasingly prevalent since FM has captured all but a few of radio's music listeners. Meanwhile, the number of nonmusic formats is significantly increasing on FM, and this trend is predicted to continue as music listeners rely more and more on other audio sources.

In the late 1990s, over 1000 stations offered the information and/or news format. This was up nearly 300% since the late 1980s. In 2008, Arbitron claimed in excess of 1500 stations aired the talk format. Over 100 stations alone concentrated on sports exclusively, and dozens of others were beginning to splinter and compartmentalize into news/info niches, such as auto, health, computer, food, business, tourism, and entertainment.

National talk networks and syndicated talk shows, mostly of a conservative nature, continued to draw huge audiences in the new millennium, as more and more Baby Boomers became engaged in the political and social dialogues of the day. Despite the fact that a liberal talk radio network (Air America) debuted in the 2000s, its reception was anything but stellar as right-wing hosts (Rush Limbaugh being the king among them) continued to rule the genre.

An indication that the information format is achieving broader appeal among younger listeners is the recent emergence on the FM dial of a new hybrid called Talk 'n' Rock. This format variation to the mainstream Talk template has yet to find a viable audience niche.

All Sports

The trend in the last few years in the proliferation of the All-Sports format has boosted the popularity of nonmusic radio and significantly contributed to the dominance of "chatter" radio in the ratings. Today, several hundred stations offer around-the-clock sports talk, among them WFAN and WEEI in the Northeast and KLAC and KJR on the West Coast. In addition, several sports networks now appear across the radio band. Since the mid-1990s, ESPN Radio Network, Fox Sports Radio, and Sporting News Radio have emerged and are now carried by stations throughout the country. If AM radio is able to claim a younger demographic at all, it is because men 18–29 are big fans of sports radio. Meanwhile, All Sports has begun to migrate to FM in significant numbers.

According to Arbitron, All Sports ranked 13th among formats at the start of 2009 with over 14 million weekly listeners. More men tune All Sports radio than women, and the audience is almost exclusively over 25 years old. It is a highly educated audience with an upper-income.

Consultant Ed Shane makes this observation regarding the success of the format. "The element of 'guy talk' is an important factor and one of the central ingredients that gives this format its special appeal."

FM Talk

Perhaps the most unique manifestation in nonmusic radio is the growing presence of talk on FM. Talent consultant Jason Insalaco gives his perspective on the rise of the *discourse* format on what has always been the dial for music: "While traditional AM talk has been profiled in recent years for its explosion onto the radio landscape, FM talk radio has become a popular format for an audience previously ignored by talk programmers. FM talk's primary audience is 25–44 years old. This demographic likely did not grow up listening to AM talk radio. In fact, the FM talk audience has very likely tuned AM very little during its lifetime. FM talk does not program itself like a traditional full-service AM talk outlet. There is not the emphasis on news and traffic, which is a staple of the AM talkers. Rather FM talk's focus is personality driven, aka Mancow, Tom Leykis, and Opie and Anthony. These FM talk stalwarts do incorporate some news into their programs, but the main focus is entertainment. FM talk programs itself more like an FM music station than an AM talk station. It features shorter segments covering a variety of issues in contrast to the 1-hour AM talk sweep. Issues discussed typically come from sources like *Rolling Stone* and *People* magazine and the local sports and entertainment section of the newspaper. Topics are not necessarily caller intensive as with most AM talkers. Listener participation is a part of FM talk radio; however, there is not the typical topic-monologue-caller participation cycle of AM talkers. Moreover, the 'bumper music' played to intro segments of FM talk comes from the latest alternative and rock artists found on the competing music stations. This gives the station a youthful sound and grabs the potential talk listener who is scanning the dial. FM talk's competition comes from Alternative/Modern Rock/AOR and Classic Rock stations. The future of FM talk looks bright. Expect the format to become more widespread in the coming years."

Clearly, the number of FM talk outlets in major markets is on the increase. A good example is 96.9 FM in Boston, which has made serious inroads into the nonmusic radio arena. In recent surveys, it has challenged the city's long-standing talk-oriented stations on AM, a feat that is being duplicated in other markets around the country.

Classic/Oldies/Nostalgia

Although these formats are not identical, they derive the music they play from years gone by. Although the Nostalgia station, sometimes referred to as *Big Band*, constructs its playlist around tunes popular as far back as the 1940s and 1950s, the Oldies outlet focuses its attention on the pop tunes of the late 1950s and 1960s. A typical Oldies quarter-hour might consist of songs by Elvis Presley, the Everly Brothers, the Beatles, Brian Hyland, Three Dog Night, and the Ronettes. In contrast, a Nostalgia quarter-hour might consist of tunes from the prerock era performed by artists like Frankie Lane, Les Baxter, the Mills Brothers, Tommy Dorsey, and popular ballad singers of the last few decades.

Nostalgia radio caught on in the late 1970s, the concept of programmer Al Ham.

Nostalgia is a highly syndicated format, and most stations go out-of-house for programming material. Because much of the music predates stereo processing, AM outlets are most apt to carry the Nostalgia sound. Music is invariably presented in sweeps, and, for the most part, deejays maintain a low profile. Similar to Easy Listening, Nostalgia pushes its music to the forefront and keeps other program elements at an unobtrusive distance. In the 1980s, Easy Listening/Beautiful Music stations lost some listeners to this format, which claimed a viable share of the radio audience.

The Oldies format was first introduced in the 1960s by programmers Bill Drake and Chuck Blore. Although Nostalgia's audience tends to be over the age of 50, most Oldies listeners are somewhat younger. Unlike Nostalgia, most Oldies outlets originate their own programming, and very few are automated. In contrast with its vintage music cousin, the Oldies format allows greater deejay presence. At many Oldies stations, air personalities play a key role. Music is rarely broadcast in sweeps, and commercials, rather than being clustered, are inserted in a random fashion between songs.

Consultant Kent Burkhart noted that in the early 1990s, "Oldies stations are scoring very big in a nice broad demographic. These stations are doing quite well today, and this should hold for a while." That said, in 2008 Arbitron reported that the Oldies format experienced the sharpest decline in audience numbers of all the vintage-oriented stations – with 30 stations dropping the sound in just 1 year. At the same time, Nostalgia has not been shown as having much growth but remains fairly solid in some markets. In the 1990s, Oldies outlets lost audience ground. However, over 700 stations still call themselves Oldies or Nostalgia. Meanwhile, a more dance/contemporary approach, called "Jammin' Oldies," has attracted additional listeners.

Meanwhile Classic Rock and Classic Hit stations emerged as the biggest winners in the late 1980s and early 1990s, and of the vintage format genres, they can boast the biggest audience shares in last part of the 2000s. These yesteryear music stations draw their playlists from the chart toppers (primarily in the rock music area) of the 1970s and 1980s (and early 1990s) and often appear in the top 10 ratings.

Classic Rock concentrates on tunes essentially featured by former AOR stations over the past two decades, whereas Classic Hit stations fill the gap between Oldies and CHR outlets with playlists that draw from 1970s, 1980s, and 1990s Top 40 charts.

Urban Contemporary

Considered the "melting pot" format, Urban Contemporary (UC), attracts large numbers of Hispanic and Black listeners, as well as white. As the term suggests, stations employ-

ing this format usually are located in metropolitan areas with large, heterogeneous populations. UC was born in the early 1980s, the offspring of the short-lived Disco format, which burst onto the scene in 1978. What characterizes UC the most is its upbeat, danceable sound and deejays who are hip, friendly, and energetic. Although UC outlets stress danceable tunes, their playlists generally are anything but narrow. However, a particular sound may be given preference over another, depending on the demographic composition of the population in the area that the station serves. For example, UC outlets may play greater amounts of music

FIGURE 3.5
Radio stations pay an annual fee to music licensing services such as BMI and ASCAP.

ASCAP is ▷

a **performing-rights organization** whose function is to protect the **rights** of our members by licensing and collecting royalties for the public performance of their copyrighted musical works.

the only U.S. society **created and controlled** by songwriters and publishers.

the only U.S. society that gives writers and publishers **a voice.** ASCAP conducts open membership meetings, issues financial reports to its members, has writer and publisher member advisory committees.

the only U.S. society that gives writers and publishers **a vote.** ASCAP is governed by an experienced Board of Directors composed of knowledgeable songwriters, composers and music publishers, each of whom is elected by the membership.

the **largest** performing-rights society in the world in terms of **license-fee collections** and writer and publisher **performance-royalty payments.** 1995 income: more than $435 million.

the **largest** performing-rights society in the world in terms of **constituency.** ASCAP has more than **75,000** U.S. writer and publisher members. Additionally, it represents more than **200,000** foreign-society writers and publishers.

the industry **leader** since 1914 in negotiating license fees with the users of music.

one of the most effective protectors of the rights of creators and music publishers. ASCAP **lobbies** in Congress and **litigates** in the courts, if necessary, on behalf of its constituents.

the only society where writers and publishers sign **identical contracts,** with **the right to resign** every year of the contract.

the only U.S. society with specific written rules covering **all types of performances on all types of media,** with all royalties distributed solely on that basis.

the only U.S. society where payment **changes have to be approved** by the Board of Directors, the Department of Justice and in some cases by a U.S. Federal Court after an open court hearing. No changes are made without notice to the membership, and rates are not subject to arbitrary change at any time, as they are at other performing-rights organizations.

the only U.S. society where your **royalties are determined objectively** over their entire copyright life and not by discretionary voluntary payments, short-term special deals or management discretion.

with a Latin or rhythm-and-blues flavor, whereas others may air larger proportions of light jazz, reggae, new rock, or hip hop. Some AM stations around the country have adopted the UC format; however, it is more likely to be found on the FM side, where it has taken numerous stations to the forefront of their market's ratings.

UC has had an impact on Black stations, which have experienced erosion in their youth numbers. Many Black stations have countered by broadening their playlists to include artists who are not traditionally programmed. Because of their high-intensity, fast-paced sound, UC outlets can give a Top 40 impression, but in contrast, they commonly segue songs or present music in sweeps and give airplay to lengthy cuts, sometimes 6–8 minutes long. Although Top 40 or CHR stations seldom program cuts lasting more than 4 minutes, UC outlets find long cuts or remixes compatible with their programming approach. Remember, UCs are very dance oriented. Newscasts play a minor role in this format, which caters to a target audience aged 18–34. Contests and promotions are important program elements.

As noted earlier, several CHR stations have adopted urban artists to offer the hybrid Churban or Rhythm Hits sound. Likewise, many Urban outlets have drawn from the more mainstream CHR playlist in an attempt to expand their listener base.

Classical

Although there are fewer than three-dozen full-time commercial Classical radio stations in the country, no other format can claim a more loyal following. Despite small numbers and soft ratings, most Classical stations do manage to generate a modest to good income. Over the years, profits have remained relatively minute in comparison to other formats. However, member stations of the Concert Music Broadcasters Association reported ad revenue increases of up to 40% in the 1980s and 1990s with continued growth, albeit modest, in the 2000s. Owing to its upscale audience, blue-chip accounts find the format an effective buy. This is first and foremost an FM format, and it has broadcast over the megahertz band for almost as long as it has existed.

In many markets, commercial Classical stations have been affected by public radio outlets programming classical music. Since commercial Classical stations must break to air the sponsor messages that keep them operating, they must adjust their playlists accordingly. This may mean shorter cuts of music during particular dayparts – in other words, less music. The noncommercial Classical outlet is relatively free of such constraints and thus benefits as a result. A case in point is WCRB-FM in Boston, the city's only full-time Classical station. Although it attracts most of

FIGURE 3.6
Dozens of other formats (often variations on those listed) have emerged since the start of program specialization in the 1950s.

Some Format Debuts						
Prior to 1950	1950s	1960s	1970s	1980s	1990s	2000s
Classical	Middle-of-	News	Adult	Arena Rock	Mix	Jammin' Oldies
Country	the-Road	Talk	Contemporary	Hot Adult	All-Children	Rhythm Hits
Hit Parade	Top 40	News/Talk	Album	Contemporary	Arrow	Active Rock
Religious	Beautiful Music	Progressive	Oriented Rock	Hit/Radio	Rap/Hip Hop	Adult Hits
Black		Acid/	Easy Listening	Urban	Digital Hits	FM Talk
Hispanic		Psychedelic	Contemporary	Contemporary	Gen X	Diversity
		Jazz	Country	New Age	Tourist Radio	Christian
		All Request	Urban Country	Eclectic	Triple A	Contemporary
		Oldies	Mellow Rock	Oriented/Rock	NAC	Rhythmic Oldies
		Diversified	Disco	All Sports	Modern Rock	Acoustic
			Nostalgia	All Motivation	Churban	Spectrum AC
			British Rock	All Comedy	Boomer Rock	Americana
			New Wave	All Beatles	Coupon Radio	Rock AC
			Public Radio	Classic Hits		Jack
				Classic Rock		Mike
				Male Adult		Spanish
				Contemporary		Contemporary
						Urban Oldies
						Contemporary
						Inspirational
						New Country

the area's Classical listeners throughout the afternoon and evening hours, it loses many patrons to public radio WGBH's classical segments. At least in part, public radio's success consists of having fewer interruptions in programming.

Classical stations target the 25–49-year-old, higher income, college-educated listener. News is typically presented at 60–90-minute intervals and generally runs from 5–10 minutes. The format is characterized by a conservative, straightforward air sound. Sensationalism and hype are avoided, and on-air contests and promotions are as rare as announcer chatter.

Religious/Christian

Live broadcasts of religious programs began while the medium was still in its experimental stage. In 1919, the U.S. Army Signal Corps aired a service from a chapel in Washington, DC. Not long after that, KFSG in Los Angeles and WMBI in Chicago began to devote themselves to religious programming. Soon dozens of other radio outlets were broadcasting the message of God. In the 1980s, over 600 stations broadcast religious formats on a full-time basis, and another 1500 stations air at least 6 hours of religious features on a weekly basis. *M Street Journal* reports that over 900 stations air the Religious format today.

Religious broadcasters typically follow one of two programming approaches. One includes music as part of its presentation, and the other does not. The Religious station that features music often programs contemporary tunes containing a Christian or life-affirming perspective. Broadcast educator Janet McMullen finds that programming Contemporary Christian is a challenge for a number of reasons. "With the broad

FIGURE 3.7
Radio programming is tuned everywhere. Courtesy Arbitron.

Listening Location

Most radio listening took place out-of-home except during evenings, and this chart shows how the distribution of radio listening logically moves around throughout the day: at home and in car led in mornings, at work dominated in middays, in car took over in afternoons and at home won again in the evenings.

For several years the story has been the consistently growing proportion of in-car tune-in. Between Spring 2002 and 2007, in-car listening share rose at a rate of 9% in mornings and middays, 6% in afternoons and weekends, and 7% in evenings. At work's segment fell at a rate of 4% in mornings, 9% in middays and evenings, 11% in afternoons and 8% on weekends. At-home was down 6% in mornings, up 4% in middays, unchanged in afternoons, down 2% in evenings and off 3% on weekends.

These figures reflect the reality of American workers' gradually longer commutes, increasing media options and more mobile lifestyles.

Distribution of AQH Radio Listeners by Listening Location
Persons 12+

	Home	Car	Work	Other
Mon-Sun, 6AM-Mid	38.9%	35.5%	23.0%	2.6%
Mon-Fri, 6AM-10AM	38.1%	37.6%	23.0%	1.3%
Mon-Fri, 10AM-3PM	29.0%	30.2%	38.6%	2.2%
Mon-Fri, 3PM-7PM	30.8%	45.1%	21.7%	2.4%
Mon-Fri, 7PM-Mid	58.3%	28.0%	10.1%	3.6%
Weekend, 10AM-7PM	48.0%	37.9%	9.6%	4.4%

Fast Fact:
It's well known that radio is the only mass medium that easily adapts to all key listening locations. But exactly what is "other" as a listening location? If you're listening to the radio at a friend's house, while at the beach or park, while working out at the gym or in a doctor's waiting room, you're in an "other" location. The new Portable People Meter™ measurement tool will also credit listening to radio stations that people hear in restaurants, stores and businesses even if their attention is not directly focused on the station. It should be noted that "at-work" listening, while frequently thought of as "office" listening, can encompass many other work locations, such as a vehicle (if you happen to drive for a living), a retail outlet, a factory or a construction site.

Source: Maximi$er® Plus National Regional Database, Spring 2007.

scope of denominations possessing varying beliefs, it is sometimes very hard to keep the listening public happy. It is a very fine line to walk. You have to be careful not to offend or alienate listeners, even in our format. This requires careful and thoughtful programming." The religious format approach also includes the scheduling of blocks of religious features and programs. Nonmusic Religious outlets concentrate on inspirational features and complementary talk and informational shows.

Religious broadcasters claim that their spiritual messages reach nearly half of the nation's radio audience, and the American Research Corporation in Irvine, California, contends that over 25% of those tuned to Religious stations attend church more frequently. Two-thirds of the country's Religious radio stations broadcast over AM frequencies.

An indication of the continued popularity of Religious radio in the latter part of the 1990s was the launch of ChristianNet, a network that offers talk shows from some of the biggest names in conservative chatter.

Black/African American

African Americans constitute the largest minority in the nation, thus making Black one of the most prominent ethnic formats. Over 300 radio stations gear themselves to the needs and desires of Black listeners. WDIA-AM in Memphis claims to be the first station to program exclusively to a non-white audience. It introduced the format in 1947. Initially, the growth of this format was gradual, but in the 1960s, as the Motown sound took hold of the hit charts and the Black Pride movement got under way, more Black stations entered the airways.

At its inception, the Disco craze in the 1970s brought new listeners to the Black stations, which shortly saw their fortunes change when All-Disco stations began to surface. Many Black outlets witnessed an exodus of their younger listeners to the Disco stations. This prompted a number of Black stations to abandon their more traditional playlists, which consisted of rhythm and blues, gospel, and soul tunes, for exclusively Disco music. When Disco perished in the early 1980s, the UC format took its

place. Today, Progressive Black stations, such as WBLS-FM, New York, combine dance music with soulful rock and contemporary jazz, and many have transcended the color barrier by including certain white artists on their playlists. In fact, many Black stations employ white air personnel in efforts to broaden their demographic base. WILD-AM in Boston, long considered the city's Black station, is an example of this trend. "We have become more of a general appeal station than a purely ethnic one. We've had to in order to prosper. We strive for a distinct, yet neuter or deethnicized, sound on the air. The Black format has changed considerably over the years," notes longtime PD Elroy Smith. The old-line R&B and gospel stations still exist and can be found mostly in the South.

Hispanic

Hispanic or Spanish-language stations constitute another large ethnic format. KCOR-AM, San Antonio, became the first All-Spanish station in 1947, just a matter of months after WDIA-AM in Memphis put the Black format on the air. Cities with large Latin populations are able to support the format, and in some metropolitan areas with vast numbers of Spanish-speaking residents, such as New York, Los Angeles, and Miami, several radio outlets are devoted exclusively to Hispanic programming. Reported Arbitron in 2008, "As their population continued to surge in the United States, Hispanics increased the percentage of their representation in 15 of the 20 non-Spanish-language formats in our report, averaging 1.1% more in audience composition than in Spring 2006. The only formats where Hispanics made up a smaller proportion of a format's listenership were UC, Oldies, Alternative and Active Rock."

Programming approaches within the format are not unlike those prevalent at Anglo stations. That is to say, Spanish-language radio stations also modify their sound to draw a specific demographic. For example, many offer contemporary music for younger listeners and more traditional music for older listeners.

Ed Shane views Hispanic radio as very diverse and vibrant. "An impressive multiplicity of programming styles and approaches are found in this format. Here in Houston, for example, we have two brands of Tejano, one of Exitos (hits), a lot of Ranchera, and a couple of Talk stations. In the Rio Grande Valley of Texas, there's a lush, instrumental-and-vocal 'Easy Listening' station in Spanish. The L.A. dial is full of Hispanic nuance. Miami, likewise, and it has a totally different slant."

Many Hispanic women are drawn to an approach called The Groove, which mixes Motown and Latin pop artists. The format is marketed by Interstar Programming.

Spanish media experts predicted that there would be a significant increase in the number of Hispanic stations through the 2000s, and they were right. Much of this growth occurred on the AM band but later spread rapidly on FM.

Ethnic

Hundreds of other radio stations countrywide apportion a significant piece of their air schedules (over 20 hours weekly), if not all, to foreign-language programs in Portuguese, German, Polish, Greek, Japanese, and so on.

Around 30 stations broadcast exclusively to American Indians and Eskimos and are licensed to Native Americans. Today, these stations are being fed programming from American Indian Radio on Satellite (AIROS), and other indigenous media groups predict dozens more Indian-operated stations by the end of the next decade. Meanwhile, the number of stations broadcasting to Asians and other nationalities is rising.

Full Service

The Full Service (FS) format (also called Variety, General Appeal, Diversified, etc.) attempts to provide its mostly middle-age listeners a mix of all programming genres – music, news, sports, and information features. Known for years as MOR, the format has attempted to strengthen its public service aspect through increased information programming. It is really one-stop shopping for listeners who would like a little bit of everything. Today, this type of station exists mostly in small markets where stations attempt to be good-citizen radio for everyone. It has been called the *bridge* format because of its "all things to all people" programming approach. However,

its large-market audience has decreased over the years, particularly since 1980, due to the rise in popularity of more specialized formats. According to radio program specialist Dick Ellis, FS now has a predominantly over-40 age demographic, several years older than just a decade ago. In some major markets, the format continues to do well in the ratings mainly because of strong on-air personalities. But this is not the format that it once was. Since its inception in the 1950s, up through the 1970s, stations working the MOR sound often dominated their markets. Yet the Soft Rock and Oldies formats in the 1970s, the updating of Easy Listening (Smooth Jazz), and particularly the ascendancy of AC and Talk formats have conspired to significantly erode MOR (now FS) numbers. For instance, *M Street Journal* cites fewer than 100 of these stations today.

FS is the home of the on-air personality. Perhaps no other format gives its air people as much latitude and freedom. This is not to suggest that FS announcers may do as they please. They, like any other announcer, must abide by format and programming policy, but FS personalities often serve as the cornerstone of their station's air product. Some of the best-known deejays in the country have come from the FS (MOR) milieu. It would then follow that the music is rarely, if ever, presented in sweeps or even segued. Deejay patter occurs between each cut of music, and announcements are inserted in the same way. News and sports play another vital function at these stations. During drive periods, FS often presents lengthened blocks of news, replete with frequent traffic reports, weather updates, and the latest sports information. Many FS outlets are affiliated with major-league teams. With few exceptions, FS is an AM format. Although it has noted slippage in recent years, it will likely continue to bridge whatever gaps may exist in a highly specialized radio marketplace.

Niche and HD² Formats

Experts say that the Alternative formats, with their narrower focus on specific demographic segments, will enjoy greater success in the coming years. In an interview in *Broadcasting and Cable*, Jeff Pollack predicted formats offering more nontraditional approaches to mainstream music (e.g., Modern Rock and Rhythmic Oldies) would be the ratings winners of the next few years. The intense fragmentation of the listening pool means that the big umbrella formats are going to lose out to the ultra-specific ones.

Alternative Rock, which has never fully enjoyed star status, was expected to move up toward the front of the pack in the new millennium. Of course, when it comes to format prognostication, the term *unpredictable* takes on a whole new meaning. Indeed, there will be a rash of successful niche formats in the coming years, due to the ever-increasing fragmentation of the radio audience, but exactly what they will be is anyone's guess.

A few years back, no one thought that All-Children's Radio (Radio Disney, Radio Aahs) would draw an economically attractive segment of the listening public, but today it is one of the most successful niches on the dial (mostly on AM at this writing), and there are many other wannabes entering the cluttered airwaves. New niche or splinter formats emerge frequently – Active Rock and Christian Talk are good examples – in an industry always on the lookout for the next best thing and competing with a myriad of other listening options. In an MP3 and iPhone world, staying fresh and current gives radio an edge – one that is more and more necessary as the audio landscape changes.

In terms of future format innovations, the rollout of HD2 side-channels may accelerate the rollout of new niche formats. Says Lynn Christian, "Unique programming ideas or concepts best suited to an audio presentation with great potential in all-size markets, while utilizing the new HD/HD[2] channels, has the greatest potential." However, some programmers, such as WIZN/WBTZ's Matt Grasso, don't expect much to change in the foreseeable future. "I don't think the formats will change much. I think the change will be within each format. Stations will focus on being more local. It's our biggest strength against satellite. We're here. Let's entrench ourselves into the community and become an important and integral part of their lives. The only format I can see changing is the so-called 'Jack' format. This knee-jerky response to iPods doesn't seem to fit the American

culture. We want specific things, not a little bit of everything. We're picky, selfish, brand loyal people. Have buffets taken over the Italian, Indian, French, Chinese, and Thai restaurants? Of course not! Jack is the radio buffet – stale, lukewarm, and boring."

At best, the preceding is an incomplete list of myriad radio formats that serve the listening public. The program formats mentioned constitute the majority of the basic format categories prevalent today. Tomorrow? Who knows? Radio is hardly a static industry, but one subject to the whims of popular taste. When something new captures the imagination of the American public, radio responds, and often a new format is conceived.

Public Radio

Like college stations, most Public radio outlets program in a block fashion. That is to say, few employ a primary (single) format, but instead offer a mix of program ingredients, such as news and information and entertainment features. National Public Radio and Public Radio International, along with state Public radio systems, provide a myriad of features for the hundreds of

Mike Janssen | On Public Radio

FIGURE 3.9
Mike Jansen.

I think the Public radio stations and networks will have to work together to figure out how they can best play a more meaningful and relevant role in the lives of listeners, given that stations, in particular, will find it more difficult to compete as new media continue to advance. Broadcast radio has long enjoyed an edge because it has few rivals in the car, to name one space for listening. But the advent of widespread broadband Internet will shatter that advantage, as listeners tune in radio stations and other audio sources from around the world. And Public radio in particular has historically claimed the franchise for thoughtful, in-depth radio news, but that, too, will fall away as competitors use the Internet to reach listeners and other media sources continue to fragment the market.

Public radio can no longer depend on the technology of radio to serve as its salvation. Instead, stations and networks will have to assess and reassess what exactly it is that they are able to provide that no one else can, given the talent in the system and their geographic reach and presence. And stations will have to learn how to survive without depending on their (until now) unchallenged claim on carrying NPR programming. Listeners will continue to bypass stations to access content from national networks. So how can stations serve local communities using their own resources in ways that make a difference and attract listener, corporate, and foundation support?

I think there's a lot of opportunity, but the system is poorly positioned to take advantage of it. Turf battles stand in the way of cooperation, and stations are too dependent on NPR. Fundraising from listeners isn't sophisticated enough to bring in the money needed to innovate on a broader level. Fortunately, the tools are out there as Web 2.0 continues to evolve. But the system needs some real visionaries and a new desire to work together to get things going.

Public radio facilities around the country. Topping the list of prominent music genres are classical and jazz. Public radio news broadcasts, among them "Morning Edition," "All Things Considered," and "The Takeaway," lead all radio in audience popularity for information focused on national and world events.

Radio Theater

Poet Stephen Vincent Benet called radio the "theater of the mind." His description was coined during the medium's heyday in the 1930s and 1940s when a myriad of original prose and verse plays were being produced and aired by the networks. The foremost radiowright of the time was Norman Corwin, whose works soared to literary heights and were tuned into and admired by millions. He was joined by many writers whose efforts were traditionally geared to the print media. These writers saw in the audio medium a chance to reach larger audiences with their works, and so they generated a significant amount of original material for it. Among the most famous print authors to ply their craft to the ethereal page were W.H. Auden, Arthur Miller, Pearl S. Buck, Archibald MacLeish, Irwin Shaw, and Edna St. Vincent Millay. The medium itself engendered other great writers besides Corwin. A close rival was Arch Oboler, whose popular thrillers brought chills and thrills to the listening audience. Perhaps the most famous of all radio dramas was Orson Welles's adaptation of H.G. Wells's *War of the Worlds*. It was so brilliantly evocative in its performances, writing, and production values that it quite literally sent its audience into a panic.

Following the arrival of television, radio dramas all but vanished from the airwaves. The networks were gone, and local stations could ill-afford their manufacture. Over the decades since, attempts have been made to revive the art form (CBS and Mutual radio networks offered short-lived series), but the radio drama was and continues to be of only passing interest to an audience with a rapidly diminishing attention span and visual orientation. In recent years, Public radio has become engaged in Radio Theater, and it is there that the medium's greatest artistic rendering makes occasional appearances.

Fortunately, dozens of Web sites on the Internet now preserve these valuable pieces of radio art and Americana. A search for "radio dramas" will result in a listing of everything from pop favorite "The Lone Ranger" to Corwin's historic "On a Note of Triumph."

The Programmer

PDs are radiophiles. They live the medium. Most admit to having been smitten by radio at an early age. "It's something that is in your blood and grows to consuming proportions," admits programmer Peter Falconi. Longtime PD Brian Mitchell recalls an interest in the medium as a small child and for good reason. "I was born into a broadcasting family. My father is a station owner and builder. During my childhood, radio was the primary topic at the dinner table. It fed the flame that I believe was already ignited anyway. Radio fascinated me from the start."

The customary route to the programmer's job involves deejaying and participation in other on-air-related areas, such as copywriting, production, music, and news. It would be difficult to state exactly how long it takes to become a PD. It largely depends on the individual and where he or she happens to be. In some instances, newcomers have gone into programming within their first year in the business. When this happens, it is most likely to occur in a small market where turnover may be high. On the other hand, it is far more common to spend years working toward this goal, even in the best of situations. "Although my father owned the station, I spent a long time in a series of jobs before my appointment to programmer. Along the way, I worked as

station janitor, and then got into announcing, production, and eventually programming," recounts Mitchell.

One of the nation's foremost air personalities and hall of famer, Dick Fatherly, whom *Billboard Magazine* has described as a "longtime legend," spent years as a deejay before making the transition. "In the 25 years that I've been in this business, I have worked as a jock, newsman, production director, and even sales rep. Eventually I ended up in program management. During my career I have worked at WABC, WICC, WFUN, WHB, to mention a few. Plenty of experience, you might say," comments Fatherly.

Experience contributes most toward the making of the station's programmer. However, individuals entering the field with hopes of becoming a PD do well to acquire as much formal training as possible. The programmer's job has become an increasingly demanding one as a result of expanding competition. "A good knowledge of research methodology, analysis, and application is crucial. Programming is both an art and a science today," observes general manager Jim Murphy. Programmer Andy Bloom concurs with Murphy, adding, "A would-be PD needs to school himor herself in marketing research particularly. Little is done anymore that is not based on careful analysis."

Publisher B. Eric Rhoads echoes this stance. "The role has changed. The PD used to be a glorified music director with some background in talent development. Today the PD must be a marketing expert. Radio marketing has become very complex, what with telemarketing, database marketing,

FIGURE 3.10
Sports radio continues to grow. Courtesy KKAM-AM.

FIGURE 3.11
Almost endless
options on satellite
radio. Courtesy
Sirius XM.

direct mail, interactive communication (fax, computer bulletin boards), and so forth. Radio is changing, and the PD must adapt. No longer will records and deejays make the big difference. Stations are at parity in music, so better ways must be found to set stations apart."

Says Shane, "The ultimate analogy for the PD is 'brand manager,' overseeing not only the product, but also the image and perception of the product. Since programmers now must work hand in hand with sellers to maximize station revenues, there's a new awareness of the marketing dimension."

Cognizant of this change, schools with programs in radio broadcasting have begun to emphasize courses in audience and marketing research, as well as other programming-related areas. An important fact for the aspiring PD to keep in mind is that more people entering broadcasting today have college backgrounds than ever before. Even though a college degree is not necessarily a prerequisite for the position of PD, it is clearly regarded as an asset by upper management. "It used to be that a college degree didn't mean so much. A PD came up through the ranks of programming, proved his ability, and was hired. Not that that doesn't still happen. It does. But more and more the new PD has a degree or, at the very least, several years of college," contends Joe Cortese, syndicated air personality. "I majored in Communication Arts at a junior college and then transferred to a four-year school. There are many colleges offering communications courses here in the Boston area, so I'll probably take some more as a way of further preparing for the day when I'll be programming or managing a station. That's what I eventually want to do," says Cortese, adding that experience in the trenches is also vital to success.

His point is well taken. Work experience does head the list on which a station manager bases his or her selection for PD. Meanwhile, college training, at the very least, has become a criterion to the extent that if an applicant does not have any, the prospective employer takes notice.

Beyond formal training and experience, Chuck Ducoty, major-market station manager, says a PD must possess certain innate qualities. "Common sense and a good sense of humor are necessary attributes and are in rather short supply, I think." Dick Fatherly adds sensitivity, patience, compassion, and drive to the list.

The PD's Duties and Responsibilities

Where to begin this discussion poses no simple problem because the PD's responsibilities and duties are so numerous and wide-ranging. Second in responsibility to

the general manager, the PD (in station clusters, the individual station programmer reports to the director of operations, who oversees all programming for the various stations) is the person responsible for everything that goes over the air. This involves working with the station manager or director of operations in establishing programming and format policy and overseeing their effective execution. In addition, he or she hires and supervises on-air music and production personnel, plans various schedules, handles the programming budget, develops promotions, monitors the station and its competition, assesses research, and may even pull a daily air-shift. The PD also is accountable for the presentation of news, public affairs, and sports features, although a news director often is appointed to help oversee these areas.

The PD alone does not determine a station's format. This is an upper management decision. The PD may be involved in the selection process, but, more often than not, the format has been chosen before the programmer has been hired. For example, WYYY decides it must switch from MOR to CHR to attract a more marketable demographic. After an in-depth examination of its own market, research on the effectiveness of CHR nationally, and advice from a program consultant and rep company, the format change is deemed appropriate. Reluctantly, the station manager concludes that he must bring in a CHR specialist, which means that he must terminate the services of his present programmer, whose experience is limited to MOR. The station manager places an ad in an industry trade magazine, interviews several candidates, and hires the person he feels will take the station to the top of the ratings. When the new PD arrives, he or she is charged with the task of preparing the CHR format for its debut. Among other things, this may involve hiring new air people, the acquisition of a new music library or the updating of the existing one, preparing promos and purchasing jingles, and working in league with the sales, traffic, and engineering departments for maximum results.

On these points, Corinne Baldasano, vice president of SW programming, observes, "First of all, of course, you must be sure that the station you are programming fills a market void, i.e., that there is an opportunity for you to succeed in your geographic area with the format you are programming. For example, a young adult alternative Rock station may not have much chance for success in an area that is mostly populated by retirees. Once you have determined that the format fills an audience need, you need to focus on building your station. The basic ingredients are making sure your music mix is correct (if you are programming a music station) and that you've hired the on-air talent that conveys the attitude and image of the station you wish to build. At this stage, it is far more important to focus inward than outward. Many stations have failed because they've paid more attention to the competition's product than they have their own."

Once the format is implemented, the PD must work at refining and maintaining the sound. After a short time, the programmer may feel compelled to modify air schedules either by shifting deejays around or by replacing those who do not enhance the format. Metro Networks president David Saperstein says, "You've got to continually fine-tune the station's sound. You must remove any and all negatives, like excessive talk, annoying commercials, technical weaknesses, and so forth. The most critical rule of thumb is that stations should always concentrate on bringing listeners to the station, keeping them tuned in, and providing the right balance of music, personalities, talk, information, and commercials so listeners do not have any reason to tune elsewhere."

The PD prepares weekend and holiday schedules as well, and this generally requires the hiring of part-time announcers. A station may employ as few as one or two part-timers or fill-in people or as many as eight to ten. This largely depends on whether deejays are on a 5- or 6-day schedule. At most stations, air people are hired to work a 6-day week. The objective of scheduling is not merely to fill slots but to maintain continuity and consistency of sound. A PD prefers to tamper with shifts as little as possible and fervently hopes that he has filled weekend slots with people who are reliable. "The importance of dependable, trustworthy air people cannot be overemphasized. It's great to have talented deejays, but if they don't show up when they are supposed to because of one reason or another, they don't do you a lot of good. You need people who are cooperative. I have no patience with individuals who try to deceive me or fail to live up to their responsibilities," says Brian Mitchell. A station that is constantly introducing new air personnel has a difficult time establishing listener habit. The PD knows that to succeed he or she must present a stable and dependable sound, and this is a significant programming challenge.

Production schedules also are prepared by the programmer. Deejays are usually tapped for production duties before or after their airshifts. For example, the morning person who is on the air from 6:00–10:00 A.M. may be assigned production and copy chores from 10:00 A.M. until noon. Meanwhile, the midday deejay who is on the air from 10:00 A.M. until 3:00 P.M. is given production assignments from 3:00–5:00 P.M., and so on. Large radio stations frequently employ a full-time production person. If so, this individual handles all production responsibilities and is supervised by the PD.

A PD traditionally handles the department's budget, which generally constitutes 30–40% of the station's operating budget. Working with the station manager, the PD ascertains the financial needs of the programming area. The size and scope of the budget vary from station to station. Most programming budgets include funds for the acquisition of program materials, such as albums, features, and contest paraphernalia. A separate promotional budget usually exists, and it too may be managed by the PD. The programmer's budgetary responsibilities range from monumental at some outlets to minuscule at others. Personnel salaries and even equipment purchases may fall within the province of the program department's budget. Brian Mitchell believes that "an understanding of the total financial structure of the company or corporation and how programming fits into the scheme of things is a real asset to a programmer."

Devising station promotions and contests also places demands on the PD's time. Large stations often appoint a promotion director. When this is the case, the PD and promotion director work together in the planning, development, and execution of the promotional campaign. The PD, however, retains final veto power should he or she feel that the promotion or contest fails to complement the station's format. When the PD alone handles promotions and contests, he or she may involve other members of the programming or sales department in brainstorming sessions designed to come up with original and interesting concepts. The programmer is aware that the right promotion or contest can have a major impact on ratings. Thus, he or she is constantly on the lookout for an appropriate vehicle. In the quest to find the promotion that will launch the station on the path to a larger audience, the PD may seek assistance from one of dozens of companies that offer promotional services.

The PD's major objective is to program for results. If the station's programming fails to attract a sufficient following, the ratings will reflect that unhappy fact. All medium and larger markets are surveyed by ratings companies, primarily Arbitron. Very few small rural markets, with perhaps one or two stations, are surveyed. If a small-market station is poorly programmed, the results will be apparent in the negative reactions of the local retailers. Simply put, the station will not be bought by enough advertisers to make the operation a profitable venture. In the bigger markets, where several stations compete for advertising dollars, the ratings are used to determine which is the most effective or cost-efficient station to buy. "In order to make it to the top of the ratings in your particular market, you have to be doing the best job around. It's the PD who is going to get the station the numbers it needs to make a buck. If he doesn't turn the trick, he's back in the job market," observes Dick Fatherly.

PDs constantly monitor the competition by analyzing the ratings and by listening. A radio station's programming is often constructed in reaction to a direct competitor's. For example, Rock stations in the same market often counterprogram newscasts by airing them at different times to grab up their competitor's tune-outs. However,

(Just a few days into the New Year, many resolutions have been broken already; but, hopefully, not the ones you made about your station. These "resolutions" first appeared in TACTICS a few years ago and are reprinted here by popular demand.)

NEW YEAR'S RESOLUTIONS FOR PDs

- Every week, I will read at least one of the magazines my target audience reads to get more in line with their tastes and interests.

- I will aircheck the morning show at least once a week.

- I will aircheck the rest of the airstaff every two weeks.

- I will schedule a meeting with the entire programming staff at least once a month.

- Every two weeks I will review liners and imaging to keep it fresh and to make sure it communicates the positioning message clearly.

- I will establish listener panels to get feedback from our core users every quarter.

- I will leave the station one day a month to listen carefully to us and the competition.

- Every three months, I will drive to small towns in my area to listen for potential air talent.

- I'll set up a promotional checklist so everybody knows what to do at live broadcasts and station events.

- I will join a sales meeting once a month to bring the account reps up to date on programming department activities.

- I will do a deep analysis of the music scheduling program each month (or ask Shane Media to do it for me).

rather than contrast with each other, pop stations tend to reflect one another. This, in fact, has been the basis of arguments by critics who object to the so-called mirroring effect. What happens is easily understood. If a station does well by presenting a particular format, other stations are going to exploit the sound in the hopes of doing well also. WYYY promotes commercial-free sweeps of music and captures big ratings, and soon its competitor programs likewise. "Program directors use what has proven to be effective. It is more a matter of survival than anything. I think most of us try to be original to the degree that we can be, but there is very little new under the sun. Programming moves cyclically. Today we're all doing this. Tomorrow we'll all be doing that. The medium reacts to trends or fads. It's the nature of the beast," notes programmer Mitchell. Keeping in step with, or rather one step ahead of, the competition requires that the PD knows what is happening around him or her at all times.

FIGURE 3.12
Advice to programmers. Courtesy Shane Media.

Probably 60% of the nation's PDs pull an airshift (go on the air themselves) on either a full-time or part-time basis. A difference of opinion exists among programmers concerning their on-air participation. Many feel that being on the air gives them a true sense of the station's sound, which aids them in their programming efforts. Others contend that the 3 or 4 hours that they spend on the air take them away from important programming duties. Major-market PDs are less likely to be heard on the air than their peers in smaller markets because of additional duties created by the size and status of the station. Meanwhile, small- and medium-market stations often expect their PDs to be seasoned air people capable of filling a key shift. "It has been my experience when applying for programming jobs that managers are looking for PDs with excellent announcing skills. It is pretty rare to find a small-market PD who does not have a daily airshift. It comes with the territory," says consultant Gary Begin.

Whether or not PDs are involved in actual airshifts, almost all participate in the production of commercials, public service announcements (PSA), and promos. In lieu of an airshift, a PD may spend several hours each day in the station's production facilities. The programmer may, in fact, serve as the primary copywriter and spot producer. This is especially true at nonmajor-market outlets that do not employ a full-time production person.

The PD must possess an imposing list of skills to perform effectively the countless tasks confronting him or her daily. There is no one person, other than the general manager, whose responsibilities outweigh the programmer's. The PD can either make or break the radio station. Summing things up, chief programmer Jimmy Steal states, "A programmer must possess balance and understanding of both the science and art of show business. A station needs someone who understands that strategies and tactics are for the conference room, and fun, engagement, buzz, innovation, and exceeding listener's expectations are for over the air and on-line. At Emmis we look for someone who understands the job description and all of the job's duties. It is incumbent upon us to give a detailed definition of what success looks like to a prospective programmer, so an inspirational leader can positively motivate their team of talent."

Programming a Cluster Operation

The widespread consolidation of the radio industry since the late 1990s has resulted in a paradigm shift in programming responsibilities. Radio clusters may consist of as many as eight stations. In this situation, one individual is usually assigned to perform the function of general supervisor of all cluster

FIGURE 3.13
A model of a station's competitive environment as conceived by Arbitron. Courtesy Arbitron.

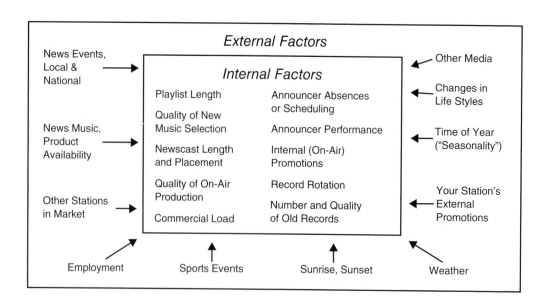

programming, and each of the stations within the cluster has a designated PD, who reports to this person – typically referred to as the director of operations. Radio corporations see it as a macrocosm/microcosm overseer design and arrangement.

As might be imagined, the challenges of programming a cluster are compounded by the very number of the stations involved. As KIMN PD Gregg Cassidy observes, "Programming a single station is very simple versus programming a cluster. In programming a single station you have all the time necessary to evaluate all areas of your station daily. You can check your air talent each week, reevaluate your music and music rotations and be very creative with your on-air promotions and take the necessary time to create clever and compelling production. Programming a cluster is like being a father of many children rather than one or two. Time becomes very valuable. In the simplest form, I would devote all my energy to one station per week."

According to WIZN/WBTZ's Matt Grasso, consolidation has created other problems for programmers: "Ironically, if not para-

doxically, many quality radio pros making top dollars were cut out in the downsizing and consolidation frenzy. This often left lesser talent in markets with clusters. Worse yet with many passionate, quality pros out of work, no one has been minding the store and developing new talent. This has become today's major challenge – finding and developing new talent. There used to be a line out the door of people wanting to be on the radio, but the perception that consolidation and downsizing have killed the job market has dramatically changed that."

Satellite Radio Programming Department

What follows is a brief sketch of the programming department's organizational structure of satellite radio, according to XM Satellite's one-time chief creative officer, Lee Abrams: "Here's how we set up the programming area. I was the head overseer of programming. For original content, we had a senior vice president of music. We

FIGURE 3.14
Music testing companies provide stations with outside expertise. Courtesy Music – Tec.

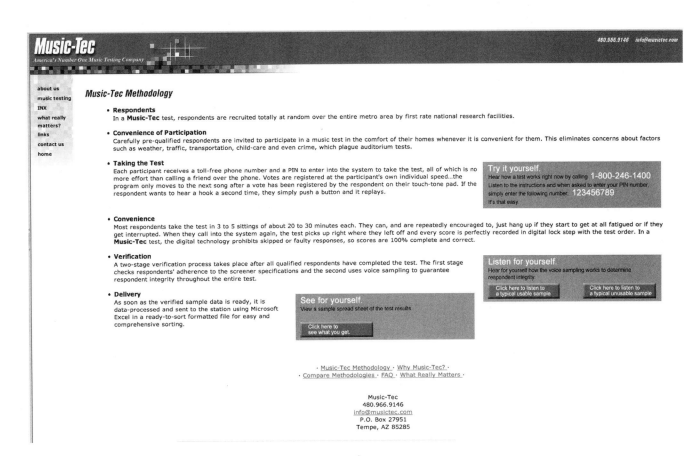

had a vice president of Talk, who handled the day-to-day operations of the nonmusic channels. Original Talk programming, such as Take 5 and XM Traffic, had a PD along with a staff of talent and producers. The vice president of Talk also spearheaded the relations with third party providers. Every cluster had a senior PD, and each channel had a PD. Channels often had music directors and deejays. A vice president also oversaw the pure operational aspects, like computer systems and production. There was a staff of senior production directors who supervised a group of producers, aka audio animators. Supporting the animators were production assistants, who often came from the internship ranks at XM. The programming department also had a music librarian and staff that oversaw the ingestion of music into the system. Keep in mind things changed as they were tweaked to enhance the efficiency of the department. As they say, it was a work in progress" (see Figure 2.7).

Elements of Programming

Few programmers entrust the selection and scheduling of music and other sound elements to deejays and announcers. There is too much at stake and too many variables, both internal and external, that must be considered to achieve maximum results within a chosen format.

It has become a very complex undertaking, observes Andy Bloom. "For instance, all of our music is tested via callout. At least one or two perceptual studies are done every year, depending on what questions we need answered. Usually a couple of sets of focus groups per year, too. Everything is researched, and nothing is left to chance." In most cases, the PD determines how much music is programmed hourly and in what rotation and when news, public affairs features, and commercials are slotted. Program wheels, also variously known as sound hours, hot clocks, and format disks, are carefully designed by the PD to ensure the effective presentation of on-air ingredients. Program wheels are posted in the control studio to inform and guide air

people as to what is to be broadcast and at what point in the hour. Although not every station provides deejays with such specific programming schemata, today very few stations leave things up to chance since the inappropriate scheduling and sequencing of sound elements may drive listeners to a competitor. Radio programming has become that much of an exacting science. With few exceptions, stations use some kind of formula in conveying their programming material.

At one time, Top 40 stations were the unrivaled leaders of formula programming. Today, however, even FS and Classic Rock outlets, which once were the least formulaic, have become more sensitive to form. The age of freeform commercial radio has long since passed, and it is doubtful, given the state of the marketplace, that it will return. Of course, stranger things have happened in radio. Depending on the extent to which a PD prescribes the content of a sound hour, programming clocks may be elaborate in their detail or quite rudimentary. Music clocks are used to plot out elements. Clocks reflect the minutes of the standard hour, and the PD places elements where they actually are to occur during the hour. Many programmers use a set of clocks, or clocks that change with each hour (see Figure 3.15).

"When I speak at college classes," Ed Shane observes, "there's always a question about why format clock hours are structured the way they are, so let me call what follows 'Clock Construction 101.' Arbitron entries show that the first quarter hour (00:00–00:15) gets the largest number of new entries, that is, when the radio is turned on for the first time or switched to a new station. The third quarter hour (00:00–30:45) gets the second largest number. The second quarter hour (00:00–15:30) gets the third largest number, and the fourth quarter hour (00:00–45:00) gets the fewest new tune-ins. That pattern is why many stations load their commercial content in the final or fourth quarter hour – trying to prevent a new listener from hearing a commercial as the first thing when tuning. Since the first quarter hour is so valuable in terms of new tune-ins, the most valuable programming elements should be placed in that segment.

A music station is advised to load the first quarter hour with Power Current or Power Gold songs, songs that test the best or are the biggest hits."

Indeed, program clocks are set up with the competition and market factors in mind. For example, programmers will devise a clock that reflects morning and afternoon drive periods in their market. Not all markets have identical commuter hours. In some cities morning drive may start as early as 5:30 A.M.; in others it may begin at 7:00 A.M. The programmer sets up clocks accordingly. A clock parallels the activities of the community in which the station operates.

Music stations are not the only ones that use program wheels; News and Talk stations do so as well. News stations, like music outlets, use key format elements to maintain ratings through the hour. Many News stations work their clocks in 20-minute cycles. During this segment, news is arranged according to its degree of importance and geographic relevance, such as local, regional, national, and international. Most News stations lead with their top local stories. News stories of particular interest are repeated during the segment. Sports, weather, and other news-related information, such as traffic and stock market reports, constitute a part of the segment. Elements may be juggled around or different ones inserted during successive 20-minute blocks to keep things from sounding repetitious.

In the Talk format, two-way conversation and interviews fill the space generally allotted to songs in the music format. Therefore, Talk wheels often resemble music wheels in their structure. For example, news is offered at the top of the hour, followed by a talk sweep that precedes a spot set. This is done in a fashion that is reminiscent of Easy Listening.

Of course, not all stations arrange their sound hours as depicted in these pages. Many variations exist, most inspired and driven by computers, but these examples are fairly representative of some of the program schematics used in today's radio marketplace.

Program wheels keep a station on a preordained path and prevent wandering. As stated, each programming element – commercial, news, promo, weather, and so

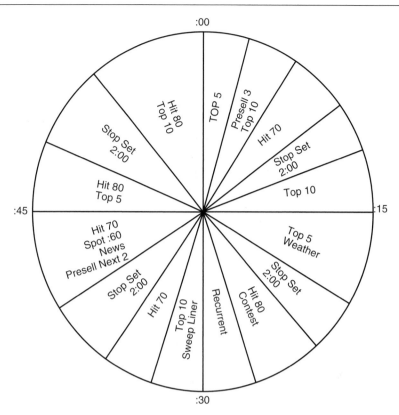

on – is strategically located in the sound hour to enhance flow and optimize impact. Balance is imperative: too much deejay patter on a station promoting more music and less talk, listeners become disenchanted; too little news and information on a station targeting the over-30 male commuter, the competition benefits. "When constructing or arranging the program clock, you have to work forward and backward to make sure that everything fits and is positioned correctly. One element out of place can become that proverbial hole in the dam. Spots, jock breaks, music – it all must be weighed before clocking. A lot of experimentation, not to mention research, goes into this," observes radio executive Lorna Ozman.

It was previously pointed out that a station with a more-music slant limits announcer discourse to schedule additional tunes. Some formats, in particular Easy Listening/Smooth Jazz, have reduced the role of the announcer to not much more than occasional live promos and IDs, which are written on liner or flip cards. Nothing is left to chance. This also is true of stations airing the super-tight hit music

FIGURE 3.15
A typical morning drive time CHR clock. It reflects a 9-minute commercial load maximum per hour. Notice the way the stop sets occur away from the quarter-hour. A Top 5 record is often aired on the quarter-hour to give the station the best ratings advantage. This is called "quarter-hour maintenance."

FIGURE 3.16
The use of podcasts
continued to grow
into the late 2000s.
Courtesy NPR.

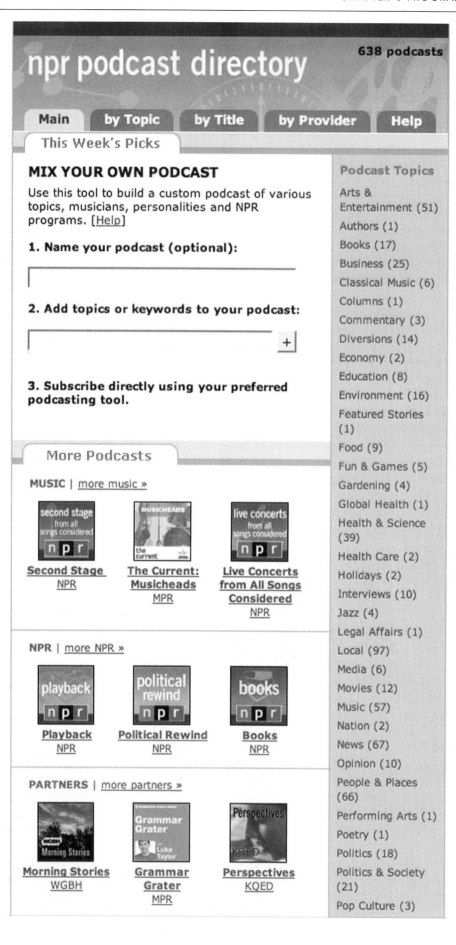

format. Deejays say what is written and move the music. At stations where deejays are given more control, wheels play a less crucial function. Outlets where a particular personality has ruled the ratings for years often let that person have more input as to what music is aired. However, even in these cases, playlists generally are provided and followed.

The radio personality has enjoyed varying degrees of popularity since the 1950s. Over the years, Top 40, more than any other format, has toyed with the extent of deejay involvement on the air. The pendulum has swung from heavy personality presence in the 1950s and early 1960s to a drastically reduced role in the mid- and later 1960s. This dramatic shift came as the result of programmer Bill Drake's attempt to stream-line Top 40. In the 1970s, the air personality regained some of his or her status, but in the 1980s, the narrowing of hit station playlists brought about a new leanness and austerity that again diminished the jock's presence. In the mid-1980s, some pop music stations began to give the deejay more to do. "There's sort of a pattern to it all. For a while, deejays are the gems in the crown, and then they're just the metal holding the precious stones in place for another period of time. What went on in the mid-1970s with personality began to recur in the latter part of the 1980s. Of course, there are a few new twists in the tiara, but what it comes down to is the temporary restoration of the hit radio personality. It's a back and forth movement, kind of like a tide. It comes in, then retreats, but each time something new washes up. Deejays screamed at the teens in the 1950s, mellowed out some in the 1960s and 1970s, went hyper again in the 1980s, and conservatism regained favor in the 1990s," observes Brian Mitchell. In the first decade of the 2000s, with the pressure from so many competing audio options, high foreground personalities are beginning to look attractive once again as an antidote to the music-intensive services.

On the subject of on-air talent, Lynn Christian observes, "Requirements have changed in the past few years. Stations are not just looking for a 'pretty voice.' Today's radio management looks for talent with facile minds who are great observers – people who can listen as well as speak, plus possess the ability to demonstrate a warm

FIGURE 3.17
Putting the program together in the 1930s. Courtesy Library of Congress.

FIGURE 3.18
Many stations
have replaced local
deejays with national
personalities. Tom
Joyner is among
the most popular.
Courtesy ABC.

Station Web Sites, Podcasts, and Blogs

In this day and age, nearly every radio station maintains a Web site. Most do so as an additional marketing tool, but many provide listeners with Web sites as a cyber-extension of their on-air signals, since so many people sit in front of their computers at work and at home for countless hours. Indeed, a station Web site is not only for listening, but it's a visual component of a radio station, a means of giving more sight to a once sightless medium. Says Ressen Design's Darryl Pomicter, "Web sites compliment all terrestrial broadcast systems, supplementing and expanding content. They give stations reach they never had before – locally, nationally, and globally."

Station Web sites hold great value for PDs for three vastly different reasons, contends Matt Grasso, WIZN.WBTZ operations manager. "First off, Pl's [dedicated listeners] spend a lot of time with your radio station, and the Web site is a way to keep things fresh and exciting for them. Games, exclusive Web-only promotions, staff blogs and bios all provide an exclusive, behind the scenes look at the product. Next, Time Spent Listening (TSL) drives the ratings bus and your online broadcast boosts it. There are a lot of people who are procrastinating at work. Plug them into your station. Give them lifestyle news and information and watch your TSL rise. And finally, the Web site constitutes new inventory. You can clutter your airwaves with so much stuff. Your Web site is a new place to do business."

Station Web sites (cyberspace display windows, if you will) literally come in all sizes, and shapes. That is to say, they can be simple offering a limited number of links, and they can be highly interactive and multitiered with dozens of links. Not all Web sites are constructed as income streams, but more and more radio stations are viewing Web sites as another good source of nontraditional revenue. Recently, stations have begun adding the iTunes Music Store link to their sites to allow their listeners to purchase the tunes they air. Emmis was the first station group to do so on its stations in Chicago, Indianapolis, Austin, and St. Louis.

and always interesting personality." On the other side of the coin, talent wants their managers to operate in a manner that makes for a positive atmosphere and experience, says Jimmy Steal. "The keys to managing talent are (1) Honesty, (2) Inspiration, (3) Creativity, and (4) Empathy."

In addition to concentrating on the role deejays play in the sound hour, the PD pays careful attention to the general nature and quality of other ingredients. Music is, of course, of paramount importance. Songs must fit the format to begin with, but beyond the obvious, the quality of the artistry and the audio mix must meet certain criteria. A substandard musical arrangement or a disc with poor fidelity detracts from the station's sound. Jingles and promos must effectively establish the tone and tenor of the format, or they have the reverse effect of their intended purpose, which is to attract and hold listeners. Commercials, too, must be compatible with the program elements that surround them.

In all, the PD scrutinizes every component of the program wheel to keep the station true to form. The wheel helps maintain consistency, without which a station cannot hope to cultivate a following. Erratic programming in today's highly competitive marketplace is tantamount to directing listeners to other stations.

Larger stations and cluster operations typically hire an individual (frequently called manager of information services – MIS) to maintain a station's Web presence. It falls to this person to maintain the appearance and relevance of the Web site. The growing role of station Web sites has made it another potential career option for those interested in entering the radio field. Clearly, computer skills would rank high on the list of attributes an applicant for this position should possess. In addition, an overall knowledge of radio programming and marketing would be of special value.

Although podcasts were originally designed for downloading to iPods and MP3s, radio stations have found them to be a value-added programming feature. Thousands of podcasts are available on the Internet, and most radio stations now offer podcasts of their on-air features on their Web sites. Some stations have created exclusive, podcast-only programs. Says consultant Jason Insalaco, "Podcasting 'exclusives' can drive Web traffic and increase the time listeners spend on the Web site. For example, Web site exclusive interviews with newsmakers, musical artists, entire unedited press conferences, or even the local high school football game can provide supplemental content for station podcasts. It's a good community

service, too." Matt Grasso adds, "Podcasts are useful to station programming because it's a way to take the station with you. At first radio programmers were afraid of iPods; now they realize that they are just another way to get even closer to the listener."

A blog is a Web page of entries from a single source/author pertaining to a particular subject or topic. Many station personalities and talk show hosts maintain blogs, which are sometimes referred to as online journals or diaries. Observes Insalaco, "Blogging has become a national phenomenon. Talk show host blogs are a popular component of a station's Web site. Consumers are processing news at a meteoric pace via the Web, cell phones, and Blackberries, so station blogs fit into this scheme. While Americans are no longer at the mercy of the network news broadcasts or the newspaper for daily information, the trend of processing news through opinion (whether a good thing or a bad thing) has developed. Radio hosts can blog about issues related to the topics discussed and the guests they have on their programs. Blogs can billboard upcoming topics and provide listeners an opportunity to interact. Also, show blogs provide additional information and links to stories discussed on the air. Radio station blogs can feature show rundowns of the day's topics

Ed Shane   Programming in a New Age

FIGURE 3.19
Ed Shane.

Radio needs to think of itself in a new way. We are content creators, content developers, and content providers. Transmission and distribution are irrelevant. That's why Internet-only radio stations show so much promise. Traditional radio is a one-way medium. For much of its reign, it seemed interactive when it engaged the imagination or stimulated phone calls for talk show feedback or contesting. The new "radio" will use a variety of means to distribute content to its constituents.

A radio station client of mine recently began streaming its audio via

the Internet. The PD was very excited, because he anticipated hearing from new listeners all over the world who could discover how good his station sounded. The president of the company who owned the station took him to the window and pointed to a house in the neighborhood nearby. "We're not streaming to be heard around the world," he told his PD. "We're streaming so the 12-year-old girl in that house will listen to our station. She doesn't listen to radio, but if she likes what you do, she'll listen on her computer."

FIGURE 3.20
Keeping track of a
song's performance
is a vital element in
retaining the edge in
music programming.
Courtesy Mediabase.

and guests so that listeners remain connected
to their favorite radio personality. Blogs are
easy to execute and maintain. In sum, stations that embrace blogs and podcasts will
gain an upper hand in the competitive radio
marketplace."

```
Page No.    1           CITISTAT - Chicago
91.01.18                    WKQX-FM/AC
                  TUNED IN-ALPHABETICAL LIST BY ARTIST

Artist                    Song Title                    Time
-------------------       -------------------------     ----


** 1
10CC                      The Things We Do For Love     12m
** A
ADAMS, OLETA              Get Here                      02a
ADAMS, OLETA              Get Here                      06a
ADAMS, OLETA              Get Here                      10a
ADAMS, OLETA              Get Here                      02p
ADAMS, OLETA              Get Here                      07p
ADAMS, OLETA              Get Here                      11p
ALIAS                     More Than Words Can Say       01a
ALIAS                     More Than Words Can Say       12n
ALIAS                     More Than Words Can Say       10p
ASTLEY, RICK             It Would Take A Strong Strong  01p
AUSTIN/INGRAM             Baby, Come To Me              02a

** B
BAD ENGLISH               When I See You Smile          01a
BANGLES                   Eternal Flame                 01a
BANGLES                   Manic Monday                  04p
BEACH BOYS                Kokomo                        07p
BERLIN                    Take My Breath Away           01a
BERLIN                    Take My Breath Away           08p
BOLTON, MICHAEL           (Sittin' On) The Dock Of The..08p
BRANIGAN, LAURA           Self Control                  01a
BROWNE, JACKSON           Doctor My Eyes                01p
BROWNE, JACKSON           Running On Empty              09p
BROWNE, JACKSON           Somebody's Baby               09a

** C
CAFFERTY, JOHN & BBB      On The Dark Side              06a
CARA, IRENE               Flashdance (What A Feeling)   01p
CAREY, MARIAH             Love Takes Time               01a
CAREY, MARIAH             Love Takes Time               05a
CAREY, MARIAH             Love Takes Time               11a
CAREY, MARIAH             Love Takes Time               04p
CAREY, MARIAH             Love Takes Time               10p
CAREY, MARIAH             Vision Of Love                10p
CARLISLE, BELINDA         Heaven Is A Place On Earth    02a
CARLISLE, BELINDA         Heaven Is A Place On Earth    11p
CARLISLE, BELINDA         I Get Weak                    06p
CARMEN, ERIC              Hungry Eyes                   09p
CHER                      If I Could Turn Back Time     12m
CHER                      The Sh
CHER                      The Sh
CHER                      The Sh
CHICAGO                   Feeli
CHICAGO                   Hard
CHICAGO                   Look Away                     11p
CHICAGO                   Old Days                      08p
```

Music is broken out alphabetically by artists with the exact hour of air noted

The PD and the Audience

The programmer, regardless of whether he
or she works for a broadcast, satellite, or
Internet radio station, must possess a clear
perception of the type of listener the station
management wants to attract. Initially, a
station decides on a given format because
it is convinced that it will make money
with the new-found audience, meaning that
the people who tune in to the station will

look good to prospective advertisers. The
purpose of any format is to win a desirable
segment of the radio audience. Just who
these people are and what makes them tick
are questions that the PD must constantly
address to achieve reach and retention. An
informed programmer is aware that different types of music appeal to different types
of people. For example, surveys have long
concluded that heavy rock appeals more to
men than it does to women, and that rock
music, in general, is more popular among
teens and young adults than it is with individuals over 40. This is no guarded secret,
and certainly the programmer who is out to
gain the over-40 crowd is doing himself or
herself and his or her station a disservice by
programming even an occasional hard rock
tune. This should be obvious.

A station's demographics refer to the
characteristics of those who tune in: sex,
age, income, and so forth. Within its demographics, a station may exhibit particular
strength in specific areas or *cells* as they have
come to be termed. For example, an AC
station targeting the 24–39-year-old group
may have a prominent cell in women over
30. The general information provided by
the major ratings surveys indicate to the
station the age and sex of those listening,
but little beyond that. To find out more,
the PD may conduct an in-house survey or
employ the services of a research firm.

Since radio accompanies listeners practically everywhere, broadcasters pay particular attention to the lifestyle activities of
their target audience. A station's geographic
locale often dictates its program offerings.
For example, hoping to capture the attention of the 35-year-old men, a radio outlet
located in a small coastal city along the
Gulf of Mexico might decide to air a series
of 1-minute informational tips on outdoor
activities, such as tennis, golf, and deep-sea
fishing, which are exceptionally popular in
the area. Stations have always catered to the
interests of their listeners, but in the 1970s,
audience research became much more oriented to lifestyle (Figure 3.21).

In the 1990s, broadcasters delved further
into audience behavior through psychographic research, which, by examining motivational factors, provides programmers with
information beyond the purely quantitative.

Perhaps one of the best examples of a station's efforts to conform to its listeners' lifestyle is *day-parting*, a topic briefly touched on in the discussion of program wheels. For the sake of illustration, let us discuss how an AC station may daypart (segmentalize) its broadcast day. To begin with, the station is targeting an over-40 audience, somewhat skewed toward men. The PD concludes that the station's biggest listening hours are mornings between 7:00 and 9:00 A.M. and afternoons between 4:00 and 6:00 P.M., and that most of those tuned in during these periods are in their cars commuting to or from work. It is evident to the programmer that the station's programming approach must be modified during drivetime to reflect the needs of the audience. Obviously, traffic reports, news and sports updates, weather forecasts, and frequent time checks are suitable fare for the station's morning audience. The interests of homebound commuters contrast slightly with those of work-bound commuters. Weather and time are less important, and most sports information from the previous night is old hat by the time the listener heads for home. Stock market reports and information about upcoming games and activities pick up the slack. Midday hours call for further modification, since the lifestyle of the station's audience is different. Aware that the majority of those listening are homemakers (in a less enlightened age this daypart was referred to as "housewife" time), the PD reduces the amount of news and information, replacing them with music and deejay conversation designed specifically to complement the activities of those tuned. In the evening, the station redirects its programming and schedules sports and talk features, going exclusively talk after midnight. All these adjustments are made to attract and retain audience interest.

The PD relies on survey information and research data to better gauge and understand the station's audience. However, as a member of the community that the station serves, the programmer knows that not everything is contained in formal documentation. He or she gains unique insight into the mood and mentality of the area within the station's signal simply by taking part in the activities of day-to-day life. A

FIGURE 3.21
Norman Corwin – one of radio's greatest program creators during the medium's golden age. Courtesy Norman Corwin.

programmer with a real feel for the area in which the station is located, as well as a fundamental grasp of research methodology and its application, is in the best possible position to direct the on-air efforts of a radio station. Concerning the role of audience research, Peter Falconi says, "You can't run a station on research alone. Yes, research helps to an extent, but it can't replace your own observations and instincts." Brian Mitchell agrees with Falconi. "I feel research is important, but how you react to research is more important. A PD also has to heed his gut feelings. Gaps exist in research, too. If I can't figure out what to do without data to point the way every time I make a move, I should get out of radio. Success comes from taking chances once in a while, too. Sometimes it's wiser to turn your back on the tried and tested. Of course, you had better know who's out there before you try anything. A PD who doesn't study his audience and community is like a racecar driver who doesn't familiarize himself with the track. Both can end up off the road and out of the race."

The PD and the Music

Not all radio stations have a music director. The larger the station, the more likely it is to have such a person. In any case, it is the PD who is ultimately responsible for the music that goes over the air, even when the position of music director exists. The duties of the music director vary from station to station. Although the title suggests that the individual performing this function would supervise the station's music programming from the selection and acquisition of records to the preparation of playlists, this is not always the case. At some stations, the position is primarily administrative or clerical in nature, leaving the PD to make the major decisions concerning airplay. In this instance, one of the primary duties of the music director might be to improve service from record distributors to keep the station well supplied with the latest releases. A radio station with poor record service may actually be forced to purchase music. This can be prevented to a great extent by maintaining close ties with the various record distributor reps.

Over the years the music industry and the radio medium have formed a mutually beneficial alliance. Without the product provided by the recording companies, radio would find itself with little in the way of programming material, since 90% of the country's stations feature recorded music. At the same time, radio serves as the principal means by which the recording industry gets word of its new releases to the general public. Succinctly put, radio sells records.

Although radio stations seldom pay for their music (CDs) – recording companies send demos of their new product to most stations – it must pay annual licensing fees to American Society of Composers, Authors, and Publishers (ASCAP), Broadcast Music Incorporated (BMI), or SESAC (Society of European Stage Authors and Composers) for the privilege of airing recorded music. ASCAP provides a "blanket" license for music stations. Fees are a percentage of a station's annual income, usually 1–1½% of gross income. According to ASCAP, non-commercial radio stations "pay an annual fee determined by the U.S. Copyright Office."

These fees range from a few hundred dollars at small, noncommercial, educational stations to tens of thousands of dollars at large, commercial, metro market stations. The music licensing fees paid by stations are distributed to the artists and composers of the songs broadcast.

When music arrives at the station, the music director (sometimes more appropriately called the music librarian or music assistant) processes them through the system. This may take place after the PD has screened them. Records are categorized, indexed, and eventually added to the library if they suit the station's format.

Programmer Jon Lutes designates music categories in the following manner: New Music, Medium Current, Hot Current, Hot Recurrent, Medium Recurrent, Bulk Recurrent, Power Gold, Secondary Gold, Tertiary Gold, and so forth. Each station approaches cataloging in its own fashion. Here is a simple example. An AC outlet receives an album by a popular female vocalist whose last name begins with an L. The PD auditions the album and decides to place three cuts into regular on-air rotation. The music director then assigns the cuts the following catalog numbers: L106/U/F, L106/D/F, and L106/M/F. L106 indicates where the album may be located in the library. In this case, the library is set up alphabetically and then numerically within the given letter that represents the artist's last name. In other words, this would be the 106th album found in the section reserved for female vocalists whose names begin with an L. The next symbol indicates the tempo of the cut: U(p) tempo, D(own) tempo, and M(edium) tempo. The F that follows the tempo symbol indicates the artist's gender: Female.

When a station is computerized (and in this day and age, few are not), this information, including the frequency or rotation of airplay as determined by the PD, will be entered accordingly.

Playlists are then assembled and printed by the computer. The music director sees that these lists are placed in the control room for use by the deejays. This last step is eliminated when the on-air studio is equipped with a computer terminal. Deejays then simply punch up the playlists designed for their particular airshifts. Ed Shane offers, "To hone the music mix for proper balance and rotation, stations use music rotation software from a variety of suppliers. The most used software program is Selector from Radio Computing Services (which also supplies music test analysis software, traffic software, and a digital studio operation system). Other popular music rotation software is Power-Gold and Music Master" (see Figure 3.22).

Without a doubt, the use of computers in music programming has become standard, especially in larger markets where the cost of computerization is absorbed more easily. The number of computer companies selling both hardware and software designed for use by programmers has soared. Among others providing computerized music systems are Halper and Associates, Jefferson Pilot Data Systems, and Columbine Systems. Also, some journals, such as *Billboard* and *Radio and Records*, provide up-to-date computerized music research on new singles and albums to assist station programmers.

In light of the extensive reliance on computers, Jon Lutes and Shane Media caution that "Music scheduling involves more than punching a few buttons on your computer keyboard. It helps to have a basic understanding of how the computer actually operates and what the particular software you are using will and will not do."

At those radio stations where the music director's job is less administrative and more directorial, this individual will actually audition and select what songs are to be designated for airplay. However, the music director makes decisions based on criteria established by the station's programmer.

Obviously, a music director must work within the station's prescribed format. If the PD feels that a particular song does not fit the station's sound, he will direct the music director to remove the cut from rotation. Since the PD and music director work closely together, this seldom occurs.

A song's rotation usually is relative to its position on national and local record sales charts. For instance, songs that enjoy top ranking, say those in the Top 10, will get the most airplay on hit-oriented stations. When songs descend the charts, their rotation decreases proportionately. Former chart toppers are then assigned another rotation configuration that initially may result in one-tenth of their former airplay, and eventually even less. PDs and music directors derive information pertaining to a record's popularity from various trade journals, such as *Billboard*, *Radio and Records*, and *Monday Morning Replay*, as well as listener surveys, area record store sales, and numerous other

FIGURE 3.22
A host of computerized music programming services is used by the stations. Courtesy RCS.

FIGURE 3.23
Computerized
logging has made
station programming
even more exacting
a science. Courtesy
WIZN-FM.

```
**REMEMBER: FORWARD MOMENTUM!! WHY SHOULD THE LISTENER KEEP LISTENING?**
                  *********************************
                  *             WIZN-FM            *
                  * 10 AM  Wednesday  10-23-02     *
                  *********************************
ARTIST/ALBUM                      TITLE                    RUNTIME  YR  CAT
===========================================================================

  --------------------------------------------------------------------------
  00:00  LEGAL I.D.                                        5025  :08
  --------------------------------------------------------------------------
  STEVE MILLER BAND               TAKE THE MONEY AND RUN              E/ 2:51
  FLY LIKE AN EAGLE
  --------------------------------------------------------------------------
  02:59  SHOTGUN                                           5050  :05
  --------------------------------------------------------------------------
  TOM PETTY                       RUNNING DOWN A DREAM               F/ 4:23
  FULL MOON FEVER                   54.00
  --------------------------------------------------------------------------
  07:27  SPEED BREAK                                       5605  :08
  --------------------------------------------------------------------------
  J. GEILS BAND                   MUST OF GOT LOST                   D/ 6:34
  LIVE BLOW YOUR FACE OUT (ON CD)   50.00
  --------------------------------------------------------------------------
  14:09  POSITIONER                                        5035  :08
  --------------------------------------------------------------------------
  PRETENDERS                      BRASS IN POCKET(I'M SPECI          E/ 3:01
  THE PRETENDERS                    50.00
  --------------------------------------------------------------------------
  17:18  SHOTGUN                                           5050  :05
  --------------------------------------------------------------------------
  HEART                           CRAZY ON YOU                       D/ 4:54
  DREAMBOAT ANNIE                   69.00
  --------------------------------------------------------------------------
  22:17  BOTTOM HOUR                                       5016  :08
  --------------------------------------------------------------------------
  CLASH                           TRAIN IN VAIN                      E/ 3:13
  LONDON CALLING                    43.00
  --------------------------------------------------------------------------
  25:38  BREAK ONE/BACKSELL/LIVE PROMO                     5606 1:00
  --------------------------------------------------------------------------
  ERIC CLAPTON                    FOREVER MAN                        F/ 3:12
  BEHIND THE SUN
  --------------------------------------------------------------------------
  29:50  BOTTOM HOUR                                       5016  :08
  --------------------------------------------------------------------------
  MANFRED MANN'S EARTH BAND       BLINDED BY THE LIGHT               E/ 7:07
  HIGHS OF 70'S CD                  80.00
  --------------------------------------------------------------------------
  37:05  BREAK TWO/PRE-SELL 10-IN-A-ROW                    5607 1:00
  --------------------------------------------------------------------------
  DEEP PURPLE                     HUSH                               D/ 4:26
  WHEN WE ROCK WE ROCK, WHEN WE ROLL    49.00
  --------------------------------------------------------------------------
  42:31  SHOTGUN                                           5050  :05
  --------------------------------------------------------------------------
```

sources. Stations that do not program from the current charts compose their playlists of songs that were popular in years gone by. In addition, these stations often remix current hit songs to make them adaptable to their more conservative sound. While Easy Listening stations do not air popular rock songs, they do air softened versions by other artists, usually large orchestras. Critics of this technique accuse the producers of lobotomizing songs to bring them into the fold. In nonhit formats, there are no "power-rotation" categories or hit positioning schemata; a song's rotation tends to be more random, although program wheels are used.

On the CHR front, Shane notes that "There's a major change in the way charts are constructed. The original *Billboard* Hot 100 chart was based substantially on record sales. *The Gavin Report* and other "tipsheets" used reports from radio station music directors who fed information on the positions on their own local charts, some validated by record sales and requests – some not."

"When *R&R* was launched in 1974, its charts were also compiled from reports from radio station programmers. *R&R*, however, mixed industry news and commentary to create a niche for itself as the most important of the music trade publications in the eyes of the music (record) industry. Because the charts were based on verbal reports from local stations, the system was too easily manipulated by a station programmer who might report play but not actually play the song. This practice was known as a "paper add" because the record was added to the playlist only on paper and did not receive airplay. In 1989, *Billboard* became the first trade publication to track radio airplay as it happened and to count "spins," or plays, in compiling charts. *Billboard* and its companion publication, *Airplay Monitor*, used Broadcast Data Systems (BDS) to electronically detect airplay by matching segments of songs called "footprints" to actual play on stations monitored over the air. The practice of paper adds decreased because a song reported to *R&R* could be tracked in BDS detections. In mid-1999 both *R&R* and *The Gavin Report* (now defunct) began using charts based on airplay detection with information compiled by MediaBase, a monitoring service owned by Premiere Radio Networks."

Constructing a station playlist is the single most important duty of the music programmer. What to play, when to play it, and how often are some of the key questions confronting this individual. The music director relies on a number of sources, both internal and external, to provide the answers but also must cultivate an ear for the kind of sound the station is after. Some people are blessed with an almost innate capacity to detect a hit, but most must develop this skill over a period of time.

With the advent of station Web site streaming, the relationship between the

---

_____ce to Programmers

FIGURE 3.24
Frank Bell.

Rule 1: *Follow the listeners, not the format.* So many people in radio get caught up in terms like *CHR, New AC, Alternative,* and *AAA* that they lose track of their goal: finding listeners.

Consumers of radio think in terms of "what I like" and "what I don't like." By researching your listeners' tastes and giving them what they want (as opposed to what fits the industry's definition of what they should have), you'll maximize your chances for success.

Rule 2: *Think outside in, not inside out.* The fact that one company may now own several stations in a market and is capable, for example, of skewing one FM toward younger females and the other toward older females does not mean that you will automatically "dominate females."

The only reality that counts is that of the listener. If listeners feel your station serves a meaningful purpose for them, they will happily cast their Arbitron vote in your favor. If they believe you are simply duplicating what is already available elsewhere on the dial, you will be doomed to ratings obscurity.

Rule 3: *Early to bed, early to rise, Advertise, Advertise, Advertise.* In the Arbitron game of unaided recall, the dominant issue is Top-of-Mindness.

The best way to get that is through advertising your name and your station's benefits on your own air and on any other medium you can afford. Just for fun, here's a diagram I sometimes use to show first-time PDs the various factors that influence their station's ratings:

$$\frac{X - Y}{A} \times B = \text{Your Ratings}$$

X is what your station does.
Y is what your direct competitors do.
A represents "environmental" factors in the market, such as what's on TV during the survey, riots, floods, earthquakes, and (in some cases) the OJ trial.
B is what the rating service does. In the case of Arbitron, this would include the response rate, editing procedures, and distribution of diaries by race, age, and sex.

The most important thing to understand is that as PD, the only part of the equation you can control is X. Do the best you can to keep your station sounding compelling, entertaining, and focused on its target audience, and don't get an ulcer over those elements you can't control.

medium and the recording industry got more contentious in the 2000s. The recording industry insisted on greater compensation for its licensed music when a station offered songs via cyberspace, while broadcasters argued that their Web site music streaming was simply an extension of their on-air signal, which was already under a fee schedule. The recording industry feared Web site users would burn or download music free of charge from the station sites, and it anticipated this to be a major issue as the medium transitioned to digital. As of this writing, progress had been made in resolving this issue.

The PD and the FCC

The government is especially interested in the way a station conducts itself on the air. For instance, the PD makes certain that his or her station is properly identified once an hour, as close to the top of the hour as possible. The ID must include the station's call letters and the town in which it has been authorized to broadcast. Failure to properly identify the station is a violation of FCC rules.

Other on-air rules that the PD must address have to do with program content

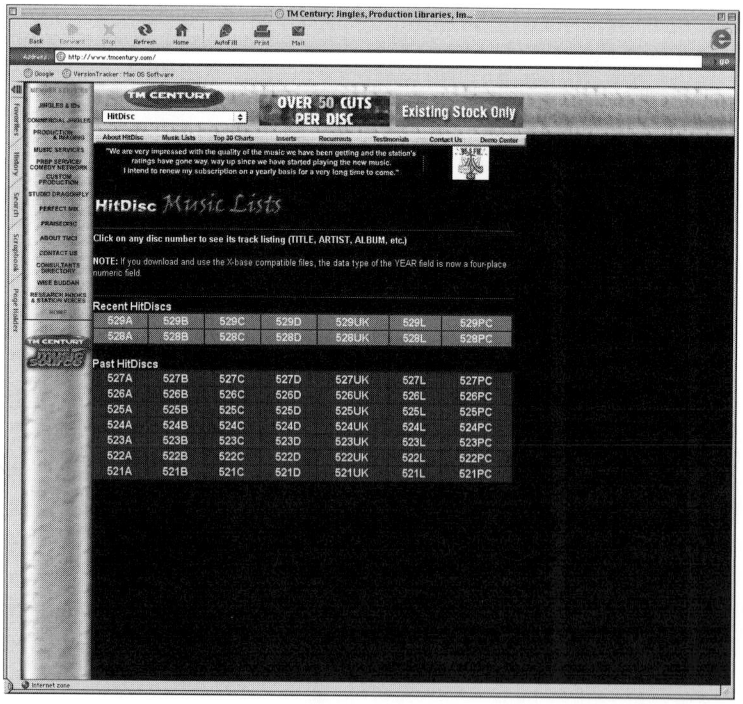

FIGURE 3.25
A station's music library in a box. Courtesy WIZN-FM.

and certain types of features. For example, profane language, obscenity, sex- and drug-related statements, and even innuendos in announcements, conversations, or music lyrics jeopardize the station's license. The FCC prohibits indecent and profane broadcasts, and the cost for violating this rule can cost the station dearly. For example, in 2006, the Commission raised the maximum charge for offenses in this category from $32,500–$325,000 per violation. Fines have been on a dramatic rise for infractions surrounding on-air indecency since the early 2000s as the result of some highly publicized incidents perpetrated by radio personalities like Bubba the Love Sponge, Opie & Anthony, and Howard Stern (now beyond the reach of these rules on satellite radio).

Political messages and station editorials are carefully scrutinized by the programmer. On-air contests and promotions must not resemble lotteries in which the audience must invest to win. A station that gets something in return for awarding prizes is subject to punitive actions. Neither the deejays, PD, music director, nor anyone associated with the station may receive payment for plugging a song or album on the air. This constitutes "payola" or "plugola" and was the cause of great industry upheaval in the late 1950s. Today, PDs and station managers continue to be particularly careful to guard against any recurrence, although there have been charges that such practices still exist.

In fact, in the mid-2000s, the FCC began a formal investigation into payola allegations against four major radio groups: CBS Radio, Clear Channel, Entercom, and Citadel. It was the largest federal inquiry since the payola scandals prompted congressional hearings in 1960. Indeed, PDs must be vigilant of this illegal practice, which seems impervious to eradication.

The PD must monitor both commercial and noncommercial messages to ensure that no false, misleading, or deceptive statements are aired, something the FCC staunchly opposes. This includes any distortion of the station's ratings survey results. A station that is not number one and claims to be is lying to the public as far as the FCC is concerned, and such behavior is not condoned.

License renewal programming promises must be addressed by the PD. The proportion of nonentertainment programming, such as news and public affairs features, pledged in the station's renewal application must be adhered to, even though such requirements have been all but eliminated. A promise is a promise. If a station claims that it will do something, it must abide by its word.

The PD helps maintain the station's Emergency Alert System (EAS), making certain that proper announcements are made on the air and that the EAS checklist containing an authenticator card is placed in the control room area. PDs also instruct personnel in the proper procedures used when conducting on-air telephone conversations to guarantee that the rights of callers are not violated.

The station log (which ultimately is the chief engineer's responsibility) and program log (no longer required by the FCC but maintained by most stations anyway) are examined by the PD for accuracy, and he or she also must see to it that operators have permits and that they are posted in the on-air studio. In addition, the station manager may assign the PD the responsibility for maintaining the station's Public File. If so, the PD must be fully aware of what the file is required to contain. The FCC and many broadcast associations will provide station operators with a Public File checklist upon request. This information is available in the *Code of Federal Regulations* (73.3526) as well.

Additional programming areas of interest to the FCC include procedures governing rebroadcasts, simulcasts, and subcarrier activities. The PD also must be aware that the government is keenly interested in employment practices. The programmer, station manager, and other department heads are under obligation to familiarize themselves with equal employment opportunity (EEO) and affirmative action rules. An annual employment report must be sent to the FCC.

The preceding is only a partial listing of the concerns set forth by the government relative to the PD's position. For a more comprehensive assessment, refer to the CFR appendix at the end of Chapter 2.

The PD and Upper Management

The pressures of the PD's position should be apparent by now. The station or cluster programmer knows well that his or her job entails satisfying the desires of many – the audience, government, air staff, and, of course, management. The relationship between the PD and the station or corporation's upper echelon is not always serene or without incident. Although their alliance is usually mutually fulfilling and productive, difficulties can and do occur when philosophies or practices clash. "Most inhibiting and detrimental to the PD is the GM who lacks a broad base of experience but imposes his opinions on you anyway. The guy who has come up through sales and has never spent a minute in the studio can be a real thorn in the side. Without a thorough knowledge of programming, management should rely on the expertise of that person hired who does. I don't mean, 'Hey, GM, get out of the way!' what I'm saying is, don't impose programming ideas and policies without at least conferring with that individual who ends up taking the heat if the air product fails to bring in the listeners," says Dick Fatherly.

Station manager Chuck Ducoty contends that managers can enhance as well as inhibit the programmer's style. "I've worked for some managers who give their PDs a great deal of space and others who attempt to control every aspect of programming. From the station manager's perspective, I think the key to a good experience with those who work for you is to find excellent people from the start and then have enough confidence in your judgment to let them do their job with minimal interference. Breathing down the neck of the PD is just going to create tension and resentment."

Programmer Peter Falconi believes that both the PD and the manager should make a sincere effort to get to know and understand one another. "You have to be on the same wavelength, and there has to be an excellent line of communication. When a manager has confidence and trust in his PD, he'll generally let him run with the ball. It's a two-way street. Most problems can be resolved when there is honesty and openness."

Programmer Andy Bloom offers this observation: "Great upper management hires the best players, gives them the tools to do their job, and then leaves them alone. A winning formula."

An adversarial situation between the station's PD and upper management does not have to exist. The station that cultivates an atmosphere of cooperation and mutual respect seldom becomes embroiled in skirmishes that deplete energy – energy better spent raising revenues and ratings.

FIGURE 3.27
Many stations ultraniche (position) their programming. Courtesy WPAT.

WPAT 930 AM Metro NY	
****ALL JEWISH ALL THURSDAY NIGHT****	
10:00–10:30 PM	**INNER MEANING WITH KIM CHEROVSKY.** Interviews on Judaism and spirituality with special guest Rabbi Jacob Jungreis
10:30–11:00 PM	**THE TOP TEN JEWISH MUSIC COUNTDOWN.** FAVORITE Jewish music of the week.
11:00–12:00 AM	**TALKLINE WITH ZEV BRENNER.** *AMERICA'S LEADING JEWISH PROGRAM. LIVE CALL IN WITH NEWSMAKER GUESTS AND CELEBRITIES MAKING HEADLINES IN THE JEWISH WORLD.*
12:00–12:30 PM	**BETWEEN THE LINES: THE TORAH CODES.** With Dr. Robert Wolf and Joel Gallis.
12:30–2:00 AM	**THE VOICE OF JERUSALEM WITH AVI. THE LATEST NEWS, SHMOOZ, AND CONTESTS LIVE FROM ISRAEL.**
2:00–3:00 AM	**THE TED SMITH SHOW.** Interview show on health and social issues.
3:00–4:30 AM	**THE TOP TEN JEWISH MUSIC COUNTDOWN.**
4:30–5:00 AM	**LIVE FROM ISRAEL.** The latest up to date news from Israel with Dov Shurin.

CHAPTER HIGHLIGHTS

1. The AC format features recent (since the 1970s) and current pop standards. It appeals to the 25–49-year age group, which attracts advertisers. It often utilizes music sweeps and clustered commercials. AC has spawned a variety of subgenres, including Adult Hits, Adult Standards, and iPod imitators Jack and Mike.

2. CHR features current, fast-selling hits from the Top 40. It targets teens, broadcasts minimal news, and is very promotion/contest oriented. Some CHRs have redirected their playlists to create a Modern Hit or Churban sound.

3. Country is the fastest growing format since the 1970s. More prevalent in the South and Midwest, it attracts a broad age group and offers a variety of subformats.

4. Easy Listening/Smooth Jazz stations evolved from the Beautiful Music stations of the 1960s and 1970s. Featuring mostly instrumentals and minimal talk, many stations have become automated and use prepackaged programming from syndicators. The primary audience is over age 50. Its following has dwindled in recent years owing to myriad softer AC formats.

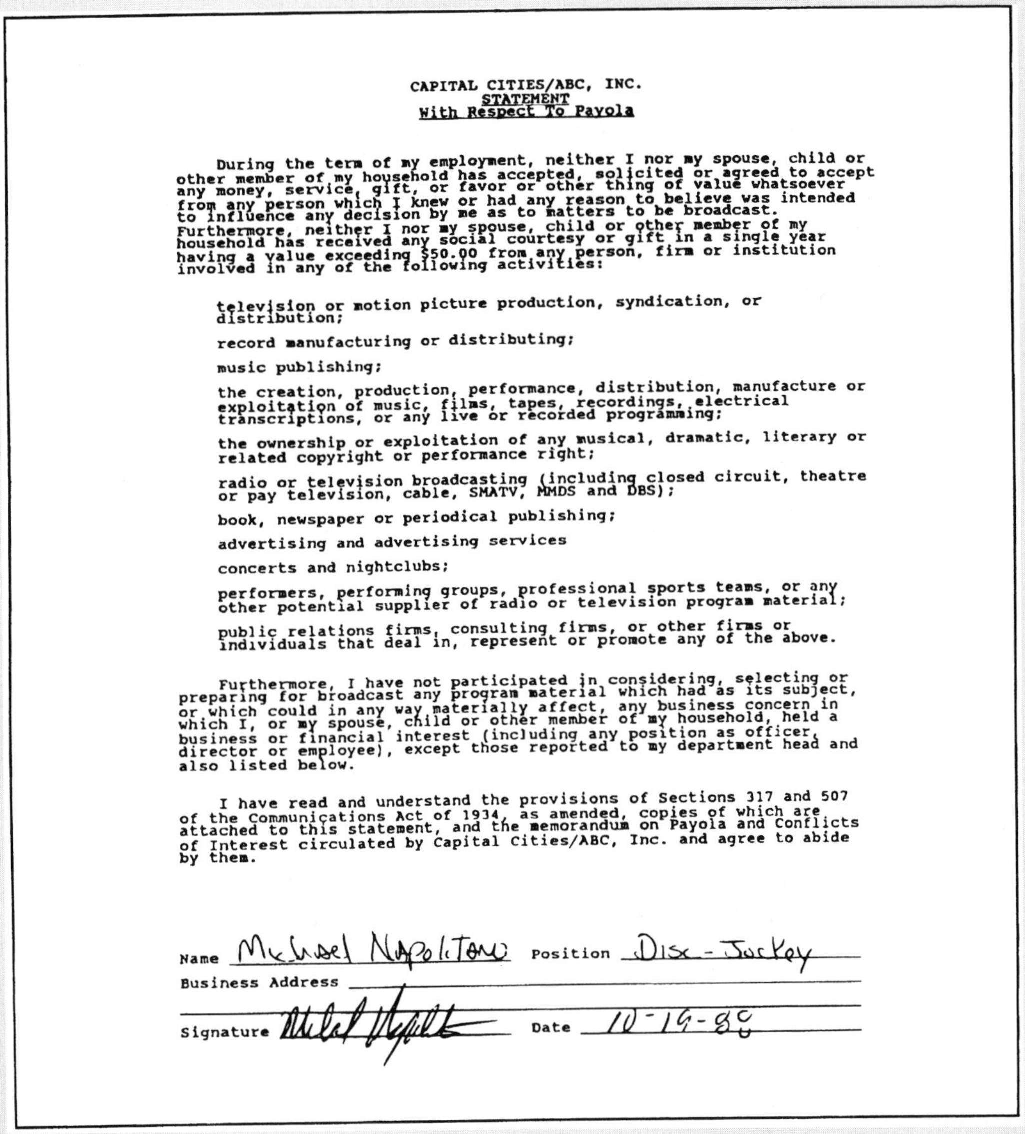

CAPITAL CITIES/ABC, INC.
STATEMENT
With Respect To Payola

During the term of my employment, neither I nor my spouse, child or other member of my household has accepted, solicited or agreed to accept any money, service, gift, or favor or other thing of value whatsoever from any person which I knew or had any reason to believe was intended to influence any decision by me as to matters to be broadcast. Furthermore, neither I nor my spouse, child or other member of my household has received any social courtesy or gift in a single year having a value exceeding $50.00 from any person, firm or institution involved in any of the following activities:

television or motion picture production, syndication, or distribution;

record manufacturing or distributing;

music publishing;

the creation, production, performance, distribution, manufacture or exploitation of music, films, tapes, recordings, electrical transcriptions, or any live or recorded programming;

the ownership or exploitation of any musical, dramatic, literary or related copyright or performance right;

radio or television broadcasting (including closed circuit, theatre or pay television, cable, SMATV, MMDS and DBS);

book, newspaper or periodical publishing;

advertising and advertising services

concerts and nightclubs;

performers, performing groups, professional sports teams, or any other potential supplier of radio or television program material;

public relations firms, consulting firms, or other firms or individuals that deal in, represent or promote any of the above.

Furthermore, I have not participated in considering, selecting or preparing for broadcast any program material which had as its subject, or which could in any way materially affect, any business concern in which I, or my spouse, child or other member of my household, held a business or financial interest (including any position as officer, director or employee), except those reported to my department head and also listed below.

I have read and understand the provisions of Sections 317 and 507 of the Communications Act of 1934, as amended, copies of which are attached to this statement, and the memorandum on Payola and Conflicts of Interest circulated by Capital Cities/ABC, Inc. and agree to abide by them.

Name Michael Napolitano Position Disc-Jockey

Business Address

Signature Date 10-19-88

FIGURE 3.28 Payola statement signed by a station employee. Courtesy Michael Napolitano and Capital Cities/ABC, Inc.

5. Rock or AOR stations began in the mid-1960s to counter Top 40 stations. They featured music sweeps with a large airplay library, and they played rock album cuts. News was minimal. The format attracted a predominantly male audience aged 18–34. Today, these stations are usually referred to simply as Rock stations.

6. All-News stations rotate time blocks of local, regional, and national news and features to avoid repetition. The format requires three to four times the staff and budget of most music operations.

7. All-Talk combines discussion and call-in shows. It is primarily a medium- and major-market format. Like All-News, All-Talk is mostly found on AM (and is the domain of conservative talkers) but is now finding a home on the FM band. All-Sports has boosted the nonmusic format's numbers and now is offered by several networks.

8. The Nostalgia playlist emphasizes popular tunes from the 1940s and prerock 1950s, presenting its music in sweeps with a relatively low deejay profile.

9. The Oldies playlist includes hits between the 1950s and 1960s, relying on fine air personalities. Commercials are placed randomly and songs are spaced to allow deejay patter.

10. Classic Rock concentrates on tunes once primarily featured by AOR stations. Meanwhile, Classic Hit stations fill the gap between Oldies and CHR outlets with play-lists that draw from 1970s' and 1980s' Top 40 charts.

11. UC is the "melting pot" format, attracting a heterogeneous audience. Its upbeat, danceable sound, and hip, friendly deejays attract the 18–34-year age group. Contests and promotions are important.

12. Classical commercial outlets are few, but they have a loyal audience. Primarily an FM format appealing to a higher income, college-educated (upscale, 25–49 years old) audience, Classical features a conservative, straightforward air sound.

FIGURE 3.29
Rules for success.
Courtesy Shane
Media.

13. Religious stations are most prevalent on the AM band. Religious broadcasters usually approach programming in one of two ways.

One includes music as a primary part of its presentation, whereas the other does not.

14. Ethnic stations serve the listening needs of minority groups. Black and Hispanic listeners constitute the largest ethnic audiences.

15. FS stations (formerly MOR) rely on the strength of air personalities and features. Mostly an AM format, FS attempts to be all things to all people, attracting an over-40 audience.

16. Niche formats, like All-Children, Business, and Tourist Radio, are popping up all over the dial as the listening audience becomes more diffused and interest grows in HD^2 stations.

17. Public and noncommercial stations typically employ a block format promoting diversity rather than a single form of programming.

18. PDs are hired to fit whatever format the station management has selected. They are chosen primarily for their experience, although education level is important.

19. The PD is responsible for everything that is aired. Second in responsibility to the general manager (except in a cluster arrangement with a director of operations), the PD establishes programming and format policy; hires and supervises on-air, music, and production personnel; handles the programming budget; develops promotions; monitors the station and its competitors and assesses research; is accountable for news, public affairs, and sports features; and may even pull an airshift.

20. The PD's effectiveness is measured by ratings in large markets and by sales in smaller markets.

21. The PD determines the content of each sound hour, utilizing program clocks to ensure that each element – commercial, news, promo, weather, music, and so on – is strategically located to enhance flow and optimize impact. Even News/Talk stations need program clocks.

22. PDs must adjust programming to the lifestyle activities of the target audience. They must develop a feel for the area in which the station is located, as well as an understanding of survey information and research data.

☑ tactics:programming

Programming Report from Shane Media Services

PROGRAM DIRECTOR - TEN TACTICS FOR SUCCESS

There are no schools to attend to become a Program Director. Many people fall into the job without a clue as to what the job really entails. Here are 10 basic points for PD success:

1. Show up. Not just for work. Show up at 2AM and visit with the overnight jock. Get to know that person in their time zone. Show up at remotes. Know how your airstaff and promotions people put on a show. Be visible both in and out of the station.

2. Listen up. You can't listen 24 hours a day, but you can tape when you must sleep. Tape the competition when you're monitoring your own shop. Don't listen as a programmer all the time. Try to slip into the attitude of your average listener to determine how well your station is delivering the format and serving your town.

3. Clean up. If you notice something wrong, why wait to make an adjustment? Eliminate small problems before they become large ones.

4. Take notes. Who's doing what in your town? Be aware of the "big picture" in your market, like an air traffic controller. If you need to make an instant adjustment, you'll be prepared.

5. Make notes. How many times have you had a brilliant idea in the middle of the night, and forgotten it by morning? Keep a note pad and pencil or mini recorder by your bed, in your car, wherever you go. A simple phrase or word jotted down quickly can bring back that concept when you've got time to develop the idea.

6. Leave notes. We are in the business of communicating, yet often do a poor job of getting a message from one end of the station to the other. Leave notes on the music log, a discrepancy sheet, a slip of paper in the phone message slot. Get in the habit of noting your thoughts to others, and watch your effectiveness as a manager improve.

© SHANE MEDIA SERVICES   HOUSTON, TX   (713) 952-9221

23. Finally, the PD must ensure that the station adheres to all FCC regulations pertaining to programming practices, anticipating problems before they occur. Indecent programming has resulted in huge fines, so PDs must be especially vigilant in this area.

24. Payola (plugola) has plagued the medium since the 1950s and continues to this day. The illegal pay-for-play practice requires careful monitoring by the station's PD and manager to ensure it does not occur. Large fines have been dealt to those stations violating the FCC laws governing this practice.

25. Web sites, podcasts, and blogs represent a way to strengthen a station's ties to its audience.

FIGURE 3.30
Many services are available to radio programmers. Courtesy McVay Media.

FIGURE 3.31
News release. In the global world, there is a need for global radio news. Courtesy Sky News.

PRESS RELEASE
DATE:25ᵗʰ March 2002 (Embargo)

Global Radio News Ltd. Announces Distribution Deal With Sky News Radio

Sky News Radio audio programme content will be available for distribution to radio stations outside the UK and South Africa via the Global Radio News network from Monday 25th March 2002.

Stations will be able to browse correspondent reports and a wide variety of material from Sky News Radio through the website (www.globalradionews.com) on a story-by-story basis. There is no subscription obligation and editors can use material that will suit their listener demographic. Stations just pay for what they use.

Henry Peirse, Director of Global Radio News Ltd. says *'this is an exciting development; stations now have the option to pick from Global Radio News correspondent reports and Sky News stories. The two complement each other well providing a comprehensive and detailed list of stories for our affiliates'.*

Andy Ivy, Editor of Sky News Radio says *'the quality of our service is proving a big hit with radio newsrooms in the UK and Global Radio News allows us to make our audio available to stations worldwide.'*

Global Radio News is a web-based audio content agency and distribution service with a network of more than 400 correspondents worldwide.

Sky News Radio is a division of Sky News. A dedicated team of radio journalists provides a news service to around 30 UK radio stations including talkSPORT, the Wireless Group and Chrysalis Radio, making it the second biggest supplier of national and international news to commercial radio stations in the UK.

Please contact: Henry Peirse at Global Radio News Ltd. – 020 7242 9192 or henry@globalradionews.com or Andy Ivy at Sky News Radio – 020 7705 3000 or andy.ivy@bskyb.com.

Note to editors:

Pictures of the Sky News Radio newsroom are available on Image Net or from the Sky Stills department on 020 7800 4271. Please contact Global Radio News Ltd. on 020 7242 9192 for pictures.

FOR IMMEDIATE RELEASE ON OR AFTER 25ᵗʰ MARCH 2002

FIGURE 3.32
A source for music
radio on the Internet.
Courtesy Pandora.

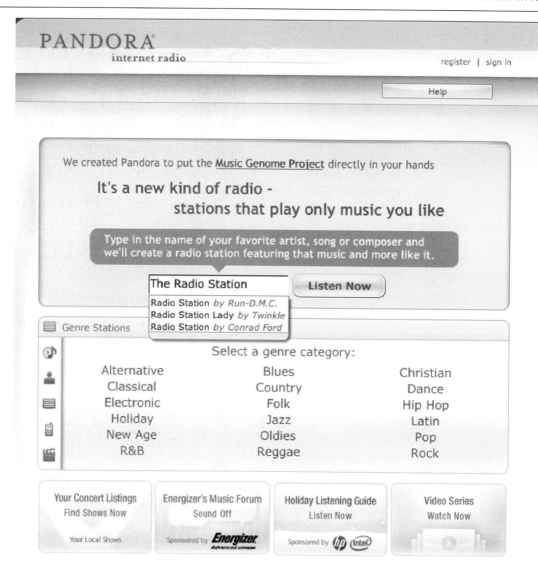

26. Stations must pay an annual music-licensing fee to ASCAP, BMI, or SESAC.

27. In the 2000s, the recording industry required that radio stations streaming music on their Web sites had to compensate it for such use.

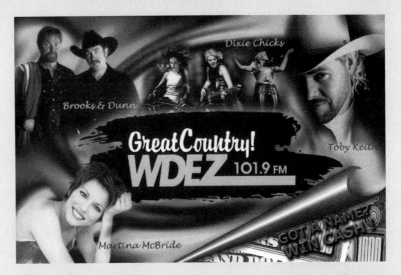

FIGURE 3.33
Radio illustrates its music format variety.
Courtesy Mix 98.5, WDEZ-FM, and KSSJ-FM.

Donald Fishman

Copyright and the Broadcast Industry

FIGURE 3.34
Donald Fishman.

One of the least discussed aspects of the broadcast industry is the role of copyright in broadcast decision making. Copyright is the area of law that protects the owner of artistic, creative, and intellectual works from unauthorized use by a second party absent the payment of a fee.

There are many examples of the type of payment required for the use of a creative work. For instance, if a radio station wants to play a song by Aerosmith, that station must pay a royalty to the owner of the musical copyright. Meanwhile, if a UHF television station wants to schedule 26 episodes of *Will and Grace*, it must pay a royalty to the syndication company that controls the right to distribute copies of the popular television comedy.

Music is a very popular area for copyright fees. Most musicians do not handle the paperwork and fee collection activities for their music. Instead, they assign the rights to a copyright clearinghouse. For broadcasters, there are three important music clearinghouses. The oldest of the clearinghouses is the ASCAP. ASCAP has satellite offices near most major cities, and it monitors radio and television station logs, visits night clubs and universities, and sells site licenses to businesses that want to play music,

such as fitness gyms and restaurants. The second most prominent music clearinghouse is BMI. BMI started in the late 1940s when ASCAP substantially raised the royalty rates for music played at radio stations. Many of the radio stations refused to pay the higher rates, and they began to sign up independent recording artists who would get exclusive play on their stations. Several of the early legends of Rock 'n' Roll, such as Elvis, Jerry Lee Lewis, and Little Richard, received extensive airtime on BMI-affiliated stations due to the feud between BMI and ASCAP. The third music clearinghouse is the SESAC. A few years ago, Bob Dylan signed an agreement with SESAC for an advance of several million dollars. SESAC will handle the authorized use of Dylan's music in European and enumerated other markets. SESAC is betting that future revenues from Dylan's music will be sufficient to offset the huge advance paid to Dylan in current dollars.

Paul Goldstein is correct: Copyright is primarily about money, and it frequently involves decision making and speculation about what creative works will provide the optimal return on an investment. The Beatles sold the rights to their most well-known music from the 1960s, seriously misjudging how popular that music would be 45 years after its release. Neil Sedaka, a prominent 1950s rock musician, sold the copyrights to his music shortly after the British musical invasion during the mid-1960s. Once Sedaka discovered that there was a lucrative market for music nostalgia and oldies concerts, the first thing he did was to repurchase the copyrights to his own songs.

Apart from money, there is a very sound philosophical rationale for maintaining a system of copyrights. Copyright laws are designed to create an incentive for authors and innovators to produce artistic, creative, and intellectual works. There is a benefit in this system for the individual as well as for society at large. For instance, if you

took a year off to produce and write a radio documentary, you would forgo a year's income and incur expenses to complete the desired project. If someone else could simply copy your work and sell it at a cheaper price because he or she had no major costs associated with creating the work, it is unlikely that any individual would write a second screenplay, book, or album. And society would be worse off because it would no longer be the beneficiary of these creative works from talented individuals.

In a word, copyright laws are designed to create incentives for individuals to produce creative works and to protect these innovators against unauthorized use of their work. The high prices that creators are able to charge is the bargain society strikes to obtain a second, third, and fourth work from creative individuals. A copyright has limitations: it lasts the life of an author plus 70 years, or in the case of a work-for-hire (something assigned to an independent contractor), 95 years. The work then goes into the public domain to be used by anyone without a fee, such as the plays of Shakespeare or the music of Beethoven.

Until recently, copyright issues did not generate interest among the general public. These questions involve a relationship between producers of creative works and the users of these materials. Moreover, the distribution of information is an expensive process undertaken primarily by large organizations that anticipate profiting from the material. In fact, it is fair to characterize the traditional copyright relationship as one between owners of copyright materials and users who typically are big media companies or major distributors.

However, this owner-user relationship has been undermined by modern technology. The development of the Internet and the digitization of intellectual property make it easier for the average person to make copies of creative works with relative ease. No special expertise is needed, and the works are verbatim copies reproduced at relatively low costs.

The development of the Internet is likely to have major implications for traditional broadcast stations and broadcasting activities. Among these developments are as follows:

- **Music File Sharing**: The use of MP3 files to exchange music has become one of the most popular activities of the millennial decade. It has been troublesome to record companies, and it will likely affect the number of listeners of traditional radio stations that continue to program music. If the record industry develops a pay-per-song satellite technology that allows anyone to listen to uninterrupted music via a radio receiver or even a cell phone, traditional radio stations are likely to see a decline of listenership. In addition, traditional radio stations have been exempted from a special performance royalty that goes directly to the performer; but web stations must still pay the fee. Understandably, there is substantial controversy over whether Internet webcasters, as they emerge, should be permitted to have a similar exemption like terrestrial stations from performance royalties.

- **Webcasting**: It is one of the growing areas of technological innovation. Radio maverick Howard Stern recently complained that traditional broadcast stations were using parts of his satellite program without paying any royalties. Stern, whose career has been associated with rebellion, not following the rules, and creative expression, wants to be compensated fairly for the work he creates. Moreover, it is likely that webcasters will want to receive royalties for the distribution of their work similar to terrestrial stations.

- **Digital Sampling**: One of the recurrent copyright issues over the past decade has been digital sampling. Sampling is taking sounds from a previous recording and placing them in a new musical work. For instance, the first note in the Beatles' well-known song, "A Hard Days Night," is so distinctive that it can be recognized as a standalone work. There are now several commercial digital samplers on the market. One of the most popular is the Fairlight CMI, or Computer Musical Instrument. It cost around $30,000 to purchase. Sampling has been especially popular within Hip-Hop music, and several Hip-Hop artists claim that sampling is a culturally expressive activity worthy of legal protection because of its rearrangements, remixes, and otherwise altered sequence and quality. However, in *Bridgeport Music v. Dimension Film* (2005), the Sixth Circuit ruled against sampling. The court stated: "Get a license or do not sample." Thus far, this is the most important ruling on sampling, but another case will surely confront the innovative applications of digital sampling. It is very unlikely that we have heard the last word on this issue.

- **Copyright Arbitration Royalty Tribune**: Although Congress is empowered to regulate the development of copyright, it has established a Royalty Tribune to set reasonable rates and to monitor emerging issues. At the same time, what rates to establish and how to handle webcasting remain unclear. Even setting reasonable rates for subscription services has proven to be difficult. In 1995, Congress passed the Digital Performance Rights in Sound Recording Act (DPRA). This act governs subscription digital audio transmissions or what we today recognize as XM Satellite Radio and Sirius. The Radio Industry Association of America (RIAA) and the organizations representing small webcasters have vigorously lobbied the Royalty Tribune for favorable rates. Interestingly, the National Association of Broadcasters (NAB) has refused to provide support for the fledgling webcasters and the new digital media providers. Instead, the NAB has focused on maintaining the rights and interests of traditional, terrestrial broadcasters. One of the emerging problems in broadcasting is the need to incorporate all relevant parties in the decision-making process with respect to copyright issues so that small, digital webcasters and the large terrestrial broadcasters can address common issues that affect their organizations.

- **Convergence**: One of the most vexing issues facing broadcasters at the end of the millennial decade is the question of convergence. Convergence refers to the ability to use information and content from one medium to another medium. Among the by-products of convergence is the ability to watch your favorite television programs on the Internet, download current movies directly to your computer, and use a wireless telephone with a GPS tracking system capable of pinpointing the exact location of a caller. In a word, convergence is the blurring of the lines between and among the existing forms of media. Convergence will provide innovative services and the "new ways of interacting with society." Existing owners of copyrights are understandably troubled. In what will be a landmark case, Viacom has sued YouTube and Google for $1 billion dollars for infringement of its copyrights. Like earlier copyright suits dealing with *Napster* and *Grokster*, *Viacom v. YouTube and Google* is a landmark case about the payment of royalties when information is distributed on the Internet. Broadcasters are attempting to be proactive with the new digital technologies by asking for the insertion of a software code (or a broadcast flag system) that regulates digital television and digital audio receivers on what programs an end user will be able to download. This is a blocking procedure that will prevent an individual without authorization from downloading the information, including the downloading of content (such as music from a radio feed) directly to a cell phone. So far, Congress has not adopted this form of technological protection, but broadcasters are rightly concerned about the long-term impact of convergence on digital rights management (DRM) and what the effect of convergence will be on their revenues.

Donald Fishman teaches at Boston College and publishes in a host of areas, including copyright.

FIGURE 3.35
Promoting the arts
on 1930s radio.
Courtesy Library of
Congress.

FIGURE 3.36
Radio honors
its legends.
Courtesy Museum
of Broadcast
Communications.

FIGURE 3.37
Protecting artists'
income and rights.
Courtesy Sound
Exchange.

SUGGESTED FURTHER READING

Adams, M.H., and Massey, K.K., *Introduction to Radio: Production and Programming*, Brown and Benchmark, Madison, WI, 1995.

Armstrong, B., *The Electronic Church*, J. Nelson, Nashville, TN, 1979.

Broady, J., *On Air: The Guide to Starting a Career as a Radio Personality*, BVI, 2007.

Busby, L., and Parker, D., *The Art and Science of Radio*, Allyn & Bacon, Boston, MA, 1984.

Carroll, R.L., and Davis, D.M., *Electronic Media Programming: Strategies and Decision Making*, McGraw-Hill, New York, 1993.

Chapple, S., and Garofalo, R., *Rock 'n' Roll Is Here to Pay*, Nelson-Hall, Chicago, IL, 1977.

Cliff, C., and Greer, A., *Broadcasting Programming: The Current Perspective*, University Press of America, Washington, DC, 1974 to date, revised annually.

Coddington, R.H., *Modern Radio Programming*, Tab Books, Blue Ridge Summit, PA, 1970.

DeLong, T.A., *The Mighty Music Box*, Amber Crest Books, Los Angeles, CA, 1980.

Denisoff, R.S., *Solid Gold: The Popular Record Industry*, Transaction Books, New York, 1976.

Dingle, J.L., *Essential Radio*, Peregrine Books, Marblehead, MA, 1995.

Eastman, S.T., *Broadcast/Cable Programming: Strategies and Practices*, 6th edition, Wadsworth Publishing, Belmont, CA, 2001.

Hall, C., and Hall, B., *This Business of Radio Programming*, Billboard Publishing, New York, 1977.

Halper, D., *Full-Service Radio*, Focal Press, Boston, MA, 1991.

Halper, D., *Radio Music Directing*, Focal Press, Boston, MA, 1991.

Halper, D., *Icons of Talk Radio*, Greenwood, Westport, CT, 2008.

Hilliar, R., and Keith, M., *Dirty Discourse: Sex and Indecency in American Radio*, Iowa State Press, Ames, IA, 2003.

Hutchings, W., *Radio on the Road*, 8th edition, Aslan Publishing, Fairfield, CT, 2006.

Johnson, T., and Burns, A., *Morning Radio*, Johnson Publishing, Washington, DC, 1999.

Keirstead, P.A., *All-News Radio*, Tab Books, Blue Ridge Summit, PA, 1980.

Keith, M.C., *Radio Programming: Consultancy and Formatics*, Focal Press, Stoneham, MA, 1987.

Keith, M.C., *Signals in the Air: Native Broadcasting in America*, Praeger Publishing, Westport, CT, 1995.

Keith, M.C., *Sounds in the Dark: All Night Radio in American Life*, Iowa State Press, Ames, IA, 2001.

Keith, M.C., *Radio Cultures: The Sound Medium in American Life*, Peter Lang, New York, 2008.

Land, J., *Active Radio: Pacifica's Brash Experiment*, University of Minnesota Press, Minneapolis, MN, 1999.

Lochte, B., *Christian Radio: The Growth of a Mainstream Force*, McFarland, Jefferson, NC, 2006.

Lujack, L., and Jedlicka, D.A., *Superjock: The Loud, Frantic, NonStop World of Rock Radio Deejays*, Regnery, Chicago, IL, 1975.

Lynch, J., and Gillispie, G., *Process and Practice of Radio Programming*, University Press of America, Lanham, MD, 1998.

MacFarland, D.T., *The Development of the Top 40 Format*, Arno Press, New York, 1979.

MacFarland, D.T., *Contemporary Radio Programming Strategies*, Lawrence Erlbaum Associates, Hillsdale, NJ, 1990.

Maki, V., and Pederson, J., *The Radio Playbook*, Globe Mack, St. Louis, MO, 1991.

Matelski, M.J., *Broadcast Programming and Promotion Worktext*, Focal Press, Boston, MA, 1989.

McCoy, Q., *No Static: A Guide to Creative Programming*, Miuller Freeman Books, Chicago, IL, 1999.

Morrow, B., *Cousin Brucie*, Morrow and Company, New York, 1987.

NAB, *The New Media Law Handbook for Radio Broadcasters*, National Association of Broadcasters, Washington, DC, 2007.

Norberg, E., *Radio Programming: Tactics and Strategies*, Focal Press, Boston, MA, 1996.

Passman, A., *The Deejays*, Macmillan, New York, 1971.

Pierce, D., *Riding the Ether Express*, University Center for Louisiana Studies, Siana, LA, 2008.

Rhoads , B.E., et al., editors, *Programming and Promotion*, Streamline Press, West Palm Beach, FL, 1995.

Routt, E., McGrath, J.B., and Weiss, F.A., *The Radio Format Conundrum*, Hastings House, New York, 1978.

Sklar, R., *Rocking America: How the All-Hit Radio Stations Took Over*, St. Martin's Press, New York, 1984.

Utterback, A.S., and Michael, G.F., *Voice Handbook: How to Polish Your On-Air Delivery*, Bonus Books, Santa Monica, CA, 2005.

Vane, E.T., and Gross, L.S., *Programming for TV, Radio, and Cable*, Focal Press, Boston, MA, 1994.

Warren, S., *Radio: The Book*, 3rd edition, NAB Books, Washington, DC, 1999.

Wilcox, J., *Voiceovers: Techniques and Tactics for Success*, Allworth Press, New York, 2007.

To: Steve
Fr: Jay
Re: WLKZ Programming

In listening over the past few days, but only to an hour or two total, it appears that much of the "big picture" programming philosophy has been lost. Perhaps Joe hasn't reviewed the old operation's manual. But some mechanical changes could dramatically help the sound of the station until the philosophy is recreated or changed.

1. One part-timer's mike was way too hot compared to the music. Music should always be dominant; personalities should never overwhelm it. The voice should be "in" the music.

2. Song titles were often announced. Oldies listeners know the song titles, and a lot more than our own people do about every record. There is also the danger that our mostly young talent will say something that reveals their age/lack of knowledge when talking about music. This is unnecessary talk and should be eliminated.

3. Conversely, there is almost no local content. This does not mean PSAs about bean suppers; this means the progress on the new building in downtown Wolfeboro, or the time the town Christmas lights will be turned on, for example. It takes more work than announcing a song title, but it's a much better reason to listen.

4. After the weather was given, the personality commented, "At least that's what it says here."

Weather is one of the principal reasons people choose a radio station. The forecast (or the Radar Weather franchise) is only as credible as we make it (the information all comes from the same place).

5. Talk between records. The music should never stop unless it has to (commercials). Stopping it down to talk, even for a liner that can be delivered over an intro, kills the momentum.

6. There are literally no prepromotes going into stop sets. The listener is not given any reasons to stick around (and forward momentum again stops).

7. There are recorded PSAs (a corporate no-no). The one I heard tells us to wear seat belts. Every media, every politician, every do-gooder is trying to tell other people what to do. Let's just be the medium that informs and entertains. Let's be an escape from all the other pointed fingers.

8. Joe signs off his show and also refers to his listener as "everybody." We should talk to only one listener at a time. And we should never end anything – keep it going, part of forward momentum. Talk about the guy coming up next.

9. Could you send Joe a memo or talk with him on a visit soon? I want to keep that station tight and happening; it's important.

10. Also, what do you think about adding some Beatles songs (over and above what we have) for the next month or so? And trading/giving away some anthology CDs? Thanks.

Commercialization: A Retrospective

As the first decade of the twenty-first century wound down, the level of radio advertising did as well, due to a decimated economy. In fact, late in 2007, the Radio Advertising Bureau (RAB) reported 18 consecutive months of decline. Still, selling commercials keeps the majority of radio stations on the air. It is that simple – yet not so simple. In the 1920s, broadcasters realized the necessity of converting the medium into a sponsor-supported industry. It seemed to be the most viable option and the key to growth and prosperity. However, not everyone approved of the method. Opponents of commercialization argued that advertising would decrease the medium's ability to effectively serve the public's good, and one U.S. senator voiced fears that advertisers would turn radio into an on-air pawnshop. These predictions would prove to be somewhat accurate. By the mid-1920s, most radio outlets sold airtime, and few restrictions existed pertaining to the substance and content of messages. Commercials promoting everything from miracle pain relievers to instant hair-growing solutions filled the broadcast day. It was not until the 1930s that the government developed regulations that addressed the issue of false advertising claims. This resulted in the gradual elimination of sponsors peddling dubious products.

Program sponsorships were the most popular form of radio advertising in the 1920s and early 1930s. Stations, networks, and advertising agencies often lured clients onto the air by naming or renaming programs after their products, such as *Eveready Hour*, *Palmolive Hour*, *Fleischmann Hour*, *Clicquot Club Eskimos*, *The Coty Playgirl*, and so on. Because formidable opposition to commercialization existed in the beginning, sponsorships, in which the only reference to a product was in a program's title, appeared the best path to take. This approach was known as *indirect* advertising.

As the outcry against advertiser-supported radio subsided, stations became more blatant or *direct* in their presentation of commercial material. Parcels of time, anywhere from 1–5, even 10, minutes, were sold to advertisers eager to convey the virtues of their labors. Industry advertising revenues soared throughout the 1930s, despite the broken economy. Radio sales people were among the few who had a salable product. World War II increased the rate of sales revenues twofold. As it became the foremost source of news and information during that bleak period in American history, the value of radio's stock reached new highs, as did the incomes of sales people. The tide would shift, however, with the advent of television in the late 1940s.

When television unseated radio as the number one source of entertainment in the early 1950s, time sellers for the deposed medium found their fortunes sagging. In the face of adversity, as well as opportunity, many radio sales people abandoned the old in preference for the new, opting to sell for television. Radio was, indeed, in a dilemma of frightening proportions, but it soon put itself back on course by renovating its programming approach. By 1957, the medium had undergone an almost total transformation and was once again enjoying the rewards of success. Sales people concentrated on selling airtime to advertisers interested in reaching specific segments of the population. Radio became extremely localized and, out of necessity, the networks diverted their attention to television.

Competition also became keener. Thousands of new outlets began to broadcast between 1950 and 1970. Meanwhile, frequency modulation (FM) started to spread its wings, preparing to surpass its older rival. Amplitude modulation (AM) music stations experienced great difficulties in the face of the mass exodus to FM, which culminated in 1979 when FM exceeded AM's listenership. FM became the medium to sell.

In the first half of the 1980s, radio programming was easily divisible. Talk was found on AM and music on FM. Today, hundreds of AM stations have become stereo in an attempt to improve their marketing potential, and some FM outlets have taken to airing nonmusic formats as a way of surviving the ratings battles.

Selling time in the new millennium is a far cry from what it was like during the medium's heyday. Observes general manager (GM) Ted Jordan, "Five years ago sales people on a call spent a lot of time separating their stations from competitors. For example "We're the contest station," "We're the office station," etc. Now, with consolidation, we gloss over the differences. "Here's what it will cost you and here's what we're willing to add" comes up much faster."

Station account executives no longer search for advertisers willing to sponsor half-hour sitcoms, quiz shows, or mysteries. Today, the advertising dollar generally is spent on spots scheduled for airing during specific dayparts on stations that attract a particular piece of the highly fractionalized radio audience pie. The majority of radio outlets program prerecorded music, and it is that which constitutes the station's product. The salesperson sells the audience, which the station's music attracts, to the advertiser or time buyer.

Rick Ducey

FIGURE 4.1
Rick Ducey.

Challenging Radio Sales

Here is what I see as the issues confronting radio sales at the present time:

1. Radio ad spending is declining due to the economy and shifting media allocation strategies.
2. Trying to ramp up Web revenues fast enough to offset loss of on-air advertising and the resulting valuation drops.
3. Managing with fewer resources – people, capital, and facilities.
4. Changing audience consumption patterns – shifts to streaming, mobile, and players.
5. With revenues and valuations declining, more owners are facing challenges as they push against debt covenants and risk defaults or at least loan workouts.

Selling Airtime

Airtime is intangible. You cannot see it or hold it in your hand. It is not like any other form of advertising. Newspaper and magazine ads can be cut out by the advertiser and pinned to a bulletin board or taped to a window as tangible evidence of money spent. Television commercials can be seen, but radio commercials are sounds flitting through the ether with no visual component to attest to their existence. They are ephemeral, or fleeting, to use words that are often associated with radio advertising. However, any informed account executive will respond to such terms by stating the simple fact that an effective radio commercial makes a strong and lasting impression on the mind of the listener in much the same way that a popular song tends to permeate the gray matter. "The so-called intangible nature of a radio commercial really only means you can't see it or touch it. There is little doubt, however, that a good spot is concrete in its own unique way. Few of us have gone unaffected or, better still, untouched by radio commercials. If a spot is good, it is felt, and that's a tangible," says radio sales manager Charles W. Friedman.

Initially considered an experimental or novel way to publicize a product, it soon became apparent to advertisers that radio was far more. Early sponsors who earmarked a small portion of their advertising budgets to the new electronic "gadget," while pouring the rest into print, were surprised by the results. Encouraged by radio's performance, advertisers began to spend more heavily. By the 1930s, many prominent companies were reallocating substantial portions of their print advertising budgets for radio. To these convinced advertisers, radio was, indeed, a concrete way to market their products.

Yet the feeling that radio is an unconventional mode of advertising continues to persist to some extent even today, especially among small, print-oriented retailers. Usually, the small market radio station's prime competitor for ad dollars is the local newspaper. Many retailers have used papers for years and perceive radio as a secondary or even frivolous means of advertising, contends Friedman. "Retailers who have used

FIGURE 4.2
Sales bullpen area. Courtesy Clear Channel.

print since opening their doors for business are reluctant to change. The toughest factor facing a radio salesperson is the notion that the old way works the best. It is difficult to overcome inertia."

Radio is one of the most effective means of advertising when used correctly. Of course, there is a right way and a wrong way to use the medium, and the salesperson who knows and understands the unique character of his or her product is in the best position to succeed. To the extent that a radio commercial cannot be held or taped to a cash register, it is intangible.

However, the results produced by a carefully conceived campaign can be seen in the cash register. Consistent radio users, from the giant multinational corporations to the so-called mom-and-pop shops, know that a radio commercial can capture people's attention as effectively as anything crossing their field of vision. A 1950s promotional slogan says it best: "Radio gives you more than you can see."

On a final note, Ed Shane says that although over-the-air advertising remains the primary source of income for most stations, "nontraditional revenue (NTR) streams (such as a Web site or special events) help stations realize financial goals."

Becoming an Account Executive

A notion held by some sales managers is that sales people are born and not made. This position holds that a salesperson either "has it" or does not, "it" being the innate gift to sell, without which all the schooling and training in the world means little. Although not all sales managers embrace this theory, many agree with the view that anyone attempting a career in sales should first and foremost possess an unflagging desire to make money, because without it, failure is almost assured.

According to RAB figures, 70% of the radio sales people hired by stations are gone within 3 years; another study shows that 73% of new radio sales people leave the business within a year. Although this sounds less than encouraging, it also must be stated that to succeed in broadcast sales invariably means substantial earnings and rapid advancement. True, the battle can be a tough one and the dropout rate is high, but the rewards of success are great.

The majority of newly hired account executives have college training. An understanding of research, marketing, and finance is important. Formal instruction in these areas is particularly advisable for persons considering a career in broadcast sales. Broadcast sales has become a familiar course offering at many schools with programs in electronic media. Research and marketing courses designed for the broadcast major also have become more prevalent since the 1970s. "Young people applying for sales positions here, for the most part, have college backgrounds. A degree indicates a certain amount of tenacity and perseverance, which are important qualities in anyone wanting to sell radio. Not only that, but the candidate with a degree often is more articulate and self-assured. As in most other areas of radio, ten or fifteen years ago fewer people had college diplomas, but the business has become so much more sophisticated and complex because of the greater competition and emphasis on research that managers actually look for sales people with college training," says general manager Richard Bremkamp.

Whether a candidate for a sales position has extensive formal training or not, he or she must possess a knowledge of the product in order to be hired. "To begin with, an applicant must show me that she knows something about radio; after all, that is what we're selling. The individual doesn't necessarily have to have a consummate understanding of the medium, although that would be nice, but she must have some product knowledge. Most stations are willing to train to an extent. I suppose you always look for someone with some sales experience, whether in radio or in some other field," says general sales manager Bob Turley.

Stations do prefer a candidate with sales exposure, be it selling vacuum cleaners door-to-door or shoes in a retail store. "Being out in front of the public, especially in a selling situation, regardless of the product, is excellent training for the prospective radio sales rep. I started in the transportation industry, first in customer service, then in sales. After that I owned and operated a restaurant. Radio sales was a whole new ball game for me when I went to work for WCFR in Springfield, Vermont, in the mid-1970s. Having dealt with the public for two decades served me well. In two years I rose to be the station's top biller, concentrating mainly on direct retail sales. In 1979, WKVT in Brattleboro hired me as sales manager," recalls Charles W. Friedman.

Hiring inexperienced sales people is a gamble that a small radio station generally must take. The larger outlets almost always require radio sales credentials, a luxury that smaller stations cannot afford. Thus, they must hire untested sales people, and there are no guarantees that a person who has sold lawn mowers can sell airtime, that is, assuming that the newly hired salesperson has ever sold anything at all. In most cases, he or she comes to radio and sales without experience, and the station must provide at least a modicum of training. Unfortunately, many stations fail to provide adequate training, and this too contributes to the high rate of turnover. New sales people commonly are given 2 to 3 months to display their wares and exhibit their potential. If they prove themselves to the sales manager by generating new business, they are asked to stay. On the other hand, if the sales manager is not convinced that the apprentice salesperson has the ability to bring in the accounts, then he or she is shown the door.

During the trial period, the salesperson is given a modest draw against sales, or a "no-strings" salary on which to subsist. In the former case, the salesperson eventually must pay back, through commissions on sales, the amount that he or she has drawn. Thus, after a few months, a new salesperson may well find himself or herself in debt for $2000 or $3000. As a show of confidence and to encourage the new salesperson who has shown an affinity for radio sales, management may erase the debt. If a station decides to terminate its association with the new salesperson, it must absorb the loss of time, energy, and money invested in the employee.

Characteristics that managers most often look for in prospective sales people include ambition, confidence, energy, determination, honesty, and intelligence. "Ambition is the cornerstone of success. It's one of the first things I look for. Without it, forget it. You have to be hungry. It's a great motivator. You have to be a quick thinker – be able to think on your feet, under pressure, too. Personal appearance and grooming also are important," says sales manager Gene Etheridge.

Station sales manager Joe Martin places a premium on energy, persistence, creativity, and organization. "Someone who is a self-starter makes life a lot easier. No manager likes having to keep after members of his sales team. A salesperson should take initiative and be adept at planning his day. Too many people make half the calls they should and could. A salesperson without organizational skills is simply not going to bring in the same number of orders as the person who does. There is a correlation between the number of pitches and the number of sales."

Metro market general sales manager Peg Kelly values people skills. "Empathy is right up there. I need someone who possesses the ability to get quick answers, learn the client's business quickly, and relate well to clients. It's a people business, really." Charles W. Friedman also looks for sales personnel who are people oriented. "My experience has proven that a prospective

> Radio has transcended current lifestyles...people today are money-rich and time-poor. 85% of all Americans are two income households complaining that they have no time to read the newspaper. Radio is the go ANYWHERE at ANYTIME medium:

> 99% of all households have radios

> 95% of all motor vehicles have radios

> 61% of all adults have radios at work

> Radio reaches people everywhere...in cars, at home, at work, on the way to and from anywhere!

> Radio appeals to each individuals own imagination...it's theater of the mind!

> Radio appeals to human emotions

> Radio convinces listeners to take action

> Radio is the IMMEDIATE medium...you can have a spot produced and be on the air with your message in as little as a few hours!

> Radio's message is easily changed...production costs are low

salesperson had better like people. In other words, be gregarious and friendly. This is something that's hard to fake. Sincerity, or the lack of it, shows. If you're selling airtime, or I guess anything for that matter, you had better enjoy talking with people as well as listening. A good listener is a good salesperson. Another thing that is absolutely essential is the ability to take rejection objectively. It usually takes several 'no's' to get to the 'yes.'"

Friedman believes that it is important for a salesperson to have insight into human nature and behavior. "You really must be adept at psychology. Selling really is a matter of anticipating what the prospect is thinking and knowing how best to address his concerns. It's not so much a matter of outthinking the prospective client, but rather being cognizant of the things that play a significant role in his life. Empathy requires

FIGURE 4.3
Courtesy Mix 105.1.

50 Ways to Leave Your Loser

The attributes, habits and characteristics America's top local Radio salespeople say make them winners.

1. Discipline
2. Attention to detail
3. Follow-through
4. Honesty
5. Listening
6. Timeliness, promptness
7. Determination
8. Thoroughness
9. Always prospecting
10. Creativeness
11. Consistently (re)discovering and fulfilling prospect/client needs
12. Flexibility
13. Love the business
14. Sincerely want their clients to succeed
15. Knowledge
16. Strong work ethic
17. 50-plus-hour workweek
18. Organized
19. Effective time/territory management
20. Priority management/crisis avoidance techniques
21. Accessible to clients/peers/management
22. Faith in God, self, product
23. Unwavering enthusiasm
24. Total personal acceptance of successes and failures
25. Focus-focus-focus. Know what you want, what you need to do, do it.
26. Understanding and application of the basics of selling
27. Persistence
28. Insistence on doing the best possible job — not just "good enough"
29. Deliver on promises
30. Very presentable personal appearance
31. Open minded — never stop growing
32. Advance preparation — no winging it
33. Rarely forget to ask for the order (as opposed to rarely remembering)
34. Regular self-improvement. Read a lot, listen to tapes. Attend seminars
35. Strong communication skills: intra-office and with clients mail/phone/in-person
36. Aggressiveness — stay with prospect/client until the job is done right
37. Empathy/sincere caring for client's results
38. Results oriented
39. Do-it-now attitude
40. Keep good records
41. In office/on street early and stay late
42. Under-promise and over-deliver
43. Get into the client's shoes, view things from client's perspective
44. Anticipate and eliminate problems before they develop
45. Don't make assumptions
46. Don't take anything for granted, especially your station's place in the buy
47. Loyalty to company, clients, self
48. Keep in touch with clients, especially during their schedules
49. Don't take rejection personally
50. Sell ideas and solutions, not spots, flights, or packages

FIGURE 4.4
Some cogent advice. Courtesy Radio Ink.

radio station itself rather than immediately looking elsewhere for sales people. For decades, it was believed that programming people were not suited for sales. An inexplicable barrier seemed to separate the two areas. Since the 1970s, however, this attitude has changed to some degree, and sales managers now give serious consideration to on-air people who desire to make the transition into sales. Consolidation and downsizing in the 1990s also inspired multiple roles playing at stations. That is to say, the morning deejay may become the afternoon salesperson. The major advantage of hiring programming people to sell the station is that they have a practical understanding of the product. "A lot of former deejays make good account reps because they had to sell the listener on the product. A deejay really is a salesperson, when you get right down to it," observes broadcaster Joe Martin.

Realizing, too, that sales is the most direct path into station management, programming people often are eager to make the shift. Since the 1980s, the trend has been greater than ever to recruit managers from the programming ranks. However, a sales background is still preferred.

The salesperson is invariably among the best-paid members of a station. How much a salesperson earns is usually left up to the individual to determine. Contrary to popular opinion, the salesperson's salary generally exceeds the deejay's, especially in the smaller markets. In the larger markets, certain air personalities' salaries are astronomical and even surpass the general manager's income, but major market sales salaries are commonly in the five- and even six-figure range.

Entry-level sales positions are fairly abundant (although station consolidation has reduced these opportunities), and stations are always on the lookout for good people. Perhaps, no other position in the radio station affords an individual the opportunities that sales does, but most sales people will never go beyond entry level in sales. Yet, for those who are successful, the payoff is worthwhile. "The climb itself can be the most exhilarating part, I think. But you've got to have a lot of reserve in your tanks, because the air can be pretty thin at times," observes Etheridge.

the ability to appreciate the experiences of others. A salesperson who is insensitive to a client's moods or states of mind usually will come away empty handed."

In recent years, sales managers have recruited more heavily from within the

The Sales Manager

The general sales manager (also called director of sales (DOS) in cluster operations) supervises the marketing of a station's or cluster's airtime. This person is responsible for moving inventory, which in the case of the radio outlet constitutes the selling of spot and feature schedules to advertisers. To achieve this end, the sales manager directs the daily efforts of the station's account executives, establishes sales department policies, develops sales plans and materials, conceives of sales and marketing campaigns and promotions, sets quotas, and also may sell as well.

A station's sales department customarily includes an emphasis on national, regional, and local sales. The station's or the cluster's general sales manager usually handles national responsibilities. This includes working with the station's rep company to stimulate business from national advertisers. The regional sales manager is given the responsibility of exploring sales possibilities in a broad geographical area surrounding the station or stations. For example, the regional person for an outlet in New York City may be assigned portions of Connecticut, New Jersey, and Long Island. The local sales manager at the same station would concentrate on advertisers within the city proper. The general sales manager oversees the efforts of each of these individuals.

The size of a station's sales staff varies according to its location and reach. A typical small-market radio station employs between two and four account executives, and the medium-market station averages about five. Large, top-ranked metropolitan outlets employ as many as eight to ten sales people, although it is more typical for the major-market station to have approximately a half-dozen account executives. Of course, in cluster operations where team selling often exists, these numbers will vary, as a salesperson may be selling the airtime of several stations. In cluster operations, it is not uncommon for there to be dozens of sales personnel.

The general sales manager/DOS reports directly to the station or station cluster's general manager and works closely with the programming department in developing salable features. Regular daily and weekly sales meetings are scheduled and headed by the sales manager, during which time goals are set and problems addressed. The sales manager also assigns account lists to members of his or her staff and helps coordinate trade and co-op deals.

As mentioned earlier, the head of the sales department usually is responsible for maintaining close contact with the station's rep company as a way of generating income from national advertisers who are handled by advertising agencies. The relationship of the sales manager and rep company is a particularly important one and will be discussed in greater detail later in this chapter. In addition, the sales manager must be adept at working ratings figures to the station's advantage for inclusion in sales promotional materials that are used on both the national and local levels.

All sales come under the scrutiny of the sales manager, who determines whether an account is appropriate for the station and

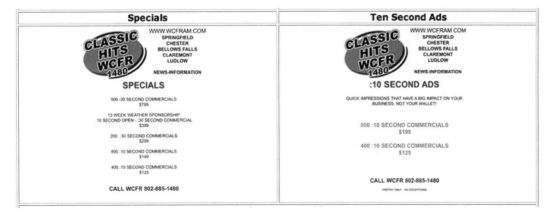

FIGURE 4.5
Special ad rates.
Courtesy WCFR.

FIGURE 4.6
Coverage map (A)
and rate card (B)
for KATL. Courtesy
KATL.

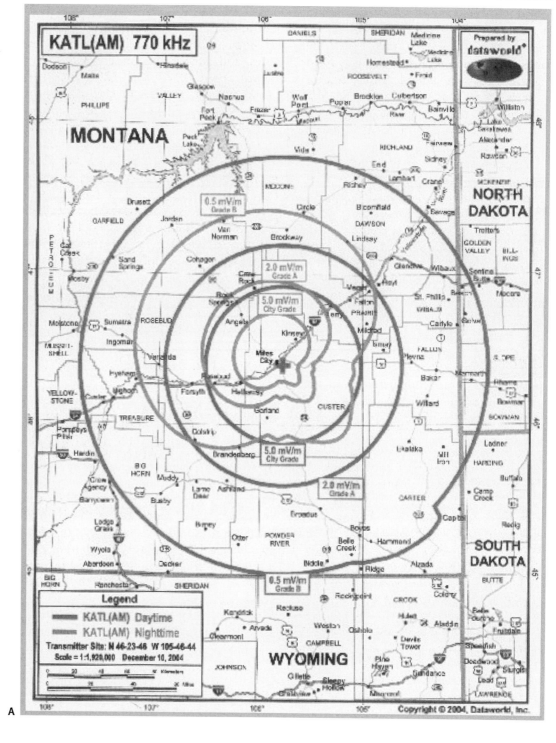

A

B

Monthly Flight Rates		
Miles City, Montana		406-234-7700
Frequency	30-Second	60-Second
1-45	$8.50	$13.60
46-100	$7.80	$12.65
101-150	$7.25	$11.80
151+	$6.65	$11.25
All Rates Net to Station		

conditions of the sale meet established standards. In addition, the sales manager may have a policy that requires credit checks to be made on every new account and that new clients pay for a portion of their spot schedule up front as a show of good faith. Again, policies vary from station to station.

It is up to the head of sales to keep abreast of local and national sales and marketing trends that can be used to the station's advantage. This requires the sales manager to constantly survey trade magazines like *Radio Ink, Radio Business Report,* and *ADWEEK*, and attend industry seminars such as those conducted by the RAB. No sales department can operate in a vacuum and hope to succeed in today's dynamic radio marketplace.

Statistics continue to bear out the fact that sales managers are most often recruited to fill the position of general manager. It is also becoming more commonplace for sales managers to have experience in other areas of a station's operations, such as programming and production, a factor that has become increasingly important to the person who hires the chief account executive.

Radio Sales Tools

The fees that a station charges for airtime are published in its rate card. Rates for airtime depend on the size of a station's listenership – the bigger the audience, the higher the rates. At the same time, the unit cost for a spot or a feature is affected by the quantity or amount purchased – the bigger the "buy," the cheaper the unit price. Clients also get discounts for consecutive week purchases over a prescribed period of time – say, 26 or 52 weeks.

The sales manager and station manager (DOS and market manager in cluster setups) work together in designing the rate card, basing their decisions on ratings and what their market can support. A typical rate card will include a brief policy statement concerning terms of payment and commission: "Bills due and payable when rendered. Without prior credit approval, cash in advance required. Commission to recognized advertising agencies on net charges for station time – 15%." A statement pertaining to the nature of copy and when it is due at the station also may be included in the rate card: "All programs and announcements are subject to removal without notice for any broadcast which, in our opinion, is not in the public's interest. Copy must be at the station 48 hours prior to broadcast date and before noon on days preceding weekends

and holidays." A station's approach to discounting must be, of practical necessity, included in the rate card: "All programs, features, and announcements are provided a 5% discount if on the air for 26 consecutive weeks and a 10% discount if on the air for 52 weeks." (See Figure 4.8)

It is important to state as emphatically and clearly as possible the station's position on all possible topics affecting a sale. Most stations provide clients with rate protection for a designated period of time should fees for airtime change. This means that if a client purchases a 3-month spot schedule in May, and the station raises its rates in June, the advertiser continues to pay the original rates until the expiration of its current contract.

The rate card also contains its feature and spot rates (see Figure 4.10). Among the most prevalent features that stations

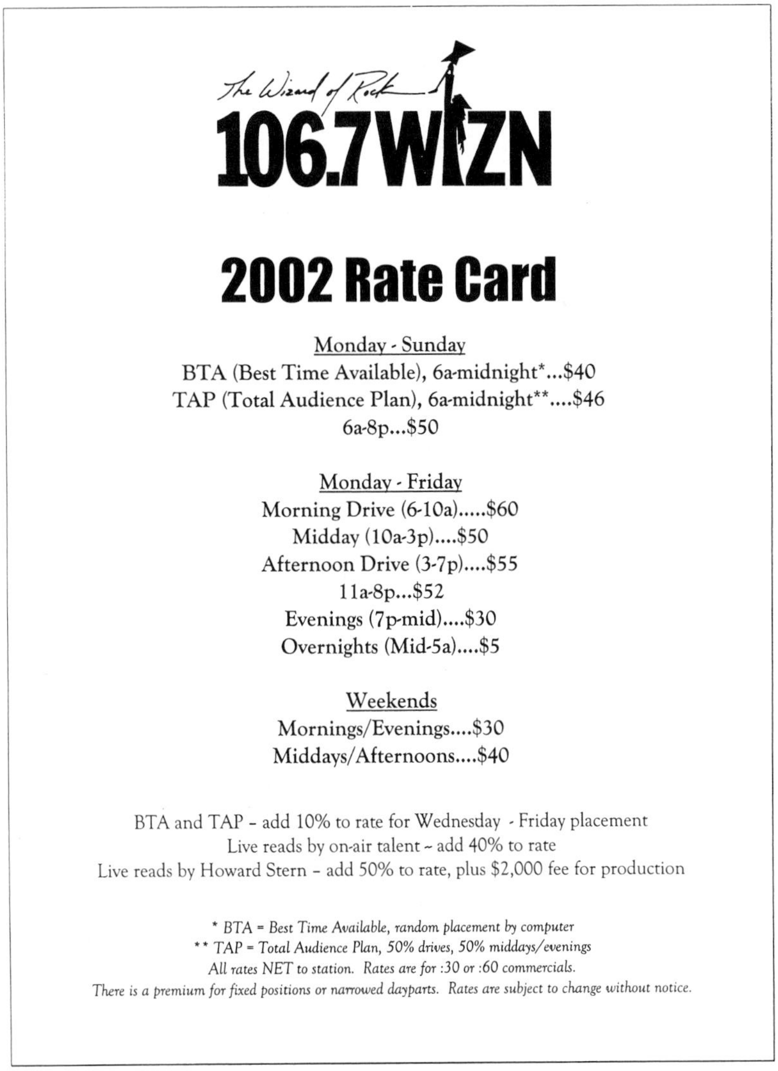

FIGURE 4.7
This early 2000s rate card shows BTA and TAP features. Courtesy WIZN.

The Wizard of Rock
106.7 WIZN

2002 Rate Card

Monday - Sunday
BTA (Best Time Available), 6a-midnight*...$40
TAP (Total Audience Plan), 6a-midnight**....$46
6a-8p...$50

Monday - Friday
Morning Drive (6-10a).....$60
Midday (10a-3p)....$50
Afternoon Drive (3-7p)....$55
11a-8p...$52
Evenings (7p-mid)....$30
Overnights (Mid-5a)....$5

Weekends
Mornings/Evenings....$30
Middays/Afternoons....$40

BTA and TAP - add 10% to rate for Wednesday - Friday placement
Live reads by on-air talent – add 40% to rate
Live reads by Howard Stern – add 50% to rate, plus $2,000 fee for production

* BTA = Best Time Available, random placement by computer
** TAP = Total Audience Plan, 50% drives, 50% middays/evenings
All rates NET to station. Rates are for :30 or :60 commercials.
There is a premium for fixed positions or narrowed dayparts. Rates are subject to change without notice.

offer are traffic, sports, weather, and business reports. Newscasts also are available to advertisers. Features generally include an open (introduction) and a 30- or 60-second announcement. They are particularly effective advertising vehicles because listeners tend to pay greater attention. Conditions pertaining to feature buys usually appear in the rate card: "All feature sales are subject to four weeks' notice for renewal and cancellation." A station wants to establish credibility with its features and therefore prefers to maintain continuity among its sponsors. A feature with a regular sponsor conveys stability, and that is what a station seeks.

Because the size of a radio station's audience generally varies depending on the time of day, rates for spots (commercials) or features must reflect that fact. Thus, the broadcast day is divided into time classifications: 6–10 A.M. weekdays is typically a station's prime selling period and therefore may be designated AAA; afternoon drive time, usually 3–7 P.M., may be called AA because of its secondary drawing power. Under this system, the midday segment, 10–3 P.M., would be given a single A designation, and evenings, 7–midnight, as B. Overnights, midnight–6 A.M., may be classified as C time. Obviously, the fees charged for spots are established on an ascending scale from C to AAA. A station

may charge $300 for an announcement aired at 8 A.M. and $45 for one aired at 2 A.M. The difference in the size of the station's audience at those hours warrants the contrast.

As previously mentioned, the more airtime a client purchases, the less expensive the cost for an individual commercial or unit. For instance, if an advertiser buys 10 spots a week during AAA time, the cost of each spot would be slightly less than if the sponsor purchased two spots a week. A client must buy a specified number of spots to benefit from the frequency discount. A 6X rate, meaning six spots per week, for AAA 60-second announcements may be $75; the 12X rate may be $71 and the 18X rate $68, and so forth. Thirty-second spots are usually priced at two-thirds the cost of a 60-second spot. Should a client desire that a spot be aired at a fixed time – say, at 7:10 A.M. daily – the station will tack on an additional charge, possibly 20%. Fixed position drive time spots are among the most expensive in a station's inventory.

Many stations use a grid structure. This gives stations a considerable degree of rate flexibility. For example, if a station has five rate-level grids, it may have a range between $20 and $50 for a 60-second spot. Clients would then be given rates at the lower grid if the station had few sponsors on the air, thus creating many availabilities (places to insert commercial messages). As business increased at the station and availabilities became scarcer, the station would ask for rates reflected in the upper grids. Gridding is based on the age-old concept of supply and demand. When availabilities are tight and airtime is at a premium, that time costs more.

Grids are inventory sensitive; they allow a station to remain viable when business is at a low ebb. Certainly, when inventory prices reach a bargain level, this encourages business. For instance, during a period when advertiser activity is sluggish, a station that can offer spots at a considerable reduction stands a chance of stimulating buyer interest.

When business is brisk at a station, because of holiday buying, for example, the situation may be exploited in a manner

FIGURE 4.8
Major market rate card. Courtesy WBZ-AM.

Rate Card 2006

Q1 and Q3

Daypart		:60's	:30's	:15's
M - F	5a – 10am	1300	800	600
M - F	10a – 3pm	425	350	300
M - F	3p – 8pm	625	450	400
M - F	8p – 12mid	200	100	N/A
M - F	12m – 5am	40	N/A	N/A
S/S	5a – 10am	200	125	100
S/S	10a – 3pm	200	125	100
S/S	3p – 8pm	200	125	100
S/S	8p – 12mid	150	100	N/A
S/S	12m – 5am	40	N/A	N/A

Q 2 and Q4

Daypart		:60's	:30's	:15's
M - F	5a – 10am	1500	950	650
M - F	10a – 3pm	500	400	350
M - F	3p – 8pm	700	500	450
M - F	8p – 12mid	250	150	N/A
M - F	12m – 5am	40	N/A	N/A
S/S	5a – 10am	250	150	125
S/S	10a – 3pm	250	150	125
S/S	3p – 8pm	250	150	125
S/S	8p – 12mid	200	125	N/A
S/S	12m – 5am	40	N/A	N/A

Rates are subject to change as inventory dictates

positive to the revenue column. Again the supply-and-demand concept is at work (one idea on which capitalism is based).

Not all stations grid their rate cards, however. Since the late 1970s, this system has gained considerable popularity because of its relevance to the ever fluctuating economy. As apparent in the rate cards exhibited in this chapter, grids are delineated by some sort of scale, usually alphabetical or numerical.

Clients are offered several spot schedule plans suited for their advertising and budgetary needs. For advertisers with limited funds, run-of-station (ROS) or best-time-available (BTA) plans are usually an option. Rates are lower under these plans because no guarantee is given as to what times the spots will be aired. However, most stations make a concerted effort to rotate ROS and BTA spots as equitably as possible, and during periods when commercial loads are light they frequently are scheduled during premium times. Of course, when a station is loaded down with spot schedules, especially around holidays or elections, ROS and BTA spots may find themselves buried. In the long run, advertisers using these plans receive a more than fair amount of choice times and at rates considerably lower than those clients who buy specific dayparts.

In *Radio Advertising's Missing Ingredient: The Optimum Effective Scheduling System* by Pierre Bouvard and Steve Marx, an innovative system is presented that improves the might of a spot schedule. According to the authors, "Optimum effective scheduling ensures that the effective reach, those hit three or more times, is at least 50% of the total reach." The idea behind optimum effective scheduling (OES) is to strengthen the impact of client buys. The OES formula is designed to heighten the efficiency of a spot buy through a system of scheduling based on ratings performance. This is accomplished by factoring a station's turnover ratio and cume.

Total audience plan (TAP) is another popular package offered clients by many stations. It is designed to distribute a client's spots among the various dayparts for maximum audience penetration, while costing less than an exclusive prime-time schedule. The rate for a TAP spot is arrived at by averaging the cost for spots in several time classifications. For example, AAA $80, AA $70, A $58, B $31; thus, the TAP rate per spot is $59. The advantages are obvious. The advertiser is getting a significant discount on the spots scheduled during morning and afternoon drive periods. At the same time, the advertiser is paying more for airtime during evenings. However, TAP is very attractive because it does expose a client's message to every possible segment of a station's listening audience with a measure of cost effectiveness.

Bulk or annual discounts are available to advertisers who buy a heavy schedule of commercials over the course of a year. Large companies in particular take advantage of volume discounts because the savings are significant.

Announcements are rotated or "orbited" within time classifications to maximize the number of different listeners reached. If a client buys three drive time spots per week to be aired on a Monday, Wednesday, and Friday, over a 4-week period, the time they are scheduled will be different each day. Here is a possible rotation setup:

	MON	WED	FRI
Week I	7:15	6:25	9:10
Week II	8:22	7:36	8:05
Week III	6:11	9:12	7:46
Week IV	9:20	8:34	6:52

Rather than purchase a consecutive week schedule, advertisers may choose to purchase time in flights, an alternating pattern of being on one week and off the next. For instance, a client with a seasonal business or one that is geared toward holiday sales may set up a plan in which spots are scheduled at specific times throughout the year. Thus, an annual flight schedule may look something like this:

Feb 13–19 Washington's Birthday Sale
   10 A 60s
Mar 14–17 St. Patrick's Day Celebration
   8 ROS 30s
Apr 16–21 Easter Parade Days
   20 TAP 30s
May 7–12 Mother's Day Sale

6 AAA and 6 AA 30s
June 1–15 Summer Sale Days
   30 ROS 60s
Aug 20–30 Back-to-School Sale
   15 A 60s
Sept. 24–Oct 6 Fall Sale Bonanza
   25 ROS 60s
Nov 25–Dec 19 Christmas Sale
   25 AAA 60s and 20 A 30s

FIGURE 4.9
An electronic rate card can change daily or weekly based on inventory pressures. Courtesy WQXA and WIOV.

Let us take a look at the wisdom behind a few of the preceding flights. The client purchases 10 spots in A time during the week that precedes Washington's Birthday to reach the home female audience. The A time on this station is 10:00 A.M.–3:00 P.M., so a schedule of spots here does a good job of targeting women who work at home. The client uses a TAP plan to move Easter inventory. This will get the client's spot in all dayparts to help her reach as many different people as possible at the best unit price. During the back-to-school days of late August, the client once again targets the strongest female daypart on the station and around Christmas time the client purchases the heaviest flight because this is the so-called do-or-die period (the time when business potential reaches its peak). The heavier spot purchase will help ensure success during this crucial time. Selling in flights makes a lot of sense to many advertisers because of its calendar relevance.

Sales people use rate cards to plan and compute buys. It is generally perceived as a poor idea to simply leave it with a prospective client to figure out, even if such a request is made. First, few laypersons are really adept at reading rate cards and, second, a station does not like to publicize its rates to its competition, which is what happens when too many station rate cards are in circulation. Granted, it is quite easy for any station to obtain a competitor's sales portfolio, but stations prefer to keep a low profile as a means of retaining a competitive edge.

Radio marketing expert Jay Williams, Jr., contends that the station rate card is on its way to obsolescence. "Most radio stations have gotten away or are getting away from using rate cards as much of the business is driven by supply and demand. Jennifer McCann, GM of Burlington Broadcasters, told me recently that 'While many small market stations still print and rely on rate cards, stations in major markets do not.' Using systems similar to 'yield management' systems first introduced by the airline industry, medium and larger stations often use programs such as Maxigrid to manage and price their spot inventory to ensure their sales goals. A radio station is usually faced with uneven and ever-changing demands on a limited amount of commercial time. Certain dayparts near the end of the week, special programming, and drive times near holidays might

WQXA FM RATE CARD (:60)

5/19/2008	M-F 5a-6a	M-F 6a-10a	M-F 10a-3p	M-F 3p-7p	M-F 7p-12m	Sat 6a-10a	Sat 10a-7p	Sun 6a-10a	Sun 10a-7p
5/19/2008	35	200	150	Sold Out	35	35	see mgr	20	35
5/26/2008	35	175	120	175	35	35	85	20	35
6/2/2008	35	120	105	130	35	35	80	20	30
6/9/2008	35	125	105	150	35	35	80	20	30
6/16/2008	35	120	105	130	35	35	80	20	30
6/23/2008	35	120	105	125	35	35	80	20	30
6/30/2008	35	120	105	120	35	35	80	20	30
7/7/2008	35	120	105	120	35	35	80	20	30
7/14/2008	35	120	105	125	35	35	80	20	30
7/21/2008	35	120	105	125	35	35	80	20	30
7/28/2008	35	120	105	120	35	35	80	20	30
8/4/2008	35	120	105	120	35	35	80	20	30

Warning	All rates beyond week of 8/4 must be cleared through mgr
:05 Rate	25% of prevailing :60 rate for the week
:10 Rate	50% of prevailing :60 rate for the week
Live Read	Add $25 to above rates then add $25 talent fee for each personality

WIOV FM RATE CARD (:60)

5/19/2008	M-F 5a-6a	M-F 6a-10a	M-F 10a-3p	M-F 3p-7p	M-F 7p-12m	Sat 6a-10a	Sat 10a-7p	Sun 6a-10a	Sun 10a-7p
5/19/2008	35	135	110	135	15	55	sold out	15	Nascar
5/26/2008	35	105	100	105	15	45	80	15	Nascar
6/2/2008	35	115	105	115	15	40	90	15	Nascar
6/9/2008	35	125	105	125	15	40	see mgr	15	Nascar
6/16/2008	35	115	105	115	15	40	90	15	Nascar
6/23/2008	35	110	100	110	15	40	85	15	Nascar
6/30/2008	35	105	100	105	15	40	80	15	Nascar
7/7/2008	35	110	100	110	15	40	80	15	Nascar
7/14/2008	35	110	100	110	15	40	80	15	Nascar
7/21/2008	35	115	105	115	15	40	80	15	Nascar
7/28/2008	35	110	100	110	15	40	80	15	Nascar
8/4/2008	35	110	100	110	15	40	80	15	Nascar

Warning	All rates beyond week of 8/4 must be cleared through mgr
:05 Rate	25% of prevailing :60 rate for that week
:10 Rate	50% of prevailing :60 rate for the week
Live Read	Add $25 to above rates then add $25 talent fee for each personality

be easily sold out, yet other time periods might have plenty of 'avails.' Using an inventory management system enables stations to continuously price their inventory by day, daypart, and even by the hour well in advance. This knowledge gives the sales department the up-to-the minute pricing and 'avail' information it needs to serve the client and allows the station to maintain the maximum control of its inventory. Even in smaller markets, rate cards are not used much except as a point for negotiating. Rate cards are often confusing and focus attention on the individual spot cost rather than the total cost of an advertising campaign. To compete against other media, radio has realized the value of creating customized presentations and programs for clients to respond to their specific needs and goals. Clients and agencies sometimes do ask to see a rate card, but they are rapidly becoming extinct."

Furthermore, observes WIZN's Matt Grasso, "We never let sales people show rate cards to clients. Rate cards force the client to try to figure out our business, radio, when radio reps should be learning about their businesses and creating customized presentations for them. Worse, clients always try to find the lowest rates on a rate card and then want to apply those rates to prime time forcing the radio salesperson to negotiate with himself. By using computerized internal rate cards, sales management can quickly and easily adjust rates to meet demand and ensure proper inventory control."

Points of the Pitch

Not all sales are made on the first call; nonetheless, the salesperson does go in with the hopes of closing an account. The first call generally is designed to introduce the station to the prospective sponsor and to determine the sponsor's needs. However, the salesperson should always be prepared to propose a buy that is suitable for the account. This means that some homework must be done relative to the business before an approach is made. "First determine the client's needs, as best as possible. Then address those needs with a schedule built to reach the client's

Radio Recruitment Plan!

Potential employees think about jobs at the beginning of the week.

Repetition works! Repetition works! Repetition works!

Suggested Radio Recruitment Schedule:

Option One:

SUN	9a- 4p	6 commercials
MON	6a-10p	10 commercials
TUE	6a-10p	9 commercials

Total: 25 commercials for $875 per week
(60 second commercials = 180 words)

Option Two:

SUN	9a- 4p	6 commercials
MON	6a-10p	10 commercials
TUE	6a-10p	9 commercials
WED	6a-10p	10 commercials

Total: 35 commercials for $1225 per week
(60 second commercials = 180 words)

Accepted for Advertiser   Date

tel: 802.860.2440 • fax: 802.860.1818 • 255 south champlain street • burlington, vermont 05401

customers. Don't walk into a business cold or without some sense of what the place is about," advises Friedman.

Should all go smoothly during the initial call, the salesperson may opt to go for an order there and then. If the account obliges, fine. In the event that the prospective advertiser is not prepared to make an immediate decision, a follow-up appointment must be made. The callback should be accomplished as close to the initial presentation as possible to prevent the impression made then from fading or growing cold. The primary objective of the return call is to close the deal and get the order. To strengthen the odds, the salesperson must review and assess any objections or reservations that may have arisen during the first call and devise a plan to overcome them. Meanwhile, the initial proposal may be beefed up to appear even more attractive to the client, and a "spec" tape (see the later section "Spec Spots") for the business can be prepared as further enticement.

FIGURE 4.10
Stations sell features to motivate advertisers. Courtesy WIZN.

Should the salesperson's efforts fail the second time out, a third and even fourth calls are made. Perseverance does pay off, and many sales people admit that just when they figured a situation was hopeless, an account said yes. "Of course, beating your head against the wall accomplishes nothing. You have to know when your time is being wasted. Never give up entirely on an account; just approach it more sensibly. A phone call or a drop-in every so often keeps you in their thoughts," says general sales manager Ron Piro.

What follows are two checklists. The Do list contains some suggestions conducive to a positive sales experience, and the Don't list contains things that will have a negative or counterproductive effect.

FIGURE 4.11
Software designed to help ad agencies make a buy. Courtesy Arbitron.

Do

- Research the advertiser; be prepared; have a relevant plan in mind.
- Be enthusiastic; think positive.

- Display self-confidence; believe in yourself and the product.
- Smile; exude friendliness, warmth, and sincerity.
- Listen; be polite, sympathetic, and interested.
- Tell of the station's successes; provide testimonial material.
- Think creatively.
- Know your competition.
- Maintain integrity and poise.
- Look your best; check your appearance.
- Be objective and keep proper perspective.
- Pitch the decision maker.
- Ask for the order that will do the job.
- Service the account after the sale.

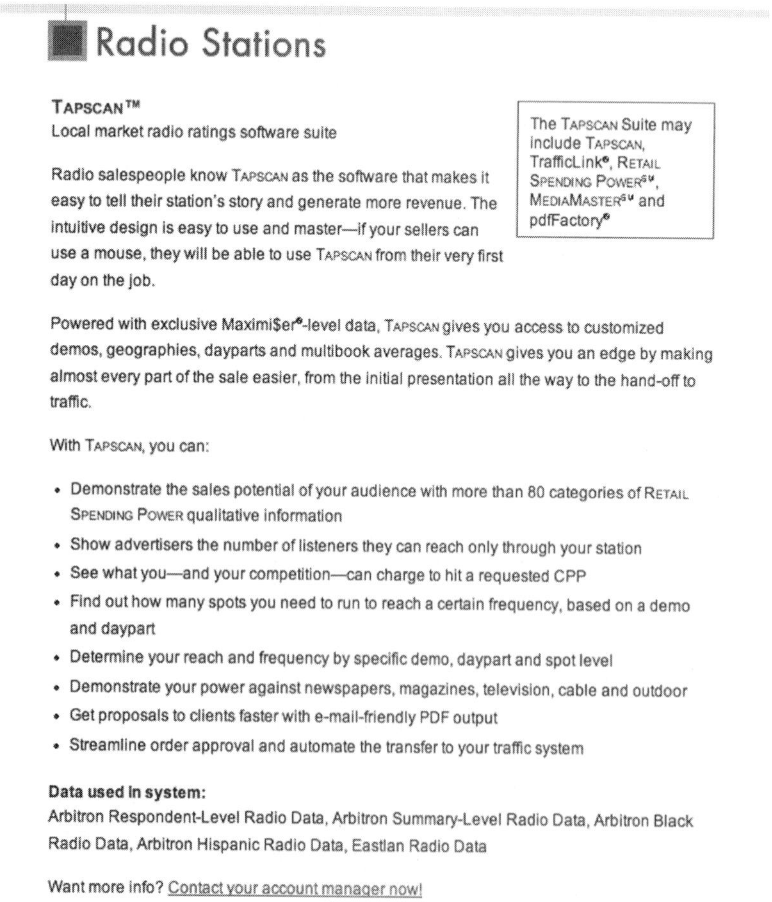

Don't

- Pitch without a plan.
- Criticize or demean the client's previous advertising efforts.
- Argue with the client. This just creates greater resistance.
- Bad-mouth the competition.
- Talk too much.
- Brag or be overly aggressive.
- Lie, exaggerate, or make unrealistic promises.
- Smoke or chew gum in front of the client.
- Procrastinate or put things off.
- Be intimidated or kept waiting an unreasonable amount of time.
- Make a presentation unless you have the client's undivided attention.
- Lose your temper.
- Ask for too little; never undersell a client.
- Fail to follow-up.
- Accept a "no" as final.

Checklists like the preceding ones can serve only as basic guidelines. Anyone who has spent time on the street as a station account executive can expand on this or any other such checklist. For the positive-thinking radio salesperson, every call gives something back, whether a sale is made or not.

Overcoming common objections is a necessary step toward achieving the sale. Here are some typical "put-offs" presented to radio sales reps:

Radio Stations

TAPSCAN™
Local market radio ratings software suite

Radio salespeople know TAPSCAN as the software that makes it easy to tell their station's story and generate more revenue. The intuitive design is easy to use and master—if your sellers can use a mouse, they will be able to use TAPSCAN from their very first day on the job.

Powered with exclusive Maximi$er®-level data, TAPSCAN gives you access to customized demos, geographies, dayparts and multibook averages. TAPSCAN gives you an edge by making almost every part of the sale easier, from the initial presentation all the way to the hand-off to traffic.

The TAPSCAN Suite may include TAPSCAN, TrafficLink®, RETAIL SPENDING POWER℠, MEDIAMASTER℠ and pdfFactory®

With TAPSCAN, you can:

- Demonstrate the sales potential of your audience with more than 80 categories of RETAIL SPENDING POWER qualitative information
- Show advertisers the number of listeners they can reach only through your station
- See what you—and your competition—can charge to hit a requested CPP
- Find out how many spots you need to run to reach a certain frequency, based on a demo and daypart
- Determine your reach and frequency by specific demo, daypart and spot level
- Demonstrate your power against newspapers, magazines, television, cable and outdoor
- Get proposals to clients faster with e-mail-friendly PDF output
- Streamline order approval and automate the transfer to your traffic system

Data used in system:
Arbitron Respondent-Level Radio Data, Arbitron Summary-Level Radio Data, Arbitron Black Radio Data, Arbitron Hispanic Radio Data, Eastlan Radio Data

Want more info? Contact your account manager now!

1. Nobody listens to radio commercials.
2. Newspaper ads are more effective.
3. Radio costs too much.
4. Nobody listens to your station.
5. We tried radio, and it didn't work.
6. We don't need any more business.
7. We've already allocated our advertising budget.
8. We can get another station for less.
9. Business is off, and we haven't got the money.
10. My partner doesn't like radio.

There are countless rebuttals for each of these statements, and a knowledgeable and skilled radio salesperson can turn such objections into positives.

Levels of Sales

There are three levels from which the medium draws its sales: retail, local, and national. Retail accounts for the biggest percentage of the industry's income, over 70%. Retail, also referred to as *direct*, sales involve the radio station on a one-to-one basis with advertisers within its signal area.

In this case, a station's account executive works directly with the client and earns a commission of approximately 15% on the airtime he or she sells. An advertiser who spends $1000 would benefit the salesperson to the tune of $150. A newly hired salesperson without previous experience generally will work on a direct retail basis and will not be assigned advertising agencies until he or she has become more seasoned and has displayed some ability. Generally speaking, the smaller the radio station, the more dependent it is on retail sales, although most medium and metro market stations would be in trouble without strong business on this level.

All stations, regardless of size, have some contact with advertising agencies. Here again, however, the larger a market, the more a station will derive its business from ad agencies. This level of station sales generally is classified as local. The number of advertising agencies in a market will vary depending on its size. A sales manager will divide the market's agencies among his reps as equitably as possible, sometimes using a merit system. In this way, an account executive who has worked hard and produced results will be rewarded for his efforts by being given an agency to work. The top billers, that is, those sales people who bring in the most business often possess the greatest number of agencies, or at least the most active. Although the percentage of commission a salesperson is accorded, typically 6–8%, is less than that derived from retail sales, the size of the agency buys usually is far more substantial.

The third category of station sales comes from the national level. In most cases, it is the general sales manager who works with the station's rep company to secure buys from advertising agencies that handle national accounts. Again, national business is greater for the metro station than it is for the rural. Agencies justify a buy on numbers and little else, although it is not uncommon for small market stations, which do not even appear in ratings surveys, to be bought by major accounts interested in maintaining a strong local or community image.

Producer Ty Ford observes that agency involvement has decreased in recent years because of intensified competition among the different media and the unpredictable national economy. "Increased competition from cable, television, radio, and print has forced many ad agencies out of business.

A medium market Cluster structure
Citadel Broadcasting, Worcester, MA
Information from Mary Ann Bolger, NSM, Citadel Broadcasting, Worcester

This group has 3 stations in a market with very few "home" stations (because of the proximity to Boston, Providence, Manchester & Springfield/Hartford).
Stations are WXLO, 104.5, WWFX, 100.1 & WORC, 98.9

They have a VP/GM for all 3 stations

They have one Sales Manager for WXLO
They have six sellers for WXLO who only sell WXLO

They have a second Sales Manager for The Fox and WORC (oldies)
They have a separate team for The Fox with 3 sellers
And another team to sell WORC Oldies 98.9 with three sellers

They have a National Sales Manager for all stations

They have one Traffic Manager for WXLO & The Fox
They have another Traffic Manager for WORC and The Cat (a station in Athol that they own—bought it to move shortspaced WWFX closer to Worcester).

FIGURE 4.12
A cluster breakdown highlighting sales organization.
Courtesy Citadel.

FIGURE 4.13
Advice to sales
people. Courtesy
Shane Media.

RESOLUTIONS FOR SELLERS

*(Now a perennial first-of-the-year TACTICS topic, these resolutions
are designed to inspire and motivate the sales staff.)*

I will have breakfast at 7:30 AM with at least two clients a week.

Each week, I will read a trade magazine from three client businesses.

I will set aside one hour a day to prepare written presentations.

One Saturday morning per month will be set aside to call on retailers.

I will read at least one book on selling and one book on advertising each month.

I'll carry a list of my top 10 prospects and call on at least one each day.

I'll follow each sales presentation with a hand-written "Thank You" note.

I will remind myself each day that 8% of sales are made after the fifth call.

I will demonstrate to my prospects that I am willing to work for their business.

I will always ask, "Is there something else you'd like to hear about?"

I will remind myself each day that I am not selling time—my business is
creating opportunities, processing ideas and distributing information.

FIGURE 4.14
Courtesy WIZN-FM.

The Wizard of Rock
106.7 WIZN **the 99.9 Buzz**

Nine Reasons to Advertise

1. **Advertising Creates Store Traffic.** Continuous store traffic is the first step toward increasing sales and expanding your base of shoppers. The more people who come into your store, the more opportunities you have to make sales.

2. **Advertising Attracts New Customers.** Your market changes constantly. Newcomers to your area mean new customers to reach. People earn more money. The shopper who wouldn't consider your business a few years ago may be a prime customer now.

3. **Advertising Encourages Repeat Business.** Shoppers don't have the store loyalty they once did. They have mobility and freedom of choice. You must advertise to keep up with your competition.

4. **Advertising Generates Continuous Business.** Your doors are open. Employees are on the payroll. As long as you're in business, you've got over head to meet, and new people to reach.

5. **Advertising is an Investment in Success.** A survey of 3,000 companies found that advertisers who maintained or expanded advertising over 5 years saw sales increase an average of 100%, while those who cut advertising grew at less than half the rate of those advertising steadily.

6. **Advertising Keeps You in the Competitive Race.** There are only so many customers in the market ready to buy at any one time. You have to advertise to keep regular customers, and to counter-balance the advertising of your competition.

7. **Advertising Keeps Your Business Top-of-Mind with Shoppers.** Many people go from store to store comparing prices, quality and service. Your name must be fresh in their minds when they decide to buy.

8. **Advertising Gives Your Business a Successful Image.** It tells your customers that your doors are open and you're ready for business. Advertising that is vigorous and positive can bring shoppers into the marketplace, regardless of the economy.

9. **Advertising Brings In Big Bucks for Your Business.** Advertising works. Businesses that succeed are usually strong, steady advertisers. Look around. You'll find the most aggressive and consistent advertisers are almost invariably the most successful. Join their ranks by advertising, and watch your business grow!

Ralph Guild

On the Future Market for Radio

The radio industry has undergone radical but positive change in recent years and will continue to experience significant evolutionary changes between now and the end of the decade. Ironically, these changes are, in many ways, the result of a constant that we have witnessed throughout the history of the medium. Radio consistently has shown a tremendous ability to adapt to a variety of market conditions, whether they be economic or competitive in nature. It is this flexibility, a by-product of intelligent industry leadership, that has fueled radio's growth in the past and will continue to elevate the industry to new heights in the years to come.

FIGURE 4.15
Ralph Guild.

Stations now frequently offer 'agency discounts' to direct-retail clients just to close the sale. Also, more retail companies are forming their own in-house agencies." Although this may be true, the ad agency is still an important factor in station revenues.

Each level of sales – retail, local, or national – must be sufficiently cultivated if a station is to enjoy maximum prosperity. Neglecting any one of these levels would result in a loss of station revenue.

Spec Spots

One of the most effective ways to convince an advertiser to use a station is to provide a fully produced sample commercial, or "spec spot." If prepared properly and imaginatively, a client will find it difficult to deny its potential. Spec tapes often are used in callbacks when a salesperson needs to break down a client's resistance. More than once, a clever spec spot has converted an adamant "no" into an "okay, let's give it a shot." Spec spots also are used to reactivate the interest of former accounts who may not have spent money on the station for a while and who need some justification to do so.

Specs also are effective tools for motivating clients to "heavy-up" or increase their current spot schedules. A good idea can move a mountain, and sales people are encouraged by the sales manager to develop spec tape ideas. Many sales managers require that account executives make at least one spec tape presentation each week. The sales manager may even choose to critique spec spots during regularly scheduled meetings.

The information needed to prepare a spec spot is acquired in several ways. If a salesperson already has called on a prospective client, he should have a very good idea of what the business is about as well as the attitude of the retailer toward the enterprise. The station sales rep is then in a very good position to prepare a spot that directly appeals to the needs and perceptions of the would-be advertiser. If a salesperson decides that the first call on a client warrants preparing a spec tape, then he or she may collect information on the business by actually browsing through the store as a customer might. This gives the salesperson an accurate, firsthand impression of the store's environment and merchandise. An idea of how the store perceives itself, and specific information such as address and hours, can be derived by checking its display ad in the Yellow Pages if it has one or by examining any ads it may have run in the local newspaper. Flyers that the business may have distributed also provide useful information for the formulation of the copy used in the spec spot. Listening to commercials the advertiser may be running on another station also gives the salesperson an idea of the direction in which to move.

Again, the primary purpose of a spec spot is to motivate a possible advertiser to buy time. A spec spot that fails to capture the interest and appreciation of the individual for which it has been prepared may be lacking in the necessary ingredients. It is generally a good rule of thumb to avoid humor in a spec spot, unless the salesperson has had some firsthand experience with the advertiser. Nothing fails as abysmally as a commercial that attempts to be funny and does not come across as such to the client – thus, the saying "What is funny to one person may be silly or offensive to another."

Although spec spots are, to some extent, a gamble, they should be prepared in such a way that the odds are not too great. Of course, a salesperson who believes in an idea must have the gumption to go with it. Great sales are often inspired by unconventional concepts.

Objectives of the Buy

A single spot on a radio station seldom brings instant riches to an advertiser. However, a thoughtfully devised plan based on a formula of frequency and consistency will achieve impressive results, contends general manager John Gregory. "It has to be made clear from the start what a client hopes to accomplish by advertising on your station. Then a schedule that realistically corresponds with the client's goals must be put together. This means selling the advertiser a sufficient number of commercials spread over a specific period of time. An occasional spot here and there doesn't do much in this medium. There's a right way to sell radio, and that isn't it."

Our lists of dos and don'ts of selling suggested that the salesperson "ask for the order that will do the job." It also said not to undersell an account. Implicit in the first point is the idea that the salesperson has determined what kind of schedule the advertiser should buy to get the results expected. Too often sales people fail to ask for what they need for fear the client will balk. Thus, they settle for what they can get without much resistance. This, in fact, may be doing the advertiser a disservice, because the buy that the salesperson settles for may not fulfill declared objectives. "It takes a little courage to persist until you get what you think will do the job. There is the temptation just to take what the client hands you and run, but that technique usually backfires when the client doesn't get what he expected. As a radio sales rep, you should know how best to sell the medium. Don't be apologetic or easily compromised. Sell the medium the way it should be sold. Write enough of an order to get the job done," says sales manager Ron Piro.

Inflated claims and unrealistic promises should never be a part of a sales presentation. Avoid "If you buy spots on my station, you'll have to hire additional sales people to handle the huge crowds." Sales people must be honest in their projections and in what a client may expect from the spot schedule he or she purchases. "You will notice a gradual increase in store traffic over the next few weeks as the audience is exposed to your commercial over WXXX" is the better approach. Unfulfilled promises ruin any chances of future buys. Too often sales people, caught up in the enthusiasm of the pitch, make claims that cannot be achieved. Radio is a phenomenally effective advertising medium. This is a proven fact. Those who have successfully used the medium can attest to the importance of placing an adequate order. "An advertiser has to buy a decent schedule to get strong results. Frequency is essential in radio," notes Piro. A radio sales axiom says it best: "The more spots aired, the more impressions made, and the more impressions made, the more impressed the client."

Prospecting and List Building

When a salesperson is hired by a radio station, he or she is customarily provided with a list of accounts to which airtime may be sold. For an inexperienced salesperson, this list may consist of essentially inactive or dormant accounts, that is, businesses that either have been on the air in the past or those that have never purchased airtime on the station. The new sales rep is expected to breathe life into the list by selling spot schedules to those accounts listed, as well as by adding to the list by bringing in new business. This is called *list building*, and it is the primary challenge facing the new account executive.

A more active list, one that generates commissions, will be given to the more experienced radio salesperson. A salesperson may be persuaded to leave one station in favor of another based on the contents of a list, which may include large accounts and prominent advertising agencies. Lists held by a station's top billers invariably contain the most enthusiastic radio users. Sales people cultivate their lists as a farmer does his fields. The more the account list yields, the more commissions in the salesperson's pocket.

New accounts are added to a sales rep's list in several ways. Once the status of the list's existing accounts is determined, which is accomplished through a series of in-person calls and presentations, a salesperson must begin prospecting for additional business. Area newspapers are a common source. When a salesperson finds an account that he wishes to add to his or her list, the account must be "declared." This involves consulting the sales manager for approval to add the account to the salesperson's existing list. In some cases, the account declared may already belong to another salesperson. If it is an open account, the individual who comes forward first usually is allowed to add it to his or her list.

Other sources for new accounts include the Yellow Pages, television stations, and competing radio outlets, and today, station sales people are also tapping the Internet and using e-mail to enhance their search for clients. Every business in the area is listed in the Yellow Pages, which contains many display ads that provide useful information. Local television stations are viewed with an eye toward their advertisers. Television can be an expensive proposition, even in smaller markets, and businesses that spend money on it may find radio's rates more palatable. On the other hand, if a business can afford to buy television, it often can afford to embellish its advertising campaign with radio spots. Many advertisers place money in several media – newspaper, radio, television – simultaneously. This is called a *mixed media* buy and is a proven advertising formula for the obvious reason that the client is reaching all possible audiences. Finally, accounts currently on other stations constitute good prospects because they obviously already have been sold on the medium.

In the course of an average workday, a salesperson will pass hundreds of businesses, some of which may have just opened their doors, or are about to do so. Sales reps must keep their eyes open and be prepared to make an impromptu call. The old saying "the early bird gets the worm" is particularly relevant in radio sales. The first account executive into a newly launched business often is the one who gets the buy.

A list containing dozens of accounts does not necessarily ensure a good income. If those businesses listed are small spenders or inactive, little in the way of commissions will be generated and billing will be low. The objective of list building is not merely to increase the number of accounts, but rather to raise the level of commissions it produces. In other words, a list that contains 30 accounts, of which 22 are active, is preferable to one with 50 accounts containing only 12 that are doing business with the station. A salesperson does not get points for having a lot of names on his list.

It is the sales manager's prerogative to shift an account from one salesperson's list to another's if he or she believes the account is being neglected or handled incorrectly. At the same time, certain

FIGURE 4.16
Computer software
lets stations
monitor their sales
success. Courtesy
RadioTraffic.com.

in-house accounts, those handled by the sales manager, may be added to a sales rep's list as a reward for performing well. A salesperson's account list also may be pared down if the sales manager concludes that it is disproportional with the others at the station. The attempt to more equitably distribute the wealth may cause a brouhaha with the account person whose list is being trimmed. The sales manager attempting this feat may lose a top biller; thus, he or she must consider the ramifications of such a move and proceed accordingly. This may even mean letting things remain as they are. The top biller often is responsible for as much as 30–40% of the station's earnings.

Planning the Sales Day

A radio salesperson should make between 75 and 100 in-person calls a week, or on the average of 15–20 each day, if possible. This requires careful planning and organization. Ron Piro advises preparing a day's itinerary the night before. "There's nothing worse than facing the day without an idea of where to go. A salesperson can spare himself that dreaded sensation and a lot of lost time by preparing a complete schedule of calls the night before."

When preparing a daily call sheet, a salesperson, especially one whose station covers a vast area, attempts to centralize, as much as possible, the businesses to be contacted. Time, energy, and gas are needlessly expended through poor planning. A sales rep who is traveling 10 miles between each presentation can get to only half as many clients as the person with a consolidated call sheet. Of course, there are days when a salesperson must spend more time traveling. Not every day can be ideally plotted. It may be necessary to make a call in one part of the city at 9 A.M. and be in another part at 10 A.M. A salesperson must be where he or she feels the buys are going to be made. "Go first to those businesses likeliest to buy.

The tone of the day will be sweetened by an early sale," contends Piro.

Sales managers advise their reps to list more prospects than they expect to contact. In so doing, they are not likely to run out of places to go should those prospects they had planned to see be unavailable. "You have to make the calls to make the sales. The more calls you make, the more the odds favor a sale," points out Gene Etheridge.

Itineraries should be adhered to regardless of whether a sale is made early in the day, says WNRI's John Gregory. "You can't pack it in at ten in the morning because you've closed an account. A salesperson who is easily satisfied is one who will never make much money. You must stay true to your day's game plan and follow through. No all-day coffee klatch at the local Ho-Jo's or movie matinee because you nailed an order after two calls."

The telephone is one of the salesperson's best tools. Although it is true that a client cannot sign a contract over the phone, much time and energy can be saved through its effective use. Appointments can be made and a client can be qualified via the telephone. That is to say, a salesperson can ascertain when the decision maker will be available. "Rather than travel twenty miles without knowing if the person who has the authority to make a buy will be around, take a couple of minutes and make a phone call. As they say, 'time is money.' In the time

spent finding out that the store manager or owner is not on the premises when you get there, other, more productive calls can be made," says Charles Friedman.

If a client is not available when the salesperson appears, a callback should be arranged for either later the same day or soon thereafter. The prospective advertiser should never be forgotten or relegated to a call 3 months hence. The sales rep should try to rearrange his or her schedule to accommodate a return visit the same day, given that the person to see is available. However, it is futile to make a presentation to someone who cannot give full attention. The sales rep who arrives at a business only to find the decision maker overwhelmed by distractions is wise to ask for another appointment. In fact, the client will perceive this as an act of kindness and consideration. Timing is important.

A record of each call should be kept for follow-up purposes. When calling on a myriad of accounts, it is easy to lose track of what transpired during a particular call. Maintaining a record of a call requires little more than a brief notation after it is made. Notes may then be periodically reviewed to help determine what action should be taken on the account. Follow-ups are crucial. There is nothing more embarrassing and disheartening than to discover a client, who was pitched and then forgotten, advertising on another station. Sales managers usually

Jason Insalaco | Selling Personality

FIGURE 4.17
Jason Insalaco.

In the quickly evolving media landscape, winning radio personalities will save radio stations from advertiser erosion. Personality cannot be duplicated. A hit music single cannot sell a product or compel a listener to patronize an advertiser. A radio personality can easily accomplish this objective. A radio personality extolling the benefits of an advertiser in a live-read commercial is always more effective than the best produced spot. A live appearance or broadcast by a radio personality

can bring throngs of listeners to a retail advertiser. The hottest chart topping single can never compel and connect like radio talent. A radio personality not only entertains the listener with fresh, compelling content every day, the person behind the mic also nurtures listener loyalty and connection. Advertisers desire this "stickiness" because the more the consumer is connected to a personality, the more likely the listener will trust and heed what he or she says about a product or service.

require that sales people turn in copies of their call sheets on a daily or weekly basis for review purposes.

Selling with and without Numbers

Not all stations can claim to be number one or two in the ratings. In fact, not all stations appear in any formal ratings survey. Very small markets are not visited by Arbitron or other rating services for the simple reason that there may be only one station broadcasting in the area. An outlet in a nonsurvey area relies on its good reputation in the community to attract advertisers. In small markets, sales people do not work out of a ratings book and clients are not concerned with cumes and shares. In the truest sense of the word, an account person must sell the station. Local businesses often account for more than 95% of a small market station's revenue. Thus, the stronger the ties with the community, the better. Broadcasters in rural markets must foster an image of good citizenship to make a living.

Civic mindedness is not as marketable a commodity in the larger markets as are ratings points. In the sophisticated multistation urban market, the ratings book is the bible. A station without numbers in the highly competitive environment finds the task of earning an income a difficult one, although there are numerous examples of low-rated stations that do very well. However, "no numbers" pretty much puts a metro area station out of the running for agency business. Agencies almost invariably "buy by the book." A station without numbers "works the street," to use the popular phrase, focusing its sales efforts on direct business.

An obvious difference in approaches exists between selling the station with ratings and the one without. In the first case, a station centers its entire presentation around its high ratings. "According to the latest Arbitron, WXXX-FM is number one with adults 24 to 39." Never out of the conversation for very long are the station's numbers, and at advertising agencies the station's standing speaks for itself. "We'll buy WXXX because the book shows that they have the largest audience in the demos we're after."

The station without rating numbers sells itself on a more personal level, perhaps focusing on its unique features and special blend of music and personalities, and so forth. In an effort to attract advertisers, nonrated outlets often develop programs with a targeted retail market in mind; for example, a home "how-to" show designed to interest hardware and interior decor stores, or a cooking feature aimed at food and appliance stores.

The salesperson working for the station with the cherished "good book" must be especially adept at talking numbers, because they are the key subject of the presentation in most situations. "Selling a top-rated metro station requires more than a pedestrian knowledge of numbers, especially

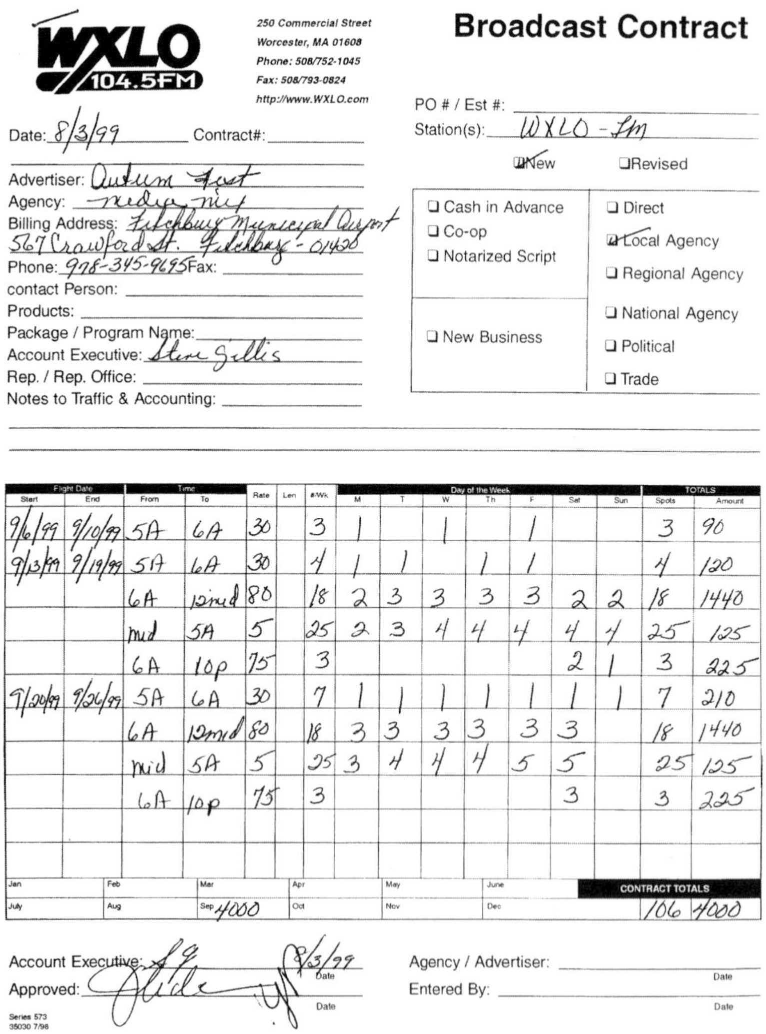
WXLO 104.5FM
250 Commercial Street
Worcester, MA 01608
Phone: 508/752-1045
Fax: 508/793-0824
http://www.WXLO.com

Broadcast Contract

PO # / Est #:
Station(s): WXLO - fm
☑ New ☐ Revised

Date: 8/3/99 Contract#:
Advertiser: Autumn Fest
Agency: media mix
Billing Address: Fitchburg Municipal Airport 567 Crawford St. Fitchburg - 01420
Phone: 978-345-9695 Fax:
contact Person:
Products:
Package / Program Name:
Account Executive: Steve Gillis
Rep. / Rep. Office:
Notes to Traffic & Accounting:

☐ Cash in Advance
☐ Co-op
☐ Notarized Script
☐ New Business
☐ Direct
☑ Local Agency
☐ Regional Agency
☐ National Agency
☐ Political
☐ Trade

Flight Date Start	Flight Date End	Time From	Time To	Rate	Len	#/Wk	M	T	W	Th	F	Sat	Sun	Totals Spots	Totals Amount
9/6/99	9/10/99	5A	6A	30		3	1		1		1			3	90
9/13/99	9/19/99	5A	6A	30		4	1	1		1	1			4	120
		6A	12mid	80		18	2	3	3	3	3	2	2	18	1440
		mid	5A	5		25	2	3	4	4	4	4	4	25	125
		6A	10p	75		3						2	1	3	225
9/20/99	9/26/99	5A	6A	30		7	1	1	1	1	1	1	1	7	210
		6A	12mid	80		18	3	3	3	3	3	3		18	1440
		mid	5A	5		25	3	4	4	4	5	5		25	125
		6A	10p	75		3						3		3	225

Jan	Feb	Mar	Apr	May	June	CONTRACT TOTALS
July	Aug	Sep 4000	Oct	Nov	Dec	106 4000

Account Executive: SG 8/3/99 Date
Approved: Date
Agency / Advertiser: Date
Entered By: Date
Series 573
35030 7/98

FIGURE 4.18
A radio sales contract written by an account executive. Courtesy WXLO-FM.

when dealing with agencies. In big cities, retailers have plenty of book savvy, too," contends Piro.

Selling without numbers demands its own unique set of skills, notes WNRI's Gregory. "There are really two different types of radio selling – with numbers and without. In the former instance, you'd better know your math, whereas in the latter, you've got to be really effective at molding your station to suit the desires of the individual advertiser. Without the numbers to speak for you, you have to do all the selling yourself. Flexibility and ingenuity are the keys to the sale."

Advertising Agencies

Advertising agencies came into existence more than a century ago and have played an integral role in broadcasting since its inception. During radio's famed heyday, advertising agencies were omnipotent. Not only did they handle the advertising budgets of some of the nation's largest businesses but also they provided the networks with fully produced programs. The programs were designed by the agencies for the specific satisfaction of their clients. If the networks and certain independent stations wanted a company's business, they had little choice but to air the agency's program. This practice in the 1920s and 1930s gave ad agencies unprecedented power. At one point, advertising agencies were the biggest supplier of network radio programming. By the 1940s, agencies were forced to abandon their direct programming involvement, and the industry was left to its own devices, or almost. Agencies continued to influence the content of what was aired. Their presence continues to be felt today, but not to the extent that it was prior to the advent of television.

Agencies annually account for hundreds of millions in radio ad dollars. The long, and at times turbulent, marriage of radio and advertising agencies was, and continues to be, based on the need of national companies to convey their messages on the local level and the need of the local broadcaster for national business. It is a two-way street.

Today, hundreds of advertising agencies use the radio medium. They range in size from mammoth to minute. Agencies such as Young and Rubicam, J. Walter Thompson, Dancer Fitzgerald Sample, and Leo Burnett bill in the hundreds of millions annually and employ hundreds. More typical, however, are the agencies scattered throughout the country that bill between one-half and two-and-a-half million dollars each year and employ anywhere from a half dozen to 20 people. Agencies come in all shapes and sizes and provide various services, depending on their scope and dimensions.

The process of getting national business onto a local station is an involved one. The major agencies must compete against dozens of others to win the right to handle the advertising of large companies. This usually involves elaborate presentations and substantial investments by agencies. When and if the account is secured, the agency must then prepare the materials – audio, video, print – for the campaign and see to it that the advertiser's money is spent in the most effective way possible. Little is done without extensive marketing research and planning. The agency's media buyer oversees the placement of dollars in the various media. Media buyers at national agencies deal with station and network reps rather than directly with the stations themselves. It would be impossible for an agency placing

FIGURE 4.19
An online pitch to potential advertisers. Courtesy Mix 102.7.

If you're interested in Advertising with New York's Classic Dance Mix or online at mix1027fm.com here is all the info you need!

Call the Mix 102.7FM Sales Department @ **212-489-1027**

or

Click here to send us an email!

a buy on 400 stations to personally transact with each.

There are basically three types of agencies: *full-service agencies*, which provide clients with a complete range of services, including research, marketing, and production; *modular agencies*, which provide specific services to advertisers; and *in-house agencies*, which handle the advertising needs of their own business.

The standard commission that an agency receives for its service is 15% on billing. For example, if an agency places $100,000 on radio, it earns $15,000 for its efforts. Agencies often charge clients additional fees to cover production costs and some agencies receive a retainer from clients.

The business generated by agencies constitutes an important percentage of radio's revenues, especially for medium and large market stations. However, compared to other media, such as television, radio's allocation is diminutive. The nation's top three agencies invest over 80% of their broadcast budgets in television. Nonetheless, hundreds of millions of dollars are channeled into radio by agencies that recognize the effectiveness of the medium.

Rep Companies

Rep companies are the industry's middlemen (see Figure 4.20). Rep companies are given the task of convincing national agency media buyers to place money on the stations they represent. Without their existence, radio stations would have to find a way to reach the myriad of agencies on their own – an impossible feat.

With few exceptions, radio outlets contract the services of a station rep company. Even the smallest station wants to be included in buys at the national level. The rep company basically is an extension of

FIGURE 4.20
A rep company explains itself. Courtesy Katz.

a station's sales department. The rep and the station's sales manager work together closely. Information about a station and its market are crucial to the rep. The burden of keeping the rep fully aware of what is happening back at the station rests on the sales manager's shoulders. Because a rep company based in New York or Chicago would have no way of knowing that its client station in Arkansas has decided to carry the local college's basketball games, it is the station's responsibility to make the information available. A rep cannot sell what it does not know exists. Of course, a good rep will keep in contact with a station on a regular basis simply to keep up on station changes.

There are far fewer radio station reps than ad agencies, and with the clustering of stations by radio corporations, the number of rep companies has dwindled dramatically as broadcasters assume the burden of representing themselves. Today, there are just a handful of major rep companies handling the 9000-plus commercial stations around the country because the huge radio companies assume this function in-house. "In their heyday in the 70s, many national and regional rep firms served individual stations and group radio owners, but because of pressures from increased costs, pressure from client stations on commission rates, and the creation of unwired network radio, an attempt to compete with the lower rates of traditional radio networks that lowered radio rates, many were forced to close or merge through the 80s and 90s. With consolidation, where one, two, or three groups now control most radio stations in a given market, the need for multiple reps evaporated," says Williams.

FIGURE 4.21
An advertising agency promotes itself in a 1953 trade magazine. Courtesy *Broadcasting Magazine*.

Adds Ed Shane about the decline of rep firms, "The demise of Katz changes the national selling landscape. With only one firm representing radio to national advertisers, national business is likely to shrink. National Business is largely transactional, and radio has allowed national advertisers to abuse the rate card or to load up 'value added' promotions in order to substantiate rates."

Major rep firms pitch agencies on behalf of hundreds of client stations. The large and very successful reps often refuse to act as the envoy for small market stations because of their lack of earning potential. A rep company typically receives a commission of between 5 and 12% on the spot buys made by agencies, and because the national advertising money usually is directed first to the medium and large markets, the bigger commissions are not to be made from handling small market outlets. Many rep companies specialize in small market stations, however, especially in the age of consolidation.

Although a small rep company may work for the agencies on behalf of numerous stations, it will seldom handle two radio outlets in the same market. Doing so could result in a rep company being placed in the untenable position of competing with itself for a buy, thus creating an obvious conflict of interest. In the past few years, many larger rep firms have taken on multiple stations in the same market due to the clustering approach of their clients.

The majority of station reps provide additional services. In recent years many have expanded into the areas of programming and management consultancy, and almost all offer clients audience research data, as well as aid in developing station promotions and designing sales materials such as rate cards.

Web Site, Podcast, and HD^2 Selling

Web sites, new HD^2 channels, and podcasts have become additional sources of revenue at many stations. Until recently station Web sites were perceived as an extension of the promotion department

more than a means for generating income. Some stations entice clients to purchase spot plans by comping them Web site ads. Web site presence is another way to add value to traditional commercial buys. This is also true for station podcasts. Contends Jason Insalaco, "Radio account executives can benefit from this source by selling additional exposure to advertisers. Another thing to keep in mind is that podcasting and streaming allow local clients of lesser means who previously could not afford a conventional broadcast schedule the chance to purchase less expensive web commercials. Account executives can attest to the difficulty of selling the intangible (sightless) nature of radio. Web advertising helps overcome this objection. Visual banner ads allow streaming listeners to click on ads that will take them directly to a client's webpage. Furthermore, radio programmers now have access to immediate data to provide advertisers the number of users streaming their station and downloading specific podcasts. The current Arbitron ratings systems provides audience data four weeks later and is arguably arbitrary due to sampling inconsistencies and often erratic results. However, streaming and podcasting is a win-win for programmers who strive to retain the fickle listener and garner additional income."

Meanwhile, it is hoped that the new HD side-channels (HD^2 channels) will provide additional revenue streams for stations. While the HD movement has been slow to launch, expectations indicate that advertiser interest in the innovative formats emerging (and predicted to emerge) will increase. In several major markets, HD^2 formats have already attracted sponsors seeking a more niche clientele.

Nontraditional Revenue

It has been estimated that over $600 million in radio revenue comes from co-op advertising – no small piece of change, indeed. However, as a consequence of a negative economy, the co-op market went a bit flat in the first half of the 1990s, says broadcaster Peter Drew. "There was less co-op. Things were tight on every level, of course. It was more difficult to qualify and collect. It was the result of higher accruals and inventory requirements. Still, co-op money is worth pursuing. A little more effort is required to acquire it." Likewise, due to the teetering economy in the late 2000s, co-op opportunities dwindled and account executives had to dig deeper to find it.

Co-op advertising involves the cooperation of three parties: the retailer whose business is being promoted, the manufacturer whose product is being promoted, and the medium used for the promotion. In other words, a retailer and manufacturer get together to share advertising expenses. For example, Smith's Sporting Goods is informed by the Converse Running Shoes representative that the company will match, dollar for dollar up to $5000, the money that the retailer invests in radio advertising. The only stipulation of the deal is that Converse be promoted in the commercials on which the money is spent. This means that no competitive product can be mentioned. Converse demands exclusivity for its contribution.

Manufacturers of practically every conceivable type of product, from lawn mowers to mobile homes, establish co-op advertising budgets. A radio salesperson can use co-op to great advantage. First, the station account executive must determine the extent of co-op subsidy a client is entitled to receive. Most of the time the retailer knows the answer to this. Frequently, however, retailers do not take full advantage of the co-op funds that manufacturers make available. In some instances, retailers are not aware that a particular manufacturer will share radio advertising expenses. Many potential advertisers have been motivated to go on the air after discovering the existence of co-op dollars. Mid-sized retailers account for the biggest chunk of the industry's co-op revenues. However, even the smallest retailer likely is eligible for some subsidy, and a salesperson can make this fact known for everyone's mutual advantage.

FORM OF TRADE AGREEMENT

FIGURE 4.22
Station trade agreement form. Courtesy WXLO-FM.

Today's Date: _____
Client Name: _____
Address: _____
_____

Account Executive: _____
Contact: _____
Title: _____
Telephone # : _____

Dear :

This letter, when signed by you and by us, will constitute our agreement relating to an exchange of goods and services for advertising time on the above named radio station.

A. ADVERTISING TIME PROVIDED BY STATION
1. We will furnish you with advertising time on our station having an aggregate *net value* at the time the ads run, of_____. All trades are at a 1-to-1 ratio.
2. Restrictions apply as to when advertising can run and are subject to availability. Your account executive has worked out the details and your trade can run as follows (or per attached sales order): _____
_____
_____

Trade Expiration date: _____
3. All advertising copy submitted to us hereunder shall be subject to our advertising and broadcast standards at the station's sole discretion.
4. In the event that such advertising incurs any talent, announcer or production charges, you will be responsible for paying the same upon receipt of our invoice, and such charges are not to be included in the value of the advertising time provided to you hereunder. Further, *there is no agency commission payable on such advertising.*

B. GOODS AND SERVICES PROVIDED TO THE STATION
1. In consideration of the advertising time provided to you hereunder, you will furnish and make available to us, within the period stated in section A.2, the following goods or services (if hotel trade, are conference rooms included?): _____
_____
_____
_____

These goods and services have a net fair market value of : _____
2. If goods are provided hereunder, you hereby warrant that the same shall be delivered new and in perfect condition.

FIGURE 4.22
Continued

3.   You shall pay sales and/or use tax on goods and services provided, as well as all shipping, delivery or handling charges associated with such goods or services.

4.   Please list any restrictions as to the use of these goods or services:

_____

_____

_____

5.   Please list any directions as to how these goods or services will be used:

_____

_____

_____

C.   MISCELLANEOUS PROVISIONS

1.   In the event you in any breach your obligations under this agreement, we have the right to immediately cease airing any advertising or time provided hereunder.

2.   We will furnish you with monthly invoices and statements setting forth the advertising time furnished hereunder, and you will furnish us with monthly invoices and statements setting forth the goods or services delivered to us each month. Such invoices and statements must be marked as "trade" and sent directly to our accounting department.

3.   In the event any of the goods or services specified in B.1 are not provided to us within the period specified in A.2, you shall be obligated to pay to us immediately upon demand and in cash an amount equal to the value of such goods or services remaining to be provided by you.

4.   Unless otherwise specifically agreed, we and you shall each have the right to terminate this agreement by giving not less than fourteen (14) days prior notice of termination to the other.

5.   This contract is subject to the terms and conditions of all licenses issued to us for the station, to all Federal, State and municipal laws and regulations, and to all rules and regulations, orders and decisions of the Federal Communications Commission nor or hereafter in effect.

6.   Each of us warrants to the other that it has the full legal power, authority, and right to enter into this agreement and perform our respective obligations hereunder.

7.   If this agreement is signed by an advertising agency, the agency and the ultimate sponsor will be jointly and severally responsible for the performance of the advertiser's obligations hereunder.

8.   You may not assign your rights and duties under this agreement to any either party without prior written consent.

Please indicate your agreement to the foregoing by signing under the words "Agreed to and Accepted."

Very truly yours,

WXLO RADIO   **AGREED TO AND ACCEPTED:**

_____   _____
General Manager   **Authorized Signature**

_____   _____
General Sales Manager   **Name**

_____   _____
Controller   **Title**

FIGURE 4.23
A call for sales interns. Courtesy WPLJ-FM.

 The ABC Radio Station Group
New York City
SALES INTERNSHIPS WITH WPLJ-FM

WPLJ-FM is a high profile, hit-driven personality radio station with lots of listener involvement, big contests and great promotions. WPLJ plays artists like Goo Goo Dolls, Sugar Ray, Alanis Morissette, Creed, Pink, Shakira, Matchbox 20, and Dave Matthews Band combined with older hits from artists like REM, Sting, Sheryl Crow and U2 to create our signature sound. WPLJ is located in Midtown Manhattan, the capitol of the entertainment and advertising industries.

The WPLJ Sales Department is looking for bright, energetic and outgoing undergraduate and graduate students who are interested in pursuing a career in radio sales or advertising. If you are team-oriented and thrive in a fast-paced environment, we want to hear from you! There is no better way to jumpstart a career in radio, communications or advertising / marketing. You will work directly with one of the top radio sales teams in New York City gaining hands-on, practical experience. College credit must be earned for the internship. Students must be enrolled in a degree program in a communications or business-related field. Hours are flexible to fit your schedule. Internships are available in all semesters. For Summer 2002, apply by April 15th.

Interested students should send their resume and a cover letter telling us a little bit about themselves and why they want to participate in our sales internship program. Email your resume and cover letter to nyradioresumes@abc.com. The subject header must read "WPLJ SALES INTERNSHIP PROGRAM". You can also send it by regular mail to Linda Wnek, Diversity Recruitment Coordinator, WPLJ-FM Sales Internship Program, Two Penn Plaza - 17th Floor, New York, NY 10121.

The sales manager generally directs a station's co-op efforts. Large stations often employ a full-time co-op specialist. The individual responsible for stimulating co-op revenue will survey retail trade journals for pertinent information about available dollars. Retail associations also are a good source of information, because they generally possess manufacturer co-op advertising lists. The importance of taking advantage of co-op opportunities cannot be overstressed. Some stations, especially metro market outlets, earn hundreds of thousands of dollars in additional ad revenue through their co-op efforts.

From the retailer's perspective, co-op advertising is not always a great bargain. This usually stems from copy constraints imposed by certain manufacturers, which give the retailer a 10-second tag-out in a 30- or 60-second commercial. Obviously, this does not please the retailer who has split the cost of advertising 50/50. In recent years, this type of copy domination by the manufacturer has decreased somewhat, and a more equitable approach, whereby both parties share evenly the exposure and the expense, is more commonplace.

Co-op also is appealing to radio stations because they do not have to modify their billing practices to accommodate the third party. Stations simply bill the retailer and provide an affidavit attesting to the time commercials aired. The retailer, in turn, bills the manufacturer for its share of the airtime. For its part, the manufacturer requires receipt of an affidavit before making payment. In certain cases, the station is asked to mail affidavits directly to the manufacturer. Some manufacturers stipulate that bills be sent to audit houses, which inspect the materials before authorizing payment.

Event marketing is another key form of nontraditional revenue generation. This involves the creation of a popular event, such as a food or arts festival, wherein merchants pay to be associated with it. This has become a very common and successful way for stations to make income without adding to their on-air spot loads. Says Jay Williams, Jr., "Stations are going outside the traditional spot load box and engaging in different ways to generate income for their stations."

Trade-Outs

Stations commonly exchange airtime for goods, although top-rated outlets, whose time is sold at a premium, are less likely to swap spots for anything other than cash. Rather than pay for needed items, such as office supplies and furnishings, studio equipment, meals for clients and listeners, new cars, and so forth, a station may choose to strike a deal with merchants in which airtime is traded for merchandise. There are advertisers who use radio only on a trade basis. A station may start out in an exclusively trade relationship with a client in the hope of eventually converting him to cash. Split contracts also are written when a client agrees to provide both money and merchandise. For example, WXXX-FM needs two new office desks. The total cost of the desks is $800. An agreement is made whereby the client receives a $1400 ROS spot schedule and $600 cash in exchange for the desks. Trade-outs are not always this equitable. Stations often provide trade clients with airtime worth two or three times the merchandise value to get what is needed. Thus, the saying "need inspires deals."

Many sales managers also feel that it makes good business sense to write radio trade contracts to fill available and unsold airtime, rather than let it pass unused. Once airtime is gone, it cannot be retrieved, and yesterday's unfilled availability is a lost opportunity.

FIGURE 4.24
Sales reps at their computers. Courtesy WIZN-FM.

CHAPTER HIGHLIGHTS

1. At the close of the first decade of the new millennium, radio advertising was down substantially. Yet, selling commercials still keeps most radio stations on the air. Between 1920 and today, advertising revenues and forms reflected the ebb and flow of radio's popularity. Today, advertising dollars are selectively spent on spots aired during times of the day and on stations that attract the type of audience the advertiser wants to reach.

2. An effective radio commercial makes a strong and lasting impression on the mind of the listener.

3. A successful account executive needs an understanding of research methods, marketing, finance; some form of sales experience; and such personal traits as ambition, confidence, honesty, energy, determination, intelligence, and good grooming.

4. Since the 1970s, programming people have made successful job transitions to sales because they have a practical understanding of the product they are selling.

5. Although an increasing number of station managers are being drawn from programming people, a sales background is still preferred.

6. The sales manager, who reports directly to the station or cluster's general manager, oversees the account executives, establishes departmental policies, develops sales plans and materials, conceives campaigns and promotions, sets quotas, works closely with the program director (PD) to develop salable features, and sometimes sells.

7. Rates for selling airtime vary according to listenership and are published on the station's rate card. The card lists terms of payment and commission, nature of copy and due dates, station's approach to discounting, rate protection policy, feature, and spot rates. Rate cards are beginning to fade from the scene as new approaches to selling airtime evolve.

8. Station listenership varies according to time of day, so rate card daypart classifications range from the highest costing AAA (typically 6–10 A.M. weekdays) to C (usually midnight–6 A.M.). Fixed-position drive time spots are usually among the most expensive to purchase.

9. Computerized rate cards allow rates to be quickly adjusted while using a grid structure allows for considerable rate flexibility. Grids are inventory sensitive and they let a station remain viable when business is slow.

10. For advertisers with limited funds, ROS, BTA, or TAP are cost-effective alternatives.

11. Because few accounts are closed on the first call, it is used to introduce the station to the client and to determine its needs. Follow-up calls are made to offset reservations and, if necessary, to improve the proposal. Perseverance is essential.

12. Radio sales are drawn from three levels: retail, local, and national. Retail sales are

FIGURE 4.25
RAB's co-op material provides pertinent facts. Courtesy RAB.

The Advertiser's Guide To Using Radio Co-op

Discover how co-operative advertising on Radio builds traffic and sales for your business, without breaking your budget.

Radio Advertising Bureau, Inc. • 304 Park Avenue South, New York, NY 10010
1 (800) 252-RADIO • FAX (212) 254-8713
New York, Atlanta, Chicago, Detroit, Houston, Los Angeles

direct sales to advertisers within the station's signal area. Local sales are obtained from advertising agencies representing businesses in the market area. National sales are obtained by the station's rep company from agencies representing national accounts.

13. A fully produced sample commercial (spec spot) is an effective selling tool. It is used to break down client resistance on callbacks, to interest former clients who have not bought time recently, and to encourage clients to increase their schedules.

14. The salesperson should commit the advertiser to sufficient commercials, placed properly, to ensure that the advertiser achieves his or her objectives. Underselling is as self-defeating as overselling.

15. New accounts are added to a salesperson's list by "prospecting" searching newspapers, Yellow Pages, television ads, competing radio station ads, and new store openings. Only open accounts may be added (those not already declared by another salesperson at the same station).

16. Because a salesperson must average 15–20 in-person calls each day, when preparing a daily call sheet it is important to logically sequence and centralize the businesses to be contacted. Also, advance telephone contacts can eliminate much wasted time.

17. Station Web sites, new HD^2 channels, and podcasts are additional opportunities for revenue at stations. The Internet and

e-mail are useful sales and prospecting tools for account executives.

18. A salesperson at a station with a high rating has a decided advantage when contacting advertisers. Stations with low or no numbers must focus on retail sales (work the street), developing programs and programming to attract targeted clients. Stations in nonsurvey areas must rely on their image of good citizenship and strong community ties.

19. Ad agencies annually supply hundreds of millions of dollars in advertising revenue to stations with good ratings. Media buyers at the agencies deal directly with station and network reps.

20. A station's rep company must convince national agency media buyers to select their station as their advertising outlet for the area. Therefore, the station's sales manager and the rep must work together closely.

21. Among NTR sources are co-op advertising, which involves the sharing of advertising expenses by the retailer of the business being promoted and the manufacturer of the product being promoted, and events marketing, wherein stations create events in which merchants invest their promotional dollars.

22. Rather than pay for needed items or to obtain something of value for unsold time, a station may trade (trade-out) advertising airtime with a merchant in exchange for specific merchandise.

FIGURE 4.26
Walls of sales materials for use by reps and clients. Courtesy WIZN-FM.

SUGGESTED FURTHER READING

Aitchison, Jim. *Cutting Edge Radio: How to Create the World's Best Radio Ads.* Englewood Cliffs, NJ: Prentice-Hall, 2002.

Astor, Brett, and Small, Jeffrey. *Direct Response Radio: The Way to Greater Profit with Measurable Advertising.* New York: Book Surge Publishing, 2008.

Barnouw, Erik. *The Sponsor: Notes on a Modern Potentate.* New York: Oxford University Press, 1978.

Bergendort, Fred. *Broadcast Advertising.* New York: Hastings House, 1983.

Bouvard, Pierre, and Marx, Steve. *Radio Advertising's Missing Ingredient: The Optimum Effective Scheduling System.* Washington, DC: NAB, 1991.

Bovee, Courtland, and Arena, William F. *Contemporary Advertising.* Homewood, IL: Irwin, 1982.

Broadcast Marketing Company. *Building Store Traffic with Broadcast Advertising.* San Francisco: Broadcast Marketing Company, 1978.

Burton, Philip W., and Sandhusen, Richard. *Cases in Advertising.* Columbus, OH: Grid Publishing, 1981.

Cox, Jim. *Sold on Radio: Advertising in the Golden Age of Broadcasting.* Jefferson, NC: McFarland, 2008.

Culligan, Matthew J. *Getting Back to the Basics of Selling.* New York: Crown, 1981.

Cundiff, Edward W., Still, Richard R., and Govoni, Norman A.P. *Fundamentals of Modern Marketing,* 3rd ed. Englewood Cliffs, NJ: Prentice Hall, 1980.

Delmar, Ken. *Winning Moves: The Body Language of Selling.* New York: Warner, 1984.

Diamond. Bob, and Frost, Jay. *Selling Air: How to Jump Start Your Career in Radio Sales.* iUniverse, 2008.

Dunn, W. Watson, and Barban, Arnold M. *Advertising: Its Role in Modern Marketing,* 4th ed. Hinsdale, IL: Dryden Press, 1978.

Gardner, Herbert S., Jr. *The Advertising Agency Business.* Chicago, IL: Crain Books, 1976.

Gilson, Christopher, and Berkman, Harold W. *Advertising Concepts and Strategies.* New York: Random House, 1980.

Heighton, Elizabeth J., and Cunningham, Don R. *Advertising in the Broadcast and Cable Media,* 2nd ed. Belmont, CA: Wadsworth Publishing, 1984.

Herweg, Godfrey W., and Herweg, Ashley P. *Making More Money Selling Radio Advertising without Numbers.* Washington, DC: NAB, 1995.

Hoffer, Jay, and McRae, John. *The Complete Broadcast Sales Guide for Stations, Reps, and Ad Agencies.* Blue Ridge Summit, PA: Tab Books, 1981.

Johnson, J. Douglas. *Advertising Today.* Chicago, IL: SRA, 1978.

Jugenheimer, Donald W., and Turk, Peter B. *Advertising Media.* Columbus, OH: Grid Publishing, 1980.

Keith, Michael C. *Selling Radio Direct.* Boston, MA: Focal Press, 1992.

Kleppner, Otto. *Advertising Procedure,* 7th ed. Englewood Cliffs, NJ: Prentice Hall, 1979.

Lipsky, Mark. *Radio Tips.* Muskegon, MI: RDR Books, 2005.

McGee, William L. *Broadcast Co-Op, the Untapped Goldmine.* San Francisco, CA: Broadcast Marketing Company, 1975.

Montgomery, Robert L. *How to Sell in the 1980s.* Englewood Cliffs, NJ: Prentice Hall, 1980.

Murphy, Jonne. *Handbook of Radio Advertising.* Radnor, PA: Chilton Books, 1980.

National Association of Broadcasters. *Think Big: Event Marketing for Radio.* Washington, DC: NAB, 1994.

Prooth, Victor. *"Radio Advertising Doesn't Work." Says Who!* New York: American Mass Media Corporation, 2006.

Rhoads, B. Eric, et al., eds. *Sales and Marketing.* West Palm Beach, FL: Streamline Press, 1995.

Shane, Ed. *Selling Electronic Media.* Boston, MA: Focal Press, 1999.

Shaver, Mary A. *Make the Sale:How to Sell Media with Marketing.* New York: Copy Workshop, 1995.

Sissors, Jack Z., and Surmanek, Jim. *Advertising Media Planning,* 2nd ed. Chicago, IL: Crain Books, 1982.

Standard Rate and Data Service: Spot Radio. Skokie, Ill.: SRDS, annual.

Warner, Charles, and Buchman, Joseph. *Broadcasting and Cable Selling,* 2nd ed. Belmont, CA: Wadsworth Publishing, 1993.

Weyland, Paul. *Successful Local Broadcast Sales.* New York: Amacom Books, 2007.

To: Rich Krezwick
Fr: Jay Williams, Jr.
Re: sales

Although I am not familiar with what happens every day, I do think I have a general idea of the sales philosophy and structure that has gotten us where we are, both positively and negatively. As I see the declining sales as a percentage of goal in a marketplace that is hotter now than at any time in the past 4 years, I think it's time we continue our discussion on a more specific level. To that end, I thought I would outline what I see from here (to see where you agree/disagree or can supply additional information) and suggest some solutions (as I have certainly seen similar trends many times before). First my suggestions:

1. Let's get Casey out of the station for a few days (your suggestion, actually). I think he needs some perspective, and there's nothing like seeing another problem to see your own better.

2. Let's give Casey a sales call quota. Sales managers learn both real problems (not self-manufactured) on the street, and they learn solutions. More importantly, they're on the front lines with their sales people and can better relate to them and teach them. He needs to be more of a player-coach. Perhaps, a minimum of 20 calls a week.

3. Let's do real meetings that teach the "consultant sell." This, in my opinion, is the philosophy that has always been missing (in the past year or so) that (a) makes us look as if we don't care about the client's problems and (b) puts downward pressure on rates. The consultant sell, which I do every day for DMR and frequently for WLKZ, talks about clients' needs and revolves around solutions. I never, as a result, and I do mean *never*, get into a rate discussion. Conversely, WXLO is now selling spots and inventory. We're like a beer distributor, competing against other beers. It's totally the wrong way to sell.

4. Let's figure out a way to hire someone to really handle vendor, interactive phones, and other nonspot revenues that you and I both know can be sold at a premium instead of the despicable "value added." Perhaps, you should be the sales manager of this special sales branch, starting with one or two people. The two-check philosophy in action. Get us in the direction you and I have talked

about – as a marketing group instead of spot sales people (or really, spot whores as I see it).

5. Let's put a stop to any sales criticism of programming, even if it's warranted. At Fairbanks broadcasting, I learned how little criticisms can become a culture if unchecked. In reality, they are more than critiquing the product they must turn around and sell, they (sales people) are giving themselves an excuse for poor sales, low rates, and giveaways to clients. I was brought up with the philosophy that only the best could sell for station XXXX; if you can't, get the hell out of the way and we'll hire someone who can. It changed the paradigm – and the success of the stations I worked with.

6. Let's hire at least one more, maybe two more, sales people and specifically target Metrowest and southern New Hampshire. I know people like Peter's Auto Sales in Nashua, and other major advertisers, that need business from south and west of Nashua. We can help, but we don't have the horses to develop that business. With not enough sales people competing for the available spots, it also lessens demand and that, in WXLO's "beer distributor" mentality, lowers rates.

As we've talked about much of this, I'm sure you will agree with much of it, but I think we must now act quickly. Fourth-quarter buys and rates are being set; too much later and the die will be cast and we won't be hitting the cash flow numbers you want and the station needs. I offer these as my first steps to change the structure. (I'm referring to a $4000/person seminar taught by a consultant to the Motorola management last week. In shorthand, most manage events. Some manage the patterns caused by the events, yet these both yield poor results as they are reactions to past events. Smart managers manage structure.) Our structure, and the philosophy you generated and that I generated in programming, is being changed in sales. This change in structure (because of the coterminous change in philosophy) is changing our patterns (sales curves) and events (individual sales, rates, complaints, bonuses to clients, low-rate packages, etc.). That's why I have proposed these solutions versus mere package or rate changes, etc. Let me know what you think.

News from the Start

Due in great part to industry consolidation and the ever-increasing availability of new media, such as the Web, iPhones, Blackberries, etc., broadcast radio news has witnessed a decline in audience size as well as the size of station news departments. Notes Ed Shane, "The diminishing number of news people and news broadcasts is alarming." It was not always that way. Indeed, the medium of radio was used to convey news before news of the medium had reached the majority of the general public. Ironically, it was the sinking of the *Titanic* in 1912 and the subsequent rebroadcast of the ship's coded distress message that helped launch a wider awareness and appreciation of the newfangled gadget called the *wireless telegraph*. It was not until the early 1920s, when the "wireless" had become known as the "radio" that broadcast journalism actually began to evolve.

A historical benchmark in radio news is the broadcast of the Harding–Cox election results in 1920 by stations WWJ in Detroit and KDKA in Pittsburgh, although the first actual newscast is reported to have occurred in California a decade earlier. Despite these early ventures, news programming progressed slowly until the late 1920s. By then, two networks, NBC and CBS, were providing national audiences with certain news and information features.

Until 1932, radio depended on newspapers for its stories. That year, newspapers officially perceived the electronic medium as a competitive threat. Fearing a decline in readership, they imposed a blackout. Radio was left to its own resources. The networks put forth substantial efforts to gather news and did very well without the wire services on which they had come to rely. Late in 1934, United Press (UP), International News Service (INS), and Associated Press (AP) agreed to sell their news services to radio, thus ending the boycott. However, by then the medium had demonstrated its ability to fend for itself.

Radio has served as a vital source of news and information throughout the most significant historical events. When the nation was gripped by economic turmoil in the 1930s, the incumbent head-of-state, Franklin D. Roosevelt, demonstrated the tremendous reach of the medium by using it to address the people. The majority of Americans heard and responded to the president's talks.

Radio's status as a news source reached its apex during World War II. On-the-spot reports and interviews, as well as commentaries, brought the war into the nation's living rooms. In contrast to World War I, when the fledgling wireless was exclusively used for military purposes, during World War II, radio served as the primary link between those at home and the foreign battlefronts around the globe. News programming during this troubled period matured while the public adjusted its perception of the medium, casting it in a more austere light. Radio journalism became a more credible profession.

The effects of television on radio news were wide ranging. While the medium in general reeled from the blow dealt it by the *enfant terrible*, in the late 1940s and early 1950s, news programming underwent a sort of metamorphosis. Faced with drastically reduced network schedules, radio stations began to localize their news efforts. Attention was focused on area news events rather than national and international. Stations that had relied almost exclusively on network news began to hire news people and broadcast a regular schedule of local newscasts. By the mid-1950s, the transformation was nearly complete, and radio news had become a local programming matter. Radio news had undergone a 180-degree turn, even before the medium gave up trying to directly compete on a program-for-program basis with television. By the time radio set a new and revivifying course for itself by programming for specific segments of the listening audience, local newscasts were the norm.

Since its period of reconstruction in the 1950s, radio has proven time and time again to be the nation's first source of information about major news events. The majority of Americans first heard of the assassination of President Kennedy, and the subsequent shootings of Martin Luther King, Jr. and Senator Robert Kennedy over radio. In 1965 when most of the northeast was crippled by a power blackout, battery-powered radios literally became a lifeline for millions of people by providing continuous news and information until power was restored.

During the 1970s through the 1990s, news on both the world and local levels reached radio listeners first. Today, despite the Internet and 24-hour cable news networks, the public still knows that radio delivers the news instantly and as it happens about occurrences at home and halfway around the world.

News and Today's Radio

More people claim to listen to radio for music than for any other reason, although studies are showing that it is changing due to a growing reliance on other audio media sources. Somewhat surprising, however, is

FIGURE 5.1

News is a prominent feature on most radio stations. Courtesy RAB.

Radio Is The First Morning News Source

Morning(6AM–10AM)	Radio	TV	News-papers	Other/None
Persons 12+	49%	29%	15%	7%
Teens 12–17	60	21	12	7
Adults 18+	48	30	16	6
Adults 18–34	53	28	13	6
Adults 25–54	50	29	16	5
College Grads.	46	27	22	5
Prof./Mgr. Males	55	19	20	6
F/T Working Women	56	27	11	6
S50K+ Income	49	28	18	5

Radio Is The First News Source At Midday

Midday(10AM–3PM)	Radio	TV	News-papers	Other/None
Persons 12+	36%	24%	14%	26%
Teens 12–17	30	24	17	29
Adults 18+	37	24	14	25
Adults 18–34	43	19	18	20
Adults 25–54	41	18	15	26
College Grads.	36	17	15	32
Prof./Mgr. Males	36	9	23	32
F/T Working Women	48	9	12	31
S50K+ Income	44	10	17	29

Radio Is The Major Source of News

Morning(6AM–10AM)	Radio	TV	News-papers	Other/None
Persons 12+	42%	31%	18%	9%
Teens 12–17	54	29	9	8
Adults 18+	41	31	19	9
Adults 18–34	45	28	20	7
Adults 25–54	43	29	20	8
College Grads.	38	24	30	8
Prof./Mgr. Males	48	16	27	9
Working Women	49	28	15	8
S50K+ Income	45	21	27	7

Radio Is The First Source For Local Emergency News

	Radio	TV	Other/None
Persons 12+	50%	48%	2%
Teens 12–17	50	49	1
Adults 18+	50	48	2
Adults 18–34	50	49	1
Adults 25–54	54	44	2
College Grads.	56	42	2
Prof./Mgr. Males	57	40	3
F/T Working Women	51	47	2

that many of these same people admit to relying on the medium for the news they receive. Recent studies have found that although most of those surveyed tuned in to radio for entertainment, three-quarters considered news and information programming important. These surveys also ascertained that radio is the first morning news source for two-thirds of all full-time working women.

According to Arbitron, 60% of the News/Talk/Information audience are men of age 18 and over while the balance are women in the same age range. Most of these listeners get their first news of the day from radio. In comparison, only 16% of adults rely on newspapers as the first source of daily news. Practically, all the nation's 9000 commercial stations program news to some extent, and there are over 2000 stations that specialize in news programming. Radio's tremendous mobility and pervasiveness have made it an instant and reliable news source for millions of Americans.

Despite all of this, however, consultant Ed Shane argues that "Radio news is in a sad state." The deregulation of the medium since the 1980s has inspired a decline in local radio news service, according to many sources. "Listen to the news on many local stations and you're hearing announcers from Metro Network's MetroSource, a linkup of Metro's local traffic services into a combination newswire and network. Because Metro has operations in 81 markets, covering 2000 radio and TV stations, the system creates a formidable presence. To its credit, Metro covers news pretty well. Presentation is not its forte. Outsourcing one of radio's essential services is a cost-cutting measure, and does not enhance quality. After the devastating Oklahoma City tornadoes in May 1999, the National Association of Broadcasters placed an ad in *USA Today* and other publications congratulating 'local broadcasters' for their fine job of informing the public about the impending storms and then covering the damage that ensued. Most of the quotations in the ad were from TV stations or about TV stations. Radio complained, of course, but a local official was quoted as saying 'radio just simulcasts TV audio.'"

Says WBZ GM (General Manager) Ted Jordan, "In one sense we suffered from the same market compression as everyone else. But in other ways, it's easier today as there

Holland Cooke | On Local Radio News

FIGURE 5.2
Holland Cooke.

What remains to be seen (heard) is how close the "actual" can come to the "theoretical." Theoretically, and logically, what would continue to value local radio stations to listeners and differentiate AM/FM broadcasters from iTunes, satellite radio, and the plethora on Internet-related content now becoming every-bit-as-portable via iPhone, WiMax, etc. is local content. But as a practical matter, debt now prohibits most radio station owners from delivering such content. Sadly, radio's biggest owners treated stations like real estate. And like real estate, stations now go-begging for buyers. Clearly, the theoretical fix would be uber-well-heeled buyers spotting the opportunity of a lifetime: radio's gazillion in-place receivers and the pre-existing listener habit of the demographic, which controls most wealth and, as a generation, is in the process of inheriting their parent's wealth. Baby Boomer's children are already radio's lost generation. But the real-life Homer and Marge Simpson characters, mega-consumers who fuel the U.S. economy, would be retrieved and maintained if stations offered programming more compelling than FM's race to go Al Christmas first and AM's self-imposed typecasting as "Not from your city/you're wrong, I'm right/bad Republicans." Whether Bill Gates or other as-wealthy folk will seize this opportunity remains to be seen.

was more AM competition. All things considered, the news quality is as good, but now the systems in place are better, the networks we use (ABC & CBS) are better and more responsive, and the stringers are better. We used to have our own Washington, DC, bureau because we didn't trust the networks to deliver the story. Now we can. They have really become responsive to the needs of the local stations. There is now a greater sharing of resources at our operations. We have a dotted line relationship with WBZ TV. Their news people give updates on our air and our anchors appear on television. We are able to co-brand the stations and get a larger share of mind."

Adds Jay Williams, "They have been able to cut costs by reallocating resources, working with their TV affiliate, using better systems, working more closely with the networks, and the like. As to the talk that there are fewer real news sources today, I know Ted believes that not to be the case. Just the opposite, in fact."

The Newsroom

The number of individuals working in a radio station newsroom will vary depending on the size of a station, whether it is part of a cluster operation or a single outlet, and its format. On the average, a station in a small market employs one or two full-time news people. Of course, some outlets find it

financially unfeasible to hire news people. These stations do not necessarily ignore news rather they delegate responsibilities to their deejays to deliver brief newscasts at specified times, often at the top of the hour. Stations approaching news in this manner make it necessary for the on-air person to collect news from the wire service during record cuts and broadcast it nearly verbatim—a practice known as "rip 'n' read." Little, if any, rewrite is done because the deejay simply does not have the time to do it. The only thing that persons at "rip 'n' read" outlets can and must do is examine wire copy before going on the air. This eliminates the likelihood of mistakes. Again, all this is accomplished while the records are spinning.

NPR reporter Corey Flintoff warns against neglecting to examine wire copy before airtime. "We've all been caught with stuff that appears to scan at first sight but turns out to be incomprehensible when you read it."

Music-oriented stations in larger markets rarely allow their deejays to do news. Occasionally, the person jockeying the overnight shift will be expected to give a brief newscast every hour or two, but in metro markets, this is fairly uncommon. There is generally a newsperson on duty around the clock. A top-rated station in a medium market typically employs four full-time news people; again, this varies depending on the status of the outlet (one of a cluster of stations) and the type of programming it airs. For example, Easy Listening stations that stress music and de-emphasize talk may employ only one or two news people. Meanwhile, an AC station in the same market may have five people as its news staff in an attempt to promote itself as a heavy news and information outlet, even though its primary product is music. Certain music stations in major markets hire as many as a dozen news employees. This figure may include not only on-air newscasters but also writers, street reporters, and technical people as well. Stringers and interns also swell the figure.

During the prime listening periods when a station's audience is at its maximum, newscasts are programmed with greater frequency, sometimes twice as often as during other dayparts. The newsroom is a hub of activity as news people prepare for newscasts scheduled every 20–30 minutes. Half a dozen people may be involved in assembling news but only two may actually enter the broadcast booth. A primetime newscast schedule may look something like this:

Drive Coverage, A.M.	Drive Coverage, P.M.
Smith 6:25 A.M.	Lopez 3:25 P.M.
Bernard 7:00 A.M.	Gardner 4:00 P.M.
Smith 7:25 A.M.	Lopez 4:25 P.M.
Bernard 8:00 A.M.	Gardner 5:00 P.M.
Smith 8:25 A.M.	Lopez 5:25 P.M.
Bernard 9:00 A.M.	Gardner 6:00 P.M.
Smith 9:25 A.M.	Lopez 6:25 P.M.

Midday and evening are far less frenetic in the newsroom, and one person per shift may be considered sufficient.

A standard-size newsroom in a medium market will contain several pieces of audio equipment, not to mention office furniture such as desks, computers, typewriters, file cabinets, and so on. Reel-to-reel recorders and cassette and cartridge machines are important tools for the newsperson. The newsroom also will be equipped with various monitors to keep news people on top of what is happening at the local police and fire departments and weather bureau. Various wire service machines provide the latest news, sports, stock, and weather information, as well as a host of other data. Depending on the station's budget, two or more news services may be used. Stations with a genuine commitment to news create work areas that are designed for maximum efficiency and productivity.

In situations where newsrooms have been combined and consolidated, more personnel, equipment, and space may be in evidence since the plant itself may be serving myriad signals. Cluster operation newsrooms accommodate reporters and news readers assigned to the various stations under the one roof.

News in Satellite Radio originates from a host of outside sources. Both Satellite services (XM and Sirius) provide feeds (channels) from ABC, NBN, CBS, CNN, Fox, ESPN, NPR, BBC, and so forth. Satellite radio is not in the business of generating news itself, so the "newsroom" (as we have been referring to it) does not exist, although this may change in the future.

The All-News Station

Stations devoted entirely to news programming arrived on the scene in the mid-1960s. Program innovator Gordon McLendon, who had been a key figure in the development of two music formats, Beautiful Music and Top 40, implemented All-News at WNUS-AM (NEWS) in Chicago. In 1965, Group W, Westinghouse Broadcasting, changed WINS-AM in New York to All-News and soon did the same at more of its metro outlets: KYW-AM, Philadelphia, and KFWB-AM, Los Angeles. While Group W was converting several of its outlets to nonmusic programming, CBS decided that All-News was the way to go at WCBS-AM, New York; KCBS-AM, San Francisco; and KNX-AM, Los Angeles.

Not long after KCBS in San Francisco began its All-News programming, another Bay City station, KGO-AM, introduced the hybrid News/Talk format in which news shares the microphone with conversation and interview features. Over the years, the hybrid approach has caught on and leads the pure All-News format in popularity.

Because of the exorbitant cost of running a news-only operation, it has remained primarily a metro market endeavor. It often costs several times as much to run an effective All-News station as it does to run one broadcasting music. This usually keeps small-market outlets out of the business. Staff size in All-News stations far exceeds that of formats that primarily serve up music. Although a lone deejay is needed at an Adult Contemporary or Top 40 station, All-News requires the involvement of several people to keep the air sound credible.

Even though the cost of running a news station is high, the payback can more than justify expenditures. However, this is one format that requires a sizable initial investment, as well as the financial wherewithal and patience to last until it becomes an established and viable entity. Considerable planning takes place before a station decides to convert to All-News, since it is not simply

a matter of hiring new jocks and updating the music library. Switching from a music format to All-News is dramatic and anything but cosmetic.

AM has always been the home of the All-News station. There are only a handful of FM news and information outlets. The format's prevalence on AM has grown considerably since the late 1970s when FM took the lead in listeners. The percentage of All-News and News/Talk formats on AM continued to increase in the 1980s as the band lost more and more of its music listeners to FM. However, All-News stations in a handful of metro markets keep AM at the top of the ratings charts. In the early 1990s, it was common to find one AM outlet among the leaders, and almost invariably it programmed nonmusic. This has changed little in the mid-2000s. Some

media observers predict that All-News will make inroads into FM as that band gives over large segments of its music audience to Internet downloading.

The Electronic Newsroom

The use of computers and online resources in the radio newsroom has increased to where they are now the norm since being introduced in December 1980 at KCBS in San Francisco. Computers linked to the various wire and Internet information services are used to access primary and background data on fast-breaking stories and features. Many stations have installed video display terminals (VDTs) in on-air studios. Instead of handheld copy, newscasters simply broadcast off the screens. Desktop computers have replaced typewriters in the newsrooms at larger stations as well as at the smaller stations since the 1990s. The speed and agility with which copy can be produced and edited makes a computer the perfect tool for broadcast journalists.

In 1986, Boston All-News station WEEI-AM installed Media Touch's Touchstone system, thus converting their entire operation to computer. News people access and store data and even activate equipment simply by touching a computer screen.

Computers have become the norm even in nonmetro market outlets. "There's not much resistance remaining against computers in the newsroom, especially, since the advent of cheaper PCs and the improvement of programs like Newspro, which is the system we use here at NPR. It allows us to access and manipulate about a half-dozen wire services. We can split screen and write stories while searching the wires and so on. There are many more sophisticated systems too. Systems like D-CART incorporate digital audio right onto the screen," comments Cory Flintoff.

Furthermore, some companies provide specifically tailored software for newsrooms. "There are computer software packages these days that a newsroom can buy. In my day we used the old file and cards and rolodex, but today newsrooms that can afford it use software to file stories, keep archives of copy, record and play actualities, and so forth." Says radio consultant Donna Halper.

Producer Ty Ford observes, "Computers are an integral part of radio newsrooms with auto-download of wire copy to word processing terminals, as well as search-by-word or topic search, auto-word count and digital archiving of sound bites with a computer database for retrieval. To put it in the contemporary lexicon, radio news is 'online.'"

More and more newsrooms use the Internet and e-mail. It make sense that the information highway be accessed by a medium determined to keep its listening public informed and up-to-date. The Internet has become the best resource for information on every conceivable topic. As a search medium, there is none better. Data of each variety are at the fingertips of all news people today. The world of cyberspace

NewsGen is your all-in-one newsroom production package.

This comprehensive, standalone newsroom software enables reporters to write newscasts, receive and revise wire copy and digitally record, edit and playback audio. Completely scalable—from an enterprise wide deployment to a server-based system serving all your reporters simultaneously to a standalone system for a single user–NewsGen can fulfill your newsroom's needs regardless of size. Whether you're writing your own newscasts for top-of-the-hour broadcast or stacking stories and audio for your show, NewsGen has the flexibility to meet your needs.

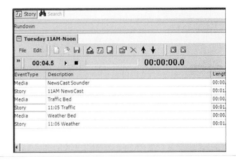

has revolutionized newsgathering. Says broadcaster and academic Larry Miller, "The evolution has been from old-fashioned teletype 'wire' by landlines, to satellites, to computers and the Internet. Even audio is accessed online."

According to broadcast scholar David Reese, "Today, newsrooms use station Web sites to deliver news, and recent studies indicate that acquiring information this way is growing in popularity. Adds Jason Insalaco, "The listener is no longer going to remain captive to a news station to learn the day's headlines. An added plus is that many station websites offer live information on traffic flow and so forth. Station websites give outlets needed additional cache in the multimedia environment."

Other technology has contributed greatly to the efficiency and performance of the electronic newsroom. For instance, in recent years, ISDN (Integrated Services Digital Network) has significantly improved the quality of phone interviews. With ISDN, technology newsrooms can create seamless reports (in terms of audio fidelity), thus creating the impression (or illusion) that all the voices on the air come from the same studio and even from the same microphone.

FIGURE 5.5
An all-in-one newsroom inside the computer. Courtesy Prophet Systems.

The News Director

News directors, like other department heads, are responsible for developing and implementing policies pertaining to their area, supervising staff members, and handling budgetary concerns. These are basic to any managerial position. However, the news department poses its own unique challenges to the individual who oversees its operation. These challenges must be met with a considerable degree of skill and know-how. Education and training are important. Surveys have concluded that station managers look for college degrees when hiring news directors. In addition, most news directors have, on the average, five years of experience in radio news before advancement to the managerial level.

The news director and program director (PD) work together closely. At most stations, the PD has authority over the news department, since everything going over the air or affecting the air product is his or her direct concern and responsibility. Any changes in the format of the news or in the scheduling of newscasts or newscasters may, in fact, have to be approved by the station's programmer. For example, if the PD is opposed to the news director's plans to include two or more recorded reports (actualities) per newscast, he may withhold approval. Although the news director may feel that the reports enhance the newscasts, the PD may argue that they create congestion and clutter. In terms of establishing the on-air news schedule, the PD works with the news director to ensure that the sound of a given newsperson is suitably matched with the time slot he or she is assigned.

Getting the news out rapidly and accurately is a top priority of the news director. "People tune radio news to find out what is happening right now. That's what makes the medium such a key source for most people. While it is important to get news on the air as fast as possible, it is more important that the stories broadcast be factual and correct. You can't sacrifice accuracy for the sake of speed. As a radio news director, my first responsibility is to inform our audience about breaking events on the local level. That's what our listeners want to hear," says Judy Smith, who functions as a one-person newsroom at the San Antonio station.

"Because I'm the only newsperson on duty, I have to spend a lot of time verifying facts on the phone and recording actualities. I don't have the luxury of assigning that work to someone else, but it has to be done."

Larry Jewett perceives his responsibilities similarly. "First and foremost, the news director's job is to keep the listener informed of what is happening in the world around him. A newsperson is a gatherer and conveyor of information. News is a serious business. A jock can be wacky and outrageous on the air and be a great success. On the other hand, a newsperson must communicate credibility or find another occupation."

Gathering local news is the most time-consuming task facing a radio news director, according to news director Cecilia Mason. "To do the job well you have to keep moving. All kinds of meetings – governmental, civic, business – have to be covered if you intend being a primary source of local news. A station with a news commitment must have the resources to be where the stories are, too. A news director has to be a logistical engineer at times. You have to be good at prioritizing and making the most out of what you have at hand. All too often, there are just too many events unfolding for a news department to effectively cover, so you call the shots the best way that you can. If you know your business, your best shot is usually more than adequate."

In addition to the gathering and reporting of news, public affairs programming often is the responsibility of the news director. This generally includes the planning and preparation of local information features, such as interviews, debates, and even documentaries. Ultimately, the news director's primary goal is to assure the credibility of the station's news operation. For the well-schooled and conscientious news director, this means avoiding advocacy and emphasizing objectivity. Says media scholar Indra de Silva, "So much of broadcast news today is opinion and commentary – infotainment – rather than dispassionate and unbiased reporting. That is a corruption of the long-held ideal that news should be fair and balanced. Editorializing a newscast essentially misleads the audience, which ultimately is a violation of the broadcaster's public trustee role."

What Makes a Newsperson?

College training is an important criterion to the radio news director planning to hire personnel. It is not impossible to land a news job without a degree, but formal education is a definite asset. An individual planning to enter the radio news profession should consider pursuing a broadcasting, journalism, or liberal arts degree. Courses in political science, history, economics, and literature give the aspiring newsperson the kind of well-rounded background that is most useful. "Coming into this shrinking field today, a college degree is an attractive, if not essential, credential. There's so much that a newsperson has to know. I think an education makes the kind of difference you can hear, and that's what our business is about. It's a fact that most people are more cognizant of the world and write better after attending college. Credibility is crucial in this business, and college training provides some of that. A degree is something that I would look for in prospective news people," says Cecilia Mason.

Even though education ranks high, most news directors still look for experience first. "As far as I'm concerned, experience counts the most. I'm not suggesting that education isn't important. It is. Most news directors want the person that they are hiring to have a college background, but experience impresses them more. I believe a person should have a good understanding of the basics before attempting to make a living at something. Whereas a college education is useful, a person should not lean back and point to a degree. Mine hasn't gotten me a job yet, though I wouldn't trade it for the world," notes Jewett. Newsman Smith agrees that "The first thing I think most news directors really look for is experience. Although I have a bachelor of arts degree myself, I wouldn't hold out for a person with a college diploma. I think if it came down to hiring a person with a degree versus someone with solid experience, I'd go for the latter."

Gaining news experience can be somewhat difficult in the age of downsizing and consolidation, at least more so than

FIGURE 5.6
Small market newsrooms are becoming scarce as the result of deregulation and consolidation.

acquiring deejay experience, which itself is more of a challenge today than it was a decade ago. Small stations, where the beginner is most likely to break into the business, have slots for several deejays but seldom more than one for a newsperson. It becomes even more problematic when employers at small stations want the one person that they hire for news to bring some experience to the job. Larger stations place even greater emphasis on experience. Thus, the aspiring newsperson is faced with a sort of Catch 22 situation, in which a job cannot be acquired without experience and experience cannot be acquired without a job.

News director Frank Titus says that there are ways of gaining experience that will lead to a news job. "Working in news at high school and college stations is very valid experience. That's how Dan Rather and a hundred other newsmen got started. Also working as an intern at a commercial radio station fattens out the resume. If someone comes to me with this kind of background and a strong desire to do news, I'm interested."

Among the personal qualities that most appeal to news directors are enthusiasm, assertiveness, energy, and inquisitiveness. "I want someone with a strong news sense and unflagging desire to get a story and get it right. A person either wants to do news or doesn't. Someone with a pedestrian interest

FIGURE 5.7
The news/talk/
information format
is a huge draw.
Courtesy Arbitron.

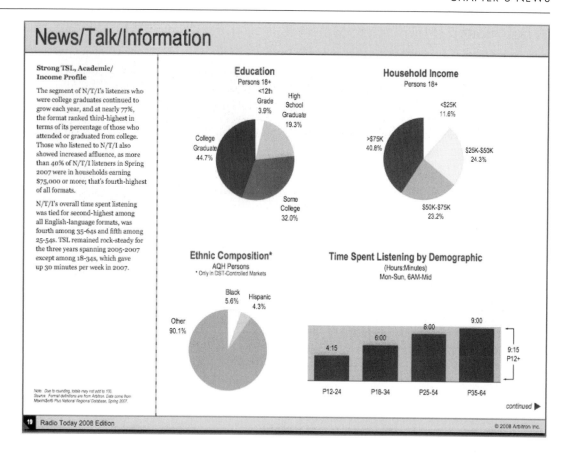

News/Talk/Information

Strong TSL, Academic/ Income Profile

The segment of N/T/I's listeners who were college graduates continued to grow each year, and at nearly 77%, the format ranked third-highest in terms of its percentage of those who attended or graduated from college. Those who listened to N/T/I also showed increased affluence, as more than 40% of N/T/I listeners in Spring 2007 were in households earning $75,000 or more; that's fourth-highest of all formats.

N/T/I's overall time spent listening was tied for second-highest among all English-language formats, was fourth among 35-64s and fifth among 25-54s. TSL remained rock-steady for the three years spanning 2005-2007 except among 18-34s, which gave up 30 minutes per week in 2007.

Note: Due to rounding, totals may not add to 100.
Source: Format definitions are from Arbitron. Data come from Maximi$er® Plus National Regional Database, Spring 2007.

Education
Persons 18+
<12th Grade 3.9%
High School Graduate 19.3%
College Graduate 44.7%
Some College 32.0%

Household Income
Persons 18+
<$25K 11.6%
>$75K 40.8%
$25K-$50K 24.3%
$50K-$75K 23.2%

Ethnic Composition*
AQH Persons
* Only in DST-Controlled Markets
Black 5.6%
Hispanic 4.3%
Other 90.1%

Time Spent Listening by Demographic
(Hours:Minutes)
Mon-Sun, 6AM-Mid
P12-24: 4:15
P18-34: 6:00
P25-54: 8:00
P35-64: 9:00
9:15 P12+

19 Radio Today 2008 Edition

© 2008 Arbitron Inc.

continued ▶

in radio journalism is more of a hindrance to an operation than a help," contends Mason. Titus wants someone who is totally devoted to the profession. "When you get right down to it, I want someone on my staff who eats, drinks, and sleeps news."

On the practical side of the ledger, newsman Sherman Whitman says that typing or keyboard skills are essential. "If you can't type, you can't work in a newsroom. It's an essential ability, and the more accuracy and speed the better. It's one of those skills basic to the job. A candidate for a news job can come in here with two degrees, but if that person can't type, that person won't be hired. Broadcast students should learn to type." Meanwhile, Jewett stresses the value of possessing a firm command of the English language. "Proper punctuation, spelling, and syntax make a news story intelligible. A newsperson doesn't have to be a grammarian, but he or she had better know where to put a comma and a period and how to compose a good clean sentence. A copy of Strunk and White's *Elements of Style* is good to have around."

An individual who is knowledgeable about the area in which a station is located has a major advantage over those who are not, says Whitman. "A newsperson has to know the town or city inside out. I'd advise anybody about to be interviewed for a news position to find out as much as possible about the station's coverage area. Read back issues of newspapers, get socioeconomic stats from the library or chamber of commerce, and study street directories and maps of the town or city in which the station is located. Go into the job interview well informed, and you'll make a strong impression."

Unlike a print journalist, a radio newsperson also must be a performer. In addition to good writing and newsgathering skills, the newsperson in radio must have announcing abilities. Again, training is usually essential. "Not only must a radio newsperson be able to write a story, but he or she has to be able to present it on the air. You have to be an announcer, too. It takes both training and experience to become a really effective newscaster. Voice performance courses can provide a foundation," says Smith. Most

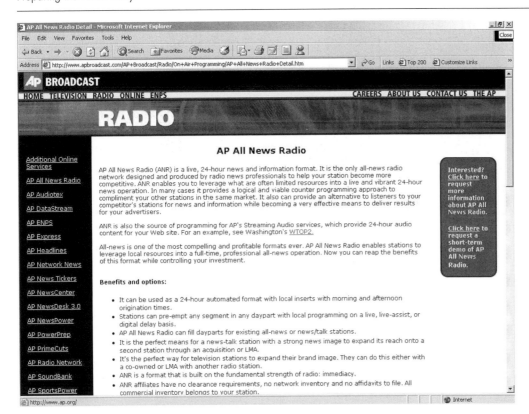

FIGURE 5.8
A press release explains the service of AP's All-News Radio. Courtesy AP

colleges with broadcasting programs offer announcing and newscasting instruction.

Entry-level news positions pay modestly, whereas news people at metro market stations earn impressive incomes. With experience come the better paying jobs. Finding that first full-time news position often takes patience and determination. Several industry trade journals, such as *Broadcasting*, the Radio-Television News Directors Association's (RTNDA) *Communicator*, *Radio and Records*, and others, list news openings.

Preparing the News Story

Observes Valerie Geller, "News programming is shorter, faster, and sharper." Given this, clean copy is essential. News stories must be legible and intelligible and designed for effortless reading by the newscaster or several different newscasters. Typos, mispunctuation, awkward phrasing, and incorrect spelling are anathema to the person at the microphone. Try reading the following news story aloud and imagine yourself in a studio broadcasting to thousands of perplexed listeners:

THE PRESIDENT STATD TODXAY THAT HE

WILL SEED RELECTION TO A SECOND TURMIN OFFICE, DEPICE ROOMERS THAT HE WILT LEAVE WASHINDON TO PURDUE A QUEER IN HOLLYWOOD.

Going on the air with copy riddled with errors is inviting disaster. The only things right about the preceding news copy are that it is typed in uppercase and double-spaced. Here are a few suggestions to keep in mind when preparing a radio news story:

1. Type neatly. Avoid typos and cross-outs. Eliminate a typing error completely. If it is left on the page, it could trip you up during a broadcast.
2. Use uppercase throughout the story. It is easier to read. Do not forget, the story you are writing is going to be read on the air.
3. Double-space between lines for the same reason uppercase is used – copy is easier to read. Space between lines of copy keeps them from merging when read aloud.
4. Use one-inch margins. Do not run the copy off the page. Uniformity eliminates errors. At the same time, try not to break up words.

5. Avoid abbreviations, except for those meant to be read as such: YMCA, U.S.A., NAACP, AFL/CIO.

6. Write out numbers under ten, and use numerals for figures between 10 and 999. Spell out thousand, million, and so forth. For example, 21 million people, instead of 21,000,000 people. Numbers can be tricky, but a consistent approach prevents problems.

7. Use the phonetic spelling for words that may cause pronunciation difficulties, and underline the stressed syllable: Monsignor (Mon-seen-yor).

8. Punctuate properly. A comma out of place can change the meaning of a sentence.

9. When in doubt, consult a standard style guide. In addition, both AP and UPI publish handbooks on newswriting.

10. Use Spellcheck or a dictionary. Misspelling causes problems and embarrassment.

Notice how much easier it is to read a news story that is correctly prepared:

THE PRESIDENT STATED TODAY THAT HE

WILL SEEK REELECTION TO A SECOND TERM IN OFFICE, DESPITE RUMORS THAT HE WILL LEAVE WASHINGTON TO PURSUE A CAREER IN HOLLYWOOD.

Since radio news copy is written for the ear and not for the eye, its style must reflect that fact. In contrast to writing done for the printed page, radio writing is more conversational and informal. Necessity dictates this. Elaborately constructed sentences containing highly sophisticated language may effectively communicate to the reader but create serious problems for the listener, who must digest the text while it is being spoken. Although the reader has the luxury to move along at his or her own pace, the radio listener must keep pace with the newscaster or miss out on information. Radio writing must be accessible and immediately comprehensible. The most widely accepted and used words must be chosen so as to prevent confusion on the part of the listener, who usually does not have the time

or opportunity to consult the dictionary. "Keep it simple and direct. No compound-complex sentences with dozens of esoteric phrases and terms. Try to picture the listener in your mind. He is probably driving a car or doing any number of things. Because of the nature of the medium, writing must be concise and conversational," contends Judy Smith.

Corey Flintoff agrees that "Copy should be adapted to a conversational style. Titles should be simplified and numbers rounded off."

News stories must be well structured and organized. This adds to their level of understanding. The journalist's five W's – who, what, when, where, and why – should be incorporated into each story. If a story fails to provide adequate details, the listener may tune in elsewhere to get what radio commentator Paul Harvey calls "the rest of the story."

When quoting a source in a news story, proper attribution must be made. This increases credibility while placing the burden of responsibility for a statement on the shoulders of the person who actually made it:

THE DRIVER OF THE CAR THAT STRUCK THE BUILDING APPEARED INTOXICATED, ACCORDING TO LISA BARNES, WHO VIEWED THE INCIDENT.

Observes Flintoff on the matter of attribution, "I prefer to identify a source at the beginning of the sentence on the theory that its more conversational. Thus, 'Lisa Barnes, a witness, said the driver...' or 'Lisa Barnes saw the car crash into the building. She said the driver....' Incidentally, I think there's a danger of legal problems using a witness's speculation that someone is drunk. I've had similar problems in the past, and I never use anything about potential intoxication unless there's a police test for drugs or alcohol."

Uncorroborated statements can make a station vulnerable to legal actions. The reliability of news sources must be established. When there are doubts concerning the facts, the newsperson has a responsibility to seek verification.

Organizing the Newscast

News on music-oriented radio stations commonly is presented in 5-minute blocks and aired at the top or bottom of the hour, During drivetime periods, stations often increase the length and/or frequency of newscasts. The 5 minutes allotted news is generally divided into segments to accommodate the presentation of specific information. A station may establish a format that allows for two minutes of local and regional stories, one minute for key national and international stories, one minute for sports, and 15 seconds for weather information. A 30- or 60-second commercial break will be counted as part of the five-minute newscast.

The number of stories in a newscast may be preordained by program management or may vary depending on the significance and scope of the stories being reported. News policy may require that no stories, except in particular cases, exceed 15 seconds. Here, the idea is to deliver as many stories as possible in the limited time available, the underlying sentiment being that more is better. In 5 minutes, 15–20 items may be covered. In contrast, other stations prefer that key stories be addressed in greater detail. As few as 5–10 news items may be broadcast at stations taking this approach.

Stories are arranged according to their rank of importance, the most significant story of the hour topping the news. An informed newsperson will know what stories deserve the most attention. Wire services weigh each story and position them accordingly in news roundups. The local radio newsperson decides what wire stories will be aired and in what order.

Assembling a five-minute newscast takes skill, speed, and accuracy. Stories must be updated and rewritten to keep news broadcasts from sounding stale.

This often requires that telephone calls be made for late-breaking information. Meanwhile, on-the-scene voicers (actualities) originating from audio news services (UPI, AP) or fed by local reporters must be recorded and slotted in the newscast. "Preparing a fresh newscast each hour can put

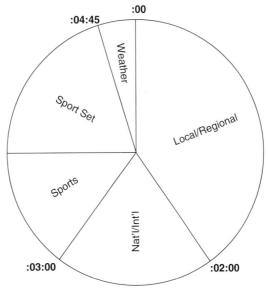

FIGURE 5.9
Five-minute newscast format clock.

FIGURE 5.10
A top market news station offers a profile of itself. Courtesy Infinity.

WBZ NEWS RADIO **1030**

1170 SOLDIERS FIELD ROAD BOSTON MASSACHUSETTS 02134 TELEPHONE (617) 787-7000

WBZ NewsRadio 1030

A BRIEF DESCRIPTION

WBZ NewsRadio, the first commercially licensed station in the country, has been broadcasting to New Englanders for almost 80 years. Our award winning coverage has earned WBZ many honors including 2000's "News Station of the Year," from the Associated Press, and three recent Marconi Awards, "The Most Prestigious Radio Award Available."

 WBZ has close to a million listeners weekly. The exclusive all news format creates a foreground listening environment, that delivers results for our advertisers.

 Our award winning news anchors and reporters have an aggregate experience level of over 100+ years in broadcasting!

 Our combined resources of both radio and television make up the largest news gathering organization in New England. Many of our radio anchors gain exposure daily on WBZ-TV 4 adding to their tremendous popularity.

 WBZ highlights advertisers' messages by airing commercials as islands surrounded by news, traffic, weather or business reports. During our news, your commercial is always the first and only sixty second commercial in a commercial break.

 WBZ's 50,000 watt clear channel signal reaches all of New England, and at night 38 states and six Canadian Providences. Our reach is unparalleled!

 We maintain a 52 week marketing campaign promoting ourselves on TV, print, web, and at countless on-site events throughout New England.

 WBZ is a leader in community involvement spearheading many events including Children's Hospital Telethon and fundraising, Call for Action, Domestic Violence and StormCenter.

 WBZ is the flagship station for the Boston Bruins and the Boston Bruins Radio Network and the only place fans can catch every game every time they play.

you in mind of what it must have been like to be a contestant on the old game show 'Beat the Clock.' A conscientious newsperson is a vision of perpetual motion," observes Cecilia Mason.

Finally, most news people read their news copy before going on the air. "Reading stories cold is foolhardy and invites trouble. Even the most seasoned newscasters at metro market stations take the time to read over their copy before going on," comments Whitman. Many news people read copy aloud in the news studio before airtime. This gives them a chance to get a feel for their copy. Proper preparation prevents unpleasant surprises from occurring while on the air.

Wire and Internet Services

Without the aid of the major broadcast news wire services and the inestimable number of news-oriented Web sites that exist (CNN, MSNBC, Fox, Drudge Report, etc.) and blogs, radio stations would find it almost impossible to cover news on national and international levels. The wire services and Internet are a vital source of news information to nearly all of the nation's commercial radio stations. Both large and small stations rely on the news copy fed them by either the AP or the UP International (UPI), the two most prominent news wire services. Meanwhile, the Internet is a primary source of data and information.

Broadcast wire services came into existence in the mid-1930s, when UP (which became UPI in 1958 after merging with INS) began providing broadcasters with news copy. Today, the UPI and AP serve over 7500 broadcast outlets.

Both news sources supply subscriber stations with around-the-clock coverage of national and world events. Over 100,000 stringers furnish stories from across the globe. The AP and UPI also maintain regional bureaus for the dissemination of local news. Each wire service transmits over 20 complete news summaries daily. In addition, they provide weather, stock market, and sports information, as well as a formidable list of features and data useful to

the station's news and programming efforts. Rates for wire service vary depending on the size of the radio market, and audio service is available for an additional fee. Some 1800 stations use UPI and AP audio news feeds.

Broadcasters are evenly divided over the question as to which is the best wire service. Each news service has about the same number of radio stations under contract.

Both major wire services have kept pace with the new technologies. In the mid-1980s, UPI alone purchased 6000 Z-15 desktop computers from Zenith Data Systems. Satellites also are used by the two news organizations for the transmission of teletype, teletext, and audio. The wire services have become as wireless as the wireless medium itself.

The audio cuts provided by the news services are an integral part of most station newscasts. Observes radio scholar Larry Miller, "When these audio clips are sent to subscribing stations, they will also send along a menu which will list the type of cut (A-actuality, V-voicer, or W-wrap), who it is, what it's about, how long it runs, and the outcue. Miller cautions that audio cuts should be used sparingly, "They should not be overused to pad out a newscast. Relevance, audio quality, and length should rule the decisions regarding how much audio to use. With the proper application of these sources, even a one-person news operation can sound like a big city newsroom."

Radio Network News

During the medium's first three decades, the terms *networks* and *news* were virtually synonymous. Most of the news broadcast over America's radio stations emanated from the networks. The public's dependence on network radio news reached its height during World War II. As television succeeded radio as the mainstay for entertainment programming in the 1950s and 1960s, the networks concentrated their efforts on supplying affiliates with news and information feeds. This approach helped the networks regain their footing in radio after a period of substantial decline. By the mid-1960s, the majority of the nation's stations used one of the four major networks for news programming.

In 1968, ABC decided to make available four distinct news formats designed for compatibility with the dominant sounds of the day. American Contemporary Radio Network, American FM Radio Network, American Entertainment Radio Network, and American Information Network each offered a unique style and method of news presentation. ABC's venture proved enormously successful. In the 1970s, over 1500 stations subscribed to one of ABC's four news networks.

In response to a growing racial and ethnic awareness, the Mutual Broadcasting System (MBS) launched two minority news networks in 1971. Though the network's Black news service proved to be a fruitful venture, its Spanish news service ceased operation within two years of its inception. Mutual discovered that the ethnic group simply was too refracted and diverse to be effectively serviced by one network and that the Latin listeners they did attract did not constitute the numbers necessary to justify operation.

In 1973, the network also went head-to-head with ABC by offering a network news service (Mutual Progressive Network) that catered to rock-oriented stations. Mutual's various efforts paid off by making it second only to ABC in number of affiliates. After years of financial difficulties, MBS went silent in 1999, ending nearly seven decades of radio news service.

The News and Information Service (NIS) was introduced by NBC in 1975 but ended in 1977. NIS offered client stations an All-News format. Fifty minutes of news was fed to stations each hour. The venture was abandoned after only moderate acceptance. CBS, which has offered its member stations World News Roundup since 1938, and NBC have under 300 affiliates apiece.

Several state and regional news networks do well, but the big three, ABC, NBC, and CBS, continue to dominate. Meanwhile, independent satellite news and information networks and the cable news services, such as CNN, have joined the field and more are planned.

FIGURE 5.11
Charles Osgood commentaries are a popular feature at News/Talk stations. Courtesy CBS.

The usual length of a network newscast is five minutes, during which time affiliates are afforded an opportunity to insert local sponsor messages at designated times. The networks make their money by selling national advertisers spot availabilities in their widely broadcast news. Stations also pay the networks a fee for the programming they receive.

According to Metro Network president David Saperstein, today "more and more stations are realizing the benefits that exist in outside news services, which provide the information that listeners would otherwise seek elsewhere. This allows the station to focus its marketing dollars, thus directing resources toward optimizing and maintaining what draws and keeps listeners." Of course, this latter trend has raised additional concerns about the decline in local news coverage as cited in recent RTNDA surveys. Station consolidations have resulted in the erosion of local news operations.

Radio Sportscasts

Sports is most commonly presented as an element within newscasts (refer back to Figure 5.9). Although many stations air sports as programming features unto themselves, most stations insert information, such as scores and schedules of upcoming games, at a designated point in a newscast and call it sports. Whether a station emphasizes sports largely depends on its audience. Stations gearing their format for youngsters or women often all but ignore

FIGURE 5.12
A provides the news
copy. Courtesy AP.

Radio

AP NewsPower MAX

Get minute-to-minute news coverage, 24 hours a day, seven days a week, with the AP NewsPower MAX wire, AP's highest level of service for radio stations.

Combining the speed and air-ready service of NewsPower+ 24 Hours with the in-depth resources of AP's print-style news and sports wires, NewsPower MAX gives you the full background on stories so you can develop your own material from our resources.

With AP NewsPower MAX, you can localize AP's state and national stories, do your own rewrites, or use the detailed information we provide to find contacts and to know where to assign your reporters. NewsPower MAX also includes two additional newsroom research tools: The Planner and the Washington Daybook.

AP Coverage Rundown is a look ahead at what stories AP Broadcast is covering and how we plan to cover them. The Rundown moves six times per day on weekdays and twice on weekends.

The Washington Daybook is an in-depth listing of all the stories on tap in Washington, including detailed contact and set-up information.

Like all AP wires, NewsPower MAX is selectable by category, so you can customize it to your newsroom's needs.

Interested? Click here to request more information about AP NewsPower Max.

Click here to request a short-term demo of AP NewsPower Max.

sports. Adult-oriented stations, such as Middle-of-the-Road, will frequently offer a greater abundance of sports information, especially when the station is located in an area that has a major league team.

Stations that hire individuals to do sports, and invariably these are larger outlets since few small stations can afford a full-time sportsperson, look for someone who is well versed in athletics. "To be good at radio sports, you have to have been involved as a participant somewhere along the line. That's for starters, in my opinion. This doesn't mean that you have to be a former major leaguer before doing radio sports but to have a feel for what you're talking about, it certainly helps to have been on the field or court yourself. A good sportscaster must have the ability to accurately analyze

a sport through the eyes and body of the athlete," contends radio sports director John Colletto.

Unlike news that requires an impartial and somewhat austere presentation, sportscasts frequently are delivered in a casual and even opinionated manner. "Let's face it, there's a big difference between nuclear arms talks between the United States and the Soviets and last night's Red Sox/Yankees score. I don't think sports reports should be treated in a style that's too solemn. It's entertainment, and sportscasters should exercise their license to comment and analyze," says Colletto.

Although sports is presented in a less heavy-handed way than news, credibility is an important factor, contends Colletto. "There is a need for radio sportscasters to establish credibility just as there is for news people to do so. If you're not believable, you're not listened to. The best way to win the respect of your audience is by demonstrating a thorough knowledge of the game and by sounding like an insider, not just a guy reading the wire copy. Remember, sports fans can be as loyal to a sportscaster as they are to their favorite team. They want to hear the stories and scores from a person they feel comfortable with."

The style of a news story and a sports story may differ considerably. Although news is written in a no-frills, straightforward way, sports stories often contain colorful colloquialisms and even popular slang. Here is an example by radio sportswriter Roger Crosley:

THE DEAN COLLEGE RED DEMON FOOTBALL TEAM RODE THE STRONG RUNNING OF FULLBACK BILL PALAZOLLO YESTERDAY TO AN 18–16 COME FROM BEHIND VICTORY OVER THE AMERICAN INTERNATIONAL COLLEGE JUNIOR VARSITY YELLOW JACKETS. PALAZOLLO CHURNED OUT A TEAM HIGH 93 YARDS ON TWENTY-FIVE CARRIES AND SCORED ALL THREE TOUCHDOWNS ON BLASTS OF 7, 2, AND 6 YARDS. THE DEMONS TRAILED THE HARD-HITTING CONTEST 16–6 ENTERING THE FINAL QUARTER. PALAZOLLO CAPPED A TWELVE-PLAY 81-YARD DRIVE WITH HIS SECOND SIX-POINTER EARLY IN THE STANZA AND SCORED THE CLINCHER WITH 4:34 REMAINING. THE DEMONS WILL PUT THEIR 1 AND 0 RECORD ON THE LINE NEXT SUNDAY AT 1:30 AGAINST THE ALWAYS TOUGH HOLY CROSS JAYVEES IN WORCESTER.

Sportscasters are personalities, says Colletto, and as such must be able to communicate on a different level than newscasters. "You're expected to have a sense of humor. Most successful sportscasters can make an audience smile or laugh. You have to be able to ad-lib, also."

The wire services, networks, and Internet are the primary source for sports news at local stations. On the other hand, information about the outcome of local games, such as high school football and so forth, must be acquired firsthand. This usually entails a call to the team's coach or a direct report from a stringer or reporter.

In August 1967, WCBS Radio became WCBS NEWSRADIO. During those 15 years, WCBS has become the station millions of people rely on for radio news. And today, WCBS is listened to by more adults than any other radio station in the country.

For radio news, the biggest...and.... the best in the business.

WCBS NEWSRADIO New York

New York Arbitron, Spring '82 TSA TOTAL WEEK CUME ESTIMATES, ADULTS 18 +

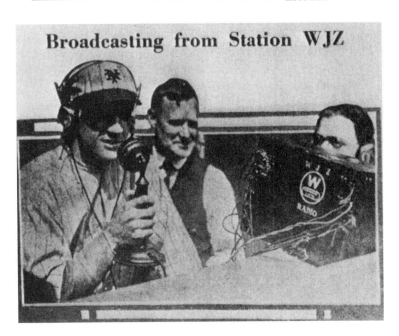

FIGURE 5.13 Network-affiliated All-News stations, such as WCBS, invest heavily in promotion in efforts to establish a strong image in their markets. Courtesy of WCBS.

FIGURE 5.14 Sports on radio in 1923. Today sports programming generates a significant percentage of the medium's annual income. Courtesy Westinghouse Electric.

Radio News and the FCC

The government takes a greater role in regulating broadcast journalism than it does print. Although it usually maintains a hands-off position when it comes to newspapers, the government keeps a watchful eye on radio to ensure that it meets certain operating criteria. Since the FCC perceives the airways as public domain, it expects broadcasters to operate in the public's interest.

The FCC requires that radio reporters present news factually and in good faith.

Stories that defame citizens through reckless or false statements may not only bring a libel suit from the injured party but action from the FCC, which views such behavior on the part of broadcasters as contrary to the public's interest. Broadcasters are protected under the First Amendment and therefore have certain rights, but as public trustees, they are charged with the additional responsibility of acting in a manner that benefits rather than harms members of society.

Broadcasters are free to express opinions and sentiments on issues through editorials. However, to avoid controversy, many radio stations choose not to editorialize even though the FCC encourages them to do so.

News Ethics

The highly competitive nature of radio places unusual pressure on news people. In a business where being first with the story is often equated with being the best, certain dangers exist. Being first at all costs can be costly, indeed, if information and facts are not adequately verified. As previously mentioned, it is the radio journalist's obligation to get the story straight and accurate before putting it on the air. Anything short of this is unprofessional.

The pressures of the clock, if allowed, can result in haphazard reporting. If a story cannot be sufficiently prepared in time for the upcoming news broadcast, it should be withheld. Getting it on-air is not as important as getting it on-air right. Accuracy is the newsperson's first criterion. News accounts should never be fudged. It is tantamount to deceiving and misleading the public.

News reporters must exhibit discretion not only in the newsroom but also when on the scene of a story. It is commendable to assiduously pursue the facts and details of a story, but it is inconsiderate and insensitive to ignore the suffering and pain of those involved. For example, to press for comments from a grief-stricken parent whose child has just been seriously injured in an accident is callous and cruel and a disservice to all concerned, including the station

the newsperson represents. Of course, a newsperson wants as much information as possible about an incident, but the public's right to privacy must be respected.

Objectivity is the cornerstone of good reporting. A newsperson who has lost his or her capacity to see the whole picture is handicapped. At the same time, the newsperson's job is to report the news and not create it. The mere presence of a member of the media can inspire a disturbance or agitate a volatile situation. Staging an event for the sake of increasing the newsiness of a story is not only unprofessional but illegal. Groups have been known to await the arrival of reporters before initiating a disturbance for the sake of gaining publicity. It is the duty of reporters to remain as innocuous and uninvolved as possible when on an assignment. Recall Indra de Silva's comment earlier about the need for news to be presented in a thoughtful and conscientious way.

Several industry associations, such as RTNDA and Society of Professional Journalists, have established codes pertaining to the ethics and conduct of broadcast reporters.

Traffic Reports

Traffic reports are an integral part of drivetime news programming at many metropolitan radio stations. Although providing listeners with traffic condition updates can be costly, especially air-to-ground reports that require the use of a helicopter or small plane, they can help strengthen a station's community service image and also generate substantial revenue. To avoid the cost involved in airborne observation, stations sometimes employ the services of local auto clubs or put their own mobile units out on the roads. A station in Providence, Rhode Island, broadcasts traffic conditions from atop a 20-story hotel that overlooks the city's key arteries. Fixed cameras at key traffic locations are also used.

Says David Saperstein, "Companies like Metro Network provide stations with outside traffic reporting services in a manner that is more cost- and quality-effective than a station handling it themselves."

Traffic reports are scheduled several times an hour throughout the prime commuter periods on stations primarily catering to adults, and they range in length from 30–90 seconds. The actual reports may be done by a station employee who works in other areas of programming when not surveying the roads, or a member of the local police department or auto club may be hired for the job. Obviously, the prime criterion for such a position is a thorough knowledge of the streets and highways of the area being reported.

News in Music Radio

In 1980s, the FCC saw fit to eliminate the requirement that all radio stations devote a percentage of their broadcast day to news and public affairs programming. Opponents of the decision argued that such a move would mark the decline of news on radio. In contrast, proponents of the deregulation commended the FCC's actions that allow for the marketplace to determine the extent to which nonentertainment features are broadcast. In the late 1980s, RTNDA expressed the concern that local news coverage had declined. This, they said, had resulted in a decrease in the number of news positions around the country. Supporting their contention they pointed out that several major stations, such as KDKA, WOWO, and WIND, had cut back their news budgets.

At that time, RTNDA's Bob Priddy noted, "There has been a perceived decline in the amount of news broadcast. I don't see this as a cold-hearted act on the part of station managers, but rather one frequently inspired by economics. The decline in news programming is particularly alarming when you realize that it is at a time when a number of new stations are entering the airwaves."

In 1992, RTNDA's president, Dave Bartlett, declared, "Deregulation really hasn't taken news off radio. News is far from dead on the medium. The vast majority do news. All deregulation did was allow the marketplace to adjust at will. A lot of shifting has occurred, but the aggregate is the same." A couple of years later, a survey published in

FIGURE 5.15
Information features are popular elements of news and public affairs programming. Courtesy CRN.

FIGURE 5.16
Traffic reports are often a central element of news broadcasts. Courtesy Metro Traffic.

the association's newsletter, *Communicator*, told a different story. The report revealed that hundreds of radio newsrooms had, in fact, closed down and it suggested that many more would likely occur. In 1994, *Radio World* reported that over 1100 radio news operations had closed since the deregulation of the medium.

FIGURE 5.17
UPI news wire providing copy to the Spanish language station. Courtesy UPI.

United Press International
News. Analysis. Insight.

| Home | Content Solutions | News and Events | Partners | About Us | Contact Us | Advertise Online |

SPANISH DESK

UPI's Spanish-language content products include UPI LatAm News Service, UPI LatAm Headlines, and UPI Chilean News Service. Correspondents in Argentina, Brazil, Chile, Colombia, Costa Rica, Mexico, Peru, Uruguay, and the United States form part of UPI's worldwide network of coverage.

The UPI LatAm News Service provides coverage of the major stories that affect the Spanish-speaking world, focusing on the affairs of Latin America and the United States. Stories from UPI's LatAm News Service are tailored to meet the needs of web sites that need frequently changing news items, publications looking for short stories and broadcasters in need of current news. UPI LatAm is also an effective source of information for corporations and financial institutions doing business in Latin America.

Areas of specialty include:

- **Latin America** – The major stories affecting politics, justice, the military and human rights issues.
- **Business** – Issues such as the regional free trade agreements, business regulations and economics.
- **Sports** – A variety of sporting events including soccer, basketball, tennis and Formula One.
- **Science** – Coverage of health, genetics and emerging technologies.
- **Entertainment** – The major stories in music, movies, television and theater.

FIGURE 5.18
A reporter in the news booth at Moscow radio station *Mayak* gives an update. Courtesy *Mayak* and Anna Yudin.

News director Sherman Whitman believes that the radio audience wants news even when a station's primary product is music. "The public has come to depend on the medium to keep it informed. It's a volatile world and certain events affect us all. Stations that aim to be full-service cannot do so without a solid news schedule."

Cecilia Mason says that economics alone will help keep news a viable entity at many radio stations. "While a lot of stations consider news departments expense centers, news is a money maker. This is especially true during drivetime periods when practically everyone tuned wants information, be it weather, sports, or news headlines. I don't see a growing movement to eliminate news. However, I do see a movement to soften things up, that is, to hire voices instead of radio journalists. In the long run, this means fewer news jobs, I suppose. Economics again. While stations, for the most part, are not appreciably reducing the amount of time devoted to airing news, I suspect that some may be thinning out their news departments. Hopefully, this is not a prelude to a measurable cutback. News is still big business, though."

"Responsible broadcasters know that it is the inherent duty of the medium to keep the public apprised of what is going on," claims Larry Jewett. "While radio is primarily an entertainment medium, it is still one of the country's foremost sources of information. Responsible broadcasters – and most of us are – realize that we have a special obligation to fulfill. The tremendous reach and immediacy that is unique to radio forces the medium to be something more than just a jukebox."

News director Frank Titus believes that stations will continue to broadcast news in the future. "There might be a tendency to invest less in news operations, especially at more music-oriented outlets, as the result of the regulation change and rampant consolidations, but news is as much a part of what radio is as are the deejays and songs. What it comes right down to is people want news broadcasts, so they're going to get them. That's the whole idea behind the commission's FCC's actions. There's no doubt in my mind that the marketplace will continue to dictate the programming of radio news."

News director Roger Nadel concurs. "As the age of the average listener increases, even people tuning in 'music' stations find themselves in need of at least minimal doses of news. So long as those stations are doing well financially, owners can be content to maintain some kind of a news operation. News is not likely to disappear; not even at music stations."

In recent years, this optimism has significantly diminished as a result of station clustering, consolidation, and downsizing and the continued elimination of radio news requirements. Competition from the wave of new audio services has also influenced the role of news in terrestrial radio.

CHAPTER HIGHLIGHTS

1. Although the first newscast occurred in 1910, broadcast journalism did not evolve until the early 1920s. The broadcast of the Harding–Cox election results in 1920 was a historical benchmark.

2. Because newspapers perceived radio as a competitive threat, UP, INS, and AP refused to sell to radio outlets from 1932 until 1934. Radio, however, proved that it could provide its own news sources.

3. The advent of television led radio outlets to localize their news content, which meant less reliance on news networks and the creation of a station news department.

4. Surveys by the National Association of Broadcasters and the Radio Advertising Bureau found that more people tune in to radio news for their first daily source of information than turn to television or newspapers.

5. The size of a station's news staff depends on the degree to which the station's format emphasizes news, the station's market size, the emphasis of its competition, and station consolidations. Small stations often have no news people and require deejays to "rip 'n' read" wire service copy.

6. Large news staffs may consist of newscasters, writers, street reporters, and tech people, as well as stringers and interns.

7. Computers in radio newsrooms are used as links to the various wire, news, audio, and database services, as display terminals for reading news copy on the air, and as word processors for writing and storing news. Software is available to newsrooms for archiving and other purposes.

8. The news director, who works with and for the PD, supervises news staff, develops and implements policy, handles the budget, ensures the gathering of local news, is responsible for getting out breaking news stories rapidly and accurately and plans public affairs programming.

9. News directors seek personnel with both college education and experience. However, finding a news slot at a small station is difficult since its news staffs are small, so internships and experience at high school and college stations are important. In addition, such personal qualities as enthusiasm, aggressiveness, energy, inquisitiveness, keyboarding skills, a knowledge of the area where the station is located, announcing abilities, and a command of the English language are assets.

10. News stories must be legible, intelligible, and designed for effortless reading. They should sound conversational, informal, simple, direct, concise, and organized.

11. Actualities (on-the-scene voicers) are obtained from news service feeds, online sources, and by station personnel at the scene.

12. Wire services and the Internet are the primary sources of national and international news for most stations. AP and UPI are the largest news wire services.

13. The FCC expects broadcasters to report the news in a balanced and impartial manner. Although protected under the First Amendment, broadcasters making reckless or false statements are subject to both civil and FCC charges.

14. Ethically, newspersons must maintain objectivity, discretion, and sensitivity.

15. The FCC's deregulation of news and public affairs programming in the 1980s, widespread station clustering in recent years due to consolidation, and emerging new information media have prompted concerns by industry officials and others that radio news service is on the decline if not on the cusp of extinction.

SUGGESTED FURTHER READING

Anderson, B., *News Flash: Journalism, Infotainment, and the Bottom-Line Business of Broadcast News*, Jossey-Bass, San Francisco, CA, 2004.

Bartlett, J., editor, *The First Amendment in a Free Society*, H. W. Wilson, New York, 1979.

Bittner, J.R., and Bittner, D.A., *Radio Journalism*, Prentice Hall, Englewood Cliffs, NJ, 1977.

Bliss, E.J., and Patterson, J.M., *Writing News for Broadcast*, 2nd edition, Columbia University Press, New York, 1978.

Bliss, E.J., *Now the News*, Oxford Press, New York, 1991.

Block, M., *Broadcast News Writing for Professionals*, Marion Street Press, Oak Park, IL, 2005.

Boyd, A., *Broadcast Journalism*, 5th edition, Focal Press, Boston, MA, 2008.

Boyer, P.J., *Who Killed CBS?* Random House, New York, 1988.

Charnley, M., *News by Radio*, Macmillan, New York, 1948.

Culbert, D.H., *News for Everyman: Radio and Foreign Affairs in Thirties America*, Greenwood Press, Westport, CT, 1976.

Day, L.A., *Ethics in Media Communications*, Wadsworth Publishing, Belmont, CA, 1991.

Fang, I., *Radio News/Television News*, 2nd edition, Rada Press, St. Paul, MN, 1985.

Fang, I., *Those Radio Commentators*, Iowa State University Press, Ames, IA, 1977.

Friendly, F.W., *The Good Guys, The Bad Guys, and the First Amendment: Free Speech vs. Fairness in Broadcasting*, Random House, New York, 1976.

Frost, C., *Reporting for Journalists*, Routledge, New York, 2002.

Garvey, D.E., *News Writing for the Electronic Media*, Wadsworth Publishing, Belmont, CA, 1982.

Gibson, R., *Radio and Television Reporting*, Allyn & Bacon, Boston, MA, 1991.

Gilbert, B., *Perry's Broadcast News Handbook*, Perry Publishing, Knoxville, TN, 1982.

Hall, M.W., *Broadcast Journalism: An Introduction to News Writing*, Hastings House, New York, 1978.

Hitchcock, J.R., *Sportscasting*, Focal Press, Boston, MA, 1991.

Hood, J.R., and Kalbfeld, B., editors, *The Associated Press Handbook*, Associated Press, New York, 1982.

Hunter, J.K., *Broadcast News*, C.V. Mosby Company, St. Louis, MO, 1980.

Johnston, C., *Election Coverage: Blueprint for Broadcasters*, Focal Press, Boston, MA, 1991.

Kalbfeld, B., *Broadcast News Handbook*, McGraw Hill, New York, 2000.

Keirstead, P.A., *All-News Radio*, Tab Books, Blue Ridge Summit, PA, 1980.

Keirstead, P.A., *Computers in Broadcast and Cable Newsrooms*, Erlbaum, Mahwah, NJ, 2005.

Mayeux, P., *Broadcast News Writing and Reporting*, Waveland Press, Chicago, IL, 2000.

Nelson, H.L., *Laws of Mass Communication*, The Foundation Press, Mineola, NY, 1982.

Raiteri, C., *Writing for Broadcast News*, Roman & Littlefield, Lanham, MD, 2005.

Shrivastava, K.M., *Broadcast Journalism in the 21st Century*, New Dawn Press, Elgin, IL, 2004.

Simmons, S.J., *The Fairness Doctrine and the Media*, University of California Press, Berkeley, CA, 1978.

Stephens, M., *Broadcast News: Radio Journalism and an Introduction to Television*, Holt, Rinehart and Winston, New York, 1980.

UPI Stylebook: A Handbook for Writing and Preparing Broadcast News, United Press International, New York, 1979.

Wenge., D., and Potter, D., *Advancing the Story: Broadcast Journalism in a Multimedia World*, CQ Press, Washington, DC, 2007.

White, T., *Broadcast News Writing*, 4th edition, Macmillan, New York, 2006.

Wulfemeyer, K.T., *Broadcast News-Writing*, Iowa State University Press, Ames, IA, 1995.

6

Research

Who Is Listening?

As early as 1929, the question of listenership was of interest to broadcasters and advertisers alike. That year Cooperative Analysis of Broadcasting (CAB), headed by Archibald M. Crossley, undertook a study to determine how many people were tuned to certain network radio programs. Information was gathered by phoning a preselected sample of homes. One of the things the survey found was that the majority of listening occurred evenings between 7:00 and 11:00 P.M. This became known as radio's "prime time" until the 1950s.

On the local station level, various methods were employed to collect audience data, including telephone interviews and mail-out questionnaires. However, only a nominal amount of actual audience research was attempted during the late 1920s and early 1930s. For the most part, just who was listening remained somewhat of a mystery until the late 1930s.

In 1938, C.E. Hooper, Inc. began the most formidable attempt up to that time to provide radio broadcasters with audience information. Like Crossley's service, Hooper also used the telephone to accumulate listener data. CAB relied on listener recall; Hooper, however, required that interviewers make calls until they reached someone who was actually listening to the radio. This approach became known as the "coincidental" telephone method. Both survey services found their efforts limited by the fact that 40% of the radio-listening homes in the 1930s were without a telephone.

As World War II approached, another major ratings service, known as the Pulse, began to measure radio audience size. Unlike its competitors, Pulse collected information by conducting face-to-face interviews. Interest in audience research grew steadily throughout the 1930s and culminated in the establishment of the Office of Radio Research (ORR) in 1937. Funded by a Rockefeller Foundation grant, the ORR was headed by Paul F. Lazarsfeld, who was assisted by Hadley Cantril and Frank Stanton. The latter would go on to assume the presidency of CBS in 1946 and would serve in that capacity into the 1970s. Over a 10-year period, the ORR published several texts dealing with audience research findings and methodology. Among them were Lazarsfeld and Stanton's multivolume *Radio Research*, which covered the periods of 1941–1943 and 1948–1949. During the same decade, Lazarsfeld also published book-length reports on the public's attitude toward radio: *The People Look at Radio* (1946) and *Radio Listening in America* (1948). Both works cast radio in a favorable light by concluding that most listeners felt the medium did an exemplary job. The Pulse and Hooper were the prevailing radio station rating services in the 1950s as the medium worked at regaining its footing following the meteoric rise of television. In 1965, Arbitron Ratings began measuring radio audience size through the use of a diary, which required respondents to document their listening habits over a seven-day period. By the 1970s, Arbitron reigned as the leading radio measurement company, whereas Hooper and Pulse faded

Ed Cohen	On Arbitron

FIGURE 6.1
Ed Cohen.

Really, the role of Arbitron is still the currency (sales) aspect tied in with Scarborough and other qualitative services to try and differentiate close competitors to agencies and major advertisers. Sure, Arbitron is used for programming and many programmers and talent (that still have jobs)

are bonused on Arbitron results, but the prime use is setting rates. The qualitative aspect is becoming more important, especially with Portable People Meter (PPM) where there is little difference in audience size between the top stations and those further down in the ranker.

from the scene. To provide the radio networks and their affiliates and advertisers with much-needed ratings information, Statistical Research, Inc., of New Jersey, introduced Radio's All Dimension Audience Research (RADAR) in 1968. The company gathers its information through telephone interviews with more than 6000 households. In the 1990s, Arbitron retained its hold on first place among services measuring radio audiences, especially since the demise of Birch/Scarborough, which gained considerable acceptance following its debut in the late 1970s. In 1991, this audience measurement company became yet another victim of the economic malaise.

Ratings companies must be reliable, and credibility is crucial to success. Therefore, measurement techniques must be tried and true. Information must be accurate, since millions of dollars are at stake. In 1963, the Broadcast Rating Council was established to monitor, audit, and accredit the various ratings companies. The council created performance standards to which rating services are expected to adhere. Those that fail to meet the council's operating criteria are not accredited. A nonaccredited ratings service will seldom succeed. In 1982, the Broadcast Rating Council was renamed the Electronic Media Planning Council to reflect a connection with the ratings services dealing with the cable television industry.

Renamed the Media Rating Council (MRC) in 1997 to include Internet constituencies, the MRC's declared purpose is (1) to secure for the industry and related

users audience measurement services that are valid, reliable, and effective, (2) to avoid and determine minimum disclosure and ethical criteria for media audience measurement services, and (3) to provide and administer an audit system designed to inform users as to whether such audience measurements are conducted in conformance with the criteria and procedures developed.

The Ratings and Survey Services

The extreme fragmentation of today's listening audience, created by the almost inestimable number of stations and formats, makes the job of research a complex but necessary one. All stations, regardless of size, must put forth an effort to acquaint themselves with the characteristics of the audience, says Edward J. Noonan, codirector, Survey Research Associates. "A station cannot operate in a vacuum. It has to know who is listening and why before making any serious programming changes." Today, this information is made available through several ratings services and research companies. More stations depend on Arbitron audience surveys than any other.

Since the collapse of Birch/Scarborough, broadcasters have had little choice but to subscribe to Arbitron – that or go without the listening estimates on which so many agencies and advertisers rely. However, the radio audience survey industry has begun

184

FIGURE 6.2
The Portable People
Meter is the newest
method for tracking
listening. Courtesy
Arbitron.

to expand, if only slowly. For example, in recent years, additional listener/ratings services have begun to emerge. AccuRatings is one example. It began to measure audiences in major metropolitan areas in the mid-1990s. Troy research is another. It relies on Internet-based research that involves online surveys pertaining to stations' music playlists. Similar companies were beginning to surface to the relief of many broadcasters concerned with Arbitron's hold. Arbitron's dominance has indeed caused anxiety in the radio community. Many managers and programmers were more than disturbed by the failure of the alternative measurement service. Arbitron covers over 250 markets ranging in size from large to small. Arbitron claims over 2700 radio clients and a staff of 3000 interviewers who collect listening information from 2 million households across the country. All markets are measured at least once a year during the spring; however, larger markets are measured on an ongoing basis year round. Until the early 1980s, metro markets traditionally were rated in the spring and fall. However, 6 months between surveys was considered too long in light of the volatile nature of the radio marketplace.

To determine a station's ranking, Arbitron follows an elaborate procedure. First, the parameters of the area to be surveyed are established. Arbitron sees fit to measure listening both in the city or urban center, which it refers to as the Metro Survey Area

(MSA), and in the surrounding communities or suburbs, which it classifies Total Survey Area (TSA). Arbitron classifies a station's primary listening locations as its Areas of Dominant Influence (ADI).

Once the areas to be measured have been ascertained, the next thing Arbitron does is select a sample base composed of individuals to be queried regarding their listening habits. Metro-mail provides Arbitron with computer tapes that contain telephone and mailing lists from which the rating company derives its randomly selected sample. Arbitron conducts its surveys over a 3- to 4-week period, during which time new samples are selected weekly.

When the sample has been established, a letter is sent to each targeted household. The replacement letter informs members of the sample that they have been selected to participate in a radio-listening survey and asks their cooperation. Within a couple of days after the letter has been received, an Arbitron interviewer calls to describe the purpose of the survey as well as to determine how many individuals aged 12 or older reside in the household. Upon receiving the go-ahead, Arbitron mails its 7-day survey diary, which requires respondees to log their listening habits. An incentive stipend of a dollar or two accompanies the document. The diary is simple to deal with, and the information it requests is quite basic: time (day/part) tuned to a station, station call letters or program name, whether AM or FM, and where listening occurred – car, home, elsewhere. Although the diary asks for information pertaining to age, sex, and residence, the actual identity or name of those participating is not requested.

Prior to the start of the survey, a representative of Arbitron makes a presurvey follow-up call to those who have agreed to participate. This is done to make certain that the diary has been received and that everyone involved understands how to maintain it. Another follow-up call is made during the middle of the survey week to ascertain if the diary is being kept and to remind each participant to return it promptly on completion of the survey. Outside the metro area, follow-ups take the form of a letter. The diaries are mailed

REPORT CONTENTS AND MAP PAGE

This is the first page of an Arbitron Radio Market Report. This page, in addition to showing a map of the Radio Market survey area and table of Report contents, contains a basic introduction to the Report, restrictions on the use of the Report, a copyright infringement warning, the survey time period, frequency of measurement and Arbitron's schedule of radio surveys for the year.

1▶ The map shows the survey area(s) included in a market definition and for which audience estimates are reported. Areas in grey are not included in a market definition (unless it is a part of an ADI to be reported for that particular market) and will have no audience estimates included in the Report.

2▶ The Metro Survey Area (MSA) of the reported market is shown by horizontal hatching.

3▶ The Total Survey Area (TSA) of the reported market is shown in white.

4▶ The Areas of Dominant Influence (ADI) of the reported market, if applicable, is shown by diagonal hatching.

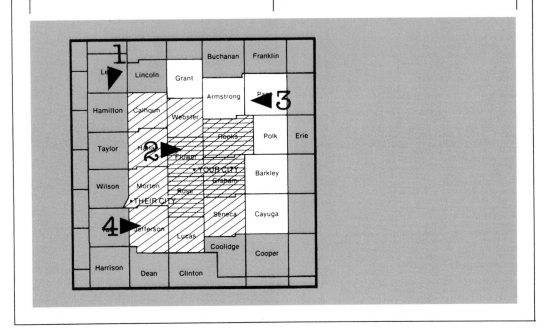

FIGURE 6.3
First page of an Arbitron Radio Market Report containing an explanation of what constitutes the survey area. Courtesy Arbitron.

to Beltsville, Maryland, for processing and computation.

Arbitron claims that 65 of every 100 diaries it receives are usable. Diaries that are inadequately or inaccurately filled out are not used. Upon arriving at Arbitron headquarters, diaries are examined by editors and rejected if they fail to meet criteria. Any diary received before the conclusion of the survey period is immediately

FIGURE 6.4
Arbitron sample
explanation.
Courtesy Arbitron.

POPULATION ESTIMATES AND SAMPLE DISTRIBUTION BY AGE/SEX GROUP

1▶ The estimated populations of reported demographic categories within survey area(s) are reported for the Metro Survey Area, Area of Dominant Influence (where applicable), and the Total Survey Area.

2▶ The ratio (expressed as a percentage) of each reported demographic's estimated population to the estimated population of all persons age 12 or older within the relevant survey area.

3▶ The number of unweighted diaries in-tab, from persons in reported demographics, expressed as a percentage of the total number of unweighted in-tab diaries from all persons age 12 or older.

4▶ The distribution of in-tab diaries after weighting for reported demographics expressed as a percentage of the total number of tabulated diaries from all persons age 12 or older.

5▶ The total persons age 12 or older in the Metro and the percent of those persons living in military housing, college dormitories and other group quarters.

6▶ The number of estimated residences in the predesignated sample, number of homes contacted, number of homes in which diaries were placed, number of persons with whom diaries were placed and the number of persons who returned usable diaries (see The Sample, Section II, for further definition of these terms) are reported for Metro, ADI (if applicable), and TSA. Standard and ESF sample statistics are reported separately along with a total sample.

Total Survey Area

	1 Estimated Population	**2** Estimated Population as Percent of Tot. Persons 12+	**3** Percent of Unweighted In-Tab Sample	**4** Percent of Weighted In-Tab Sample
Men 18-24	115,900	7.2	6.4	7.2
Men 25-34	139,900	8.7	8.5	8.7
Men 35-44	107,300	6.6	6.7	6.6
Men 45-49	49,400	3.1	2.5	3.1
Men 50-54	54,600	3.4	2.9	3.4
Men 55-64	96,300	6.0	7.0	6.0
Men 65 +	94,700	5.9	4.2	5.9

Area of Dominant Influence

Men 18-24	104,200	7.2	6.3	7.2
Men 25-34	124,900	8.6	8.1	8.6
Men 35-44	96,500	6.6	7.1	6.6
Men 45-49	44,800	3.1	2.3	3.1
Men 50-54	49,300	3.4	2.7	3.4
Men 55-64	86,300	5.9	7.0	5.9
Men 65 +	84,000	5.8	4.1	5.8

Metro Survey Area

Men 18-24	74,800	7.2	6.8	7.1
Men 25-34	90,900	8.6	8.5	8.6
Men 35-44	71,500	6.8	7.3	6.8
Men 45-49	33,500	3.2	2.4	3.2
Men 50-54	36,800	3.5	2.5	3.5
Men 55-64	62,300	5.9	6.7	5.9
Men 65 +	57,600	5.4	3.8	5.4

Metro Persons Living in Group Quarters

	5▲		
	% Military	% College	% Other Group Quarters
Total Persons 12 + 13,476,300	.1	.4	1.7

Diary Placement and Return Information

6▶	Metro	ADI	TSA
Standard Residential Listings in Designated Sample	751	1,033	1,185
ESF Residential Listings in Designated Sample	359	380	383
Total Residential Listings in Designated Sample	1,110	1,413	1,568
Standard Contacts (homes in which telephone was answered)	740	1,023	1,568
ESF Contacts (homes in which telephone was answered)	353	359	374
Total Contacts (homes in which telephone was answered)	1,093	1,382	11,514
Standard Homes in Which Diaries Were Placed	657	920	1,037
ESF Homes in Which Diaries Were Placed	253	257	283
Total Homes in Which Diaries Were Placed	910	1,177	1,320
Standard Individuals Who Were Sent a Diary	1,562	2,210	2,487
ESF Individuals Who Were Sent a Diary	588	600	625
Total Individuals Who Were Sent a Diary	2,150	2,810	3,112
Standard Individuals Who Returned a Usable Diary (In-Tab)	1,031	1,421	1,610
ESF Individuals Who Returned a Usable Diary (In-Tab)	360	374	398
Total Individuals Who Returned a Usable Diary (In-Tab)	1,391	1,795	2,008

voided, as are those that arrive more than 12 days after the end of the survey period. Diaries with blank or ambiguous entries also are rejected. Those diaries that survive the editors' scrutiny are then processed through the computer, and their information is tabulated. Computer printouts showing audience estimates are sent to subscribers.

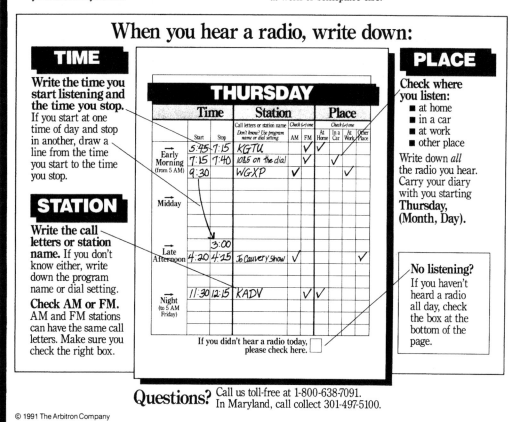

FIGURE 6.5
Instructions for filling out a diary. Accuracy is important. Courtesy Arbitron.

Stations receive the "book" within a few weeks after the last day of the survey.

Arbitrends, a computerized service designed to feed data to stations, has been made available to subscribers since the 1990s. Information regarding a station's past and current performances and those of competitors is available at the touch of a finger. Breakouts and tailor-made reports are provided on an ongoing basis by Arbitrends to assist stations in the planning of sales and marketing strategies. The survey company has over 13 billion characters reserved on computer disk packs. Arbitron also makes available its Arbitrends Rolling Average Printed Reports to those stations without computers. To date, Arbitron has prepared over 380,000 radio market reports.

Ever evolving its services, Arbitron rolled out another online product for its radio clients in 2006. In an announcement on its Web site, it stated "Arbitron Inc., in conjunction with comScore Media Metrix, a division of comScore Networks, Inc., has established a new audience measurement system designed to provide traditional broadcast ratings for the online radio industry. The service provides customers with Average Quarter-Hour and Cume audience estimates for standard dayparts and demographics. The comScore Arbitron Online Ratings service is based on approximately a quarter of a million U.S. participants within the comScore global consumer panel. Using proprietary and patent-pending technology, comScore passively and continuously captures the online behavior of these panelists, including online radio listening behavior."

Arbitron's most formidable rival in recent years was Birch/Scarborough, headquartered in New Jersey. As a radio audience measurement service, Birch provided clients with both quantitative and qualitative data on local listening patterns, audience size, and demographics. Birch interviewers telephoned a prebalanced sample of households during the evening hours, 7 days a week, to acquire the information they needed. "Respondents aged twelve or older were randomly selected from both listed and nonlisted telephone households. These calls were made from highly supervised company WATTS facilities," notes Phil Beswick, vice president of the defunct Birch/Scarborough broadcast services. The sample sizes varied depending on the size of the market being surveyed. For example, Birch/Scarborough contacted approximately 1100 households in

FIGURE 6.6
Diary log sheet. This current sheet includes a checkmark box for "at work," a feature not found in earlier sheets. Courtesy Arbitron.

4

THURSDAY

	Time		Station			Place			
			Call letters or station name *Don't know? Use program name or dial setting.*	*Check (✓) one*		*Check (✓) one*			
	Start	Stop		AM	FM	At Home	In a Car	At Work	Other Place
1 Early Morning 5 AM to 10 AM									
2 Midday 10 AM to 3 PM									
3 Late Afternoon 3 PM to 7 PM									
4 Night 7 PM to 5 AM (Early Fri.)									

If you didn't hear a radio today, please check here. ☐

a medium market and between 2000 and 8000 in major metro markets.

A wide range of reports were available to clients, including the *Quarterly Summary Report*, estimates of listening by location, county by county, and other detailed audience information; *Standard Market Report*, audience analysis especially designed for small market broadcasters; *Capsule Market Report*, listening estimates in the nation's smallest radio markets; *Condensed Market Report*, designed specifically for radio outlets in markets not provided with regular syndicated measurements and where cost was a key consideration; *Monthly Trend Report*, an ongoing picture of the listening audience so that clients might benefit from current shifts in the marketplace; *Prizm*, lifestyle-oriented radio ratings book that defined radio audiences by lifestyle characteristics in more than 85 markets; and BirchPlus, a microcomputerized system (IBM-PC) ratings retrieval and analysis. Fees for Birch/Scarborough services were based on market size. Birch provided subscribers with general product consumption and media usage data. In late 1994, Arbitron purchased 50% of the Scarborough Research Corporation, with plans to offer stations expanded data about their listeners.

Dozens of other research companies throughout the country (among them Coleman Research, Bolton Research Corporation, Mark Kassof & Company, Spectrum Research, Frank N. Magid Associates, DIR, Star, Paragon Research, Shane Media, Hagan Media Research, Gallup Services, Mediabase, TAPSCAN, Rantel Research, and others cited herein) provide broadcasters with a broad range of useful audience information. Many use approaches similar to Arbitron (and formerly Birch) to collect data; still others use different methods. "Southeast Media Research offers four research methods: focus groups, telephone studies, mail intercepts, and music tests," explains Don Hagen, the company's president. Christopher Porter, associate director of Surrey Research, says that his company uses similar techniques.

Meanwhile, audience researcher Dick Warner claims that the telephone recall method is the most commonly used and effective approach to radio audience surveying. "The twenty-four-hour telephone recall interview, in my estimation, yields the most reliable information. Not only that, it is quick and current – important factors in a rapidly moving and hyperdynamic radio marketplace."

In her book *Listening In*, scholar Susan Douglas presciently noted that new technologies have been developed to more effectively track listening. For instance, she cites databases such as MapMAKER that "can map the geography of a radio station's listeners and correlate their location with retailer trading areas." Says Douglas, "The company is developing a pocket people meter, based on the 'latest military technology,' designed to track radio listening electronically no matter where the person is and to eliminate the [Arbitron] diary altogether."

On the subject of music testing, Coleman Research's Rebecca Reising notes that her company's approach is unique. "We developed F.A.C.T., short for Fit Acceptance and Compatibility Test. F.A.C.T.'s proprietary research methods and sophisticated databases make it much more powerful, reliable, and useful than old-fashioned music testing methods. As quick and efficient as old tests, F.A.C.T. provides a sophistication of interpretation of music tests not offered by any other research company."

In the hyperactive radio industry arena, both traditional and novel audience survey techniques must ultimately prove themselves by assisting stations in their unrelenting quest for stronger ratings numbers.

Qualitative and Quantitative Data

Since their inception in the 1930s, ratings services primarily have provided broadcasters with information pertaining to the number of listeners of a certain age and gender tuned to a station at a given time. It was on the basis of these quantitative data that stations chose a format and advertisers made a buy.

Due to the explosive growth of the electronic media in recent years, the audience is presented with many more options, and the radio broadcaster, especially in larger markets, must know more about his intended listeners to attract and retain them. Subsequently, the need for more detailed information arose. In the 1990s, in-depth research was available to broadcasters from numerous sources. In this age of highly fragmented audiences, advertisers and agencies alike have become less comfortable with buying just numbers and look for audience qualities, notes Surrey's Christopher Porter. "The proliferation of stations has resulted in tremendous audience fragmentation. There are so many specialized formats out there, and many target the same piece of demographic pie. This predicament, if it can be called that, has made amply clear the need for qualitative, as well as quantitative, research. With so many stations doing approximately the same thing, differentiation is of paramount importance."

Today, a station shooting for a top spot in the ratings surveys must be concerned with more than simply the age and sex of its target audience. Competitive programming strategies are built around an understanding and appreciation of the lifestyles, values, and behavior of those listeners sought by a station.

Portable People Meter

Another approach to measuring station listenership has emerged in the form of the PPM created by Arbitron. The plan is to have this small mobile device replace the conventional paper diary method of tabulating audience size. Says Jeff Smulyan, "Electronic measurement is long overdue. We are finally getting credit for the huge audience we felt we had all along in Arbitron's previous methodology. In Los Angeles, for example, one of our Emmis station's cume was up 70% and our other Emmis station cume has almost quadrupled. That's a lot of people listening to us that we were not getting credit for." No longer will survey participants take an active role in recording their listening patterns. The PPM does it by detecting codes embedded in radio broadcasts. This cell phone size device will be carried by Arbitron measurement panelists for an agreed upon period of time, and the information it records can be accessed

by the company to create timely reports to radio station subscribers.

In 2006, Arbitron announced that it would begin the transition to the PPM. It's use of the traditional 7-day paper diary commenced in 1965, so its conversion to this new measurement technology represented an historic landmark. Five years in development yielded a positive response to the rollout of the PPM as CBS contracted the use of the device in 35 of its markets. Beasley Broadcast Group and Spanish Broadcasting System did likewise. On the heals of these deals, four other major radio groups – Bonnevile International Corporation, Emmis Communications Corporation, Greater Media, Inc., and Lincoln Financial Media – signed multiyear contracts for PPM radio ratings. Recently, PPM received approval from the Media Ratings Council, which signaled to the industry that the device was likely here to stay.

Ed Shane says the PPM may never be employed in small markets. "I daresay small markets will never see PPM because of the cost of implementation. It's a much more important element in the sales process in large markets because of the transactional nature of buying. The smaller the market, the more selling is based on relationships and – most importantly – on results at the cash register."

Tripp Eldredge, president of Direct Marketing Research, explains how the PPM works, "To reiterate, it's a small pager-like device that survey panelists keep with them during their daily activities. The unit records inaudible codes emitted from any encoded audio source (including radio stations, television stations, and in-store audio). The meter captures a near-continuous stream of data as whenever and for as long as the panelist is exposed to the encoded media. The media needs to be audible for the meter to pick up the encoded audio. The meters are 'docked' at night and the data collected are transmitted to Arbitron's data center."

Eldredge offers his views as to why the PPM is superior to the old paper method of gathering audience data. "The PPM is both passive and longitudinal. Both qualities lead to a superior methodology. Because it's passive, it doesn't rely on the memory or

FIGURE 6.7
The Portable People
Meter is a major
departure in the
gathering of listening
data. Courtesy
Arbitron.

The Portable People Meter
NEXT GENERATION ELECTRONIC RATINGS℠
The Portable People Meter System in Action

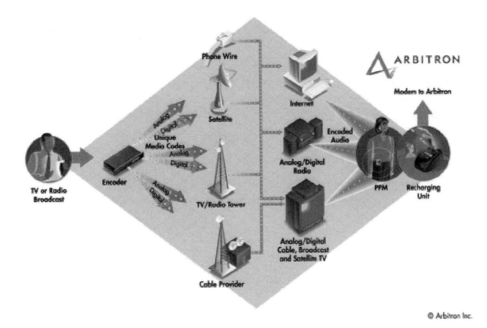

© Arbitron Inc.

consciousness of the respondent to gather data and more importantly report it correctly. The diary relies on proper station identification as well as proper reporting of behavior on a quarter-hour by quarter-hour basis. Because it's longitudinal, it provides much more stable results for the time periods most relevant to advertisers and broadcasters. Much of the differences in the diary methodology can be a result of sampling error, depending on the time period in question. The meter eliminates much of the instability due to randomness because it's kept for an average of six months. Also, the long-term nature of the meter may serve to eliminate the survey bias inherent in the diary process."

"There are some important new insights the PPM will provide that result from its longitudinal nature. One very important new benefit is the ability to track loyalty and brand-switching over time. The diary process would infer the preferred station through the week-long measurement. The First Preference (P1) is the station that gets the majority of a consumer's listening. P1 drives the majority of a station's AQH (average quarter hour listening). However, the diary could not track the changes in P1 from week to week or month to month. The meter can because it tracks the same consumers from day to day, etc. This new metric will provide new and better feedback to programmers and potentially advertisers as they begin to understand how loyalty impacts listening and how it is impacted by programming and marketing components."

Eldredge observes that the PPM is not without its shortcomings, "Currently, the PPM shows an approximately 20% decrease in AQH listening to many stations. In a related note, the overall time spent listening to radio is lower, although there are about double the total audiences of stations. The meter shows that there are far more people tuning into a station than the diary has shown. Because there are more people identified, the average time spent listening is lower. That's not necessarily a shortcoming of the PPM as much as it is an indication that the diary was not able to pick up about half of the actual stations tuned, resulting in consumers inadvertently overstating their listening volumes to the stations they remembered."

Other devices may challenge the PPM. Cell phones are being touted as potential media measurement devices given their ubiquity and expanding service capabilities. In 2006, The Media Audit/Ipsos company entered the test phase to determine the

FIGURE 6.8
Arbitron estimates show where a station stands in its market. Courtesy Arbitron.

AVERAGE SHARE TRENDS

The Trends section provides an indication of individual station performance and the relative standing among stations for periods prior to the most recent survey. The duration reported in this section may include as many as five discrete Arbitron survey rating periods, always including the most recent. Trends may not always reflect actual changes over time due to changes in methodology, station operations, etc.

1▶ The estimates reported are average persons shares in the Metro Survey Area, by individual stations, on the basis of broad demographics in specific dayparts. A share is the percent of all listeners in a demographic group that are listening to a specific station. This percent is calculated by dividing the Average Quarter-Hour Persons to a station by the Average Quarter-Hour Persons to all stations.

2▶ Total listening (Metro Totals) in the market, expressed as a rating, is also reported. This is the sum of all reported stations' Average Quarter-Hour estimates plus those for stations not meeting Minimum Reporting Standards and unidentified listening.

3▶ Reported dayparts are as follows:
Monday-Sunday 6AM-Midnight
Monday-Friday 6AM-10AM
Monday-Friday 10AM-3PM
Monday-Friday 3PM-7PM
Monday-Friday 7PM-Midnight

4▶ Reported demographics are as follows:
Total Persons 12+
Men 18+
Women 18+
Teens 12-17

5▶ A " + " indicates station changed call letters.

6▶ A " * * " indicates station not reported for that survey.

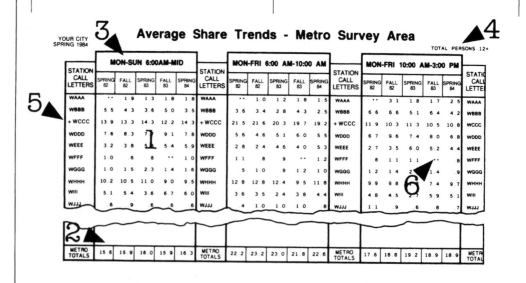

Average Quarter-Hour Listening Estimates

PHILADELPHIA   SUNDAY
3:00PM–7:00PM

AVERAGE PERSONS—TOTAL SURVEY AREA, IN HUNDREDS

TOT PERS 12+	MEN 18-24	25-34	35-44	45-54	55-64	WOMEN 18-24	25-34	35-44	45-54	55-64	TNS 12-17	STATION CALL LETTERS
392		13	27	27	27	3	6	30	21	65	6	KYW
-1												WBCB
625	15	38	42	59	106	3	31	47	23	66	9	WCAU
562	59	16	41	5	26	65	78	53	8		178	WCAU FM
100		23				4	8	8	9			WDAS
437	107	38	7	25	13	48	107	11	13	15	53	WDAS FM
358		7	19	41	28	3	28	4	58	47		WEAZ
108	11	6	4	35		5	20	8	12		3	WFIL
12					3							WFLN
166			13	12	14	3	18	10	28	9		WFLN FM
178			13	15	14	3	18	10	28	9		TOTAL
109		10			8		5	14	33	26	13	WHAT
52		1				18					33	WIFI
269	14	99	31			28	74	1	6		16	WIOQ
172		4	12	4	20		15	24	16	40	27	WIP
96		2	5	19		13	10	30	17			WKSZ
427	18	94	11	34		29	100	33	38	14	30	WMGK
423	95	93	3	2	6	73	75	15			61	WMMR
551		15	13	70	65	16	28	39	73	41		WPEN
3				1							2	WSNI
146		28	21			23	49				25	WSNI FM
149		28	22			23	49				27	TOTAL
32	11					9	4				3	WSSJ
585	116	116	31		12	69	79	43	5	7	107	WUSL
19								19				WVCH
270	15			26		5	28	27	13	55	1	WWDB
97	10	4	8	11		2	15	14	20	4	2	WWSH
432	88	86		2	10	124	40	3	9	5	65	WYSP
40			17					17		4	2	WZZD
122				40	30			2			32	WJBR FM
113	12	20		2		54					27	WPST
52	12	11		2		16		8			3	WSTW
24			18		6							WTTM
55								17	13			WOR

AVERAGE PERSONS—METRO SURVEY AREA, IN HUNDREDS

TOT PERS 12+	MEN 18-24	25-34	35-44	45-54	55-64	WOMEN 18-24	25-34	35-44	45-54	55-64	TNS 12-17	STATION CALL LETTERS
350		13	22	14	24	3	6	26	11	62	6	KYW
-1												WBCB
570	15	38	42	50	86	3	31	47	17	46	9	WCAU
420	59	16	27	5	26	59	51	28			126	WCAU FM
91		23				4	8	8				WDAS
343	32	38	7	25	13	48	88	11	13	15	53	WDAS FM
239		7	2	5	23	3		4	34	42		WEAZ
100	11	6	4	29		5	18	8	12		3	WFIL
12					3							WFLN
144			13	12	14	3	5	10	28	9		WFLN FM
156			13	15	14	3	5	10	28	9		TOTAL
109		10			8		5	14	33	26	13	WHAT
23		1				14					8	WIFI
263	14	94	31			28	74		6		16	WIOQ
144		4	12	4	20		13	24		30	27	WIP
76		2	5	10		9	10	30	10			WKSZ
374	18	83	11	27		29	70	28	38	14	30	WMGK
352	74	88	3	2	6	71	47	15			46	WMMR
533		15	13	70	47	16	28	39	73	41		WPEN
3				1							2	WSNI
146		28	21			23	49				25	WSNI FM
149		28	22			23	49				27	TOTAL
32	11					9	4				3	WSSJ
466	75	87	31		12	51	79	38	5	7	81	WUSL
-1												WVCH
237	15			26		5	28	27		55	1	WWDB
68	10	4	8	11		2	15	7	5	4	2	WWSH
289	63	52		2	10	75	17	3	9	5	62	WYSP
40			17					17		4	2	WZZD
67		12	20			20		2			3	WJBR FM
67	12	20				20					15	WPST
18					2	16						WSTW
24			18		6							WTTM
13											13	WOR

SHARES—METRO SURVEY AREA

TOT PERS 12+ %	MEN 18-24 %	25-34 %	35-44 %	45-54 %	55-64 %	WOMEN 18-24 %	25-34 %	35-44 %	45-54 %	55-64 %	TNS 12-17 %	STATION CALL LETTERS
5.7		1.9	6.7	3.9	6.5	6	.8	6.3	3.6	16.2	1.1	KYW
												WBCB
9.3	3.1	5.5	12.8	13.9	23.3	.6	4.4	11.4	5.6	12.0	1.7	WCAU
6.9	12.2	2.3	8.2	1.4	7.0	11.3	7.2	6.8			23.4	WCAU FM
1.5			3.4				.8	1.1	1.9			WDAS
5.6	6.6	5.5	2.1	7.0	3.5	9.2	12.4	2.7	4.2	3.9	9.9	WDAS FM
3.9		1.0	.6	1.4	6.2	.6		1.0	11.1	11.0		WEAZ
1.6	2.3	.9	1.2	8.1		1.0	2.5	1.9	3.9		.6	WFIL
.2												WFLN
2.4			4.0	3.3	3.8	.6	.7	2.4	9.2	2.3		WFLN FM
2.6			4.0	4.1	3.8	.6	.7	2.4	9.2	2.3		TOTAL
1.8		1.5			2.2		.7	3.4	10.8	6.8	2.4	WHAT
.4		1				2.7					1.5	WIFI
4.3	2.9	13.7	9.4			5.4	10.4		2.0		3.0	WIOQ
2.4		.6	3.6	1.1	5.4		1.8	5.8		7.8	5.0	WIP
1.2		.3	1.5	2.8		1.7	1.4	7.2	3.3			WKSZ
6.1	3.7	12.1	3.3	7.5		5.5	9.9	6.8	12.4	3.7	5.6	WMGK
5.8	15.3	12.8	.9		1.6	13.6	6.6	3.6			8.6	WMMR
8.7		2.2	4.0	19.5	12.7	3.1	3.9	9.4	23.9	10.7		WPEN
												WSNI
2.4		4.1	6.4			4.4	6.9				4.6	WSNI FM
2.4		4.1	6.7			4.4	6.9				5.0	TOTAL
2.4	5.2	3				1.7	.6				.6	WSSJ
7.6	15.5	12.7	9.4		3.3	9.8	11.1	9.2	1.6	1.8	15.1	WUSL
												WVCH
3.9	3.1			7.2		1.0	3.9	6.5		14.4	.2	WWDB
1.1	2.1	.6	2.4	3.1		.4	2.1	1.7	1.6	1.0	.4	WWSH
4.7	13.0	7.6			6	2.7	14.3	1.1		7	2.9	1.3	11.5	WYSP
.7			4.7					2.4		1.0	.4	WZZD
.3				3.5				5		8		WJBR FM
1.1	2.5	2.9		3.8							2.8	WPST
.3				.6		3.1						WSTW
4			5.5	1.6								WTTM
2										3.4		WOR

TOTAL LISTENING IN METRO SURVEY AREA	6102	484	686	329	359	369	523	710	414	306	383	538

PAGE 84

Footnote Symbols: (*) means audience estimates adjusted for actual broadcast schedule.

ARBITRON RATINGS

application of the cell phone for audience measurement purposes. Also in 2006, Mediamark Research developed a beeper-size portable device designed to calculate audience shares for radio stations. Jump ahead to 2009 and Arbitron announced plans to sample listening via cell phones. Obviously, the next edition of this book will have more to say about the PPM's effectiveness and application, as well as other new portable ratings devices, which may be embraced by the market.

In terms of what the PPM means to on-air personnel, Jason Insalaco posits the view that "early results indicate music is winning over deejay patter. Consequently, programmers of struggling morning shows are pulling back their personalities from the usual bits, interviews, and banter and offering more music-intensive morning programming. However, PPM data also indicates that strong morning show personalities are continuing to exhibit success equal to, if not greater, AQH compared to the old diary methodology. The early lessons of PPM are that the new measurement device highlights the strengths and weaknesses of the station. If a morning show was underperforming according to the diaries, it will likely become even more flaring under PPM. Programmers have a large amount of weekly data at their fingertips with PPM. It also is showing that midday and afternoon drive listening is reaching audience levels sometimes equal to morning drive. As programmers become more comfortable with PPM, they will take more risks on the air. If the early data shows that something new is not working, programmers can quickly change course

FIGURE 6.9
Sample page from an Arbitron *Radio Report*. Courtesy Arbitron.

without having to wait months to discern a trend as they did under the previous diary system."

In-House Research Techniques

Research data provided by the major survey companies can be costly. For this reason and others, stations frequently conduct their own audience studies. Although stations seldom have the professional wherewithal and expertise of the research companies, they can derive useful information through do-it-yourself, in-house telephone, face-to-face, and mail surveys.

Telephone surveying is the most commonly used method of deriving audience data on the station level. It generally is less costly than the other forms of in-house research, and sample selection is less complicated and not as prone to bias. It also is the most expedient method. There are, however, a few things that must be kept in mind when conducting call-out surveys. One, not everyone has a phone and many numbers are unlisted. People also are wary of phone interviews for fear that the ultimate objective of the caller is to sell something. The public is inundated by phone solicitors (both human and computerized). Finally, extensive interviews are difficult to obtain over the phone. Five to 10 minutes usually is the extent to which an interviewee will submit to questioning. Call-out interview seminars and instructional materials are available from a variety of sources, including the telephone company itself.

Internet and e-mail services provide another valuable means for those radio stations that survey their audiences. Many stations employ computers for call-out research purposes. There are many obvious benefits, interactivity and archiving foremost among them. The face-to-face or personal interview also is a popular research approach at stations, although the cost can be higher than call-out, especially if a vast number of individuals are being surveyed in an auditorium setting. The primary advantages of the in-person interview are that questions can be more substantive and greater time can be spent with

the respondees. Of course, more detailed interviews are time consuming and usually require refined interviewing skills, both of which can be cost factors.

Mail surveys can be useful for a host of reasons. To begin with, they eliminate the need to hire and train interviewers. This alone can mean a great deal in terms of money and time. Because no interviewers are involved, one source of potential bias also is eliminated. Perhaps most important is that individuals questioned through the mail are somewhat more inclined toward candor since they enjoy greater anonymity. The major problem with the mail survey approach stems from the usual low rate of response. One in every five questionnaires mailed may actually find its way back to the station. The length of the questionnaire must be kept relatively short and the questions succinct and direct. Complex questions create resistance and may result in the survey being ignored or discarded.

Large and major market outlets usually employ someone to direct research and survey efforts. This person works closely with upper management and department heads, especially the program director (PD) and sales manager. These two areas require data on which to base programming and marketing decisions. At smaller outlets, area directors generally are responsible for conducting surveys relevant to their department's needs. A case in point would be the PD who plans a phone survey during a special broadcast to help ascertain whether it should become a permanent program offering. To accomplish this task, the programmer enlists the aid of a secretary and two interns from a local college. Calls are made, and data are collected and analyzed.

The objective of a survey must be clear from the start, and the methodology used to acquire data should be as uncomplicated as possible. Do-it-yourself surveys are limited in nature, and overly ambitious goals and expectations are seldom realized. However, in-house research can produce valuable information that can give a station a competitive edge. Today, no radio station can operate in a detached way and expect to prosper.

Every station has numerous sources of information available to it. Directories containing all manner of data, such as population statistics and demographics, manufacturing and retailing trends, and so on, are available at the public library, city hall, chamber of commerce, and various business associations. The American Marketing Association and American Research Foundation also possess information designed to guide stations with their in-house survey efforts.

Research Deficits

Although broadcasters refer deferentially to the ratings surveys as the "book" or "bible," the stats they contain are audience-listening estimates – no more, and, it is hoped, no less. Since their inception, research companies have been criticized for the methods they employ in collecting audience listening figures. The most prevalent complaint has had to do with the selection of samples. Critics have charged that they invariably are limited and exclusionary. Questions have persisted as to whether those surveyed are truly representative of an area's total listenership. Can 1% of the radio universe accurately reflect general listening habits? The research companies defend their tactics and have established a strong case for their methodology.

In the 1970s, ratings companies were criticized for neglecting minorities in their surveys. In efforts to rectify this deficiency, both Arbitron and Birch established special sampling procedures. The incidence of non-telephone households among Blacks and Hispanics tends to be higher. The survey companies also had to deal with the problem of measuring Spanish-speaking people. Arbitron found that using the personal-retrieval technique significantly increased the response rate in the Spanish community, especially when bilingual interviewers were used. The personal-retrieval technique did not work as well with Blacks, since it was difficult to recruit interviewers to work in many of the sample areas. Thus, Arbitron used a telephone retrieval procedure that involved callbacks to selected households over a 7-day period to document listening habits. In essence, the interviewer filled out the diaries for those being surveyed. In 1982, Arbitron implemented Differential Survey

Treatment (DST), a technique designed to increase the response rate among Blacks. The survey company provides incentives over the customary 50¢–$1 to certain Black households. Up to $5 is paid to some respondents. DST employs follow-up calls to retrieve diaries.

During its years of operation, Birch/Scarborough Research employed special sampling procedures and bilingual interviewers to collect data from the Hispanic population. According to the company, its samples yielded a high response rate among Blacks. Thus, Birch did not use other special sampling controls. Ethnic listening reports containing average quarter-hour and cume estimates for Hispanics, Blacks, and others were available from the company in a format similar to that of its Capsule Market Report.

FIGURE 6.10
Radio station promotional pieces often reflect research and survey data provided by Arbitron and other companies. Courtesy WBMX.

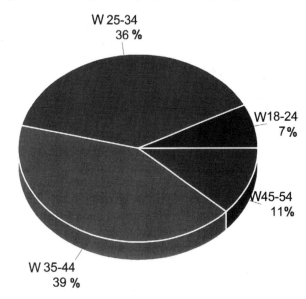

MIX 105.1

AUDIENCE COMPOSITION

W 25-34
36 %

W18-24
7%

W45-54
11%

W 35-44
39 %

94% of MIX's Female Audience is W18-54!

Source: ARBITRON WINTER 2000, W12+ Audience omposition (M-Sun 6a-12m) AQH

ORLANDO

Both survey companies employed additional procedures to survey other nontelephone households, especially in markets that have a large student or transient population. In the late 1970s, a Boston station targeting young people complained that Arbitron failed to acknowledge the existence of over 200,000 college students who did not have personal phone listings. The station, which was rated among the top five in the market at the time, contended that a comprehensive survey of the city's listening audience would bear out the fact that they were, in fact, number one.

Similar complaints of skewed or inconclusive surveys persist today, but the procedures and methods used by the major radio audience research companies, although far from perfect, are more effective than ever. Christopher Porter says the greatest misconception about research data is that they are absolutes etched in granite. "The greatest fallacy is that research findings are gospel. This goes not only for the quantitative studies but for focus groups as well. Regardless of the methodology, any findings should be used as a 'gut adjuster,' rather than a 'gut replacer.' Sampling error is often ignored in a quantitative study, even in an Arbi-

FIGURE 6.11
The Radio Advertising Bureau provides radio station data for use in attracting advertisers. Courtesy RAB.

About the Radio Advertising Bureau

RAB Mission:

The RADIO ADVERTISING BUREAU mission is to lead industry initiatives and provide organizational, educational, research and advocacy programs and services that benefit the RAB membership and the Radio industry as a whole.

To that end, RAB will endeavor to...
Share knowledge.
Facilitate Consensus.
Drive Revenue.

RAB Objectives:

- ☒To enhance the perception of Radio as a primary medium for all advertisers.
- ☒To increase Radio's advertising and marketing revenue
- ☒To organize the industry to set standards and guidelines that make Radio an easier medium for agencies and marketers to buy and capture value

RAB is the sales and marketing arm of the Radio industry. Today our constituents number nearly 7,000 members including some 6,000 stations in the U.S., and over 1,000 associate members in networks, representative firms, sales and international organizations.

tron report. When we report that 25% of a sample feels some way about something, or when a station with a 4.1 beats one with a 3.8 in a book, most station managers and PDs take all these statistics at face value."

Rip Ridgeway, former vice president of Arbitron Ratings, believes that stations place too much emphasis on survey results. "I think that station hierarchy puts too much credence on the ratings estimates. They're an indicator, a sort of report card on a station's performance. They're not the absolute end all. To jump at the next numbers and make sweeping changes based on them generally is a big mistake."

Radio executive Lorna Ozman concurs with both Porter and Ridgeway and warns that research should help direct rather than dictate what a station does. "I use research, rather than letting it use me. The thing to remember is that no methodology is without a significant margin of error. To treat the results of a survey as gospel is dangerous. I rely on research to provide me with the black-and-white answers and depend on myself to make determinations on the gray areas. Research never provided a radio station with the glitter to make it sparkle."

Station general manager (GM) Richard Bremkamp also expresses concern over what he perceives as an almost obsessive emphasis on survey statistics. "The concern for numbers gets out of hand. There are some really good-sounding stations out there that don't do good book, but the money is in the numbers. Kurt Vonnegut talks about the 'Universal Will to Become' in his books. In radio that can be expanded to the Universal Will to Become Number One. This is good if it means the best, but that's not always what it means today."

The proliferation of data services has drawn criticism from broadcasters who feel that they are being oversurveyed and over-researched. When Arbitron introduced its computerized monthly ratings service (Arbitrends), the chairman of its own radio advisory council opposed the venture on the grounds that it would cause more confusion and create more work for broadcasters. He further contended that the monthly service would encourage short-term buying by advertisers. Similar criticism was lodged against Birch/Scarborough's own comput-

erized service, BirchPlus. However, both services experienced steady growth.

Compounding the task of audience surveying, says Ed Shane, is the fact that "lower response rates are affecting all research." Continues Shane, "Telephone research operations have the same problem because people are burned out on solicitation by phone. For a recent research project, we made 20,100 phone calls to yield 405 respondents. As already indicated, some researchers suggest turning to the Internet for surveys. It's sure convenient, because the respondents come to the researcher. However, until Internet usage levels are as ubiquitous as the telephone, the sample generated from Internet surveys is not projectable across the population as a whole."

David Pearlman concurs. "Audience research is increasingly hard to acquire. Response rates are the foremost issue facing Arbitron, or any one else measuring listening or consumer habits." Adds, consultant Gary Begin, "Until PPM or some other methodology is fully realized, getting diary keepers to make accurate entries will largely depend on their remembering a station's name or frequency, and that, as we well know, is a dubious business."

Adding to all this, notes Shane, is the fact that "radio research has been all but eliminated from station budgets as simply too costly. That leaves little understanding of the audience and its needs and desires."

FIGURE 6.12
The more a station knows about its audience, the more effectively it can program itself. Courtesy DMR.

How Agencies Buy Radio

The primacy of numbers perhaps is best illustrated through a discussion of how advertising agencies place money on radio stations. It is the media buyer's job to effectively and efficiently invest the advertiser's money – in other words, to reach the most listeners with the budget allotted for radio use. According to media buyer Lynne Price, the most commonly employed method determines the cost per point (CPP) of a given station. Lynne explains the procedure: "A media buyer is given a budget and a gross rating point (GRP) goal. Our job is to buy to our GRP goal, without going over budget, against a predetermined target audience, i.e., adults 25 to 54, teens, men 18 to 34, etc. Our CPP is derived by taking the total budget and dividing by the GRP goal, or total number of rating points we would like to amass against our target audience. Now, using the CPP as a guideline, we take the cost per spot on a given station, and divide by the rating it has to see how close to the total CPP the station is. This is where the negotiation comes in. If the station is way off, you can threaten not to place advertising until they come closer to what you want to spend."

The other method used to justify station buys is cost per thousand (CPM). Using this technique, the buyer determines the cost of reaching 1000 people at a given station. The CPM of one station is then compared with that of another's to ascertain efficiency. To determine a station's CPM, the buyer must know the station's average quarter-hour audience (AQH persons) estimate in the daypart targeted and the cost of a commercial during that time frame. The following computation will provide the station's CPM: by dividing the number of people reached into the cost of the commercial, the CPM is deduced.

$$\frac{\$30 \text{ for } 60 \text{ seconds}}{25 \text{ (000) AQH}} = \$1.20 \text{ CPM}$$

Thus, the lower the CPM, the more efficient the buy. Of course, this assumes that the station selected delivers the target audience sought. Again, this is the responsibility of the individual buying media for an agency. It should be apparent by now that many things are taken into consideration before airtime is purchased.

Careers in Research

The number of media research companies grew rapidly since the late 1960s but slowed in the post-Telecom Act 1990s as station consolidation became the rule of the land. Today dozens of research houses nationwide offer audience measurement and survey data to the electronic media and allied fields. Job opportunities in research have increased proportionately. Persons wanting to work in the research area need sound educational backgrounds, says Surrey's Porter. "College is essential. An individual attempting to enter the field today without formal training is at a serious disadvantage. In fact, a master's degree is a good idea." Dr. Rob Balon, president of Balon and Associates, agrees with Porter. "Entering the research field today requires substantial preparation. College research courses are where to start."

Researcher Ed Noonan is of the same opinion. "It is a very competitive and demanding profession. Formal training is very important. I'd advise anyone planning a career in broadcast research to get a degree in communications or some related field and heavy-up on courses in research methodology and analysis, statistics, marketing, and computers. Certain business courses are very useful, too."

To Don Hagen of Southeast Media Research, a strong knowledge of media is a key criterion when hiring. "One of the things that I look for in a job candidate is a college background in electronic media. That's the starting point. You have to know more today than ever before. Audience research has become a complex science."

As might be expected, research directors also place considerable value on experience. "The job prospect who offers some experience in the research area, as well as a diploma, is particularly attractive," notes researcher Dick Warner. Ed Noonan concurs. "Actual experience in the field, even if it is gained in a summer or part-time job, is a big plus." Christopher Porter advises aspiring researchers to work in radio to get a firsthand feel for the medium. "A hands-on knowledge of the broadcast industry is invaluable, if not vital, in this profession."

In the category of personal attributes, Dick Warner puts inquisitiveness at the top of the list. "An inquiring mind is essential. The job of the researcher is to find and collect facts and information. Curiosity is basic to the researcher's personality." Don Hagen adds objectivity and perceptiveness to the list, and consultant Dwight Douglas emphasizes interactive skills. "People skills are essential, since selling and servicing research clients are as important as the research itself."

Although not everyone is suited for a career in audience research, those who are find the work intellectually stimulating and financially rewarding.

Ted Bolton

FIGURE 6.13
Ted Bolton.

Bolton is a quantitative research company – our main objective is to get the opinions of radio listeners on virtually anything having to do with the sound of a given station (or future station). There are several methods we use to get the info:

• **Perceptual studies.** These are in-depth surveys that gather opinions on issues such as music preferences, station personalities, competitors. All respondents are included based

What a Research Company Does

on their age, listening habits (e.g., favorite station), favorite music types, ethnicity, county of residence, and anything else of importance to the station (client). These surveys run 15–20 minutes.

Respondents are selected at random. We also do tracking studies, which include respondents from the original survey and which measure changes in opinion (usually 6 months out from the original survey).

Perceptual studies are the foundation of research, because they provide overall market information: perceptions of the client's station and its competitors, which the station uses to make programming, marketing, and sales decisions. The information gathered also aids us in designing a research program for the station.

• **Music and program testing.** There are several commonly used methods for testing music and program elements.

1. *Auditorium testing.* This is the industry standard for testing music that may be aired on the station. Respondents are screened according to station listenership, and paid an incentive between $35 and $50, depending on the market size. The typical test involves 100–150

respondents; they are usually split into two groups. Each group gathers at a hotel, where they listen on speakers to 350–400 hooks (5–10 seconds of a song, the most memorable part). In total, 700–800 hooks will be tested. The respondents score each hook, using a 1–5 (or similar) scale. They also note if they are familiar with the song, and give it a burn score if they're tired of hearing the song.

Bolton does "Personalized Music Tests" (PMT) instead of auditorium tests. Respondents in a PMT come to a facility at a time of their choice, and they test the hooks on Walkman-style cassette players with headphones. We've found that we have a better turnout than the auditorium tests and that the results are better because each respondent hears the hooks the same way (in an auditorium, respondents are at different distances from the speakers) without distractions from other listeners. Auditorium tests are still the industry standard, however.

2. *Perceptual analyzer tests.* In both of the previous methods, responders typically score hooks with paper and pencil. The data then must be coded and tabulated before the client sees the results. A recent development, perceptual analyzer tests, gives a

client instant information. As the scores are given, the computer produces an instant, continuous EKG-like graph that shows averages for different groups – a station's "core" listeners and its competitors' listeners, for instance. We've found this method (we call the test "BoltScan") to be most useful in testing music in the original order that it actually aired, thereby showing us both popular songs that keep listeners tuned in, and the stuff that causes tune-out. It works the same way for testing morning shows, comedy bits, and so on.

3. *Call-out music research*. This is a staple of radio programming. Respondents of a specific age and listening group – typically core listeners in a tight age range – are called at home and asked to score 25–30 hooks. The test is obviously short and can be conducted biweekly or even weekly. This information is most useful for trending the familiarity, popularity, and burnout of songs (usually new songs) over time. Callout is a task often assigned to station interns, but a number of research companies offer the service as well.

4. *Focus groups and listener panels*. Focus groups are, of course, used for all kinds of consumer product testing, and radio is no exception. Again, respondents are screened for age and listenership. Chosen participants are paid a small incentive and come to a focus group facility or hotel room in groups of 8–12. Station staff observe while the moderator asks respondents about their likes and dislikes of station attributes, including music preferences, personalities, competing stations, etc.

Listener panels are more informal and are usually done in-house by the station. Respondents are recruited on the air or from the station's database. Again, respondents are asked for their opinions about the station.

5. *Statistics*. Although some complicated statistical methods are sometimes used, the vast majority of data analysis involves "descriptive" statistics: frequency and average scores. Frequency is a computation of how many people fit into a category or choose a given response to a question. Averages (mean, median, mode) are measures of average or typical performance. For most research reports, these basic statistics are enough.

Some more sophisticated statistics are used to look for relationships and differences between groups: correlation ANOVA (analysis of variance) t-tests, chi-square, and cluster and factor analysis. For instance, we often use cluster analysis to separate respondents into distinct groups, such as Modern Rock and Classic Rock lovers. This helps a station to determine which artists are unique elements in a specific audience's tastes.

FIGURE 6.14
Research companies aid station efforts to locate advertisers. Courtesy Mercury Research.

What Mercury does

What Mercury Does

Brand Development

Ratings lackluster? Does your brand stand for a little bit of everything rather than a whole lot of something? Mercury can help you focus your strategy and exceed your expectations.

Online Research

Mercury has all the online tools to you need, not only to ask the questions but to interpret the answers and map a smart strategy.

Telephone Research

Mercury specializes in **Perceptual Research** and **Format Studies** in radio, television, and new media.

Focus Groups

"Masterful." That's how one client described a recent round of focus groups moderated by Mercury.

In-Depth interviews

When only a deep dive into consumer attitudes will do, we've got your needs covered.

Contact Mark Ramsey

Email
Or call 858-485-6372.

Phone:
858.485.MERC (6372)
858.485.6373 (fax)

Address:
11828 Rancho Bernardo Road,
Suite 211
San Diego, CA 92128 USA

Email Mercury

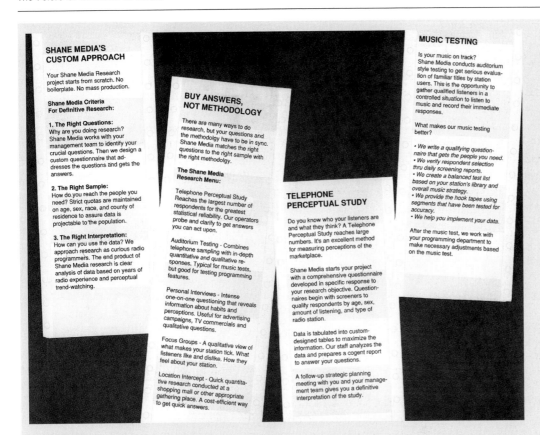

FIGURE 6.15
Many consultants provide a host of research services to their clients. Courtesy Shane Media.

Why do research? Not every radio programmer is a convert to the gospel of research. It is expensive, and stations are always on a tight budget. Many programmers have done just fine using experience and their gut to get them through. In addition, as people become more guarded with their privacy, both in terms of personal information and home invasion with the telephone, research becomes a more difficult and expensive proposition.

Yet, the market intelligence research provides is vital to the stations. As deregulation approaches, and station values skyrocket, gut feelings alone won't be enough to keep a multimillion dollar station on top. Research provides information that can make the gut feeling more of a sure thing or tell you that your gut is all wrong. But it is a tool, much as a computer or a tape recorder is. Even the best research is useless if it's not studied and properly applied. Also, shoddy research *can do* a lot more harm than good.

Bolton Research Director Doug Keith assembled the preceding material.

The Future of Research in Radio

Most experts agree that the role of research in radio will continue to grow despite the trend toward downsizing and clustering. They base their predictions on the ever-increasing fragmentation and niching of the listening audience, which makes the jobs of targeting and positioning more complex. "The field of broadcast research has grown considerably in the last two decades, and there is every reason to suspect that the growth will continue. As demographic targets and formats splinter, there will be an increasingly greater need to know. Much of the gut feel that has propelled radio programming will give way to objective research that is based on a plan," contends Dwight Douglas.

Christopher Porter sees the fragmentation and niching as creating a greater demand for research. "With the inevitability of more competition in already overcrowded markets, the need to stay abreast of market developments is critical. Yes, the role of research will continue to grow."

Although the role of research in the programming of large-market stations is significant to in-house methods, claims Ed Noonan. "Professional research services can be very costly. This will keep research to a minimum in lesser markets, although there will be more movement there than in past. Call-out research will continue to be a mainstay for the small station."

"Cost-effective ways to perform and utilize sophisticated psychographic data have made the computer standard equipment at most stations, small and large alike. Research is becoming a way of life everywhere, and computers and station Web site are an integral part of the information age. Computers encourage more do-it-yourself research at stations, as well, and Web sites allow for the collection of data and the interaction with audience," contends WGAO station manager Vic Michaels.

Gary Begin contends that advances in research technology also will continue to improve the nature and quality of research. "As with the portable ratings devices now being touted, we'll see more improvement in methodology and a greater diversity of applicable data as the result of high-tech innovations. I think the field of research will take a quantum leap in the years to come. It has in the past, but the size of the leap will be greater into the 2000s."

Today it is common for stations to budget 5–10% of their annual income to the research, and Christopher Porter believes it will probably increase. "As it evolves," he says, "it is likely that the marketplace will demand that more funds be allocated for research purposes. Research may not guarantee success, but it's not getting any easier to be successful without it."

Research has been a part of radio broadcasting since its modest beginnings in the 1920s, and it appears that it will play an even greater role in the operations of stations as the new century deepens.

CHAPTER HIGHLIGHTS

1. Beginning in the late 1920s, surveys were conducted to determine the most popular stations and programs with various audience groupings. Early surveys (and their methods) included C.E. Hooper, Inc. (telephone), CAB (telephone), and The Pulse (in-person). In 1968, RADAR (telephone to 6000 households) began to provide information for networks. The current leader among local market audience surveys is Arbitron (week-long diary).

2. In 1963, the Broadcast Rating Council was established to monitor, audit, and accredit ratings companies. In 1982, it was renamed the Electronic Media Planning Council to reflect its involvement with cable television ratings. Renamed the Media Rating Council in 1997, it now represents Internet constituencies, as well as radio, TV, cable, and print.

3. Arbitron measures listenership in the MSA, that is, the city or urban center, and the TSA, which covers the surrounding communities.

4. A station's primary listening locations are called ADI.

5. The Arbitron daily diary logs time tuned to a stations; station call letters or program name; whether AM or FM; where listening occurred; and the listener's age, sex, and area of residence.

6. From the late 1970s to the early 1990s, Birch/Scarborough gathered data by calling equal numbers of male and female listeners aged 12 and over. Clients were offered seven different report formats, including a computerized data retrieval system. The company went out of business on December, 31, 1991.

7. With today's highly fragmented audiences, advertisers and agencies are less comfortable buying just ratings numbers and look for audience qualities. Programmers must consider not only the age and sex of the target audience but also their lifestyles, values, and behavior.

8. The PPM is a pager-size device that records radio audience listening patterns. Its creator, Arbitron, hopes it will eventually replace its long-used 7-day paper diary. The cell phone may well serve to record radio-listening habits as well.

9. Station in-house surveys use telephone, computer, Web site, face-to-face, and mail methods.

10. In response to complaints about "missed" audiences, the major survey companies adjusted their survey techniques to ensure

Radio Reaches All Ages

These figures testify to radio's remarkable ability to attract listeners in every demographic group, and Radio's Cume rating has been consistently strong for the decade between Spring 1997 and 2007, declining less than 3%, and just 0.1% in the three years from Spring 2005 to 2007.

Among Men, nearly all of the decline occurred among Teen boys and 18-24 Men, with whom the decline was 6% over the 10-year span. Meanwhile, radio's Cume rating among Men 25-34, 35-44, 45-54 and 55-64 increased in Spring 2007 to their best numbers in three or more years.

Among Women, the erosion was less, with the Cume rating among Teen girls and Women 18-24 down only 4% during the decade, and 2% among Women 25-34. The Cume rating with Women 35-44 was its highest since Spring 2004, and reach among Women 45+ has remained virtually unchanged for years.

Weekly Cume Rating

	P12-17	P18-24	P25-34	P35-44	P45-54	P55-64	P65+
Men	87.2	89.7	94.5	95.3	95.1	94.0	87.5
Women	93.5	93.2	95.6	96.1	95.3	93.2	85.1

92.7 P12+

■ Men
□ Women

How to Read:
These figures represent "weekly Cume ratings." For example, slightly more than 93% of 18-24 Women in the U.S. tune in to the radio at least once during an average week, between the hours of 6AM-Midnight, Monday through Sunday. The blue-green background represents the average of all Americans, at least 12 years old, who listen to the radio at least once during the week. You can then see how radio reaches various demographic groups compared to the national average.

Source: MediaMark Plus National Regional Database, Spring 2007, Mon-Sun, 6AM-Mit

continued ▶

85 Radio Today 2008 Edition

© 2008 Arbitron Inc.

FIGURE 6.16
Arbitron data gives radio stations information to attract advertisers. Courtesy Arbitron.

MARK KASSOF & CO.

SUCCESS STRATEGIES FOR RADIO

RX......WLTQ.......KRMG........

📞 Call Us: (734) 662-5700

- Home
- Custom Strategic Research
- WINAMT™ Music Testing
- Kassof *PSI*™
- Focus Groups
- "Slog"
- Principles of Radio Research
- Research Insights '93-'05
- Quotations of Chairman Mark
- About Mark Kassof
- Contact Us

Mark Kassof & Co. is a radio audience research firm, specializing in THE MOST POWERFUL, ACTIONABLE RESEARCH IN RADIO to give your station a competitive edge. We conduct format research, strategic surveys, focus groups and music testing.

MARK KASSOF & CO.
SUCCESS STRATEGIES FOR RADIO
THE MOST POWERFUL, ACTIONABLE RESEARCH.

FIGURE 6.17
Web sites offer stations enormous research opportunities. Courtesy Mark Kassof & Company.

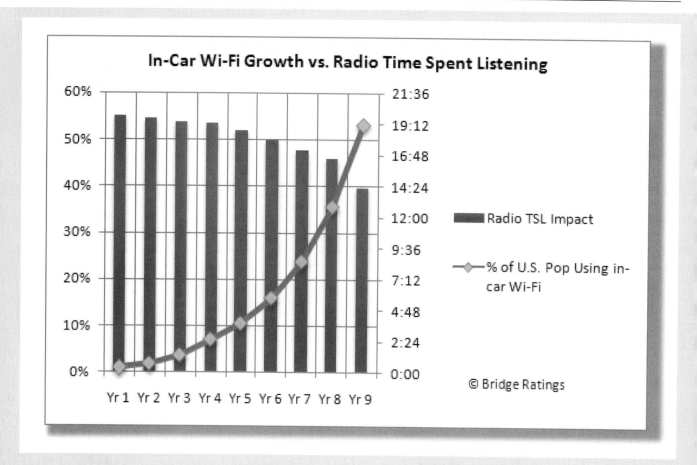

FIGURE 6.18
Bridge Ratings examine the growth of competitive media. Courtesy Bridge Ratings.

inclusion of minorities and nontelephone households. Today's survey results are more accurate.

11. Ratings data should only direct, not dictate, what a station does.

12. Media buyers for agencies use station ratings to determine the most cost-effective buy for their clients. Two methods they use are the cost per rating point (CPP) and the CPM.

Radio Research

FMR Associates, Inc. is an international media research firm that has worked with more than 400 radio stations since its inception in 1981 by founder and president Bruce Fohr. This includes extensive experience in commercial radio in virtually every format, including clients like Citadel Broadcasting, ABC Radio Networks, Infinity/CBS Radio, Lincoln Financial, Saga Communications, Fisher Broadcasting and Lotus Communications.

FMR has also conducted numerous projects for public broadcasting companies, including Corporation for Public Broadcasting (CPB), National Public Radio (NPR), Public Radio International (PRI), Public Radio Program Directors (PRPD) and Minnesota Public Radio (MPR) - as well as many individual public radio stations (such as KCFR, KUSC, KPLU, WBUR, WNYC, WXPN, KNAU and WBNI) and numerous program producers.

Internationally, FMR has worked with broadcasters like The British Broadcasting Company, Australian Broadcasting Company, Europe 2 (France), Multimundo (Mexico) and Telemedia Radio Network (Canada).

Contact us and we'll be happy to provide references of the most current and relevant radio clients.

Objective Research

While consolidation has been going on in the radio and research businesses, FMR remains one of the few still independently-owned companies (not part of another broadcast group or involved in other types of non-research services). FMR works on a competitive market-exclusive basis, with fee discounting available for multi-methodology and station cluster clients.

Independent and Affordable Research

Since FMR does not farm out any of its survey work, it is able to maintain high quality, cost-efficient services and provide exceptionally fast turnaround on projects. Contact us to discuss your research needs.

Innovative Research

FMR Associates offers a variety of custom radio research services to meet your needs, including:

[Home] [Company Profile] [Radio Research] [Media Research] [Market Research Services]
[Servicios en español] [Servicios de música en español] [Secure Client Area] [Contact Info]

FIGURE 6.19
Companies such as FMR Associates provide radio stations with important research data. Courtesy FMR Associates.

FIGURE 6.20
The electronic music testing graph shows audience reaction to specific songs. Even the ID is tested. Courtesy FMR Associates.

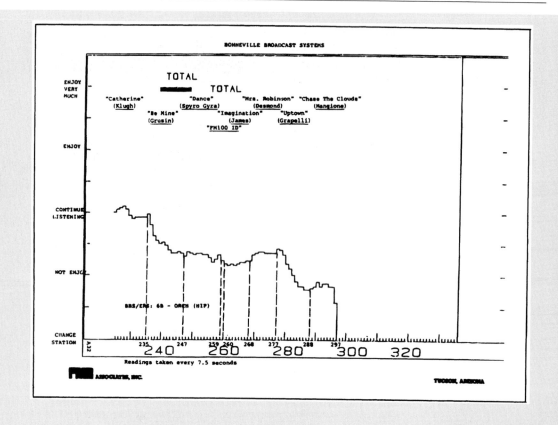

FIGURE 6.21
Demographic information is still the coin of the realm in audience research despite a much more qualitative orientation by advertisers. Courtesy Arbitron.

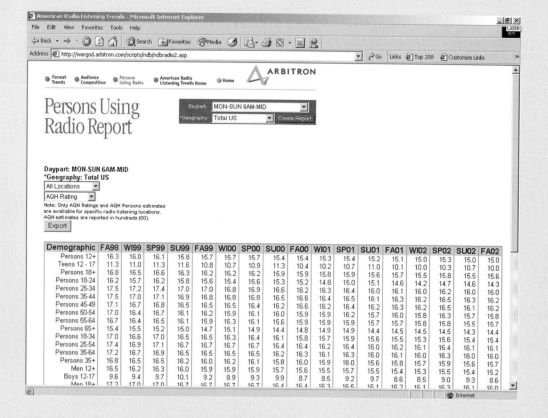

13. Although the significant increase in the numbers of broadcast research companies (several dozen nation wide) has created a growing job market, a college education is necessary. Courses in communications, research methods, statistics marketing, computers, and business are useful. Beneficial personal traits include inquisitiveness, objectivity, perceptiveness, and interpersonal skills.

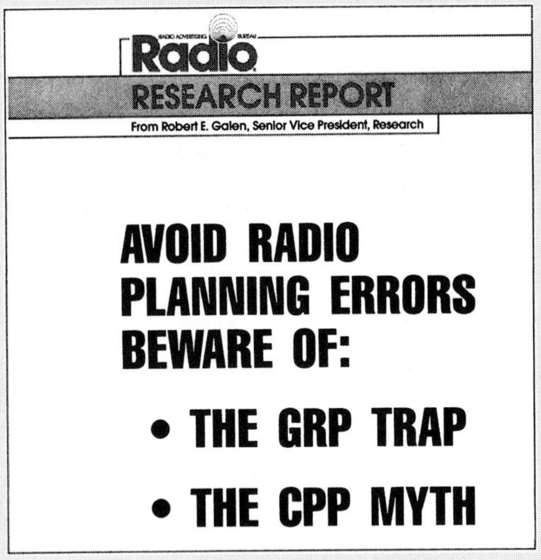
Radio
RESEARCH REPORT
From Robert E. Galen, Senior Vice President, Research

AVOID RADIO PLANNING ERRORS BEWARE OF:

- THE GRP TRAP
- THE CPP MYTH

FIGURE 6.22 Some broadcasters contend that there are inherent failures in across-the-board GRP/CPP buying by agencies. RAB publishes this report to caution against the pitfalls of buying formulas. Courtesy RAB.

SUGGESTED FURTHER READING

Arbitron Company, *The Comprehensive Resource Guide to Next Generation Electronic Management*, 2006. URL: http://www.arbitron.com/portable_people_meters/industry_main.htm.

Balon, R.E., *Radio In the '90's*, NAB Publishing, Washington, DC, 1990.

Bartos, R., *The Moving Target, What Every Marketer Should Know about Women*, The Free Press, New York, 1982.

Berger, A.A., *Media and Communication Research Methods*, Sage, Beverly Hills, CA, 2008.

Broadcast Advertising Reports, Broadcast Advertising Research, New York, periodically.

Broadcasting Yearbook, Broadcasting Publishing, Washington, DC, 1935 to date, annually.

Bryant, J., *Media Effects: Advances in Theory and Research*, 3rd edition, Routledge, New York, 2008.

Buzzard, K., *Electronic Media Ratings*, Focal Press, Boston, MA, 1992.

Chappell, M.N., and Hooper, C.E., *Radio Audience Measurement*, Stephen Day Press, New York, 1944.

Compaine, B., et al., *Who Owns the Media? Confrontation of Ownership in the Mass Communication Industry*, 2nd edition, Knowledge Industry Publications, White Plains, NY, 1982.

Duncan, J., *American Radio*, Author, Kalamazoo, MI, twice yearly.

Duncan, J., *Radio in the United States: 1976–82. A Statistical History*, Author, Kalamazoo, MI, 1983.

Eastman, S.T., *Research in Media Promotion*, LEA, Mahwah, NJ, 2000.

Electronic Industries Association, *Electronic Market Data Book*, EIA, Washington, DC, annually.

Fletcher, J.E., editor, *Handbook of Radio and Television Broadcasting: Research Procedures in Audience, Programming, and Revenues*, Van Nostrand Reinhold, New York, 1981.

Gunter, B., *Media Research Methods*, Sage Publishing, Beverly Hills, CA, 2000.

Jamieson, K.H., and Campbell, K.K., *The Interplay of Influence: Mass Media and Their Publics in News, Advertising, and Politics*, Wadsworth Publishing, Belmont, CA, 1983.

Jensen, K.B., *Handbook of Media and Communications Research*, Routledge, New York, 2002.

Katz, H., *The Media Handbook*, 3rd edition, LEA, New York, 2006.

Lazarsfeld, P.F., and Kendall, P., *Radio Listening in America*, Prentice Hall, Englewood Cliffs, NJ, 1948.

McDowell, W., *Troubleshooting Audience Research*, NAB, Washington, DC, 2000.

National Association of Broadcasters, *Audience Research Sourcebook*, NAB Publishing, Washington, DC, 1991.

National Association of Broadcasters, *Radio Financial Report*, NAB, Washington, DC, 1955 to date, annually.

Park, D.W., and Pooley, J., editors, *The History of Media and Communication Research*, Peter Lang, New York, 2008.

Radio Facts, Radio Advertising Bureau, New York, published annually.

Shane, E., *Selling Electronic Media*, Focal Press, Boston, MA, 1999.

Webster, J.G., Phelan, P., and Lichty, L.W., *The Theory and Practice of Audience Research*, 3rd edition, Lawrence Erlbaum Associates, Mahwah, NJ, 2006.

Wimmer, R.D., and Dominick, J., *Mass Media Research: An Introduction*, 5th edition, Wadsworth Publishing, Belmont, CA, 2002.

APPENDIX 6A: Radio Advertising Bureau's (RAB) Radio Research Glossary

FIGURE 6.23
RAB'S Radio
Research Glossary.

Glossary of Terms

Audience Composition: The age, sex and/or ethnic makeup of a station's listening audience.

Average Quarter-Hour (AQH): The average number of people listening in any quarter hour during a particular time period.

> For example: If you worked for a store instead of a radio station, the Cume would be the number of different people who shopped in your store each week, while the AQH would be the average number of people in the store during any fifteen minute period.

Choice: Exclusive listeners choose only one station. First Choice listeners choose other stations, but they choose your station at least as much if not more than any others. 2nd/3rd choice listeners select at least one if not more than one other station before your station. Adding the Exclusive and First Choice categories reported in the Loyalty and Choice analysis yields "core" listeners. The remaining percentages added together are also known as "fringe" listeners.

Composition answers the question: What percentage of my listeners...?

Cume: The estimated number of different listeners that tune in during a daypart in an average week, sometimes called "reach" or "circulation."

Dayparts: Industry-accepted time periods for radio listening; e.g., Monday-Friday 6AM-10AM or Saturday 3PM-7PM. May also be "custom" Dayparts such as a time period for a particular program.

Demographics: Population groups identified by age, sex and/or ethnicity. There are two types: Discrete Demographics, which do not overlap (e.g., Men and/or Women 18-24, 25-34 and 35-44), and Target Demographics, which are broader and indicate the audience group to which the station's programming is aimed (e.g., Men and/or Women 18+, 18-34 and 25-49).

Designated Market Area (DMA): A Nielsen geography defined by television viewing, not radio listening, patterns. It may or may not include all counties in the Metro or TSA.

Gross Quarter-Hours (Impressions): The total quarter-hours of listening to a station by its audience.

Index answers the question: Are my station's listeners more likely or less likely than the total market to...?

> 100 = more likely
< 100 = less likely

Use this guide to help determine which are your best opportunities:

Opportunities	Index	% Composition
Best	High	High
Good	High	Medium
Average	Medium	Medium
Low	Low	Low

Loyalty: A measure of the amount of quarter-hours listeners contribute to a station as a percentage of their listening to all radio; a station's share of its listeners' radio use.

Metro Survey Area (MSA or Metro): Generally corresponds to a government-defined county configuration for a market. There are exceptions, based on historical usage of radio in a market, or other marketing considerations.

Non-metro: Those counties in a market not part of the metro, but included as part of the DMA or TSA. Non-Metro counties are surveyed only in the Spring and Fall surveys.

Persons: The total count, Cume or AQH, of the number of people listening. Rounded to the nearest one-hundred persons, with the last two zeroes dropped for display purposes.

Persons Using Radio (PUR): The total Average Quarter-Hour audience for all radio in any particular time period and demographic in the Metro Survey Area of a market.

Rating: The persons estimate expressed as a percent of the population. AQH and Cume ratings are reported.

Share: The most commonly used and cited estimate, it's a station's Average Quarter-Hour audience in the context of the Average Quarter-Hour audience for all radio (otherwise known as **Persons Using Radio**). It's your station's percentage of all radio listening.

Note: *Persons* estimates are absolute measurements; *rating* and *share* are relative measurements expressed as percentages.

Time Spent Listening (TSL): The amount of time the average person spends listening during a particular time period. Expressed in hours or quarter-hours.

Total Market: Includes all counties in any of the above market definitions.

Total Survey Area (TSA): Includes those counties penetrated significantly by signals from stations licensed to the Metro Survey Area. The Metro Survey Area definition plus the non-metro counties yields the Total Survey Area.

FIGURE 6.24
Arbitron's Glossary
of Terms.

MARKETING GOALS

There are several objectives stations strive to reach when executing a marketing campaign. For example:

STRATEGY

With the introduction of PPM, there are now two rating methodologies by which stations are evaluated. PPM confirms much of our understanding of radio listening that came from the diary methodology. At the same time, the panel-based nature of PPM yields new insights into how consumers use radio over time compared to the results from the 1-week diary.

Both methodologies reveal the importance of core listeners to radio stations. In both diary and PPM, P1's provide, on average, nearly two-thirds of the listening to a station. For all intents and purposes, these P1's are relatively loyal to their given station. As goes the P1, so go the ratings. As a result, the most important strategic objective of the marketing campaign continues to be directed at reinforcing the loyalty of existing P1's and building more. Effective marketing campaigns, whether PPM or diary-based are

- highly targeted to existing and potential P1's;
- focused, with a clear, benefit-driven message and call-to-action;
- reinforced through varied, frequent, and repeated communications.

PPM also provides new insights into consumers over time. For example, in the White Paper, "P1's In A PPM World," published by dmr, The University of Wisconsin's A.C. Nielsen Center for Marketing Research and Arbitron, all P1's are not created equal. Some P1's are very light users of radio and some are very heavy users of radio. In fact, the heavy radio listeners contribute 80–90% of the total amount of listening to the market, even though they represent just 50% of the population. In addition, P1's aren't as loyal as we originally assumed. Most P1's switch with one other station, if they switch at all. Finally, PPM panels are ongoing and reported monthly, as compared to quarterly with diaries. The ongoing nature of PPM also serves to change the strategic planning of the marketing plan.

Based on our new understanding of radio users through PPM, the following criteria should be considered as part of an effective marketing campaign in PPM markets:

- identify and focus the message and media plan primarily on HEAVY radio listeners;
- develop a monthly or semimonthly plan to build and reinforce loyalty;
- develop and ongoing and interactive relationships with the Heavy and Loyal listeners.

The success of every marketing campaign is driven by its ability to

- target the appropriate and likely core listeners;
- present a message that provides a compelling and salient benefit;
- delivered using a multilayered, multimedia approach designed to build loyalty.
- Consistent and directed toward developing an ongoing and interactive relationship

TARGETING IS KEY

The key to any marketing communications plan is reaching the correct audience. No matter what the composition of elements one uses, if the campaign is directed to the

FIGURE 6.25
Direct Marketing Results rely on research data to present its marketing goals. Courtesy DMR.

Figure 6.25
Continued

wrong consumer, it will waste time and money. In radio, there are several sophisticated tools that help to precision-target the right consumers by their listening over a defined geographic area and in some cases by psychographical model. For the diary markets, these tools include Arbitron's PD-Advantage, MapMaker, and Maximizer. Additionally, Nielsen's PRIZM-coding classification is also available. In PPM markets, Arbitron's new PDA-web and the PPM Analysis tool provide substantial insight into geographic targeting.

TARGETING GOALS

The targeting goal is threefold: (1) reach the best prospects for WXXX to produce new P1's or potential P1's for the station in the targeted households; (2) maintain the current level of P1's, and (3) cultivate more loyalty among the existing P1's.

Before we talk about the steps in the targeting analysis, let's first review the value of WXXX and the competitors' heavy listeners. The concept of heavy users applies across many different consumer categories. In his book, *The End of Marketing As We Know It*, Coca-Cola Chief Marketing Officer, Sergio Zyman said that much of the 50% increase in Coca-Cola sales in just 5 years was driven by their strategy to gain and maintain heavy users of soft drinks (not just Coke P1's). Zyman writes, "Heavy users are obviously more profitable than light users. So once you recognize them as a specific segment, you can tailor your marketing to maintain and increase the usage of your heavy consumers and win your competitors' heavy consumers... develop programs that address heavy users." As we noted earlier, PPM underscores the strength and importance of heavy radio listeners because while they are only 50% of the population, they account for nearly 90% of all radio listening. With limited dollars and time, your marketing plan should be targeting the very small portion of the market who are P1's and potential P1's for your station and are heavy users of radio.

THE MESSAGE

Consumers receive, on average, more than 5000 commercial messages per day. To break through, your message needs to be clear, benefit-driven and action-oriented. In addition, it should be anticipated, relevant, and expected. It is a waste of time to simply push unwanted ads at consumers and expect them to embrace your marketing communications. Today, it is more critical than ever to begin a relationship with your listeners or potential listeners. The more personalized and relevant the message, the greater the likelihood that the consumer will engage with it. In addition, marketing messages and communications must be authentic (believable and provable) and consistent across every touchpoint of your station brand. Too often marketing communications are separate and different from the overall brand message or promise. Not only do those messages fall short of engagement, they may ultimately devalue the brand in the mind of the consumer.

THE PLAN

Many marketing plans aren't planned at all. They result from a short burst of necessity, budget availability, and or competitive behavior. As a result, they focus on a tactical medium (TV, billboards, direct mail, etc.) rather than a strategic plan. To break through to the consumer, your plan must have frequency, which reinforces the message you are communicating. It also aids learning and engagement if it is delivered via multiple media. Multiple component campaigns have a much greater likelihood of success. For example, Arbitron uses a multivaried approach to recruiting ratings households (in both diary and PPM) beginning first with a postcard or letter survey, then following up with a live phone call or voicemail, continuing with a confirmation letter or postcard, etc. An effective plan employs multiple elements to ensure the message is noticed and attended to by the target consumer.

Figure 6.25
Continued

PERSONAL PHONE CALLS

Personal, live phone calls continue to be an efficient and cost-effective way of identifying, targeting, and developing a relationship with P1's and potential P1's on a large scale over a relatively short time period. The phone provides for the achievement of four steps quickly: (1) impression, (2) awareness, (3) recall, and (4) sampling. For PPM, the value of the phone call is particularly significant because of its ability to create a "take-action-now" immediate usage occasion, which will immediately register in PPM.

The personal call element of an integrated campaign can also capture radio usage level and perceived loyalty as well as purchase habits, opinions, preferences, and other lifestyle information. Once a station commits to obtaining this information, it will have initiated an active database of loyal, heavy listeners – the foundation for an on-going interactive relationship. Unlike the shotgun approach of "everyone's a target" from TV or billboards, personal phone calls are much more effective because it essentially filters for the households and consumers who are phone-responsive, rather than all people everywhere. This is particularly important in PPM because of the added importance of the heavy loyal P1's who while representing just a small percentage of the cume contribute and drive as much as half the audience.

DIRECT MAIL

Direct mail is another valuable tool to include in an integrated marketing campaign. Direct mail is personal, specific, and targeted to reinforce a station's marketing position and brand with a strong visual message. Direct mail can provide the continuity with print, billboards, and web-based promotions. Types of direct mail include personalized laser-printed letters with enclosures like magnets, coupon packets, reply cards, personalized billboards, videos and DVDs, CDs, newsletters, calendars, and birthday and thank-you cards. New technologies and web integration have provided a whole new area of direct mail called Personalized Domains which allow the consumers name to be the foundation of the Web site they're directed to on the printed piece.

E-MAIL MARKETING

By using an e-mail marketing system, you can send individualized focused messages instantly, with powerful attention-getting graphics or flash animation to your database. Some systems provide a built-in bounce-back and reply management to simplify the backend operations. With database-driven e-mail systems, you can track activity levels and engagement levels of your key listeners and segment those who are connectors.

TEXT MESSAGING

Many campaigns today employ a text messaging component. Texting is particularly valuable because it allows a consumer to take action immediately, not wait to send in a card or log-in to a Web site, or call and try to get through. The key to adding a successful text messaging component to your marketing campaign is to ask for a quick registration at some point so that you can determine which members of your database are actively using that channel. That can be done with a special bounce-back text driving the texting phone to a mobile Web site and/or a conventional site for a short entry.

WEBFORM

Webforms are a critical component of a strong relationship marketing campaign and initiative. By creating an enrollment form, you allow the listeners the chance to engage

Figure 6.25
Continued

and interact with the station. It's also a perfect way to quickly gather usage and loyalty information to help segment the database and focus on those heavy listeners. Once active, you can use the data to create more personalized domains as discussed in the direct mail section above. Webforms are commonplace today, but it's critical to keep them short and relatively easy. It may also be important to have a mobile version depending on your audience demographics.

INTERNET AND SEARCH MARKETING

The Internet enables delivery of personalized messages within targeted content and real-time interaction. It's an essential component to any effective marketing campaign because of the interactivity and immediacy it provides. In particular, search marketing provides a unique platform to connect and engage targeted consumers while online at work or at home and engage quickly with the station and easily register for the station database. The Internet also provides an excellent vehicle for word-of-mouth and pass-along advertising particularly with its new social media component.

SOCIAL MEDIA

With the advent of MySpace and Facebook, social media has rocketed to the top of the marketers' tool kit. However, it's relatively unknown or not well used by radio stations. The basis for success of social media marketing is allowing your consumers or the community to control part, or all, of the message instead of forcing or broadcasting what you believe the message should be. Including a social media component to your marketing plan is becoming more important because of the power and value of the community. The objective of a social media component is to "join the conversation" that consumers are (or can be) having about your brand and how it relates to their life. In many cases, this rich and fertile sharing can be more valuable and far-reaching than any conventional research you're conducting. At the very least, it provides an avenue into the natural patterns of communities that center around a radio station brand.

One particular social media tool that is growing dramatically with the ubiquitous nature of the mobile phone is Twitter. Twitter provides a simple, yet powerful platform to enable like-minded individuals to converse in 160-character bursts. Twitter conversations about virtually anything (and in many cases, about radio stations) are happening right now on Twitter. To see if they're talking about a station you know, just go to search twitter.com

Promotion 7

Past and Purpose

In the fiercely competitive audio marketplace, radio stations must of necessity resort to heavy-handed self-aggrandizement. "WXXX – the station without equal," "For the best in music and news tune WXXX," or "You're tuned to the music giant – WXXX" certainly illustrate this point. Why must stations practice self-glorification? The answer is simple: to keep the listener interested and tuned. The highly fragmented radio marketplace has made promotion a basic component of station operations. Five times as many stations vie for the listening audience today as did when television arrived on the scene. It is competition that makes promotion necessary.

Small and large stations alike promote and market themselves. In the single-station market, stations promote to counter the effects of other media, especially the local newspaper, which often is the archrival of small-town outlets. Since there is only one station to tune to, promotion serves to maintain listener interest in the medium. In large markets, where three stations may be offering the same format, promotion helps a station differentiate itself from the rest. In this case, the station with the best promotion often wins the ratings war.

Radio recognized the value of promotion early. In the 1920s and 1930s, stations used newspapers and other print media to inform the public of their existence. Remote broadcasts from hotels, theaters, and stores also attracted attention for stations and were a popular form of promotion during the medium's golden age. Promotion-conscious broadcasters of the pretelevision era were just as determined to get the audience to take notice as they are today. From the start, stations used whatever was at hand to capture the public's attention. Call letters were configured in such a way as to convey a particular sentiment or meaning: WEAF/ New York, Water, Earth, Air, Fire; WOW/ Omaha, Woodmen Of the World; and WIOD/Miami, Wonderful Isle Of Dreams. In addition, placards were affixed to vehicles, buildings, and even blimps as a means of heightening the public's awareness.

As ratings assumed greater prominence in the age of specialization, stations became even more cognizant of the need to promote. The relationship between good ratings and effective promotion became more apparent. In the 1950s and 1960s, programming innovators such as Todd Storz and Gordon McLendon used promotions and contests with daring and skill, even a bit of lunacy, to win the attention of listeners.

The growth of radio promotion has paralleled the proliferation of frequencies. "The more stations you have out there, the greater the necessity to promote. Let's face it, a lot of stations are doing about the same thing. A good promotion sets you apart. It gives you greater identity, which means everything when a survey company asks a listener what station he or she tunes. Radio is an advertising medium in and of itself. Promotion makes a station salable. You sell yourself so that you have something to sell advertisers," observes Las Vegas radio station promotion director (also called promotion manager) Charlie Morriss. Stations that once confined the bulk of their

215

FIGURE 7.1
Stations promote
their image. Courtesy
KUDL.

promotional effort to spring and fall to coincide with rating periods now find it necessary to engage in promotional campaigns on an ongoing basis throughout the year, notes Morriss. "More competition and monthly audience surveys mean that stations have to keep the promotion fire burning continually, the analogy being that if the flame goes out you're likely to go cool in the ratings. So you really have to hype your outlet every opportunity you get. The significance of the role of promotion in contemporary radio cannot be overstated."

The vital role that promotion plays in radio is not likely to diminish as hundreds of more stations enter the airways by the turn of the century.

"Promotion has become as much a part of radio as the records and the deejays who spin them, and that's not about to change," contends promotion director John Grube.

Promotions – Practical and Bizarre

The idea behind any promotion is to win listeners. Over the years, stations have used a variety of methods, ranging from the conventional to the outlandish, to accomplish this goal. "If a promotion achieves top-of-the-mind awareness in the listener, it's a winner. Granted, some strange things have been done to accomplish this," admits Mississippi broadcaster Bob Lima.

Promotions designed to captivate the interest of the radio audience have inspired some pretty bizarre schemes. In the 1950s, Dallas station KLIF placed overturned cars on freeways with a sign on their undersides announcing the arrival of a new deejay,

Johnny Rabbitt. It would be hard to calculate the number of deejays who have lived atop flagpoles or in elevators for the sake of a rating point.

In the 1980s, the shenanigans continued. To gain the listening public's attention, a California deejay set a world record by sitting in every seat of a major league ballpark that held 65,000 spectators. In the process of the stunt, the publicity hungry deejay injured his leg. However, he went on to accomplish his goal by garnering national attention for himself and his station. Another station offered to give away a mobile home to contestants who camped out the longest on a platform at the base of a billboard. The challenge turned into a battle of wills as three contestants spent months trying to outlast each other. In the end, one of the three was disqualified, and the station, in an effort to cease what had become more of an embarrassment than anything else, awarded the two holdouts recreational vehicles.

Today, promotions have gotten edgier, especially on those stations featuring shock jock shows. Things can and do get out of hand when personalities go to the extreme to draw listeners' attention with on-air pranks and giveaways. Prior to migrating to satellite, Howard Stern held all manner of scatological promotions and contests, many centered around women removing their clothes, and Opie and Anthony asked listeners to have sex in public places. This ultimately got them removed from the air, thus proving there are limits to what a station can do to get attention from an audience. Of course, after a successful stint (or exile) on satellite radio, the duo was hired back by terrestrial radio – proving again that ratings matter most. The tone and tenor of station promotions have certainly changed over the decades, notes Larry Miller. "Although occurring in what now seems a gentler and kinder world, my personal favorite is the one about a station in LA in the early 1950s that sent out a 'free Valhalla Oil credit card' to listeners. Well, there was no such oil company, but loyal listeners nevertheless spent a good deal of time searching for a Valhalla gas station. Everybody had a laugh."

Reporter Peg Harney offers testimony that the bizarre still occurs in radio promotions.

FIGURE 7.2
Stations showcase their superstars. Courtesy WOR.

WOR NewsTalk Radio 710

Click HERE to book today.

Amtrak.com

BLOGS   FOOD   ENERGY   POLITICS   NEWS   AUTO

WOR PERSONALITIES

The John Gambling Show
Weekdays 5:30am-9:00am
The John Gambling Show is New York's <u>only</u> local News/Talk program in the mornings! John's experience, his deep understanding of the tri-state area and its residents, and his legendary pragmatic approach to the day's headlines make this show a must for your morning!

Joan Hamburg
Weekdays 9am-11am
Joan Hamburg has been covering the scene as a journalist and broadcaster for many years, and is known throughout the country for her award-winning consumer affairs reporting.

Food Talk with Michael Colameco
Weekdays 11am-Noon
Sundays 10am-Noon
Listen for delicious recipes, cooking techniques, interviews with the top chefs in the industry, & wine and restaurant recommendations - call to ask for suggestions!

Bill O'Reilly
Weekdays Noon-2pm
Originating from the FOX News Channel in New York, The Radio Factor With Bill O'Reilly will focus on a specific topic each day generated from the events and people making headlines. The Radio Factor With Bill O'Reilly will also feature special guests and phone calls from listeners nationwide.

"As a publicity stunt and also to get people to use the local public library, a station in Ft. Worth, Texas, a couple years back announced it had hidden cash in small denominations in the fiction section. Approximately 800 people descended on the library and proceeded to pull books off the shelves looking for the money. The library had not been notified that the station was going to make the announcement, and it was totally taken by surprise. The librarian said that approximately 4000 books were pulled from the shelves – some of them had pages torn out – and that people were climbing on the bookcases and making a tremendous mess. The station was forced to make a public apology, and it promised full financial restitution."

One of the most infamous examples of a promotion gone bad occurred when a station decided to air-drop dozens of turkeys to a waiting crowd of listeners in a neighborhood shopping center parking lot. Unfortunately, the station discovered too late that turkeys are not adept at flying at heights above 30 feet. Consequently, several cars were damaged and witnesses were traumatized as turkeys plunged to the ground. This promotion-turned-nightmare was depicted in an episode of the television sitcom WKRP in Cincinnati.

The list of glitches is seemingly endless. In the late 1960s, a station in central Massachusetts asked listeners to predict how long its air personality could ride a carousel at a local fair. The hardy airman's effort was cut short on day 3 when motion sickness got the best of him and he vomited on a crowd

of spectators and newspaper photographers. A station in California came close to disaster when a promotion that challenged listeners to find a buried treasure resulted in half the community being dug up by overzealous contestants. In Massachusetts, a station invited listeners to retrieve money-filled balloons dropped by helicopters into the surf, and contestants came close to drowning as the balloons floated out to sea.

These promotions did indeed capture the attention of the public, but in each case, the station's image was somewhat tarnished. The axiom that any publicity, good or bad, is better than none at all can get a station into hot water, contends station promotion director Chuck Davis. "It's great to get lots of exposure for the station, but if it makes the station look foolish, it can work against you."

The vast majority of radio contests and promotions are of a more practical nature and run without too many complications. Big prizes, rather than stunts, tend to draw the most interest and thus are offered by stations able to afford them. In the mid-1980s, WASHAM, Washington, DC, and KSSK-AM, Honolulu, both gave a lucky listener a million dollars. Cash prizes always have attracted tremendous response. Valuable prizes other than cash also can boost ratings. For example, Los Angeles station KHTZ-AM experienced a sizable jump in its ratings when it offered listeners a chance to win a $122,000 house (this was a decade ago). Increased ratings also resulted when KHJ-AM, Los Angeles, gave away a car every day during the month of May.

Promotions that involve prizes, both large and small, spark audience interest, says Rick Peters, vice president of programming, Sconnix Broadcasting. "People love to win something or, at least, feel that they have a shot at winning a prize. That's basic to human nature, I believe. You really don't have to give away two city blocks, either. A listener usually is thrilled and delighted to win a pair of concert tickets."

Although numerous examples can be cited to support the view that big prizes get big audiences, there is also ample evidence that low-budget giveaways, involving T-shirts, albums, tickets, posters, dinners,

FIGURE 7.3
Getting noticed is the key. Courtesy WGH.

and so forth, are very useful in building and maintaining audience interest. In fact, some surveys have revealed that smaller, more personalized prizes may work better for a station than the high-priced items. iPods, concert tickets, and dinners-for-two rank among the most popular contest prizes, according to surveys. Cheaper items usually also mean more numerous or frequent giveaways.

The Promotion Director's/Manager's Job

Not all stations employ a full-time promotion director. But most stations designate someone to handle promotional responsibilities. At small outlets, the program director (PD) or even the general manager (GM) assumes promotional chores. Larger stations and station clusters with bigger operating budgets typically hire an individual or individuals to work exclusively in the area of promotion. "At major-market stations, you'll find a promotion department that includes a director and possibly assistants. In middle-sized markets, such as ours, the promotion responsibility is often designated to someone already involved in programming," says Bob Lima.

Observes Ed Shane: "Some promotion managers consider themselves 'marketing directors.' There are two levels of job responsibility for promotion people. Some are glorified 'banner hangers,' who make sure the grunt work is done at a station promotion or a live broadcast. Others are true department heads who exhibit leadership and vision within their operations."

Indeed the promotion director's responsibilities are manifold. Essential to the position are a knowledge and understanding of the station's audience. A background in research is important, contends Grube. "Before you can initiate any kind of promotion you must know something about who you're trying to reach. This requires an ability to interpret various research data that you gather through in-house survey efforts or from outside audience research companies, like Birch and Arbitron. You don't give away beach balls to 50-year-old

men. Ideas must be confined to the cell group you're trying to attract."

Writing and conceptual skills are vital to the job of promotion director, says Morriss. "You prepare an awful lot of copy of all types. One moment you're composing press releases about programming changes, and the next you're writing a 30-second promo about the station's expanded news coverage or upcoming remote broadcast from a local mall. Knowledge of English grammar is a must. Bad writing reflects negatively on the station. The job also demands imagination and creativity. You have to be able to come up with an idea and bring it to fruition."

Chuck Davis agrees with Morriss and adds that although the promotion person should be able to originate concepts, a certain number of ideas come from the trades and other stations. "When this is the case, and it often is, you have to know how to adapt an idea to suit your own station. Of course, the promotion must reflect your location. Lifestyles vary almost by region. A promotion that's successful at a station in Louisiana may bear no relevance to a station with a similar format in Michigan. On the other hand, with some adjustments, it may work as effectively there. The creativity in this example exists in the adaptation."

Promotion directors must be versatile. A familiarity with graphic art generally is necessary, since the promotion director will be involved in developing station logos and image IDs for advertising in the print media

FIGURE 7.4
Stations use point of purchase posters to promote their contests. Courtesy WENS-FM.

FIGURE 7.5
Cautionary words
from a consultant.
Courtesy Shane
Media.

tactics: promotions

A Promotions Report from Shane Media

January 28, 2008

PROMOTIONAL PITFALLS

If you don't consider every detail when putting a promotion together, expect headaches. Here are common promotion mistakes encountered by the Promotion Marketing Association:

Contradiction between the selling copy and the official rules.

> If your promo copy says "win a trip to anywhere in America," and the rules say "continental U.S.," you're in trouble when the winner opts for Hawaii.

The photo or illustration of the prize doesn't match the prize exactly.

> In a printed ad or Web promotion page, show the prize you intend to give away. Even a change of color (especially on a car) can cause a problem when the winner comes to claim the prize.

Expenses are not explained.

> If you say "all expenses paid," the winner may expect a new wardrobe or to have the pets boarded while they take the prize trip. Name specific expenses you'll cover or set a dollar limit to avoid ambiguity.

Over-estimating the value of a prize.

> Whatever you pay for the prize, there's always the possibility that the winner could get it cheaper. Airfare's a good example. A cross-country trip at $3,000 could be had for $2,000 and the consumer might demand full value. Report a $3,000 prize to the IRS and the winner claims $2,000, there's more trouble. Use a phrase like "full retail value."

Using descriptive words without knowing the established meanings.

> "Luxury" and "deluxe" are travel industry words that set a standard for expectations. Don't give a stay at a "luxury" hotel and book a Day's Inn.

Copy rules from someone else's contest or using last year's rules.

> There's always a minor detail that is unique to the situation. Check the law and whether it has changed since the last play of the contest.

Allowing retailers to handle entries without guidance.

> A promotional partner needs to be as vigilant about security and abuse as you do. Provide detailed instructions on how to handle entry boxes and forms.

Launching the promotion before you have the prizes.

> Secure the prize first and you never worry about a product that's behind on production, a retailer who fails to deliver, or a winner who shows up sooner than you expected.

and billboards. The promotion department also participates in the design and preparation of visuals for the sales area.

The acquisition of prize materials through direct purchase and trades is another duty of the promotion person, who also may be called on to help co-ordinate sales co-op arrangements. "You work closely with the sales manager to arrange tie-ins with sponsors and station promotions," contends Morriss.

Like other radio station department heads, it is the promotion director's responsibility to ensure that the rules and regulations established by the FCC, relevant to the promotions area, are observed. This will be discussed further later in the chapter, in the section Promotions and the FCC.

Of course, it is important that a promotion director maintains a high level of communication with other station personnel, particularly the program director and sales manager, who are almost always an integral part of a promotion's execution and implementation. Everyone should be in the know-about contests and promotions.

On a final note (corroborating Ed Shane's preceding contention), Lynn Christian observes that "The word marketing has become the rallying cry today. At a BPME meeting the question was raised as to whether a promotion director should be designated 'marketing director,' and given upgraded status in a station – that is, parity with the program director and sales manager. In the light of the horrendous competition and the need to survive in what has been a very soft market, it makes sense to acknowledge the value and importance of an effective promotion (marketing) director."

Who Promotion Directors Hire

In each section devoted to hiring in preceding and subsequent chapters, college training is listed as a desirable, if not necessary, attribute. This is no less true in the area of radio station promotion. "My advice to an individual interested in becoming a promotion person would be to get as much formal training as possible in marketing, research, graphics, writing, public relations, and, of course, broadcasting. The duties of

FIGURE 7.6
Remote broadcasts from sponsor sites generate buzz. Courtesy WIZN.

❖HALL COMMUNICATIONS REMOTE/APPEARANCE CHECKLIST

HAVE YOU: ____ APPROVED DATE WITH STEVE/MATT? ____ RESERVED THE DATE WITH A POST-IT ON THE CALENDAR?

CIRCLE STATION: **WOKO   WIZN   WKOL   WBTZ   WJOY**

EVENT DATE: _____   TIME: _____

CLIENT/EVENT NAME: _____

EVENT DESCRIPTION: _____

CLIENT/EVENT ADDRESS: _____

TOWN/CITY:_____   STATE: _____

CONTACT INFORMATION:

ON-SITE NAME: _____   ON-SITE PHONE: _____

SALES REP NAME: _____   SALES REP CEL PH: _____

TALENT REQUEST: _____

ARE THERE ANY "OUT OF THE ORDINARY" DUTIES TALENT WILL BE ASKED TO PERFORM:___YES ___NO IF YES, WHAT? _____

_____

WILL CLIENT BE PROVIDING GIVEAWAYS AT EVENT:___YES ___NO

IF YES, WHAT? _____

ARE ADDITIONAL SPONSORS INVOLVED? _____ YES _____ NO

IF YES, WHO/HOW? _____

HAVE THEY BEEN PROMISED MENTIONS IN EVENT PROMOS? ____ YES ____ NO

HAVE THEY BEEN PROMISED MENTIONS DURING CALL IN'S? ____ YES ____ NO

ADDITIONAL CHECKLIST ITEMS TO BE COMPLETED BY SALES:
____ HAS AN ORDER BEEN TURNED INTO TRAFFIC FOR THIS EVENT?
____ HAS INFORMATION FOR A WEB SITE LISTING FOR THIS EVENT BEEN TURNED IN?
____ IS THE CLIENT/EVENT CONTACT AWARE THAT STEVE/MATT MAY BE CALLING TO SET UP LOGISTICS?
____ HAVE YOU GIVEN A COPY OF THIS FRONT PAGE TO MATT/STEVE FOR SCHEDULING?

the promotion director, especially at a large station, are diverse," notes Rick Peters of TK Communications.

Charlie Morriss agrees with Peters and adds, "A manager reviewing the credentials of candidates for a promotion position will expect to find a statement about formal training, that is, college. Of course, nothing is a substitute for a solid track record. Experience is golden. This is a very hands-on field. My advice today is to get a good education and along the way pick up a little experience, too."

Familiarity with programming is important, contends Lima, who suggests that prospective promotion people spend some time on the air. "Part-timing it on mic at a station, be it a small commercial outlet or a college facility, gives a person special insight into the nature of the medium that he or she is promoting. Working in sales also is valuable. In the specific skills department, I'd say the promotion job candidate should have an eye for detail, be well organized, and possess exemplary writing skills. It goes without saying that a positive attitude and genuine appreciation of radio are important as well."

Both John Grube and Chuck Davis cite wit and imagination as criteria for the job of promotion. "It helps to be a little wacky and crazy. By that I mean able to conceive of entertaining, fun concepts," says Grube. Davis concurs, "This is a convivial medium. The idea behind any promotion or contest is to attract and amuse the listener. A zany, off-the-wall idea is good, as long as it is based in sound reasoning. Calculated craziness requires common sense and creativity, and both are qualities you need in order to succeed in promotion."

The increasing competition in the radio marketplace has bolstered job opportunities in promotion. Thus, the future appears bright for individuals planning careers in this facet of the medium.

Types of Promotions

There are two primary categories of station promotions: on-air and off-air. The on-air category will be examined first since it is the most prevalent form of radio

promotion. Broadcasters already possess the best possible vehicle to reach listeners, and so it should come as no surprise that on-air promotion is the most common means of getting the word out on a station. The challenge confronting the promotion director is how to most effectively market the station so as to expand and retain listenership. To this end, a number of promotional devices are employed, beginning with the most obvious – station call letters. "The value of a good set of call letters is inestimable," says KGLD's Bremkamp. "A good example is the call letters of a station I once managed which have long been associated with the term rich and all that it implies: 'Hartford's Rich Music Station – WRCH.'"

Call letters convey the personality of a station. For instance, try connecting these call letters with a format: WHOG, WNWS, WEZI, WODS, WJZZ, WIND, and WHTS. If you guessed Country, News, Easy Listening, Oldies, Jazz, Talk, and Hits, you were correct. The preceding call letters not only identify their radio stations but they literally convey the nature or content of the programming offered.

Larry Miller adds, "Anything that can be made to spell 'KISS' is always a favorite with listeners, starting with a KISS station in the Northwest back in the 1950s. Other similar calls include 'Magic' for a soft AC, 'Zoo' for a wild and crazy CHR or Hot AC, or 'Rock' as in K-Rock. In Hawaii, calls that spell Hawaiian words have always been popular, such as K-POI. In the early 1970s, the ABC group of O&O FMs changed call letters to reflect 'hip' or local culture with calls like KLOS in LA or KSFX in San Francisco or WRIF in Detroit or WPLJ (white port and lemon juice) in New York."

When stations do not possess call letters that create instant recognition, they often couple their frequency with a call letter or two, such as JB-105 (WPJB-FM 105) or KISS-108 (WXKS-FM 108). This also improves the retention factor. Slogans frequently are a part of the on-air ID. "Music Country – WSOC-FM, Charlotte," "A Touch of Class – WTEB-FM, New Bern," and "Texas Best Rock – KTXQ-FM, Fort Worth" are some examples. Slogans exemplify a station's image. When effective, they capture the mood and flavor of the station and leave a strong impression in the listener's mind. It is standard programming policy at many stations to announce the station's call letters and even its slogan each time a deejay opens the microphone. This is especially true during ratings sweeps when survey companies ask listeners to identify the stations they tune into. "If your calls stick in the mind of your audience, you've hit a home run. If they don't, you'll go scoreless in the book. You've got to carve them into the listener's gray matter and you start by making IDs and signatures that are as memorable as possible," observes Rick Peters.

Jay Williams, Jr., observes that call letters are being used less and less in the digital age. "Stations identify themselves using their frequencies (92.5) today more than their call letters. This has become the case since the radio dial became digitized. The emphasis is now more numerical than alphabetical. Even the alphanumeric approach (Magic 92) has faded in favor of simply stating the station's frequency."

It is a common practice for stations to "bookend" – place call letters and/or frequencies before and after all breaks between music. For example, "WHJJ. Stay tuned for a complete look at local and national news at the top of the hour on WHJJ." Deejays also are told to graft the station call letters onto all bits of information: "92.9 Time," "102.5 Temperature," "102.5 Weather," and so on. There is a rule in radio that call letters can never be overannounced. The logic behind this is clear. The more a station tells its audience what it is tuned to, the more apt it is to remember, especially during rating periods.

On-air contests are another way to capture and hold the listener's attention. Contests must be easy to understand (are the rules and requirements of the contest easily understood by the listener?) and possess entertainment value (will nonparticipants be amused even though they are not actually involved?). A contest should engage the interest of all listeners, players and nonplayers alike.

A contest must be designed to enhance a station's overall sound or format. It must fit in, be compatible. Obviously, a mystery sound contest requiring the broadcast of loud or shrill noises would disrupt the tranquility and continuity of an Easy Listening station and result in tune-out.

Successful contests are timely and relevant to the lifestyle of the station's target audience, says Bob Lima. "A contest should offer prizes that truly connect with the listener. An awareness of the needs, desires, and fantasies of the listener will help guide a station. For example, giving away a refrigerator on a hot hit station would not really captivate the 16-year-old tuned. This is obvious, of course. But the point I'm making is that the prizes that are up for grabs should be something the listener really wants to win, or you have apathy."

The importance of creativity already has been stated. Contests that attract the most attention often are the ones that challenge the listener's imagination, contends Morriss. "A contest should have style, should attempt to be different. You can give away what is perfectly suitable for your audience, but you can do it in a way that creates excitement and adds zest to the programming. The goal of any promotion is to set you apart from the other guy. Be daring within reason, but be daring."

FIGURE 7.7
Listeners love to win money. Courtesy Froggy.

On-air promotion is used to inform the audience of what a station has to offer: station personalities, programs, and special features and events. Rarely does a quarter-hour pass on any station that does not include a promo that highlights some aspect of programming:

"Tune in WXXX's News at Noon each weekday for a full hour of …"

"Irv McKenna keeps 'Nightalk' in the air midnight to six on the voice of the valley – WXXX. Yes, there's never a dull moment …"

"Every Saturday night WXXX turns the clock back to the fifties and sixties to bring you the best of the golden oldies …"

"Hear the complete weather forecast on the hour and half hour throughout the day and night on your total service station – XXX …"

On-air promotion is a cost-efficient and effective means of building an audience when done correctly, says John Grube. "There are good on-air promotions and weak or ineffective on-air promotions. The latter can inflict a deep wound, but the former can put a station on the map. As broadcasters, the airtime is there at our disposal, but we sometimes forget just how potent an advertising tool we have."

Marketing expert Andrew Curran points to another area of promotion. "A stealth promotion might include members of the station database and is something that only the people eligible to win know is going on. For example, a station might announce a name three times a day for a chance to win $1000. 'We'd like to thank John Smith for listening to Classic Rock WXYZ.' Then this person would have 20 minutes to call in and win and since only he can win, he's not competing with the whole city to get through on the phone. Plus, he feels important that he's eligible to win a special contest from the station. In the end, of course, a great promotion makes people want to tune the station."

Radio stations employ off-air promotional techniques to reach people not tuned in. Billboards are a popular form of outside promotion. To be effective, they must be both eye-catching and simple. Only so much can be stated on a billboard, since people generally are in a moving vehicle and have only a limited amount of time to absorb a message. Placement of the billboard also is a key factor. To be effective, billboards must be located where they will reach a station's intended audience. Although an All-News station would avoid the use of a billboard facing a high school, a rock music outlet may prefer the location.

Bus cards are a good way to reach the public. Cities often have hundreds of buses on the streets each day. Billboard companies also use benches and transit shelters to get their client's message across to the population. Outside advertising is an effective and fairly cost-efficient way to promote

FIGURE 7.8
Billboards catch the attention of commuters. Courtesy Rock102.

a radio station, although certain billboards at heavy traffic locations can be extremely expensive to lease.

Newspapers are the most frequent means of off-air promotion. Stations like the reach and targeting that newspapers can provide. In large metro areas, alternative newspapers, such as the *Boston Phoenix*, are very effective in delivering certain listening cells. The *Phoenix* enjoys one of the largest readerships of any independent press in the country. Its huge college-age and young professional audience makes it an ideal promotional medium for stations after those particular demographics. Although the readership of the more conventional newspapers traditionally is low among young people, it is high in older adults, making the mainstream publications useful to stations targeting the over-40 crowd.

Newspapers with large circulations provide a great way to reach the population at large, but they also can be very costly, although some stations are able to trade airtime for print space. Newspaper ads must be large enough to stand out and overcome the sea of advertisements that often share the same page. Despite some drawbacks, newspapers usually are the first place radio broadcasters consider when planning an off-air promotion.

Television is a costly but effective promotional tool for radio. A primary advantage that television offers is the chance to target the audience that the station is after. An enormous amount of information is available pertaining to television viewership. Thus, a station that wants to reach the 18–24 year olds is able to ascertain the programs and features that best draw that particular cell.

The costs of producing or acquiring ready-made promos for television can run high, but most radio broadcasters value the opportunity to actually show the public what they can hear when they tune to their station. WBZ-AM in Boston used local television extensively to promote its former morning personality, Dave Maynard, and its current sunrise news team. Ratings for the Westinghouse-owned station have been consistently high, and management points

to their television promotion as a contributing factor.

Bumper stickers are manufactured by the millions for distribution by practically every commercial radio station in the country. The primary purpose of stickers is to increase call letter awareness. Over the years, bumper stickers have developed into a unique pop-art form, and hundreds of people actually collect station decals as a hobby. Some station bumper stickers are particularly prized for the lifestyle or image they portray. Youths, in particular, are fond of displaying their favorite station's call letters. Stations appealing to older demographics find that their audiences are somewhat less enthusiastic about bumper stickers.

Stations motivate listeners to display bumper stickers by tying them in with on-air promotions:

WXXX WANTS TO GIVE YOU A THOUSAND DOLLARS. ALL YOU HAVE TO DO IS PUT AN X-100 BUMPER STICKER ON YOUR CAR TO BE ELIGIBLE. IT'S THAT SIMPLE. WHEN YOUR CAR IS SPOTTED BY THE X-100 ROVING EYE, YOUR LICENSE NUMBER WILL BE ANNOUNCED OVER THE AIR. YOU WILL THEN HAVE THIRTY MINUTES TO CALL THE STATION TO CLAIM YOUR ONE THOUSAND DOLLARS....

Hundreds of ways have been invented to entice people to display station call letters. The idea is to get the station's name out to the public, and 10,000 cars exhibiting a station's bumper sticker is an effective way to do that. Says Ed Shane, "Visibility is part of the answer. Station promotion has reached new levels of creativity and intrusion – skateboard jumpers, rolling radios, inflatables in the boots, guitars, frogs."

Stations give away thousands of items displaying station call letters and logos annually. Among the most common promotional items handed out by stations are posters, T-shirts, calendars, key chains, coffee mugs, music hit lists, book covers, pens, and car litter bags. The list is vast.

Plastic card promotions have done well for many stations. Holders are entitled to a variety of benefits, including discounts at various stores and valuable prizes. The bearer is told to listen to the station for

FIGURE 7.9
Bumper stickers
visually convey
a station's sound
and image.
Courtesy Mo Money
Associates.

FIGURE 7.10
The more
extravagant the
giveaway, the more
interest it generates.
Courtesy Star-FM.

information as to where to use the card. In addition, holders are eligible for special on-air drawings.

Another particularly effective way to increase a station's visibility is to sponsor special activities, such as fairs, sporting events, theme dances, and concerts. Hartford's Big Band station, WRCQ-AM, has received significant attention by presenting an annual music festival that has attracted over 25,000 spectators each year, plus the notice of other media, including television and newspapers.

Personal appearances by station personalities are one of the oldest forms of off-air promotion but still a very effective one.

Remote broadcasts from malls, beaches, and the like also aid in getting the word of the station out to the public.

One last means of marketing a station is offered by Jay Williams, Jr., CEO, Direct Marketing Results: "Promotion and marketing have never been more critical. In the current economy, stations have to do everything they can to draw and hold an audience. Direct marketing through mail and/or by telephone is a very cost-effective way to target an audience and to keep a station in front of radio listeners, especially during rating periods. Telepromoting is becoming more prevalent. Directed or targeted

Randy Michael | Selling Promotions

Marketing is changing. Twenty years ago, 70% of marketing was advertising. It's now 40%. It may be 20% in 10 years. Direct to consumer, B to B, events, and branding are replacing advertising in many cases. Radio needs to get more of the promotion dollars and not rely on just advertising. Radio can deliver results for advertisers, and it can promote effectively if it reaches a desirable audience. Radio stations must select a target audience available to them given the constraints of the signal and competition environment. The best stations feature programming that is different, desirable, and difficult to duplicate. Too many managers have made stations generic in an effort to cut costs. This is a mistake. I can hear my favorite music on a personal device without commercials.

FIGURE 7.11
Randy Michael.

marketing makes sense because stations must be more effective with what they have. The business of radio is changing. Audiences are fragmenting, brand loyalties are eroding. Mass marketing is losing its impact. Person-to-person or individualized marketing delivers tangible results."

Ed Shane concurs with Williams, adding, "Direct marketing is the wave of the one-to-one future. More direct mail, telemarketing, database management, and computer interaction."

Sales Promotion

Promoting a station can be very costly, as much as half a million dollars annually in some metro markets. To help defray the cost of station promotion, advertisers are often recruited. This way both the station and the sponsor stand to benefit. The station gains the financial wherewithal to execute certain promotions that it could not do on its own, and the participating advertiser gains valuable exposure by tying in with special station events. Stations actually can make money and promote themselves simultaneously if a client purchases a substantial spot schedule as part of a promotional package. Says Larry Miller, "An effective promotional campaign should try to include a sales component, in part to help allay the costs of advertising. If it's done right, it will bring in new business for the station."

There are abundant ways to involve advertisers in station promotion efforts. They run the gamut from placing advertisements and coupons on the back of bumper stickers to joining the circus for the day; for example, "WXXX brings the 'Greatest Show on Earth' to town this Friday night, and you go for half price just by mentioning the name of your favorite radio station – WXXX." The ultimate objective of a station/sponsor collaborative is to generate attention in a cost-efficient manner. If a few dollars are made for the station along the way, all the better.

As stated previously, the promotion director also works closely with the station's sales department in the preparation and design of sales promotion materials, which include items such as posters, coverage maps, ratings breakouts, flyers, station profiles, rate cards, and much more.

FIGURE 7.12
Direct marketing helps increase audience awareness of a radio station. Courtesy DMR.

Research and Planning

To effectively promote a station, the individual charged with the task must possess a thorough knowledge of the station and its audience. This person must then ascertain the objective of the promotion. Is it the aim of the promotion to increase call letter awareness, introduce a new format/feature/personality, or bolster the station's community service image? Of course, the ultimate goal of any promotion is to enhance listenership.

Effective promotions take into account both internal and external factors. An understanding of the product, consumer, and competition is essential to any marketing effort,

including radio. Each of these three areas presents the promotion director with questions that must be addressed before launching a campaign. As stated earlier in this chapter, it is imperative that the promotion or contest fit the station's sound – in other words, be compatible with the format. This accomplished, the next consideration is the relevancy of the promotion to the station's audience. For example, does it fit the listener's lifestyle? Third, is the idea fresh enough in the market to attract and sustain interest?

Observes programming executive Corinne Baldassano, "You must institute ongoing research to make sure your target audience is happy with what it's hearing. You can make adjustments depending on the feedback you get from the research. Those stations that have succeeded have been single-minded in their desire to achieve their goals. They establish a market position and do everything they can to fulfill audience expectations. The other major ingredient for success with promotions is fun. You have to have fun with the promotion while you're doing all the work. If you and your staff have a good time, it is conveyed to the listeners and potential advertisers. It makes a station hard to beat."

Concerning the basic mechanics of the contest, the general rule is that if it takes a long time to explain, it is not appropriate for radio. "Contests that require too much explanation don't work well in our medium. That is not to say that they have to be thin and one-dimensional. On the contrary, radio contests can be imaginative and captivating without being complicated or complex," notes John Grube.

The planning and implementation of certain promotions may require the involvement of consultants who possess the expertise to ensure smooth sailing. Contests can turn into bad dreams if potential problems are not anticipated. Rick Sklar, who served as program director for WABC in New York for nearly 20 years, was responsible for some of the most successful radio promotions ever devised, but not all went without a hitch. In his autobiographical book, *Rocking America* (St. Martin's Press, 1984), Sklar told of the time that he was forced to hire, at great expense, 60 office temporaries for a period of 1 month to count the more than

170 million ballots received in response to the station's "Principal of the Year" contest. The previous year the station had received a paltry 6 million ballots.

On another occasion, Sklar had over 4 million WABC buttons manufactured as part of a promotion that awarded up to $25,000 in cash to listeners spotted wearing one. What Sklar did not anticipate was the huge cost involved in shipping several million metal buttons from various points around the country. The station had to come up with thousands of unbudgeted dollars to cover air freight. Of course, both miscalculations were mitigated by the tremendous success of the promotions, which significantly boosted WABC's ratings.

An even more bizarre experience befell Dallas deejay Ron Chapman when he jokingly asked listeners to send $20 without explaining why. The listening faithful, assuming Chapman's request to be a part of a legitimate station promotion, mailed in nearly a quarter of a million dollars. This left the station (KVIL-FM) with the interesting problem of what to do with the money. "We're flabbergasted," exclaimed Chapman. "We never expected this to happen." The moral to this tale is never underestimate the power of the medium. Plan before implementing.

Careful planning during the developmental phase of a promotion generally will prevent any unpleasant surprises, says Bob Lima. "Practical and hypothetical projections should be made. Radio can fool you by its pulling power. If a promotion catches on, it can exceed all expectations. You've got to be prepared for all contingencies. These are nice problems to have, but you can get egg on your face. Take a good look at the long and short of things before you bolt from the starting gate. Don't be too hasty or quick to execute. Consider all the variables, then proceed with care."

Lima tells of a successful promotion at WVMI that required considerable organization and planning. "We called it 'The Great Easter Egg Hunt.' What was basically an Easter egg hunt at a local park here in Biloxi attracted over 11,000 people. A local bottler co-sponsored the event and provided many of the thousands of dollars in prizes. The station hyped the event for several weeks over the air, and a little off-air promotion was done. The reason the promotion worked so well is that there actually was a need for a large, well-organized Easter event. We did our homework in selecting and executing this promotion, which turned out to be a big winner."

Charlie Morriss shares an account of a successful promotion at radio station KOMP.

SHANE MEDIA PROGRAM DIRECTOR'S CHECKLIST

We all know what it takes to be a good program director — develop and direct your station's on-air sound, conduct or oversee research, develop and reinforce a positive station image in the community, accept responsibility for air staff … the list goes on and on. The difficulty, however, is getting it all done. We've broken the program director's many jobs into daily, weekly, bi-weekly and monthly increments. It's a checklist that'll help you get things done.

DAILY
A. Direction of on-air sound
❏ Morning Show Meeting
 ○ Review day's high and low points
 ○ Evaluate talent plans for next day
 ○ Plan next day's benchmarks
 ○ Brainstorm ideas for topicality
❏ Casual feedback to each air talent in other dayparts
❏ Check at least one daypart at competitor
❏ Listen to your station 15 minutes outside drive times
❏ Check announcer activity schedule
 ○ Shifts
 ○ Promotions
❏ Give assignments to
 ○ Music director
 ○ Production director
 ○ Promotion director

❏ Music logs for next day
 ○ Create
 ○ Review
❏ Review commercial discrepancy report

B. Liaison with Sales Department
❏ Provide creative copy and scheduling input
❏ Make decisions on new promotional opportunities
❏ Talk to a client to see how the station is working

WEEKLY
A. Direction of on-air sound
❏ Listen to one hour of your station *uninterrupted*
 ○ Rotate times until you've heard every daypart
 ○ Check positioning, call letter delivery, contest play and enthusiasm, relatability
 ○ Check music flow
❏ Monitor competition for an hour *uninterrupted*
 ○ Know key positioning
 ○ Review contesting
 ○ Track promotions
 ○ Evaluate music
 ○ Review findings with GM and/or GSM
❏ Music meeting
 ○ Discuss adds and moves with MD
 △ Do adds and moves reflect station mission and music research?
 ○ Have MD circulate an internal list and provide new records for jocks to audition

○ Check music software system
○ Check turnovers of all rotations
○ Check histories on selected songs
○ Review Selector's "Most Frequently Played Analysis" or Powergold's "History"
❏ Promotion meeting
 ○ Brief post-mortem on last week's promotions
 ○ Review calendar for this weekend, next week
 ○ Be sure all promotions fit station image and accomplish cume or TSL goals
 ○ Ask promotion director for follow-up summary (or circulate one you create)
 ○ Make sure assignments are clear
❏ Production meeting
 ○ Discuss needs for coming promotions
 ○ Evaluate image promos & schedule new ones
 ○ Review announcer scheduling
 ○ Brainstorm ideas
❏ Engineering meeting
 ○ Review previous week's discrepancy reports
 ○ Advise chief of anything that needs repair
 ○ Review technical side of remotes
 ○ Discuss costs & savings ideas

EVERY TWO WEEKS
A. Direction of on-air sound
❏ Aircheck session with talent other than morning
 ○ Recap in writing
❏ Be sure you've listened to every announcer in every daypart at direct competitor

FIGURE 7.13
A checklist designed to keep a station in the hearts and minds of its audience. Courtesy Shane Media.

"Jocks flew around the Las Vegas skies in several World War II fighter planes owned by Miller Beer while our call letters were written by a skywriter. The effect was stunning. This promotion worked because skywriting is so rare these days and not many people have seen a squadron of vintage warplanes. It also worked because it didn't cost us a penny. It was a trade agreement with Miller. We gave them the exposure, and they gave us the air show. Of course, a lot of details had to be worked out in advance."

The most effective promotion in recent years at New London's WSUB involved awarding contestants an elaborate night out on the town. Chuck Davis relates: "Our 'Night Out' promotion has been popular for some time. The station gets premium concert tickets through a close alliance with a New York concert promoter. It then finds a sponsor to participate in the giveaway and provides him with counter signs and an entry box so that people may register in his store. The sponsor then becomes part of the promotion and in return purchases an air schedule. Contestants are told to go to the store to register for the 'Night Out,' thus increasing store traffic even more. In addition, the sponsor agrees to absorb the expense of a limousine to transport the winners, who also are treated to a preconcert dinner at a local restaurant that provides the meals in exchange for promotional consideration – a mention on the air in our 'Night Out' promos. In the end, the station's cost amounts to a couple of phone calls, a cardboard sign, and a box. Reaction has always been great from all parties. The sponsor likes the tie-in with the promotion. The restaurant is very satisfied with the attention it receives for providing a few dinners, and the concert promoter gets a lot of exposure for the acts that he books simply by giving the station some tickets. It works like a charm. We please our audience and also put a few greenbacks in the till."

In the end, making certain that everything is kosher with the execution of a promotion or contest is absolutely crucial, notes Larry Miller. "Another perhaps apocryphal tale of things going amiss is the San Francisco Top 40 station that did a Lucky License Plate contest during morning drive. Everybody listening stopped and got out of their car to check their license plate to see if they had won. This caused a monumental traffic jam, and the authorities were not pleased."

The point already has been made that a station can ill afford not to promote itself in today's highly competitive marketplace. Promotions are an integral part of contemporary station operations, and research and planning are what make a promotion a winner.

Budgeting Promotions

Marketing expert Andrew Curran opens this section with his views on the challenges of finding resources to promote a station: "In my experience, since revenue growth in radio has been relatively flat in recent years, marketing budgets are often the first thing to cut, especially in the third and fourth quarters of the year when a company needs to hit its financial numbers. In addition, it seems that stations seem to get the most marketing money when the ratings are down and instant results need to be delivered to get revenue up. Certainly this makes for some tense campaigns and often – if the promotion is successful and ratings go up – marketing dollars are moved to another station that is in need of help rather than allowing the original station to strengthen its position with additional marketing."

Obviously, cost projections are included in the planning of a promotion. The promotion director's budget may be substantial or all but nonexistent. Stations in small markets often have minuscule budgets compared with their giant metro market counterparts. But then again, the need to promote in a one- or two-station market generally is not as great as it is in multistation markets. To a degree, the promotion a station does is commensurate with the level of competition.

A typical promotion at an average-size station may involve the use of newspapers, plus additional handout materials, such as stickers, posters, buttons, and an assortment of other items depending on the nature of the promotion. Television and billboards

mix 98-5   mix 98-5   mix 98-5   mix 98-5   mix 98-5

Van Appearance

The MIX 98-5 Expedition can be spotted throughout New England at MIX 98-5 station appearance! At every appearance, the **MIX WHEEL OF PRIZES CLOSET** is on-site for contestants to win great prizes. Lucky winners get to choose a gift off the shelf that corresponds with the color on the wheel.

During each appearance, the MIX 98-5 promotion coordinators arrive in the MIX Expedition ready to give away great station premium and create excitement while supporting your marketing message to your target consumers.

Sponsor receives:

1. 2 hour station appearance with Wheel of Prizes, Sound System, Station Van, and giveaways.

2. On-air promotional announcements to run prior to the appearance.

3. Inclusion on MIX 98-5 Web Site - www.mix985.com

Source: Arbitron Spring 2002/Scarborough 2002

may also be utilized. Each of these items will require an expenditure unless some other provision has been made, such as a trade agreement in which airtime is swapped for goods or ad space.

The cost involved in promoting a contest often constitutes the primary expense. When WASH-FM in Washington, DC, gave away a million dollars, it spent $200,000 to purchase an annuity designed to pay the prize recipient $20,000 a year for 50 years. The station spent nearly an equal amount to promote the big giveaway. Most of the promotional cost resulted from a heavy use of local television.

A decade ago KHTZ-FM in Los Angeles spent over $300,000 on billboards and television to advertise its dreamhouse giveaway. The total cost of the promotion approached a half million dollars. The price tag of the

FIGURE 7.15
Promoting
on-air contests
online. Courtesy
KORN-AM.

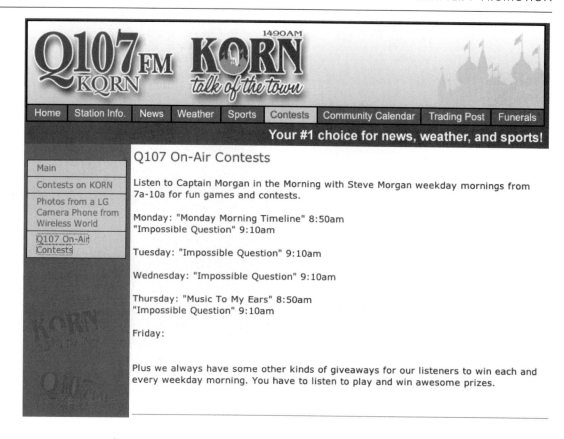

house was $122,000. Both of these high-priced contests accomplished their goals – increased ratings. In a metro market, one rating point can mean a million dollars in ad revenue. "A promotion that contributes to a two- or three-point jump in the ratings is well worth the money spent on it," observes Rick Peters.

The promotion director works with the station manager in establishing the promotion budget. From there, it is the promotion director's job to allocate funds for the various contests and promotions that are run throughout the station's fiscal period. Just as in every other area of a station, computers are becoming a prominent fixture in the promotion department. "If you have a large budget, a computer certainly makes life a lot easier. The idea is to control the budget and not let it control you. Obviously computers have been a big help in this respect," states Marlin R. Taylor, who also contends that large sums of money need not be poured into promotions if a station is on target with its programming. "In 1983, the Malrite organization came to New York and launched Z-100, a con-

temporary hit-formatted outlet, moving it from 'worst to first' in a matter of months. They did a little advertising and gave away some money. I estimate that their giveaways totaled less dollars than some of their competitors spent on straight advertising. But the station's success was built on three key factors: product, service, and employee incentives. Indeed, they do have a quality product. Second, they are providing a service to their customers or listeners, and, third, the care and feeding of the air staff and support team are obvious at all times. You don't necessarily have to spend a fortune on promotion." Larry Miller agrees, "A really good promotion director can do effective promotions without spending a lot of money. First, utilize 'on air' promotions; second, trade out for stuff like contest prizes and newspaper advertising. You can do much for very little through a combined effort with programming."

Since promotion directors frequently are expected to arrange trade agreements Promotions and the FCC with merchants as a way to defray costs, a familiarity with and understanding of the station's rate structure is necessary. Trading airtime for use in promotions is less popular at highly rated stations that can demand top dollars for spots. Most stations, however, prefer to exchange available airtime for goods and services needed in a promotion, rather than pay cash.

Promotions and the FCC

Although the FCC has dropped most of its rules pertaining to contests and promotions, it does expect that they be conducted with propriety and good judgment. The basic obligation of broadcasters to operate in the public interest remains the primary consideration. Section 73.1216 of the FCC's rules and regulations (as printed in the *Code of Federal Regulations*) outlines the do's and don'ts of contest presentations.

Stations are prohibited from running a contest in which contestants are required to pay in order to play. The FCC regards as lottery any contest in which the elements of prize, chance, and consideration exist. In other words, contestants must not have to risk something to win.

Contests must not place participants in any danger or jeopardize property. Awarding prizes to the first five people who successfully scale a treacherous mountain or swim a channel filled with alligators certainly would be construed by the FCC as endangering the lives of those involved. Contestants have been injured and stations held liable more than once. In the case of the station in California that ran a treasure hunt resulting in considerable property damage, it incurred the wrath of the public, town officials, and the FCC. In a more tragic example of poor planning, a listener was killed during a "find the disk jockey" contest. The station was charged with negligence and sustained a substantial fine.

Stations are expected to disclose the material terms of all contests and promotions conducted. These include the following:

- Entering procedures
- Eligibility requirements

- Deadlines
- When or if prizes can be won
- Value of prizes
- Procedure for awarding prizes
- Tie-breaking procedures

The public must not be misled concerning the nature of prizes. Specifics must be stated. Implying that a large boat is to be awarded when, in fact, a canoe is the actual prize would constitute misrepresentation, as would suggesting that an evening in the Kon Tiki Room of the local Holiday Inn is a great escape weekend to the exotic South Seas.

The FCC also stipulates that any changes in contest rules must be promptly conveyed to the public. It makes clear, too, that any rigging of contests, such as determining winners in advance, is a direct violation of the law and can result in a substantial penalty, or even license revocation.

Although the FCC does not require that a station keep a contest file, most do. Maintaining all pertinent contest information, including signed prize receipts and releases

FIGURE 7.17
Stations are expected to make contest rules clear to the public. Courtesy 97 Rock.

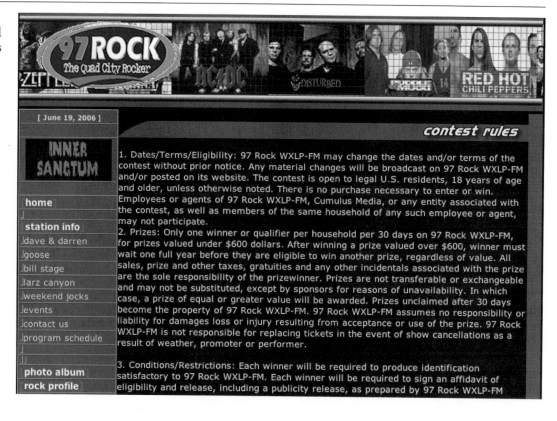

by winners, can prevent problems should questions or a conflict arise later.

Stations that award prizes valued at $600 or more are expected by law to file a 1099-MISC form with the IRS. This is done strictly for reporting purposes, and stations incur no tax liability. However, failure to do so puts a station in conflict with the law.

Broadcast Promotion and Marketing Executives

The Broadcasters Promotion Association (BPA) was founded in 1956 as a nonprofit organization expressly designed to provide information and services to station promotion directors around the world. In the late 1980s, its name was changed to Broadcast Promotion and Marketing Executives (BPME). In the 1990s, the organization became Promax International. Its objectives are as follows:

- Increase the effectiveness of broadcast promotion personnel.
- Improve broadcast promotion methods, research principles, and techniques.
- Enhance the image and professional status of its members and members of the broadcast promotion profession.
- Facilitate liaison with allied organizations in broadcasting, promotion, and government.
- Increase awareness and understanding of broadcast promotion at stations, in the community, and at colleges and universities.

Promax conducts national seminars and workshops on promotion-related subjects. Further information about the organization may be obtained on its Web site: www.promax.org.

CHAPTER HIGHLIGHTS

1. To keep listeners interested and tuned, stations actively promote their image and call letters. Small-market stations promote themselves to compete for audience with other forms of media. Major-market stations use promotion to differentiate themselves from competing stations.

2. Radio recognized the value of promotion early and used print media, remote broadcasts, and billboards to inform the public. Later, ratings surveys proved the importance of effective promotions.

3. Greater competition because of the increasing number of stations and monthly audience surveys means today's stations must promote themselves continually.

4. The most successful (attracting listenership loyalty) promotions involve large cash or merchandise prizes.

5. A successful promotion director possesses knowledge and understanding of the station's audience; a background in research and marketing, writing, and conceptual skills; the ability to adapt existing concepts to a particular station; and a familiarity with graphic art. The promotion director is responsible for acquiring prizes through trade or purchase and for compliance with FCC regulations covering promotions.

6. On-air promotions are the most common method used to retain and expand listenership. Such devices as slogans linked to the call letters and contests are common.

7. To "bookend" call letters means to place them at the beginning and conclusion of each break. To "graft" call letters means to include them with all informational announcements.

8. Contests must have clear rules and must provide entertainment for players and non-players alike. Successful contests are compatible with the station's sound, offer prizes attractive to the target audience, and challenge the listener's imagination.

9. Stealth promotions include members of a station's database and are known only to the people eligible to win.

10. Off-air promotions are intended to attract new listeners. Popular approaches include billboards, bus cards, newspapers, television, bumper stickers, discount cards, giveaway items embossed with call letters or logo, deejay personal appearances, special activity sponsorship, remote broadcasts, direct mail, faxing, and telemarketing. Station Web sites are promotional tools.

11. To offset the sometimes-substantial cost of an off-air promotion, stations often collaborate with sponsors to share both the expenses and the attention gained.

12. FCC regulations governing promotions are contained in Section 73.12116. Basically, stations may not operate lotteries, endanger contestants, rig contests, or mislead listeners as to the nature of the prize.

13. Promax International provides information and services to station promotion directors.

SUGGESTED FURTHER READING

Bergendorff, F.L., *Broadcast Advertising and Promotion: A Handbook for Students and Professionals*, Hastings House, New York, 1983.

Dickey, L., *The Franchise: Building Radio Brands*, NAB Publications, Washington, DC, 1994.

Donnelly, W.J., *Planning Media: Strategy and Imagination*, Pearson Education, New York, 1995.

Eastman, S.T., Klein, R.A., and Ferguson, D., *Promotion and Marketing for Broadcasting, Cable, and the Web*, 5th edition, Focal Press, Boston, MA, 2006.

Gompertz, R., *Promotion and Publicity Handbook for Broadcasters*, Tab Books, Blue Ridge Summit, PA, 1977.

Johnson, A., *The Radio Sponsorship and Promotions Handbook: Creative Ideas for Radio Campaigns*, Saland Publishing, New York, 2007.

Macdonald, J., *The Handbook of Radio Publicity and Promotion*, Tab Books, Blue Ridge Summit, PA, 1970.

Matelsi, M., *Broadcast Programming and Promotion Work Text*, Focal Press, Boston, MA, 1989.

National Association of Broadcasters, *Best of the Best Promotions, III*, NAB Publications, Washington, DC, 1994.

National Association of Broadcasters, *Casinos, Lotteries, and Contests*, NAB Publications, Washington, DC, 2007.

Nickels, W., *Marketing Communications and Promotion*, 3rd edition, John Wiley & Sons, New York, 1984.

Peck, W.A., *Radio Promotion Handbook*, Tab Books, Blue Ridge Summit, PA, 1968.

Ramsey, M., *Fresh Air: Marketing Gurus on Radio*, iUniverse, Lincoln, NE, 2005.

Rhoads, B.E., et al., editors, *Programming and Promotions*, Streamline Press, West Palm Beach, FL, 1995.

Roberts, T.E.F., *Practical Radio Promotions*, Focal Press, Boston, MA, 1992.

Savage, B., *Perry's Broadcast Promotion Sourcebook*, Perry Publications, Oak Ridge, TN, 1982.

Shane, E., *Selling Electronic Media*, Focal Press, Boston, MA, 1999.

Stanley, R.E., *Promotions*, 2nd edition, Prentice Hall, Englewood Cliffs, NJ, 1982.

Traffic and Billing

8

The Air Supply

What was printed here nearly a quarter of a century ago remains a fact today: a station sells airtime – that is its inventory, its product. The volume or size of a given station's inventory depends chiefly on the amount of time it allocates for commercial matter. For example, some stations with Easy Listening and Adult Contemporary formats deliberately restrict or limit commercial loads as a method of enhancing overall sound and fostering a "more music, less talk" image. Other outlets simply abide by commercial load stipulations as outlined in their license renewal applications.

A full-time station has more than 10,000 minutes to fill each week. This computes to approximately 3000 minutes for commercials, based on an 18-minute commercial load ceiling per hour. In the eyes of the sales manager, this means anywhere from 3000 to 6000 availabilities or slots – assuming that a station sells 60- and 30-second spot units – in which commercial announcements are inserted.

From the discussion in the first seven chapters, it should be apparent that inventory control and accountability at a radio station are no small job. They are, in fact, the primary duty of the person called the traffic manager.

The Traffic Manager

A daily log is prepared by the traffic manager (also referred to as the traffic director). This document is at once a schedule of programming elements (commercials, features, and public service announcements [PSAs]) to be aired and a record of what was actually aired. It serves to inform the on-air operator of what to broadcast and at what time, and it provides a record for, among other things, billing purposes.

Let us examine the process involved in logging a commercial for broadcast beginning at the point at which the salesperson writes an order for a spot schedule.

1. The salesperson writes an order and returns it to the station.
2. The sales manager then checks and approves the order.
3. The sales secretary types the order.
4. Copies of the formalized order are distributed to the traffic manager, sales manager, billing, salesperson, and client.
5. The order is placed in the traffic scheduling book or entered into the computer for posting to the log by the traffic manager.
6. The order is logged, commencing on the start date according to the stipulations of the buy.

Although the preceding is both a simplification and generalization of the actual process, it does convey the basic idea. Keep in mind that not all stations operate in exactly the same manner. The actual method for preparing a log will differ also from station to station depending on whether it is done manually or by computer. Those outlets using the manual system (very few remain) often simplify the process by preparing a master or semipermanent log containing fixed program elements and even long-term advertisers. Short-term sponsors and other changes will be entered on an ongoing basis. This method significantly reduces typing. The master may be imprinted on plastic or Mylar, and entries can be made and erased according to need. Once the log is prepared, it is then copied and distributed.

It is the traffic manager's responsibility to see that an order is logged as specified and that each client is treated fairly and equitably. A sponsor who purchases two spots, 5 days a week, during morning drive, can expect to receive good rotation for maximum reach. It is up to the traffic manager to schedule the client's commercials in as many quarter-hour segments of the daypart as possible. The effectiveness of a spot schedule is reduced if the spots are logged in the same quarter-hour each day. If a spot is logged at 6:45 A.M. daily, it is only reaching those people tuned at that hour each day. However, if on one day it is logged at 7:15 A.M. and then at 8:45 A.M. on another, and so on, it is reaching a different audience each day. It also would be unfair to the advertiser who purchased drivetime to have spots logged only prior to 7:00 A.M., the beginning of the prime audience period.

The traffic manager maintains a record of when a client's spots are aired to help ensure effective rotation. Another concern of the traffic manager is to keep adequate space between accounts of a competitive nature. Running two restaurants back-to-back or within the same spot set likely would result in having to reschedule both at different times at no cost to the client.

It also falls within the traffic manager's purview to make sure that copy and production tapes are in on time. Most stations have a policy, often stated in their rate card, requiring that commercial material be on hand at least 48 hours before it is scheduled for broadcast. Traffic manager Carol Bates of Providence, Rhode Island, says that getting copy before the air date can be a problem. "It is not unusual to get a tape or copy a half-hour before it is due to air. We ask that copy be in well in advance, but sometimes it's a matter of minutes. No station is unfamiliar with having to make up spots due to late copy. It's irritating but a reality that you have to deal with."

Station traffic manager Jan Hildreth says that holiday and political campaign periods can place added pressure on the traffic person. "The fourth quarter is the big money time in radio. The logs usually are jammed, and availabilities are in short supply. The workload in the traffic department doubles. Things also get pretty chaotic around elections. It can become a real test for the nerves. Of course, there's always the late order that arrives at 5 P.M. on Friday that gets the adrenaline going."

There are few station relationships closer than that of the traffic department with programming and sales. Programming relies on the traffic manager for the logs that function as scheduling guides for on-air personnel. Sales depends on the traffic department to inform it of existing availabilities and to process orders onto the air. "It is crucial to the operation that traffic have a good relationship with sales and programming. When it doesn't, things begin to happen. The program director (PD) has to let traffic know when something changes; if not, the system breaks down. This is equally true of sales. Traffic is kind of the heart of things. Everything passes through the traffic department. Cooperation is very important," observes radio station traffic manager Barbara Kalulas.

The Traffic Manager's Credentials

A college degree usually is not a criterion for the job of traffic manager. This is not to imply that skill and training are not

FIGURE 8.1
A station's traffic department has nothing to do with the highway conditions. Courtesy WIZN-FM.

necessary, and more and more everybody at a radio station has at least some college education. Obviously, the demands placed on the traffic manager are formidable, and not everyone is qualified to fill the position. "It takes a special kind of person to effectively handle the job of traffic. Patience, an eye for detail, plus the ability to work under pressure and with other people are just some of the qualities the position requires," notes radio executive Bill Campbell.

Typing or keyboard skills are vital to the job. A familiarity with computers and word processing has become necessary, because most stations have given up the manual system of preparing logs in favor of the computerized method.

Many traffic people are trained in-house and come from the administrative or clerical ranks. It is a position that traditionally has been filled by women. Even though traffic salaries generally exceed that of purely secretarial positions, this is not an area noted for its high pay. Although the traffic manager is expected to handle many responsibilities, the position generally is perceived as more clerical in nature than managerial.

Traffic managers frequently make the transition into sales or programming. The considerable exposure to those particular areas provides a solid foundation and good springboard for those desiring to make the change.

FIGURE 8.2
A handheld check of station availabilities. Courtesy RadioTraffic.com.

FIGURE 8.3
Working a station's ad traffic online. Courtesy RadioTraffic.com.

Directing Traffic

Computers vastly enhance the speed and efficiency of the traffic process. Computers store copious amounts of data, retrieve information faster than humanly possible, and schedule and rotate commercials with precision and equanimity, to mention only a few of the features that make the new technology especially adaptive for use in the traffic area (see Figures 8.2–8.4).

Computers are an excellent tool for inventory control, contends former broadcast computer consultant Vicki Cliff. "Radio is a commodity not unlike a train carload of perishables, such as tomatoes. Radio sells time, which is progressively spoiling. The economic laws of supply and demand are classically applied to radio. Computers can assist in plotting that supply-and-demand curve in determining rates to be charged for various dayparts at any given moment.

"Inventory control is vital to any business. Radio is limited in its availabilities and seasonal in its desirability to the client. In a sold-out state, client value priorities must be weighted to optimize the station's billing. All things being equal, the credit rating of the client should be the deciding factor. Computers can eliminate the human subjectivity in formulating the daily log."

The cost of computerizing traffic has kept a small percentage of stations from converting from the manual system, notes Cliff. "Purchasing a personal computer for

```
WXLO-FM  Fitchburg, MA              Saturday, August 7, 1999
                  ANNOUNCER'S PAGE

                     MISSED SPOTS:
Len    Advertiser          Reason   1  2  3  4  5  6  7  8  9 10
 |                          |        |  |  |  |  |  |  |  |  |  |
 |                          |        |  |  |  |  |  |  |  |  |  |
 |                          |        |  |  |  |  |  |  |  |  |  |
 |                          |        |  |  |  |  |  |  |  |  |  |
 |                          |        |  |  |  |  |  |  |  |  |  |
 |                          |        |  |  |  |  |  |  |  |  |  |
 |                          |        |  |  |  |  |  |  |  |  |  |
 |                          |        |  |  |  |  |  |  |  |  |  |
 |                          |        |  |  |  |  |  |  |  |  |  |
 |                          |        |  |  |  |  |  |  |  |  |  |
 |                          |        |  |  |  |  |  |  |  |  |  |
 |                          |        |  |  |  |  |  |  |  |  |  |
 |                          |        |  |  |  |  |  |  |  |  |  |
 |                          |        |  |  |  |  |  |  |  |  |  |
 |                          |        |  |  |  |  |  |  |  |  |  |
 |                          |        |  |  |  |  |  |  |  |  |  |

                  COMMENTS:
```

FIGURE 8.4

The form used by on-air people to cite missed commercials. Courtesy WXLO-FM.

the traffic function is okay, but if a station desires to perform several functions, it may find itself out of luck. There are limits as to what can be done with a personal computer. On the other hand, a larger capacity, mainframe computer can be a major expense, although the functions it can perform are extraordinary. An online, real-time system can be costly also. Line expenses can really add up. Those station managers considering computerizing must gather all possible data to determine if the system they're considering will cost justify itself."

In an interview in *Radio Ink*, WPOC-FM's Jim Dolan observed that "The move right now is toward putting your sales force in the field armed with laptops and instantaneous online access to inventory, availability, and contract information. And the PC-based systems seem to be evolving faster than the minicomputer systems in this regard."

Various types of traffic and billing software are available. Dozens of companies, most notably Radio Traffic, Marketron, Columbine, Bias Radio, Custom Business Systems, Jefferson Pilot, and The Management, specialize in providing broadcasters with software packages. Prices for computer software vary depending on the nature and content of the program.

Compatible hardware is specified by the software manufacturer. Most software is IBM-PC compatible, however. Companies and consultants specializing in broadcast computerization are listed in *Broadcasting Yearbook*.

According to the NAB, the majority of stations were utilizing computers, especially in the area of traffic, in the 1990s. Notes Jay Williams, Jr., "Traffic and accounting for many affiliated stations are now being done by modem from corporate offices. Even sales is becoming more computer-powered. It won't be long before avails and pricing will be offered to stations, acceptance of an order will be confirmed by a keystroke, and the commercial downloaded on command."

Traffic in Clusters

In the age of widespread station clustering, it is common for a centralized traffic (and billing) department to handle the work of several outlets that are owned by the same company or group. In this case, the staff of the "hub" department (the one handling all of the work) may be enlarged to accommodate the increased demands. Obviously, this also means that the traffic departments at the various stations in the cluster are no longer necessary and therefore are typically eliminated.

Williams adds, "Consolidation and technology have provided opportunities for savings in traffic, bookkeeping, engineering, production, and other internal operations. Technology soon will allow stations to automatically accept and schedule orders directly from approved clients and agencies; the acceptance of this 'offer-buy-schedule' software will streamline the traffic-billing process even more."

Dave Scott, CEO of RadioTraffic.com, further discusses the impact of consolidation of radio station traffic operations. "In the era when an owner could only have two stations in a market (prior to the Telecom Act), one traffic person often did all the 'back room' commercial scheduling and billing for two stations. So six or seven stations would have had three or four people. After consolidation, it's not usual for seven stations to have one or two people handling all commercial scheduling and billing. This has been possible partly through combination sales (where one or two sales people handle sales of ads for six, seven, or eight stations) and partly through more efficient traffic and billing software (made so one order entry process could get all the details into all six, seven, or eight stations).

Some of this has been due to the multitasking aspect of Windows software and some due to faster and more powerful desktop computers, along with the advent of networking of several computers together so all sales people could do some order entry.

What we do at our company is take multiple station operation two steps further. First, RadioTraffic.com software is Internet enabled, so sales people don't have to phone in to find out about unsold availabilities. This is important because ad time is perishable. You can't sell the time a few minutes ago if you didn't sell it in advance.

Internet connectivity also means sales people don't have to drive back to the station to get new orders or change orders entered by traffic people. They can do so with any computer or the Internet anywhere. That includes laptop computers with wireless Internet access, any computer at an Internet café, and any PDA with wireless Internet. Station people and clients have secure access to full account information from any Internet computer, just the way as one has account info from their bank or credit card company. Here at RadioTraffic.com we also offer client invoices, affidavits, and statements that talk. Merely click on the day and time of any commercial and you can hear an aircheck playback of it along with what came before and after, all over the Internet. All this makes traffic run smoothly in cluster situations."

Billing

At most stations, advertisers are billed for the airtime they have purchased after a portion or all of it has run. Few stations require that sponsors pay in advance. It is the job of the billing department to notify the advertiser when payment is due. Al Rozanski, former business manager of WMJX-FM, Boston, explains the process involved once a contract

has been logged by the traffic department. "We send invoices out twice monthly. Many stations bill weekly, but we find doing it every 2 weeks cuts down on the paperwork considerably. The first thing my billing person does is check the logs to verify that the client's spots ran. We don't bill them for something that wasn't aired. Occasionally a spot will be missed for one reason or another, say a technical problem. This will be reflected on the log because the on-air person will indicate this fact. Invoices are then generated in triplicate by our computer. We use an IBM System 34 computer and Columbine software. This combination is extremely versatile and efficient. The station retains a copy of the invoice and mails two to the client, who then returns one with the payment. The client also receives an affidavit detailing when spots were aired. If the client requests, we will notarize the invoice. This is generally necessary for clients involved in co-op contracts." The billing procedure at WMJX-FM is representative of that at many stations.

Not all radio stations have a full-time business manager on the payroll. Thus, the person who handles billing commonly is responsible for maintaining the station's financial records or books as well. In this case, the services of a professional accountant may be contracted on a regular periodic basis to perform the more complex bookkeeping tasks and provide consultation on other financial matters.

Accounts that fail to pay when due are turned over to the appropriate salesperson for collections. If this does not result in payment, a station may use the services of a collection agency. Should its attempt also fail, the station likely would write the business off as a loss at tax time.

Dave Scott adds the cluster angle to the preceding, "In the era of group ownership a seamless automatic consolidation of financial reporting from clusters of stations in different cities, states, and regions, as well as national totals, is needed. Previously, clusters would combine their stations and fax weekly reports to headquarters. Now, group owners know their own pacing on an hour-by-hour basis, just the way a chain retailer would have their cash registers tied together for consolidated sales pacing and restocking."

FIGURE 8.5
Enhanced logging
through computer
software. Courtesy
RadioTraffic.com.

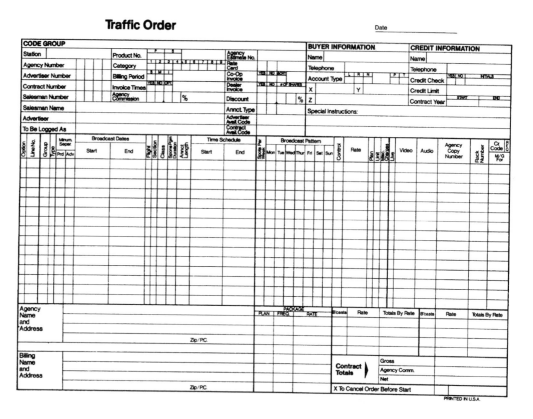

FIGURE 8.6
Spot schedule order
form. Courtesy
WMJX-FM.

The FCC and Traffic

The FCC eliminated program log requirements in the early 1980s as part of the era's formidable deregulation movement. Before then the FCC expected radio stations to maintain a formal log, which – in addition to program titles, sponsor names, and length of elements – reflected information pertaining to the nature of announcements (commercial material, PSA), source of origination (live, recorded, network), and the type of program (enter tainment, news, political, religious, other). Failing to

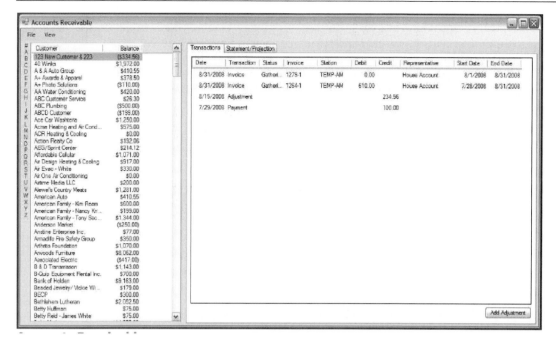

FIGURE 8.7
Keeping track of accounts is a vital station function. Courtesy, RadioTraffic.com.

STANDARD TERMS AND CONDITIONS

1 Approvals. Station reserves the right to approve all advertising, which approval shall not be unreasonably withheld. Advertiser agrees that advertisements and promotions which it runs in accordance with this Agreement shall be in accordance with applicable rules and policies established from time to time by Station.

2. Commercial Content. Station assumes no responsibility, obligation or liability with respect to the content or style of the advertising provided by the Advertiser and Advertiser agrees to indemnify Station for any liability which may result from broadcasting said commercial. In an effort to provide the community with wholesome entertainment, Station reviews all programming and commercials which it places for broadcast, and reserves the right to reject any particular advertisement provided by Advertiser. See station's production guidelines for a thorough detail of stations commercial policies.

3. Additional Requested Broadcasts. Except as otherwise agreed to in writing, if Advertiser continues to request that Station broadcast advertising beyond that specified herein, additional broadcasts shall be considered a part of this contract, at the rate established by the Station from time to time, and otherwise subject to these terms and conditions, until otherwise agreed to in writing.

4. Confirmations and Cancellations. All contracts and revisions are scrutinized for accuracy prior to mailing. Upon receipt of station contracts by Advertiser, it is Advertiser's responsibility to notify Station of any possible discrepancy. If Station receives no notice within seven (7) days of issue, the contract or revision will be considered correct and Advertiser will be responsible for payment. Station requires two (2) weeks notice of cancellation.

5. Trademarks and Non-Exclusivity. This Agreement does not grant Advertiser the rights to use tradenames, trademarks or service marks of Station. No merchandising, promotional or other special consideration, nor any product category exclusivity or other protection regarding any broadcast, will be provided by Station in connection with the scheduled advertising unless specifically set forth in this Agreement.

6. Failure to Broadcast Commercials. Advertiser acknowledges that commercials occasionally may not be broadcast when scheduled due to events beyond the reasonable control of Station. in the event scheduled advertising is not broadcast when scheduled. Station shall be entitled to place advertising on a subsequent, comparable broadcast, on a "make good" basis. In no event shall Station be liable for any consequential or incidental damages relating to its failure to air scheduled advertising.

7. Execution by Agency. If this Agreement is entered into by an Advertising Agency on behalf of an Advertiser, said Agency jointly and severally undertakes the obligations of Advertiser hereunder.

8. Massachusetts Law. This Agreement is made and entered into in Massachusetts and shall be interpreted, construed and enforced in accordance with the laws of the Commonwealth of Massachusetts.

CREDIT POLICY

1. Extension of Credit. Standard Station credit policy is cash in advance for Advertiser's first order, pending approval of credit, and said credit will not be extended without a completed and signed credit application from Advertiser on file.

2. Credit limits. Individual credit limits are established at the sole discretion of Station and are subject to review from time to time.

COMMISSIONS AND DISCOUNTS

1. Agency Commissions. Commissions will be paid by Station only to established Advertising Agencies in good standing.

PAYMENTS

1. Payments. Standard Station payment policy is that all invoices are due and payable net thirty (30) days from receipt of invoice.

2. Late Charges. Any amounts due Station from Advertiser not paid within (30) days of receipt of invoice are subject to a five percent (5%) late payment charge.

3. Collections. In the event of any collection action or litigation to collect amounts due from Advertiser, Station shall be entitled to reasonable cost of collection and attorneys fees as determined by the Court.

FIGURE 8.8
Terms and conditions of an advertising buy. Courtesy WXLOFM.

FIGURE 8.9 The designated placement of spots in 4-minute sets (clusters). Courtesy RadioTraffic.com.

include this information on the log could have resulted in punitive actions against the station by the FCC.

Although stations no longer must retain a program log under existing rules, some sort of document is still necessary to inform programming personnel of what is scheduled for broadcast and to provide information for both the traffic and billing departments pertaining to their particular functions. A log creates accountability. It is both a programming guide and a document of verification.

Stations are now at liberty to design logs that serve their needs most effectively and efficiently. The WMJX log form shown in Figure 8.11 is an example of a log that has been designed to meet all of its station's needs in the most economical and uncomplicated way.

There are no stipulations regarding the length of time that logs must be retained. Before the elimination of the FCC program log regulations, stations were required to retain logs for a minimum of 2 years. Today most stations still hold onto logs for that amount of time for the sake of accountability, and with computers as archive sources, logs may be kept indefinitely without creating physical space issues.

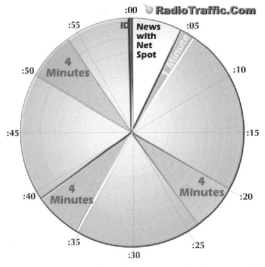

FIGURE 8.10 Traffic and billing receive copies of orders written by sales reps. Courtesy WIZN-FM.

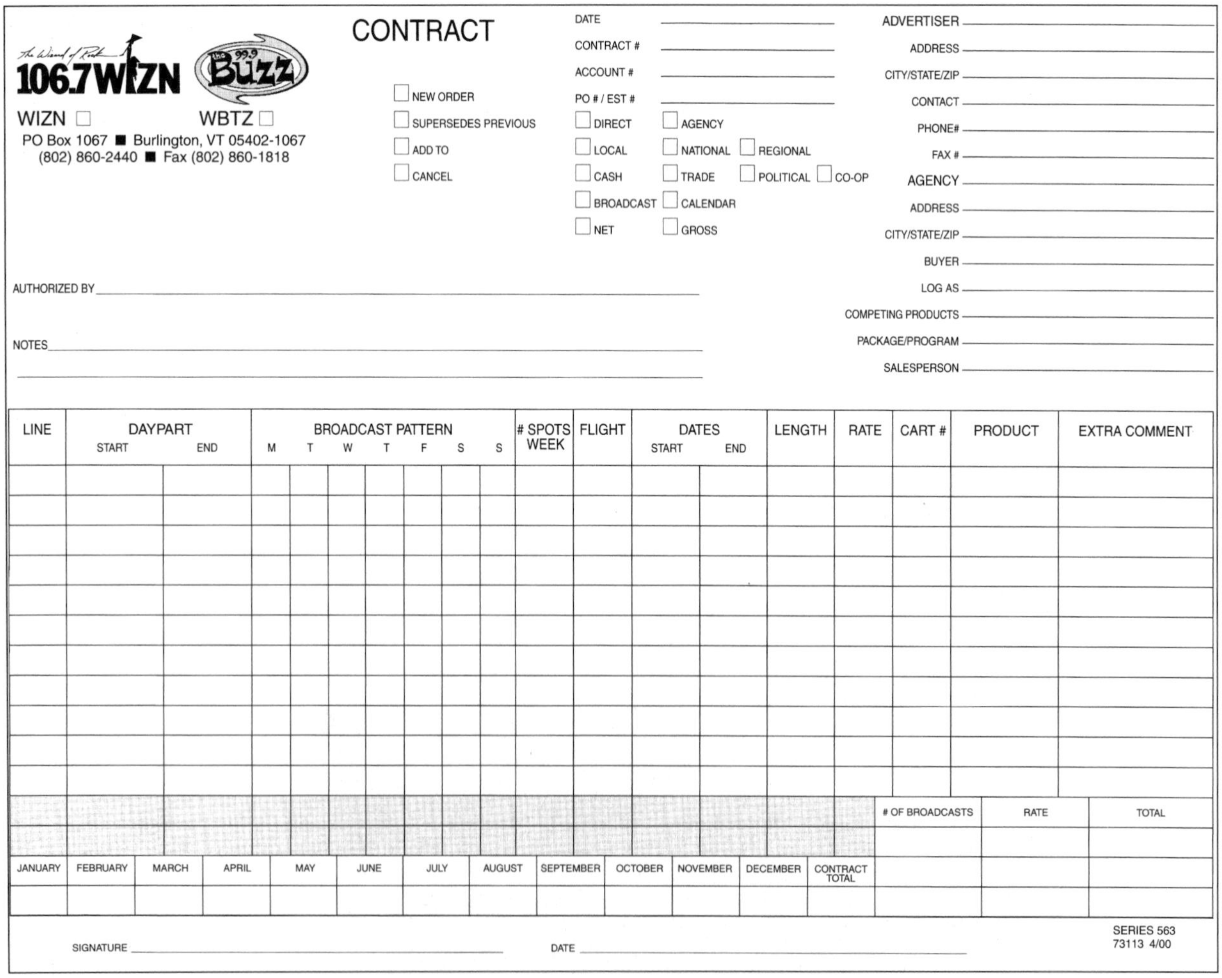

CONTRACT

106.7 WIZN The Buzz 99.9

WIZN ☐ WBTZ ☐

PO Box 1067 ■ Burlington, VT 05402-1067

(802) 860-2440 ■ Fax (802) 860-1818

☐ NEW ORDER
☐ SUPERSEDES PREVIOUS
☐ ADD TO
☐ CANCEL

DATE
CONTRACT #
ACCOUNT #
PO # / EST #

☐ DIRECT ☐ AGENCY
☐ LOCAL ☐ NATIONAL ☐ REGIONAL
☐ CASH ☐ TRADE ☐ POLITICAL ☐ CO-OP
☐ BROADCAST ☐ CALENDAR
☐ NET ☐ GROSS

ADVERTISER
ADDRESS
CITY/STATE/ZIP
CONTACT
PHONE#
FAX #
AGENCY
ADDRESS
CITY/STATE/ZIP
BUYER
LOG AS
COMPETING PRODUCTS
PACKAGE/PROGRAM
SALESPERSON

AUTHORIZED BY

NOTES

LINE	DAYPART START	DAYPART END	M	T	W	T	F	S	S	# SPOTS WEEK	FLIGHT	DATES START	DATES END	LENGTH	RATE	CART #	PRODUCT	EXTRA COMMENT

BROADCAST PATTERN

# OF BROADCASTS	RATE	TOTAL

JANUARY	FEBRUARY	MARCH	APRIL	MAY	JUNE	JULY	AUGUST	SEPTEMBER	OCTOBER	NOVEMBER	DECEMBER	CONTRACT TOTAL

SIGNATURE DATE

SERIES 563
73113 4/00

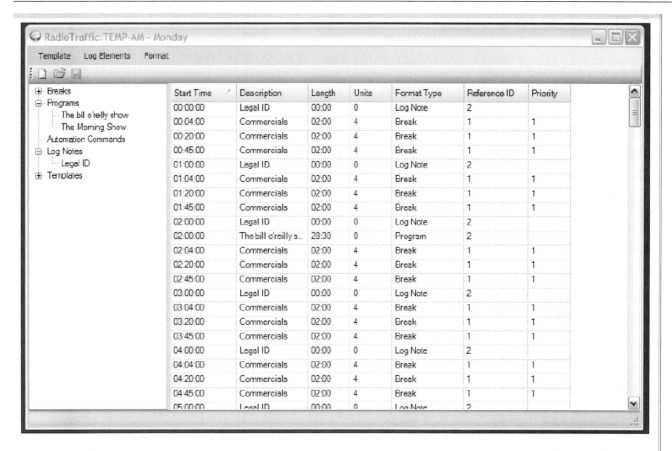

Log Templates

Log templates are easy to set up in RadioTraffic.com. Commercial avails and limits go in here. Certain stop sets can be set to always get filled, then others are filled based on priorities. Automation codes are normally kept off edit screens and printed logs but can be viewed if desired.

FIGURE 8.11
Accounts are entered to a log at the time they have purchased. Courtesy RadioTraffic.com.

FIGURE 8.12
Traffic department in cluster operation. Courtesy Clear Channel.

FIGURE 8.13
When spots are to appear in a log after it has been printed, they are hand-entered. Courtesy WXLO-FM.

WXLO-FM Fitchburg, MA Saturday, August 7, 1999

OFFICE PAGE

HAND-ENTERED SPOTS THAT NEED TIMES:

Name:____________ Length:________ Number:______

Name:____________ Length:________ Number:______

Name:____________ Length:________ Number:______

Name:____________ Length:________ Number:______

Name:____________ Length:________ Number:______

Name:____________ Length:________ Number:______

ENTERED SPOTS THAT DO NOT NEED TIMES:

FIGURE 8.14
Standard form used for clients involved in co-op agreements. Courtesy WMJX-FM.

ANA/RAB FORM FOR SCRIPT (IF TAPE IS USED, PREPARE SCRIPT FROM TAPE)

wmjx 106 fm
The magic is the music.®

ANA/RAB RADIO "TEAR-SHEET"
FORM AT BOTTOM OF SCRIPT PERMITS KNOWING HOW MANY TIMES THIS SCRIPT RAN, AT WHAT COST.

Client:	For:	
Begin:	End:	Date:

STATION DOCUMENTATION STATEMENT APPROVED BY THE CO-OPERATIVE ADVERTISING COMMITTEE OF THE ASSOCIATION OF NATIONAL ADVERTISERS

This announcement was broadcast________times, as entered in the station's program log. The times this announcement was broadcast were billed to this station's client at our invoice(s) number/dated ________at his earned rate of:

$________each for________announcements, for a total of $________
$________each for________announcements, for a total of $________
$________each for________announcements, for a total of $________

Signature of station official

(Notarize above) Typed name and title Station

Marketron Traffic

The Marketron Radio Traffic solution manages all station spot scheduling and billing via a single, intuitive interface. It automates workflow, electronically tracks contract data and revisions and provides detailed spot information to improve productivity.

Marketron offers a hosted solution that provides all of the features and functionality of our client-server applications via the Internet. Marketron clients benefit from unmatchable performance, time-to-market and reach.

Marketron Radio Traffic

Marketron Radio Traffic offers the following features and benefits:

Streamlined Order Processing - Reduces data entry errors and eliminates communication lapses. With a single database, all traffic processes such as assigning approvals, conversion to contract, spot scheduling and generation of invoices, are completed electronically.

Advanced Inventory Controls - Enable traffic managers to easily review inventory and manipulate spot placement so as to maximize revenue and reduce makegoods. Through powerful inventory query features, traffic managers can quickly identify and reschedule lower rate spots to accommodate higher paying advertisers.

Multi-Market and Multi-Station Capabilities - Enable large station groups to easily manage the scheduling and billing of advertising orders across multiple stations via one central location. Multiple station contracts are handled seamlessly from order entry through to single invoice billing.

Automated Reporting for Station Management - Provides up-to-the-minute, custom reports, enabling station management to monitor progress and make immediate corrections to maximize revenue. Review of station revenue streams and inventory sales allows corporate management to accurately design group-wide or regional goals.

Marketron Hosting

Marketron Hosting provides the following features and benefits:

Competitive Advantage - Because we maintain the application suites centrally, all enhancements, upgrades and new releases are deployed immediately and automatically. As a result, sales, traffic and management personnel using our hosted solutions always utilize the most advanced applications and technology, giving them the capability to out-strategize, out-sell and out-execute the competition.

Mission Critical Focus - Marketron Hosting frees corporate and IT resources from ongoing application implementation and support demands, freeing them for other mission critical functions. Moreover, Marketron Hosting eliminates IT budgeting for application deployment.

Unsurpassed Reach - If you can get to the Internet, you can use Marketron's hosted applications.

Outstanding Performance - Marketron's state-of-the-art back-end server equipment scales quickly and on demand.

Advanced Technology - Marketron Hosting provides the latest technology at a fraction of the cost to develop in-house. Economies of scale allow us to give Marketron Hosting customers the ultimate in infrastructure, failover and security.

More Information

▸ **Schedule a Live Demo**

▸ **Brochure**

▸ **Why Switch to Marketron Traffic?**

▸ **Hosting Benefits**

▸ **Traffic Requirements**

▸ **Hosting Requirements**

▸ **Contact Sales**

Copyright Marketron © 2008

Privacy   Legal

FIGURE 8.15
Traffic management services are of great assistance to stations. Courtesy Marketron.

CHAPTER HIGHLIGHTS

1. Each commercial slot on a station is called an *availability*. Availabilities constitute a station's salable inventory.

2. The traffic manager (or traffic director) controls and is accountable for the broadcast time inventory.

3. The traffic manager prepares a log to inform the deejays of what to broadcast and at what time.

4. The traffic manager is also responsible for ensuring that an ad order is logged as specified, that a record of when each client's spots are aired is maintained, and that copy and production tapes are in on time.

5. Programming relies on the traffic manager for the logs that function as scheduling guides for on-air personnel; the sales department depends on the traffic manager to inform them of existing availabilities and to process orders onto the air.

6. Although most traffic people are trained in-house and are drawn from the administrative or clerical ranks, they must possess patience, an eye for detail, the ability to work under pressure, and keyboarding skills.

7. Most traffic departments have been computerized to enhance speed and efficiency. Therefore, traffic managers must be computer knowledgeable.

8. In many instances, consolidation (clustering) has eliminated individual station traffic and billing departments and a single traffic hub within the cluster prepares logs and sponsor invoices for all the stations. In some cases, outside companies have assumed the task.

9. Based on the spots aired, as recorded and verified by the traffic department, the billing department sends invoices weekly or biweekly to each client. Invoices are notarized for clients with co-op contracts.

10. Since the FCC eliminated program log requirements in the early 1980s, stations have been able to design logs that inform programming personnel of what is scheduled for broadcast and that provide necessary information for the traffic and billing departments.

SUGGESTED FURTHER READING

Diamond, S.Z., *Records Management: A Practical Guide*, AMACOM, New York, 1983.

Doyle, D.M., *Efficient Accounting and Record Keeping*, David McKay and Company, New York, 1977.

Heighton, E.J., and Cunningham, D.R., *Advertising in the Broadcast and Cable Media*, 2nd edition, Wadsworth Publishing, Belmont, CA, 1984.

Hunter, J., and Thiebaud, M., *Telecommunications Billing Systems*, McGraw-Hill, New York, 2002.

Keith, M.C., *Selling Radio Direct*, Focal Press, Boston, MA, 1992.

Muller, M., *Essentials of Inventory Management*, American Management Association, New York, 2002.

Murphy, J,. *Handbook of Radio Advertising*, Chilton, Radnor, PA, 1980.

Schreibfeder, J., *Achieving Effective Inventory Management*, Effective Inventory Management, Dallas, TX, 2005.

Shane, E., *Selling Electronic Media*, Focal Press, Boston, MA, 1999.

Slater, J., *Simplifying Accounting Language*, Kendall-Hall Publishing, Dubuque, IA, 1975.

Warner, C., and Buchman, J., *Broadcast, Cable, Print, and Interactive*, Iowa State University Press, Ames, IA, 2003.

Wild, T., *Best Practice in Inventory Management*, John Wiley & Sons, New York, 1998.

Zeigler, S.K., and Howard, H.H., *Broadcast Advertising: A Comprehensive Working Textbook*, 2nd edition, Grid Publishing, Columbus, OH, 1984.

Every radio station has a person who manages "traffic." Traffic management is the scheduling of commercials. Client orders are entered into the traffic software specifying the dates, times, length, and rate of the requested commercials.

Once the order is entered, the questions "Who wants to advertise?" and "When do they want to be on the air?" are answered. Clients can choose to run a certain number of commercials over a period of days, or they can opt for a specific number of commercials on specific days. In general, the more detailed the client specifications for placement, the greater the cost of the commercial.

After deciding when they want to run and how much flexibility they have in day placement, the client must choose the scheduling plan. Every radio station has a "run of station" plan that means the client's commercials will be placed randomly by the computer in whatever openings are available. This is generally called ROS or BTA (best times available) and is the least expensive placement option. A client may want to ensure that his commercials will run throughout the day. A plan that guarantees an even distribution throughout the dayparts is the next step up from an ROS schedule. Clients who specifically want a certain number of commercials in a particular daypart on a chosen day will pay the highest rate for the individual commercial unit. The customary dayparts are 6 A.M.–10 A.M., 10 A.M.–3 P.M., 3 P.M.–7 P.M., 7 P.M.–Mid.

The next question after "Who" wants to advertise and "When" is "What do they want to advertise?" The two most common reasons for advertising are "image" and "event."

Clients may want to advertise on a consistent basis to have their name and message in the public awareness, or they may want to hype a particular event or sale.

Commercials may be produced by the radio station production department from a script or copy points provided by the client. Finished commercials can be sent in the form of reel, over the Internet (MP3), or through commercial delivery systems. However the commercial arrives, the information about how to run that commercial must go to the traffic manager. The acceptable dates and times for each commercial are entered into the computer as well as rotation instructions if there are multiple commercials running for a client. Code numbers or information about the commercials that must be provided on the invoice are also entered.

Once all the contracts and traffic instructions are input, the traffic manager assembles and arranges a daily log. A multilevel priority system is used to ensure that the clients specifying the most detailed placement are scheduled first. If the traffic and in-studio computers are linked, the commercial log is immediately in place and ready to be merged with the music log. Any additions, deletions, or adjustments are registered as they occur. If the traffic and in-studio computer systems are not linked, the completed commercial log is transferred by disk and changes are entered manually into the traffic software.

Invoices specifying the date and time that each commercial aired are generated from the finalized log information.

Courtesy WIZN/WBTZ

Production 9

A Spot Retrospective

Radio has entered a new era in mixing and sound imaging. Still, a typical broadcast radio station produces thousands of commercials, public service announcements (PSAs), and promos annually. Meanwhile, satellite radio stations will mix a vast array of liners, voicers, promos, and features, and Web radio operations frequently do likewise.

Initially, commercials were aired live, due to a lack of recording technology. In the 1920s, most paid announcements consisted of lengthy speeches on the virtues of a particular product or service. Perhaps the most representative of the commercials of the period was one of the first ever to be broadcast, which lasted over 10 minutes and was announced by a representative of a Queens, New York, real estate firm. Aired live over WEAF in 1922, by today's standards the message would sound more like a classroom lecture than a broadcast advertisement. Certainly, no snappy jingle or ear-catching sound effects accompanied the episodic announcement.

Most commercial messages resembled the first until 1926. On Christmas Eve of that year the radio jingle was introduced, when four singers gathered for a musical tribute to Wheaties cereal. It was not for several years, however, that singing commercials were commonplace. For the most part, commercial production during the medium's first decade was relatively mundane. The reason was twofold: the government had resisted the idea of blatant or direct commercialism from the start, which fostered a low-key approach to advertising, and the medium was just in the process of evolving and therefore lacked the technical and creative wherewithal to present a more sophisticated spot.

Things changed by 1930, however. The austere, no-frills pitch, occasionally accompanied by a piano but more often done a cappella, was gradually replaced by the dialogue spot that used drama or comedy to sell its product. A great deal of imagination and creativity went into the writing and production of commercials, which were presented live throughout the 1930s. The production demands of some commercials equaled and even exceeded those of the programs they interrupted. Orchestras, actors, and lavishly constructed sound effects commonly were required to sell a chocolate-flavored syrup or a muscle liniment. By the late 1930s, certain commercials had become as famous as the favorite programs of the day. Commercials had achieved the status of pop art.

Still, the early radio station production room was primitive by today's standards. Sound effects were mostly improvised show by show, commercial by commercial, in some cases using the actual objects with which sounds were identified. Glass was shattered, guns fired, and furniture overturned as the studio's on-air light flashed. Before World War II, few sound effects were available on records. It was just as rare for a station to broadcast prerecorded commercials, although 78 rpm and wire recordings were used by certain major advertisers. The creation of vinyl discs in the 1940s inspired more widespread use of electrical transcriptions for radio advertising purposes. Today, sound effects are taken from CDs and downloaded from the Internet.

FIGURE 9.1
Sirius Satellite
Radio's "live" studio.
Courtesy Sirius.

The live spot was the mainstay at most stations into the 1950s, when two innovations brought about a greater reliance on the prerecorded message. Magnetic recording tape and 33 LPs revolutionized radio production methods. Recording tape brought about the greatest transformation and, ironically, was the product of Nazi scientists who developed acetate recorders and tape for espionage purposes. The adoption of magnetic tape by radio stations was costlier and thus occurred at a slower pace than 33 rpm, which essentially required a turntable modification.

Throughout the 1950s, advertising agencies grew to rely on LPs. By 1960, magnetic tape recorders were a familiar piece of studio equipment. More and more commercials were prerecorded. Some stations, especially those automated, did away with live announcements entirely, preferring to tape everything to avoid on-air mistakes.

Commercials themselves became more sophisticated sounding since practically anything could be accomplished on tape. Perhaps, no individual in the 1960s more effectively demonstrated the unique nature of radio as an advertising medium than did Stan Freberg. Through skillful writing and the clever use of sound effects, Freberg transformed Lake Michigan into a basin of hot chocolate crowned by a 700-foot-high mountain of whipped cream, and no one doubted the feat.

Today, the sounds of millions of skillfully prepared commercials trek through the ether and into the minds of practically every man, woman, and child in America. Good writing and production are what make the medium so successful.

Formatted Spots

In the 1950s the medium took to *formatting* to survive and prosper. Today listeners are offered myriad sounds from which to choose; there is something for practically every taste. Stations concentrate their efforts on delivering a specific format, which may be defined as Adult Contemporary, Country, Easy Listening, or any one of a dozen others. As you will recall from the discussion in

FIGURE 9.2
Today mixing is done
in the digital box.
Courtesy Sirius.

Chapter 3, each format has its own distinctive sound, which is accomplished through a careful selection and arrangement of compatible program elements. To this end, commercials attempt to reflect a station's format. In the age of consolidation, says Larry Miller, "There is a tendency to do one size fits all at the agency level. In-house local retail may be more customized to fit the format. We used to make a point of avoiding loud rock 'n' roll spots at the classical station I worked for, but I'm not sure if that's still a consideration."

The Production Room

In general, metro market stations and clusters employ a full-time production person (known variously as production director, production manager, production chief, and more recently as chief imager or head audio animator). This individual's primary duties are to record voice-tracks and mix commercials and PSAs. Other duties involve the maintenance of the bed and sound effects library and the mixdown of promotional material and special programs, such as public affairs features, interviews, and documentaries.

Stations that do not have a slot for a full-time production person divide work among the on-air staff. In this case, the program director (PD) often oversees production responsibilities, or a deejay may be assigned several hours of production duties each day and be called the production director.

At most medium and small outlets, on-air personnel take part in the production process. Production may include the simple transfer of an agency spot into the computer system, a mixdown that requires a single bed (background music) under a 30-second voicer, or a multielement mixdown of a 60-second two-voicer with sound effects and several bed transitions. Station production can run from the mundane to the exciting and challenging (mixing a commercial without words conveyed through a confluence of sounds).

Most production directors, in this digital age often called imaging directors, are recruited from the on-air ranks, having acquired the necessary studio dexterity and know how to meet the demands of the position. In addition to the broad range of mixdown skills required by the job, a solid knowledge of editing is essential. The production director routinely is called on to make rudimentary edits or perform more complex editing chores, such as the rearrangement of elements in a 60-second concert promo. (Editing is covered in more detail later in this chapter.)

The production/imaging director works closely with many people but perhaps most closely with the program director. The person responsible for production is expected to have a complete understanding of the station's programming philosophy and objective. This is necessary because commercials constitute an element of programming and therefore must fit in. A production person must be able to determine when an incoming commercial clashes with the station's image. When a question exists as to the spot's appropriateness, the program director will be called on to make the final judgment, because it is he or she who is ultimately responsible for what gets on the air. In the final analysis, station production is a product of programming. In most broadcast organizations, the production director answers to the program director. It is a logical arrangement given the relationship of the two areas.

The production/imaging director also works closely with the station copywriter. Their combined efforts make or break a commercial. The copywriter conceives of the concept, and the producer brings it to fruition. The traffic department also is in close and constant contact with production, because one of its primary responsibilities is to see that copy gets processed and placed in the on-air studio where it is scheduled for broadcast.

Once again the extensive clustering of station facilities in the age of consolidation finds many production responsibilities centralized. By now many radio groups have established one production hub to mix the spots of their other outlets, especially when in the same market. Typically, this has resulted in the downsizing of individual station production staffs and the elimination of comprehensive mixdown studios at these sites.

The Studios

A radio station has two kinds of studios: on-air and production. Both share basic design features and have comparable equipment. In cluster operations where stations are colocated, there is often a single primary production facility. For ease of movement and accessibility, audio equipment commonly is set up in a U-shape within which the operator or producer is seated.

The standard equipment found in radio studios includes microphones, an audio console (commonly referred to as the "board"), computer workstations (on-air studio usually networked to production studio – this computer would also contain automation software, such as Audio Vault), video display monitors, compact disc machines, mini-disc machines, digital effects boxes, patch panel (digital consoles typically have these built in), and a distribution amplifier (see Figure 9.4).

FIGURE 9.3
This cutting-edge digital studio is state of the art. Courtesy RTBF.

FIGURE 9.4
Although each production studio is unique, the basics of layout are fairly consistent from station to station. For the sake of ease and accessibility, most studios are developed in a U-shape or a variation thereof. However, computer workstations have had an effect on equipment layout, since most work is done on the mouse and keyboard. Courtesy Clear Channel.

Audio Console

The audio console is the centerpiece, the very heart of the radio station. Dozens of manufacturers produce audio consoles, and although design characteristics vary, the basic components remain relatively constant. Consoles come in all different sizes and shapes and all contain inputs that permit audio energy to enter the console, outputs through which audio energy is fed to other locations, VU meters that measure the amount or level

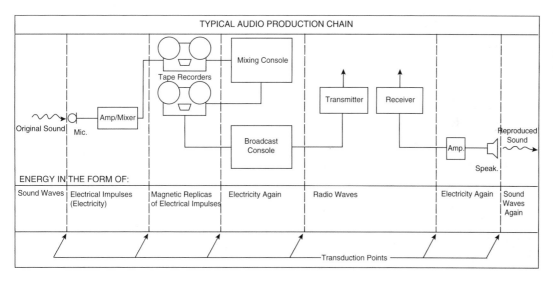

FIGURE 9.5
Transduction points in a typical audio chain.

FIGURE 9.6
Multichannel board.
Courtesy Auditronics.

FIGURE 9.7
Audio console
with linear faders,
popularly referred
to as a "slide" board.
Courtesy Auditronics.

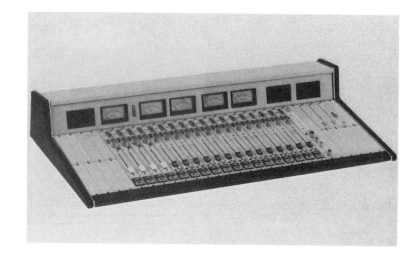

FIGURE 9.8
A digital console.
Courtesy Solid State
Logic.

FIGURE 9.9
Audio mixing
requires special
skills and dexterity.
Courtesy Danmarks
Radio.

of sound, pots (faders) that control gain or the quantity of sound, monitor gains that control in-studio volume, and master gains for the purpose of controlling general output levels (see Figures 9.6–9.8).

Since the late 1960s, the manufacture of consoles equipped with linear faders has surpassed those with rotary faders. *Slide* (another term used) faders perform the same function as the more traditional pots, and they are easier to read and handle.

Cue Mode

A low-power amplifier is built into the console so that the operator may hear audio from various sources without it actually being distributed to other points. The

FIGURE 9.10
Mic setup in a Moscow radio studio. Courtesy Echo Musika.

purpose of this is to facilitate the setup of certain sound elements, such as records and tapes, for eventual introduction into the mixdown sequence (see Figure 9.9).

Computers

Computers have become the soul of the audio studio – both on-air and production. Observes Vic Michaels, "Studio computers would contain editing software, like Pro Tools or Adobe Audition. The on-air computer would also contain automation software, such as Audio Vault. It would also possess Selector, which is needed to tell the Audio Vault system what to play. At my station, we have three computers in production: one is for Audio Vault automation, the second is for Selector music software, and the third is for editing on Pro Tools. All three are networked to the on-air computer. Everything now is "audio files." When one makes a commercial or records a song off a CD, it becomes an audio file that can be moved from computer to computer."

FIGURE 9.11
An integrated console environment. Courtesy Digidesign Icon.

FIGURE 9.12
Multitrack reel-to-reel recording is used but the computer has mainly taken over this task. This is a 32-track recorder, using 2-inch audio tape. Courtesy Otari.

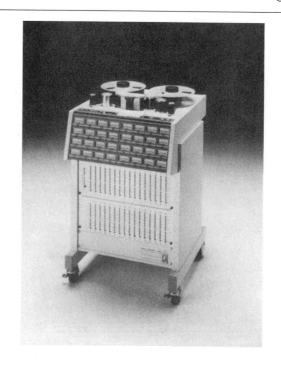

FIGURE 9.13
A typical on-air and production combination. Courtesy WIZN.

FIGURE 9.14
Monitoring the sound wave on the screen. Courtesy WIZN.

Digital (Mini) Disc Machines

Analog cart machines were replaced by random-access mini-disc (record/playback) technology. These machines have not become as popular as the cart machines they replaced, because of other studio innovations. The so-called new-age cart machine allows producers to digitally archive vast amounts of audio on mini reusable discs. Says station manager Vic Michaels, "They replaced the old-line carts, because they were faster, programmable, visual, digital, and competitively priced." Companies like Sony, 360 Systems, Harris, Denon, and Otari manufactured the mini-disc machine, which replaced the traditional analog cart machine at most stations – another victim of the computer age.

Among other things, digi-disc machines offer instant start (there is none of the hesitation or drag common in its analog

FIGURE 9.15
Production elements and their mixing are centered in the workstation. Courtesy WIZN.

Specifications & Details:

- A minimum of 2 gigabytes of hard drive space.
- Extract audio from more than 7 approved CD-ROMs with the appropriate workstation configuration simultaneously, with the power to support multiple SCSI drives.
- CD-ROM drives may be either EIDE or SCSI devices and must be connected to the workstation.
- Minimum of 256 megabytes of RAM, more if you will be importing from multiple CD devices or importing audio over 20 minutes long.
- Designed to run as an integrated component of the NexGen Digital system. Windows 98, Windows 2000 or Windows NT required.

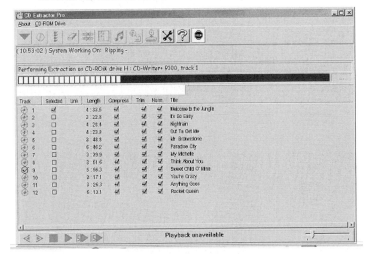

FIGURE 9.16
Computer-driven production tools have greatly enhanced mixdown. Courtesy Prophet Systems.

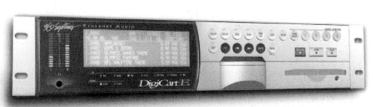

DigiCart/E Ethernet Audio™ Recorder

FIGURE 9.17
The old-line analog cart machine is now an all-function, digital recording source. Courtesy 360 Systems.

FIGURE 9.18
Production studio
equipment rack.
Courtesy WIZN.

predecessor), back cueing, track selection, end marking, automatic fade-in, visual ID and cueing, digital editing, and so forth.

Compact Discs

Compact disc players entered the radio production studio in the 1980s. Although CD players have become less and less evident in studios, their value as a piece

FIGURE 9.19
To clean a CD, use a piece of lint free cloth. Never touch the encoded surface and handle the disc at its edges.

of production equipment has not entirely vanished. Observes Skip Pizzi: "Digital audio had its greatest initial acceptance as CD hardware, to the point where it was estimated that over half of the radio stations in the USA used CD to some extent. In major markets, this figure rose steeply. Many of these stations programmed music exclusively from CD, or nearly so. The practice of providing promotional copies of new releases on CD by record companies (following an earlier period of general reluctance to do so) became common practice. Second- and third-generation professional CD players aided in the process of acceptance" (see Figure 9.20).

CD players employ a laser beam to read encoded data at a rate of 4.3218 million bits per second. A compact disc is 4.7 inches wide and 1.2 mm thick, and players are quite light and compact as well. This feature alone makes them attractive to broadcasters. But what makes a CD player most appealing to broadcasters is its superior sound. Compact disc players offer, among other features, far greater dynamic range than standard turntables and a lower signal-to-noise ratio. They also eliminate the need for physical contact during cueing, and wowing and distortion are virtually gone.

Because digital discs are specially coated, they are much more resistant to damage than are analog discs. This is not to suggest that CDs are impervious; they are not. In fact, the majority of CD-related problems stem from the discs themselves and not the players.

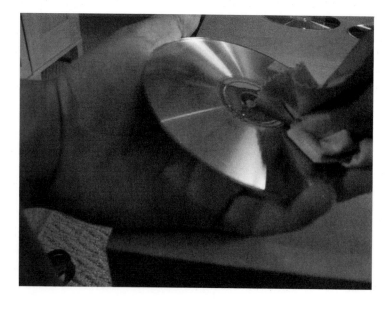

FIGURE 9.20
CD players cart players continue to be used in some studios. Courtesy Denon.

Despite initial claims of the invincibility of the digital disc, experience has shown that mishandling of discs is courting disaster. CDs cannot be mistreated – that is, used as Frisbees or placemats for peanut butter sandwiches – and still be expected to work like new. The simple fact is that although compact discs are more resistant to damage, they can be harmed.

A CD reads a disc from its core outward, moving from 500 rpm on the inside to 200 rpm on the outer edge of the disc. Most CD players feature a variety of effect options, which can be of particular use to a production mix. Accessing cuts on a CD player is quick and simple, though excerpting segments from a track for inclusion in a mixdown can be somewhat less expedient. Nonetheless, CD players are still useful in the production studio. Compact discs are a wonderful source for bed music (music that serves as background under voiced copy) and sound effects.

Working with a CD unit is anything but complicated. Press a button and a tray ejects (on top-loaded models a door pops open). A disc is placed into the tray, and the press of the same button returns the tray and disc into the player. The operator then selects the track to be played and presses the appropriately numbered button. The audio rolls.

Burnable CD units (CD-R and CD-RW) are prominent in the production room.

CD-Rs allow one time burning, whereas CD-RWs allow multiple burnings.

Compressors, Equalizers, and Audio Processing

"There are three domains of audio," says producer Ty Ford. "They are amplitude, frequency, and time." Some stations alter amplitude to create the illusion of being louder without actually changing level. This is called compressing the signal. Production people use compressors to enhance loudness as well as to eliminate or cut out ambient noise, thus focusing on specifics of mix. Compression often is used as a method of getting listeners to take greater notice of a piece of production and as a remedy to certain problems (see Figure 9.22).

Equalizers (EQs) work the frequency domain of audio by boosting and/or cutting lows (hertz\obHz\cb range) and highs (kilohertz\obkHz\cb range). EQs allow producers to correct problems as well as to create parity between different elements of production. They are also useful in creating special effects. EQs are available in-board (part of the audio console) and out-of-board (stand-alone unit) and as part of certain integrated audio effects processors.

FIGURE 9.21
Screens, screens
everywhere. The
modern studio.
Courtesy Afan FM.

FIGURE 9.22
Digital effects
processor. Courtesy
Lexicon.

Most audio processors (also called effects processors or simply boxes) are time-domain devices. Stations use these digital boxes to create a wide range of effects such as reverb, echo, and flange.

In the last few years, radio stations have become increasingly interested in what audio processors have to offer their mixes. Today these boxes are a familiar, often integral, item in production rooms at the majority of stations. Their value in the creation of commercials, PSAs, promos, and features is inestimable. The use of samplers and synthesizers is common in radio production rooms too. Samplers let a production person load a studio audio source (recorder, live mike) into its built-in microprocessor and then manipulate the digitized data with the aid of a musical keyboard to create a multitude of effects. Samplers employ magnetic microfloppies

and are wired to an audio console so that the sounds they produce may be integrated into mixdown. Samplers are also found in certain audio effects processors with musical instrument digital interface (MIDI). A sample is a digital recording of a small bit of sound.

"A lot of musical instrument (MI) gear has been introduced into the radio production studio. Synths, samplers, and sequencers are pretty commonplace today," notes Ty Ford.

Many software applications, such as Cool Edit Pro and Pro Tools, have these and other signal processing built in.

Patch Panels and ISDNs

A patch panel consists of rows of inputs and outputs connected to various external sources – studios, equipment, remote locations, network lines, and so forth. Patch panels essentially are routing devices that allow for items not directly wired into an audio console to become a part of a broadcast or production mixdown. Today, says Vic Michaels, "Patch panels are still utilized but not as frequently as before. Use is based on a station's needs. Digital consoles now have internal patch capabilities built right into the console so one can patch in certain effects or sources to any channel" (see Figure 9.23).

ISDNs are digital phone lines that bring voices and other audio to studios with near perfect sound quality. Because voice tracking has become the means by which so many stations fill their airwaves, ISDN connections have become invaluable.

As production director Matt Grasso observes, "The day of the scratchy cell phone or muddy dedicated line is over. Your talent sounds like they are right in the studio. If they are at a club, not only can they talk, but they can broadcast the music they are playing there right over the air with the same quality you would get from a CD player in the main studio. ISDN means no reel to reels or DATS coming to a station via snailmail either."

Microphones

Microphones are designed with different pickup patterns. Omnidirectional microphones are sensitive to sound from all directions (360°), whereas bidirectional microphones pick up sound from two directions (180°). The unidirectional microphone draws sound from only one path (90°), and because of its highly directed field of receptivity, extraneous sounds are not amplified. This feature has made the unidirectional microphone popular in both the control and production studios, where generally one person is at work at a time. Most studio consoles possess two or more microphone inputs so that additional voices can be accommodated when the need arises (see Figure 9.25).

Omnidirectional and bidirectional microphones often are used when more than one voice is involved. For instance, an omnidirectional may be used for the broadcast or recording of a round-table discussion, and the bidirectional during a one-on-one interview.

FIGURE 9.23
Digital switching systems for connection from one source (studio/equipment) to another. Courtesy Wheatstone.

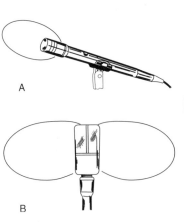

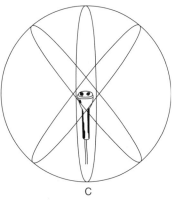

FIGURE 9.24
The look of microphones in the 1920s. Courtesy Jim Steele.

FIGURE 9.25
Microphone pickup patters: (A) unidirectional, (B) bidirectional, and (C) omnidirectional.

FIGURE 9.26
Sound pressure level (SPL) chart depicting volume of different sounds in relation to human aural perception.

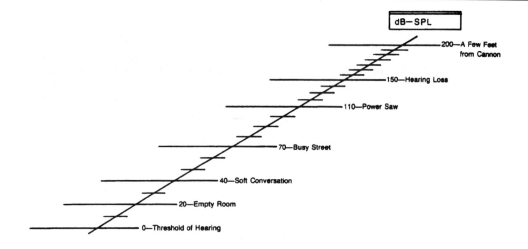

Announcers must be aware of a microphone's directional features. Proper positioning in relation to a microphone is important. Being outside the path of a microphone's pickup (off-mike) affects sound quality. At the same time, being too close to a microphone can result in distortion, known as popping and blasting. Keeping a hand's length away from a microphone will usually prevent this from occurring. Windscreens and blast filters may be attached to a microphone to help reduce distortion.

Digital Editing

Old time tape editing is a lost art that ranged from a simple repair to a complicated rearrangement of sound elements. Today the old razor approach to editing and splicing tape is all but ancient history, having lost ground to "nondestructive" tapeless digital methods.

Computers handle the bulk of editing in the production room. This tapeless approach involves loading audio into a RAM or hard disc and making edits via a monitor (with the aid of a mouse, a keyboard, or a console). Although this technology has been costly in the past, today prices are quite affordable, motivating more and more stations to convert to the tapeless studio. Computerized audio workstations were once perceived as the studio of the future, but they are the studio of today (see radio production expert David Reeses' discussion and advice on digital editing in this chapter).

David Reese | Basic Digital Audio Editing (and a few tips)

FIGURE 9.27
David Reese.

Today, nearly all audio-production employs a computer (or computer-based audio equipment) with audio editing software and involves four basic processes: recording, editing, mixing, and mastering.

Step 1: Recording Audio. This can be accomplished by recording with a microphone, by opening an existing audio file, or by extracting audio from a CD. If you're live recording, watch volume levels and err on the low side. *TIP: Record around –10 db on the VU*

meter. Low audio levels can generally be raised with the editing software: over-modulated, high-volume audio can't be fixed and will leave you with distorted audio.

Step 2: Editing Audio. Audio editing is similar to word processing – you are using a lot of cut, paste, and copy functions. Not only can you hear the audio, but you can "read" the audio waveform. You see a visual representation of the audio with a vertical axis showing volume level and a horizontal axis showing time. It's usually easy to see groups of words and the spaces between words. Editing often involves making an "edit in" point and an "edit out" point and then cutting out a word, several words, or a chunk of music. *TIP: Always make your edit in point just before the first word you want to cut out and your edit out point just before the first word you want to leave in.* This will maintain proper phrasing and the natural flow of words; however, if you make a mistake, remember, most editing functions include an "Undo" command.

Step 3: Mixing Audio. Most audio production uses two "tracks" (stereo) or several tracks (multitrack). Once you've edited the various tracks, mixing is the blending of those tracks together. One aspect of the mix is balancing levels. For example, a simple radio spot might include an announcer vocal track and a music bed. In mixing them together, you would want to lower the volume of the music when the vocal is playing. Mixing also involves panning tracks to the left or right channel or somewhere in between. *TIP: Use audio processing, like echo or reverb, to add "depth" to the sound track.* You can also use equalization to enhance specific tracks or segments giving them brighter highs or a bass boost. Don't forget to save your mix so you can go back and make changes, if necessary.

Step 4: Mastering Audio. The final step is to listen critically to your work several times and make any fine-tuning adjustments. *TIP: If you hear any "plosives" (those "pops" on p, t, b sounds), you usually can't eliminate them, but you can diminish them. With your editor, select just the plosive part and slightly decrease the volume to reduce the impact of the plosive sound.* In most cases, a multitrack production will be mastered down to stereo and saved as the finished product. You may need to transfer your audio file from the production computer to another server for eventual playback or you may need to burn a copy onto CD for playback, to give a client, or just to archive.

Digital editing gives you almost unlimited ways to manipulate audio and to build a creative, finished product. Don't be afraid to experiment; you never know what unique effect you might come up with.

Copywriting

As stated earlier, poet Stephen Vincent Benet, who wrote for radio during its heyday, called the medium *the theater of the mind.* Indeed, the person who tunes into radio gets no visual aids but must manufacture images on his or her own to accompany the words and sounds broadcast. The station employee who prepares written material is called a copywriter. A copywriter job consists primarily of writing commercials, promos, and PSAs, with the emphasis on the first of the three.

Not all stations employ a full-time copywriter. This is especially true in small

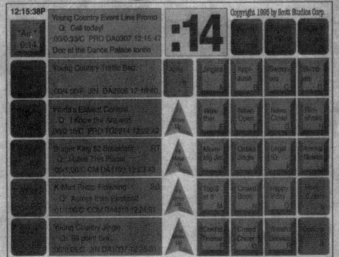

FIGURE 9.28
Digital audio puts the next-generation studio in a box. A world of production sound at your fingertips. Courtesy Scott.

FIGURE 9.29
A digital mixing
board. Courtesy
Orban.

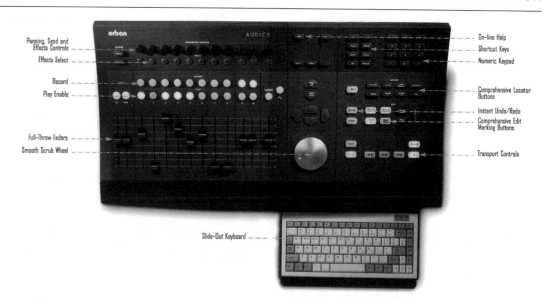

FIGURE 9.30
Today most audio
editing is done
on the screen.
Waveforms are
altered and
manipulated to
create the sound
sought. Reprinted
with permission from
GoldWave.

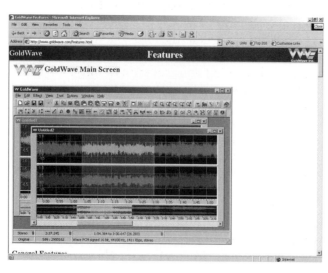

markets where economics dictate that the salesperson write for his or her own account. Deejays also are called on to pen commercials. At stations with bigger operating budgets, a full-time copywriter often will handle the bulk of the writing chores.

Copywriters must possess a complete understanding of the unique nature of the medium, a familiarity with the audience for which the commercial message is intended, and knowledge of the product being promoted. A station's format will influence the style of writing in a commercial; thus, the copywriter also must be thoroughly acquainted with the station's particular programming approach. Commercials must be compatible with the station's sound. For instance, copy written for Lite AC usually is more conservative in tone than that written for Modern Rock stations, and so on.

WXXX

"Home of the Hits" (SFX: Bed in)
TJ'S ROCKHOUSE, MARK STREET, DOWNTOWN BOISE, PRESENTS CLEO AND THE GANG ROCKING OUT EVERY FRIDAY AND SATURDAY NIGHT. AT TJ'S THERE'S NEVER A COVER OR MINIMUM, JUST A GOOD TIME. SUNDAY IDAHO'S MONARCHS OF ROCKABILLY, JOBEE LANE, RAISE THE ROOF AT TJ'S. YOU BETTER BE READY TO SHAKE IT, BECAUSE NOBODY STANDS STILL WHEN JOBEE LANE ROCKS. THURSDAY IS HALFPRICE NIGHT, AND LADIES ALWAYS GET THEIR FIRST DRINK FREE AT BOISE'S NUMBER ONE CLUB FOR FUN AND MUSIC. TAKE MAIN TO MARK STREET, AND LOOK FOR THE HOUSE THAT ROCKS, TJ'S ROCK-HOUSE.
(SFX: Stinger out)

WYYY

"Soothing Sounds"
ELEGANT DINING IS JUST A SCENIC RIDE AWAY. (SFX: Bed in and under) THE CRITICALLY ACCLAIMED VISCOUNT (VYCOUNT) INN IN CEDAR GLENN OFFERS PATRONS AN EXQUISITE MENU IN A SETTING WITHOUT EQUAL. THE VISCOUNT'S 18TH CENTURY CHARM WILL MAKE YOUR EVENING OUT ONE TO REMEMBER. JAMISON LONGLEY OF THE WISCONSIN REGISTER GIVES THE VISCOUNT A FOURSTAR RATING FOR SERVICE, CUISINE, AND ATMOSPHERE. THE VISCOUNT (SFX: Royal fanfare) WILL SATISFY YOUR ROYAL TASTES. CALL

675-2180 FOR RESERVATIONS. TAKE ROUTE 17 NORTH TO THE VISCOUNT INN, 31 STONY LANE, CEDAR GLENN.

Some basic rules pertain to the mechanics of copy preparation. First, copy is typed in uppercase and is double-spaced for ease of reading. Next, left and right margins are set at 1 inch. Sound effects are noted in parentheses at that point in the copy where they are to occur. Proper punctuation and grammar are vital, too. A comma in the wrong place can throw off the meaning of an entire sentence. Be mindful, also, that commercials are designed to be heard and not read. Keep sentence structure as uncomplicated as possible. Maintaining a conversational style will make the client's message more accessible.

Timing a piece of copy is relatively simple. There are a couple of methods: one involves counting words, and the other counting lines. In the first approach, 25 words would constitute 10 seconds; 65 words, 30 seconds; and 125 words, 1 minute. Counting lines is an easier and quicker way of timing copy. This method is based on the assumption that it takes, on average, 3 seconds to read one line of copy from margin to margin. Therefore, 9 to 10 lines of copy would time out to 30 seconds, and 18–20 lines to 1 minute. Of course, production elements such as sound effects and beds must be included as part of the count and deducted accordingly. For example, 6 seconds worth of sound effects in a 30-second commercial would shorten the amount of actual copy by 2 lines.

Because everything written in radio is intended to be read aloud, it is important that words with unusual or uncommon pronunciations be given special attention. Phonetic spelling is used to convey the way a word is pronounced. For instance: "DINNER AT THE FO'C'SLE (FOKE-SIL) RESTAURANT IN LAITONE (LAY-TON) SHORES IS A SEA ADVENTURE." Incorrect pronunciation has resulted in more than one canceled account. The copywriter must make certain that the announcer assigned to voice-track a commercial is fully aware of any particulars in the copy. In other words, when in doubt spell it out.

Excessive numbers and complex directions are to be avoided in radio copy. Numbers, such as an address or telephone number, should be repeated and directions should be as simple as possible. The use of landmarks ("ACROSS FROM CITY HALL . . .") can reduce confusion. Listeners are seldom in a position to write down something at the exact moment they hear it. Copy should communicate, not confuse or frustrate.

Of course, the purpose of any piece of copy is to sell the client's product. Creativity plays an important role. The radio writer has the world of the imagination to work with and is limited only by the boundaries of his own.

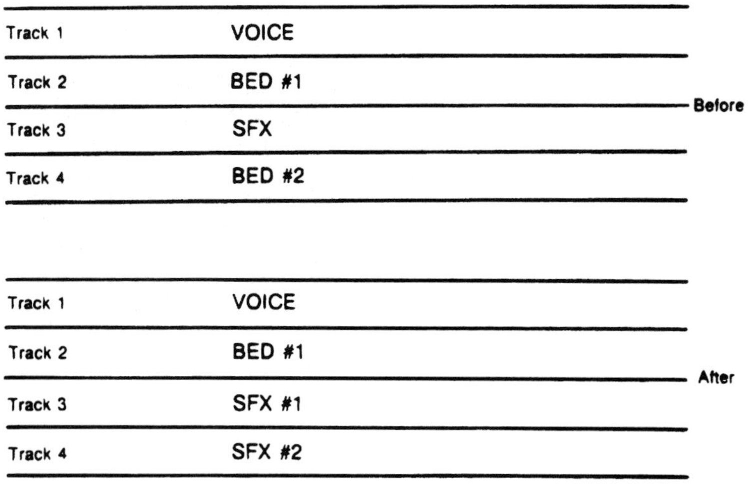

Track 1	VOICE
Track 2	BED #1
Track 3	SFX
Track 4	BED #2

Before

Track 1	VOICE
Track 2	BED #1
Track 3	SFX #1
Track 4	SFX #2

After

FIGURE 9.31
Editing a multitrack involves adding or deleting tracks. Here BED 2 is replaced by SFX 2 on track 4.

Announcing Tips

Although the radio announcer ranks have dwindled as radio companies consolidate and downsize their staffs and employ voice-tracking to serve multiple stations, thousands of men and women in this country still make their living before the microphone. In few other professions is the salary range so broad. A beginning announcer may make little more than minimum wage, whereas a seasoned professional in a major market may earn a salary in the six-figure range.

Although announcer salaries can be very modest in smaller markets, the financial rewards tend to be substantial at metro market stations, which can afford to pay more. Of course, competition for the metro market station positions is keener, and expectations are higher. "You have to pay your dues in this profession. No one walks out of a classroom and into WNBC. It's usually a long and winding road. It takes time to develop the on-air skills that the big stations want. It's hard work to become really good, but you can make an enormous amount of money, or at least a very comfortable income, when you do," says radio personality Mike Morin.

The duties of an announcer vary depending on the size or ranking of a station. In the small station, announcers generally fill news and/or production shifts as well. For example, a midday announcer at WXXX, who is on the air from 10 A.M. until 3 P.M., may be held responsible for the 4 and 5 P.M. newscasts, plus any production that arises during that same period. Meanwhile, the larger station may require nothing more of its announcers than the taping of voiceovers. Of course, the preparation for an airshift at a major-market station can be very time consuming.

An announcer must, above all else, possess the ability to effectively read copy aloud. Among other things, this involves proper enunciation and inflection, which are improved through practice. Programmer Bill Towery contends that the more a person reads for personal enjoyment or enrichment, the easier it is to communicate orally. "I'd advise anyone who aspires to the microphone to read, read, read. The more the better. Announcing is oral interpretation of the printed page. You must first understand what is on the page before you can communicate it aloud. Bottom line here is that if you want to become an announcer, first become a reader."

Having a naturally resonant and pleasant-sounding voice certainly is an advantage.

Voice quality still is very important in radio. There is an inclination toward the voice with a deeper register. This is true for female announcers as well as male. However, most voices possess considerable range and with training, practice, and experience even a person with a high-pitched voice can develop an appealing on-air sound. Forcing the voice into a lower register to achieve a deeper sound can result in injury to the vocal chords. "Making the most of what you already have is a lot better than trying to be something you're not. Perfect yourself and be natural," advises Morin.

Relaxation is important. The voice simply is at its best when it is not strained. Moreover, announcing is enhanced by proper breathing, which is only possible when one is free of stress. Initially, being "on-mike" can be an intimidating experience, resulting in nervousness that can be debilitating. Here are some things announcers do to achieve a state of relaxation:

1. Read copy aloud before going on the air. Get the feel of it. This will automatically increase confidence, thus aiding in relaxation.
2. Take several deep breaths and slowly exhale while keeping your eyes closed.
3. Sit still for a couple of moments with your arms limp at your sides. Tune out. Let the dust settle. Conjure pleasant images. Allow yourself to drift a bit, and then slowly return to the job at hand.
4. Stand and slowly move your upper torso in a circular motion for a minute or so. Flex your shoulders and arms. Stretch luxuriously.
5. When seated, check your posture. Do not slump over as you announce. A curved diaphragm impedes breathing. Sit erect, but not stiffly.
6. Hum a few bars of your favorite song. The vibration helps relax the throat muscles and vocal chords.
7. Give yourself ample time to settle in before going on. Dashing into the studio at the last second will jar your focus and shake your composure.

In most situations, an accent – regional or otherwise – is a handicap and should be eliminated. Most radio announcers in the

FIGURE 9.32
Digital audio workstations mark a new era in radio production mixing, editing, and storage. Courtesy Ardour.

South do not have a drawl, and the majority of announcers in Boston put the "r" in the word *car*. A noticeable or pronounced accent will almost always put the candidate for an announcer's job out of the running. Accents are not easy to eliminate, but with practice they can be overcome.

Voice-Tracking

In the age of station consolidation and clusters (station malls), radio corporations are finding it cost efficient to feed their stations prerecorded voices. In other words, these days as much station announcing takes place away from the station as it does at the station. Radio companies hire announcers to provide their stations with their voicing needs, so there is less and less on-sight voice origination. One announcer may be the voice of a hundred stations. Through satellite feeds and ISDN lines, local station airwaves are filled with out-of-town voices. When voice-tracking is done at the station level, it is to allow more multitasking opportunities for the announcer. Says Ed Shane, "Voice-tracking is an ideal productivity tool, allowing air talent to prerecord their air shifts in order to use their work time producing commercials, appearing live at sponsor locations, or doing a variety of jobs other than waiting for songs to end in order to deliver a 10-second talkover."

Voice-tracking has generated concern because the ranks of announcers are being thinned down. Jackie O'Brien, Metro Networks director of operations, observes, "The field of radio broadcasting has changed tremendously over the past few years. Many positions have been lost due to the innovation of voice-tracking. While this may be a cost-efficient way to run a radio group, it has taken away the personality of the service. When I started in broadcasting, I felt the position was more than the sound of my own voice. There was a commitment made to service the public with news, information, and a little entertainment. This meant staying on through a snowstorm or covering local elections. It also meant talking the occasional lonely heart out of suicide. I've been at Metro Networks for four years. In that time, I've watched old positions I held in radio disappear to voice-tracking."

Despite concern for the impact voice-tracking has on the announcing profession and radio localism, more and more stations are using it, and the future would suggest that this practice – for better or worse – will grow.

The Sound Library

Music is used to enhance an advertiser's message – to make it more appealing, more listenable. The music used in a radio commercial is called a *bed* simply because it backs the voice. It is the platform on which the voice is set. A station may bed thousands of commercials over the course of a year. Music is an integral component of the production mixdown.

FIGURE 9.33
Production order. Courtesy WBTZ.

106.7 WIZN **PRODUCTION ORDER** 99.9 Buzz

Client SMITH HDWARE AE KEITH

STATION: WIZN (WBTZ) (:30) :60

START DATE 9-14 END DATE 11-21

ROTATION INSTRUCTIONS Equal
(How many versions? 2)

✓ PRODUCE USING ATTACHED COPY
___ ADD TAG TO EXISTING SPOT
___ SPEC SPOT
___ NEED A CASSETTE

DUB FROM: ✓
MP3 ✓
DGS ___
Spot Taxi ___
Other ___

SEND DUB TO: KALO
(via MP3) via reel
Address: ___

APPROVALS:
___ NO APPROVAL NEEDED
✓ NEEDS APPROVAL
CONTACT: ___
PHONE NUMBER: ___
___ OK TO LEAVE ON VOICE MAIL AND PUT ON THE AIR

OTHER INSTRUCTIONS Use Bill on VT

FOR PRODUCTION USE ONLY
Music/SFX ___
Date/Time Produced ___
Date/Time Approved ___

CART NUMBERS
WIZN ___
Buzz ___

Today, sound libraries are almost always delivered via downloads. However, many stations still derive bed music from other sources. Demonstration CDs (demos) sent by recording companies to radio stations are a familiar source, since few actually make it onto playlists and into on-air rotations. These CDs are particularly useful because the music is unfamiliar to the listening audience. Known tunes generally are avoided in the mixdown of spots because they tend to distract the listener from the copy. However, there are times when familiar tunes are used to back spots. Nightclubs often request that popular music be used in their commercials to convey a certain mood and ambiance.

Movie soundtrack CDs are another good place to find beds because they often contain a variety of music, ranging from the bizarre to the conventional. They also are an excellent source for special audio effects, which can be used to great advantage in the right commercial.

On-air CDs are screened for potential production use as well. Although several tracks may be placed in on-air rotation and thereby eliminated for use in the mixdown of commercials, some cuts will not be programmed and therefore will not be available for production purposes.

Syndicated bed music libraries are available at a price and are widely used at larger stations. *Broadcasting Yearbook* contains a complete listing of production companies offering bed music libraries. Similarly, a search of the Internet will yield lists of audio production sources. The majority of stations continue to lift beds from in-house CDs (see Figure 9.34).

Music used for production purposes is catalogued so that it can be located and reused. Syndicated libraries come fully catalogued. An old system employed index cards, which could be stored for easy access in a container or on a rotating drum. At most stations today, computers are used to store production library information and files.

If a file exists for a bed that is not in current use and the bed is appropriate for a new account, then either a fresh file will be prepared or the new information will be added into the existing file.

No production studio is complete without a commercial sound effects library, but in the digital age, many effects are made in-house. Sound effects libraries can be purchased for as little as $100, or they can cost thousands. The quality and selection of effects vary accordingly. Specially tailored audio effects also can run into the thousands but can add a unique touch to a station's sound.

FIGURE 9.34
CD library in studio.
Courtesy WIZN.

WRITE GREAT COPY

Good copy is essential for successful advertising. To make certain the ad will attract customers for your client, remember these points:

1) Make your first sentence count. Does it provoke interest? Does it demand attention? Does it create a mood? If your first sentence doesn't have it, you've lost your best chance at getting the listeners' attention.

2) Keep your copy simple. The most eloquent thoughts are expressed in few words. If good writers can express complex emotions such as "love" simply, why are convoluted sentences needed to sell a leather coat? Cogent copy takes time and effort. The results are worth it.

3) Write for one person. Don't use words like "many of you" that refer to a lot of people listening. Radio isn't TV; people listen and respond to radio as individuals. Make your copy personal.

4) Eliminate the details. Store hours, telephone numbers, the credit cards they accept are useful in newspaper ads, not on radio. People don't listen to radio with a scratch pad handy. These details take up space and won't motivate anyone to buy anything.

5) Use a "locator." Store addresses are hard to remember, harder to visualize where they might be. Listeners relate better to "locators"—places they know or can easily find. "Across from the fairgrounds" will be remembered, "1365 N. King Street" likely won't be.

6) Focus on one thought or idea. What is the single most important thing you want the listener to know? Make it personal, make it entertaining, make it exciting—but concentrate on one theme idea. Never resort to a laundry list of services or use cliches.

7) Create and consistently use a phrase that "positions" the business or product. This will help the listener recall the business and why he/she should go there. Examples: Chevy Trucks: "Like a Rock"; Fox News Channel, "Fair and Balanced"; "Dude, you're gettin' a Dell."

8) After you've written the copy, read it aloud to someone else. Find out what they remembered. You may need to revise it.

BROADCAST MARKETING CONSULTANTS • 35 Main Street, Wayland, Massachusetts 01778 • 508/653-7200 • Fax 508/653-4088

FIGURE 9.35
Tips on writing effective copy. Courtesy Broadcasting Unlimited.

CHAPTER HIGHLIGHTS

1. The first radio commercials aired in 1922.

2. Early commercials were live readings: no music, sound effects, or singing.

3. Dialogue spots, using drama and comedy to sell the product, became prominent in the 1930s. Elaborate sound effects, actors, and orchestras were employed.

4. With the introduction of magnetic recording tape and 33 LPs in the 1950s, live commercial announcements were replaced by prerecorded messages.

5. The copy, delivery, and mixdown of commercials must be adapted to match the station's format to avoid audience tune-out.

6. The production director (imaging director) records voice tracks, mixes commercials and PSAs, maintains the bed music and special effects libraries, mixes promotional material and special programs, and performs basic editing chores.

7. At smaller stations the production responsibilities are assigned part-time to on-air personnel or the program director.

8. The production director (increasingly referred to as the imaging director at stations mixing with computers), who usually answers to the program director, also works closely with the copywriter and the traffic manager.

9. For ease of movement and accessibility, both on-air and production studio equipment are arranged in a U-shape.

10. The audio console (board) is the central piece of equipment. It consists of inputs, which permit audio energy to enter the console; outputs through which audio energy is fed to other locations; VU meters, which measure the level of sound; pots (faders), which control the quantity (gain) of sound; monitor gains, which control in-studio volume; and master gains, which control general output levels.

11. When operating the console in cue mode, the operator can listen to various audio sources without channeling them through an output.

12. Digital cart audio devices (360 Systems) have replaced the standard analog cart deck. They let producers digitally mix and archive extensive amounts of audio.

13. Compact disc players use a laser beam to decode the disc's surface, which eliminates stylus and turntable noises, distortion, and record damage. Recordable CDs are now in use.

14. Audio processors, samplers, digital carts, and MIDI enhance a radio production studio's product. Software such as Cool Edit Pro and Pro Tools have these features built in.

15. A patch panel is a routing device, consisting of inputs and outputs, connecting the audio console with various external sources.

16. Microphones are designed with different pickup patterns to accommodate different functions: omnidirectional (all directions), bidirectional (two directions), and unidirectional (one direction).

17. Audio editing ranges from simple repairs to complicated rearrangements of sound elements. Today the once conventional razor-cut approach to tape editing has been replaced by nondestructive computer and multitrack methods.

18. Digital audio workstations, which rely on computer technology and software (Pro Tools is very popular), are currently used in a vast number of radio production studios.

19. The station copywriter, who writes the commercials, promos, and PSAs, must be familiar with the intended audience and the product being sold. The station's format and programming approach influence the style of writing. Copy should be typed in uppercase, be double-spaced, and have 1-inch margins. Sound effects are noted in parentheses, and phonetic spellings are provided for difficult words.

20. Aspiring announcers must be able to read copy aloud with proper inflection and enunciation. A naturally resonant and pleasant-sounding voice without a regional accent is an advantage.

21. The practice of voice-tracking is reducing the number of announcing jobs. More and more, local station announcing

FIGURE 9.36
The production person remains the station's true artist whether the studio be cutting-edge digital or old-world analog. Courtesy WIZN.

originates elsewhere, especially in cluster operations and when stations are a part of major station groups.

22. Every station maintains a sound library for use in spot mixdowns. Commercially produced sound effects, bed music collections, and unfamiliar cuts from CDs and the Internet (and even LPs) are common source materials. Digital equipment and computer workstations allow producers to create their own in-house effects.

FIGURE 9.37
At many stations, Pro Tools is the new sound and effects library. Courtesy Digidesign.

FIGURE 9.38
The book's author sits in what was regarded as a state of the art studio in 1960. Courtesy Boston College.

SUGGESTED FURTHER READING

Adams, M.H., and Massey, K., *Introduction to Radio: Production and Programming*, Brown and Benchmark, Madison, WI, 1995.

Alburger, J.R., and Hall, M., *The Art of Voice Acting*, Focal Press, Boston, MA, 2002.

Alten, S.R., *Audio in Media*, 8th edition, Wadsworth Publishing, Belmont, CA, 2007.

Bartlett, B., *Stereo Microphone Techniques*, Focal Press, Boston, MA, 1991.

Campbell, T., *Wireless Writing in the Age of Marconi*, University of Minnesota, Minneapolis, MN, 2006.

Ford, T., *Advanced Audio Production Techniques*, Focal Press, Boston, MA, 1993.

Gross, L., Reese, D.E., and Gross, B., *Radio Production Worktext: Concepts, Techniques, and Equipment*, 6th edition, Focal Press, Boston, MA, 2009.

Hausman, C., et al., *Modern Radio Production*, Wadsworth Publishing, Belmont, CA, 2006.

Hilliard, R.L., *Writing for Television, Radio, and New Media*, 9th edition, Wadsworth Publishing, Belmont, CA, 2007.

Hoffer, J., *Radio Production Techniques*, Tab Books, Blue Ridge Summit, PA, 1974.

Hyde, S.W., *Television and Radio Announcing*, 7th edition, Houghton Mifflin, Boston, MA, 1995.

Kaempfer, R., and Swanson, J., *The Radio Producer's Handbook*, Allworth Press, New York, 2004.

Keith, M.C., *Broadcast Voice Performance*, Focal Press, Boston, MA, 1989.

Keith, M.C., *Radio Production: Art and Science*, Focal Press, Boston, MA, 1990.

Labelle, B., *Background Noise: Perspectives on Sound Art*, Continuum International Publishing, London, UK, 2006.

McLeish, R., *Radio Production*, 5th edition, Focal Press, Boston, MA, 2005.

Mott, R.L., *Radio Sounds Effects*, McFarland Publishing, Jefferson, NC, 2005.

National Association of Broadcasters, *Guidelines for Radio Continuity*, NAB Publishing, Washington, DC, 1982.

National Association of Broadcasters, *Guidelines for Radio Copywriting*, NAB Publications, Washington, DC, 1993.

Nisbet, A., *The Technique of the Sound Studio*, 4th edition, Focal Press, Boston, MA, 1979.

Nisbet, A., *The Use of Microphones*, 3rd edition, Focal Press, Boston, MA, 1989.

O'Donnell, L.B., Hauseman, C., and Benoit, P., *Announcing: Broadcast Communication Today*, 5th edition, Wadsworth Publishing, Belmont, CA, 2000.

O'Donnell, L.B., Hauseman, C., and Benoit, P., *Modern Radio Production*, 5th edition, Wadsworth Publishing, Belmont, CA, 2003.

Oringel, R.S., *Audio Control Handbook*, 6th edition, Focal Press, Boston, MA, 1989.

Orlik, P.B., *Broadcast/Cable Copywriting*, 7th edition, Allyn & Bacon, Boston, MA, 2003.

Pohlmann, K.C., *Advanced Digital Audio*, SAMS, Indianapolis, IN, 1991.

Priestman, C., *Web Radio: Radio Production for Internet Streaming*, Focal Press, Boston, MA, 2002.

Reese, D.E., et al., *Broadcast Announcing Worktext*, Focal Press, Boston, MA, 2005.

Rumsey, F., *Digital Audio Operation*, Focal Press, Boston, MA, 1991.

Rumsey, F., *Tapeless Sound Recording*, Focal Press, Boston, MA, 1990.

Watkinson, J., *Digital Audio and Compact Disc Technology*, 3rd edition, Focal Press, Boston, MA, 1995.

Engineering 10

Pioneer Engineers

Radio at its core is a technology. Therefore, anyone who has ever spoken into a microphone or sat before a radio receiver owes an immense debt of gratitude to the many technical innovators who made it possible. Guglielmo Marconi, a diminutive Italian with enormous genius, first used electromagnetic (radio) waves to send a message. Marconi made his historical transmission, and several others, in the last decade of the nineteenth century. Relying, at least in part, on the findings of two earlier scientists, James Clerk Maxwell and Heinrich Hertz, Marconi developed his wireless telegraph, thus revolutionizing the field of electronic communications.

Other wireless innovators made significant contributions to the refinement of Marconi's device. J. Ambrose Fleming developed the diode tube in 1904, and 2 years later Lee de Forest created the three-element triode tube called the Audion. Both innovations, along with many others, expanded the capability of the wireless.

In 1906, Reginald Fessenden demonstrated the transmission of voice over the wireless from his experimental station at Brant Rock, Massachusetts. Until that time, Marconi's invention had been used to send Morse code or coded messages. An earlier experiment in the transmission of voice via the electromagnetic spectrum also had been conducted. In 1892, on a small farm in Murray, Kentucky, Nathan B. Stubblefield managed to send voice across a field using the induction method of transmission, yet Fessenden's method of mounting sound impulses atop electrical oscillations and transmitting them from an antenna proved far more effective. Fessenden's wireless voice message was received hundreds of miles away.

Few pioneer broadcast technologists contributed as much as Edwin Armstrong. His development of the regenerative and superheterodyne circuits vastly improved receiver efficiency. In the 1920s Armstrong worked at developing a static-free mode of broadcasting, and in 1933 he demonstrated the results of his labor – FM. Armstrong was a man ahead of his time. It would be decades before his innovation would fully be appreciated, and he would not live to witness the tremendous strides it would take.

Had it not been for these men, and many others like them, there would be no radio medium. Today's broadcast engineers and technologists continue in the tradition of

FIGURE 10.1
Assembling the technology. Courtesy Library of Congress.

275

their forebears. Without their knowledge and expertise, there would be no broadcast industry because there would be no medium. Radio is first and foremost an engineer's medium. It is engineers who put the stations on the air and keep them there.

Radio Technology

Radio broadcasters utilize part of the electromagnetic spectrum to transmit their signals, and they are obliged to pay spectrum fees of up to $1500 annually (depending on their size) for this privilege. A natural resource, the electromagnetic spectrum is composed of radio waves at the low-frequency end and cosmic rays at the high-frequency end. In the spectrum between are infrared rays, light rays, X rays, and gamma rays. Broadcasters, of course, use the radio wave portion of the spectrum for their purposes.

Electromagnetic waves carry broadcast transmissions (radio frequency) from station to receiver. It is the function of the transmitter to generate and shape the radio wave to conform to the frequency the station has been assigned by the FCC. Audio current is sent by a line from the control room to the transmitter. The current then modulates the carrier wave so that it may achieve its authorized frequency. A carrier wave that is undisturbed by audio current is called an unmodulated carrier.

The antenna radiates the radio frequency. Receivers are designed to pick up transmissions,

convert the carrier into sound waves, and distribute them to the frequency tuned. Thus, in order for a station assigned a frequency of 950 kHz (a kilohertz equals 1000 hertz [Hz]) to reach a radio tuned to that position on the dial, it must alter its carrier wave 950,000 cycles (Hz) per second. The tuner counts the incoming radio frequency.

AM/FM

AM and FM stations are located at different points in the spectrum: AM stations are assigned frequencies between 540 and 1700 kHz on the Standard Broadcast band, and FM stations are located between 88.1 and 107.9 MHz (megahertz equals 1 million hertz) on the FM band.

Ten kilocycles (kc) separate frequencies in AM, and there are 200 kc between FM frequencies. FM broadcasters utilize 30 kc for over-the-air transmissions and are permitted to provide subcarrier transmission (SCA) to subscribers on the remaining frequency. The larger channel width provides FM listeners a better opportunity to fine-tune their favorite stations as well as to receive broadcasts in stereo. To achieve parity, AM broadcasters developed a way to transmit in stereo, and by 1990 hundreds were doing so. The fine-tuning edge still belongs to FM, because its sidebands (15 kc) are three times wider than AM's (5 kc).

FM broadcasts at a much higher frequency (millions of cycles per second) compared to AM (thousands of cycles per second). At such a high frequency, FM is immune to low-frequency emissions, which plague AM. Although a car motor or an electric storm generally will interfere with AM reception, FM is static free. Broadcast engineers have attempted to improve the quality of the AM band, but the basic nature of the lower frequency makes AM simply more prone to interference than FM. FM broadcasters see this as a key competitive advantage and refer to AM's move to stereo as "stereo with static."

Signal Propagation

The paths of AM and FM signals differ from one another. Ground waves create AM's primary service area as they travel across

FIGURE 10.2
Station engineering operations in the digital age. Courtesy Clear Channel.

iTunes® Tagging

Hear it. Tag it. Download it. Never forget it.

How many times have you heard a song on the radio you'd really like to hear
again? Wouldn't it be great
if you could tag that song
and buy it?

With an iTunes Tagging
enabled HD Radio™
receiver you can. When you
hear a song you like on
your local FM HD Radio
station, you simply hit the
"tag" button. The song's
info will be saved from
your HD Radio receiver to
your iPod®. The songs will

Video Demo

show up in a playlist called "Tagged" in iTunes the next time you sync your iPod
to your computer. So you can click, download and buy the songs you want
directly from the Apple® iTunes Music Store.

With a brand new HD Radio receiver, you will be able to tag songs while you
listen to your favorite music in pure crystal-clear digital sound. And if that isn't
enough, many HD Radio stations now are broadcasting additional digital
channels called HD2 and HD3, all subscription-free.

---

the earth's surface. High-power AM stations are able to reach listeners hundreds of miles away during the day. At night AM's signal is reflected by the atmosphere (ionosphere), thus creating a skywave that carries considerably farther, sometimes thousands of miles. Skywaves constitute AM's secondary service area.

In contrast to AM signal radiation, FM propagates its radio waves in a direct or line-of-sight pattern. FM stations are not affected by evening changes in the atmosphere and generally do not carry as far as AM stations. A high-power FM station may reach listeners within an 80- to 100-mile radius because its signal weakens as it approaches the horizon. Because FM outlets radiate direct waves, antenna height becomes nearly as important as power. In general, the higher an FM antenna, the farther the signal travels.

Skywave Interference

The fact that AM station signals travel greater distances at night is a mixed blessing. Although some stations benefit from the expanded coverage area created by the skywave phenomenon, many do not. In fact, over 2000 radio stations around the country must cease operation near sunset, and thousands more must make substantial transmission adjustments to prevent interference. For example, many stations must decrease power after sunset to ensure noninterference with others on the same frequency: WXXX-AM is 5000W (5 kW) during the day, but at night it must drop to 1000 W (1 kW). Another measure designed to prevent interference requires that certain stations direct their signals away from stations on the same frequency. Directional stations require two or more antennas to shape the pattern of their radiation, whereas a nondirectional station that distributes its signal evenly in all directions needs only a single antenna. Because of its limited direct wave signal, FM is not subject to the post-sunset operating constraints that affect most AM outlets.

Station Classifications

To guarantee the efficient use of the broadcast spectrum, the FCC established a classification system for both AM and FM stations. Under this system, the nation's 10,000 radio outlets operate free of the debilitating interference that plagued broadcasters prior to the Radio Act of 1927.

AM classifications are as follows:

- **Class A**: Clear channel stations with power not exceeding 50 kW. Their frequencies are protected from interference up to 750 miles. Among the pioneer, or oldest, stations in the country are KDKA, WBZ, WSM, and WJR.

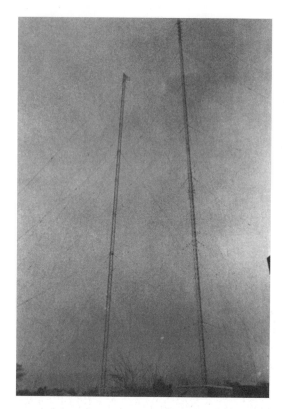

FIGURE 10.4
Antennas (towers) propagate station signals.

- **Class B**: Stations with power ranging from a minimum of 250 W to a maximum of 50 kW. They must protect Class I outlets by altering their signals around sunset. As a Class B station, WINZ-AM in Miami is required to reduce power from 50 kW to 250 W so as not to intrude on other stations at 940 kHz. These stations also operate on regional channels. If a station is authorized to operate in the expanded band (1610–1700), the maximum power is 10 kW.
- **Class C**: Stations that operate on local and regional channels with power between 250 and 1000 W. They may operate without time restrictions.
- **Class D**: Stations that operate either daytime, limited time, or unlimited time with a nighttime power less than 250 W. Daytime-only stations are Class D.

Section 73.21 of the *Code of Federal Regulations*, Part 73, provides more details on AM station classifications.

New AM band space (1605–1705 kHz) is currently being allocated, and the FCC is encouraging existing AM license holders to shift to the new space as a means of reducing interference on the clogged band.

FM classifications include the following:

- **Class C**: The most powerful FM outlets with the greatest service parameters, these stations may be assigned a maximum ERP of 100 kW and a tower height of up to 2000 feet. Class C radio waves carry, on average, 70 miles from their point of transmission.
- **Class B**: These stations operate with less power – up to 50 kW – than Class Cs and are intended to serve smaller areas. The maximum antenna height for stations in this class is 500 feet, and signals generally do not reach beyond 40–50 miles.
- **Class A**: The least powerful of commercial FM stations; they seldom exceed 3 kW ERP (except in select cases where a ceiling of 6 kW is imposed) and 328 feet in antenna height. The average service contour for stations in this category is 10–20 miles.
- **Class D**: Set aside for noncommercial stations with 10 W ERP, this type of station is most apt to be licensed to a school or college.

FIGURE 10.5
A 3-kW FM transmitter. Courtesy Broadcast Electronics.

FM Station Class	Reference (Maximum) Facilities for Station Class (see 47 CFR Section 73.211) ERP (in kW) / HAAT (in meters)	FM Protected or Primary Service Contour		Distance to Protected or Primary Service Contour (km)	Distance to 70 dBu (or 3.16 mV/m) City Grade or Principal Community Coverage Contour (see 47 CFR Section 73.315) (km)
		dBu	mV/m		
Class A	6.0 kW / 100 meters	60 dBu	1.0 mV/m	28.3 km	16.2 km
Class B1	25.0 kW / 100 meters	57 dBu	0.71 mV/m	44.7 km	23.2 km
Class B	50.0 kW / 150 meters	54 dBu	0.50 mV/m	65.1 km	32.6 km
Class C3	25.0 kW / 100 meters	60 dBu	1.0 mV/m	39.1 km	23.2 km
Class C2	50.0 kW / 150 meters	60 dBu	1.0 mV/m	52.2 km	32.6 km
Class C1	100.0 kW / 299 meters	60 dBu	1.0 mV/m	72.3 km	50.0 km
Class C0 (C-zero)	100.0 kW / 450 meters	60 dBu	1.0 mV/m	83.4 km	59.0 km
Class C	100.0 kW / 600 meters	60 dBu	1.0 mV/m	91.8 km	67.7 km

FIGURE 10.6
FM station classes. Courtesy Federal Communications Commission.

In the 1980s, the FCC introduced three new classes of FM stations under Docket 80–90 in an attempt to provide several hundred additional frequencies, and more subclasses were added later. They are as follows:

- **Class C1**: Stations granted licenses to operate within this classification may be authorized to transmit up to 100 kW ERP with antennas not exceeding 984 feet. The maximum reach of stations in this class is about 50 miles.
- **Class C2**: The operating parameters of stations in Class C2 are close to Class Bs. The maximum power granted Class C2 outlets is 50 kW, and antennas may not exceed 492 feet. Class C2 stations reach approximately 35 miles.
- **Class C3**: These stations operate with shorter antennas and with power that typically exceeds 6 kW ERP.
- **Class B1**: The maximum antenna height permitted for Class B1 stations (328 feet) is identical to Class As; however, Class B1s are assigned at least 25 kW ERP. Class B1 signals carry 25–30 miles.

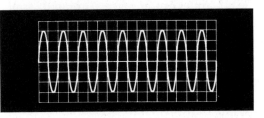

FIGURE 10.7
Stations receive their power from conventional utility companies. From *FCC Broadcast Operator's Handbook*, Figure 3–1.

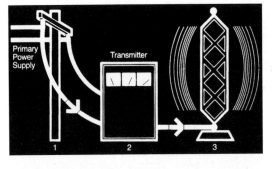

FIGURE 10.8
Unmodulated (undisturbed) carrier. *From FCC Broadcast Operator's Handbook*, Figure 5–1.

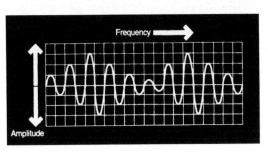

FIGURE 10.9
Amplitude modulated (AM) carrier. From *FCC Broadcast Operator's Handbook*, Figure 5–2.

LPFM classifications include the following:

Class L1: 50–100 W ERP
Class L2: 1–10 W ERP

In view of the ongoing revisions made to FM classifications, we suggest you consult Section 73.210 of the current *Code of Federal Regulations*, Part 73.

FIGURE 10.10
Frequency modulated (FM) carrier. From *FCC Broadcast Operator's Handbook*, Figure 5–4.

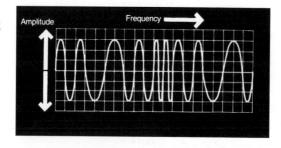

FIGURE 10.11
Standard AM and FM band. From *FCC Broadcast Operator's Handbook*, Figures 4–7 and 4–8.

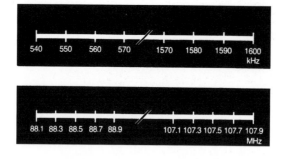

Boeing HS 702 satellites) were set aloft in a geostationary orbit, Sirius Satellite Radio's birds (three SS/L-1300 satellites) rotate in an elliptical pattern ensuring that each satellite spends around 16 hours over the United States. Offering CD-quality digital radio, these satellite radio signals are beamed to nearly 10 million receiving dishes located in cars and homes. Satellite radio uses the S-band (2.3 GHz) for its digital audio radio service (DARS). Both services keep a satellite ready for launch in the event one of their satellites malfunctions. Program origination from ground stations are uplinked to the satellites and then relayed to terrestrial end users (subscribers). Receivers unscramble the incoming signals, which offer over 100 channels each. In addition, the signals contain encoded data for display on receivers allowing listeners to see what is being broadcast (artist, song, etc.). Ground repeaters are employed when needed to strengthen incoming satellite signals. An international satellite radio service called WorldSpace utilizes the L-band to provide digital audio to Africa and Asia. According to former XM Satellite's chief programmer, Lee Abrams, the operation's technical department consists of four key areas: studios, hardware development, satellites and repeaters, and IT.

Satellite and Internet Radio

Satellite Radio

Satellite radio signals come from over 22,000 miles out in space. Although former XM Satellite Radio's transponders (two

Internet Radio

Since the 1990s, radio has been available over the Internet. There are two types of Internet radio stations: those generated by broadcast stations and those that are Web-only in origin. In the case of the first

FIGURE 10.12
Radio spectrum table.

VLF (Very Low Frequency) 30 kHz and below	—Maritime use
LF (Low Frequency) 30 kHz to 300 kHz	—Aeronautical/maritime
MF (Medium Frequency) 300 kHz to 3000 kHz	—AM, amateur, distress, etc.
HF (High Frequency) 3 MHz to 30 MHz	—CB, fax, international, etc.
VHF (Very High Frequency) 30 MHz to 300 MHz	—FM, TV, satellite, etc.
UHF (Ultra High Frequency) 300 MHz to 3000 MHz	—TV, satellite, CB, DAB (proposed), etc.
SHF (Super High Frequency) 3 GHz to 30 GHz	—Satellite, radar, space, etc.
EHF (Extreme High Frequency) 30 GHz to 300 GHz	—Space, amateur, experimental, etc.

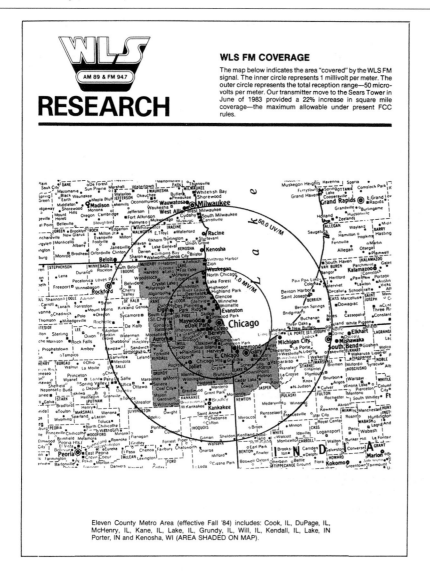

WLS FM COVERAGE

The map below indicates the area "covered" by the WLS FM signal. The inner circle represents 1 millivolt per meter. The outer circle represents the total reception range—50 microvolts per meter. Our transmitter move to the Sears Tower in June of 1983 provided a 22% increase in square mile coverage—the maximum allowable under present FCC rules.

Eleven County Metro Area (effective Fall '84) includes: Cook, IL, DuPage, IL, McHenry, IL, Kane, IL, Lake, IL, Grundy, IL, Will, IL, Kendall, IL, Lake, IN, Porter, IN and Kenosha, WI (AREA SHADED ON MAP).

FIGURE 10.13
Coverage maps show where a station's signal reaches. Courtesy WLS.

category, stations typically simulcast their broadcast signals over the Web. The second category of Internet station is typically more eclectic in its programming offerings, because the formatting constraints prevalent in broadcast radio do not exist in the independent, cyber-only outlets. Unlike traditional terrestrial stations, whose reach and operating parameters are limited, there are no geographical limitations in Internet radio. With Web access, anyone anywhere can enjoy the medium. A Web station emanating from Dayton, Ohio, may be heard in Bangkok, Thailand, and tens of thousands of broadcasts are available. Unlike terrestrial and satellite radio, Internet radio has the capability of providing a full range of visual data, such as photos, text, and links. Interactivity also adds further cache to the medium's appeal, which has been battling copyright issues concerning the use of music through the decade.

The process of distributing an Internet radio signal is not complex. Internet radio operations possess an encoding computer, which converts the audio in a stream. The audio is then sent to a server and it routes the audio data over the Internet to the computer plug-in of the end-user/listener.

Digital Audio Broadcasting (HD Radio)

Radio has been undergoing a metamorphosis as analog signal processing is being supplanted by digital processing. The reason for

FIGURE 10.14
The difference
between the two
bands. Courtesy
Brian Belanger,
Radio and Television
Museum.

FM vs. AM: Technical Considerations

If electrical signals could be seen, they would look like the figures shown here. (Actually, they *can* be seen, on an instrument called an oscilloscope, which resembles a small television set.) If one were to whistle into a microphone with a pure low-frequency audio tone, the microphone would convert the voice into an electrical signal like Fig. 1.

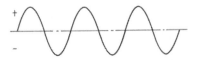

Figure. 1. A pure audio tone converted into an electrical signal.

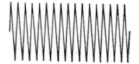

Figure. 2. A carrier wave produced by a radio transmitter.

An essential portion of a radio transmitter produces a much higher frequency electrical signal called the carrier wave like Fig. 2. To transmit intelligence, the radio transmitter must somehow superimpose the voice signal on the carrier wave, a process called modulation. (The radio receiver *demodulates*, or separates the desired audio signal from the carrier wave.)

Amplitude modulation or AM was the first type of modulation developed, early in the 20th century. When the amplitude or height of the carrier is changed in time with the audio signal, the result would look like Fig. 3

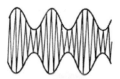

Figure 3. An amplitude modulated radio signal.

TIME ⟶

Figure 4. A frequency modulated radio signal, modulated by the same audio signal as in Fig. 3.

Instead of modulating the amplitude of the carrier, one can use the audio signal to change the *frequency* of the carrier, and that is frequency modulation. If the carrier were frequency modulated by the same audio signal as in Fig. 3, the result would look like Fig. 4. The frequency increases and decreases, but the amplitude of the modulated signal stays constant. The same intelligence has been transmitted. Of course a symphony concert with its multitude of sounds would produce a much more complicated looking waveform.

Questions About AM vs. FM:

Why is FM more static-free than AM?

Static is caused by things like lightning discharges or electrical discharges from nearby motors or other electrical devices, and those discharges produce small bursts of radiated energy. The

the transformation is simple: the demand for better and more evolved sound is at an all-time high. Broadcast stations must convert to digital, or they will not be competitive with audio alternatives, such as MP3 players, satellite radio, and mobile music services.

The full conversion to digital broadcasting is being planned and is likely to be completely realized within a few years. At the 1992 World Administrative Radio Conference (WARC), conducted by the International Telecommunications Union (ITU) in Spain, the FCC proposed use of the S-band

FIGURE 10.14
Continued

AM receiver picks up the bursts of static along with the desired signal and adds them together. Static shows up as sharp vertical peaks (spikes) on the modulated waveform, and AM radios respond to them. However, in an FM receiver, the amplitude of the signal does not matter— only changes in frequency matter—so there is no static with FM.

If it is better, why didn't people use FM in the early days of radio?

AM was discovered first, and tends to be simpler. In the early days of radio, mathematicians thought they had "proved" that FM would not work as well as AM, but their analyses were oversimplified. E. H. Armstrong showed that if one used a sufficiently wide bandwidth, FM works just fine. For FM to work well, a much wider channel (bandwidth) is required than with an AM station. At the frequencies used in the AM broadcast band (roughly 550 to 1700 kilohertz) there is insufficient spectrum "space" to permit the wide channels needed for FM, but there is sufficient channel space available at the higher frequencies now used for FM (88 to 108 Megahertz). Another problem was that in the early days of radio, the vacuum tubes then available did not work well at the high frequencies where FM needed to operate. Another benefit of FM: the wider channels occupied by FM stations can accommodate modulation with wider frequency excursions than those from AM stations, so FM stations broadcast with much higher fidelity.

Why can you sometimes hear far away stations on AM but not on FM?

That has to do <u>not</u> with the difference between AM and FM, but rather *the different radio propagation conditions* in the AM band vs. the FM band. At the frequencies used in the AM broadcast band, signals can bounce off the ionosphere, especially at night, and be reflected back to earth at considerable distances from the transmitter, as shown in the figure below. But signals at the much higher frequencies used for FM generally do *not* bounce off the ionosphere, and so FM reception is limited to more or less a line-of-sight path.

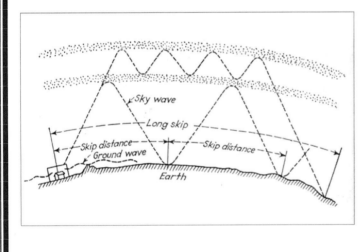

Figure 5. Charged particles in the ionosphere can reflect radio signals, which can then come back to earth quite some distance away from the transmitter. These reflected signals often shows up at the frequencies used in the AM broadcast band, especially at night, but NOT at the much higher frequencies used for FM.

(2310–2360 MHz) for the propagation of DAB signals.

Although some things remain to be resolved, in-band on-channel (IBOC) digital radio, as created by iBiquity, has been given the go-ahead. This is something the NAB has long supported as a way of maintaining a station's brand identity as established by its frequency numbers.

Although the present system of analog broadcasting essentially replicates sound waves (with inherent shortcomings), digital converts sound waves into a bit-stream of 1's and 0's for processing into a low bandwidth.

FIGURE 10.15
AM signal radiation. From *FCC Broadcast Operator's Handbook*, Figure 3–2.

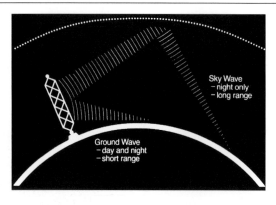

FIGURE 10.16
Nondirectional and directional antenna radiation. From *FCC Broadcast Operator's Handbook*, Figure 7–2.

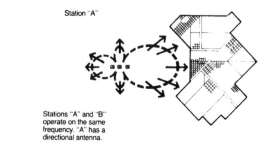

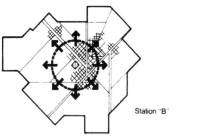

FIGURE 10.17
In digital processing of sound, an analog waveform is quantified, that is, given a numeric binary value.

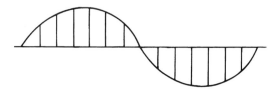

In digital, sound waves are assigned numeric values and become coded pulses.

Simply put, in digital, sounds are quantified. This allows a more accurate representation of audio signals. Unlike analog, which is limited in what it can reproduce, digital provides greater frequency response and dynamic range. Thus, more audio information is conveyed to the listener, who hears more. Another positive feature from the broadcast operator's perspective is the fact that digital signals do not require as much power as do analog signals.

Obviously, the transition to digital requires the manufacture of new receivers, and several companies now offer such

products. Part of their appeal, according to telecommunications professor Ernest Hakanen, is the fact that they "will allow for much more faithfulness of signal reproduction. High-definition (HD) receivers are designed to use reflected signals as alternative sources of information when the primary signal deteriorates. Using receivers that correct the fading and interference problems associated with AM and FM broadcasts, DAB signals that include specific information that can 'tell' the receiver how to compensate for information lost between transmitter and receiver can be received."

Eventually, the existing analog system of AM and FM broadcasting will be passé. It is not likely, however, that the conversion to digital will occur overnight. Some predict that analog broadcasting will be around for a few more years and that, even when digital is the preeminent broadcasting system, analog AM and FM stations will still be out there – that is, until the FCC no longer perceives them as providing a viable service. In any event, the switch to digital is mandated, and so digital is inevitable. Analog broadcasting will go the way of the turntable.

Radio engineer Aaron Reed expresses his views on the issues that will confront the full implementation of digital radio. "Dealing with the political boondoggle and the necessary paradigm shift in how 'radio' will be done after its implementation (from the technical changes necessary to augment the programming delivery to the altering of the way people think of radio as a mostly one-way medium) will prove a major challenge to any engineer. Couple that with station managers demanding they be digital because 'the other guy is' but then balking at the hefty price and you can see the problems. It won't be easy, and inevitably many stations will try to do it on the cheap and fail because DAB is not something that can be done incrementally. Just saying your station is digital is not going to get the listeners. Something far more radical in the programming services that stations offer will be required. The potential is there. Whether engineers and their moneymen are willing to do it is the big question."

Smart Receivers

It is now possible to get more than just audio from a radio receiver. The new HD sets and satellite radio receivers are programmable and provide visual screens offering copious data. In fact, consumers are able to format scan without actually having to listen to stations. These so-called smart receivers feature emergency alerting capabilities, traffic announcements, advertisements and promos, music tagging options, and other informational services via a built-in LCD display panel. This was proposed in the early 1990s by Radio Broadcast Data Systems but never realized. Now with the existence of digital and satellite radio it has come to fruition.

Some programmers opposed the idea of "sightradio" (a throwback term used to describe television at its onset) because they felt that it was difficult to categorize a format given the existing options, especially with a limited number of letters. The thought of a quasi-teletext component to radio inspires mixed emotions in many broadcasters. Will people be *watching* radio, and what exactly will that mean? In the main, however, "screen" radio is perceived as an important value-added feature for the medium, and something it must offer in the computer age.

Although it is difficult at this time to predict the future impact and role of these innovations, it is certain, with the conversion to digital, that eventually receivers will do more than simply tune frequencies.

One other plus offered by smart-receiver technology is that it will allow car radios to automatically retune a different station offering the same format when a vehicle leaves the coverage area of the first station.

Becoming an Engineer

Most station managers or chief engineers look for experience when hiring technical people. Formal training such as college ranks high but not as high as actual hands-on technical experience. "A good electronics background is preferred, of course. This doesn't necessarily mean 10 years of experience or an advanced degree in electronic engineering,

HD Radio: How HD Radio Works

1
Stations bundle analog and digital audio signals (with textual data, such as artist and song information, weather and traffic, and more).

2
The digital signal layer is compressed using iBiquity's HDC compression technology.

3
The combined analog and digital signals are transmitted.

4
The most common form of interference, multipath distortion, occurs when part of a signal bounces off an object and arrives at the receiver at a different time than the main signal. HD Radio receivers are designed to sort through the reflected signals and reduce static, hiss, pops and fades.

5
The signal will be compatible with HD Radio receivers and analog radios.

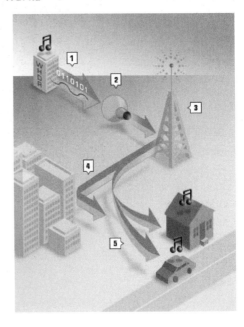

FIGURE 10.18
How HD Radio works. Courtesy iBiquity.

but rather a person with a solid foundation in the fundamentals of radio electronics, perhaps derived from an interest in amateur radio, computers, or another hobby of a technical nature. This is a good starting point. Actually, it has been my experience that people with this kind of a background are more attuned to the nature of this business. You don't need a person with a physics degree from MIT, but what you do want is someone with a natural inclination for the technical side. Ideally speaking, you want to hire a person with a tech history as well as some formal in-class training," contends Kevin McNamara, Director of Engineering, Beasley Broadcasting Group.

Chief engineer Jim Puriez concurs. "A formal education in electronics is good, but not essential. In this business if you have the desire and natural interest, you can learn from the inside out. You don't find that many broadcast engineers with actual electronics degrees. Of course, most have taken basic electronics courses. The majority are long on experience and have acquired their skills on the job. While a college degree is a nice credential, I think most managers hire tech people on the basis of experience more than anything else."

Station engineer Sid Schweiger also cites experience as the key criterion for gaining

FIGURE 10.19
Station engineer
at the workbench.
Courtesy WMJX-FM.

FIGURE 10.20
A station
engineer must be
knowledgeable about
the sophisticated
state-of-the-art
audio processing
equipment (such
as the limiter and
processor shown
here) used by many
stations, especially in
metro markets where
great sound gives a
station an important
competitive edge.
Courtesy CRL
Audio and Broadcast
Electronics.

a broadcast engineer's position. "When I'm in the market for a tech person, I'll check smaller market stations for someone interested in making the move to a larger station. This way, I've got someone with experience right from the start. The little station is a good place for the newcomer to gain experience."

In his column in *Radio World* (June 9, 1999), editor Paul J. McLane lamented the dearth of young people entering the field and the need for specialists with various technical and computer skills. Wrote McLane, "Fluency never stops. People I respect say radio engineers should learn to think large, and that goes for digital audio and data training."

Numerous schools and colleges offer formal training in electronics. The number shrinks somewhat when it comes to those institutions actually providing curricula in broadcast engineering. However, a number of technical schools do offer basic electronics courses applicable to broadcast operations.

Before August 1981, the FCC required that broadcast engineers hold a First Class Radiotelephone license. To receive the license, applicants were expected to pass

an examination. An understanding of basic broadcast electronics and knowledge of the FCC rules and regulations pertaining to station technical operations were necessary to pass the lengthy examination. Today a station's chief engineer (also called chief operator) need possess only a Restricted Operator Permit. Those who held First Class licenses prior to their elimination now receive either a Restricted Operator Permit or a General Radiotelephone license at renewal time.

It is left to the discretion of the individual radio station to establish criteria regarding engineer credentials. Many do require a General Radiotelephone license or certification from associations, such as the Society of Broadcast Engineers (SBE) or the National Association of Radio and Telecommunications Engineers (NARTE), as a preliminary means of establishing a prospective engineer's qualifications. The appendix at the end of this chapter contains a reproduction of SBE's membership application form.

Communication skills rank highest on the list of personal qualities for station engineers, according to McNamara. "The old

stereotype of the station 'tech-head' in white socks, chinos, and shirt-pocket pen holder weighed down by its inky contents is losing its validity. Today, more than ever, I think, the radio engineer must be able to communicate with members of the staff from the manager to the deejay. Good interpersonal skills are necessary. Things have become very sophisticated, and engineers play an integral role in the operation of a facility, perhaps more now than in the past. The field of broadcast engineering has become more competitive, too, with the elimination of many operating requirements."

Because of a number of regulation changes in the 1980s, most notably the elimination of upper-grade license requirements, the prospective engineer now comes under even closer scrutiny by station management. The day when a "1st phone" was enough to get an engineering job is gone. There is no direct "ticket" anymore. As in most other areas of radio, skill, experience, and training open the doors the widest.

Because the very landscape of radio has changed as the result of the Telecommunications Act of 1996, station clusters abound. This means a chief engineer or director of a cluster's technical operation has formidable responsibilities. Instead of keeping one station on the air, this person may have as many as eight signals to watch over. In cluster operations, there may be several experienced engineers on site or one senior engineer who directs the duties of several techs and producers.

also is available should a technical problem arise. Larger stations and cluster operations with more studios and operating equipment often employ an engineer on a full-time basis. It is a question of economics. The small station can little afford a day-to-day engineer, whereas the larger station or cluster usually finds that it can ill afford to do without one.

Beasley Broadcast Group's McNamara considers protecting the station's license his number one priority. "A station is only as good as its license to operate. If it loses it, the show is over. No other area of a station is under such scrutiny by the FCC as is the technical. The dereg movement in recent years has affected programming much more than engineering. My job is to first keep the station honest, that is, in compliance with the commission's rules. This means, keep the station operating within the assigned operating parameters, i.e., power, antenna phase, modulation, and so on, and to take corrective action if needed."

Chief engineer Steve Church says that maintenance and equipment repairs consume a large portion of an engineer's time. "General repairs keep you busy. One moment you may be adjusting a pot on a studio console and the next replacing a part on some remote equipment. A broadcast facility is an amalgam of equipment that requires care and attention. Problems must be detected early or they can snowball. The proper installation of new equipment eliminates the chance of certain

FIGURE 10.21
Station engineers must possess a high level of proficiency with computer technology. Courtesy BE.

The Engineer's Duties

The FCC requires that all stations designate someone as chief operator. This individual is responsible for a station's technical operations. Equipment repairs and adjustments, as well as weekly inspections and calibrations of the station transmitter, remote control equipment, and monitoring and metering systems, fall within the chief operator's area of responsibility.

Depending on the makeup and size of a station or cluster, either a full-time or part-time engineer will be contracted. Many small outlets find they can get by with a weekly visit by a qualified engineer who

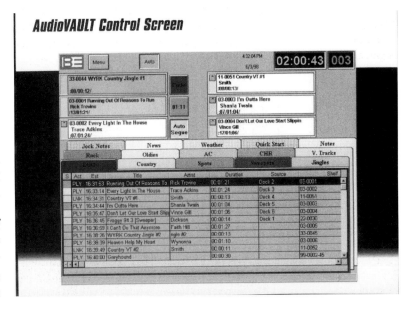

problems later on. The station's chief must be adept at a whole lot."

Other duties of the chief engineer include training techs, monitoring radiation levels, planning maintenance schedules, and handling a budget. Many stations hire outside engineering firms to conduct performance proofs, but it is ultimately the responsibility of the chief operator to ensure that the outlet meets its technical performance level. Proofs ascertain whether a station's audio equipment performance measurements fall within the prescribed parameters. A station's frequency response, harmonic distortion, FM noise level, AM noise level, stereo separation, crosstalk, and subcarrier suppression are gauged. If found adequate, the proof is passed. If not, the chief sees to it that necessary adjustments are made. Although the FCC no longer requires Proof of Performance checks, many stations continue to observe the practice as a fail-safe measure.

The duties of a station engineer are wide ranging and demanding. It is a position that requires a thorough grasp of electronics relative to the broadcast environment, knowledge of FCC rules and regulations pertaining to station technical operations, and, especially in the case of the chief engineer, the ability to manage finances and people.

Station Log

In 1983, the FCC dispensed with its requirement that radio stations keep maintenance and operating logs. In their place the commission created a new and considerably modified document called the Station Log, which stations must maintain. The new log requires that information pertaining to tower light malfunctions, Emergency Alert System (EAS) tests, and AM directional antenna systems be entered. Station Logs are kept on file for a period of 2 years.

Despite the fact that the FCC has eliminated the more involved logging procedures, some stations continue to employ the old system. "I like the accountability that maintenance and operating logs provide. We still use them here, and they are inspected daily. Despite the elimination

of certain requirements, namely, the tech logs, a station is still required to meet the operating stipulations of their license. Actually, enforcement action has been on the rise at the FCC, perhaps in reaction to the deregs. The commission is really interested in station technical operations. Keeping daily logs ensures compliance," says McNamara.

§ 73.1820 Station Log

(a) Entries must be made in the station log either manually by a properly licensed operator in actual charge of the transmitting apparatus, or by automatic devices meeting the requirements of paragraph (b) of this section. Indications of operating parameters that are required to be logged must be logged prior to any adjustment of the equipment. Where adjustments are made to restore parameters to their proper operating values, the corrected indications must be logged and accompanied, if any parameter deviation was beyond a prescribed tolerance, by a notation describing the nature of the corrective action. Indications of all parameters whose values are affected by the modulation of the carrier must be read without modulation. The actual time of observation must be included in each log entry. The following information must be entered:

(1) *All* stations: (i) Entries required by § 17.49 of this chapter concerning any observed or otherwise known extinguishment or improper functioning of a tower light:

(A) The nature of such extinguishment or improper functioning.

(B) The date and time the extinguishment or improper operation was observed or otherwise noted.

(C) The date, time and nature of adjustments, repairs or replacements made.

(ii) Any entries not specifically required in this section, but required by the instrument of authorization or elsewhere in this part.

(iii) An entry of each test of the EAS procedures pursuant to the requirement of Subpart G of this part and the appropriate EAS checklist. All stations may keep EAS test data in a special EAS log, which shall be maintained at any convenient location; however, such log should be considered a part of the station log.

(2) Directional AM stations without an FCC-approved antenna sampling system (see § 73.68): (i) An entry at the beginning of operations in each mode of operation, and thereafter at intervals not exceeding 3 hours, of the following (actual readings observed prior to making any adjustments to the equipment and an indication of any corrections to restore parameters to normal operating values):

(A) Common point current.

(B) When the operating power is determined by the indirect method, the efficiency factor F and either the product of the final amplifier input voltage and current or the calculated antenna input power. See § 73.51(e).

(C) Antenna monitor phase or phase deviation indications.

(D) Antenna monitor sample currents, current ratios, or ratio deviation indications.

(ii) Entries required by § 73.61 performed in accordance with the schedule specified therein.

(iii) Entries of the results of calibration of automatic logging devices (see paragraph (b) of this section), extension meters (see § 73.1550) or indicating instruments (see § 73.67) whenever performed.

(b) Automatic devices accurately calibrated and with appropriate time, date and circuit functions may be utilized to record entries in the station log provided:

(1) The recording devices do not affect the operation of circuits or accuracy of indicating instruments of the equipment being recorded;

(2) The recording devices have an accuracy equivalent to the accuracy of the indicating instruments;

(3) The calibration is checked against the original indicators as often as necessary to ensure recording accuracy;

(4) Provision is made to actuate automatically an aural alarm circuit located near the operator on duty if any of the automatic log readings are not within the tolerances or other requirements specified in the rules or station license;

(5) The alarm circuit operates continuously or the devices that record each parameter in sequence must read each parameter at least once during each 30-minute period;

(6) The automatic logging equipment is located at the remote control point if the transmitter is remotely controlled or at the transmitter location if the transmitter is manually controlled;

(7) The automatic logging equipment is located in the near vicinity of the operator on duty and is inspected periodically during the broadcast day. In the event of failure or malfunctioning of the automatic equipment, the employee responsible for the log shall make the required entries in the log manually at that time;

FIGURE 10.22
A satellite beams down program channels to subscribers. Courtesy XM Satellite Radio.

FIGURE 10.23
Maintaining prescribed technical parameters is one of many engineering responsibilities.

(8) The indicating equipment conforms to the requirements of § 73.1215 (indicating instruments – specifications) except that the scales need not exceed 2 inches in length. Arbitrary scales may not be used.

(c) In preparing the station log, original data may be recorded in rough form and later transcribed into the log. (43 FR 45854, Oct. 4, 1978, as amended at 44 FR 5873, Oct. 11, 1979; 47 FR 24580, June 7, 1982; 48 FR 38481, Aug. 24, 1983; 48 FR 4480, Sept. 30, 1983; 49 FR 33603, Aug. 23, 1984)

§ 73.1835 Special Technical Records

The FCC may require a broadcast station licensee to keep operating and maintenance records as necessary to resolve conditions of actual or potential interference, rule violations, or deficient technical operation. (48 FR 38482, Aug. 24, 1983)

§ 73.1840 Retention of Logs

(a) Any log required to be kept by station licensees shall be retained by them for a period of 2 years. However, logs involving communications incident to a disaster or which include communications incident to or involved in an investigation by the FCC and about which the licensee has been notified, shall be retained by the licensee until specifically authorized in writing by the FCC to destroy them. Logs incident to or involved in any claim or complaint of which the licensee has notice shall be retained by the licensee until such claim or complaint has been fully satisfied or until the same has been barred by statute limiting the time for filing of suits upon such claims.

(b) Logs may be retained on microfilm, microfiche, or other data-storage systems subject to the following conditions:

1. Suitable viewing-reading devices shall be available to permit FCC inspection of logs pursuant to § 73.1226, availability to FCC of station logs and records.

2. Reproduction of logs, stored on data-storage systems, to full-size copies, is required of licensees if requested by the FCC or the public as authorized by FCC rules. Such reproductions must be completed within two full work days of the time of the request.

3. Corrections to logs shall be made:

(i) Prior to converting to a data storage system pursuant to the requirements of § 73.1800 (c) and (d) (§ 73.1800, General requirements relating to logs).

(ii) After converting to a data-storage system by separately making such corrections and then associating with the related data-stored logs. Such corrections shall contain sufficient information to allow those reviewing the logs to identify where corrections have been made, and when and by whom the corrections were made.

4. Copies of any log required to be filed with any application; or placed in the station's local public inspection file as part of an application; or filed with reports to the FCC must be reproduced in full-size form when complying with these requirements. (45 FR 41151, June 18, 1980, as amended at 46 FR 13907, Feb. 24, 1981; 46 FR 18557, Mar. 25, 1981; 49 FR 33663, Aug. 24, 1984)

The Emergency Alert System

In 1994, the FCC established the EAS, which replaced the old Emergency Broadcast System (EBS). The EBS came into existence following World War II as the nation and the world entered the nuclear age. The system was designed to provide the president and heads of state and local government with a way to communicate with the public in the event of a major emergency.

In the 1990s, EBS was viewed as outmoded due to the revolution in technology, and it was significantly revamped. EAS is intended to upgrade the effectiveness of broadcast warnings by employing digital equipment and sophisticated automation. Its speed and timeliness are greatly enhanced under the new protocol. Stations were expected to have the new EAS system fully installed by mid-1997. At present, stations take the following steps should the president and/or heads of state and local government agencies deem it necessary to alert the public of a potential or imminent disaster:

1. Receive Emergency Action Notification (EAN) via AP/UPI feeds, network feed,

or EAS decoder display. Continue to monitor for further instructions.
2. Discontinue normal programming.
3. Transmit EAN announcement.
4. Transmit EAN header codes followed by the attention signal.
5. Monitor Local Primary Source (LP), State Relay Source (SR), any other broadcast station for further instructions.
6. Transmit emergency messages as soon as they are available.
7. Announce termination of EAN.

Allen Myers

The FCC and Radio

FIGURE 10.24
Allen Myers.

In evaluating the service to the radio medium provided by the Federal Communications Commission, it is necessary to understand that the Commission was created by Congress in the Communications Act of 1934 and that the agency, therefore, carries out the wishes of that body. If the Commission wants to implement regulations for which it lacks the statutory authority, it must first obtain the approval of Congress.

The Commission's service to the radio medium is twofold. First, it sets the technical standards under which the medium operates. Second, it ensures an adequate and equitable distribution of radio services throughout the United States. The Commission was created by Congress to specifically carry out these objectives. Prior to the existence

of the Commission and its predecessor, the Federal Radio Commission, radio broadcasting in this country was in a state of chaos. There was no spectrum planning. Operators put the stations on the air wherever they wanted. If a new station caused interference to a station already on the air, the operator of the older station often would just increase power – sort of an electronic shouting match. There were also no standards for radio receivers to prevent them from causing radiofrequency interference. So when Congress created the FCC, it charged it with making the radio medium "serve the public interest need and necessity."

The Commission's principal missions are accomplished with this objective in mind. Some of the agency's rules set minimum and maximum power requirements for radio stations; others set interference and distance standards – all with the objective of making sure that when a listener tunes to a radio station, he or she will be able to hear it clearly. The Commission's role in setting technical standards also extends to the equipment used in the transmission of radio signals. Manufacturers of transmitters and receivers are required to receive FCC "type acceptance" approval before putting their products on the market. This insures that a clean signal is transmitted and received and that the equipment does not cause interference to other stations or electronic services. Other Commission rules deal with spectrum planning and are intended to ensure an equitable distribution of radio stations throughout the country so that as many communities as possible

will have a local radio station and possibly access to several different stations to provide a multitude of voices.

The Commission recognizes the different types of services that radio stations provide to listeners. To this end, it will often establish rules to foster the growth of a group of stations providing a unique service. For example, in 1945 the Commission reserved the first 20 channels in the FM band (88.1–91.9 MHz) for radio stations licensed to nonprofit, educational institutions and organizations to be operated as noncommercial, educational radio stations. The Commission then established a set of rules for this type of station, including both technical standards and spectrum planning. Similarly, in 2000 the Commission accepted applications for the first Low Power FM ("LPFM") stations to further enhance the public's access to local, noncommercial FM radio stations.

Finally, in looking at the Commission's service to the radio medium, one must realize that the Communications Act is a living document. It has been amended many times to allow for new technologies in the radio medium, and the Commission has implemented regulations to carry out these changes. There is no doubt that the Communications Act will continue to be amended to take into consideration future changes in radio service and the Commission will proscribe regulations implementing these changes.

The views expressed by the author are not necessarily those of the Federal Communications Commission.

FIGURE 10.25
Operating log
currently in use at
WFBQ-FM. Courtesy
WFBQ-FM.

WFBQ-FM operating log

DAY _____

DATE _____

Time	Plate Volts	Plate Amps	Power Out

1. All times are EST.
2. Unless otherwise noted, all operations are continued from previous day.
3. WFBQ leases its subcarrier to Comcast, Inc. for the operation of a background music service. Unless otherwise noted, subcarrier program material is background music provided by the Muzak Corp., subcarrier is on continuously when modulation present, and, with the exception of short breaks between music segments modulation is continuous.
4. Responsibility for tower maintenance and light checks delegated to WRTV
5. Po = Ep x Ip x Eff
   Eff= 74.12% as ind. in mfrs instr.

Comments:

POWER TOLERANCE: Low Limit = 18,000 w / High Limit = 21,000 w

EBS TEST SENT	EBS TEST RECEIVED	EBS RECEIVER CHECK
	VIA _____	
____ ____	____ ____	____ ____
time initial	time initial	time initial

Operator on	Time	Operator off	Time

Ch.Op.Review:

_____

Date _____

Stations not designated to remain in operation in the event of an EAN then remove their carriers from the air after advising listeners where to tune for further information. Those participating stations continue to broadcast information as it is received from the nation's base of operations. Every radio station is required to install and operate an EAS monitor. Failure to do so can result in a substantial penalty imposed by the FCC.

Stations are also required to test the EAS by airing both an announcement and an attention signal. EAS tests are documented in the Station Log when they are broadcast. The entry must include the time and the date of the test.

The Federal Emergency Management Agency (FEMA) makes funds available to stations designated to remain on the air during an authentic emergency through the Broadcast Station Protection Plan. Under this provision the government provides financial assistance to EAS stations for the purpose of constructing and equipping a shelter designed to operate for at least 14 days under emergency conditions.

In the 1990s, the FCC began an inquiry into whether the system needed updating or replacement. Critics of the old EBS claimed that the system had become obsolete. In late 1992, proposed EBS revisions included the following:

- Replacement of the existing emergency alerting system.
- Updating of EBS equipment.
- Cable media involvement in emergency alerting.
- Self-testing of the system.
- Mandated equipment standards.
- Rules to prohibit false and deceptive use of the system.
- Revised EBS test script.

Today EAS embraces many of these revisions, as well as additional innovations and procedures. It is always a system under evaluation as world events, such as 9/11 and Hurricane Katrina, increase the need for an effective emergency alert system.

Automation

The FCC's decision in the mid-1960s requiring that AM/FM operations in markets with populations of more than 100,000 originate separate programming 50% of the time provided significant impetus to radio automation. Before then combo stations, as they were called, simulcast their AM programming on FM primarily as a way of curtailing expenses. FM was still the poor second cousin of AM. (In the late 1980s, the FCC dropped most of its simulcast requirements. Since then many stations have resorted to simulcasting as a means of dealing with the realities of fierce competition and a declining AM market.)

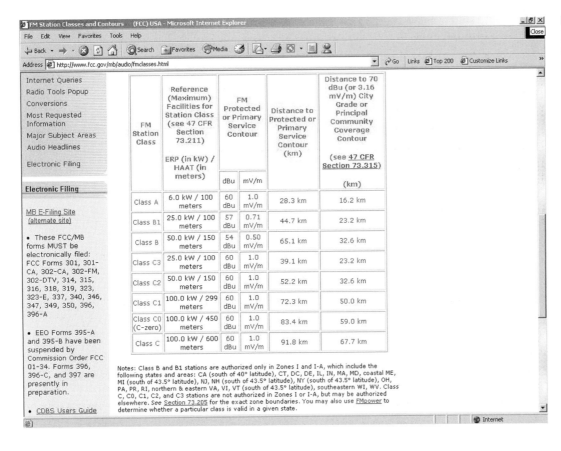

FIGURE 10.26
FM station classification table. Courtesy FCC.

Responding to the rule changes, many stations resorted to automation systems as a way to keep expenses down. Interestingly enough, however, automation for programming, with its emphasis on music and deemphasis on chatter, actually helped FM secure a larger following, resulting in increased revenue and stature.

FIGURE 10.27
Satellite networks may interface with station automation systems. Courtesy SMN.

SET UP SUGGESTIONS FOR BROADCAST OF SMN FORMATS
Examples of how some SMN affiliates have set up simple broadcast systems that are effective in delivering a high quality sound.

#1 AUTOMATION SYSTEMS
In the 60's and 70's many stations purchased automation systems that gave the station operator hours of walk-away time. The good news is that with Satellite Music Network (SMN) you can put that system back to work for you.
Treat the SMN format as another source. If you have a network source input use us there or as you would any tape machine or cartridge machine. You can use the contact closures for the spot breaks as an end of message (EOM) pulse for that particular source. Your contact closures for the liners, sweepers and I.D.'s should be hooked up to separate cartridge machines to fire them individually. We call these dedicated carts.
All dedicated carts should be connected with their audio outputs paralleled to the audio going out over the air at all times. A good place to insert the dedicated cart audio is at the audio processor input by using a combining pad or some other audio combining device. The dedicated cart audio can also be combined at the output of the automation system.

#2 REEL AND AUDIO SWITCHER
Another set up utilizes a reel to reel machine and a switcher.
Basically all an audio switcher needs to do is turn off or isolate the network audio while you take a local spot break. You can build a latching relay using the contact closure going into the spot break to latch the audio off the air signal line. When the break is done they use the contact closure for the liner cart machine, but release the latch and return the network audio to the on-air buss (connection).
The reel to reel machine can be loaded with commercial spots that are timed for each break. Some stations can have as much as 12 hours walk away time with this system depending on their spot load. It is necessary to provide a function to stop your reel after each spot break so you do not get out of sequence. The liners, I.D.'s and sweepers need to be on dedicated carts with the cart audio paralleled with the on-air audio buss. This is called the old sound on sound concept.

#3 CART MACHINES AND AUDIO SWITCHER
Basically the same as example #2 except the reel to reel is replaced with sequenced cart machines that can handle the spot breaks. The only difference in this system is that the carts need to be changed out after each spot break. All other functions remain the same.

Today, over a third of all commercial stations are automated. Some are fully automated (computer driven); others rely on automation for part of their broadcast day. Automation is far more prevalent on FM, but in the late 1970s and 1980s many AM outlets were employing automation systems to present Nostalgia and Easy Listening programming. The advent of AM stereo also generated some use of automation on the Standard Broadcast band, but since AM stereo all but fizzled, this specific application of automation remained minuscule.

Although a substantial initial investment usually is necessary, the basic purpose of automation is to save a station money, and this it does by cutting staffing costs. Automation may also reduce the number of personnel problems. However, despite early predictions that automation eventually would replace the bulk of the radio workforce, very few jobs have actually been lost. In fact, new positions have been created.

Automated stations employ operators as well as announcers and production people (unless satellite-fed by syndicators). The extent to which a station uses automation often bears directly on staffing needs. Obviously, a fully automated station will employ

FIGURE 10.28
Rack rooms in cluster operation. Courtesy Clear Channel.

FIGURE 10.28
Continued

fewer programming people than a partially automated outlet.

An automation system consists of a computer that also produces logs, music sheets, invoices, affidavits, and so on. Automated operations typically consist of a fully loaded computer system containing all of a station's music and announcement inventory. Indeed, the day of in-house loading of format elements is all but gone. Satellite syndicators using computers control local station ingredients (news, weather, promos, spots) remotely from the uplinks.

Today, thanks to the prevalence of computers, larger stations may employ a manager of information systems (MIS), who serves the computer tech needs of an outlet or entire cluster operation. This is another example of the so-called station in a box trend.

Posting Licenses and Permits

The FCC requires that a station's license and the permits of its operators be posted. What follows are the rules pertaining to this requirement as outlined in Subpart H, § 73.1230, of the FCC's regulations.

§ 73.1230 Posting of Station and Operator Licenses

(a) The station license and any other instrument of station authorization shall be posted in a conspicuous place and in such a manner that all terms are visible at the place the licensee considers to be the principal control point of the transmitter. At all other control or ATS monitoring and alarm points a photocopy of the station license and other authorizations shall be posted.

(b) The operator license of each station operator employed full-time or part-time or via contract shall be permanently posted and shall remain posted so long as the operator is employed by the licensee. Operators employed at two or more stations, which are not colocated, shall post their operator license or permit at one of the stations, and a photocopy of the license or permit at each other station. The operator license shall be posted where the operator is on duty, either:

(1) At the transmitter; or

(2) At the extension meter location; or

(3) At the remote control point, if the station is operated by remote control; or

(4) At the monitoring and alarm point, if the station is using an automatic transmission system.

(c) Posting of the operator licenses and the station license and any other instruments of authorization shall be done by affixing the licenses to the wall at the posting location, or by enclosing them in a binder or folder which is retained at the posting location so that the documents will be readily available and easily accessible. (43 FR 45847, Oct. 4, 1978, as amended at 49 FR 29069, July 18, 1984)

CHAPTER HIGHLIGHTS

1. Guglielmo Marconi first used electromagnetic (radio) waves to send a message at the end of the nineteenth century. Marconi used earlier findings by James C. Maxwell and Heinrich Hertz.

2. J. Ambrose Fleming developed the diode tube (1904), and Reginald Fessenden transmitted voice over the wireless (1906).

3. Edwin Armstrong developed the regenerative and superheterodyne circuits, and first demonstrated the static-free FM broadcast signal (1933).

4. Broadcast transmissions are carried on electromagnetic waves. The transmitter creates and shapes the wave to correspond to the "frequency" assigned by the FCC.

5. Receivers pick up the transmissions, converting the incoming radio frequency (RF) into sound waves.

6. AM stations are assigned frequencies between 535 and 1705 kHz, with 10 kc separations between frequencies. AM is disrupted by low-frequency emissions, can be blocked by irregular topography, and can travel hundreds (along surface level ground waves) or thousands (along nighttime sky waves) of miles.

7. Because AM station signals travel greater distances at night, to avoid skywave interference, over 2000 stations around the country must cease operation near sunset. Thousands more must make substantial nighttime transmission adjustments (decrease power), and others (directional stations) must use two or more antennas to shape the pattern of their radiation.

8. FM stations are assigned frequencies between 88.1 and 107.9 MHz, with 200 kc separations between frequencies. FM is static free, with direct waves (line-of-sight) carrying up to 80–100 miles. Both AM and FM stations are licensed for 8 years as of this writing.

9. To guarantee efficient use of the broadcast spectrum and to minimize station-to-station interferences, the FCC established four classifications for AM stations and eight classifications for FM. Lower classification stations are obligated to avoid interference with higher classification stations. Recent FCC actions have created more subclassifications.

10. Satellite radio employs both geosynchronous (former XM) and elliptical (Sirius) orbits from over 22,000 miles in space. When necessary, ground repeaters are used to strengthen signals.

11. Analog is being replaced by digital audio (DAB/HD) because digital audio provides superior frequency response and greater dynamic range. New spectrum space may be allocated to accommodate the digital service.

12. A station's chief engineer (chief operator) needs experience with basic broadcast electronics, as well as a knowledge of the FCC regulations affecting the station's technical operation. The chief must repair and adjust equipment, and perform weekly inspections and calibrations. Other duties may include installing new equipment, training techs, planning maintenance schedules, and handling a budget.

FIGURE 10.29
Stations that generated 50 kw promoted their greater coverage areas. Courtesy WHAS.

13. A Proof of Performance involves checking the station's frequency response, harmonic distortion, FM noise level, AM noise level, stereo separation, crosstalk, and subcarrier suppression.

14. Although the FCC dispensed with the maintenance and operating log requirements (1983), a Station Log must be maintained. The log lists information about tower light malfunctions, EAS tests, and AM directional antenna systems.

15. The EAS (formerly the EBS), implemented after World War II, provides the government with a means of communicating with the public in an emergency. Stations must follow rigid instructions both during periodic tests of the system and during an actual emergency.

16. Over one-quarter of today's commercial stations are fully or partially automated. More prevalent in FM stations, automation reduces staffing costs but requires a significant equipment investment. Automated programming elements are aired when a trip mechanism is activated by a cue tone, which is impressed on all program material. Either an operator or a computer can maintain the programming chain.

At many stations, satellite programming services use computers (at both uplink and downlink sites) to control station automation systems.

17. A MIS maintains a station's computer systems.

18. Direct satellite-fed stations need little equipment because programming originates at the syndicator's studios.

19. The FCC requires that a station's license and the permits of its operators be accessible in the station area.

FIGURE 10.30
A 1970s PC-based program controller running an automation system. Courtesy IGM Communications.

FIGURE 10.31
Satellite-linked automation systems are available in certain formats. Diagram shows how the system works. Courtesy Broadcast Electronics.

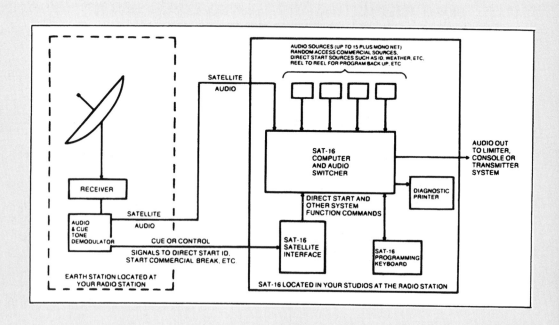

SUGGESTED FURTHER READING

Abel, J.D., and Ducey, R.V., *Gazing into the Crystal Ball: A Radio Station Manager's Technological Guide to the Future*, NAB, Washington, DC, 1987.

Antebi, E., *The Electronic Epoch*, Van Nostrand Reinhold, New York, 1982.

Butler, A., *Practical Tips for Choosing and Using Consulting and Contract Engineers*, NAB Publications, Washington, DC, 1994.

Cheney, M., *Tesla: Man out of Time*, Prentice Hall, Englewood Cliffs, NJ, 1983.

Considine, D.M., editor, *Van Nostrand's Scientific Encyclopedia*, Van Nostrand Reinhold, New York, 1983.

Davidson, F.P., *Macro: A Clear Vision of How Science and Technology Will Shape Our Future*, William Morrow, New York, 1983.

Ebersole, S., *Broadcast Technology Worktext*, Focal Press, Boston, MA, 1992.

Grant, A.E., *Communication Technology Update*, Focal Press, Boston, MA, 1995.

Hilliard, R.L., *FCC Primer*, Focal Press, Boston, MA, 1991.

Hoeg, W., and Lauterbach, T., editors, *Digital Broadcast Audio: Principles and Application of Digital Radio*, 2nd edition, Wiley, Hoboken, NJ, 2003.

Hong, S., *From Marconi's Black-Box to the Audion*, The MIT Press, Cambridge, MA, 2001.

Mirabito, M., and Morgenstern, B., *The New Communication Technologies*, 2nd edition, Focal Press, Boston, MA, 1994.

Morton, D.L., Jr., *Sound Recording: The Life Story of a Technology*, Johns Hopkins University Press, Baltimore, MD, 2006.

National Association of Broadcasters. *Broadcast Engineering*, NAB Publications, Washington, DC, 2008.

Noll, E.M., *Broadcast Radio and Television Handbook*, 6th edition, Howard Sams, Indianapolis, IN, 1983.

Priestman, C., *Web Radio: Radio Production for Internet Streaming*, Focal Press, Boston, MA, 2005.

Reed, J.H., *Software Radio: A Modern Approach to Radio Engineering*, Prentice-Hall, Englewood Cliffs, NJ, 2002.

Regal, B., *Radio: The Life Story of a Technology*, Greenwood, Westport, CT, 2005.

Reitz, J.R., *Foundations of Electromagnetic Theory*, Addison-Wesley, Reading, MA, 1960.

Roberts, R.S., *Dictionary of Audio, Radio, and Video*, Butterworths, Boston, MA, 1981.

Sarkar, T.K., et al., editors. *History of the Wireless*, Wiley-Interscience, New York, 2006.

Starr, W., *Electrical Wiring and Design: A Practical Approach*, John Wiley & Sons, New York, 1983.

Watkinson, J., *The Art of Digital Audio*, Focal Press, Boston, MA, 1992.

Wilson, D., *A Broadcast Engineering Tutorial for Non-Engineers*, NAB, Washington, DC, 1999.

Wurtzler, S.J., *Electronic Sounds: Technological Changer and the Rise of Corporate Mass Media*, Columbia University Press, New York, 2007.

APPENDIX: Federal Communications Commission

Fact Sheet: Hints on Filing Comments with the FCC

The FCC is interested in any experiences, knowledge, or insights that outside parties may have to shed light on issues and questions raised in the rule-making process. The public and industry have the opportunity to comment upon Petitions for Rule Makings, NOIs, NPRMs, Further NPRMs, Reports and Orders, and others' comments on the aforementioned documents. It is a common misconception that only a lawyer can file comments with the FCC, but all that is necessary is an interest in an issue and the ability to read and follow directions.

Prior to drafting comments it is crucial to read and understand fully the item on which you wish to comment. Usually, the NPRM, NOI, or other item will specify and invite comment upon the issue(s) that the Commission is interested in studying further. Examination of the issue(s) and relevant documents is the most important part of the comment process. Comments may take any form, but the following hints may assist you in writing them.

Format. There is no required format for informal comments, although if you plan to file formally, it is required that they be typed, double-spaced, and on 8.5" × 11" paper. Additional requirements for formal filings are set forth in Sections 1.49 and 1.419 of the FCC Rules. The Docket Number or Rule Making Number of the item at hand should be included on your comments and can be found on the front page of the Commission document or public notice. You should also include your name and complete mailing address.

Content. Your comments should state who you are and what your specific interest is. (You do not need to represent yourself in an official capacity. You may, for example, express your opinion as a concerned consumer, concerned parent, etc., and sign your name.) State your position and the facts directly, as thoroughly but as briefly as possible. Explain your position as it relates to your experience and be explicit. Make clear if the details of a proposed rule or only one of several provisions of the rule are objectionable. If the rule would be acceptable with certain safeguards, explain them and why they are necessary.

Support. Statements of agreement or dissent in comments should be supported to the best extent possible by factual (studies, statistics, etc.),

logical, and/or legal information. Support should illustrate why your position is in the public interest. The more support made, the more persuasive the comments will be.

Length. Comments may be any length, although it is preferred that they be succinct and direct. If formal comments are longer than 10 pages, a summary sheet is required.

Time frame. Your comments should be submitted well within the time frame designated on the original document or public notice. It is almost always included on the first page of an NPRM or NOI. However, if the deadline has passed, you can still submit your views informally in a permissible ex parte presentation.

Filing. Send your written comments to Secretary, Federal Communications Commission, 445 Twelfth Street, S.W., Washington. D.C. 20554. If you wish your comments to be received as an informal filing, submit the original and one copy. If you want your comments to be received as a formal filing, you should submit an original and four copies. For more specific filing information, please refer to the FCC Public Notice "Guidelines for Uniform Filings" available from the same address.

Reply comments. As the name implies, reply comments are used to respond to comments filed by other parties. You may file reply comments even if you did not submit comments initially. When drafting reply comments use the same guidelines expressed earlier regarding content and be careful not to raise additional or irrelevant issues.

Tracking your comments. After you have properly filed your comments with the FCC, they will be part of the official Commission record. To track the progress of proceedings in which you have filed comments, you may check the *Daily Digest* or *Federal Register* for releases and notices. The *Daily Digest* can be obtained from the Office of Public Affairs, 445 Twelfth Street, S.W., Washington, D.C. 20554 or from a daily recorded listing of texts and releases at 202-418-2222.

For further information. For further information, you may contact the Secretary's office at the FCC directly, at 202-418-0300. Explicit information about filings in rulemaking proceedings can be found in Sections 1.49 and 1.419 of the

FCC Rules. Copies of any FCC documents can be obtained through the FCC's duplicating contractor, Best Copy and Printing, Inc. www.bcpiweb.com 1-800-378-3160 or from one of the private distributors of FCC releases. A list of distributors is available from the Public Service Division, 445 Twelfth Street, S.W., Washington, D.C. 20554, 202-418-0190.

FIGURE 10.32
SBE application.

An invitation to join SBE

Who are we?

The Society of Broadcast Engineers, formed in 1963 as the Institute of Broadcast Engineers, is a non-profit organization serving the interests of broadcast engineers. We are the only society devoted to all levels of broadcast engineering.

Our membership, which is international in scope, is made up of studio and transmitter operators and technicians, supervisors, announcer-technicians, chief engineers of large and small stations and of commercial and educational stations, engineering vice presidents, consultants, field service and sales engineers, broadcast engineers from recording studios, schools, CCTV and CATV systems, production houses, advertising agencies, corporations, audio-visual departments, and all other facilities that utilize broadcast engineers.

What can we do for you?

Help you keep pace with our rapidly changing industry through educational seminars, and a look at new technology through industry tours and exhibits at monthly chapter meetings, regional conventions, and our national meeting held in conjunction with the National Association of Broadcasters (NAB).

Give you national representation. To serve as a voice for you in the industry; a liaison for you with governmental agencies as well as other industry groups.

To provide a forum for the exchange of ideas and sharing of information with other broadcast engineers and industry people.

To promote the profession of broadcast engineering.

To establish standards of professional education and training for broadcast engineering, and to recognize achievement of these standards.

In addition to the intangible benefits of membership in the SBE, the tangible benefits of an insurance program, communications through **The SBE Signal**, certification and re-certification opportunities, and a readily available network of specialized professionals.

All this adds up to an increase in your worth as a broadcast engineer to your employer.

Where does your money go?

A small office staff handling membership, certification, and the day-to-day business of the Society. Many duties of the SBE are handled by officers and board members who volunteer their time with no remuneration.

A library of videotape training material for loan from the national headquarters.

The production of our bi-monthly newsletter, **The SBE Signal**.

Allows SBE representation—through a professionally designed informational booth at state and regional meetings as well as NAB and NRBA.

A portion of your annual dues returns to subsidize the local chapter.

Supplements expenses for special events such as NAB, Chapter Chairman and Certification Chairman Meetings, and invitational opportunities to represent the SBE.

How to be one of us

Membership categories include Student, Associate Member, Member, Senior Member, Honorary Member, and Fellow.

Qualification for Member grade requires that the individual be actively engaged in broadcast engineering or have an academic degree in electrical engineering or its equivalent in scientific or professional experience in broadcast engineering or a closely related field or art.

The cost of membership is $20 annually for member and associate member grades, and $10 for student memberships.

What do we want from you?

First, we'd like to have your name on the SBE roster.

Strength in numbers gives us additional clout. And we want and need your participation and input at the regional and national levels as well as at the local level.

Certification Program

The program issued its first certificates on January 1, 1977, and now conducts tests at various times and places for those people, either members or non-members, who wish to have a certificate attesting to their competence as broadcast engineers. The certificates are issued for two different levels of achievement in either radio or TV and are valid for five years from date of issue. Recertification may be accomplished by earning professional credits for activities which maintain competence in the state-of-the-art or by re-examination.

Emphasis in the tests is on practical working knowledge rather than general theory. The tests are as valid for people in related industries as they are for broadcasters.

An entry-level certificate was added to the certification program in January 1982 to attract new technical talent to the broadcast industry and provide incentive for them to grow with technology.

The certification program is conducted by the SBE to benefit everyone in the industry. The program recognizes professional competence as judged by one's peers, and encourages participation in seminars, conventions, and meetings to help keep abreast of the constantly changing technology in broadcast engineering.

If you ever wanted to meet the people who design the equipment you use,
■ to talk with your fellow engineers and technicians,
■ to tour the many facilities that employ engineers and technicians,
■ to keep abreast of the state-of-the-art equipment,
■ to upgrade your skills for certification,
■ here is the opportunity to become a member of the most prestigious society in its field.

SOCIETY OF BROADCAST ENGINEERS, INC.
P.O. Box 50844, Indianapolis, Indiana 46250

Group Insurance Program

When you join the SBE, you have the opportunity to participate in the Group Insurance Program for SBE members and their dependents, which offers a wide range of coverage to suit your individual needs. The low rates are made possible through the economics of group administration and by the fact that SBE does not profit from the insurance program. Please note that requests for coverage under some of the plans are subject to insurance company approval.

■ Term Life Insurance Plan offers options of up to $195,000 for eligible members, with lesser amounts for dependents.

■ High-Limit Accident Insurance provides protection wherever you go, 24 hours a day, and eliminates the need for special accident insurance every time you travel.

■ Disability Income Plan protects your income by providing monthly benefit payments when you are unable to work due to a disabling illness or accident.

■ Excess Major Medical Plan supplements your regular hospital/medical coverage in the event of a catastrophic illness or accident, paying up to $1,000,000 after you satisfy your deductible.

■ In-Hospital Plan pays up to $100 per day for every day you spend in the hospital—up to 365 days—directly to you, to spend as you wish.

■ Major Medical Expense Insurance is designed for members who have little or no basic medical coverage.

For further information concerning membership, certification, application, regional meetings and conventions, contact the Society of Broadcast Engineers, Inc., P.O. Box 50844, Indianapolis, IN 46250, (317) 842-0836.

FIGURE 10.32
Continued

MEMBERSHIP APPLICATION

SOCIETY OF BROADCAST ENGINEERS
P.O. Box 50844 • Indianapolis, Indiana 46250 • 317/842-0836

(Please type or print)

Application For:
- □ New Member $20.00
- □ Associate Member $20.00
- □ Student Member $10.00
  - □ Change in Grade
  - □ To Member
  - □ Sr. Member
- Reinstate:
  - □ Former Member #_____

Name: _____

Full home Address: (don't abbreviate)
_____

_____ Receive SBE Mail here? _____

_____ Home Phone ( )_____

Full Company Name and Address: _____ or here?

_____

_____ Business Phone ( )_____

If accepted, please consider me a member of _____ Chapter

SBE Certification # _____ (if applicable)

Date of Birth _____

Current Job Title: _____   Date Employed: _____

Type of Facility: _____

Description of Duties: _____

Total years of responsible   Field of   Radio _____
Engineering Experience: _____   Activity: Television _____
                                               Other _____

PROFESSIONAL LICENSES OR CERTIFICATES

_____
_____

Additional Information Requested on Reverse Side

ADMISSIONS COMMITTEE ACTION

Date: _____

Action deferred for more information _____

Admissions Committee Chairman's

Signature: _____

Approved for Grade _____

Candidate Notified _____

Entered in Records _____

EXPERIENCE RECORD

List in chronological order, beginning with the most recent, all formal experience in Broadcast Engineering or related employment. Indicate field or fields of specialization under 'Position.' Please do not limit yourself to the four spaces below. ATTACH A BRIEF DESCRIPTION OF DUTIES.

From Mo. Yr.	To Mo. Yr.	Company Name and Location	Position or Title	Type of Facility

EDUCATION

College, University, or Technical Institute	From Mo. Yr.	To Mo. Yr.	Credits or Yrs. Compl.	Course or Major	Degree

List Short Courses, Seminars Related to Broadcast-Communications Technology

SPECIAL ACHIEVEMENTS
List awards, patents, books, articles, etc.

REFERENCES
List two references - familiar with your work

Name	Company	Address	Phone

Have you ever been convicted of a violation of the Communications Act of 1934, as amended. Yes □ No □. If so, describe in full.
(Use additional space if necessary) _____

_____ I have enclosed the required application fee.

Signed _____ Date _____ 19__

I agree to abide by the By-Laws of the Society if admitted.

Consultants and Syndicators

Radio Aid

Two things directly contributed to the rise of radio consultants: more stations – from 2000 in the 1950s to 12,000 in 2000 – and more formats – from a half dozen to several dozen during the same period. Broadcast consultants have been around almost from the start, but it was not until the medium set a new course following the advent of television that the field grew to real prominence. By the 1960s, consultants were directing the programming efforts of hundreds of stations. In the 1970s, over a third of the nation's stations enlisted the services of consultants. Today, the field of radio consultancy has shrunk substantially due to the corporatization of the radio industry. The ranks have dwindled to half of its former number. Says former top radio consultant Kent Burkhart, "Since consolidation many of the small consulting companies have shut their doors. Most of the large consulting companies with lots of assets (meaning an exclusive format, research partners, marketing connections, etc.) have done well financially…but not as well as before. Prior to consolidation our company (Burkhart/Abrams) was charging a certain fee for each station in a group. However, since consolidation many groups have hired one chief programming executive for a lot less money than the aforementioned fee per station. I thought consolidation would change the face, operations, and efficiency our consulting company and others. It didn't sound like fun to me, so prior to the consolidation rollout I sold our consulting company in 1995."

Consultant Donna Halper shares a similar view of the impact of consolidation on her profession, "It's certainly affected radio consulting. With fewer independent stations that means radio conglomerates are relying more on voice-tracking and syndication. It used to be that consultants trained and developed talent in small and medium markets, but these days a company might simulcast the same programs on two or more of their stations or use voice-tracking from another city to give the impression that a live and local personality is on the air. They may also have an in-house person who oversees the stations. Yet, this saves the companies money on hiring talent (and also saves them from hiring a consultant), but it also presents a problem. Many of these companies are not planning for the future. Rush Limbaugh and Howard Stern will not live forever, and without developing new talent, who will take their place? As we witnessed during the 9/11 and Hurricane Katrina crises, people DO want live and local radio, yet in many markets, there are no local personalities at all. Sooner or later somebody will have to start developing talent again and creating radio stations that are unique. We are already raising a generation of young adults who don't rely on radio the way their parents did. To get these people back (and I do believe it can be done) radio needs to return to its roots and get involved with the community again. As a consultant and someone who loves radio, I hope we will see more local personalities and more local programming. Radio needs to get back to being a friend again."

Echoing Halper's sentiments, consultant Doug Erickson says, "The biggest challenge for radio consultants today is the corporate resistance to new ideas. As radio has become a consolidated industry, it has become more conservative in many ways. General managers (GM) and program directors (PDs) feel more pressure to make the 'right' choice and this often leads to making the 'safest' choice – which is not always in the best interest of the station. As a consultant I try to make station management aware of the risks of doing nothing innovative. If terrestrial radio is to continue to be a part of the daily lives of most people, it must find a new way to remain personal and relevant, and it must do as much to touch the hearts of listeners as it does their ears." Meanwhile, consultant Gary Berkowicz says that consolidation has not impacted his business greatly but admits it has taken its toll on the field, "I still fly over 100,000 miles a year, so I'd say things are pretty good. In all seriousness, there is no doubt that it has changed. There are fewer consultants today, and somewhat fewer opportunities and stations to work for." Also, from the perspective of Juan Carlos Hidalgo, who

consults Spanish radio, the market for his services is strong. "It's been a fascinating experience working for stations in major markets, such as Los Angeles, Chicago, and San Francisco, where you have all the tools, like research and marketing budgets to compliment programming efforts. At the same time in the smaller markets that I consult, I have to rely more on creativity due to the limited budgets and tools. The dynamic of these two different situations keeps me on the cutting edge of doing new and exciting things to improve the performance of my client radio stations. Consolidation hasn't impacted my business. Maybe in the future."

Whether the radio consultancy function will be completely absorbed by corporations remains to be seen. However, consultants continue to play an important role in the shaping and management of the medium today. Observes prominent radio consultant George Burns, "The principal role of radio consultants has evolved considerably since Mike Joseph started the whole thing in the 1950s. We began by being very specifically task oriented. A consultant was assumed to have greater expertise at the job

FIGURE 11.1
There are an abundance of radio consulting services from which stations can choose. Courtesy Lund Consultants.

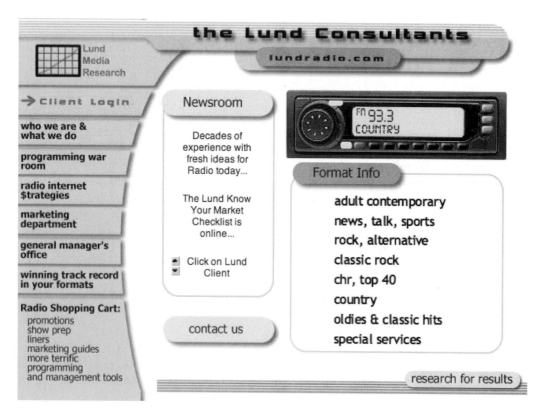

FIGURE 11.1

Continued

Specialized services for your Station(s) and individual Cluster(s)

• 24/7 phone and email access at no additional charge.

• Bi-weekly scheduled phone conferences.

• Music scheduling.

• Weekly Personality critique with confidential written reports to you, the station management.

• Talent recruitment and coaching.

• Music testing preparation, with interpretation for burn and making sure that each title is familiar to your P1's. Increasing CUME and TSL listenership and driving AQH!

• Branding/Imaging preparation, writing and creation of Imaging that stands above the crowd. Making you unique.

• Voiceover talent located, retainer price negotiated and management made easy.

• Arbitron interpretation, with straightforward, easy to interpret reports, showing your strengths as well as your station's weaknesses in the market. This is a different approach from what your PD "spins" and thinks you want to hear.

than anyone that the station could afford fulltime. Currently consultants serve primarily as outside (and, it is hoped, impartial) monitors of station progress. The job is to assure management that everything possible is being done to maximize the station's potential. If something is not functioning properly or needs to be changed, consultants are expected to give voice to these concerns. Over the years, the job has become infinitely more complex. Musical and nonmusical aspects of programming have spread widely apart. Research has become a separate discipline. And lately, the marketing side of radio has achieved a 'life of its own.' Different consultants approach each station's progress from varying points of view. Specialization was inevitable."

Stations use consultants for various reasons, says Fred Jacobs, president of Jacob's Media: "Stations realize that they need an experienced, objective ear to make intelligent evaluations. Consultants are also exposed to ideas and innovations from around the country that they can bring to their client stations. As radio has become more competitive, stations understand that their need for up-to-date information about current trends in programming and marketing has increased."

Dave Scott, former president of Century 21 Programming (now TM Century), Dallas, Texas, adds that a lack of research expertise on the local station level prompts many stations to use consultants. "We're well into the information age, the age of highly sophisticated research techniques and computerized data. It takes a lot of resources to assess a market and prescribe a course of action. Most stations do not have the wherewithal. At the former Century 21 Programming, each of our consultants went through more ratings surveys and research data than most station owners, managers, or program directors did in a lifetime. The way the marketplace is today, using a consultant generally is a wise move. Radio stations that attempt to find their niche by trial and error make costly mistakes. A veteran consultant can accelerate a station's move on the road to success."

Donna Halper agrees with Scott and adds, "Consultants give their client stations an objective viewpoint and another experienced person's input. Consultants are support people, resource people, who bring to a situation a broader vision rather than the purely local perspective. Consultants, and not just out-of-work PDs who call themselves consultants but in reality aren't, have a lot of research, information, and expertise they can make available to a client with an ailing station."

Mikel Hunter of Mikel Hunter Broadcast Services, Las Vegas, says consultants' help stations develop a distinctiveness that they need to succeed. "Unfortunately most station PDs are bandwagon riders. Many watch what other stations do around the country and clone them in their markets. Sometimes this works. Often it doesn't. It likely was a consultant who helped design the programming of that successful station being copied, and the consultant did so based on what was germane to that particular market, not one a thousand miles away. Therein lies the problem. Simply because a station in Denver is doing great book by programming a certain way does not guarantee that a station in Maryland can duplicate that success. A good consultant brings originality and creativity to each new situation, in addition to the knowledge and experience he possesses. The follow-the-leader method so prevalent among programmers actually creates a lot of the problems that consultants are called on to remedy."

Fewer than 100 broadcast consultants are listed in the various media directories around the country. More than half of this number specializes in radio. Says Ed Shane, "I remember a time when there were 250 programming consultants listed in the *R&R* directory. The number has tumbled since consolidation. One-man shops that couldn't make it as clients were swallowed by competing companies. Some consulting firms merged (Holland Cooke and McVay Media, for example). Others folded to go in-house at major companies (Jack Taddeo to Capstar, for instance)."

In general, consultancy companies average around 20–30 employees but may be composed of as few as two or three and in some cases are a one-person operation. Many successful program directors also provide consultancy to stations in other markets in addition to their regular programming duties. A growing number of station rep companies provide their client stations consultancy services for an additional fee.

Again, in the age of station consolidation and massive radio groups, consultancy often originates in-house.

Consultant Services

Successful consultant Valerie Geller believes that station concentration actually creates a need for her services and expertise. "Programmers and managers tend to be stretched very thin these days because of consolidation; thus experienced consultants are more needed than ever." Stations hire program consultants to improve or strengthen their standings in the ratings surveys. An outside consultant may share general program decisions with the station's PD or may be endowed with full control over all decisions affecting the station's sound, contends Halper. "I have as little or as much involvement as the client desires. Depending on the case, I can hire and train staff (or fire staff), design or fine-tune a format, or simply motivate and direct deejays, which is actually anything but simple. Whatever a station wants, as a professional consultant I can provide. Usually, I make recommendations and then the owner or GM decides whether or not I will carry them out. At some of my stations, I've functioned as the acting PD, for all intents and purposes. At other client stations, I've been sort of the unofficial mother figure, providing support, encouragement, and sometimes a much-needed kick in the behind."

Among other services, Fred Jacobs says his company offers "in-market visits for monitoring and strategizing; ongoing monitors of client competition from airchecks or station 'listen lines'; critiques of on-air talent, assistance/design of music scheduling and selection; computer programs that assist with promo scheduling, database marketing, and morning show preparation; design of off-air advertising and coordination with production; and design/implementation of market research for programming, image, and music."

Most consultant firms are equipped to provide either comprehensive or limited support to stations. "In some cases, consultants offer a packaged 'system for success'

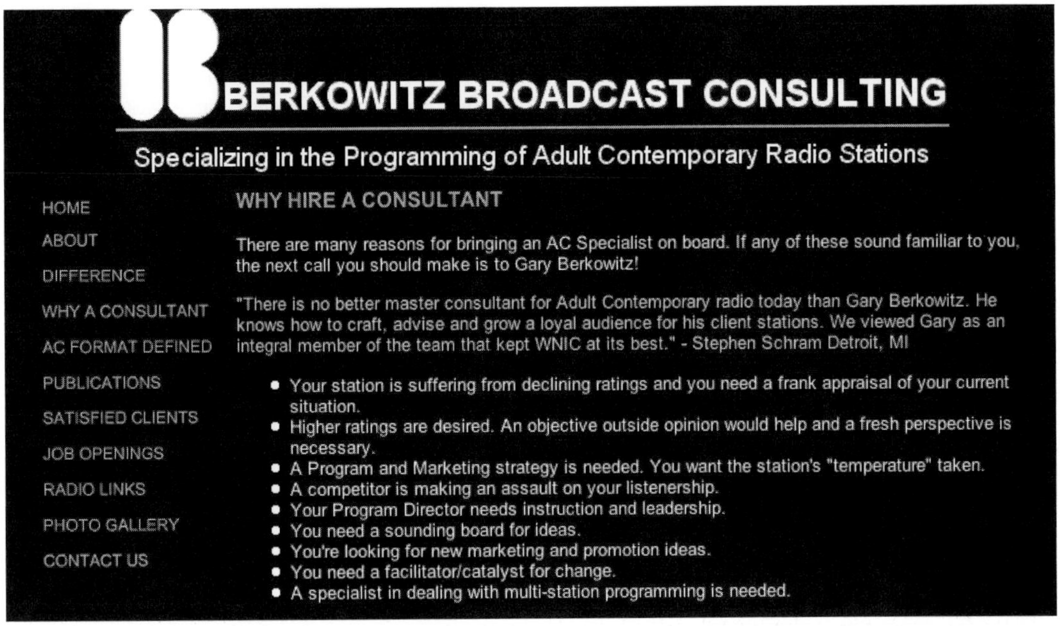

FIGURE 11.2
Consultants
make a dramatic
difference at many
stations. Courtesy
Berkowitz Broadcast
Consultants.

in the same way a McDonald's hamburger franchise delivers a 'system for success' to an investor. The consultant gets control. In other instances, consultants deliver objective advice or research input to a station more on a one-to-one basis. This parallels the role of most accountants or attorneys in that the decisions are still made by the station management, not the consultant," notes Dave Scott.

In the mid-1990s, niche consultants came into vogue. For example, a consulting service called Air Support focuses on improving the ratings of station morning shows by working on "talent development, preparation, creativity, and performance," reports *Radio Ink*.

Program consultants diagnose the problems that impair a station's growth and then prescribe a plan of action designed to remedy the ills. For example, station WXXX, located in a 20-station market, is one of three that programs current hits, yet it lags behind both of its competitors in the ratings. A consultant is hired to assess the situation and suggest a solution. The consultant's preliminary report cites several weaknesses in WXXX's overall programming. The consultant's critique submitted to the station's general manager may be written like this:

Dear GM:
Following a month-long analysis of WXXX's on-air product, here are some initial impressions. A more extensive report on each of the areas cited herein will follow our scheduled conference next week.

1. Personnel: Morning man Jay Allen lacks the energy and appeal necessary to attract and sustain an audience in this daypart. Although Allen possesses a smoothness and warmth that would work well in other time slots, namely midday or evenings, he does not have the "wake-up and roll" sound, nor the type of humor listeners have come to expect at this time of day. The other "hot hit" stations in the market offer bright and lively morning teams. Allen does not stand up against the competition. His contrasting style is ill-suited for AM drive, whereas midday man Mike Curtis would be more at home during this period. His upbeat, witty, and casual style when teamed with news people Chuck Tuttle and Mark Fournier would strengthen the morning slot.

Tracy Jessick and Michelle Jones perform well in their respective time periods. Overnight man Johnny Christensen is very adequate – potential as midday man should Curtis be moved into morning slot. Weekend personnel uneven. Better balance needed. Carol Mirando, 2:00–7:00 P.M. Sunday, is the strongest of the part-timers. Serious pacing problems with Larry Coty in 7:00 P.M. to midnight slot on Saturday. Can't read copy.

2. Music: Rotation problems in all dayparts. Playlist narrowing and updating necessary. Better definition needed. As stands, station verges on Adult Contemporary at certain times of the day, especially during A.M. drive. On Monday the fourteenth, during evening daypart, station abandoned currents and assumed Oldies sound. More stability and consistency within format essential. Computerized music scheduling possible solution. Separate report to follow.

3. News programming: General revamping necessary. Too heavy an emphasis during

both drive periods. Cut back by 20–30% in these two dayparts. Fifteen-minute "Noon News" needs to be eliminated. Tune-out factor in targeted demos. Same holds true for half-hour, 5:00–5:30 P.M., "News Roundup." Hourly 5-minute casts reduced to minute headlines after 7:00 P.M. Both content and style of newscasts presently inappropriate for demos sought. Air presentations need adjusting to better, more compatibly suit format. Tuttle and Fournier of morning show are strong, whereas P.M. drive news would benefit from a comparable team. Ovitt, Hart, and Lexis do not complement each other. Van Sanders is effective in evening slot. More sounders and actualities in hourly newscasts. Greater local slant needed, especially on sports events.

FIGURE 11.3
Consultants offer various services to stations. Courtesy Shane Media.

They're the consultants for companies that "don't use consultants."

They're our station's secret weapon.

- Today's # 1 stations choose Shane Media for programming.

- Now, a full menu of research services, too.

- Our 20th Year of thinking ahead!

SHANE MEDIA
(713) 952-9221
Radio Programming
and Research
www.shanemedia.com

4. General programming: Too much clutter! A log-jam in drive dayparts. Spots clustered four deep in spot sets, sometimes at quarter hour. So much for maintenance. Rescheduling needed for flow purposes as well. "Consumer Call" at 8:00 A.M., noon, and 5:00 P.M. not suitable for demos. "Band News" good, but too long. One-minute capsule versions scheduled through day would be more effective. Friday evening "Oldies Party" too geriatric – breaks format objective. Sends target demos off to competition by appealing to older listeners with songs dating back to 1960s. Public affairs programs scheduled between 9:00 A.M. and noon on Sundays delivers teens to competition that airs music during same time period. Jingles and promos dated. Smacks of decade ago. New package would add contemporary luster needed to sell format to target demo.

5. Promotions: "Bermuda Triangle" contest aimed at older demos. Contest prizes geared for 25–39-year-old listener. Ages station. Concert tie-in good. Album giveaway could be embellished with other prizes. Too thin as is. Response would indicate lack of motivation. True also of "Cash Call." Larger sums need to be awarded. Curtis's "Rock Trivia" on target. Hits demos on the money. Expand into other dayparts. Bumper stickers and "X-100" calendar do not project appropriate image. New billboards and bus-boards also need adjusting. Paper ads focus on weak logo. Waiting to view TV promo. Competition promos are very weak. A good "X-100" TV promo would create advantage in this area. Opportunity.

6. Technical: Signal strong. Reaches areas that competition does not. Significant null in Centerville area. Competition's signals unaffected. Occasional disparity in levels. Spots sometimes very hot. Promos and public service announcements (PSAs), especially UNICEF and American Cancer Society, slightly muddy. In general, fidelity acceptable on music. Extraneous noise, possibly caused by scratches or dirt, on some power rotation cuts. Stereo separation good. Recommend compressor and new limiter. Further plant evaluation in progress. A more detailed report to follow.

Following an extensive assessment of a station's programming, a consultant may suggest a major change. "After an in-depth evaluation and analysis, we may conclude that a station is improperly positioned in its particular market and recommend a format switch. Sometimes station management disagrees. Changing formats can be pretty traumatic, so there often is resistance to the idea. A critique more often

Gary Berkowitz | Station Consulting

The principal reason stations hire consultants is the experience, knowledge, and wisdom that are not necessarily available to them on a local basis or in a market that is smaller. Today's program directors can be responsible for multiple stations, pull airshifts, and also do the job of a few other people. I can focus in on one station, develop a strategy, and make sure that strategy is being followed. In terms of the effect of consolidation on the field of radio consultancy, if one of the large companies likes you, it's good. If not, it can be tough to get new clients. Many of the larger companies don't use outside consultants, so that has also added some interesting twists. There are still many broadcasters who need the savvy of solid consultants. As far as the effects of all the new audio technologies on the consultancy profession, it has not been as significant as one might think. Radio stations are still judged by the ratings and ratings are still determined by having the best sounding and best-marketed product. Terrestrial radio still fights for every ad dollar available, so the ratings are now more important than ever.

FIGURE 11.4
Gary Berkowitz.

recommends that adjustments be made in an existing format than a changeover to a different one. There are times when a consultant is simply called upon to assist in the hiring of a new jock or newsperson. Major surgery is not always necessary or desired," says Halper.

Today, the majority of stations in major and medium markets switching formats do so with the aid of a consultant (or an in-house programming executive in cluster situations). According to the National Association of Broadcasters (NAB), 3–5% of the nation's stations change formats each year. Consultant fees range from $500 to more than $1200 a day, depending on the complexity of the services rendered and the size of the station.

Consultant Qualifications

Most consultants begin as broadcasters. Some successfully programmed stations before embarking on their own or joining consultancy firms. According to fabled programmer Rick Sklar, deceased president of Sklar Communications, consultants who have a background in the medium have a considerable edge over those who do not. "The best way to fully understand and appreciate radio is to work in it. As you might imagine, radio experience is very helpful in this business." Jacobs agrees with Sklar. "Ideally a consultant should have a successful background in programming, with expertise in a number of areas, including research, sales, marketing, and promotion. The key word is *success* – a solid track record in a number of different market situations is invaluable. Consultants also need to have strong communication and tracking skills to best work with a variety of clients in markets around the country." Not all consultants have extensive backgrounds in the medium. Most do possess a thorough knowledge of how radio operates on all its different levels, from having worked closely with stations and having acquired formal training in colleges offering research methodology, audience measurement, and broadcast management courses. "A solid education is particularly important for those planning to become broadcast consultants. It is a very complex and demanding field today, and it is becoming more so with each passing day. My advice is to load up. Get the training and experience up front. It is very competitive out there. You make your own opportunities in this profession," says Dave Scott.

Both Halper and Scott rate people skills and objectivity highly. "Consulting requires an ability to deal with people. Decisions – for example, changing formats – sometimes result in drastic personnel changes. A consultant must be adept at diplomacy but must act with conviction when the diagnosis has been made. Major surgery invariably is traumatic, but the idea is to make the patient, the station, healthy again. You can't let your own personal biases or tastes get in the way of what will work in a given market," observes Halper. Dave Scott shares Halper's sentiments. "A consultant, like a doctor, must be compassionate and at the same time maintain his objectivity. It is our intention and goal as a program consultant service to make our client stations thrive. As consultants, we're successful because we do what we have to do. It's not a question of being mercenary. It's a question of doing what you have to do to make a station prosper and realize its potential."

Consultant company executives also consider wit, patience, curiosity, sincerity, eagerness, competitiveness, and drive – not necessarily in that order – among the other virtues that the aspiring consultant should possess. Adds Gary Berkowitz, "All of those things are important. Indeed experience, integrity, and honesty top the list, as does the ability to tell clients what you really think versus what they might want to hear."

Consultants: Pros and Cons

There are as many opponents of program consultants within the radio industry as there are advocates. Broadcasters who do not use consultants argue that local flavor is lost when an outsider comes into a market to direct a station's programming. Donna Halper contends that this may be true to some degree but believes that most professional consultants are sensitive to a station's local identity. "Some consultants do clone their stations. Others of us do not. In fact, I'd say most do not. For those of us who recognize local differences, there need not be any loss whatsoever as a consequence of consultant-recommended changes. But the hits are pretty much the hits, and good radio is something that Tulsa deserves as well as Rochester. So I do try to localize my music research and acquire a good feel for the market I'm working in. But as far as basic rules of good radio are concerned, those don't vary much no matter what the market is. It's important for a station to reflect the market it serves, and I support my clients in that. Because I work out of Boston doesn't mean that my AOR client in Duluth should sound like a Boston album rocker. It should sound like a solid AOR station that could be respected in any city but fits the needs of Duluth."

Consultant Dwight Douglas says that localization is essential for any radio station and that consultants are amply aware of this fact. "It is an industry axiom that a station must be a part of its environment. An excellent station will be uniquely local in relating to its audience. That tends to take the form of news, weather, sports, public service, general information, and jock talk. A good consultant will free a station from music worries and allow it to concentrate on developing local identity. We work hard at customizing formats to suit the geodemographics or lifestyles of the audiences of our client stations."

A station has an obligation to retain its sense of locality regardless of what a consultant may suggest, contends Mikel Hunter. "No station should simply turn itself over body and soul to a consultant. Local flavor does not have to be sacrificed if a station has a strong PD and a general manager who doesn't insist that the PD merely follow the consultant's suggestions. A station should not let itself become a local franchise. Consultants are a valuable resource, but both the station and the consultant must pool their wisdom to make the plan work."

Jacobs strikes a similar note of caution regarding the importance of local connection. "With a consultant, a station can conceivably lose some of its localness if there isn't adequate effort to give it a hometown flavor. But the loss of local presence is far more likely with satellite-delivered formats. Consultants need to work closely with station management (and vice versa) to find local ties and signposts, because listeners care most about what's happening in their town. It's always important to understand that there are regional differences in taste, personalities, and music. Many high-powered on-air personalities would be hard-pressed to duplicate their success in another market."

The cost factor is another reason why some stations do not use consultants. "Consultants can be expensive, although most consultants scale their fees to suit the occasion, that is, the size of the market. A few hundred dollars a day can be exorbitant for many smaller stations. But the cost of the research, analysis, and strategy usually is worth the money. I believe that a station, in most cases, gets everything it pays for when it uses a consultant. It's worth investing a few thousand to make back a million," contends Dwight Douglas.

Dave Scott believes that certain stations can become too dependent on consultants. "A consultant is there to provide support and direction when needed. If a station is infirm, it needs attention, perhaps extensive care. However, when a station regains its health, an annual or semi-annual checkup is usually sufficient. A checkup generally can prevent problems from recurring."

Mikel Hunter agrees with Scott, adding, "A radio doctor needs the cooperation of his client. On the other hand, a station must insist that a consultant do more than diagnose or critique. Positive input, that is, a remedying prescription, is what a consultant should provide. Conversely, a station should be willing to use the aid that the consultant provides."

Statistically, those stations that use programming consultants more often than not experience improved ratings. In case, after case consultants have taken their client stations from bottom to top in many of the country's largest markets. Of course, not all succeed quite so dramatically. However, a move from eleventh place to sixth in a metro market is considered a noteworthy achievement and has a very invigorating effect on station revenue. "The vast majority of consultants benefit their clients by increasing their position in the book. This means better profits," notes Halper, who has improved the ratings of 90% of her client stations.

FIGURE 11.5 Consultant's response to commonly asked questions. Courtesy Donna Halper and Associates.

Donna Halper & Associates
Radio Programming Consultants
304 Newbury St., #506
Boston, MA 02115
(617) 786-0666

QUESTIONS I AM OFTEN ASKED ABOUT HIRING A CONSULTANT

1. What kind of station would hire a consultant?

All kinds! From major market #1 stations that want to stay that way to new stations that need help choosing a format or hiring staff.

2. Aren't most consultants just out-of-work Program Directors?

Not today. Competition is too intense. Most of us who have stayed in the consulting field have years of experience in one thing: CONSULTING.

3. Should I hire a 'big name' consultant?

Since the majority of consultants today are experienced, you should choose one based on what his/her areas of expertise are. Interview a few consultants and you will see that each has some specialty-- whether it's a certain format (some consultants prefer to do only one format) or a certain market size. Choosing the right consultant for your station is an important decision, and you shouldn't do it on name alone.

4. What can a consultant offer my station that my own people can't provide?

First, consultants aren't there to replace your people, nor do they want them to look bad. While staff changes may result from the recommendations of a consultant, our first purpose is to offer you an UNBIASED, outside overview of how your station sounds, both its strengths and its weaknesses. We work WITH your people, providing research, guidance, training, market studies, etc. Often, because we are not caught up in the day-to-day circumstances, we can offer a fresh, objective point of view.

5. What are the benefits of HALPER & ASSOCIATES?

I'm glad you asked. We've been in business since 1980. (Before that, Donna Halper spent 13 years in major markets as an announcer, Music Director, PD, news reporter, and writer/producer of special programming.) Our specialties include critiques/positioning studies, staff training and motivation, and talent development. We work in markets of all sizes, but we are best-known for our ability to turn around failing small and medium market stations. We also do motivational seminars, and are expert at handling morale problems. Unlike some consultants who only do one format, Halper & Associates can show success stories in AC, Gold, CHR, Urban, Classic Rock, Full-Service/M-O-R, and Country. SINCE 1980, OVER 90% OF OUR CLIENTS HAVE SHOWN RATINGS GROWTH. And, our critiques and market studies have been used by some of the biggest and best companies. Also, Halper and Associates has experience with Canadian radio, and we have consulted in Puerto Rico.

6. Can you promise results for every client?

No consultant wins 'em all, although we'd like to. But, our slogan has always been "NO PROMISES...JUST RESULTS." We are proud of our many satisfied clients and our renewal rate is quite high. Many of our clients say they would never use another consultant. So, when it's time to think about a consultant, choose DONNA HALPER & ASSOCIATES. We can get results for you. To find out more, call us at 617-786-0666. We'll give you the attention you might not get from the "big names," affordable rates, and, most important, you can count on us to make a positive impact on your station and its staff! DONNA HALPER GETS RESULTS!!!

A Good Consultant Can Make A Difference...

With so many good consultants out there, it can be a difficult task to choose the one who is right for your station. To help you make such an important decision, **HALPER & ASSOCIATES** offers a few facts about what we can do for you:

1. **HALPER & ASSOCIATES** has gotten results for our clients since 1980. Our staff and our reputation are solid.
2. **HALPER & ASSOCIATES** has success stories in nearly every format, from CHR to Urban, Gold to Classic Rock, Country to AC, News and MOR. We've helped turn around many stations — both AM's and FM's. Recently, for example, we took a declining Urban/CHR from a 5.3 to an 8.4 in one year. An AC client of ours has grown from a 13.0 to a 17.1 in two years. Since 1980, over 90% of our clients have shown ratings increases. Many are now #1 or #2.
3. **HALPER & ASSOCIATES** gets results in markets of all sizes, from the East Coast to the West Coast, Canada and Puerto Rico. We have clients in major and large markets, but we have become known for our work in small and medium markets. We understand the special challenges of these markets and can make an impact even if you don't have a huge promotion budget or a legendary air staff.
4. **HALPER & ASSOCIATES** offers more than just better ratings. Our specialty is motivation and talent development. We can help to bring out the best in your staff, handle morale problems, or give your department heads the training and input they need to do their jobs more effectively. We are also known for our thorough market analyses, critiques and positioning studies. We can help you find the right format, or fine tune the one you now have.
5. **HALPER & ASSOCIATES** never clones stations or deals in fad formats. Each of our clients is unique. We are there whenever you need us.

No promises. Just results.

Donna Halper and Associates
Radio Programming Consultants
304 Newbury Street #506
Boston, Mass. 02115
(617) 786-0666

FIGURE 11.6 Consultant promotional piece. Courtesy Donna Halper and Associates.

About the future of radio consultancy, George Burns says, "I see the role of consultants undergoing considerable change in the next few years. The rules of ownership and the very principles under which our industry is organized are altering radically. Consultants will probably take even more of an advisory role and have less involvement in the day-to-day operations of a station. The new and larger broadcasting companies, in all size markets, will keep expertise in-house and rely less on outside input in these areas. I see consultants operating at 'higher levels' in the future. They will be working on organization, continuing education, motivation, compensation, human resources, and other 'top management' concerns. Consultants, I believe, will become more policy oriented and less concerned with ground level activities."

Program Suppliers

The widespread use of automation equipment commencing in the 1960s sparked significant growth in the field of programming syndication. Initially, the installation of automation systems motivated station management to seek out syndicator services. Today, the highly successful and sophisticated program formats offered by myriad syndicators often inspires stations to invest in automation equipment. Of course, many of the large radio corporations create programming for distribution to their own stations, and this has had an effect on the number of program suppliers still in operation. Observes Jay Williams, "The syndication business has changed because of consolidation, which reduced the opportunities for selling programs by syndication companies on the one hand and on the other made the larger companies aware that they should be syndicating programs on their own. I think some of the most innovative syndication is being done now by News Corp, which has taken their TV personalities, most recently 'Brian and the Judge,' who have individually made a name for themselves on the Fox News Channel, and developed new radio programs for them (even though they don't actually appear together on television). Formats like Adult Contemporary (where product is becoming more generic and less innovative) are declining in numbers across the country, whereas the numbers of News/Talk and Sports stations are increasing, so there are opportunities for syndicating talk programming. Short form programming syndication appears to have very limited appeal. On the other hand, long form program syndication, which can garner ratings over time, appears to be increasing. Finally, advertisers believe ads work better in talk programming since they blend with the format and the spot clusters don't have to be as long."

It is estimated that over half of the country's radio outlets purchase syndicated programming of some type, which may consist of as little as a series of one- or two-minute features or as much as a 24-hour, year-round station format. Longtime program specialist Dick Ellis cites economics as the primary reason why stations resort to syndicators. "When I programmed for Peters Productions they supplied high-quality programming and engineering at a relatively low cost. For instance, for a few hundred dollars a month a small market operator gets a successful program director, a highly skilled mastering engineer, all the music he'll ever need (no service problems with record companies) recorded on the highest quality tapes available. It takes a programmer eight hours to program one twenty-four-hour cut reel. It takes a mastering engineer eight hours to remove all the pops and clicks found on even brand new records, plus place the automation tones. All of this frees the local operator to concentrate his efforts on promotion and, of course, sales."

William Stockman, who led Schulke Radio Productions (SRP was purchased by Bonneville Broadcasting System in the mid-1980s), says that stations are attracted to syndicators because of the highly professional, major market sound they are able to provide. "By using SRP's unique programming service, a smaller station with limited resources can sound as polished and sophisticated as any metro station."

Both economics and service motivate radio stations to contract syndicators, contends former Satellite Music Network (now part of ABC Radio) programmer Lee Abrams (now heading the programming effort of XM Satellite). "Stations are attracted to our affordable, high-quality programming. It's just that simple. Syndies provided an excellent product within a cost-effective context. Their expertise in delivering niche concepts was very appealing to radio operators."

The late and great Rick Sklar observed, "In today's cost-conscious economic climate, more and more radio station operators are turning to suppliers of twenty-four-hour formats for their programming. Whether delivered via satellite, conventional tape, CD or DAT, these increasingly sophisticated

```
Pro's and con's of using a consultant:

     +'s                              -'s

* Objective, experienced view    * Overreliance on consultant
* Exposure to new ideas            and not enough local input
* Ongoing evaluation of the      * Program director gets too
  station                          much advice from too many
* Input about stations from        sources
  around the country
* National research and information
* Experience/assistance in a wide
  range of areas including music,
  promotion, marketing, talent
  management, etc.
```

FIGURE 11.7
Courtesy Jacobs Media.

products are not only penetrating new markets but larger markets as well, where until now, traditional thinking has held that locally originated programming was the only way to go."

The demand for syndicator product has paralleled, if not exceeded, the increase in the number of radio outlets since the 1960s. Again, the new millennium has brought a change in the field of program syndication with the large radio corporations often assuming the chore of program generation in-house.

Every part of the broadcast day is served by syndicators, and morning drive in particular, observes Ed Shane. "Syndicated morning shows are widespread and proliferating. There are almost too many to keep track of. At a quick glance, you've got Bob and Sheri, John Boy and Billy, Bob and Tom, Mark and Brian, Steve and DC, Big D and Bubba, Mancow, Opie & Anthony, and on and on."

Syndicator Services

The major program syndicators usually market several distinctive, fully packaged radio formats. "In its heyday, Peters Productions made available a complete format service with each of their format blends. They were not merely a music service. Their programming goal was the emotional gratification of the type of person attracted to a particular format," says Dick Ellis, whose former company offered a dozen different formats, including Beautiful Music, Easy Listening, Standard Country, Modern

Country, Adult Contemporary, Standard MOR, Super Hits, Easy Contemporary, and a country and contemporary hybrid called Natural Sound.

Century 21 Programming also was a leader in format diversity, explains Dave Scott. "Our inventory included everything from the most contemporary super hits sound to several Christian formats. We even offered a full-time Jazz format. We had programming to fit any need in any market."

Drake-Chenault Enterprises (now owned by Jones Satellite Networks) was among the oldest and largest of syndicators and specialized in Beautiful Music. Today, Classical Music Network, TM Century, Jones Satellite Network, Westwood One, United Station Radio Network, and NBG Radio Networks also are among the most successful of those syndicators marketing several program formats. Some syndicators prefer to specialize in one or two programming areas. For example, Bonneville Broadcasting and Churchill Productions primarily specialize in the adult Easy Listening format.

Syndicator formats are fully tested before they are marketed, explains Stockman. "At Schulke our strategy was to reorient the music from essentially a producer-oriented to a consumer-oriented product. Music was tested on a cut-by-cut basis in several markets coast-to-coast. Using patented and proven methodology, music was carefully added or selectively deleted. By determining what songs the listeners like to hear and which songs they dislike, SRP assembled a totally researched library that has been on the air via our subscriber stations since March 1983. Every song played on our stations has been rated by the listeners as a 'winner' and all the 'stiffs' that have a high dislike factor have been eliminated altogether."

Customized sound hours are designed for each format to ensure consistency and compatibility on the local station level. "An exact clock is tailored for our client station after our market study. The format we provide will perfectly match the station in tempo, style, music mix, announcing, promos, news, weather, and commercial load," says program syndicator

Dave Scott. Observes Ed Shane, "The key to using syndicator or network programming is to make it sound like it belongs to the station. Even big personality shows like Rush and Dr. Laura can make use of local avails and bumpers for personalized call letters and promos."

Audience and market research and analysis are conducted by syndicators before implementing a particular format. "Our clients receive comprehensive consulting services from our seasoned staff. We begin with a detailed study of our client station's market. We probe demographics, psychographics, and population growth trends of a station's available audience. We analyze a client's competition quantitatively through available ratings and qualitatively from airchecks. Then the programming our service provides is professionally positioned to maximize our client's sales, ratings, and profits. All of our programming is solidly backed by systematic studies of the listening tastes of each format's target audience. Our research includes call-out and focus group studies, in-depth market analysis, attitudinal audience feedback, psychographic patterns and tests, and several in-house computers with ratings data online," says Dave Scott.

Format programming packages include hundreds of hours of music, as well as breaks, promos, and IDs, by seasoned metro market announcers. Customized identity elements, such as jingles and other special formatic features (taped time checks), are made available by the majority of syndicators. "We try to cover all bases to ensure the success of our clients. We back each of our formats a dozen different ways. For example, image builders in the form of promotions, contests, and graphics also are an element of our programming service at Radio Arts," says programmer Larry Vanderveen.

To stay in step with the ever-changing marketplace, syndicators routinely update the programming they provide their subscribers. "When you want people to listen to a station a lot, you've got to keep them interested in it. To do so you have to air a sound that's always fresh and current. Tape updates are plentiful. We give stations the most extensive initial collection

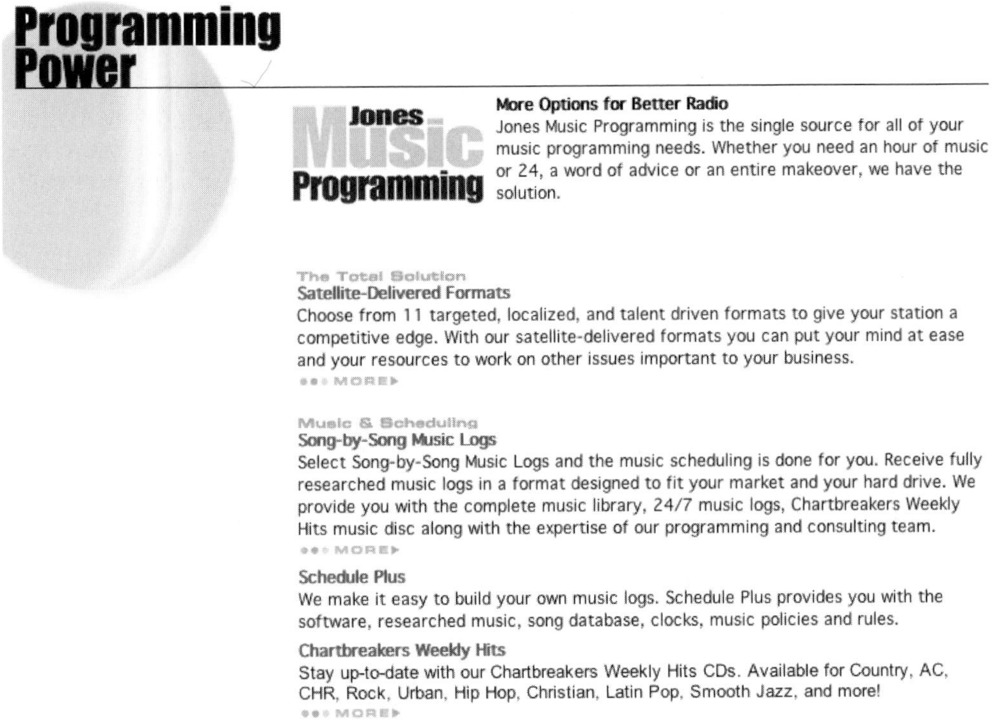

Programming Power

Jones Music Programming

More Options for Better Radio
Jones Music Programming is the single source for all of your music programming needs. Whether you need an hour of music or 24, a word of advice or an entire makeover, we have the solution.

The Total Solution
Satellite-Delivered Formats
Choose from 11 targeted, localized, and talent driven formats to give your station a competitive edge. With our satellite-delivered formats you can put your mind at ease and your resources to work on other issues important to your business.
●●● MORE▶

Music & Scheduling
Song-by-Song Music Logs
Select Song-by-Song Music Logs and the music scheduling is done for you. Receive fully researched music logs in a format designed to fit your market and your hard drive. We provide you with the complete music library, 24/7 music logs, Chartbreakers Weekly Hits music disc along with the expertise of our programming and consulting team.
●●● MORE▶

Schedule Plus
We make it easy to build your own music logs. Schedule Plus provides you with the software, researched music, song database, clocks, music policies and rules.

Chartbreakers Weekly Hits
Stay up-to-date with our Chartbreakers Weekly Hits CDs. Available for Country, AC, CHR, Rock, Urban, Hip Hop, Christian, Latin Pop, Smooth Jazz, and more!
●●● MORE▶

FIGURE 11.8
"Full-service syndicators for every programming need. Courtesy Jones Radio Networks."

of music tapes available. Then we follow them up with hundreds more throughout the year. For instance, our CHR, AOR, and Country subscribers receive over 100 updates annually. All categories have frequent updates, so our client's sound stays fresh and vital," says Dave Scott, who adds that the lines of communication are kept open between the client and syndicator long after the agreement has been signed. "Since the success of our clients is very important to us, continuing consultation and assistance via a toll-free hotline is always available twenty-four hours a day. Automation-experienced broadcasters are in our production studios around the clock, and consultants can be reached at work or home any time. Help is as close as the phone."

Syndicators assist stations during the installation and implementation stage of a format and provide training for operators and other station personnel. Comprehensive operations manuals are left with subscribers as a source of further assistance.

Syndicators offer programs on a barter basis, for a fee without presold spots or for a fee containing spots. Leasing agreements generally stipulate a minimum 2-year term and assure the subscriber that the syndicator will not lease a similar format to another station in the same market. Should a station choose not to renew its agreement with the syndicator, all material must be returned unless otherwise stipulated.

The majority of format syndicators also market production libraries, jingles, and special features for general market consumption.

What is the difference between a network and a syndicator? Ed Shane explains, "Networks and syndicators are essentially or almost the same. Premiere calls Rush Limbaugh a 'network' and Dr. Laura a 'syndicated show.' United Stations Radio Network works the same way. (It has more to do with the way spots are sold than the realities of programming.) Westwood One is more of a network, combining CBS News, CNN Radio, long form music programs, Metro Traffic and News with syndicated programming like country music specials. ESPN is networked for all talk shows and live sports (NFL football play-by-play, for example) by ABC."

FIGURE 11.9
Century 21s catalog
of syndicated
formats in the 1990s.
Courtesy Century 21.

Chris Witting's
Syndication.net

Home Page
Latest News
Syndicate Now!
Our Shows
Products
The Database
Suggest a Link
Grow Your Show
About Us
Site Map

Syndication.net Shows List

Here are just some of the shows we represent. Click on an image to learn more.

Sign up for our FREE Syndication E-mail Newsletter!

Your E-Mail Address:

Go!
Unsubscribe Info

Billy Bush

Interviewed by Jay Williams Syndication

FIGURE 11.10
Billy Bush.

Jay Williams – Billy, although you're best known as a TV star, you began your career in radio. What attracted you to radio?

Billy Bush – The intimacy of radio. I got to talk with people in a one-on-one conversation and that was extremely cool and it still is.

JW – What kinds of jobs did you have in radio, and which were the most rewarding for you?

BB – I had the luxury of starting in a small market where I had every job. I was a sales guy during the day, and boy is that a humbling experience, and I was on the air one night a week, and on the weekends I did promotions. I pumped up the station balloon and I handed out hundreds of fliers. There is not a job in radio I have not done outside of management, and I never want to do that.

JW – With "Access Hollywood" and your syndicated "Billy Bush Show," you shift from one medium to the other every day. Is that difficult? Also, what are the major differences as a performer between the two mediums?

BB – In radio, the greatest preparation is just knowledge. It's just

knowing what you're talking about. It's about drawing on life experiences. In TV, you have a lot of people helping you. You've got a lot of people preparing and editing and all that. In radio, you need to be your own research department. So radio's a lot more difficult.

JW – Tell us about radio. What makes radio unique in your view?

BB – The car, because the car is a unique environment, and radio will always be the easiest and best choice for people. People who are texting and using the Internet in their car are very few and far between. The automobile is ideal for radio and that single invention years ago is what makes radio unique, and it's what will insure that radio will be there forever.

JW – As we are talking, radio is going through technological changes, facing new competition and economic distress. Yet, your well-received syndicated show is rapidly expanding across the country. How do you see radio's future?

BB – Radio's future is secure because of the car. I said that. But my syndicated show is a great answer for people who are facing economic problems because it's cost effective. I don't cost them anything. They just have to give me some inventory. They give me 4 minutes an hour, and that's it. So it's an opportunity cost and not an actual outlay of cash.

JW – Syndication seems to be growing, too. From the old network programs such as Paul Harvey news to later off-network radio syndication, such as Howard Stern, Bob and Tom, Rush Limbaugh, more stations seem to be embracing syndication. Do you see that as a growing trend and why?

BB – Yes, because syndication makes sense. If you have great talent and content, then you're just giving up time. If the ratings are big, then you'll be able to charge more for the commercials that you do get revenue for. So it's all about choosing the right talent, the biggest will survive and I believe we are in that direction.

JW – Your show is marketed by Westwood One, one of the largest syndication companies. Tell us about your role verses theirs, how much are you personally involved, and how much control do you have over your own show?

BB – I have entire control over editorial, what I put out there is what goes on the air. In that regard it's great. I'm very personally involved and I control all the content. As for the sales and marketing of the show, I weigh in whenever I want to, but we agree between Westwood and me. If I feel strongly about anything, I'm confident my voice is heard and I'll usually prevail because at the end of the day the talent has to be happy to provide. However, having done every job in radio, I have total respect for the people who do things outside of what I do, and I'm totally open to whatever they have to say.

JW – It must be demanding preparing and voicing a new show every day. Who and what does it take to produce your show?

BB – I have a broadcast producer, Michelle Salvatore, who takes in all my content and who arranges and organizes our schedule and lays out what the show is going to be each day. I have five bookers who book guests for me on the radio show. I book a lot myself because my BlackBerry has gotten pretty deep over the years. We have three editors on the other side of things who package the show at the end of the day. We are spread out perfectly.

JW – You are heavily involved with getting new station clients. Tell us a bit about how that process works.

BB – Everything is sales in life, and each client, each station I'm on needs to feel that if they need to get in touch with me they can. The truth is, they can. Anyone can call and set up a time to talk on the phone through Michelle or anybody else or my assistant, Marla, and I will talk to any station clients. There are walls because it makes it easier for everyone, but if someone needs to weigh in with me, they can.

JW – "The Billy Bush Show" competes with locally produced shows in many markets. How do you react to objections from potential clients that your show "won't work in this market because it isn't local"?

BB – Entertainment is everywhere. There is an insatiability for celebrity content. What I do is provide an everyman's perspective to it. I tell people about what it's like behind the scenes. I make it personally relatable for them because they hear someone they trust and listen to and connect with deal with celebrities in these situations and they love it. Also I'm honest; I tell it like it is. If someone is difficult, I share that.

JW – How do you position your show against other syndicated shows? What makes "The Billy Bush Show" unique or better?

BB – My main competition, I think, is probably Ryan Seacrest, although there are others. I'm not positive how Ryan does his show, but I do believe there's a lot of people taking his existing content and putting it out there. What I do is a totally new and original show for my stations every single day. A lot

of syndicated shows are packaged. They do three, four, or five shows at a time. I do a new show every day with new analysis, new insights, and new guests.

JW – Do you think more radio stations will embrace syndicated shows because it gives them access to better on-air talent than they can find locally or because, in some cases, syndicated shows may save them money?

BB – The answer is a little bit of both, absolutely. The best on-air talent will survive and grow, and those particular people will continue to survive. The better known you are, the better chance you have out of the gate. Although that doesn't mean local people can't rise to that level. And yes, my show saves a lot of money for stations because they're not paying me. They're giving me commercial time and if my ratings are good, they're going to get more money for the commercial time that they do have left.

JW – Does syndication help or hurt radio?

BB – I think syndication helps radio because you want to have big names in your field. You want to be as relevant and taken as seriously as everyone else. The bigger stars you have on radio, I think, the higher the profile of radio but the trap is – and I hope radio stations don't fall into it – to go for the biggest name you can get just because of the name. At the end of the day, they have to deliver, they have to work, they have to have that strong ethic. And the biggest radio names are really hardworking people.

JW – You're a big TV star, you travel the world to do pageants, events, even the Olympics, and you certainly don't need extra work. So why did you launch "The Billy Bush Show" and get back into radio?

BB – Because I love radio, and because radio gives me the opportunity to expand upon my thoughts. It gives me a chance to walk a tightrope without a net. I love being able to express my opinions. I know Hollywood and understand it very well and I have an insider's perspective, and I love being able to share that with people.

Hardware Requirements and Quality

FIGURE 11.11
Sample customized
sound hour. Courtesy
Century 21.

Everything is computer-based now, and the use of satellites by syndicators has grown enormously since 1980. An NAB survey concluded that over three-quarters of the nation's stations receive some form of satellite programming. The majority of stations with satellite dishes use them to draw network feeds. However, the percentage of stations receiving product from syndicators and other programming services has more than doubled during the past couple of decades, and the use of station hardware (other than computers) for syndicator programming is nearly extinct. It is more cost effective and efficient to catch the digital satellite signals than it is to handle actual product on the local station level. In fact, the majority of program syndicators have ceased to mail material to stations, opting to beam it to them instead.

Satellite-fed syndicator programs are often archived for later replay. Drew Carey of Clear Channel Communications discusses the procedure for doing so for one of his company's shows: "The Bob & Tom Show is designed to air in its entirety for the full four hours as sent with no editing. Stations in the Central, Mountain, and Pacific time zones run the show either at 5 to 9 A.M. or 6 to 10 P.M. depending upon their competitive situation. Stations use one of three methods to delay broadcast of the show: 1. Station automation systems (record to system, such as Audio Vault, then replay automatically), 2. Record to DAT then replay (requires the station be staffed overnight and during playback), and

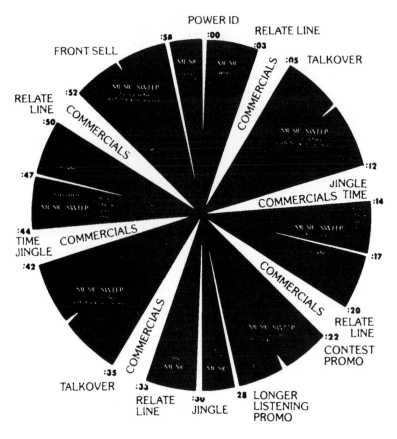

FIGURE 11.12
Satellite program
services. Courtesy
WFMT.

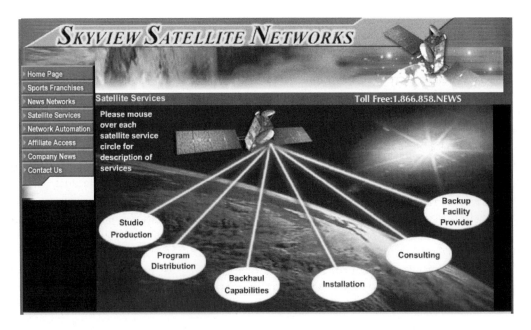

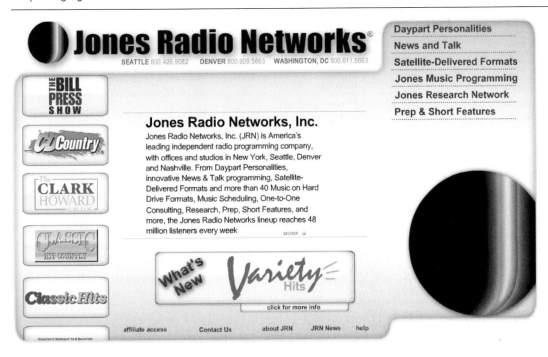

3. Record to mini-disc the replay (requires the station be staffed overnight and during playback)."

Concerning audio quality, syndicators are very particular about sound quality and make every effort to ensure that their programming meets or exceeds fidelity standards. "TM Century uses the finest quality recording studio equipment. Actually, it's far superior to most broadcast-grade gear. Therefore, it is quite important that subscribers have adequate hardware, too. We utilize a number of highly regarded audio experts to make the sound and the client's are the very best possible. In fact, we use special audiophile 'super disks,' master tapes from record companies, noise reduction, click editing, and precise level control or slight equalization, if needed," says Scott.

Periodic airchecks of subscriber stations are analyzed from a technical perspective to detect any deficiencies in sound quality.

CHAPTER HIGHLIGHTS

1. The significant increase in stations and formats created a market for consultants. Today, the ranks of radio consultants has been reduced due to consolidation and major radio companies typically have their own in-house consultant in the form of an experienced programming executive.

2. Consultants provide various services, including market research, programming and format design, hiring and training of staff, staff motivation, advertising and public relations campaigns, news and public affairs restructuring, and technical evaluation (periodic airchecks of sound quality).

3. Aspiring consultants should acquire background experience in the medium, solid educational preparation, and strong interpersonal skills.

4. Station executives opposed to using consultants fear losing the station's local flavor, becoming a clone of other stations, and the substantial cost.

5. Statistically, stations using programming consultants more often than not experience improved ratings.

6. Increased use of programming syndication is related to the increased use of computers and satellites. Most of the nation's stations purchase some form of syndicated programming.

7. Syndicated programs are generally cost effective, of high quality, and reliable, thus allowing smaller stations to achieve a metro station sound.

8. Program syndicators provide a variety of test-marketed, packaged radio formats—from Country to Top 40 to Religious. Packages may include music, breaks, promos, customized IDs, and even promotions. Package updates are frequent.

9. Networks and syndicators are essentially one and the same.

10. The number of syndicators using satellites to deliver programming is at an all-time high. Many deliver programming only via satellite.

SUGGESTED FURTHER READING

Broadcasting Yearbook, Broadcast Publishing, Washington, DC, 1935 to date, annually.

Crouch, S., *No Static: A Guide to Creative Radio Programming*. Backbeat Books, San Francisco, CA, 2002.

Deweese, S.B., *Radio Syndication: How to Create, Produce, and Distribute Your Own Show*, Elfin Cove Press, Bellevue, WA, 2001.

Fornatale, P., and Mills, J., *Radio in the Television Age*, Overlook Press, Woodstock, NY, 1980.

Geller, V., *Creating Powerful Radio*, Focal Press, Boston, MA, 2007.

Hall, C., and Hall, B., *This Business of Radio Programming*, Billboard Publishing, New York, 1977.

Howard, H.H., and Kievman, M.S., *Radio and Television Programming*, Grid Publishing, Columbus, OH, 1983.

Inglis, A.F., *Satellite Technology*, Focal Press, Boston, MA, 1991.

Keith, M.C., *Radio Programming: Consultancy and Formatics*, Focal Press, Boston, MA, 1987.

Kempner, M.A., *Can't Wait Til Monday Morning: Syndication in Broadcasting*, Rivercross Publishing, Orlando, FL, 1998.

Mirabito, M.M., and Morgenstern, B.L., *New Communication Technologies: Applications, Policy, and Impact*, 4th edition, Focal Press, Boston, MA, 2000.

The Radio Programs Sourcebook, 2nd edition, Broadcast Information Bureau, Syosset, NY, 1983.

Series, Serials, and Packages, Broadcast Information Bureau, Syosset, NY, annually.

Shane, E., *Selling Electronic Media*, Focal Press, Boston, MA, 1999.

Vane, E.T., and Gross, L.S., *Programming for TV, Radio, and Cable*, Focal Press, Boston, MA, 1994.

Wasserman, P., *Consultants and Consulting Organization Directory*, 3rd edition, Gale Research, Detroit, MI, 1976.

To: GM/BRadio
Fr: Donna L. Halper, Halper & Associates
Re: Critique of tapes of B

Thanks for sending along the latest batch of tapes for me to critique. I do hear some improvements since I last visited the station. On the other hand, I am still hearing some areas that we need to work on. Most of what I noticed are problems with formatics, although a few little things stood out. In no particular order,

1. Bet is back to being too close to the mic, causing her to pop her *P*s again. The good news is that on this tape, her voice is now VERY midrange – and not high-end or "cutesy," and she sounds more natural. The bad news is that she seems determined to use verbal clichés (however, she is not the only one with this habit). For example, when she reads the liner about "playing the music that made FM great," she repeatedly says "and here's another great example" when she introduces the next song. She is also trying too hard to make simple format elements sound enthusiastic: the school lunch menu basically just needs to be read, rather than embellished upon for two minutes. I know she is *trying*, but it just sounds artificial to get *that* excited about school lunches. The entire staff seems stuck on the phrases *keep it locked* and *music from* . . . ("that was music from the Beatles; now here's music from Steely Dan"). In real life, do we really talk

FIGURE 11.14
Many syndicators use satellites to feed programming to client stations. This greatly simplifies the distribution process. Handling of tapes and mailing is eliminated. Satellite syndication also keeps station equipment costs down. Courtesy IDB.

that way, or do we talk about great SONGS, or use phrases like "a classic from. . . . " We need to VARY what we say, or else we sound like robots. Thus, if I just said "Now, here's a classic from Bob Dylan," I don't want to use that phrase for every front-sell. Ditto for "keep it locked" – it's a rather overused AOR phrase as it is, but boy, do our jocks say it a lot . . . can't we find some other ways to invite people to listen?

2. Virtually everyone seems to have acute lineritis. It's a disease where you want to read a lot of liners all at once. I heard "the all-new

FIGURE 11.15
Satellite Music Network program clock. Courtesy SMN.

B-, the station that plays the classic hits and the music that made FM great!!!" ONE LINER PER BREAK IS JUST FINE, THANKS. If we just used "the all-new B-" or "your station for Classic Hits," we don't need to add in two more liners. A good front-sell might be as simple as "on the home of classic hits, B-, here's Cat Stevens." Or "playing the music that made FM great, we're B-, with Fleetwood Mac." Simple is better, in other words.

3. How much weather do we need in middays? During morning drive, the announcer should give time, temp, and say good morning to the audience each break; that isn't necessary the rest of the day. Unless there are major storms coming, I wouldn't have so many

FIGURE 11.16
Syndicator features provide stations with the seasoning to keep programming interesting. Courtesy Shane Media.

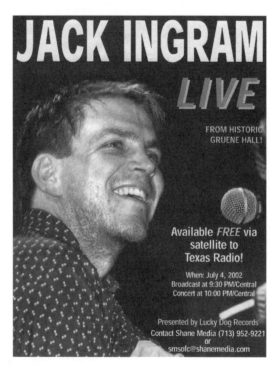

FIGURE 11.17
Syndicators are especially sensitive to quality control. Here, a commercial CD is enhanced by a syndicator's computer prior to shipment to a client. Courtesy Century 21.

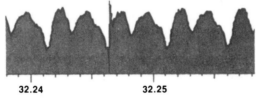

Waveform of commercial CD with clicks and tape hiss.

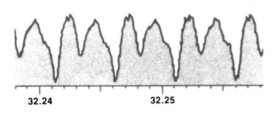

weather forecasts during the workday – folks already got there, the kids are in school, etc. But we should still be friendly: I seldom heard Dave say his name (I assume it was Dave?), and I like a liner that thanks people for listening or invites them to tell a friend about the All-New B-.

4. Although I agree that call letters are crucial, I heard them used way too much at some times: It is not conversational to say "on the all- new B-, here's Bob Seger on the all-new B-." That just sounds repetitious. My training has been to use call letters going into a song and use them when coming out of a long music set ("That was Traffic on the All-New B-, and we also heard Joan Baez and Dan Fogelberg.") But to use them two or three times within the same front-sell strikes me as too much of a good thing. Also, I'm hearing B- a lot more than I'm hearing Classic Hits. And a final grammatical note – you CAN'T say "the classic hits of all time" – you can play the greatest hits, but *classic hits* are a format description and a positioning statement. I'd suggest "playing ALL the classic hits" or "playing nothing but classic hits" or "playing the classic hits of the past and the classic hits of today" – you get the idea.

5. More clichés – why is Wednesday called *hump day*? Again, do we really talk that way? And in several of the forecasts I heard various people do, I heard about *scattered rain* – I knew that showers could be scattered, but rain? I remind everyone to keep being CONVERSATIONAL – how would you talk to a FRIEND? Would you really say "It's 52 minutes past the hour of 6 o'clock"? I also like consistency – some jocks, as mentioned earlier, said their name often, some said it repeatedly, some seldom said it at all. Some used one liner over and over, some used a variety. These elements must be formatted in so that all the liners are rotated evenly. Also, I'm not sure if it was the skimmer, but I heard some problems with levels when a song ended. The jock's voice sounded much louder or much softer than the song at certain times. A request – could you tape an hour of each jock and NOT scope it down – in other words, just put a tape in a boom-box and let it run, so that I can hear an uninterrupted hour, commercials and all? I'd like to hear what the audience heard.

More critique later – I'll go over the music in more detail in my next memo. What I heard sounded basically hit-oriented, which is good, but let's stress CLASSIC HITS too, because we are getting to a point where the variety of the music is right on target! I'll be in touch.

P.S. I meant to mention that the PSA or Street-Sheet outro may be too long, although it may also be the jock ad-libbing. The ending of a PSA should be brief and to the point. What I heard was over a MINUTE of numbers and advice – "If your church, social club, or nonprofit organization has a message you want to be publicized, just send the who-what-when-where-how-and-why, etc." – boy, that's wordy!!! It's better to be simple, without tons of addresses and phone numbers. You are wiser to advise those with something to send to call B- for our fax number, rather than taking up so much time telling them they can phone it or fax it or mail it, then giving the address on top of everything. This slows the station down too much. It also goes without saying that the way something is sent to us on a press release may not sound good read verbatim on the air. What *I* heard B- reading sounded as if we had just put the press release right into the studio with no rewrite. Local news and local PSAs should be rewritten for clarity, and it helps that they be conversational. (I would also like to hear our local news, by the way, plus how Chris sounds.) Perhaps the announcers were nervous because they were doing an aircheck, but they do need to become accustomed to taping themselves regularly so that they can eliminate the verbal crutches they use and make their show sound smoother.

FIGURE 11.18
This interview with Ron Hartenbaum was conducted by Jay Williams, Jr. Courtesy same.

Interview with: Ron Hartenbaum, CEO, Jones Radio Networks (New York)

Difference between network and syndication? "You can't separate them, there is no difference. It's a fallacy to think there is; the same thing is happening" with network and syndication. In the old model, the Federal Communications Commission (FCC) used to separate networks as they distributed programming regularly using dedicated telephone lines (and that distribution method was how a network was described). That was done throughout the 30s, 40s, and 50s. "That's an ancient way of distribution, with bad fidelity, and no longer applies. Now network-syndication programming is distributed in a variety of ways . . . CD, the Internet, wired and wireless, satellite . . . it's based on which method is the most 'cost effective' for them."

"There is no difference between syndication and network – it's all national programming. A Matchbox 20 Concert or a Tony Bennett special for the Thanksgiving Weekend might be distributed by CD, as there is not an urgent time constraint. Breaking news, though, wouldn't go out on CD. You would use the distribution method that is best and most cost efficient for the product you're sending out. If it's live, immediate, and interactive (with phone calls) such as Rush Limbaugh, it's delivered via satellite; if it's not time sensitive, it may be mailed out on CD. But it's all national radio."

"It's all audio. It's how do we deliver a signal to as many ears as we can. How do we deliver an audience to an advertiser." And the trend is to deliver increasingly specific audiences that can appeal to specific types of advertisers. "National radio and network radio are the same."

Even the old radio networks have changed, although they retain part of their names. CBS/Viacom Radio is now handled by Westwood One, itself a division of Viacom. The GE/NBC Network is also distributed by Viacom. ABC/Disney is still the ABC Radio Network.

Current Example. Jones Radio works with the CNN Radio Network "en Espanol." CNN creates the news, but Jones Radio Network handles all the advertising and all the affiliate sales. Programming is delivered on the Internet. And using the special client feature, in a special password protected part of the Web site – called Ala Carta – stations can pick the items and information that best suits their specific mix of Hispanics in their individual communities. For example, New York might want programming for Puerto Rican and Cuban Hispanics that would not be needed in Los Angeles where most of the population consists of Mexican and Central American Hispanics. This distribution flexibility and choice are both the present and future of syndication.

National radio revenues are over $1 billion annually. There are only four major companies: Westwood One (the largest with almost half that revenue), ABC, Premier, and Jones; there once were over a dozen.

"But how do you look at Sirius and XM? These are national radio stations just using a different model." In other words, people looking to buy national radio would include these two satellite radio systems in their plans.

Ron also believes that "streaming media" could have been part of national radio but was killed by the "greed of music publishing and actor's union's rights fees. Internet radio was economically squashed before it could get started – everybody ended up losing."

The future: There probably won't be much more consolidation and there could even be more producers and distributors of content in the future.

FIGURE 11.18
Continued

The distribution model is always changing. Ron used the example of mail . . . moving from horseback to rail, truck, airplanes, and the Internet. But it's still mail.

He suggests that a triangle is the best way to show the business model. At the top is product/program/content. At the lower left corner is the audience/circulation/distribution. At the lower right side is generation of ad sales revenue. If you make a good product (program) then "people will want it," they'll want to listen to it or watch it. If they watch, you can generate ad sales revenue (and then, "if you're smart, you'll put some of that revenue back into the product"). Jones is in all three parts of this model – programming, distribution and sales. Ron adds: "You learn in business school that if you're standing still, you're losing. You have to constantly evolve your product and your product lines" and that means you have to invest in them.

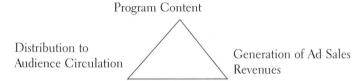

Program Content

Distribution to
Audience Circulation

Generation of Ad Sales
Revenues

Ron also believes that there are only three ways that programming/content is being distributed: Pay/subscription, Ad supported, or a blend of the two. "Someone has to make money. There are costs to generate news and to develop music programming."

[He has this analogy for college students who think music is free and should remain that way – "What if you went to college, went to all the classes, took all the tests, wrote all the papers, and handed in the work and didn't get a grade? "Where's my grade?" you'd say; we'd say that we've downloaded all your information on the Internet and we don't need to give you a grade."]

[We also discussed news programming and Ron gave some thoughts you may want to use in a separate section. There is increasing pressure on these big companies to eliminate money-losing divisions. Either you amortize your costs over a variety of channels and outlets (as NBC) or you look to mergers to be able to reduce those costs (ABC's talks with CNN). Rupert Murdoch was one of the first to work with a "global platform" and "by having papers and networks all over the world, he doesn't have to open a foreign bureau, he's already there. A Fox News anchor can get information from a New York *Post* reporter in New York or a co-owned newspaper in Sydney in seconds. You must either get more customers for your programming or reduce your costs."]

Interview with Tom Griswold, of the Bob & Tom Show, Indianapolis "Quotations" are from Tom Griswold

Show is delivered to 125 stations nationwide via satellite.

It's distributed by Premier Radio Network (owned by Clear Channel).

Interesting note . . . Premier used to have separate salespeople for certain shows and they are now moving to a model where all the sales people will sell all the shows.

Shows are fed live from 6:00 to 10:00 A.M. Eastern time . . . with three 6 minute breaks per hour for local programming (commercials, news updates, etc). Some stations, mostly in the Mountain States or on the West Coast, will tape delay the broadcast to fit their morning time slots.

Bob and Tom try to entertain . . . and don't focus on their local area at all. "If you listen to the show, you wouldn't know where we were here" (Indianapolis). Tom doesn't think syndicated shows like Bob and Tom will replace local shows but believes "there will be a mix of local and syndicated shows. There is still a big demand for a lot of local content."

"We tip-toed into it (syndication) starting out with three affiliates. But the show took off quickly. One magazine had voted us as one of the 'most stolen-from radio shows in America,' and it was great to be able to get our show out there."

Preparing for a show. "There's at least one aspect that's easier. If you make a comment about a local institution, it could cost your station billings from some advertiser who gets upset. But when you're getting material from all over the nation, rarely do you get negative feedback. And there's a lot more ammo to choose from nationally – you don't have to rely on what happened at the local school board."

Live is very important. "I could listen to tapes or CD's, but I listen to radio just to keep in touch."

XM and Sirius – "both of them will make it" . . . maybe not with the same stockholders, but they will be able to produce great shows and have great talent. These national satellite radio networks "are delivering variety with low commercial loads; local radio stations have lots of commercials and all sound the same. XM even went after Howard Stern – they know the next step is to get great talent on the air." John considers satellite radio, national radio, or syndicated radio, just in a slightly different form.

APPENDIX 11D: Syndication

Interview with John H. Garabedian

Radio and TV entrepreneur, former president of Superadio Networks, and current host of "Open House Party." John also started V66 in Boston, probably the first music video television station.
"Quotation marks" are from John Garabedian

Much of the live programming is done using C-Band satellite distribution (vs. the less reliable KU satellite systems). The costs of satellite distribution keeps coming down and a satellite uplink only costs about $150,000, so programming can come from almost anywhere.

Hundreds of successful programs are distributed nationally . . . including Delilah, Paul Harvey news, Rush Limbaugh, and Howard Stern. It's over a $1 billion business.

John says there's not much difference between network radio and syndication but suggests the difference is that Network programs are rated by RADAR, a national service (now owned by Arbitron) that produces ratings for radio network programming. He says that other than that, there is really no difference.

He says that Superadio, now owned by Access One Communications (also owners of American Urban Radio Network and individual radio stations), sends out over 5000 CDs a week!

John believes that "live and local shows" are overrated in radio.

"Everyone in radio thinks you have to have a local morning show to win. That radio is local. That's wrong. Don't waste your time with the 'Bob and Debbie' show. The people who control radio in the future will be the people who have the talent . . . " "Howard Stern died for our (syndicators') sins. He said, 'Don't put on local shows – just put on the Howard Stern Show and you'll be #1,' and he was right."

The goal of the big radio groups is "to control all their own programming. There will be more centrally programmed live shows." If they don't do it nationally, they'll probably start doing it regionally. "They can take the best talent from all of their classic rock stations and make one really great radio station" that people will really want to listen to and save a fortune in costs in the process. "And local PD's won't screw up making bad music decisions." All programming, he believes, will become more national.

FIGURE 11.20
This interview with John H. Garabedian was conducted by Jay Williams, Jr. Courtesy same.

327

Afterword

Jay Williams, Jr.

The cliché, "The future's just not what it used to be," applied to radio, is also true. The radio industry is experiencing wrenching structural upheaval, sea changes in operating philosophies, painful personnel layoffs, plunging revenues and business valuations, and uncertainty about its future. But this 85-year-old medium has been counted out before, and it came back stronger than ever.

Two Breathtaking Inventions

Radio, Marconi's invention that magically reproduced sound from thin air, was an instant success. From the early

The Future of Radio

1920s, families gathered around the large consoles to hear drama, news, orchestras, and FDR's "Fireside Chats." Late into the night, kids listened to stations from far-away cities, mesmerized by the mysterious glowing tubes that created the staticky sound. Television arrived to a war-weary country in the 1950s, and TV's explosive impact cannot be overstated! TV was radio with pictures. Universally loved radio stars like Jack Benny jumped to this new medium, and experts predicted radio's demise. But radio adapted and innovated, dropping network dramas for live news, personalities, and music. Programming innovations, coinciding with the rise of rock 'n' roll music and the invention of inexpensive, portable battery-powered transistor radios, gave radio a new life and future.

Technology Changed Consumer Expectations

In the early 70s, another invention upended the very concept of broadcasting. Before the VCR, families had to watch the "Carol Burnett Show" at 8 P.M. on Wednesday, or miss it entirely. The VCR changed how media was used by transforming "real time" into "my time." The VCR marked the beginning of a new era of consumer

control of media. Another 20 years later, computer and digital technology spawned a tsunami of innovations that have changed the media landscape completely.

Digital technology has transformed the way we live and work, propelled by systems and devices only dreamed of a few years ago. Once meaningless letter and alphanumeric combinations such as MP3, DVD, iPod, PDA, Ti-Vo, SMS, and GPS are now digital necessities. The fierce battle to supply consumers with entertainment, information, and communication options is having its impact on all media, including radio. One battle for the keys into the consumers' homes is evidenced by competing ads for cable, satellite TV, and "bundled" fiber optics telephone services. But the critical battle is for control of enhanced digital handheld devices that have become more versatile and powerful even as they shrink. Portability, the once unique edge radio owned, is making handhelds indispensable for consumers.

Technology itself has become its own force driving listening and media decisions. Technology precipitated the growth of the Internet, huge numbers of distribution channels, wireless communications, and social networking that, along with increasingly flexible and glamorous devices, lure consumers with boundless content choices, and on-demand capabilities.

Technology, Regulation, and New Competition

Digital technology, coupled with the Telecom Act of 1996 that legalized publicly traded radio companies and the consolidation of the industry, revolutionized radio operations. Unattended operations, digital workstations, ISDN lines, and centralized billing and traffic systems streamlined radio operations. Voice-tracking hour-long music programs in minutes enhanced personnel productivity and flexibility. Group operators utilized digital technology to reduce costs by putting their best on-air people and syndicated products on multiple stations. But while technology delivered new efficiencies, it also gave rise to new competition and challenges.

Until the 1990s, "radio" described the AM and FM stations licensed to a limited number of frequencies in a given city or market because of the limitations of the radio spectrum. Technology demolished those limitations. The term "radio" now encompasses new distribution channels that encompass thousands of Internet stations, Sirius-XM and other satellite radio services, web-based "personalization technology-powered" stations such as Pandora, low-power FM stations (soon to become more prolific), and HD (high definition) channels. Not only are all these "stations" vying for their share of the listeners and ultimately revenues, they compete for consumers' time and minds with an immense number of global providers shoving content through an endless stream of devices: TV, computers, iPods, BlackBerrys, Xbox, Kindle, and many more.

The Impact on Radio

Traditional or "old media" is under siege. Newspapers, some published for 200 years, are in rapid economic decline, battered by free, up-to-the second online versions and an economic crisis that demolished advertising budgets. Yellow pages, television, magazines, and radio have all felt the impact; even "new media" including satellite and Internet radio are suffering. This new choice-filled environment arrives at an inopportune time for terrestrial radio. Too much talk, too many commercials, lack of compelling content, flagging community involvement, homogenized music, absence of exciting head-to-head competition, and staff reductions have contributed to radio's vulnerability. Radio has been too content to simply "broadcast," spending few resources on listener feedback or relationships. Revenue and valuation declines, accelerated by a weakened economy, forced many debt-stressed operators to slash overhead well beyond "streamlining." Hundreds of personalities, news and sportscasters, salespeople, and managers nationwide have been axed from payrolls. Although locally programmed stations operated by dedicated broadcasters still exist, those numbers are declining. The golden age of local radio has passed.

Radio Reacts

Terrestrial radio broadcasters view the future with trepidation, but they are making changes to meet it. High definition, HD radio, rapidly launched in 2006, uses digital technology to create new "side channels" from existing terrestrial signals. Although listeners must buy a new HD radio to receive these new stations, listeners can receive them free. Promising more unique programming, broadcasters see HD radio as a new way forward.

Many broadcasters are pressing for the expansion of more precise electronic audience measurement technologies such as the PPM, the Personal People Meter, to replace the diary system of listening "estimates" to establish more credibility with advertisers and agencies determined to get better value for their advertising dollars. Other broadcasters are striving to develop new sources of revenue by updating and monetizing station websites, developing promotional and event marketing tie-ins, and targeting new sources of advertising such as government programs and recruitment.

In this choice-filled environment, it is not surprising that people have become more "atomized" than ever before. Traditional social institutions such as the church, town meetings, fraternal and service organizations are disappearing; humans, who require social interaction for enjoyment and health, are progressively drawn toward "causes" and social networking to supply the "communities" that they need. This presents an opportunity for radio to nurture social involvement on a local level.

Radio Requires Renewal and Reinvestment

Radio's core strengths remain; expanding on them is the best course to ensure terrestrial radio's future. Radio has well-known personalities, personalities so influential that President Obama chided political opponents by saying, "You can't just listen to Rush Limbaugh and get things done." Like Limbaugh or not, the president's comment is testimony to radio's power and influence. From Don McNeill, to Larry Lujack, Howard Stern, and Mark Levin, personalities have made radio compelling through generations. These familiar voices serve as companions and friends, commanding enduring loyalties unlike any other media. That's because listening to radio, even in a carpool, is a personal, one-on-one experience. Radio is the perfect multitasking medium that is often used surfing the web, studying, or in the workplace. Radio has the best opportunity to be local, be integrated in the community and provide a social network. With the decline of newspapers, magazines, yellow pages, and other media, radio also has a renewed opportunity to capture new local advertising revenue. Radio serves as an editor. In this world of expanding choice and complexity, radio serves as a personal filter, eliminating the necessity of wading through limitless material by selecting the most interesting, entertaining, and popular sources of music and information. Unlike an iPod, radio continuously refreshes and edits content for the listener, adding the benefit of "surprise." Radio is free, easy to use, portable, and universally accessible. Almost 95% of all Americans listen to radio once a week, amazingly loyal to radio's relatability, reliability, personalities, and content. The industry must now press to ensure that radio is included in as many handheld devices as possible.

Focus on the Future

Radio's future requires reinvestment. This will mean finding, training, and promoting on-air talent to rebuild radio's product and appeal. Radio must reframe itself for the advertiser and abandon its antiquated "mass appeal" approach. Radio should focus on its exceptional efficiency as a targeted, personal medium that reaches age 25+ working consumers in a local market. Gone are the days of competing with TV or newspapers on a mass scale; that's no longer relevant. The radio industry knows too little about its own customers; fixing this will require a commitment to identify, target, and develop a relationship with radio's core listeners to enable it to be more responsive, useable, and relatable.

Radio must quickly look outside itself to expand its reach and brand by integrating into far reaching social networking communities. Radio's leaders must oppose the so-called Fairness Doctrine, issue-strangling legislation that failed in the 60s. Under the principle that every station must broadcast "opposing views," virtually impossible to administer in a political environment with multiple positions, this proposal ignores the existence of the "unregulated" media marketplace that includes satellite, Internet, cable TV, and other distribution channels. If the "Fairness Doctrine" is revived, the loser will be local terrestrial radio that, financially unable to hire enough lawyers or pay government fines, will forfeit politically oriented personalities to other outlets. Given the decline of newspapers with their free press guarantees, any government regulation of broadcast content will cast a chilling pall on Free Speech. Importantly, it will take reinvigorated confidence and belief in the medium by a breed of radio leaders who see possibilities, not obstacles. With a new infusion of leadership, radio, even in its most traditional form, will still be there to inform, stimulate, and entertain in more ways than ever before.

A Personal Note

If you're a student, inquisitive, observant, and willing to work, you can be an important part of radio's future. Radio, as with all media, needs intelligent young people at all levels who can communicate clearly and knowledgeably. Editing and filtering information to listeners are important, thoughtful processes requiring a familiarity with history to give events proper context and the ability to write interestingly and concisely. Understanding business and observing consumer trends is important for sales and sales managers who are ultimately successful by helping their advertising clients become successful. A desire to become involved in shaping and serving the needs of a community and its organizations, charities, and infrastructure is essential to radio's mission and continued importance. An understanding of technology, what it can do, and an ability to imagine what it might do in the future will also serve you well. Sherlock Holmes once said to Dr. Watson, "You see, but you do not observe. There is a distinction." Successful radio reflects its community; this cannot be done by those who do not observe what they see around them.

Glossary

ABC American Broadcasting Company; network.

AC Adult Contemporary format.

Account executive Station or agency salesperson.

Actives Listeners who call radio stations to make requests and comments or in response to contests and promotions.

Actuality Actual recording of news event or person(s) involved.

ADI Area of Dominant Influence; Arbitron measurement area.

Adjacencies Commercials strategically placed next to a feature.

Ad lib Improvisation; unrehearsed and spontaneous comments.

Affidavit Statement attesting to the airing of a spot schedule.

AFTRA American Federation of Television and Radio Artists; union composed of broadcast performers: announcers, deejays, and newscasters.

Aircheck Tape of live broadcast.

AM Amplitude modulation; method of signal transmission using Standard Broadcast band with frequencies between 535 and 1605 (1705) kHz.

AMAX Enhanced AM receiver developed by the NAB.

Analog Continuous variation in quantity of soundwaves and current.

Announcement Commercial (spot) or public service message of varying length.

AOR Album-Oriented Rock radio format.

AP Associated Press; wire and audio news service.

Arbitron Audience measurement service employing a 7-day diary to determine the number of listeners tuned to area stations.

ASCAP American Society of Composers, Authors, and Publishers; music licensing service.

Attenuate Reduce signal; decrease levels or output.

Audio Sound; modulation.

Audio animator Term used by satellite radio for production person.

Audition tape Telescoped recording showcasing talents of air person.

Automation Equipment system designed to play prepackaged programming.

Average quarter-hour (AQH) persons See the research glossaries in the Appendices of Chapter 6.

AWRT American Women in Radio and Television.

Back announce Recap of preceding music selections.

Barter Exchange of airtime for programming or goods.

BEA Broadcast Education Association.

Bed Music behind voice in commercial.

Blasting Excessive volume resulting in distortion.

Blend Merging of complementary sound elements.

Blog Internet journal or diary page of personality or talk host.

Book Term used to describe rating survey document; "bible."

BM Beautiful Music radio format.

BMI Broadcast Music Incorporated; music licensing service.

Branding Establishing station identity and value.

Bridge Sound used between program elements.

BTA Best-time-available, also run-of-station (ROS); commercials logged at available times.

Bulk eraser Tool for removing magnetic impressions from recording tape.

Bumper Music played to intro segments on talk programs and features.

Call letters Assigned station identification beginning with "W" east of the Mississippi and "K" west.

Capstan Shaft in recorder that drives tape.

Cart Plastic cartridge containing a continuous loop of recording tape.

CCC Clear Channel Communications

CFR *Code of Federal Regulations*.

Chain broadcasting Forerunner of network broadcasting.

CHR Contemporary Hit Radio format.

Clock Wheel indicating sequence or order of programming ingredients aired during one hour.

Clustering Combining the operations of several stations.

Cold Background fade on last line of copy.

Combo Announcer with engineering duties; AM/FM operation.

Commercial Paid advertising announcement; spot.

Compact disc (CD) Digital recording using laser beam to decode surface.

Compression Manipulation of audio dynamic range; control frequency range.

Console Audio mixer consisting of inputs, outputs, toggles, meters, and pots; board.

Consolidation. See *Clustering*.

Consultant Station advisor or counselor; "radio doctor."

Control room Center of broadcast operations from which programming originates; air studio.

Cool out Gradual fade of bed music at conclusion of spot.

Co-op Arrangement between retailer and manufacturer for the purpose of sharing radio advertising expenses.

Copy Advertising message; continuity; commercial script.

Cost per point (CPP) See the research glossaries in the Appendices of Chapter 6.

Cost per thousand (CPM) See the research glossaries in the Appendices of Chapter 6.

CPB Corporation for Public Broadcasting.

CRB Copyright Review Board.

CRMC Certified Radio Marketing Consultant.

Crossfade Fade-out of one element while introducing another.

Cue Signal for the start of action; prepare element for airing; queue.

Cue burn Distortion at the beginning of a record cut resulting from heavy cueing.

Cume See the research glossaries in the Appendices of Chapter 6.

DAB Digital audio broadcasting.

DARS Digital Audio Radio Service.

DAT Digital audio tape.

Dayparts Periods or segments of broadcast day: for example, 6 to 10 A.M., 10 A.M. to 3 P.M., 3 to 7 P.M.

Daytimer AM station required to leave the air at or near sunset.

Dead air Silence where sound usually should be; absence of programming.

Deejay Host of radio music program; announcer; disk jockey.

Demagnetize See *Erase*.

Demographics Audience statistical data pertaining to age, sex, race, income, and so forth.

Digital Convergence of analog waveform to numerical code.

Direct Broadcast Satellite (DBS) Powerful communications satellite that beams programming to receiving dishes at earth stations.

Directional Station transmitting signal in a preordained pattern so as to protect other stations on similar frequency.

Distortion Audio garble.

DMX Digital music satellite service.

Dolby Noise reduction system.

Donut spot Commercial in which copy is inserted between segments of music.

DOS Director of Sales.

Double billing Illegal station billing practice in which client is charged twice.

Downloading Gathering audio or video from the Internet for storing on a portable device.

Downsizing Reducing staff by combining functions and departments.

Drivetime Radio's prime time: 6 to 10 A.M. and 3 to 7 P.M.

Dub Copy of recording; duplicate (dupe).

EBS/EAS Emergency Broadcast System/Emergency Alert System.

Edit To alter composition of recorded material; splice.

ENG Electronic news gathering.

Equalization Manipulation of frequency spectrum.

Erase Wipe clean magnetic impressions; degauss, bulk, deflux, demagnetize.

ERP Effective radiated power; tape head configuration: erase, record, playback.

ET Electrical transcription.

Ethnic Programming for minority group audiences.

Fact sheet List of pertinent information on a sponsor.

Fade To slowly lower or raise volume level.

FCC Federal Communications Commission; government regulatory body with authority over radio operations.

Feedback Recycling of audio signal; reamplification.

Fidelity Trueness of sound dissemination or reproduction.

Fixed position Spot routinely logged at a specified time.

Flight Advertising air schedule.

FM Frequency modulation; method of signal transmission using 88 to 108 MHz band.

FMX System used to improve FM reception.

Format Type of programming a station offers; arrangement of material, formula.

Frequency Number of cycles-per-second of a sine wave.

Fulltrack Recording utilizing entire width of tape.

Gain Volume; amplification.

Generation Dub; dupe.

Grease pencil Soft-tip marker used to inscribe recording tape for editing purposes.

Grid Rate card structure based on supply and demand.

Gross rating points (GRP) See the research glossaries in the Appendices of Chapter 6.

Ground wave AM signal traveling the earth's surface; primary signal.

HD High-definition radio.

HD2 An HD radio frequency side-channel.

Headphones Speakers mounted on ears; headsets, cans.

Hertz (Hz) Cycles per second; unit of electromagnetic frequency.

HLT Highly leveraged transaction.

Hot Overmodulated.

Hot clock Wheel indicating when particular music selections are to be aired.

Hype Exaggerated presentation; high intensity, punched.

IBEW International Brotherhood of Electrical Workers; union.

IBOC In Band On Channel.

ID Station identification required by law to be broadcast as close to the top of the hour as possible; station break.

Imager Audio production person.

Input Terminal receiving incoming current.

Institutional Message promoting general image.

iPod Portable media player.

IPS Inches per second; tape speed: 1, 3, 15, 30 IPS.

IRT Internet radio tuner.

ISDN Integrated Services Digital Network.

ITU International Telecommunications Union; world broadcasting regulatory agency.

Jack Plug for patching sound sources; patchcord, socket, input.

Jack format Programming emulating iPod sound mix.

Jingle Musical commercial or promo; signature, logo.

Jock See *Deejay*.

JRAM *Journal of Radio and Audio Media*.

KDKA Radio station first to offer regularly scheduled broadcasts (1920).

Kilohertz (kHz) One thousand cycles per second; AM frequency measurement, kilocycles.

Leader tape Plastic, metallic, or paper tape used in conjunction with magnetic tape for marking and spacing purposes.

Level Amount of volume units; audio measurement.

Licensee Individual or company holding license issued by the FCC for broadcast purposes.

Line Connection used for transmission of audio; phone line.

Line-of-sight Path of FM signal; FM propagation.

Liner cards Written on-air promos used to ensure adherence to station image; prepared ad-libs.

Live copy Material read over air; not prerecorded.

Live tag Postscript to taped message.

LMA Local marketing (or management) agreement.

Local channels Class D AM stations found at high end of band: 1200 to 1600 kHz.

LPFM Low power FM.

Make-good Replacement spot for one missed.

Market Area served by a broadcast facility; ADI.

Master Original recording.

Master control See *Control room*.

MBS Mutual Broadcasting System; radio network.

Megahertz (MHz) Million cycles per second; FM frequency measurement, megacycles.

Mergers Consolidation or combining of assets and resources.

Mini-disc machines Digital cart decks employing floppy disc technology for audio reproduction and archiving.

MIS Manager of Information Systems.

Mixdown Integration of sound elements to create desired effect; production.

MMD Mobile multimedia device.

MMS Mobile music services.

Monitor Studio speaker; aircheck.

Mono Single or full-track sound; monaural, monophonic.

MOR Middle-of-the-Road radio format.

Morning Drive radio's primetime daypart: 6 to 10 A.M.

MP3 Digital audio player.

MSA Metro Survey Area; geographic area in radio survey.

Multitasking Performing several duties.

Multitracking Recording sound-on-sound; overdubbing, stacking tracks.

Music sweep Several selections played back-to-back without interruption; music segue.

NAB National Association of Broadcasters.

NAEB National Association of Educational Broadcasters.

Narrowcasting Directed programming; targeting specific audience demographic.

NBC National Broadcasting Company; network.

Network Broadcast combine providing programming to affiliates: NBC, CBS, ABC, MBS.

Network feed Programs sent via telephone lines or satellites to affiliate stations.

News block Extended news broadcast.

NPR National Public Radio.

NRSC National Radio Systems Committee.

NTR Nontraditional revenue.

O & Os Network or group owned and operated stations.

OES Optimum effective scheduling.

Off-mike Speech outside normal range of microphone.

Out-cue Last words in a line of recorded copy.

Output Transmission of audio or power from one location to another; transfer terminal.

Overdubbing. See *Multitracking*.

Overmodulate Exceed standard or prescribed audio levels: pinning VU needle.

Packaged Canned programming; syndicated, prerecorded, taped.

Pandora Internet music source.

Passives Listeners who do not call stations in response to contests or promotions or to make requests or comments.

Patch Circuit connector; cord, cable.

Patch panel Jack board for connecting audio sources: remotes, studios, equipment; patch bay.

PBS Public Broadcasting System.

PDA Personal digital assistant.

Pinch roller Rubber wheel that presses recording tape against capstan.

Playback Reproduction of recorded sound.

Playlist Roster of music for airing.

Plug Promo; connector

P1, P2, P3 Arbitron scale of a station's time spent listening (TSL).

Podcast Online archived/posted audio available for downloading.

Popping Break-up of audio due to gusting or blowing into mic; blasting.

Positioner Brief statement used on-air to define a station's position in a market.

Pot Potentiometer; volume control knob, gain control, fader, attenuator, rheostat.

PPM Portable People Meter.

Production. See *Mixdown*.

Promax Broadcast promotion and marketing executives association.

PSA Public Service Announcement; noncommercial message.

Psychographics Research term dealing with listener personality, such as attitude, behavior, values, opinions, and beliefs.

Punch Emphasis; stress.

Quadraphonic Four-speaker/channel sound reproduction.

RAB Radio Advertising Bureau.

Rack Prepare or set up for play or record: "rack it up"; equipment container.

RADAR Nationwide measurement service by Statistical Research, Inc.

RAIN *Radio and Internet Newsletter.*

Rate card Statement of advertising fees and terms.

Rating Estimated audience tuned to a station; size of listenership, ranking.

RCA Radio Corporation of America; NBC parent company.

RDS/RBDS Technology that enables AM and FM stations to send data to "smart" receivers, allowing them to perform several automatic functions.

Recut Retake; rerecord, remix.

Reel-to-reel Recording machine with feed and take-up reels.

Remote Broadcast originating away from station control room.

Reverb Echo; redundancy of sound.

Rewind Speeded return of recording tape from take-up reel.

Ride gain Monitor level; watch VU needle.

Rip'n read Airing copy unaltered from wire.

rpm Revolutions per minute: $33\frac{1}{3}$, 45, and 78 rpm.

R&R *Radio & Records* magazine

RTNDA Radio and Television News Directors Association.

Run-of-station (ROS) See *BTA.*

Satellite Orbiting device for relaying audio from one earth station to another; DBS, Comsat, Satcom.

SBE Society of Broadcast Engineers.

SCA Subsidiary Communication Authority; subcarrier FM.

Secondary service area AM skywave listening area.

Segue Uninterrupted flow of recorded material; continuous.

SESAC Society of European Stage Authors and Composers; music licensing service.

SFX Abbreviation for sound effect.

Share Percentage of station's listenership compared to competition; piece of audience pie.

Side-channel An additional HD channel or frequency.

Signal Sound transmission; RF. Signature Theme; logo, jingle, ID.

Simulcast Simultaneous broadcast over two or more frequencies.

SiriusXM Satellite radio service; subscriber-based audio source.

Sound Imager Audio producer, animator.

Spec spot Specially tailored commercial used as a sales tool to help sell an account.

Splice To join ends of recording tape with adhesive; edit.

Splicing bar Grooved platform for cutting and joining recording tape; edit bar.

Sponsor Advertiser; client, account, underwriter.

Spot set Group or cluster of announcements; stop set.

Spots Commercials; paid announcements.

Station Broadcast facility given specific frequency by FCC.

Station identification See *ID.*

Station log Document containing specific operating information as outlined in Section 73.1820 of the FCC *Rules and Regulations.*

Station rep Company acting in behalf of local stations to national agencies.

Stereo Multichannel sound; two program channels.

Stinger Music or sound effect finale preceded by last line of copy; button, punctuation.

Straight copy Announcement employing unaffected, nongimmicky approach; institutional.

Stringer Field or on-scene reporter.

Subliminal Advertising or programming not consciously perceived; below-normal range of awareness, background.

Sweep link Transitional jingle between sound elements.

Syndicator Producer of purchasable program material.

Tag See *Live tag.*

Tagging device Allows listener to buy songs they hear on radio.

Talent Radio performer; announcer, deejay, newscaster.

Talk Conversation and interview radio format.

TAP Total audience plan; spot package divided between specific dayparts: AAA, AA, A.

Tape speed Movement measured in inches per second: 3, 7, 15 IPS.

Telescoping Compressing of sound to fit a desired length; technique used in audition tapes and concert promos, editing.

TFN Till further notice; without specific kill date.

Trade-out Exchange of station airtime for goods or services.

Traffic Station department responsible for scheduling sponsor announcements. Transmit to broadcast; propagate signal; air.

TSA Total survey area; geographic area in radio survey.

Underwriter See *Sponsor*.

Unidirectional mic Microphone designed to pick up sound in one direction; car-dioid, studio mic.

UPI United Press International; wire and audio news service.

VOA Voice of America.

Voicer Voice of another news reporter.

Voiceover Talk over sound.

Voice-tracking Prerecorded announcer.

Volume Quantity of sound; audio level.

Volume control See *Pot*.

VU Meter gauge measuring units of sound.

WARC World Administrative Radio Conference; international meeting charged with assigning spectrum space.

Web radio Online radio station.

Web site Station Internet site.

Wheel See *Clock*.

Wifi Wireless Internet access.

Windscreen Microphone filter used to prevent popping and distortion.

Wireless telegraphy Early radio used to transmit Morse code.

Wow Distortion of sound created by inappropriate speed; miscue.

Wrap Open and close voicers in actuality.

XM Satellite Former independent satellite radio service; subscriber audio source.

Index